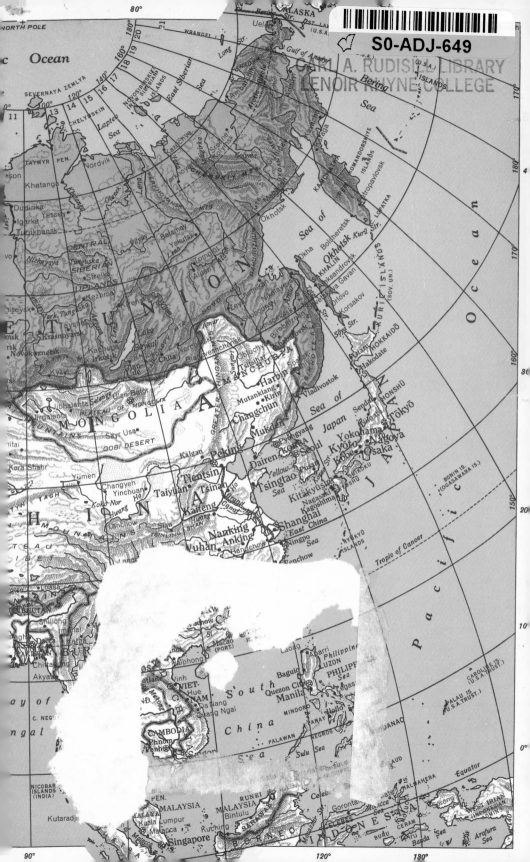

COMMUNIST EDUCATION

Communist Education :

Its History, Philosophy and Politics

by

WASYL SHIMONIAK
Marquette University

RAND McNALLY & COMPANY   Chicago • New York • San Francisco

To my wife, Alexandra (Nadia), and children,
Michael, Ann, Roman and Doreen.

ACKNOWLEDGEMENTS

In any scholarly work, many factors must be coordinated to accomplish the desired end. Three factors, or areas of assistance, contributed greatly to this work: financial aid, research facilities and personal encouragement.

I am grateful for the financial help provided by the Slavic Institute of Marquette University—particularly to the secretary of the Institute, Professor Alfred J. Sokolnicki, and to His Excellency, the late Roman Atkielski, for providing funds to type the manuscript. Further, my sincere thanks go to Professor Adrian M. Dupuis for his advice and assistance in organizing the manuscript; to the late Professor Roman Smal-Stocki for providing valuable research material; to Professor George F. Donovan for advice on the nature of school and society, and to Professor George Z. F. Bereday for his valuable suggestions concerning the content of the manuscript.

I wish to express appreciation to the Library of Congress, the New York Public Library, the University of Michigan Graduate Library, and to the Russian, Polish, Czech and Yugoslavian Academies of Science for making necessary sources available.

Patience was exhibited by many persons—especially by my family. My wife receives my sincere thanks for encouraging this work. Finally, sincere appreciation goes to the editor of this book, Mrs. Laurette Hupman of Rand McNally, who indeed put in extra efforts to make this work clear and legible.

W.S.

INTRODUCTION

It is said that experience is the best teacher. At any rate, the author of these lines was born and educated in the Carpathian district of Ukraine and had the experience of living under the communist way of life. During World War II the Western Ukraine was occupied by the Hungarians, allies of Nazi Germany. Due to political discrimination under Hungarian rule, the Ukrainians of this region viewed the Russians as liberators since they were of the same Slavic origin although not of the same political affiliation. "Liberation" policies of the Russians, however, severely disappointed the entire population of the occupied areas. Because of this personal experience and in an attempt to illuminate these events the author decided to explore further the educational-cultural policies of communism in general and Russian communism in particular.

The main objective of this work is to present important communist educational policies and practices and to analyze their role in social change. Obviously, education is important in the social structure of any nation, but in a communist society it plays the role of regenerating society.

An endeavor is made to present the total picture of Soviet education, that is, the Soviet-Russian system and the Soviet non-Russian systems. Obviously, it is impossible to cover each nationality (there are over 180), but an attempt is made to obtain a representative sample by studying the following: 1) Russian educational and cultural policies in terms of new educational demands, 2) Ukrainian educational status in the Soviet educational system, and 3) the Muslim education, society and culture during the Soviet period. This distribution is important because of the 230 million Soviet people, the Russians comprise about 114 million; Ukraine embodies 45 million and the Muslims another 30 million. An analysis of the educational and cultural efforts of the Russian communists and the two national groups provides insight into Soviet theory and practice in education as well as political cultural patterns.

The school, of course, is the environment where scientists as well as revolutionists are educated. Therefore, the second part of this book relates major developments in Soviet linguistic policies, the attitude of Soviet government toward organized religion and the position of women in the communist society.

The third part of the book focuses on educational plans and practices in other communist countries. The description of other non-Russian communist countries deserves much more study and space than can be given in this work, but, again, the aim of this book is to present the Soviet type of education and its impact on all other communist countries.

Naturally, the communist states of today are different from those that existed in the early 1920s and in the late 1930s. There are many causes for the varying structures within the communist countries, but the causes are predominantly political ones. Although many of these communist nations have different cultures and histories, they share one aspect of development: a big power has imposed ideas upon every small power in the communist block.

Changes in the educational structure are very important because in the framework of the communist ideas the school is the most important agency for raising a new generation in the spirit of communistic ideas and in spreading those ideas among the population. By imposing a new system upon a new society the Russians expected the school to educate a new generation—a generation capable of transmitting the new ideas to the people and implanting in them a completely new set of principles based on a materialistic philosophy. The children were taught the supremacy of Russian culture and the 'hazards' of religion. This philosophy is well planned. It is designed to create a myth of Russian messianism—regardless of the form it takes—and a myth of 'independent' cultural developments of non-Russian nationalities.

It was in the Soviet Union during the period 1918-1939 that the whole set of philosophical principles and ideas underlying communist education were studied by the Russian-communist educators and social scientists. The impact of the Russian communist educational ideas and policies on non-Russian societies has hardly been explored, although considerable information is available on early Marxian philosophy and the aims of such thinkers as Shulgin, Krupskaia, Pinkevitch, Lunacharski, Makarenko and on various programs of the communist party and the Soviet government. These sources show that Soviet theories and practices in education were the products of European (Russian as well as non-Russian) educational developments and as such were no part of the historical, cultural, or educational practices of many non-European peoples. In most of the countries which the communists have taken over the general forms and ideas underlying social institutions differ significantly from the Russian ones.

An important feature of Soviet educational philosophy is its revolutionary approach to changing the traditional values of ethnic groups inhibiting various parts of the Soviet Union. It is common practice to impose Russian ideas on many nationalities regardless of the fact that these nationalities may have entirely different views regarding the structure of their particular social institutions. In the early period of the Bolshevik regime, for example, the communists in power promised free education to all ethnic groups in their own languages without any interference by the Russian people. They also predicted that the school, like the state, would wither away because organized educational institutions would not be necessary once the full stage of communism was realized. Later these ideas were rejected and the people who promulgated them were either liquidated or removed from responsible positions or offices.

By 1967 almost all of the communist countries had educated a new generation. There is no question that the communist philosophy of education and culture represents a real challenge to Christianity. The Russian communist party has clearly stated that the aim of the Russian communists is the complete liquidation of any religion. This pattern, unfortunately, has been imposed upon many other communist countries.

The Soviet, as well as the non-Soviet, nations try to reduce the parental influences upon children. They are not satisfied merely with the prohibition of religious instructions in schools; they want to dominate the minds of all young children and they go about it with all the psychological and educational techniques that modern science can provide. Therefore, the education of the new man, whether he be Russian, Chinese, Polish, etc., is not merely limited to the conquest of an unknown; most of all it is dedicated to the conquest of the human mind.

Finally, technical terms and last names have been given in their English equivalents wherever this has contributed to clarity; in such cases the standard spellings from Webster's Third dictionary have been used. In some instances where exact translation was either unclear or where the Russian would be readily recognized, the foreign terms were retained.

W.S.

TABLE OF CONTENTS

                                                                          Page

ACKNOWLEDGEMENTS vii

ABBREVIATIONS xviii

INTRODUCTION ix

LIST OF FIGURES xxiii

LIST OF TABLES xix

PART I.   SCHOOL AND SOCIETY IN THE U.S.S.R.

Chapter

   I. THE POPULATION OF RUSSIA–U.S.S.R.   3
     Historical Trends of Russian-Soviet Population
     Major Characteristics of Soviet Population
     The Problem of Many Nationalities • Fate of Ethnic Groups
     Other Communist Countries

  II. SCHOOL AND SOCIETY BEFORE 1917 23
     Kievan "Window to Europe"
     The Academy of Peter Mohyla
     Students of Peter Mohyla and Peter I
     Cultural Development of Moscow after Peter I
     The Russian Enlightenment
     Educational Ideas of Slavophils
     The Westernites
     The Progressive Period: K. Ushinski
     Education of Non-Russians: Ukraine
     The Muslim Schools Before 1917

 III. GOALS OF SOVIET EDUCATION 51
     The Leading Role of the Party
     The Creed in Matter Only
     The Creed in the Communist Morality
     The Necessity of Class Struggle
     Russian Patriotism
     The Principle of Hate
     To Surpass America
     Respect for Authority

 IV. SOVIET EDUCATIONAL AND CULTURAL REFORMS . 67
     Problems of Illiteracy
     Development of Elementary and Secondary Education
     Educational Development in the Soviet Ukraine
     Educational Development in Central Asia

V. NEW TYPES OF SCHOOLS vs. NEW DEMANDS 97
Pre-school Education
Schools for General Education
Schools for Working Youth, Rural Youth and Technicums
Workers' Faculties (Rabfak)
Boarding Schools
Higher Education
New Demands Facing Teachers' Institutes
Other Areas of Higher Education
Adult Education

VI. ADMINISTRATION AND CONTROL 119
The Role of the Party
The Federal Centralized Structure
The Narkompros and the Ministry of Education
Functions of the Ministry of Education
School Administration
The Teacher
The Student
School and Society
Educational Expenditures

VII. CURRICULUM POLICIES 143
Organization and Curriculum Policies in
General Schools, 1918–1941
Curriculum in Non-Russian Schools
General Educational Changes After World War II.
Curriculum Structure at Institutions of Higher Learning

VIII. METHODS OF TEACHING 159
Makarenko's Method
Subject Matter vs. Teacher
Methods of Teaching History
Teaching of Ukrainian History
Teaching of Central Asian History

IX. DIALECTICAL MATERIALISM vs. EDUCATION 183
General Background
Basic Criteria of Russian Dialectical Materialism
Marxism and the Nature of Reality
The Nature of Truth
Philosophy and Science
Impact of Dialectical Materialism on Educational Practices
Makarenko's System

X. SOME CONCEPTS OF SOVIET EDUCATIONAL
PSYCHOLOGY 199
General Background
Characteristics of Educational Psychology

Child Development
Recent Experiments in Learning
The Subject of Personality
Political Psychology

PART II. IMPACT OF COMMUNIST POLICIES ON SOCIETY

XI. BOLSHEVIK LINGUISTIC POLICIES 215
Language and the Nation
The Ukrainian Reforms
Linguistic Reforms in Central Asia

XII. RELIGION AND COMMUNISM 235
Foundation of Atheism
Legal Limitations of Religious Freedom
The Scope of Anti-Religious Propaganda
The Fate of Individual Religions
Is Religion Dead?

XIII. WOMEN AND COMMUNISM 253
Theoretical Foundations
Women and the Propaganda Apparatus
Women in the National Economy
Is the Soviet Woman Happy?

XIV. SOME CONCEPTS OF SOVIET CULTURE 273
Soviet Culture vs. National Culture
Literature in the Soviet Society
Scientific Communism
The Class Struggle
Soviet Intelligentsia
Conclusions

PART III. SCHOOL AND SOCIETY IN OTHER COMMUNIST COUNTRIES

XV. EDUCATION IN CZECHOSLOVAKIA 291
Historical Background
Culture and Education
Social Foundations of Communist Education
Religious and Other Reforms

XVI. EDUCATION IN POLAND 303
Historical Background
Education Before the Communist Take-over
Education Under Communism
Higher Education and Training of Teachers
Other Reforms

XVII. EDUCATION IN BULGARIA 315
General Background
Education Before 1945
The Period of Reconstruction
The Period of Socialist Education
Other Reforms

XVIII. EDUCATION IN YUGOSLAVIA 329
Historical Background
Education Before the Communist Take-over
Education After World War II
General Education
Higher Education
Other Developments

XIX. EDUCATION IN EAST GERMANY 345
General Polytechnical Education
Problems Beyond the Secondary Level
Moral Education
Religion and School
Women In East German Society

XX. EDUCATION IN COMMUNIST HUNGARY 357
Historical Background
Educational Before 1945
Education Under the Communists
General and Secondary Schools
Higher Education
Other Reforms

XXI. EDUCATION IN ROMANIA 371
Historical Background
Education Before 1948
The 1948 Reforms
General Education
Vocational Education
Higher Education
Teaching Profession
Other Reforms

XXII. EDUCATION IN ALBANIA 385
Historical Background
Education and Culture Before 1945
Education After 1945
Policies Toward Religion

XXIII. THE SCHOOLS OF CHINA 397
General Background
Education Before 1949

Communist Educational Reforms
Social Foundations of Chinese Education
Organization and Control
Types of Schools
Spare Time Education
Teacher Training
Methodological Problems
Other Reforms

XXIV. EDUCATION IN OTHER COMMUNIST COUNTRIES . 415
  A. EDUCATION IN CUBA 415
    Historical Background
    Castro's Reforms
    General Education
    Higher Education
    Propaganda and Education
  B. EDUCATION IN THE MONGOLIAN PEOPLES'
    REPUBLIC 422
    Russian Intervention
    Educational Developments Since 1920
    Higher Education
    Religious Reforms
  C. EDUCATION IN NORTH KOREA 427
    General Background
    The Communist Educational Reforms
    Educational System After 1960
    The Position of Women
  D. EDUCATION IN NORTH VIETNAM 432
    General Background
    The Russian Influence
    Social Foundations of Education
    Types of Schools
    Political Indoctrination

XXV. SUMMARY AND CONCLUSIONS 439
    Communism and the People
    Administration and Control
    Statistical Reliability
    Education and Marxism
    Communist Youth Organizations
    Curricular Changes
    Methods of Research and Teaching
    Social Foundations of Education
    Linguistic Problems
    Religion and Communism
    Culture and Communism

APPENDIX (Comparative Tables) 449

BIBLIOGRAPHY 469

ABBREVIATIONS

AN: Akademiia Nauk (Academy of Sciences).

APN: Akademiia Pedagogicheskikh Nauk (Academy of Pedagogical Sciences).

ASSR: Autonomous Soviet Socialist Republic.

FUZ: Fabrychno-uchebnye Zavedeniia (Factory Educational Establishments).

Gosstatizdat: Gosudarstvenno-statisticheskoe Izdatel'stvo (State Statistical Publishing House).

Gosizda: Gosudarstvennoe Izdatel'stvo (State Publishing House).

GPO: Government Printing Office.

Komsomol: Kommunisticheskii Soiuz Molodezhi (Communist Youth League).

KPSS: Kommunisticheskaia Partiia Sovetskogo Soiuza (Communist Party of the Soviet Union).

Kul'tstroi: Kul'turnoe Stroitel'stvo (Cultural Construction).

NEP: New Economic Policy.

Narkompros: Narodnyi Komissariat Prosveshcheniia (People's Commissariat of Education).

NKVD: Narodnyi Komissariat Vnutrennykh Del (People's Commissariat of Internal Affairs: Security Police).

Rabfak: Rabochie Fakul'tety (Workers' Faculties).

RSFSR: Russian Soviet Federated Socialist Republic.

Sovnarkom: Sovet Narodnykh Komissarev (Soviet of People's Commissars).

VKP(b): Vsesoiuznaia Kommunisticheskaia Partiia (Bol'shevikov) (All-Union Communist Party: Majority Group [b]).

VTsIK: Vsesoiuznyi Tsentral'nyi Ispol'nitel'nyi Komitet (All-Union Central Executive Committee).

VUZ: Vysshie Uchebnye Zavedeniia (Higher Educational Establishments).

ZMNP: Zhurnal Ministerstva Narodnogo Prosveshcheniia (Journal of the Ministry of Public Education).

LIST OF TABLES

Table   *Text Tables*   *Page*

1. Population of Asiatic Russia According to Major Nationalities, 1897, 1911 .   5
2. Population of the Soviet Union According to Major Nationalities,
   1926, 1939, 1959   9
3. Distribution of Population in Turkestan, 1897, 1911 14
4. Total Population Change: Russia-USSR, 1926–1939 16
5. Changes in the Distribution of the Soviet Population, 1940, 1959 17
6. Population of the USSR by Republics: 1965 19
7. Distribution of the Population in Communist Countries 20
8a. Development of Elementary and Secondary Education in Turkestan
   and Steppe, 1893–1897 42
8b. Distribution of Schools, Teachers and Students in Muslim Schools of
   Russia, 1893/94 46
9. Number of Schools and Students in the USSR: 1925 71
10. Increase in Number of Schools, Children and Teachers, 1928, 1935 76
11. Data On Tashkent District: Number of Public Schools, Teachers, and
   Childrens' Movements (1925–1927) 89
12. Increase in Number of Schools, Students and Teachers in the
   Uzbek SSR, 1929–1935 91
13. Composition of Student Body at Factory Schools, Technicums and
   Universities: By Nationalities 92
14. Number of Schools, Teachers and Students: Selected Republics, 1965 . . . 102
15. Curriculum of the Soviet Ten-Year Program School: Distribution of
   Hours per Subject Matter: RSFSR, 1927, 1929 109
16. Higher Educational Establishments and Number of Students, 1914–1965 . . 112
17. Number of Students at Higher Educational Institutions According to
   Specialty, 1965 113
18. Distribution of Students at VUZ According to Time of Studies 116
19. Expenditures of the Ministry of Public Education on Elementary and
   Secondary Schools, 1893 139
20. Expenditures of the Soviet Government on Education, in Selected
   Republics, 1932, 1934 141
21. Expenditures of the Soviet Government on Education: 1950, 1965 142
22. Comparison of Curriculum of Boys' Gymnasium (1914) and Soviet
   Curriculum of 1920, 1927 146
23. Curriculum of the Soviet Ten-Year Program School, RSFSR, 1927, 1929 . 147
24. Curriculum for Grades IX and X in Soviet Ukraine, 1967 150
25. Courses for Teachers in Pskovsk Guberniia, 1923 155
26. Structure of Lectures in Pedagogy and Number of Hours per Week 164
27. Soviet "Commandments" of Moral Behavior 165
28. Distribution of Class-Hours per Uzbek and Russian Languages, 1939 . . . 231
29. Nationalities of the Uzbek SSR According to Language 233
30. Distribution of Population of the UzSSR According to Major Occupations
   and Per cent of Women in the National Economy, 1926, 1939 264

Table	Text Tables	Page
31. Composition of Students and the Per cent of Women, 1928, 1935		266
32. Composition of Students in Rabfak, Technicums and Universities, By Nationality, 1928, 1935		269
33. Number of Women Specialists with Higher and Secondary Special Education		270
34. Number of Students in Communist Countries as Compared to Some Other non-Communist Countries		271
35. Educational Development in Czechoslovakia, 1937, 1964		299
36. General Development of Education in Poland, 1964		310
37. General Development of Education in Bulgaria, 1940, 1957, 1965		321
38. General Educational Polytechnical Schools of Bulgaria, 1940, 1957, 1965		322
39. Development of Higher Education in Bulgaria: 1940, 1957, 1965		323
40. Educational Development in Yugoslavia: 1939, 1964		338
41. Number of Schools, Students and Teachers in Yugoslavia, 1939, 1964		339
42. Development of Elementary and Secondary Education in East Germany, 1955, 1965		348
43. Development of Higher Education in East Germany: 1965		349
44. Educational Development in Hungary, 1949, 1965		366
45. Development of Education in Romania, 1939, 1960, 1964		378
46. Number of Students at Romanian Universities, 1939, 1954, 1960		380
47. Elementary and Secondary Education in Romania: 1939, 1960		383
48. Educational Development in Albania, 1938, 1965		390
49. Higher Education in Albania and Number of Women in Higher Schools, 1964/65		391
50. Number of Men and Women Graduated from Higher Educational Institutions in Albania, 1955, 1965		392
51. Development of Education in Cuba, 1953, 1963		420
52. Development of Education in North Korea, 1946, 1953, 1964		430
53. Development of Education in North Vietnam, 1952, 1962, 1965		435

Tables in Appendix

1. Distribution of the Available Total Population of the Russian Empire and the USSR, 1897–1959		451
2. Estimated Deficit of the Population of the Soviet Union, By Age and Sex: 1926, 1939		455
3. Rate of Literacy of the Uzbek SSR (Major Ethnic Groups Only), 1926		458
4. Per Cent of Literates in the Age Group 9–49 in Selected Republics, 1897, 1936		461
5. Development of Public Education in Selected Republics, 1914–1940		462
6. Distribution of Students in Higher Educational Institutions According to Nationality and the Per Cent of Women: 1960, 1966		467
7. Distribution of Students in Soviet Higher Educational Establishments by Republics: 1915–1966		468

LIST OF FIGURES

Figure   *Page*

1. Number of Students in Schools for Illiterates and Secondary Schools . . . 69
2. Literacy of the Population of the USSR, Nine Years of Age and Older, 1926. 70
3. Relative Proportion of College Students in Ukraine 81
4. Russification of Ukraine: Per Cent of Students in Russian Schools,
   Major Cities only, 1959 83
5. Decrease of Scientific Workers in Ukraine 84
6. Distribution of Communist Party Membership According to Social
   Classes of Turkestan, 1924–1930 87
7. Distribution of Administrative Personnel in the Uzbek SSR, 1930 88
8. Per Cent of Turkestanian Students in Colleges, 1960 94
9. Per Cent of Students at Secondary Special Schools and at Higher
   Educational Institutions: Selected Nationalities Only, 1965. 115
10. Educational Administration of the Russian SFSR 126
11. Educational Administration of the USSR 127
12. Administrative Structure of the Ministry of Education of a Union
    Republic 128
13. The Structure of the Academy of Pedagogical Sciences 130
14. Educational Council for Schools of General Education 135
15. The Structure of the Student Government 137
16. Relative Proportion of Women Among Students of Higher Educational
    Institutions, 1926, 1936 267
17. Per Cent of Women in Higher Educational Institutions, 1961 268

Part One

SCHOOL AND SOCIETY
IN THE U.S.S.R.

Chapter 1

THE POPULATION
OF RUSSIA—U.S.S.R.

HISTORICAL TRENDS OF RUSSIAN-SOVIET POPULATION

The Union of Soviet Socialist Republics occupies the largest territory
of the world, over 22 million sq. km., which is equal to the entire territory of Canada, the United States, Central America, and Mexico.[1] From

---

[1] N. P. Nikitin (ed.); and others, *Ekonomicheskaia geografiia SSSR* (Moscow:
Izdat. "Prosveshcheniie," 1966), p. 18. See also Pervaia Obshchaia Perepis'
Naseleniia Rossiskoi Imperii, *Obshchei svod po imperii rezul'tatov razrabotky
fannykh pervoi vseodshei perepisi naseleniia, 28-go ianvaria, 1897,* (S. Petersburg:
Tipografiia N. L. Nyrkina, 1905, vol. 1), p. 1; Frank Lorimer, *The Population of
the Soviet Union: History and Prospects* (Geneva: League of Nations, 1946), p.
209; Walter Kolarz, *Russia and her Colonies* (London: George Philip and Sons,
Ltd., 1952), p. 3; Pereselencheskoe Upravlenie Glavnogo Upravleniia Zem-
leustroistva i Zemledeliia, *Aziatskaia Rossiia,* vol. II (S. Petersburg: Izdatel'stvo
Pereselencheskogo Upravleniia, 1914), p. 4; Ivan Mirchuk, *Ukraine and Its
People* (Munich: Ukrainian Free University Press, 1949), pp. 72–94; Ivan
Mirchuk, *Geschichte der Ukrainischen Kultur* (Munich: Isar Verlag, 1957), p.
120; M. Hrushevskyj, *A History of Ukraine* (New Haven: Yale University Press,
1941), pp. 265 ff.; Oscar Halecki, *Borderlands of Western Civilization* (New York:
The Ronald Press Co., 1952), pp. 130–234.

east to west its borders spread over 10,000 km. and from north to south, 4,500 km. In the arctic regions, all islands except the Spitsbergen Islands belong to the U.S.S.R.

The Asiatic parts of the Soviet Union play an important part in the Soviet economy. They are very rich in mineral resources, but of even more importance, they provide natural protection for the Russian borders, which are more than 60,000 km. long. Over three-quarters of the Soviet Union is surrounded by water—a natural barrier.

After World War II the borders of Russia were strengthened by Russian expansion into European territories. All the Slavs then fell under Russian control and the non-Slavs, like the Hungarians, Romanians, and Prussians, were entirely encircled by the Soviet Empire.

The communist countries of today occupy over 26 per cent of the globe with 35 per cent of its population. The Soviet Union itself occupies 16.6 per cent of the territorial expansion of our earth and embodies 7.2 per cent of the population.

A consideration of the historical development of czarist Russia and the Soviet Union necessitates mention of an important date—1552, the year when Ivan the Terrible defeated the Tatars at Kazan and laid the foundation for Russian expansion to the east and to the south. From that time on Russia began occupying small ethnic groups in far northern regions as well as Asiatic areas (which in reality represented a military vacuum at that time) ; thus almost all the Asiatic parts of the present Soviet Union were left to the mercy of the Russian rulers. The Russian expansion to the west was decided, at first, not on the battle field but on a voluntary union with the hetman of Ukraine, Bohdan Khmelnitski. In 1654 he signed the treaty between the two countries, both as equal members, but united only by the crown of Moscow. The strategy of Khmelnitski was to prevent further wars with Poland. Such a treaty, he thought, would reduce danger of future wars and at the same time safeguard the peaceful development of cultural endeavors in eastern Europe. However, in 1709, Peter the First defeated the Ukrainian armies of Mazepa and the ally of Mazepa, Charles XII. This put an end to the equality of the two nations and, furthermore, opened the door to Russian expansion to the Baltic and to the subsequent ruin of Poland. In the eighteenth century Poland was divided among Russia, Austria and Prussia.

The area beyond the Ural Mountains was not entirely colonized during the reign of Peter I since only initial steps were taken to transfer the Slavic population into the new areas. Fewer than a half million Russian-Belorussian-Ukrainians lived in the Asiatic parts as of 1724, but this number increased to 3.4 million in 1859; 5.3 million in 1897; and 10 million in 1911 (see Table 1).

TABLE 1

Population of Asiatic Russia According to Major Nationalities
1897–1911

Nationalities	1897	1911
A. Russians	5,341,745	9,945,732
B. Natives–total	7,762,525	9,090,294
Of which:		
Kirgiz	4,082,748	4,692,384
Sarts	1,458,128	1,847,420
Uzbeks	534,825	592,150
Tadzhiks	338,279	396,529
Buriats	289,001	332,554
Turkmen	248,651	290,170
Iakuts	225,773	245,406
Tatars	175,735	208,133
Kara-kalpaks	111,799	134,313
Taranch	60,999	83,000
Tungiz	76,504	75,204
Kipchaks	45,353	60,785
Kashgirs	41,312	54,832
Osetins	17,221	18,591
Indo-Europeans	98,690	174,462
Tatars (Nomads)	94,909	124,468
Chinese	43,225	101,430
Dungans	14,132	20,600
Koreans	26,159	59,577
Kalmiks	2,849	1,825
Mordva	40,838	53,935
Total in Asiatic Russia . .	13,506,887	19,693,368

Pereselencheskoe Upravlenie Zemleustroistva i Zemledeliia, *Aziatskaia Rossiia, Liudi i poriadki za Uralom,* (St. Petersburg: Tipografiia A. F. Marksa, 1914), vol. 1, pp. 79–80.

In the second half of the nineteenth century Russia gained substantial territorial advantages over other imperial powers, especially England, by occupying the central Asian territories known as Turkestan and expanding 'trade' to the khanates of Khiva and Bukhara. About 20 million Muslims became the subjugated peoples of the czarist expansion. During the same period most of Siberia was taken.

More than 160 million inhabitants representing over 180 different nationalities lived within the present boundaries of Russia—U.S.S.R., just before World War I. If one considers the territorial and the population loss—over 24 million people—during the Bolshevik Revolution, then the second stage of the Russian Soviet empire constitutes another story. For the first time in the history of Russia, the borders of the Soviet state reached from the Tisa and Danube rivers to the Far Eastern regions.

The population of Russia increased very rapidly. In 1897, it amounted to 125 million people; in 1926 it reached 147 million; in January of 1939 it was 170 million and by December of that same year (occupation of the Western Ukraine and parts of Poland) the population reached the 190 million mark (see Appendix, Table 1). In 1959, the population of the Soviet Union amounted to 208 million and the Soviet estimate for 1965 indicated 230 million.[2]

MAJOR CHARACTERISTICS OF THE SOVIET POPULATION

Before World War I, the Russian empire was predominantly agricultural in economy. After the revolution of 1917, the Bolshevik regime attempted to industrialize and at the same time urbanize the nation.

When the Soviets launched their economic plans beginning in 1928, the pastoral life and small scale agricultural enterprises were threatened by these new reforms. The new government demanded voluntary abandonment of private property, and from 1928 on, continuous efforts were made to industrialize the Soviet Union even in the remote parts of Siberia and the Ural regions. Peasants left their rural settlements and moved to the city, either voluntarily or forcibly. During the ten year period, 1928-1939, more than 23 million people moved to the cities. As a result, the urban population increased 112 per cent. During the period of Stalin and Hitler's friendship, the Russians occupied another 453,000 sq. km. of the western regions (mainly the territories of western Ukraine, Bukovina and the Baltic states totaling more than 22 million inhabitants). The urban population increased even more because the Bolsheviks introduced the same policies to the occupied territories as they introduced earlier to their own people.

The process of urbanization took place very rapidly and during a very short period of time. The United States of America witnessed a similar

<hr>

[2]Tsentral'noe Statisticheskoe Upravlenie pri Sovete Ministrov SSSR, *Narodnoe khoziaistvo SSSR v 1960 g.* (Moscow: Gosstatizdat, 1961), p. 16; Nikitin, *op. cit.,* pp. 25–85; B. Ts. Urlanov (ed.); and others, *Naselenie mira* (Moscow: Gospolitizdat, 1965), p. 114.

rapid transformation from rural to urban areas (on a voluntary basis, of course). In the Soviet Union this transformation took various steps—force and violence, deportation, colonization and dictatorial administrative practices. Today more than 118 million Soviet people live in urban areas. This number constitutes more than one-half of the total population and in 1980, according to Soviet estimation, the number in urban centers will increase to 144 million and in 1990 to 190 million. In 1926, there were 31 cities with more than 100,000 inhabitants, and in 1966 there were 178 such cities, or 51 per cent of the total Soviet population. Further, in 1926, only three cities had a population of 500,000 or more; in 1966 there were 28 such cities. Clearly, nineteenth century agrarian Russia is being transformed into a twentieth century industrial nation.

The density of population depends largely upon the geographical area. The average density is ten people per 1 sq. km. and, of course, is much higher in industrial centers, e.g., in Moscow, the density is 100 per sq. km., in the Ukrainian SSR, 74 per sq. km., and in Kazakhstan four people per 1 sq. km. In Siberia the density depends on the area of settlement or the number of labor camps which change in population from time to time.

The Soviet source states that colonization of Siberia began in the seventeenth century, but it has achieved a high tempo during the Soviet regime. Whatever the circumstances (and there were many), the population of the eastern Siberian regions increased by 94 per cent during the period of 1927-1947, and the density of population increased to 10 people per sq. km. The Soviet Union, in this respect, is still far from overpopulated—as are many European countries today. In Belgium the average density is 302 people per sq. km., in Malta, 1,096 people per sq. km., and in Britain the density is 219 people per sq. km.

Soviet population study according to age groups is rather complicated, especially during periods of collectivization and industrialization. As many Western studies have indicated, deportation to Siberian regions of Soviet "unsympathetic" persons is never mentioned by Soviet statistical sources. We know, however, that the Soviets have estimated the total population of 12-year-olds and under as over 63 million persons by 1939, and the actual census revealed only 48,089,000 or about a 15 million deficit (see Appendix, Table 2).

THE FATE OF MANY ETHNIC GROUPS

The population of the Soviet Union comprises many different ethnic groups and nationalities. It would be quite wrong to call the Soviet

Union "Russia" (as many friends of Russian communists do) because there are almost the same number of non-Russians in the U.S.S.R. The term Soviet Union is, of course, a better one.

A clear picture of the Soviet nationalities has never been determined. The imperial sources list only major groups and the Soviet sources either completely change the name of an ethnic group (Sarts to Uzbek, for instance) or assimilate it into a major ethnic unit. The 1926 Soviet census listed 169 different ethnic groups, and in 1949 Fedeev listed only seventy ethnic groups. In 1966 there were 100 "fully independent ethnic groups."

Before the Bolshevik Revolution of 1917, there was never an actual majority of Russian people in the empire. Many sources, Soviet and non-Soviet, have determined this case. Even Lenin himself stated in 1921 that the nationality question must be treated very gently because there were more than 57 per cent non-Russian people in the Soviet Union.[3] This ratio remained constant until the end of the 1920s. At that time the Soviets prohibited many religious practices, thus *ipso facto* liquidating a national unity because many ethnic groups identified themselves first by their religious affiliation and second by their ethnic ties. The Russian majority is clear now since the 1959 census estimated about 54 per cent of Russian nationals while the Jewish population dropped 44 per cent in favor of the Russian (prohibition of the Jewish religion). The Ukrainian population similarly dropped in favor of the Russian (physical liquidation during the period of 1932-1950). As Table 2 shows, the number of the Ukrainian people dropped from 31 million in 1926 to 28 million in 1939. Many nationalities of the Asiatic regions, as well as 600,000 Volga Germans, either perished during the Soviet regime or were not listed by the Soviet demographic data. One should note that there were two census reports during the 1930s which made the Soviet statistical publications of 1937-1939 less significant. In the first place, the second Soviet census was undertaken February 6, 1937, but according to a Soviet source, "because of difficulties involved in dealing with enemies of the people, the central statistical administration was unable to apply basic statistical method."[4] There was a different reason.

[3]Institute Marksa, Englesa, Lenina i Stalina, *Kommunisticheskaia Partiia Sovetskogo Soiuza v rezoliutsiiakh, postanovleniiakh i resheniiakh s'iezdov, 1898–1953,* vol. I (Moscow: Izdat. "Politicheskoi Literatury," 1953), pp. 533–563; see also L. Dobrianskyj, W. Shimoniak, *Study of Population and Migration Problems* (Washington: U. S. Government Printing Office, Committee on the Judiciary, House of Representatives, Hearings, Special Series No. 17 [b], pp. 60–89).

[4]J. Santin, *Vsesoiuznaia perepis' naseleniia 1937 g.* (Moscow: Gospolitizdat, 1938), pp. 18–19.

TABLE 2

Population of the Soviet Union According to Nationality,
Major Groups Only: 1926, 1939, 1959
(In Thousands)

Nationality	1926[1]	1939[2] (January)	1959[3]
Total	147,027	170,467	208,827
Russian	77,791	99,019	114,114
Ukrainian	31,191	28,070	37,233
Belorussian	4,738	5,267	7,913
Uzbek	3,954	4,844	6,015
Tatar	3,477	4,300	4,968
Kazakh	3,968	3,098	3,622
Jewish	2,672	3,020	2,268
Azerbaidzhanian	1,706	2,274	2,940
Georgian	1,821	2,248	2,619
Armenian	1,567	2,151	2,782
Mordva	1,340	1,451	1,285
German	1,246	1,423	1,620
Chuvash	1,117	1,367	1,420
Tadzhik	980	1,228	1,397
Kirghiz	762	884	963
Dagestanian	669	857	944
Bashkir	741	842	989
Turkmen	763	811	1,002
Polish	792	626	1,380
Udmurt	504	605	625
Mari	428	481	504
Komi	375	408	431
Chechin	318	407	419
Osetin	272	354	413
Greek	259	285	309
Moldavian	278	260	2,214
Karelian	248	252	167
Karakalpak	146	185	173
Kabardin	139	164	204
Estonian	155	142	989
Latvian	154	126	1,400
Lithuanian	42	32	2,236

[1] Frank Lorimer, *The Population of the Soviet Union: History and Prospects* (Geneva: League of Nations, 1946), pp. 208–209.

[2] Tsentral'noe Statisticheskoe Upravlenie, *Sorok let sovetskoi vlasti v tsifrakh* (Moscow: Gosstatizdat, 1957), p. 8.

[3] Tsentral'noe Statisticheskoe Upravlenie, *Narodnoe khoziaistvo SSSR v 1960 g.* (Moscow: Gosstatizdat, 1962), pp. 14 ff.

In 1937 Stalin estimated that the population of the Soviet Union was close to 180 million, but the actual census of 1937 revealed that the population had decreased instead of increased as a result of the 1932-1933 famine, purges, and the forced collectivism of agriculture (the birth rate declined even in the cities).[5] Because these facts were so startling, Stalin ordered the data destroyed and assigned another "census" in 1939.

The Soviets made various excuses—that the losses were due to the effects of war and revolution—without mentioning, of course, the post-revolutionary losses totaling 29 million people, an estimate based on the preceding prediction. From 1926-1939, again, the Soviets predicted 191 million people (by 1939), but the census showed only 170 million people, i.e., a loss of more than 20 million (see Appendix, Table 1).

In terms of ethnic distribution, the Russian communists tabulated all kinds of ethnic increases as compared to the Russians. For example, the Soviet data stated that the net reproduction ratio of Ukraine, 1924-1927, was 1.70 as compared to that in Leningrad of 1.11; and that the gross reproduction ratio in Ukraine urban areas was 2.773 (births per 1,000 women in the 15-49 age group) and in rural areas, 1.530, as compared to Moscow, 1.167. The question arises: How is it possible that Ukraine, having a "greater natural increase," lost a great number of its people during peaceful conditions while the population of the U.S.S.R. increased during the same period by 15.9 per cent and the population of Russia increased by 16.9 per cent?[6]

The status of the other Soviet nationalities, Slavic and non-Slavic, depended on the shift in Russian policies. The Poles, for instance, represented over 9 million people as of 1897, and after World War I, when Poland regained her independence, only 792 thousand remained in the Soviet Union. In January, 1939, the number of Poles dropped still further—626 thousand—indicating a ratio of only 0.719 from 1926 to 1939 while the ratio of the Russian people showed an increase of 1.273 (see Table 2). The Baltic nationalities, similar to the Ukrainians and Poles, witnessed a drastic change during the Soviet administration, as did the Finnish groups living in the territory of the RSFSR. The natural increase of the Estonian population was 1.7 per 1,000 in 1938 and 0.6 per 1,000 in 1940, Latvians, 4.9 in 1938 and 3.7 in 1940. The Finns,

---

[5]B. Wolfe, *Six Keys to the Soviet System* (Boston: The Beacon Press, 1956), p. 126.

[6]Institute for the Study of the USSR, *Reports on the Soviet Union in 1956* (Munich: Institute Press, 1961), pp. 48 ff.; Lorimer, *op. cit.*, pp. 89–92, 216; Kolarz, *Russia and Her Colonies*, p. 112.

besides their natural decrease as compared to the Russian increase, were displaced from their native lands and the Russian people were moved in. Mordvian ASSR in 1939, for instance, had 1.4 million people of which 785,000 were Russians; in Mari the population in 1939 was over 400,000 of which 40 per cent were Russians; Udmur ASSR had 42.3 per cent Russians; Karelia was over 70 per cent Russian; and the northern regions in general dropped their majority in favor of Russian population—from 56 per cent in 1926 to 35 per cent in 1935. When the Soviets captured Vilbrog, the second largest town in Finland, in 1940, 6,000 Russian families were brought to that city.

The central Asian nationalities did not escape the "new reforms" of the Kremlin on the redistribution of "unsympathetic" elements. Even *Pravda* admitted that during one year only, 1920, more than 1 million Kirghiz were killed by the Russian settlers in Turkestan. Sorokin, the secretary of Turkestan Soviets, stated:

> Everything is taken away from the Moslems, but not only that, our soldiers kill them, too. Instead of protecting them, they carry on the slaughter of the people still, and do many immoral things. The Moslem population is terrified in towns and villages, they try to escape ... The Moslem population asks for help from Russia, but we (Russians) reply that we do not trust them. Their women and children suffer and how can they like us? We make them nationalists.[7]

The population of Turkestan, using the imperial demarcation of the Turkestanian territory, was 5,221,936 as of 1920; by 1924 the population increased only to 5,254,000, an actual increase of 32,037. This increase might be still lower if other sets of complete data were available.

After the termination of the New Economic Policy (1928) and the introduction of forceful collectivization, the terror and liquidation of the opposition continued to an even larger extent. The Muslim population of central Asia met the same fate as the Ukrainians. Some sources indicate that during the famine of 1932-33 about 3 million Muslims of Turkestan died of starvation.

Another example of Soviet ethnic policies is noted in the data given by the 1926 and 1939 Soviet censuses of Kazakhstan. The 1926 population of the Kazakh SSR was 6.2 million, but dropped to 6.1 million in

---

[7]Mustafa Chokaev, *Turkestan pod vlastiu sovetov* (Paris: Iam Turkestan, 1935), p. 16; *Pravda*, June 20, 1920; *Foreign Policy Report*, February 1960; A. Ryskulov, *Revoliutsiia i korennoe naselenie Turkestana* (Tashkent: 1925), pp. 84 ff.; see also Wasyl Shimoniak, *A Study of the Soviet Educational Policies in Uzbekistan and Their Implications for Social and Educational Change* (Ann Arbor: Unpublished Ph. D. Dissertation, The University of Michigan, 1963), pp. 117 ff.

1939. The total number of Kazakhs living in the U.S.S.R. was 3,968,000 in 1926 and 3,099,000 in 1939, a 21.9 per cent decrease.

It is evident that the losses of non-Russian nationalities during the 'peaceful' times by far exceeded the losses of wars and revolutions. As an example, the *Basmachi* movements and their revolutionary uprisings between the years of 1920 and 1924 lost approximately 700,000 men (dead and wounded) and an additional 270,000 people were arrested or sent to Siberia during the post-revolutionary period, 1924-26.

As a result of the above policies, the Russian population increased from 77.7 million in 1926 and to 114 million in 1959;[8] and the Ukrainian population dropped from 33 million in 1926 to 28 million in 1939.

Deportation and Migration

The method of deportation, first of all, is the newest application of imperial power designed to get rid of undesirable elements. Such methods were applied by the imperial administration, but not on the scale the Russian communists used. Second, the Soviets initiated the policy of industrialization in the 1920s, and one of the least expensive industrial investments was the investment of human capital (free labor). These laborers were deprived of medical care, housing and sufficient food, which resulted in a massive death rate among the deported prisoners.

There was also another kind of deportation designed to separate a given nationality from its culture, language and traditional ways of life cherished by ethnic groups. Many families in the western parts of the Soviet Union—Ukrainians, Poles, Baltic people—were deported to places like Kazakhstan, Eastern Siberia, or Sakhalin, making it impossible for them to educate their children in their own languages and traditions which *ipso facto* contributed to the "natural" increase of the Russian population.

The difference between family deportation and individual deportation is that the first method followed the old principle of Russification, that of relocating ethnic groups in such regions as Siberia or Mongolia. Those who were deported individually were placed in slave-labor camps and were entirely at the mercy of the Russian administrators of these camps.

The number of Ukrainians living outside their ethnographic terri-

---

[8] Akademiia Nauk UzSSR, *Istoriia sovetskogo gosudarstva i prava Uzbekistana* (Tashkent: AN UzSSR, 1960), pp. 37, 187; for further information see Baymirza Hayit, *Turkestan im XX. Jahrhundert* (Darmstadt: W. Leske Verlag, 1956), pp. 264–281; Olaf Caroe, *Soviet Empire: The Turks of Central Asia and Stalinism* (London: Macmillan Co., 1953), pp. 163–167.

tory illustrates the point: well over a million live in the Kazakh SSR; very nearly another million in Western Siberia; half a million in the lower Volga regions; and three and a half million in northern Caucasus. From 1926-1939, the cities of Vinnitsia and Poltava lost 15 per cent of their population, but the percentage of Ukrainians in Siberia increased to 33 per cent.

More important, however, is the population redistribution and the ratio of increase between Russian and non-Russian nationalities. As we can see from Table 5, the population increase in Siberia and the northern regions of the U.S.S.R. is much higher, proportionately, than that of the European parts of the Soviet Union. It is not likely that people of the European regions, Ukraine, Belorussia, and the Baltic states, would voluntarily migrate to places that have no cultural attractions nor climatic conditions suitable for their development. As Table 3 indicates, the number of Russian and non-Russian settlers from European parts of the empire increased steadily. In 1897, for example, there were 640,432 Russian settlers in the territories of Turkestan and the Steppe—out of the total population of 7.7 million; and by 1911 the number of European settlers increased to nearly 2 million. In the whole of Asiatic Russia, as it was called at that time, the number of Russians and non-Russians from European parts of the country increased to 9,090,294. (See also Table 3.)

The so-called virgin land of Kazakhstan lost 21 per cent of its own people by 1939, but gained 25 per cent of the Russian and Ukrainian settlers by 1959. The Soviet sources explain this by saying that the population of the western regions of the U.S.S.R., primarily of the Ukraine, Belorussia and the Baltic states lost population during the period of 1939-1959 'because of the poor harvest,' and that part of the U.S.S.R., Belorussia, for instance "is still behind the pre-war figures of the Belorussian population."[9]

---

[9]There were various methods used by the Communists to liquidate the opposing population. Beside the artificial famine in Ukraine, the Russian Communists used tortures of various kinds. For example, in Vinnitsa (1938–39) more than 12,000 people have been murdered. The graves discovered showed that 9,439 people were shot and buried in 95 separate graves and 1,390 in another 14 graves. Also in 1939, more than 12,000 people were murdered in one prison of Lvov; 5,000 were burned alive in Kharkov; over 5,000 murdered in Chortkiv, 752 in Solochiv, 4,500 in Stri and Uman and many other places. See Ukrainian Congress Committee of America, *Massacre in Vinnitsa* (New York: The Ukrainian Congress Committee Press, 1953), pp. 3–10; *Russischer Kolonialismus in der Ukraine: Berichte und Dokumente* (Munich: Ukrainischer Verlag, 1962), pp. 48–149. Note that parts of this section have been printed by the Committee on the Judiciary in Special Series, No. 17 (B), House of Representatives, Washington, D. C., 1964. Testimony was given by Dr. Lev Dobrianskyj and the section of testimony, The Population of Russia-U.S.S.R., 1897–1959, was written by the author of this book.

TABLE 3
Distribution of Population in Turkestan: 1897–1911

Oblast'	1897 Total Population Male	Total Population Female	Total	Of which Russians	1911 Total Population	Of which Russians
Zakaspeisk	212,638	169,849	382,487	33,273	472,500	41,671
Urban	31,305	10,572	41,877	21,724	68,871	27,176
Rural	181,333	159,277	340,610	11,549	403,629	14,495
Syr-Dar'ia	803,411	674,987	1,478,398	44,834	1,816,550	103,500
Urban	117,259	88,337	205,596	25,789	319,267	66,982
Rural	686,152	586,650	1,272,802	19,045	1,497,283	36,518
Samarkand	472,443	387,578	860,021	14,006	960,202	22,929
Urban	75,289	60,024	135,313	10,530	179,352	16,783
Rural	397,154	327,554	724,708	3,476	780,850	6,146
Fergana	852,919	719,295	1,572,214	9,842	2,041,900	34,200
Urban	158,189	126,169	284,358	9,168	384,612	16,565
Rural	694,730	593,126	1,287,856	674	1,657,288	17,635
Semirechie	529,215	458,648	987,863	95,465	1,201,540	204,307
Urban	35,291	27,683	62,974	28,730	100,392	49,868
Rural	493,924	430,965	924,889	66,735	1,101,148	154,439
Total for Turkestan	2,870,626	2,410,357	5,280,983	197,420	6,492,692	406,607
Urban	417,333	312,785	730,118	95,941	1,052,494	177,374
Rural	2,453,293	2,097,572	4,550,865	101,479	5,440,198	229,233
Total for Turkestan and Steppe	4,164,551	3,582,167	7,746,718	640,432	10,327,033	1,950,112
Urban	525,070	409,300	934,370	240,289	1,423,099	459,159
Rural	3,639,481	3,172,867	6,812,348	450,143	8,903,934	1,490,953

Pereselencheskoe Upravlenie Zemleustroistva i Zemledeliia, *Aziatskaia Rossiia, liudi i poriadki za Uralom* (St. Petersburg: Tipografia A. F. Marksa, 1914), vol. 1, p. 87.

Slave Labor. It is difficult to give precise data on the number of people in the slave-labor camps since Soviets do not list the number of people deported to these camps. Some sources, however, give the following figure for persons deported to Siberia for slave labor: In 1930, the number of people in concentration camps amounted to 1.5 million; 1932, 2.5 million; 1936, 6.5 million; 1938, 11.5 million; and 1941, 13.5 million. Kravchenko, in a book *I Chose Freedom,* estimated that the number of prisoners in the slave labor camps was about 15 million in 1938. Stalin himself told Sir Winston Churchill that more than 10 million families were "dealt with" during the period of forceful collectivization.

In short, a consideration of Soviet demographic data, even though the number of people killed, liquidated or deported is not listed, shows that the most populated areas of the Russian empire (1897)—Ukraine, Baltic regions and western parts of Belorussia—have decreased in expected population (e.g., western Ukraine as much as 20 per cent). The Far Eastern regions, the subarctic regions and Siberia increased as much as 100 per cent or more by 1940 (see Tables 4 and 5). Such a condition can be explained only by the genocide designed by the communists to conquer the opposition.

The Zig-Zag Techniques. From the theoretical point of view, the Soviet Union is a union of fifteen republics and its government is the government of workers and peasants. If a western reader studies the Soviet laws and the Soviet Constitution, he can find nothing wrong with the written form. These constitutions promise more than any constitution, per se. These are clauses in the Soviet Constitution that imply separatism, such as the complete independence of a nationality, its fully-independent internal and external structure, the secession from the union of any republic at any time, complete linguistic and religious freedom, freedom of speech, etc. In practice, however, no republic has been able to separate itself from the union.

The communists initiated an entirely new administrative division of the empire. The old system disappeared together with the czarist regime. The *guberniia,* regardless of their location—in Russia or the territories occupied by the Russians like central Asia or Poland—had one motto: "Russia is for the Russians and the language in school must be Russian." The Bolsheviks, on the other hand, promised full cultural self-determination in all areas.

In 1917, Lenin said to all the people inhabiting the old Russian empire "on our banners we bring liberation to all the people . . ." but as soon as these banners entered a given country, the old policy of terror

TABLE 4

Total Population Change: U.S.S.R., 1897–1926 and 1926–1939[1]
(In Thousands)

Area	1897	1926	Redistribution Increment (+) or Decrement (−)	
			1897–1926	1926–1939
USSR	106,070	147,028	..	..
European Part, except Ural,				
Bashkir, but inc. Dagestan . .	78,739	105,459	−3,684	−5,258
Belorussia	3,722	4,983	−176	−209
Ukraine[2]	21,246	29,043	−407	−2,712
Central Black Soil	9,328	12,667	−263	−2,576
Western	4,801	6,275	−380	−1,372
Old Industrial Area	12,201	16,704	−208	+2,666
Northern (Leningrad				
Karelia-Murmansk) . .	5,985	7,754	−542	+1,388
Viatka & Tatar	6,222	7,161	−1,462	−279
Central Volga	6,666	8,600	−639	−1,903
Lower Volga & Don	3,689	5,203	+89	−629
Crimea	524	714	−12	+299
North Caucasus &				
Dagestan	4,355	6,354	+316	+69
Transcaucasus	4,493	5,872	−356	+1,227
Ural, Bashkir and				
Asiatic RSFSR	12,702	22,026	+4,419	+3,257
Ural & Bashkir	6,951	9,508	−127	+1,194
West Siberia	3,361	7,612	+2,953	+83
Central Siberia	1,073	2,340	+853	+514
East Siberia	968	1,325	−17	+567
Far East	349	1,241	+757	+899
Kazakhstan	4,248	6,074	+186	−897
Central Asia	5,888	7,597	−565	+1,671

[1] Frank Lorimer, *The Population of the Soviet Union: History and Prospects* (Geneva: League of Nations, 1946), p. 170.

[2] This figure is very low because the Soviet statistical publications did not include over five million Ukrainians who perished during the famine, 1932–1933 (see *Russischer Kolonialismus in der Ukraine, Berichte und Dokumente*, Munich: Ukrainischer Verlag, 1962), p. 37; also, Ukrainians represent more than 33% of the total population of Siberia, and over 60% in the North Caucasus (see Walter Kolarz, *Russia and Her Colonies*, London: George Philip & Son, 1952), p. 126.

TABLE 5

Changes in the Distribution of the Soviet Population,
1940–1959

Area	Population in Millions		Change in Per cent
	Estimate, End of 1940	Census Jan. 1959	1940 to 1959
U.S.S.R.: Total	191,80	208,80	+9.0
Baltic States & Belorussia	15,13	14,67	−3.0
Russian SFSR (excluding			
Kaliningrad Oblast)	108,39	116,88	+8.0
Valdai Region	7,19	4,63	−36.0
Subarctic Region	2,18	3,30	+51.0
Central Industrial Area	18,39	20,54	+12.0
South (Mordva ASSR, etc.) . . .	19,95	16,25	−16.0
NE Urals	6,42	10,03	+56.0
SW Siberia	5,75	6,60	+15.0
NW Siberia	0,15	0,34	+127.0
Central Siberia	7,12	9,76	+37.0
Eastern Siberia	2,80	3,32	+13.0
Far Eastern Region	1,84	3,55	+176.0
Rostov Oblast'	3,09	3,31	+7.0
Ukraine and Moldavia	43,53	44,86	+3.0
NE Ukraine (Kharkiv, etc.) . . .	7,93	7,21	−9.0
Vinnitsa Oblast'	2,29	2,14	−7.0
Odessa Oblast'	2,10	2,03	−3.0
Western Ukraine	10,31	9,43	−17.0
Moldavian SSR	2,50	2,88	+12.0
Transcaucasus	8,06	9,52	+18.0
Kazakh SSR	6,10	9,30	+52.0
Central Asia	10,53	13,68	+30.0

Calculated from: Demitri B. Shimkin, "Demographic Changes and Socio-Economic Forces within the Soviet Union, 1939–1959," in *Population Trends in Eastern Europe, the USSR and Mainland China* (New York: Milbank Memorial Fund, 1960), pp. 247–253. Note: Not all provinces of the Soviet Union are included. For further information see Shimkin, *Ibid.*, pp. 224–258.

and Russification would take place. In central Asia, for example, the natives believed the Bolshevik slogans of 1917 and cooperated with the communists at first. But by 1918, the Russian communists took over all the important positions in the government and destroyed those natives who opposed the new order. The Red terror, acknowledged by recent Soviet sources, became evident.[10] Although Lenin said in his speeches that any unification of two nations would be valid only if it is voluntary, this voluntary union was shaped by the same Lenin who said "we do not have to be sorry for it (terror) or to give it up," because to give up terror would mean to give up power—and the Bolsheviks would not hesitate to use terror again if it became necessary.

On June 25, 1918, Lenin signed a declaration of self-determination for each nationality of the union. This declaration promised to any ethnic group complete independence if it would support the communist regime of Lenin and his government. Since the Russian nationalities were disillusioned with previous promises, they were reluctant to act on Lenin's proposal. Lenin then found it necessary to promise more than an autonomous or cultural way of life; he invented another proposal— independent republics bound by nothing except the communist ideology. This propaganda had a better effect. Revolutionary groups that were fighting each other began to change their position about the war against the Soviets. Officially, the Union of Soviet Socialist Republics was established in December 1922, and in 1968, was comprised of fifteen republics.

Administrative Changes. Several so-called republics appeared and disappeared during the Soviet rule, e.g., the Tadzhik people were under the Uzbek administrative division until 1930; from 1930 on they were told they were an independent Tadzhik SSR. German and Tatar independent Soviet republics disappeared before World War II; Karelo-Finnish SSR decided to join the Russian SFSR in 1956 after having enough of "independent" SSR; thus the number of republics was reduced to the present number—fifteen (see Table 6).

The division of Turkestan into five separate republics had an important politico-international significance because the Russians neutralized any internal or external efforts of the Muslim people to unite themselves

---

[10]Winston Churchill, *The Second World War*, vol. IV (London: 1951), pp. 447–448; Leonard Schapiro, *The Communist Party of the Soviet Union* (New York: Random House Press, 1960), p. 385; The World Federation of Ukrainians, Former Political Prisoners and Victims of the Soviet Regime, *The Black Deeds of the Kremlin: The Great Famine in Ukraine, 1932–1933* (Detroit: Dobrus Press, 1955), vol. II, *passim.*

TABLE 6

Population of the U.S.S.R. by Republics: 1965
(Numbers in Thousands)

Republic	Area in km²	Population	Capital	No. of People
USSR—Total	22,402,2	230,508	Moscow	6,384
Russian SFSR	17,075,4	126,229	Moscow	6,384
Ukrainian SSR	601,0	45,300	Kiev	1,348
Belorussian SSR	207,6	8,570	Minsk	717
Uzbek SSR	449,6	10,300	Tashkent	1,106
Kazakh SSR	2,715,1	11,985	Alma-Ata	623
Georgian SSR	69,7	4,515	Tiblis	812
Azerbaidzhanian SSR	86,6	4,590	Baku	1,147
Latvian SSR	65,2	2,967	Vilno	298
Moldavian SSR	33,7	3,326	Kishinev	282
Lithuanian SSR	63,7	2,247	Riga	658
Kirghiz SSR	198,5	2,609	Frunze	360
Tadzhik SSR	143,1	2,535	Dushanbe	316
Armenian SSR	29,8	2,164	Erevan	633
Turkmenian SSR	488,1	1,893	Ashkhabad	226
Estonian SSR	45,1	1,278	Tallin	330

Tsentraal'noe Statisticheskoe Upravelenie pri Sovete Ministrov SSSR, *Narodnoe Khoziaistvo SSSR v 1964 g.* (Moscow: Gosstatizdat, 1965), p. 783.

into one Turco-Islamic state. Stalin said in 1924 that this division was of the utmost importance and praised the Bolsheviks for finding the key to ethnic and national dissolution. The communist union, said Stalin, was a voluntary union and "in order to unite Poland, the bourgeoisie required a few revolutionary wars; in order to unite Turkmenia and Uzbekistan the Bolsheviks required only a few months of explanatory propaganda."[11] He, of course, did not mention that more than 3 million Turkestanians were killed before this "voluntary" union was established.

In theory each Soviet republic has a constitution, its own laws, etc., but in practice all major decisions are settled in Moscow. Even economic and educational problems are decided in Moscow and executed in local districts or republics. In theory, each republic can also have its own army and diplomatic missions, but in practice, again, all these functions

[11]Akademmia Obshcheobrazovatel'nykh Nauk pri TsKP of the Soviet Union, *O programe KPSS* (Moscow: VPS i AON, 1961), p. 358; V. I. Lenin, *Sochineniia* (Moscow: Gospolitizdat, 1952), vol. XIV, p. 146, vol. XXII, p. 314, vol. XXV, p. 38, vol. XXVII, p. 194.

belong to the Russian SFSR. Only two Soviet republics, Ukraine and Belorussia, have puppet representatives in the United Nations. All others are represented by the Russians.

There are three main types of economic administration: higher, middle, and lower. The educational structure and administrative division will be described in a later chapter.

OTHER COMMUNIST COUNTRIES

As Table 7 indicates, there are over 1 billion people living under the communist regime. This equals 35 per cent of the total population of the globe.

World War II ended very favorably for the Soviet Union since its borders expanded far into western European regions and occupied the Japanese lands of Sakhalin, part of Manchuria, and all the surrounding islands. All of this happened while England lost her colonies and the

TABLE 7

Distribution of the Population in Communist Countries
(Numbers in Thousands)

Country	Area in km²	Year	Population	Capital	No. of People
Albania	28,7	1963	1,762	Tirana	152
Bulgaria	110,9	1965	8,206	Sofia	822
China	9,597,0	1957	656,630	Peking	4,010
Cuba	114,5	1965	7,630	Havana	2,024
Czechoslovakia	127,9	1964	14,107	Prague	1,020
East Germany	108,3	1964	17,012	Berlin	E.B.1,071
Hungary	93,0	1965	10,135	Budapest	1,900
Mongolia	1,565,0	1963	1,050	Ulan-Bator	239
North Korea	121,2	1965	11,568	Pyongyong	495
Poland	312,5	1964	31,339	Warsaw	1,241
Rumania	237,5	1965	18,980	Bukarest	1,239
Soviet Union	22,402,2	1965	230,508	Moscow	6,384
Vietnam-North	159,0	1963	17,850	Hanoi	1,096
Yugoslavia	56,0	1965	19,393	Belgrad	960

Tsentral'noe Statisticheskoe Upravlenie pri Sovete Ministrov SSSR, *Narodnoe Khoziaistvo SSSR v 1964 g.* (Moscow: Gosstatizdat, 1965), pp. 782–793. Note that there are 1,046,170,000 people under the communist rule while the population of the whole world is 3.2 billion of which 621 million live in Europe; 1.9 billion in Asia; 276 million in Africa; 442 million in America (in North America there are 285 million and in South America 157 million); Australia and other Pacific countries (not including Philippines and Indonesia) 19 million. *Op. cit.*, p. 781.

United States maintained a status quo. The China of today has a population of over 700 million, which represents a threat not only to Christian civilization but to the Soviet Union as well.

The Soviet satellites are semi-independent nations in economic terms but completely dependent on the Kremlin from the political and military point of view. All major political and military decisions are not decided in Prague, Budapest, Warsaw or other capitals, but in Moscow.

The Slavic people are truly united; not a single Slavic nation is outside Russian domination. Today there are 114 million Russians living in the Soviet Union, 37 million Ukrainians, 10 million Belorussians, and outside the Soviet Union there are 14 million Czecho-Slovaks, 19 million southern Slavs (Serbians, Croations, Slovenians, Macedonians), 29 million Poles and 7 million Bulgarians totaling over 230 million Slavic people under the communist regime (see Table 7).

Additional References

Some important sources concerning the Russian occupation of Central Asia are: L. F. Kostenko, *Turkestanskii krai*, vol. I (St. Petersburg: Tipografiia Transbeliia, 1880), pp. 400–450; O. Olufsen, *The Emir of Bukhara and his Country* (London: W. Heinemann, 1911), pp. 268–352; Tolstov, S. P., and Others, *Narody Srednei Azii i Kazakhstana* (Moscow: AN SSSR, 1962), *passim.;* Mary Holdsworth, *Turkestan in the 19th Century: A Brief History of the Khanates of Bukhara, Kokand and Khiva* (Oxford: ʼSt. Antonyʼs College Press, 1959), pp. 33–35; Geofrey Wheeler, *Racial Problems in Soviet Muslim Asia* (London: Oxford University Press, 1960), *passim.;* Emanual Sarakisyanz, *Geschichte der Orientalischen Voelker* (Munich: R. Oldenbourg Verlag, 1961), pp. 200–210.

Important sources concerning the ethnic composition of the Soviet Union are: L. V. Oshanin, *Antropologicheskii sostav naseleniia Srednei Azii i etnogenez ee narodoy* (Erevan: Eravanskii Universitet, 1957), pp. 16–59; S. A. Tokarev, *Etnografiia narodov SSSR: istoricheskie osnovy byta i kyl'tury* (Moscow: Izdat. Moskovskogo Universiteta, 1958), pp. 30–351; S. A. Tokarev, S. P. Tolstov, *Podrevnym del'tam Oksa i Iaksarta* (Moscow: Izdat. Vostochnoi Literatury, 1959), pp. 47–294; V. V. Bartold, *Turkestan Down to the Mongol Invasion* (London: Oxford University Press, 1928), pp. 1–14; N. G. Bakabov, and Others, *Istoriia uzbekskoi SSR,* vol. I (Tashkent: Akademiia Nauk UzSSR, 1956), *passim.*

One of the best sources describing the methods of the Russian Communist policies in regard to the people of the USSR is the book by B. Iakovlev, *Kontsentratsionnye lageri SSSR* (Concentration Camps of the USSR) (Munich: Institute for the Study of the USSR, 1955), *passim.* Not only are the methods described in the above book but also exact location (with maps) of the concentration camps and the number of people in them. See also *Russische Kolonialismus, passim,* especially p. 317; Akademiia Pedagogicheskikh Nauk RSFSR, N. Bakaev (ed.), *Natsional'ney shkoly RSFSR* (Moscow: Izdat. APN RSFSR, 1961), p. 304; Akademiia Obshchestvennykh Nauk pri TsKKP, *Lenin o druzhbe s narodami vostoka* (Moscow: Gospolitizdat, 1961), pp. 261–263; Akademiia Obshchestvennykh Nauk, Kafedra istorii KPSS, *Lenin i nekotorye voprosy stroitel'stva partii* (Moscow: Gospolitizdat, 1961), p. 108; see also Wasyl Shimoniak, "Bolshevism in Turkestan," in *The Ukrainian Quarterly,* vol. XXII, no. 4, pp. 351 ff.

Chapter 2

SCHOOL AND SOCIETY
BEFORE 1917

In Russia general cultural enlightenment took place somewhat later than in other European countries. Historically, no data are available on the status of cultural activities before the acceptance of Christianity, but there is good reason to believe that eastern Europe was far behind the cultural accomplishments of the early Greco-Roman civilization. In Ukraine, especially in the Kievan principality, some excellent attempts were made to introduce a solid Christian educational system based on the accomplishments of the West as well as the accomplishments of the Kievan princes, particularly Vladimir the Great and Yaroslav the Wise (Yaroslav Mudrii). However, all efforts were heavily influenced by two forces: the Mongol invasion and the struggle among the princes.

During the Mongol invasion, the people of the Moscovite principality came out much better than the rest of the Slavic peoples. The Mongols put the Moscovites in charge of tax collections and the maintenance of order among other principalities. In the cultural area, of course, little was done to raise the level of education. Only after the Mongol invasion were initial steps taken to build an educational system.

KIEVAN WINDOW TO EUROPE

The Kievan principality from its very beginning kept in constant contact with the West and purposely avoided any dogmatic quarrels evident elsewhere in western Europe. Marriages between the Kievan royal families and the royal families of western Europe included those of France, England and Hungary. Cultural development took place in a very similar manner. Kievan culture was traditionally attached to Byzantine culture but intellectually oriented toward Latin Europe. This was unique in the Byzantine sphere since the Moscovite principalities purposely kept away from any western European cultural penetration.

In Ukraine the shaping of cultural history, which the dynasty of Rurik initiated, took a somewhat different path since cultural development was shifted from Kiev to Halich—a Volynian principality, which later united with the Ukrainian-Lithuanian state. Thus it had nothing in common with the dynasty of Romanovs and the development of Russian culture via Kiev-Moscow. It should be clear that the development of East-European culture went through Kiev, Halich and Lvov. Only after these steps did the Moscovite development follow. The Ukrainian scholars, keeping in mind cultural opportunities in western Europe, were able to go to Italy, France and several other countries to study and learn Latin culture, e.g., in 1481, Yurij Drohobitski, a Ukrainian, was rector of the famous Bologna University and in 1483 he published a scientific work on astronomic problems and the development of astronomy to that time.[1]

The fifteenth century was also a century of religious diplomacy, i.e., an endeavor was made to unite two Christian churches which had been separated by the Photian schism. The union of churches also played an important part in the cultural enlightenment since for the first time a significant effort was made to elevate the cultural level of eastern Christians to that of western Christians. Through the unification of churches, the Slavs from the East had direct contact with more culturally advanced Slavic groups, namely the Czechs and Moravians. There are no exact data on the extent of these cultural relations between the western and eastern Slavs, but the fact is that in 1457 the Czechs established an important educational system, the Moravian Brothers. This group was designed by Chelcicky to prevent a Germanification of the Czech people and to raise the educational standards of the Czech-

---

[1]*Zhovten'* (October, a Journal of Social and Literary Affairs in Ukrainian), No. 2, 1965, p. 147 (Lvov).

Moravian nation. Here it is important to note that in Ukraine similar schools (known as the Brotherhood Schools—*Bratskie shkoly*) were established and played an important part in the development of the Ukrainian and the Russian educational system.

These schools were located at the monasteries as in the West, but the important thing was not their location but the ideas and the structure under which they developed. These schools were in some ways different from those of western Europe because the language of the school was not Latin but Church-Slavonic, the language of the Greek Orthodox religion.

The Brotherhood Schools were established in the Western Ukraine at a time when it was under Polish domination. Because of religious and political differences between the Poles and the Ukrainians and since the union of Florence had not been successful, in 1595 a second endeavor, known as the Union of Brest, was made to unite the two churches.

There were several reasons for the union beside the obvious religious goals. First, in Poland there was always a danger of Turkish invasion. Second, the Ukrainian Orthodox clergy felt somewhat inferior since the political power was in Roman Catholic hands. It was believed that the unification of the two churches would also strengthen the cultural position of the Ukrainians and give them educational opportunities equal to those of the Poles.

THE ACADEMY OF PETER MOHYLA

Having been motivated by the religious spirit, the Ukrainian clergy took another look at the differences between the two Christian churches. Among other things, they could see that the educational level in the western European schools was far beyond that of their own country. The Moscovite principality had little to offer since the Moscovites were engaged in wars conquering Siberia and other regions and were doing very little in the area of education.

The most important person in the development of education at that time in Ukraine and Russia was the metropolitan of Kiev, Peter Mohyla. Mohyla, contrary to other reformers, began to build the educational system on the basis of the Jesuit schools. His *Weltanschauung* (world outlook) was based on the philosophy of St. Thomas. Meanwhile the other Orthodox nation, Russia, was trying to reject any Catholic influence upon its schools and society. Of particular interest were two bishops, Nikon and Avacuum, who wanted to modernize not the educational system but the Orthodox religion per se. The story of these two bishops was overly publicized—in reality they had nothing to offer the cultural enlightenment of the Russian people.

The Kievan metropolitan attracted distinguished teachers by means of a new educational system. He also sent promising new scholars and teachers abroad for the continuation of their academic studies. Many of these students accepted Catholicism while they were in Europe and went back to Orthodoxy when they returned. The metropolitan allowed this practice since the Jesuit schools of that time did not admit non-Catholics to higher educational institutions.

Mohyla also began to change the curriculum of the Brotherhood schools. He introduced scientific subjects and the Jesuit philosophy while keeping the basic tenets of the Orthodoxy. After these steps were achieved, the metropolitan began to work on the foundations of an academy. Success was realized in 1633 when the first institution of higher learning was established in Kiev. The academy was soon recognized by the Polish king, Wladyslaw IV, as an equal to Polish universities.

As mentioned before, Mohyla established the academy on the basis of the Jesuit educational practices and also wrote the most important book on the principles of the Orthodox religion, known as the *Orthodox Confession*. He met some opposition to his theories, but he realized that the West could not be fought with ignorance. He emphasized that the East must first learn what the Western schools, in particular the Jesuit schools, had accomplished. It was this stimulus that motivated the metropolitan and other cultural leaders of Kiev to write and translate Latin books into Church-Slavonic, thus giving a sound foundation to a modern culture for that time. During the period of 1635-1643, eleven books were published, each containing from 500 to 1,000 pages.

The curriculum of the academy was divided into four areas of study: (1) languages—Old-Slavonic, Latin, Polish and German; (2) philosophy —including logic, rhetoric, and dialectics; (3) natural philosophy— physics, mathematics and chemistry; (4) metaphysics—concentrating upon the study of the Bible, the works of church fathers and the philosophy of Greek and Roman scholars—chiefly Aristotle, Plato and Quintilian.

Thus, the Kievan Academy became the first higher educational institution in eastern Europe, and the city of Kiev became the cultural center for the Eastern Slavs. In 1654 a treaty was signed between the Ukrainian hetman, Bohdan Klmelnitski, and the Russian czar, Aleksi, whereby Ukraine became a federate state of the Moscovite principality. The treaty of 1654 was important because the cultural acquisitions of Kiev were taken by Moscow.

The Kievan Academy did not lock itself within the walls of a monastery. On the contrary, it became a cultural platform for many areas of Ukrainian life. The students, especially during vacations, participated in social programs and often gave theatrical performances dealing with various aspects of human life. The founder of the academy, Mohyla, stated: "I have decided to establish a school where not only religious subjects will be taught but also the liberal arts." Thus the general orientation of scholastic and intellectual endeavors took a different position than was usual. We can find many examples during this period where the metropolitan tried to improve social conditions or tried to change the legal system (laws, civil procedures of the time) in order to educate those who were willing to be educated.

Mohyla also took an important step toward the re-union of the two churches and kept in constant contact with Rome (Pope Urban VI) hoping to unite the two Christian religions.

Finally, the academy attempted to establish a scientific foundation for Slavic studies. The first study successfully finished and published was the *Lexicon of Slavic Affairs,* a book which became a prime reference source not only in the Slavic world but in the non-Slavic as well. There is no question that the Russians benefited from this academy; many Russian scholars acknowledge this fact.[2]

STUDENTS OF MOHYLA AND PETER I

After the death of Mohyla and the annexation of Ukraine to Russia, the Kievan Academy played a most important role in establishment of the higher educational system in Russia. Two students of the Kievan Academy, S. Polotski and T. Prokopovich, helped Peter the Great estab-

---

[2]Wasyl Shimoniak, *Reforms of Peter Mohyla* (Milwaukee: Marquette University Press, Slavic Institute Papers, No. 20, 1965), pp. 1–20. See also E. N. Medynski, *Bratskie shkoly Ukrainy i Belorussii* (Moscow: Akademiia Nauk RSFSR, 1954), pp. 8ff.; V. Z. Smirnov, *Khrestomatiia po istorii pedagogiki* (Moscow: Gospedizdat, 1961), pp. 278ff.; H. E. Johnson, *Russia's Educational Heritage* (Pittsburgh: Congress Press, 1950), pp. 3–20,; A. Jablonowski, *Akademija Kijowsko-Mohylanska* (Krakow: 1900), passim.; Akademiia Nauk UkSSR, *Istoriia Kieva* (Kiev: AN UkSSR, 1960), pp. 160ff.; M. Hrushevskyj, *Istoriia Ukrainy,* Vol. 6 (New York: Knyhospilka, 1955), p. 314.; Teofie Ionesco, *La vie et l'oeuvre de Pierre Movila* (Paris: 1944), passim; Mirchuk, *Geschichte der Ukrainischen Kultur* (Munich: Isar Verlag, 1958), pp. 17–70.; V. V. Vinogradov, *Velikii russkii iazyk* (Moscow: Ogiz, 1945), p. 74.

lish an institute in Moscow to which was transferred the knowledge acquired at Kiev. The means of transforming the Kievan culture to Moscow were typical of Peter I. He used persuasion, voluntary actions, force—all that could help elevate the cultural level of the Moscovite kingdom. When Peter I won the battle at Poltava in 1709, most of the cultural institutions were forced to work for the Petrovian reforms. Scholars enrolled in the task included the following: Filalet, Yavorski, Lopatinski, Kopistenski and Rostovski. There were many others whose mission was to help Russia build a so-called Third Rome.

The epoch of Peter I is generally described as the era of Europeanization of Russia and a massive colonization of the Baltic and Eastern regions of the empire. Peter I was quite interested in science and education of all kinds. He went abroad, himself, and invited many European scholars to come to Russia to establish the initial stages of the Russian enlightenment. He organized elementary and secondary education in all major urban centers as well as military academies of many kinds and laid the foundation of higher education in Russia.

As mentioned before, Polotski was one of the most important educational reformers in Moscow. Although his methods were not exciting, they were new. He proposed a tri-level educational structure: (1) the child should be educated as early as possible in his native language; (2) he should be taught about his natural surroundings next and this should be mastered during the period from seven to fourteen years of age; (3) he should learn fear before God, as Polotski called it, which should be the highest category of education and this should be a continuous process. He believed that religio-philosophical topics could not be learned in terms of time intervals since one should never stop studying supernatural values.

In 1697, with the help of the previously mentioned men, Peter I established the Greco-Russian-Latin Institute, designed to study other cultures and disciplines, which became the first Russian higher educational establishment. In 1701, Peter I further established the Mathematical-Navigational Research Institute and invited many foreign scholars to teach in Russia. In 1725, one year after his death, the Academy of Sciences was established in Moscow, the first such institution in the world.

To enforce his reforms, Peter I used a variety of methods. He did not hesitate to use force on anyone or any organization. When the clergy opposed his ideas, he forced the entire Orthodox Church to obey his rules. He thus put an end to a free democratic religious Synod and directed the subordination of the Orthodox Church to the state's autocratic rule. He was excommunicated by the Orthodox Church and pronounced anti-Christ. As an example of his dealings with the Church, Peter I forbade marriage licenses to those who did not learn how to read and write. No priest was allowed to witness a marriage contract involving illiterate parties or to seek any further recourse on their part. In reality, however, this rule was never implemented.

CULTURAL DEVELOPMENT IN MOSCOW AFTER PETER I

The decision of Peter I to subordinate the Orthodox Church under political rule had its consequences on freedom of religion and equally affected the devolopment of Russian education. Most European educational systems of that time were religiously oriented and most of the early discoveries were the fruits of monastery schooling.

During the reign of Catherine II, extensive pressure was placed on all cultural establishments to serve as informer-type of institutions, i.e., the duty of every teacher was to report to the authorities any anti-governmental act or teaching against the empire. There were various discriminations, e.g., a special law was passed prohibiting any Ukrainian language publications. The Ukrainians were not even allowed to sing songs in Ukrainian.

Since the religious schools of the Holy Synod were under state jurisdiction any attempt to separate the school from political influences was very dangerous. The children were educated on the premise that God and czar are equally significant and that the czar was sent by God to rule over the people. Those religious leaders who tried to change the conditions of the church were persecuted in a similar manner as the two previously mentioned bishops, Nikon and Avacuum.[3]

Still another barrier of Russian cultural development was the language problem in Russia itself. The aristocracy and the religious leaders believed that plain Russian should not be used in literature or any area of higher intellectual endeavor. Michael Lomonosov was the first man in Moscow to write a Russian grammar which was known as the Grammar of the Three Styles (*Gramatika trekh stilei*). Lomonosov's grammar was actually based on Smotritski's grammar, a Kievan product of the Mohylian Academy.

Russian literature did, however, play an important part in the general development of Russian culture and education. Although in the be-

---

[3] N. A. Konstantinov; E. N. Medynski, *Istoriia pedagogiki* (Moscow: AN SSSR, 1959), p. 66; I. I. Shchipanov (ed.), *Russkie prosvititeli ot Radishcheva do dekabristov* (Moscow: Izdatel'stvo "Mysl," 1966), pp. 217ff.

ginning of the eighteenth century this literature represented the upper classes of society and was basically foreign-oriented, it did produce some initial works in the Russian language. Translation and imitation of other literary products was probably the most important achievement during the period of the eighteenth century. For instance, Trediakovski translated Fenelon's *Telemague,* Sumarokov translated German literary works, Khersakov wrote *Rossiada* imitating *Henriada* of Voltaire, Bogdanovich literally copied LaFontaine's *Psyche et Cupidon.*

As we can see there were no important educational philosophies during the seventeenth and the early part of the eighteenth centuries. Russian schools depended on other areas of cultural endeavors, such as literature, political writings and some general ideas stated by men like Lomonosov, Sumarokov or Derzhavin. Literary people, as well as progressive intelligentsia, saw the main evil of Russian misery in the educational system of that time. Simultaneously they demanded more extensive efforts on the part of the government to improve the cultural level of the Russian people. It was a general belief that the Russian aristocracy was not really bad and the only thing needed was educational reform which presumably would change their attitudes toward the other classes of society.

THE RUSSIAN ENLIGHTENMENT

Before Alexander I (1801), Russian educational and cultural thought more or less existed on borrowed culture. The problem was not only that education was designed for a special class, but that in Russia, education for even the select did not produce sufficient results. Until the end of the nineteenth century we find four types of educational planning: (1) education for agricultural needs—the poorest in all respects; (2) education for vocational trades—primarily concentrated in industrial centers rather provincial in character; (3) education for nobility—well supported and organized; and (4) education for religious purposes—strictly Greek Orthodox in its context.

Very little was done about education for peasants. Peasants worked as serfs and had no opportunity to improve their position. The government had no intention of introducing any reforms regarding them, and the progressive intelligentsia who wanted to improve the social position of the people were persecuted.

During the reign of Czar Alexander I, who was more or less a liberal ruler, many societies were founded. They were heavily influenced by French cultural ideas and the general philosophical ideas of the West.

Most of these organizations tried to publish journals dedicated to propagating the new ideas in terms of the modern cultural trends existing in all modern states except Russia. The most important journal, an adult educational magazine, was the *Saint Petersburg Mercury.*

A significant feature began to appear on the Russian intellectual scene. The literary people, poets and novelists, became the revolutionary cultural force. Viazemski, Batiushkow, Pushkin and others were dissatisfied with merely foreign imitation. They began to construct something new; something that they could call their own. A typical representative of the Russian mind of that time was Pnin, who tried to reconcile the natural phenomena with that of the social phenomena by stating that the people have to achieve a state of conformity between their feeling and the logical rules.

Due to the efforts made by men like Pnin and Zhukovski the peasants of Russia gained their freedom from serfdom and with it gained some right to education.

Pnin believed in an evolutionary development of Russian culture—man must first educate his fellowman before any improvement would become possible. To him the word *muzhik* (peasant) was not only a linguistic term but also an enslaved man.

Pnin and other educators of that time believed in the separate education of classes, but none developed an exact procedure for achievement of these ends. They did write that there should be a different education for the class of artisans or skilled workers who were responsible for the maintenance and operation of the machinery than for the peasants who should preserve what the machine has developed. Most of these men believed that the czar was good by nature and that the duty of the school was to work for the country and the czar.

The city population in contrast to the peasants was to be well educated. They were to receive a well-rounded education not only in their particular skills but also a general knowledge of the business of the state, since they worked not only in their particular professions but also represented the nation.

In education of nobility, a detailed plan and the distribution of work was not the most important item—the emphasis was on the education of a gentleman. Since this class would represent Russia on one hand and protect her citizens at home on the other, a knowledge of philosophy and law was of utmost importance. So were the social habits (or the psychology of the masses in a modern term), the local traditions, etc. Children in this class were educated in the spirit of international cooperation, knew the foreign languages and began their educational training at the age of seven while others attended schools on an irregular basis.

Education of religious persons was entirely subject to the religious schools which were supported by funds of the Ministry of Education and controlled by the Holy Synod.

A special curriculum was developed for political[4] and moral education. The idea was to train Russian nobility in religious doctrines because the nobility would exercise power over others. The school, therefore, should be aware of the danger of educating a tyrant or despot who would abuse his power. Children were to be trained in moral outlook because they easily imitate their respected heroes regardless of the moral qualities these heroes possess.

EDUCATIONAL IDEAS OF THE SLAVOPHILS

Slavophils were the people who desired to maintain old Russian traditions and insisted on faithfulness to the Russian Orthodox Church. This movement began to function in the early 1830s although the spirit of it always existed in many Russian minds. At the beginning of Slavophilism most of its admirers were Russian nationalists, who later changed to a liberal philosophy but not without an anarchic element. S. T. Aksakov is considered the most representative leader of the Slavophils.

The Slavophils were trying to find the solution to all cultural and educational problems in the Russian Church, the Russian national traditions, Russian history and the national psychology. Most of the Slavophils saw a "Godless West" and envisioned Russia as the savior of mankind and Moscow as the Third Rome. In Catholic Europe, if the worst had come to pass, they would have preferred the Protestant religions probably because England was a royal-Protestant fortress and a friend (here and there) of Russia. Their leaders like A. S. Khomiakov, Kirejevski (brothers, Peter and Paul) tried to picture Russia in the most beautiful manner, an idealistic relationship between the monarch and the people. A very good example of this "excellent" relationship between the ruler and the people is the book written by N. Danilevski, *Russia and Europe* (1869), where Russia is represented as the messiah of the new Christianity and the carrier of the new culture into the "Godless West."

On education, the Slavophils were never progressive social intelligentsia. They sincerely supported the administration and continued the policy

---

[4]D. S. Myrsky, *A History of Russian Literature* (New York: Vantage Books, 1958), pp. 27–49,; Shchipanov, *op. cit.,* pp. 9–29, 218; A. A. Maksymov, *Ocherki po istorii bor'by za materializm v russkom estestvoznanii* (Moscow: AN SSSR, 1947), pp. 11–33.

of Russification. There were many examples of nationalistic policies among the Slavophils who opposed any aid to non-Russian schools.

Liberal Slavophils. This movement was represented mainly by three people, Samarin, Kostelev and Cherkaski. Although they all considered themselves members of the general Slavophil front, they differed radically in the sphere of cultural and educational reforms.

The aim of their philosophy was to persuade the government to adopt more liberal policies toward the cultural development of underprivileged people. They based this philosophy on the natural rights of man. Samarin, in particular, was deeply concerned with both the emancipation of serfs and the introduction of liberal cultural philosophy into the social and educational system.

The Westernites

As the term itself indicates, the philosophy of these people was entirely Western. They were influenced by French socialism and English liberalism. They saw very little in the Russian political and social structure that could influence a modern man or could create a progressive type of social system. As the West produced many philosophical thoughts, so did the Russian Westernites. There were Russian Westernites anarchically oriented; there were also Western-nihilists, Western-nationalists, socialists, liberalists, etc. One of the leaders of these Westernites in the second half of the nineteenth century was V. Belinski, an idealistically oriented man somewhat influenced by Hegel. He was an extremely well educated man and the promoter of liberal reforms in education, which he considered primitive in Russia.

The Growth of Materialistic Philosophy among the Westernites. The most influential man in this area was N. G. Chernishevski. Although not known as a philosopher, he did write and work in the context of materialism. His work, *Chto delat'* (What to Do), is more socio-political than socio-educational. Similarly, other Westernites—men like Dobroliubov, Pisarev and others—took the matter as the prime mover rather than the Hegelian absolute.

The general trends of Russian philosophical thought seemed to go side by side with the nationality problem and the socio-historical evolution. Russia, by far different from the West, could not see the difference between sole philosophical judgments and historical events. In Europe a definite separation existed between power-politics and philosophy per se. Several philosophical schools—German idealism, or English and French realism, for instance—tried to give certain logical foundations to the nature of man and his place in society as well as the relationship of man to his government, God, social norms and values. All this took an entirely different form in Russia. Social condition became the pivotal point of Russian philosophy, Russian history and Russian literature.

The communists now try to take advantage of past socio-economic conditions and try to group every distinguished Russian reformer of pre-revolutionary Russia into the socialistic or at least the materialistic camp. Such a man as Belinski is also listed as materialistically oriented and a man who could not do much during the czarist regime because, the Soviets say, the czars were against the materialistic philosophy of life.

One such philosophical work is the philosophy of Shchipanov, who tries to prove that Belinski was a forerunner of communism and a man atheistically oriented. Here the communists purposely select citations that fit their design and omit anything that is religious or idealistic in nature.

The Russian philosophy of the nineteenth century generally did not see the difference between the ideal, per se, and the Russian nation. The leading Russian intelligentsia also kept far away from the common people, or as Dobroliubov described them: "the intelligentsia of no progress and inertia."[5]

Not only that, but even the socialist intelligentsia, like Plekhanov, believed that the Russian czars would allow a liberal cultural and political development inside the Russian empire.

THE PROGRESSIVE PERIOD: USHINSKI

After the Napoleonic Wars the Russians had numerous opportunities to visit European countries and to get first hand experience about the European way of life. We can appreciate this fact from the outstanding quality of nineteenth century Russian literature.

Russian teachers also had opportunities to get acquainted with the more advanced European educational systems, particularly those of Switzerland, France, and Germany.

One man in particular was important: Konstantin Ushinski (1824-1870). He is considered to be not only the most important Russian pedagogue before the Revolution, but also might be considered one of the most important men in the history of Russian education.

---

[5] O. P. Kuzmin, *Iz istorii revoliutsionnoi mysli v Rossii* (Moscow: AN SSSR, 1961), p. 48; Shchipanov, *op. cit.,* pp. 169–229; Konstantinov, *op. cit.,* p. 101.

Ushinski was born in the city of Tula, where he completed his general education. At the age of twenty-two, he finished his studies at the University of Moscow and soon afterward received a position as a teacher of Russian language and jurisprudence in the town of Yaroslav. Soon after his graduation and some teaching experience, he visited several European countries. He became quite impressed with the Swiss educational system.

His importance in the Soviet system is such that there is a special medal of Ushinski that is awarded annually to the best teachers. In this section we shall discuss Ushinski from three main viewpoints: (1) the significance of labor; (2) the significance of the method; and (3) the significance of language.

Significance of Labor. Ushinski analyzed the value of work under the aspect of psychological importance rather than under the aspect of practical experience. It is interesting to note that he divided labor into two kinds: free labor and involuntary or slave labor. Describing slave labor he took as an example a Negro worker. Ushinski states that this man might work hard; yet because he does not get a proper reward for his work, his main objective will be to avoid the boss. Therefore, any meaningful, beneficial work must be voluntary work.

A child must be educated in terms of love toward labor which must be the unconditional step for physical and mental development. A man who does not like to work falls into the following dilemma: Either he will be constantly dissatisfied with and apathetic toward life or he will be destroyed by his own compassion and loneliness. Mental labor, according to Ushinski, is just as important as physical labor because it stimulates the nervous system into action and supplies an unusual liveliness. In order to appreciate work and to develop an enthusiastic attitude toward nature—both the body and the soul must be in an emotionally active state. Furthermore, education should not strive solely for a state of happiness, but it should be the means for the accomplishment of hard and useful work. Therefore, work is not something temporary in nature. It must be a habit-forming process, otherwise it may be dangerous. As an example Ushinski described a peasant-worker who is used to very hard work, but once he gets his pot of gold, he automatically feels a sense of security and with it the lack of necessity for labor because personal security has been achieved. This is not educational and this man will soon become a dishonest man poisoning his mind with only money and the luxuries that money might bring him. Not only will he try to surpass the millionaire, but he will come to hate his fellow peasants.

Therefore, the value of work with all of its varieties must be taught in schools from the viewpoint of "knowing oneself" as an immortal being.

In comparing Ushinski's educational ideas to those of Rousseau, we find a drastic difference. Ushinski, for example, stated that one can teach a child in terms of playing only until the child is about seven years of age. Later on learning should be approached from a serious point of view. Here, however, it is not a matter of military seriousness but rather a matter of logical demands. Parents and teachers alike should not be concerned over frightening a boy away from school because they teach him the difference between work and play, but they should be afraid of indifference or hate toward school. The courage, according to Ushinski, will come by itself, but the seed of indifference or unwillingness toward work planted in the child's heart will produce bad fruit. To be a daydreamer one does not have to be taught, but to think and work constructively one must be taught.

The value of a break or a recess during a school day is necessary not because the child is tired, but because he wants to do other things. Similarly, physical work is not dangerous for child development; it is very useful.

Significance of the Method. Ushinski approached the problem of methodology in terms of age groups and levels of achievement. It is important to note that Ushinski did not favor an accelerated program for advanced students. He felt that such an approach would do more harm than good in the case where the child finds his social environment not in his age group or the educational tasks beyond his ability to solve. This may create an inferiority complex in later years.

In teaching first grade children the basic concepts of reading and writing, Ushinski did not favor the old phonetical methods of learning. Instead, he tried to use a whole-word approach, i.e., recognition of a picture rather than a symbol. As far as the time of study was concerned, it was not a good practice, according to Ushinski, to keep a child more than two hours in school before noon and one hour after noon. Only after the child was 9 years old should he stay in school a little longer.

It was very important to assign material to young children but by no means was extensive copying of books or memorization of poems to be encouraged. Here the child does not learn anything, wastes his whole day and psychologically becomes unbalanced because he keeps thinking constantly about his inability to recite certain poems in front of the class, or his running out of time in recopying certain passages of books. The assignment must be meaningful and useful in his future life or daily routine. The teacher should make sure that pupils understand his explanations; otherwise homework assignments might not be done properly. Ushinski was against corporal punishment. He opted for other persuasive methods of teaching and disciplining. In the ethical problems of discipline, Ushinski elaborated each area of subject matter, its relative importance to the child's world and its usefulness for his education.

Teaching of a Language. To Ushinski there was nothing more important than the mastery of one's native language. Language is the basis for further mental development and understanding other subjects, people and things.

Ushinski in his educational works approached the problem of teaching and learning languages from the level of educational achievements as well as from the age group of a child. Considerable attention is given to lectures, class plans, the explanation of material, the comparison of a lecture-type teaching *vs.* group cooperation, the selection of linguistic material for educational purposes and the beneficial use of Russian poetry and religious writings, especially the Bible. All these topics are related to the development of the speaking ability of a child. Ushinski felt that the language of a nation portrays its spirit, expresses its history and feelings and describes the facts created by the human mind.[6]

Other Educators: Lev N. Tolstoi (1828-1910). Tolstoi is known throughout the world as a great Russian writer, but very little attention is given to his pedagogical writings. While his main concern was literary activities, in the field of education he tried to contribute something new or rather what he observed in many schools abroad, especially in Switzerland and Italy.

Tolstoi's major pedagogical creed was expressed in his own journal, *Yasnaia Poliana* (*A Clear Valley,* the name of the town where he was born) where he tried to introduce some modern ideas of the European educators, chiefly Rousseau and Pestalozzi. The schools of *Yasnaia Poliana* soon became known throughout Russia for having a student population of various social classes and from various parts of the country. They were the first Russian schools giving equal opportunities to both sexes and to the peasants of the realm. The schools themselves were rather unusual; only two or three teachers worked in two classrooms.

---

[6]K. Ushinski, *Sobranie sochinenii,* vol. 8 (Moscow: APN RSFSR, 1950), pp. 333–361; *Zhurnal Ministerstva Narodnogo Prosveshcheniia,* No. 7, 1860 , pp. 330 ff. See also George Counts, *The Challenge of Soviet Education* (New York: McGraw Hill Press, 1957), p. 20.

Tolstoi tried to introduce the French ideas of naturalism into his school. He wrote this about it:[7]

> We do not have any beginners. The children of the lower class are busy reading and writing while others are trying to solve problems, recite religious stories ... No one carries any books or notebooks. There is no homework. Not only they do not carry anything in their hands, they have nothing to carry in their heads. The child does not worry about forgetting his homework and does not have to think about yesterday's assignment. He carries to school only himself, his nature being convinced that he will have fun today in school as he had yesterday ... There are no punishments or exact times for the beginning of classes ... They are completely free and this (freedom) is what brings them to school.

Tolstoi's pedagogical ideas, however, were known only among high society; he was not known to the average Russian teacher. Also, his ideas were not new. They were to be found in the writings of French naturalists and practiced in Pestalozzian project-method schools.

Other more important Russian educators were A. Korf (1834-1893), N. I. Pirogov (1810-1881). Vakhterov, Sechenev and Pavlov will also be mentioned in the psychological section of this book.

EDUCATION OF NON-RUSSIANS: UKRAINE

The imperial educational policies toward non-Russian nationalities were entirely based on nationalistic principles: no significant cultural media were allowed to exist in the territory of the Russian Empire. We shall take two examples: the Ukrainians, a Slavic group, which is a representative sample of imperial aims toward all Slavs and the Muslims. These two groups comprise over 70 million people out of the total population of the Soviet Union.

The Russian educational authorities paid special attention to other Slavs, aiming at a possible assimilation of all Slavs into the Russian cradle. In addition to the Ukrainians, Belorussians, Poles and those Czechs who lived in Volin were subjected to a complete assimilation in due process of time. Russian was the only official language in schools and there were no higher educational institutions of other origins before 1917. The Russian language was the language of culture and communication. The Russification of the Ukrainians, Poles and the Belorussians was designed to increase the geographical area of the Russian nation. Georgians, Armenians, Azerbaidzhanians, and many Turkish and Mongolian tribes lived in a cultural vacuum and in primitive cultural conditions.

---

[7]Smirnov, *op. cit.*, pp. 257-407.

In Ukraine the struggle for instruction in their native language never ended. As of 1917 there were 30 million Ukrainians in Russia, but Ukrainian was not spoken as the official language in any of the schools. Those Ukrainians who could afford it attended either Russian schools or went abroad to further their education. Those who had access to important Russian journals and periodicals tried to persuade leading Russian administrators of the necessity for the vernacular in schools the national minorities attended. They published their articles in Russian magazines such as *Vestnik Evropy (European News), S-Peterburgskie Vedomosty (St. Petersburg News), Vestnik Vospitaniia (Educational Journal)* and others.

Suppression of Printing

In 1863, the imperial administration of Ukraine prohibited any printing in the Ukrainian language. This and other decisions aroused the Ukrainians to active defense for their own culture. During the following years demonstrations and written petitions were sent to St. Petersburg to try to persuade the emperor to intervene in the cultural policies of his administrators. However, all such maneuvers resulted in one negative reply to those making such demands. In fact many were persecuted for their efforts. Many teachers were released from their teaching positions because they insisted on the Ukrainian language in schools. Even worse, Ukrainian teachers and students were expelled from universities for reasons like translating the Bible into Ukrainian.

The leading Ukrainian intelligentsia demanded that at least some subject matter be taught in Ukrainian. They argued that it was impossible to teach the children and the adult population basic concepts of literacy in a foreign language. At various meetings the teachers, writers and social intelligentsia who hoped to improve the situation prepared resolutions and sent them to St. Petersburg. Such resolutions with the signatures of many leading reformers were prepared in 1875, 1881 and again in 1895. They demanded that the "little Russian" language be taught in elementary schools together with the Russian language. The teachers argued that they could attain a better student-parent relationship by teaching in the native language and using Russian as an important administrative language. They also claimed that the forceful introduction of Russian into every phase of cultural activity would only harm the purity of the Russian language since the people would misuse any language taught by force.

Ukrainian culture and literature was the concern of another drive. It was thought that it would be better to request these rights on the grounds that by studying literary work one could develop a better national feeling for his own people and the state. Educators insisted that any positive result could only be accomplished when the teaching was in the vernacular.

After the revolution of 1905, more pressure was put on the Russian government to change its official position toward the non-Russian schools. The request was made in the Russian *Duma* (parliament) by Representative Saiko, who demanded the following: 1) the language in schools of the South (Ukraine) should be Ukrainian; 2) elementary and secondary education in the territory of Ukraine should be free; 3) all textbooks and educational materials should be written in Ukrainian; 4) immediate steps should be taken to train the teachers in Ukrainian so they would later be able to teach in Ukrainian schools as well as establish constructive cultural relations with the population; and 5) that the universities of Kiev and Odessa should establish professorial chairs in the study of the Ukrainian language and culture.

In reality these efforts were nullified since the answers on the demands either never came or were bluntly denied as unconstitutional. Many leading Russians and social reformers wanted to change the situation. They saw the introduction of the Ukrainian language into the schools of the 'south' as an urgent necessary change. Among such men was Ushinski.

Repression of Language Study

Ushinski insisted that a school which represses the national language has little or no value for educational programs and purposes. Children exposed to such a type of education will go to school as "a transition from heaven to hell" and after finishing the day of schooling a child will run home as if chased by some evil spirit. He wants to go home to his father and mother and speak the language he understands. He sees the school as a place incomprehensible to his little mind. This child never hears any Russian words in his home. At school he tries hard to speak a broken Russian which will psychologically remain in his system for the rest of his life. Consequently, he will have a very negative approach to the study of foreign languages. According to Ushinski, such an approach served no useful purpose because children exposed to such instruction only spoiled the Russian language. Such a school can only ruin the educational opportunities of an individual by bringing him from one strange place to another and keeping him far away from his own people and culture.

Other progressive Russian teachers and educators, like Ushinski, insisted on the establishment of non-Russian schools on the territory of the Russian Empire. They insisted that the policy of repudiation of all that is not of Russian origin can only lead to the decrease of educational standards and the creation of national opposition toward the Russian rule.

Russian statistical data before 1914 did not indicate a precise number of Ukrainian students at any educational level. It merely divided the European parts of the empire into administrative districts and disregarded the nationality of the school. In 1914, for example, it listed 105 higher educational institutions with 127,000 students for the whole empire, and 9.6 million students in the elementary and secondary schools.[8] If we were to try to calculate the data for the Ukrainian territory only, we could not piece together a representative picture because the school population in the Ukraine, particularly in higher schools, was by no means homogeneous.

The Soviet data concerning the pre-revolutionary period are also not accurate since they do not list many religious schools. They purposely omitted such statistical calculations to make the data on the accomplishments of the public school system less impressive. They divided the educational system according to territorial regions. For example, they state that there are in present day Ukraine 48,403 teachers (see Appendix, Table 4), 20,197 schools and 1.7 million students. But the status of ethnic schools is not indicated by this data; only Russian accomplishments in education are noted.

THE MUSLIM SCHOOLS

Before the Bolshevik Revolution and a few years after it, there were two kinds of Muslim schools in the Russian Empire: (1) *mektab*—the elementary Muslim school, and (2) *medressa*—the secondary school.

After occupying central Asia, the Russians decided to maintain the poor quality of the Muslim educational system because it did not represent any cultural threat to the empire.

The precise number of schools and students is difficult to determine because only those schools that were registered (many were not) were included in the Russian statistical reports. We know that there were 7,009 Muslim schools in Russian central Asia (almost all of them at the elementary level) and over 100 thousand students in these schools (see Table 8). In large cities like Tashkent, for instance, there was also a

---

[8] I. Krylov, *Sistema osvity v Ukraini,* 1917–1931 (Munich: Institute for the Study of the USSR, 1956), pp. 2–20; Tsentral'noe Statisticheskoe Upravlenie pri Sovete Ministrov SSSR, *SSSR v 1960 godu* (Moscow: Gosstatizdat, 1960), p. 305.

TABLE 8A

Development of Elementary and Secondary Education in Turkestan and Steppe,
All Types: 1893–1897[1]

Region	No. of Schools	No. of Teachers[5]	Number of Students:			No. of Students per 1000 People[3]
			Male	Female	Total	
1. Ural'sk						
Muslim Schools	118	119	2,515	491	3,006	21
Russian Schools[2]	389	..	6,988	2,856	9,844	
Khadera[4]	..	..	..	..	..	
Schools for Illiterates	23	23	321	162	483	
Total	530	142	9,824	3,509	13,333	
2. Turgaisk						7
Muslim Schools	59	59	362	95	457	
Russian Schools	83	..	1,847	433	2,280	
Khadera	..	..	..	..	..	
Schools for Illiterates	9	9	240	87	327	
Total	151	68	2,449	615	3,064	
3. Akmolinsk						21
Muslim Schools	295	299	3,376	865	4,241	
Russian Schools	196	..	7,619	2,902	10,521	
Khadera	3	3	38	..	38	
Schools for Illiterates	8	8	80	24	104	
Total	502	310	11,113	3,791	14,904	

TABLE 8A (Continued)

Development of Elementary and Secondary Education in Turkestan and Steppe,
All Types: 1893–1897[1]

Region	No. of Schools	No. of Teachers[5]	Number of Students:			No. of Students per 1000 People[3]
			Male	Female	Total	
4. Semipalatinsk						
Muslim Schools	92	94	1,498	253	1,751	
Russian Schools	107	..	3,861	1,039	4,900	
Khadera	..	..	..	..	..	
Schools for Illiterates						
Total	199	94	5,359	1,292	6,651	10
5. Zakaspeisk						
Muslim Schools	233	258	2,933	331	3,264	
Russian Schools	42	..	1,322	503	1,825	
Khadera	..	..	..	..	..	
Schools for Illiterates						
Total	275	258	4,255	834	5,089	13
6. Syr-Dar'ia						
Muslim Schools	2,546	2,743	25,867	4,478	30,345	
Russian Schools	77	3	2,506	1,156	3,662	
Khadera	3	..	49	..	49	
Schools for Illiterates						
Total	2,626	2,746	28,421	5,634	34,056	22

(Continued on next page)

TABLE 8A (Continued)

Development of Elementary and Secondary Education in Turkestan and Steppe, All Types: 1893–1897[1]

Region	No. of Schools	No. of Teachers[5]	Number of Students:			No. of Students per 1000 People[3]
			Male	Female	Total	
7. Samarkand						
Muslim Schools	1,813	1,945	19,331	536	19,867	25
Russian Schools	18	..	605	240	845	
Khadera	11	11	325	1	326	
Schools for Illiterates	..	..	..	..	..	
Total	1,842	1,956	20,261	777	21,038	
8. Fergana						
Muslim Schools	1,685	1,734	30,995	2,295	33,290	22
Russian Schools	16	..	405	169	574	
Khadera	8	8	228	..	228	
Schools for Illiterates	..	..	..	..	..	
Total	1,709	1,742	31,628	2,464	34,092	
9. Semirechie						
Muslim Schools	168	166	3,228	989	4,217	10
Russian Schools	78	..	3,558	1,388	4,976	
Khadera	..	..	..	..	..	
Schools for Illiterates	11	11	293	147	440	
Total	257	177	7,109	2,524	9,633	

TABLE 8A (Continued)

Development of Elementary and Secondary Education in Turkestan and Steppe, All Types: 1893–1897[1]

Region	No. of Schools	No. of Teachers[5]	Number of Students:			No. of Students per 1000 People[3]
			Male	Female	Total	
Total for Turkestan and Steppe						18
Muslim Schools	7,009	7,417	90,096	10,333	100,429	
Russian Schools[2]	1,006	...	28,711	10,686	39,397	
Khadera[4]	25	25	640	1	641	
Schools for Illiterates	51	51	934	420	1,354	
Total	8,091	7,493	120,381	21,440	141,821	
Turkestan only						20
(Includes Five Oblasti: Fergana, Syr-Dar'ia, Samarkand, Semirechie and Zakaspeisk)						
Muslim Schools	6,445	6,846	82,354	8,629	90,983	
Russian Schools	231	...	8,396	3,456	11,852	
Khadera	22	22	602	1	603	
Schools for Illiterates	11	11	293	147	440	
Total	6,709	6,879	91,645	12,233	103,878	

[1] Calculated from: Imperatorskoe Vol'noe Ekonomicheskoe Obshchestvo, *Nachal'noe narodnoe obrazovanie v Rossii*, edited by I. Fal'bork i V. Chornolutskii (St. Petersburg: Tipografiia Narodnaia Pol'za, vol. 1, 1900), pp. 361–62.

[2] Pereselencheskoe Upravlenie Zemleustroistva i Zemledeliia, *Aziatskaia Rossiia*, liudi i poriadki za Uralom (St. Petersburg: Tipografiia A. F. Marksa, 1914), vol. 1, pp. 260 ff.

[3] Number of students per 1,000 people in the years 1883 and 1897 was calculated on the basis of the 1897 census.

[4] The Khadera schools were religious establishments, predominantly Jewish, designed only for boys (see *Entsiklopedicheskii Slovar'*, Moscow: Izdatel'stvo Russkogo Bibliograficheskogo Instituta "Grant", 1935, vol. 17, pp. 167–68).

[5] The total number of teachers does not include the number of Russian teachers (data are not available).

TABLE 8B

Distribution of Schools, Teachers, and Students in Muslim Schools of Russia:
1893–94 School Year[1]

Administrative Region	No. of Schools	No. of Teachers	Number of Students:		
			Male	Female	Total
Regions of Zemstvo[2]	2,974	3,654	93,587	32,348	125,935
Urban	118	151	3,406	789	4,195
Rural	2,856	3,503	90,181	31,559	121,740
Four Non-Zemstvo Regions of European Russia	320	358	10,347	540	10,887
Urban	40	42	1,640	35	1,675
Rural	280	316	8,707	505	9,212
Caucasus	2,590	2,633	26,818	4,529	31,347
Urban	136	142	3,668	14	3,682
Rural	2,454	2,491	23,150	4,515	27,665
Siberia	61	65	1,688	751	2,439
Urban	3	4	195	30	225
Rural	58	61	1,493	721	2,214
Steppe Krai	732	737	10,979	2,693	13,672
Urban	82	88	2,160	405	2,565
Rural	650	649	8,819	2,288	11,107

TABLE 8B (Continued)

Distribution of Schools, Teachers, and Students in Muslim Schools of Russia: 1893–94 School Year[1]

Administrative Region	No. of Schools	No. of Teachers	Number of Students:		
			Male	Female	Total
Turkestan	6,277	6,680	79,126	7,640	86,766
Urban	986	1,050	26,264	2,236	28,500
Rural	5,291	5,630	52,862	5,404	58,266
European Russia	3,294	4,012	103,934	32,888	136,822
Urban	158	193	5,046	824	5,870
Rural	3,136	3,819	98,888	32,064	130,952
Russian Empire	12,954	14,127	222,545	48,501	271,046
Urban	1,365	1,477	37,333	3,509	40,842
Rural	11,589	12,650	185,212	44,992	230,204

[1] Imperatorskoe Vol'noe Ekonomicheskoe Obshchestvo, *Nachal'noe narodnoe obrazovanie v Rossii*, edited by I. Fal'bork i V. Chrnolitskii (St. Petersburg: Tipografiia Narodnaia Pol'za, vol. 2, 1900), pp. 366–68.

[2] The source did not indicate which four of the *zemstvo* were not included in the total number of zemstvo. However, as of 1914 there were forty three zemstvo gubernii in Russia (see *Bol'shaia Sovetskaia Entsiklopediia*, vol. 17, p. 44).

large net of Muslim secondary schools, *medressas*. Over 100 medressas were located in the Muslim part of the city and 1,100 in the whole of central Asia. The total number of students in medressas as of 1899 was 8,000.

Although considered a secondary school, the medressa curriculum was almost exclusively religious, and the level was actually no more than the first few years of elementary school. Mathematics, for instance, never exceeded arithmetic.

Russian-Native Schools (Russko-tuzemnye shkoly). In this section we shall concentrate on the other type of Muslim schools, the *Russian-Native Schools.* These were a Russian creation aimed at the Russification of the native population. These schools were by far more important than the mektabs and medressas because they were on a higher educational level.

A few years after the Russians had completed their occupation of Turkestan, an imperial decree of March 26, 1870, provided for a new type of school, *Russko-tuzemnaia shkola.*[9] It was a primary school designed to re-educate the natives in an effort to bring them closer to Russian culture and its social system. However, such schools were first proposed by Muslims such as Sayyid Azin, a Tashkent merchant, in 1867, and officially, this school began in 1884 in the home of Sayyid Ghani, Azin's son. Nalivkin, the prominent Russian orientalist, was its first teacher. The aim of the Russian-Native school was not only to achieve cultural unity but also to accomplish such aims as Russification, the goal of converting Muslims to Christianity (a movement headed by Prof. Ilminski at Kazan), and the practical goal of facilitating the Russian administration's transactions with the natives. In spite of the fact that the schools were founded primarily for the natives of Turkestan, they were very beneficial for the Russian population because the children of Russian settlers also were able to attend. These schools were not widely attended by the natives, however, because the Muslim clergy did not want their people in the Russian schools.

To avoid any antagonism arising from conflict with native traditions, the Russians introduced religion in these schools. Both the Orthodox and Muslim religions were offered in the curricula. For example, the first Governor of Turkestan, General von Kaufman, favored religious

---

[9]R. Sharafudinova, *Shkol'noe obrazovanie v uzbekskoi SSR* (Tashkent: Gosizdat UzSSR, 1961), p. 8; Henry Lansdel, *Russian Central Asia,* vol. II (Boston: Houghton and Mifflin, 1885), pp. 123ff; V. Bartold, *Istoriia kul'turnoi zhizni Turkestana* (Leningrad: 1927), pp. 130ff; *Zhurnal Ministerstva Narodnogo Prosveshcheniia,* No. 6, 1913, p. 195.

instruction in Russian-native schools, and the next governor, General Rosenbach, even permitted the study of Muslim laws. The Muslims nonetheless remained hostile although the law of 1870 made some provisions for their religion and laws to be taught. It did state, however, that these educational programs should be in line with Russian interests.

The imperial decree of June 20, 1886, called for learning both the Russian and the native language, but the indigenous people were still unenthusiastic. The situation improved in 1906 when the Governor of Turkestan, N. N. Teviashev, assured the natives that it was not in Russia's interest to interfere with the Muslim religion.

The Russian administration had taken several measures to improve the educational status of the natives. But the general tendency was not to impose any rapid changes since Muslims could not adjust quickly to Russian culture. For obvious reasons the Russian language was emphasized. Only after learning Russian could one continue his education at the higher educational institutions in European Russia.

The Russian-Native school had a four-year program and Russian, taught mainly by oral and visual methods without texts, was emphasized in every grade. Many words were taken directly from the immediate environment to build the child's vocabulary. Writing skills were developed in the last year. In 1906, the Russians proposed to increase the number of native students in pedagogical schools and to offer more scholarships. The last proposition presented difficulties because in European Russia itself scholarships were few, e.g., during 1863-1875, the number of scholarships for each university—and there were only six Russian universities—did not exceed four or five per university.

In practice, however, the progress of *Russko-tuzemnye shkoly* was not as rapid as the administration expected. By 1911, there were only 89 such schools in Turkestan.

In general, then, the native population did not have the facilities for educational advancement because of this complex state of affairs. This situation is evident from the composition of the school population of Turkestan. For instance, the number of people living in Syr-Dar'ia province consisted of 1.5 million natives and 44,844 Russians (1897). The number of Russian children in schools was 2,326—well over 90 per cent of school age children—whereas only a little over 2 per cent of the total native children were in schools. The percentage of Russians in the whole of Turkestan in 1897, was only 2.8 per cent. (See also Table 1.)

The number of natives in Russian secondary schools, such as gymnasiums and seminaries, also was insignificant. (See Tables 8A and 8B).

The end result of both Muslim and Russian educational efforts was not brilliant. The literacy rate among the Turkestan population in 1897 was correspondingly low, 7.9 per cent for men and 2.2 per cent for women. By 1916, according to Soviet data—and they varied substantially from the Imperial—literacy among Tadzhiks was 0.3 per cent; among the Kara-Kalpaks, 0.2 per cent; or an average for the present boundaries of Uzbekistan, 1 per cent.

The status of other cultural efforts, such as libraries, book production, museums, etc., showed little if any improvement during the imperial period. Even bookstores witnessed some decrease in number instead of an increase. There were thirty-seven such stores in Tashkent in 1904, and only thirty-one by 1912. In 1913, the number of books published in Turkestan was fifty-nine with a total of 100,000 copies. Also, the region had one playhouse, three museums and twenty-five cinemas.[10]

Schools for other nationalities had a limited opportunity to develop, e.g., the Jewish schools were able to offer only one year of religious instruction, and this too, was prohibited in cities like St. Petersburg and Moscow. The *khadera,* Jewish Talmudic schools, were non-accredited schools designed strictly for Jewish boys. Other nationalities, German, Baltic, Polish all had to study in Russian since there was no higher educational system other than the Russian before 1917.

Additional References

The Orthodox Confession of Peter Mohyla, in *Orientale Christiane,* vol. X, No. 39, 1927, CXXXII, pp. 6, 349; *Svod zakonov rossiiskoi imperii,* vol. XI (St. Petersburg: Gosudarstvennaia Tipografiia, 1896), pp. 245ff.; D. I. Pirogov, *Polnoe sobranie sochinenii,* vol. V (Moscow: Gospolitizdat, 1949), especially pages 120–130; F. F. Aleksandrov, *Dialekticheskii materializm* (Moscow: AN SSSR, 1954); Imperatorskoe Vol'noe Ekonomicheskoe Obshchestvo, *Nachal'noe obrazovanie v Rossii* (St. Petersburg: Izdat. Fol'borka, 1900), pp. 180–350; N. P. Semenov, *Osvobozhdenie khrestian v tsarstvovanie imperatora Aleksandra II* (St. Petersburg: 1889); A. A. Kornilov, *Obshchestvennoe dvizhenie pri imperatore Aleksandre II* (Paris: 1905); Y. Samarin, *Sochineniia,* vol. VII (Moscow: 1877); N. Berdyeev, *The Russian Idea* (New York: The Macmillan Press, 1948); V. G. Belinskii, *Sochineniia,* vol. I. (Moscow: Izdatel'stvo Momontove, 1888); N. G. Chernishevskii, *Chto dielat'* (Moscow: Gosizdat, 1963); S. Y. Shchipanov, *Iz istorii russkoi filosofii* (Moscow: Gospolitizdat, 1951); D. I. Dobroliubov, *Polnoe sobranie sochinenii,* vol. I (Moscow: 1894); Hans Kohn, *Nationalism in the Soviet Union* (London: Routledge Ltd., 1933); V. P. Eliutin, *Vysshaia shkola strany sotsializma* (Moscow: Sotsekonomizdat, 1959); R. Pierce, *Russian Central Asia* (Berkeley: University of California Press, 1959); S. Zenkovski, *Pan-Turkism and Islam in Russia* (Cambridge: Harvard University Press, 1960); Franz Schwarz, *Turkestan das Wiege der Indogermanischen Voelker* (Vienna: 1900); *Revoliutionnyi Vostok,* No. 1, 1934, pp. 160ff; S. Z. Urazov, *Turkestanskaia ASSR* (Tashkent: AN UzSSR, 1958).

---

[10] *Zhurnal Ministerstva Narodnogo Prosveshcheniia,* No. 10, 1906, pp. 143 ff; K. T. Galkin, *Vysshoe obrazovanie i podgotovka narodnykh kadrov* (Moscow: Sovetskaia Nauka, 1958), p. 3.

Chapter 3

GOALS OF
SOVIET EDUCATION

The objectives and goals of Russian communist education can be found partially in the philosophy of Marx-Engels, partially in the social philosophy of Lenin but most of all in Soviet history and in the decisions and aims of the communist party of Russia. An accumulation of events made the communist philosophy vivid, a so-called philosophy of the workers and peasants.

There is nothing permanent in the communist philosophy of education. Even ethical and moral laws have no definite or infinite ends. It is not a matter of education for classless society, nor of the solidarity of the working classes but primarily the matter of Russian objectives in political fields using education only as a means of bringing up the so-called New Soviet Man.

The Soviet government and the Soviet educational authorities take quite seriously the theoretical and practical applications necessary for changing human nature in such a way that this new man becomes the tool of their political aims and desires. The aim of the Communist Party of Russia is to educate this new man by any means deemed necessary as quickly and as well as possible. In this section we shall try to present

51

a few "commandments" of Russian communist education—an education which strives to control the human mind as early as possible, the mind which will act and think as it is told.

THE LEADING ROLE OF THE PARTY

From Lenin to the present leader of Bolshevik Russia, the aim of Soviet education is to educate active workers of communism, workers who foresee and understand the plans of the party and execute these in their lives. The school, therefore, is nothing other than the ideological arm of the revolution, the revolution which will last until Soviet workers achieve the state of communism, or the world revolution of the proletariat. An engineer, doctor or any other professional is not only to work for the sake of science but more importantly to be a conscious fighter for communism in helping the party to "regenerate the society."

In the process of this social and educational endeavor, the individual is not working as he pleases. He always finds the "helping hand" of the party. Of course, education is one of the most important social institutions because it raises the new people, the new intelligentsia. Stalin, in referring to the problem of the intelligentsia, stated that "no ruling class has ever managed without intelligentsia of its own." The same Stalin indicated that the construction of communism all over the world is not the task of the communist party alone but the task of all other social organizations, particularly educational ones. The party officially stated that the upbringing of the young generation cannot be allowed in a spirit of indifference to politics and to the Soviet regime. In other words, the man who takes a neutral position is just as dangerous as the enemy. In such an all-around cultural and educational approach the myth of the infallibility of the communist party and the supernatural ability of its leaders is developed among the young Soviet generation. Similarly developed beliefs existed among the old communists and noncommunists who saw in the party a type of phenomenon through which one can get "forgiveness of sins" or through which one can perish.

From the very beginning of the Bolshevik regime in Russia the communists wanted to replace a belief in God with a belief in the party. They used diversified maneuvers to accomplish this end according to the various political events which transpired. During the 1920s the Soviet teachers were reminded constantly about the greatness and uniqueness of the party and its leaders. The duty of the school was to educate the youth in the spirit of communism. Lenin and Stalin alike demanded that education should be the striking force of the party.

There is one peculiar feature of the Russian educational policy—a feature that the imperial regime did not apply—that forces non-Russian nationalities to educate their children in Russian patriotism before they can say anything about Polish, Ukrainian, Turkish, etc., patriotism. All non-Russian nationalities are forced to glorify Soviet-Russian history and Russian communist (or any Russian) achievements. Only after fulfilling this obligation can one talk about a local-national-patriotism. Only in an exceptional situation such as during World War II (when Stalin needed local nationalism to win the war) were the Soviet nationalities allowed to write something about their own patriotism. However, soon after the war, the order reverted to previous lines. For example, a Ukrainian writer, Sosiura, was ordered by Stalin to write a poem about love for the Ukraine, which he did. After the war ended, Sosiura was arrested for writing a "nationalistic" poem. Many writers, teachers and artists (especially during the Stalin-Postishev rule in Ukraine) were forced to glorify the party and the Russian liberation. All the Ukrainian intelligentsia were ordered to praise the achievements of the Russian Communist Party and were liquidated if they chose otherwise.

In this politico-educational work, the party said that it was striving to achieve firm followers for the communist regime. *Narodnoe Obrazovanie* puts it this way:

> It is just in the growth of the communist consciousness, in the Soviet people, and above all, in the younger generation that our success in the further advancement along the road to communism will depend.[1]

Another example: the Soviet government makes all efforts to create a so-called "light-house of communism" of the Uzbek SSR. A variety of methods are used to persuade the outsiders, in particular the Muslims, that the Soviet government is really a friend of the Muslim people. However, at the same time, they eliminate those Uzbek who are not entirely pro-Russian, together with the Muslim clergy and religious believers. Sending some of the Uzbek to school and others to Siberia apparently works well for the Soviets because no foreigner is allowed to visit Siberian camps. Again, no one can visit a place like Fergana which

---

[1]*Narodnoe obrazovanie,* February 1962, vol. II, No. 4, p. 14. See also J. V. Stalin, "On the Problem of Technological Intelligentsia in the USSR," in *Soviet Cultural Bulletin,* No. 5, September 1931, p. 2; N. Leites, *Ritual of Liquidation* (Glencoe: The Free Press, 1956), passim; N. I. Boldyrev, *Direktivy VKP (b) i postanovleniia sovetskogo pravitel'stva o narodnom obrazovanii* za 1917–1947 g. (Moscow: AN RSFSR, 1947), vypusk 1, pp. 20, 98, 100; F. F. Korolev and Others, *Ocherki po istorii sovetskoi shkoly i pedagogiki* (Moscow: AN RSFSR, 1961), p. 14; *Pravda,* January 1, 1922.

is 100 per cent Muslim and tell the true story of Uzbek SSR. Instead the Russians show a foreigner the new construction sites, contrasting them with the old city of Tashkent and underlining the point that this is what the Soviets are doing for the Uzbeks and what the communist party of Russia is doing for other nationalities. The Muslims, themselves, are forced to condemn their own national traditions, their own history and their own middle-class.

All other nationalities have to prove before the party their devotion to Moscow; and in time, they might also be equally devoted to Tashkent, Kiev, Vilno, etc. There is not a single textbook published in the Soviet Union which does not glorify and give thanks to the party for the "happy and joyful" life. As one Soviet Ukrainian journal put it: "Oh, Party! Oh, Party! How happy we are to feel your hand upon our shoulders."[2]

THE CREED IN MATTER ONLY

The communists in Russia do not want to have a division of power, i.e., one person serving God and another serving the government. There can be no other belief than belief in the Russian communist party and belief in the ability of the party to direct the Soviet sciences which in time (they say) will substitute for all the supernatural values. In their view, science is the creator of miracles.

Lenin and other Bolshevik leaders saw in religious beliefs a danger to the state. In 1917, Lenin issued his first public law, completely separating church from state. By virtue of this law, all churches were confiscated and church property was nationalized.

Extensive force and propaganda were used by the regime to exterminate religious beliefs. The writers, poets and artists were compelled to write and produce works about the dangers of religious beliefs. Here is one poem:

> Away, begone, you cheating priests
> With holydays devoted to the saints,
> Away with ancient, vain deceiving lies
> That should not shadow our young eyes.[3]

This atheistic propaganda included all branches of the social and educational apparatus. The New Soviet Man is not to be handicapped by

---

[2] *Radianska Ukraina* (Kiev), January 16, 1965; Vitchizna (Kiev, monthly), June 1961, p. 60; A. P. Kuchkin (ed.), *SSSR v period vostanovleniia narodnogo khoziaistva*, 1920–1925 (Moscow: AN SSSR, 1955), p. 547.

[3] Thomas Woody, *New Minds: New Men?* (New York: The Macmillan Press 1932), p. 59.

religious prejudices, as the party labels them, and by no means need he feel a sense of guilt when committing a religious crime in the name of Lenin and Stalin. In this process the school is to help the student to arrive at the "right" *Weltanschauung* and the "right" ideology. A good education, the Soviets theorized, should unite the school with politics and all spiritual values—a process which no nation had yet done.

The communist party of Russia clearly stated that the aim of the party is the complete destruction of any religious beliefs. Therefore, the Soviet youngster is told that there is no supernatural existence; man is the creation of natural occurrences which, in time, the Soviet laboratories will be able to duplicate. The Soviet sciences try to prove that the nature of man is the same as the nature of any other creature, plant or animal, and that religious practices are dangerous not only to society but also to one's own well-being.

Recent Soviet writers have frequently selected topics of the Dr. Zhivago type. A young boy is pictured as being spiritually lost because of the death of his father. Naturally, in such a tragedy the young mind will think about the nature of man and the worth of life. The young boy, according to Soviet teaching, never should be allowed to become estranged. Seeing his father dead, the child might conclude that there is no purpose in attending school or taking examinations because sooner or later he too will fade away. Here the task of the school is to reorientate the child's mind—keep him busy, give him extra homework or special assignments where he can show his own initiative, give him examples of the party's teaching about the nature of man and life, etc. Furthermore, the school should try to develop in a child the sense of belonging here and not "out there."

The communist party always supplies educational institutions with a variety of literature to fight the religious beliefs. Besides lectures in schools about 'scientific' atheism, special propagandists are trained and sent among the parents to lecture on various religious topics. Anti-religious associations never ceased to function in the U.S.S.R. They work in a variety of educational institutions, evening schools, arts clubs and in adult education. Churches, especially Christian ones, are either converted into museums or destroyed. If the propaganda staff cannot handle the opposition to the communist creed, the usual methods of force are used to subdue the people.

Important religious centers, like Muslim Bukhara for instance, are the centers of communist propaganda. The Soviets believe that once the symbolic value of such cities is destroyed, atheism will follow among the populace. Bukhara for the Muslim population was known for a long time as Bukhara the Holy. It symbolized the great historical events of the Muslim people and attracted Muslim believers with its variety of mosques and theological schools.

In other Soviet cities, educational institutions, including the Academy of Sciences, established special departments to deal with the topic of atheism. The party announced that Soviet society had almost reached the stage of full communism. They theorize that a man should be able to find answers to his daily problems in the communist ideology and the practices of the communist government of Russia. At the same time they call upon every individual to produce as much as he can for the society. A man should give the society the best he possesses and take, in return, what he needs.[4]

THE CREED IN THE COMMUNIST MORALITY

Lenin said before the revolution that the proletariat must be taught to distrust the bourgeoise and that the most important duty of the new communist education was the indoctrination of children in communist ethics and the new principles of morality.

At the Third Congress of the Communist Youth Association Lenin said it was necessary that all educational activities be focused around the new values which ultimately will destroy the old exploitatory society and traditions.

The Soviet pedagogical textbooks emphasize the structuring of new moral laws and principles. Makarenko (who will be mentioned later) underlined the importance of moral education in school. The families themselves do not always know the moral demands which will be placed on the new generation. One always can hear the phrases of the conscious discipline and the conscious cultural education of the working classes. This conditioning is expected to form a politically conscious youth with broad world outlooks, one who can subordinate his will to a friend or who can order the friend to obey the social rules, a man with a great respect for the collective values, a man who should be happy, etc.

Medysnki, a well known Soviet educator, says that the Soviet educational system is trying to educate a man who will be able to understand and appreciate the beauty of nature and the beauty of society based on Soviet economic planning. Education during the Soviet reconstruction, as

---

[4]*Narodnoe obrazovanie*, No. 10, 1961, pp. 11 ff. See also Gustav Krist, *Alone Through Forbidden Land: Russian Central Asia*. Translated by O. E. Lorimer (London: Faber and Faber Press, 1939), p. 83; *Zvezda* (Moscow, monthly), June 1961, p. 196.

the official communist party source states, involves all strata of the population. It teaches old-fashioned peasants about the values and ethics of the new epoch. It fundamentally changes the old traditions. It introduces a new psychological process of shaping the mind, a mind free from exploitation by others. All these accomplishments are achieved thanks to the communist party.

The old Christian love for neighbors and the brotherhood among mankind are replaced by the brotherhood among the communist countries and the socialistic societies. There can be no brotherhood among communists and non-communists since only the Russian communists are striving for a complete "liberation" of other nations and this makes the question of the national liberation a commandment of the century. Furthermore, the communist party asserts that true friendship now exists among the Russian minorities because in the past there were many small capitalistic states existing on the principles of force and violence, on the principle of enslavement of small nations—all of this, according to communists, does not exist in Russia now.

A new type of culture, the Soviets theorized, will replace the belief in God or any supernatural values. It is the "highest" type of contemporary culture and is characterized by the following: humanism, progressivism, and self-determination. In the process of the above work old forms of culture are rejected—those forms that are anti-scientific, anti-socialistic . . . "such a gigantic work no other social class accomplished and cannot accomplish."[5]

The capitalistic way of life with its ethics and morals cannot bring happiness to the people, Soviet propaganda claims. Happiness is only *true* possible under the leadership of the communist party which gives to the working people unlimited wealth and happiness.

The Soviet government, the communists say, promotes the new set of values, and provides many means of prolonging the life-span of the population. When the Soviets compare statistical data of this kind, they always include the U.S.A. and England, who are pictured as examples *true* of the worst social systems. The communist party claims that the life-span in old Russia was twice as long as in the U.S.A. (before the revolution) and "is substantially longer during the Soviet regime."[6]

Another concept of the communist morality is the idea that the Soviet Russians care for other people. They use the term humanism, "a humanism which is possible only in the Russian communist state." Furthermore, the Soviets say that the traditionally used means of force and

---

[5]B. N. Ponomarev, *Istoriia KPSS* (Moscow: Gospolitizdat, 1959), p. 664.
[6]*Ibid.*, p. 667.

violence are absent from the Soviet scene. Not only that, force and violence never were applied by the Russians. Only capitalists apply the force, prepare wars, etc.

Any work dealing with foreign or spiritual values other than communist ones is prohibited. A good example is the John Dewey society in Russia after the revolution. Once the important points of Dewey's theories were utilized by the Soviets he was needed no more. Consequently, his works were prohibited. A special meeting of the top echelon of the communist party was called to discuss the influences of Deweyism on Soviet education. His theories were rejected and were explained by the party as "theories based on lies and are anti-Marxist."

It is clear that the educational theories of the West which are based on the free development of the human mind and free initiative were rejected by the dictatorial regime. As George Counts expressed it, everything that contributes to the communist society is moral and what does not is immoral. In 1945, Kalinin said that the Great October Revolution raised the moral standards of Russia to the highest degree—Communist morality was the highest of all human society.[7]

The communist party realizes the fact that the school is the most important social institution for inculcating the principles of communism. They recognize that the teacher is primarily the one to shape the views and beliefs of the young generation. In 1959, Krushchev called upon the schools to start then to educate the future leaders of full-scale communism. He insisted that the work of educating a new generation in the communist principles of morality must begin right then ... the communist morality must be developed in the Soviet people. Such morality is based on devotion to communism and irreconcilability to its enemies, consciousness of public duty ... "and intolerance towards disturbers of public order."

The communist universities are called upon to play a large part in fostering the communist dogmas of the young generation. They seem to divide ethical principles into two categories: one before the communist revolution and the other after the revolution.

Pravda and other Soviet newspapers devote a substantial amount of space to the principles of communist morality. They ask all the people, particularly the intelligentsia, to cooperate with (or follow) the party's ideas. The artists, for example, are asked to arrange the necessary conditions for fulfillment of the ideas of socialistic realism.

---

[7]Counts, op. cit., p. 112. See also Ponomarev, op. cit., pp. 665–667; Boldyrev, Direktivi VKP (b) i sovetskogo pravit el'stva po narodnom obrazovanii, p. 193.

THE NECESSITY OF A CLASS STRUGGLE

The communist philosophy of government is built upon the struggle among classes, and this concept is constantly before students and the Soviet people in general. The Soviet man should always be aware that there could be no progress without class-struggle and that this progress requires sacrifices from time to time in the name of communism. This is important because, according to the Soviets, there is a natural process of Marxian development which would accomplish nothing without struggle between classes. In order that this struggle be continuous, an enemy of some kind is always existing in the Soviet society. The Soviet citizens know very well that the concept of the class-struggle need not be connected with a real enemy. Even an imaginary enemy will fulfill the desired function.

The communist party of Russia tirelessly produces all kinds of "evidences" of the inability of the capitalistic countries to establish a proper cultural relationship between the workers and other classes. They say that in the capitalistic countries the political and social structures are designed to deprive the average person of the cultural advantages that one might have at a particular time—always supporting these statements by citations from Lenin such as: "in the capitalistic countries the whole brain of a man is designed only for one purpose, i.e., to give everything to one man depriving the others of the basic needs of education and culture."[8]   true

The Russian communists say that contemporary capitalism is unable to provide definite cultural means and is unable to serve the cause of progress because it treats the working class as its enemy and that the number of unsatisfied people is growing rapidly among all strata of the population including physicians, teachers, engineers, etc. But in the socialistic societies, there is quite another story. Here everything is running smoothly, everybody is happy and satisfied.

The Soviet sources go to an extreme in praising their own accomplishments. For instance, Zhirnov insists that the most important feature of the socialistic culture is its idealistic way of approaching every individual and every group. Marxism, according to Zhirnov, is a mixture of two philosophies: materialism and idealism.

The principle of the class-struggle must involve all the people regard-

---

[8] V. E. Zhirnov, *Voprosy planirovaniia kul'turnogo stroitel'stva v SSSR* (Moscow: Gospolitizdat, 1958), pp. 5–6; Akademiia Nauk SSSR, *Osnovi marksiskoi filosofii* (Moscow: AN SSSR, 1959), p. 463.

less of age or sex. Khrushchev said at the 20th Party Congress that "education divorced from life and politics is a hypocrisy and a lie."

The school, most of all, must teach the basic Marxian steps of the class-struggle as the conscious and ideological foundation of the Marxian dialectics. These stages are described as having their origin in primitive societies. The initial stage is primitive communism when the people divide their profits among themselves on an equal basis. The second stage is known as the period of slavery; later comes the period of feudalism followed by capitalism; then socialism. Finally the highest stage of social development is to be found in the final stage of communism. No society and no nation striving to reach the perfect society is able to avoid this process. If necessary, the Soviets will even support nationalism just to maintain the class-struggle on the one hand and to fulfill the Marxian prophecy on the other.

The Soviets explain the existence of the American two-party system thus: the democrats and republicans are capitalistic creations to deprive the workers of their rights and daily bread.

It is for these reasons that the importance of the class-struggle is so strongly underlined by the Soviet authorities. The school must educate the conscious workers of communism and the world revolution, always teaching class structure not from the scientific point of view but from their own elaborated concepts.

RUSSIAN PATRIOTISM

Dostoevski once wrote that the Russian people were fortunate because Europe did not know anything about Russia, but once the Europeans understood Russia, the Russians would be in danger.

Although Dostoevski's comment applied to pre-revolutionary Russia, nevertheless it characterizes the present general spirit in Russia. Today the communists maintain that they are working for international friendship and solidarity. At the same time that friendship requires a huge military build-up and readiness of the Russian people to defend that friendship toward other nations. Of course, the duty of the school is to educate an all-around individual. That individual cannot afford to be indifferent to the Soviet political and social system. The Soviet citizen must be educated in the framework of Soviet patriotism and be blindly obedient to the rules of the party.

As mentioned before, the aim of Soviet education is to educate a new man, a man who devotes himself to spreading communism throughout the world. He loves all fellow communists but hates non-communists.

In the process of this transformation one principle is very important for all teachers: the New Soviet Man cannot be a product of some kind of ghost; the New Soviet Man first of all must be a new Russian who 'liberates' others and tries to teach other nations Russian culture, history and traditions. Therefore, it is much safer for citizens of the Soviet Union to forget their own cultures, like Uzbek, Tatar, Finnish, etc. The Soviet patriotism is nothing more than the Russian patriotism devoted entirely to the previous imperial policies.

Soviet nationalities are not allowed to celebrate their national holidays or honor their national heroes, unless those heroes were collaborating with the Russian empire or the communist regime. The Ukrainian Mazepa (who fought Peter I for the establishment of the independent Ukraine) is considered a traitor because he was against the czar. For Turkestanians, the national movements and liberation wars during the imperial regime "were nationalistic because they were against the Russian empire." A famous Russian writer, A. Blok, once wrote the following:

> Yea, Russia is a sphinx, exulting, grieving,
> And sweating blood she cannot sate.
> Her eyes that gaze, and gaze and gaze
> At you with stone-lipped love for you, and hate.[9]

Soviet indoctrination has no limits for achievement of the desired patriotic education. The children are educated in the spirit of love for Russia—regardless of their nationality—and about "unconquered" (nepobedimaia) Moscow. This method of educating the Soviet-Russian patriots is much more elaborate than during the Romanovs. The czars at least said clearly that they did not allow any national cultures. The Soviets make a great deal out of national culture, but in reality they apply more intensely oppressive techniques toward the non-Russian people of the Soviet Union than did the czars. Furthermore, in almost every country of the world the Russian communists are trying to subvert existing governments and promote national revolutions, promising political independence. The English colonies suffered the final blow not from national uprisings but from people trained and supported by the Kremlin. Here was the major key of the English end of colonialism. In satellite countries, too, the Russians were able to promise more than any other power. Once the situation was under control, they gave nothing in return.

Inside the Soviet Union, particularly in the Soviet Ukraine, the indoctrination in the spirit of the Soviet Russian patriotism is unavoidable.

---

[9]Woody, *op. cit.*, p. 19.

As an 'independent' state, the Soviet Ukraine had no national anthem or national flag. It was only after World War II when the Russians demanded several seats in the United Nations that the problem of the national flag and a national anthem was raised by some Western diplomats, who objected to seats for the Ukraine and Bellorussia on these grounds. It did not take long for the Russians to print in Soviet newspapers necessary emblems for these countries. Moscow then presented to the Ukraine a "national anthem and flag." The national anthem is worded as follows:

> Live my Ukraine, beautiful and strong,
> You found your happiness in the Soviet Union
> Being the freest among the free
> Flourishing like a flower under the free sun.[10]

These national symbols are fixed only for foreigners. Inside Russia a tremendous drive for promoting the Russian language and culture is taking stronger steps from day to day. After Sputnik was launched, Khrushchev commented with pride that Russian words need no interpretation anymore.

In conclusion, the aim of the Soviet school is to educate a type of Soviet patriot who does not see the difference between tenderness and brutality or between love and hate as long as these ideas are concentrated around "Mother Russia."

THE PRINCIPLE OF HATE

Hate is a very necessary thing in the Soviet social philosophy. Without this concept, according to the Soviets, one cannot love his own country or be a fighter for Marxism. It goes even beyond the broad love for one's country. The Soviet child is obligated to report to the police when he thinks his parents are not thinking properly. Many cases regarding this peculiar parent-state-child relationship are recorded in Soviet history.

The party often sponsors social gatherings where the young children are taught how to fight the incoming western ideas.

As an example, *Komsomolskaia Pravda* accused certain Soviet writers of having committed a crime against socialism because they based their literary subjects on "imported" bourgeois ideas.

The Soviet newspapers frequently defend the methods used by Stalin in the past, e.g., the leading Soviet journal, *Kommunist,* criticized those

---

[10]F. Virnyk, *Ukrainskaia SSR* (Moscow: Gospolitizdat, 1956), pp. 94–96.

people in literature and arts who are against the methods used by Stalin in building the socialist state. The journal accuses them of trying to defame the first socialist state in the world.

The communist party also attempts to set the younger generation against the older: the former as the progressive builder of communism and the latter as the regressive type of people who do not adjust themselves to the present situations. The Soviet writers who dare to follow strict literary lines (literary style, movements, pattern of writing, etc.) rather than imposed party lines often fall under the latter heading. This, in itself, brings psychological confusion to the young generation since they read and hear contradictions on the part of the party and historical events. They ask themselves questions: "How are we to live in the future? Are we to continue repeating the mistakes of our fathers?"

In 1964, a young writer, Simonenko, in his diary accused the Kremlin of immorality and repression against non-Russians. Simonenko wrote that during his twenty-eight years of existence he did not learn nor was he taught anything other than hate toward his fellowman. He said, "I learned how to drink, smoke, to tell lies . . . and lies are defended by the authorities if they are in the name of communism."[11]

Such people as Evtushenko are often criticized by the party for not giving youth the example of their own solidarity to the party.

Briefly, the aim of education is to educate the youth in the principle of hate toward the West and Anglo-American imperialism.

TO SURPASS AMERICA

The Soviet goal of surpassing the United States has many facets including hard work by Soviet citizens as well as some imaginary successes claimed by the communist statistical publications. From the very beginning of the Soviet regime the drive was on to change an agricultural country into a huge industrial power using the slogan: "We shall surpass America." To achieve this aim at least partially the communist authorities have employed about 20 million slave laborers at one time or another.

A planned socialist economy is another endeavor of the communists to

---

[11] *Pravda,* March 9, 1963. See also *Kommunist,* No. 1, 1963, p. 94; *Komsomolskaia pravda,* March 12, 1963, *Kommunist,* No. 4, 1963, pp. 8–9; Komsonolskaia pravda, March 2, 1962, *Iunost,* vol. II, 1963, pp. 47 ff.; V. Symoneneko, "A Diary Which Horrified Moscow," in *The Ukrainian Quarterly* (New York), vol. XXII, No. 2, 1966, pp. 162 ff.

improve their economic conditions. The Kremlin initiated many plans: the Five-Year Plan, the Seven-Year Plan and lately even a Twenty-Year Plan. If these plans do not work, they usually blame the United States for their failure, saying that the need for rearmament against the bourgeois who are preparing for war does not allow completion of the various plans.

Still another method of "surpassing" the capitalistic nations is statistical publications in all important languages, especially English, aimed at supplying impressive data on the Soviet economy. Ridiculous as it may seem, the success is such that many times the Russian government has to ask for wheat from Canada or the United States.

Educational statistics are therefore designed to serve the party goals of showing the superiority of the socialistic system over any other systems. Sometimes it is confusing even to the Soviets because the Soviet press occasionally allows criticism on the lack of certain professional workers or on the incompetence of teachers. On the other hand the statistical publications report that there are more than enough Soviet engineers and scholars, in fact more than in the United States. For instance in 1959, the Soviets reported that 80,000 engineers graduated from Soviet universities as compared to 34,000 engineers graduated in the United States. Also, the number of students at higher educational institutions is always higher in the Soviet Union than it is in the United States.

RESPECT FOR AUTHORITY

In Soviet society an individual is punishable by law when he or she is twelve years of age. The laws of 1930 together with some 1956 revisions provide severe measures against children who violate the rules of the social order.

The principle of fear, of course, applies more to the adult population than it does to children. There is always tension, real persecution or psychological warfare which serves to remind the Soviet people of the dictatorial regime.

The aim of the Soviet authorities in education is, therefore, not only to enforce discipline in the classroom but also to inculcate respect for Soviet authorities. The directives of the communist party of Russia concerning youth clearly state that only a well-disciplined youth can help the spread of communism. Students are reminded that 130,000 well-disciplined people ran the empire during the czarist regime. Lenin did the same with 240,000 devoted communists.

Additional References

Tsentral'noe Statisticheskoe Upravlenie pri Sovete Ministrov SSSR, *Dostizhenie sovetskoi vlasti za sorok let* (Moscow: Gosstatizdat, 1957), p. 231; V. I Lenin, *Sochineniia,* vol. 31, pp. 261–274; Akademiia Nauk SSSR, *Kommunisticheskoe vospitanie v sovetskoi shkole* (Moscow: AN SSSR, 1950), especially pages 8–83; E. N. Medynskii, *Narodnoe obrazovanie v SSSR* (Moscow: APN RSFSR, 1952; Anton S. Makarenko, *Izbrannye pedagogicheskie sochineniia* (Moscow: Uchpedgiz, 1946), pp. 33–60; *Vestnik vysshei shkoly,* No. 11, 1959, p. 3; George Bereday and Others, *The Politics of Soviet Education* (New York: F. Praeger Press, 1960); B. Hayit, "Turkestan as Example of Soviet Colonialism," in *Studies on the Soviet Union,* vol. II, 1961, pp. 1–18; Narkompros UzSSR, *Nauka v Uzbekistane za 15 let* (Tashkent: Izdatel'stvo Narkomprosa, 1939, passim; John Gunther, *Inside Russia Today* (London: Hamilton Press, 1958), pp. 207 ff.; Leon Trotsky, *The Real Situation in Russia* (New York: Harcourt Brace and Co., 1928); Gustav Wetter, *Dialectical Materialism* (London: Routledge and Kegan Ltd., 1958), passim.

Chapter 4

SOVIET EDUCATIONAL
AND CULTURAL REFORMS

The Bolshevik Revolution of 1917 was quite different from any other revolution in the history of mankind. It touched the political structure of the government and involved many phases of social and educational life, including national traditions, habits, ways of life of various ethnic groups and religious beliefs. Most of all, it aimed at a complete change of the human mind. The methods of force and violence used in political affairs were also the methods of implementation in educational and social affairs.

As far as educational opportunity before the revolution is concerned, there is little to praise in the imperial regime for the Russian or the non-Russian people. In order to have a better idea about Soviet educational reforms, we shall illustrate the general trends in Soviet educational reforms for non-Russian people, taking as examples the two largest non-Russian groups, the Ukrainians and the Muslim-Turcic group.

PROBLEMS OF ILLITERACY

Soviet and imperial sources classified literacy in two categories—*gramotnyi* (literate) and *malogramotnyi* (semi-literate). To the first

67

category belonged those who could read or write without any help, and to the second category, those who needed some help in either reading or writing. The Soviets demanded that a literate man should be familiar with his socio-cultural development.

A more complicated problem than the definition of literacy was the lack of precise estimation. Neither the imperial statistical publications nor the Soviet ones included a careful study of the rate of literacy among the entire population. For example, imperial publications as of 1897 estimated that the literacy among people of Turkestan was 7.5 per cent among men and 2 per cent among women. The Soviets included a variety of estimations, ranging from zero to 2 per cent for Asiatic native population and between 28 and 30 per cent for the whole empire (see also Table 4 in the Appendix).

After the 1917 Bolshevik Revolution, the situation began to change. Lenin and his government demanded that illiteracy be eliminated, stating that it was impossible to talk about politics and change as long as there was a mass of illiterates. The People's Commissariat of Education issued a decree in December of 1918, calling for the speedy establishment of educational centers aimed at liquidation of illiteracy. There was, however, a twofold task assigned to those people who were to teach others how to read and write. They had to propagate the policies of the Soviet government as well as to teach the skills of literacy. In 1919, Lenin signed another decree, this time ordering all the literate people to help those who were illiterates.

Similar demands and resolutions by the party continued after Lenin's death since the problem of illiteracy was far from over. In 1925, another decree was passed by the party with the added slogan, 'Down with Illiteracy.' In 1929, still another reminder was issued to rural and industrial centers. In 1930, the Commissariat of Education issued a statement saying that tremendous progress had been made in the area of liquidating illiteracy, but at the same time it underlined some deficiencies in the general level of education.

Reviewing historical data on the Soviet campaign against illiteracy, one can see that in 1925 there were, for example, 1.5 million students in schools for illiterates compared to a total number of 750,000 in grades 5-9. Medyski estimated that about 50 million people went through schools for illiterates during the years 1920-1940. In 1932 alone, more than 7.6 million people were taught to read and write in various parts of the Soviet Union, while in the same year there were 6.6 million people in schools for *malogramotnye* or semi-literates. (See Figures 1, 2, and Table 9).

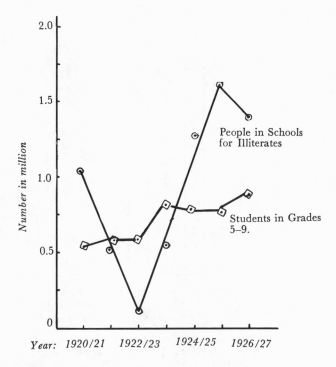

FIGURE 1. Number of students in schools for
illiterates and secondary schools

Calculated from: *Soviet Union Year-Book, 1929*
(London: George Allen and Unwin Ltd., 1929),
pp. 477–79.

These campaigns were part of the program launched throughout the
whole U.S.S.R. For example, in 1930, about 86 per cent of all the school
population were in schools for illiterates; the figure dropped to fewer
than 54 per cent by 1932. In 1897 one notes that 28 per cent of the
population of the Russian Empire was literate; in 1939—some 42 years
later—87 per cent of the population was literate, and during this same
time span, the percentage of literate women rose from 17 per cent to
82 per cent.

A comparison of the world illiteracy rate during the period 1955-1965
shows the following: the whole world 43 to 45 per cent; Western Europe
7 to 9 per cent; Asia 60 to 65 per cent; Africa 80 to 85 per cent; North

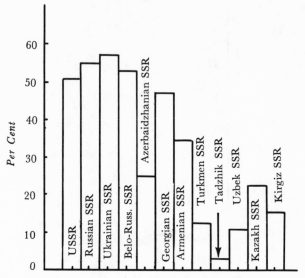

FIGURE 2. Literacy of the population in the
USSR according to union republics,
nine years of age and older, 1926.

Calculated from: E. N. Medinski, *Narodnoe
obrazovanie v SSSR* (Moscow: Izdat APN RSFSR,
1952), p. 31.

America 3 to 4 per cent; South America 42 to 44 per cent; and the
U.S.S.R. according to the Soviets 1.5 per cent.[1]

DEVELOPMENT OF ELEMENTARY AND SECONDARY EDUCATION

First Period (1917-1936) The early development of Soviet education
in general was marked by many radical ideas, policies and laws which
were substantially changed in later Soviet educational practice. To such
a radical policy belonged the announcement on 'Unified Labor Schools'
(*Edinaia Trudovaia Shkola*), which was made by the All-Russian Executive Committee on October 16, 1918. This decree was designed to replace

---

[1] Nirkin, *op. cit.*, p. 141. See also *Bol'shaia Sovetskaia Entsiklopediia*, vol. 12
(1959), pp. 433–450; *Soviet Union Yearbook*, 1926 (London: George Allen and
Unwin, 1926), pp. 477–479; Medynskii, *Narodnoe obrazovanie*, pp. 114–115;
M. M. Deineko, *Sorok let narodnogo obrazovaniia v SSSR* (Moscow: Izdat.
Ministerstva Prosveshcheniia RSFSR, 1957), p. 206; Tsentral'noe Statisticheskoe
Upravlenie pri Sovete Ministrov SSSR, *Itogi vsesoiusnoi perepisi naseleniia 1959 g.*
(Moscow: Gosstatizdat, 1962), p. 89.

TABLE 9

Number of Schools and Students in the U.S.S.R. on Jan. 1, 1925

Educational Institutions	No. of Schools	No. of Students
Pre-School Institutions	1,146	60,002
Elementary Schools	71,567	5,821,872
Schools for 7-year-olds	17,706	2,470,710
Schools for 9-year-olds	754	437,171
Secondary Schools	1,041	272,330
School Communes	195	19,960
Schools for Defectives	181	11,323
Total	91,444	9,033,366
Children's Homes and Colonies	3,531	299,504
Children's Homes and Colonies for Defectives	296	17,014
Reception, Isolation and Distribution Centers	244	16,862
Total	4,071	333,380
Grand Total	96,661	9,426,748
Technical Education Total	4,139	645,215
I. Higher Educational Institutions	167	166,928
II. Workers' Faculties	113	42,220
III. Secondary and Elementary Technical Schools	3,859	436,067
Class III includes:		
a. Technical Institutes	873	157,685
b. Trade Schools	2,017	196,674
c. Factory & Workshop	773	68,762
d. Model Workshop	196	12,946

Soviet Union Year-Book, 1926. Edited by A. A. Santalov (London: George Allen and Unwin Ltd.), p. 455.

imperial educational theories and practices promising all-around education, respect for individuality, humanism, democracy, instructional unity in all schools, active methods of instruction, etc.

More specifically, the decree listed provisions regarding teacher-student relationships, administration and structure of the school. It stated that all schools in the Russian Soviet Republic (except the higher educational institutions) would be named Unified Labor Schools, in which the first five years would be known as the first division (age of students from eight to thirteen) and the remaining four years (ages fourteen to seventeen) known as the second division. It further emphasized that education would be free and compulsory for both sexes until seventeen years of age, and also, that any religious training in public schools would be prohibited by law. The decree stated that the conceptual basis for educational activities should be the productive work of individuals, participation of children in class activities and school administration, elimination of the older forms of discipline, prohibition of punishment, omission of all examinations (entrance and passing), complete freedom of students to organize their youth centers, etc.

This policy called for repudiation of all previous official theories and practices, even though as yet, there were no new trained personnel capable of carrying out the new policies. By 1919, some additional provisions had been made (although the main principles of the *trudovaia shkola* were to be retained), and these became the guideline for future Soviet educational policies.

Foundations of the Soviet educational system are found in the 1919 program of the Eighth Congress of the Russian Communist Party in which it was stated that the task of the Soviet school was

> to fulfill the original purpose of the October Revolution of converting schools from aristocratic and bourgeois-dominated selective education to complete destruction of the division of society into classes.[2]

The school should be, according to this view, an instrument for the regeneration of communism. The school should play a leading role in influencing the semi-proletarian and non-proletarian masses through communistic ideas and should educate a generation capable of building communism.

Some important provisions of this program are:

a. The establishment of free and compulsory polytechnical education for all children of both sexes up to seventeen years of age;
b. The establishment of pre-educational schools (kindergartens) for the purpose of improving general education and emancipating women;
c. The complete realization of Unified Labor School principles, with instruction in one's native language, co-educational practices, freedom from any kind of religious influences, and tight relationships with general productive work to prepare the child to be an all-around member of the communist society;

---

[2]*KPSS v rezoliutsiiakh i resheniiakh s'iezdov,* vol. 1, p. 420; Boldyrev, *op. cit.,* (vypusk 1), p. 120.

d. The provisions to supply all students with clothing, food and educational materials;

e. The preparation of new cadres of educational workers indoctrinated with communistic ideals and ideas;

f. The complete state aid to facilitate self-education and self-development of workers and peasants—establishment of schools for adults, lectures, libraries, etc.;

g. The broad development of professional education for persons above seventeen years of age in line with general polytechnical knowledge;

h. The opportunity of a higher education for all who are willing to study—particularly workers and peasants—and financial aid to students;

i. The development of the broadest possible propaganda of communist ideas with the use of state apparatus.

But the transition from education limited to a relatively select few (before the revolution) to universal education could not be effected by merely publishing decrees. Compulsory elementary education came into existence only after 1930. In addition to the physical problems, e.g., the country had a limited supply of teachers and schools—economic and industrial development was just getting under way.

Other revisions of goals came as early as 1923, when party leaders in their resolutions proved less ambitious than they had been in 1918. For example, a decree on Unified Labor Schools by the People's Commissariat of the RSFSR, December 18, 1923, stated that the definitive aim of the Unified Labor School was to give children an opportunity to gain knowledge, habits and other necessities of a rational program pertinent to the education of the individual and working people. The decree also specified the qualifications necessary for a school administrator (unlike the decree of 1918, in which an administrative function was not properly defined; it stated only that education would be administered by a School Council); it specified that the director of a school should be chosen from the pedagogical personnel—those who are ranked as educators. By these decrees and others the introduction of compulsory elementary education began to take evolutionary rather than revolutionary steps. Experience proved that the realization of this goal could not be accomplished as readily as was thought during the early revolutionary period. This policy transition is clearly evident in subsequent decrees, which called for carefully planned programs, and specified the kinds needed by Soviet society.

Another problem that Russian educators neglected to consider in their enthusiastic planning was financial resources. Experience proved that such radical policies would not guarantee the financial needs of all schools since high expenditures had to be made for teaching facilities, equipment, preparation of teachers, students, etc. Therefore, a decree was issued by the Council of People's Commissars of the U.S.S.R. in 1929, ordering all higher and technological establishments of the Union to charge tuition for the use of books and equipment, and for attendance at class. Thus, the laws of 1918 and of April 4, 1924, were superseded by the new law of 1929. According to Korolev, the introduction of universal primary education required an enormous amount of money. For example, in 1926, 7.5 million rubles were spent on education and by 1929, 30.9 million rubles. The introduction of compulsory four year education required 2 billion and 758 million rubles in the implementation of the plan.

Taking into consideration financial problems which had to be overcome first, the *Narkompros* did not see any possible solution by which compulsory education could be introduced before 1933-1934. They repeatedly expressed this idea, holding that it would be possible to achieve this goal with a planned enrollment program and enough trained teachers to accommodate such a large expansion. According to their plan, during the school year of 1927-1928, 70 per cent of the country's children would be in schools; in 1928-1929, 80.4 per cent; and by 1933-1934, 97.1 per cent.[3]

However, in 1930, Stalin declared that the time had arrived for the introduction of compulsory universal elementary education and asked the *Narkompros* to make preparation in this direction. Therefore, in July of 1930, the party issued a resolution stating that the development of socialist construction required a speedy educational reform, namely, the introduction of compulsory education. The party also decreed that during 1930-1931 all children in the age group of eight to ten and those who had no opportunity to attend school and were in the age group of eleven to fifteen, should be given educational opportunities. A provision was also made for the school year 1931-1932, whereby all children in the age group of eight to eleven were to be enrolled in the elementary school system. On August 19, 1930, the law was passed by the *Sovnarkom* of the RSFSR; all union republics were ordered to establish compulsory instruction for all children in the age group of eight to ten.

By 1931, universal compulsory elementary education was required throughout the U.S.S.R. However, the details of the program were in-

---

[3] F. F. Korolev; A. Smirnov, *Sovetskaia shkola v period sotsialisticheskoi industrializatsii* (Moscow: Gospedizdat, 1959), pp. 36–37; Akademiia Pedagogicheskikh Nauk RSFSR, *Sbornik rukovodiashchikh materialov o shkole* (Moscow: APN RSFSR, 1952), p. 45.

sufficient. Therefore, another party decree listing basic aims and needs of the program was passed September 5, 1931. (Some of these requirements merit special attention, and they are discussed below in connection with problems of educational theory.)

Much emphasis was given to the preparation of teachers who would support the Marxist-Leninist ideology. According to the decree, the Soviet teacher was to be on a level higher than he had ever been before, "and he could not represent bourgeois values and society." Teachers had to be familiar with the industrial needs and requirements of their area and prepare their students to meet these needs.

All republics were to take definite measures to improve both the construction of schools and school equipment. A five-year plan that demanded that basic school equipment be provided by 1932 was introduced to achieve this.

Thus, for the first time in the history of Russia, universal compulsory elementary education came into being. There were, however, some weak points in the decree, particularly in the demand that teachers and schools fulfill all requirements within the prescribed time limit.

The overriding idea of Soviet authorities during that time was to implement the concepts of socialist education, especially the idea of socially useful labor. Many educators were studied before the Bolshevik Revolution, particularly Robert Owen. The Soviet educators tried to include everyone in the camp of socially useful labor, but there were no definite plans as to how to achieve these ends.

Having no exact theoretical beckground of polytechnical education, the Soviet educators searched for the answers to their problems in many countries and in many theories. Most of them were quite impressed with the educational ideas of American instrumentalists, especially John Dewey. (More about the foreign influences on the Soviet education will be presented in the chapter dealing with the philosophical foundations of Soviet education.) The problems of profiting from American educational experiences arose very soon, because the psychological and social conditions in the United States were entirely different from those in Russia. For obvious reasons the democratic ideas of American instrumentalists could not work in a dictatorial society. After many teachers complained of the lack of discipline when using American educational practices, the party decided to abolish entirely any foreign influences—thus terminating all Dewey influences on the Soviet educational scene. In 1936, a special law that prohibited any pedagogical practices of foreign derivation was passed by the Soviet government. Dewey and his associates were de-

76   Communist Education

nounced as reactionary bourgeois educators and Soviet educators were told they would be punished if they followed his ideas.[4] (See Table 10, the level of educational achievements.)

TABLE 10

Increase in Number of Schools, School Children and Teachers, 1928–35

| | Year | Schools | Teachers | Pupils | |
				Absolute figures	Per Cent of 1928–29
A	B	1	2	3	4
USSR—Total (All types of schools for genr. educ.)	1928–29	124,429	363,328	12,074,806	100.0
	1929–30	132,656	391,869	13,503,712	111.8
	1930–31	152,654	479,839	17,656,232	146.2
	1931–32	167,262	569,749	20,846,232	172.6
	1932–33	167,254	631,257	21,813,452	180.7
	1933–34	166,737	655,696	22,003,631	182.2
	1934–35	162,904	709,378	23,555,807	195.1
Cities	1928–29	11,103	133,944	3,342,767	100.0
	1929–30	11,130	136,192	3,550,887	106.2
	1930–31	10,790	139,171	3,809,228	114.0
	1931–32	11,257	149,672	4,526,201	135.4
	1932–33	11,120	166,026	4,904,161	146.7
	1933–34	11,538	167,277	5,113,005	153.0
	1934–35	12,552	193,520	6,087,836	182.1
Rural	1928–29	113,326	229,384	8,732,039	100.0
	1929–30	121,526	255,677	9,732,039	114.0
	1930–31	141,874	340,668	13,847,004	158.6
	1931–32	156,005	420,077	16,320,031	186.9
	1932–33	156,134	465,231	16,909,291	193.6
	1933–34	155,199	488,419	16,890,626	193.4
	1934–35	150,352	515,858	17,467,971	200.0

Central Administration of Economic and Social Statistics of the State Planning Commission of the USSR, *Socialist Construction in the USSR. Statistical Abstract* (Moscow: Soyuzorgouchet, 1936), p. 446.

[4] *Sbornik rukovodiashchikh materialov o shkole,* pp. 99; *O programe KPSS,* p. 499.

Second Period (1936-1956). This period was characterized by the implementation of decisions and educational ideas set forth during the late 1930s, especially by the law of 1936. There was no longer a desire to experiment with new ideas but only to continue the Russian educational heritage, changing only the names of schools but leaving the basic educational concepts unaltered. Although the Soviet sources call this period the "victory of socialism," it would be more accurate to describe it as a shift back to traditional Russian education.

The pre-revolutionary educational practices—strict discipline, the importance of subject matter, respect for the teacher—were reintroduced to the Soviet schools; any deviation from the above points was punishable by Soviet law. Insolvent or impudent student behavior toward the teachers was not tolerated. The students were required to apply themselves very seriously to school and to educators in general. The Soviet educational authorities went further than that: they reinstated the pre-revolutionary practice of regarding the secondary school as strictly a 'college preparatory school.'

Industrialization was the official policy of the Soviet state from 1928 on; the aim of education was to produce as many technological specialists as possible. The level of this education was frequently less than desirable; nevertheless, the process of changing the agricultural country into an industrial power proceeded.

Third Period (1957-1967). In 1956, Khrushchev began his famous attack on the 'cult of personality' by criticizing Stalin for all the purges of the Soviet population. At the same time Khrushchev thought that the existing educational structure was insufficient, primarily because the students lost contact with the working population. To remedy that, he introduced the *work and study plan*—all who want to enter higher educational institutions must work at least two years in the national economy.

Much was written and said about the new plan, but soon after the fall of Khrushchev it also became a subject for criticism. In 1965, Soviet education went back to that of the pre-Khrushchevian period. The eleven year program of general education was reduced to ten and the physical labor requirement was omitted.

There were many complaints against the Khrushchevian plan. It was called impractical, lacking in educational foundations, deficient in actual time spent in general school (because of the two years lost in industry), encouraging children to imitate bad habits (language, drinking after working hours, etc.) while working with the labor force.

The Soviet sources indicate that the main features of this total period were education in the spirit of physical labor, participation of students in the socialist construction, development of a multi-national socialist culture.[5] But regardless of what the Soviets write about it, the main goal of Soviet education was to overtake the Western European countries and the United States in industrial man-power by concentrating on the technological specialties that the country needed so badly.

EDUCATIONAL DEVELOPMENT IN THE SOVIET UKRAINE

The significance of the Ukrainian SSR lies not only in the agricultural sphere (it is the breadbasket of Europe) but also in political, educational and social affairs. Ukraine has 45 million inhabitants and is the second largest Soviet republic.

As mentioned before, the historical and cultural development of Ukraine was quite different from that of Moscovite Russia; the reasons are two-fold. First, Ukraine is located in the western part of the U.S.S.R. and, second, parts of Ukraine at one time or another were subjected to foreign domination. Both resulted in the assimilation of Western civilization much earlier than that of the Russian.

When the revolution broke out, the Ukrainians, as all other non-Russian nations, were afraid of Russification and tried to protect their individual national character. The Russian communists promised complete independence to the Ukrainians. Stalin, being the head of the nationality programs in Lenin's government, promised full independence if the Ukrainians would help win the war. He called for the unity of workers regardless of their nationality.

The solution of the nationality question for all people in the Russian empire was approached by the communists from the Marxian point of view, which was a new doctrine of the political and social order. The foundation of this new social order rested on the concepts of internationalism (i.e., a movement which subordinated any nationality to the abstract superstructure of internationality) and interest in the worker and peasant class. A combination of these concepts resulted in the complete Russian domination of national government. In 1920, all key positions of the Ukrainians, Turkestanians, and others were in Russian hands.

The educational development of the Ukrainian SSR could be divided similarly to the Russian. But, more properly, it should be divided into three categories: (1) education during the period of independence, 1917-

---

[5] Ponomarev, *Istoriia Kommunisticheskoi Partii Sovetskogo Soiuza*, p. 700; *Pravda*, August 14, 1959; V. Z. Smirnov, *Khrestomatiia po istorii pedagogiki*, p. 564.

1920/21; (2) education during the NEP period, known as the period of Ukrainization; and (3) the period of the Soviet Russian culture from 1930 on.

First Period (1917-1921). Together with the declaration of Ukrainian independence and the establishment of the Ukrainian Assembly under the leadership of S. Petliura, the Ukrainian educational structure began to take shape. On April 5, 1917, the Congress of Ukrainian teachers met in Kiev for the purpose of laying a foundation for Ukrainian education. This Congress established several important points:

1. In all urban and rural areas educational boards shall be organized to establish elementary and secondary public schools.

2. Priorities in such establishments shall be given to gymnasiums.

3. The publication of textbooks, especially those dealing with history, shall be sanctioned by the Educational Board. Complete freedom in methods of teaching shall be given to all teachers at all levels.

4. All citizens of the republic have the right to an education. Schools for the national minorities are guaranteed by the law.

5. The school system in Ukraine should be the same for all students regardless of the social origin.

Further recommendations and decisions of the educational authorities stressed that the Ukrainian language was to be used in schools, especially at the elementary and secondary levels; a library system was to be organized in the republic; and short range pedagogical courses were to be organized for elementary and secondary school teachers.

During the period of independence, which lasted only three years, fundamentals were set that later became the foundation of the Russian school system. The type of school which the Russians especially copied was the *Iedina Trudova Shkola* (Unified Labor School). The Ukrainian school of this type operated under the following laws: all education must be compulsory and free for children eight to sixteen years of age; all books and food for children while in school should be free of charge; all financial matters must be in line with the socialistic programs; the language in school should be the native language of the child.

Elementary education consisted of two levels, the lower and the upper grades. Each lasted four years. (The Russian program consisted of four and three years; the three years in Soviet Russia were called a semi-secondary school.) Religion was a compulsory subject in the school curriculum.

As far as secondary and higher education were concerned, there were no significant changes made either in terms of structure or curriculum.

Second Period (1921-1931). The Ukrainians call this period the Enlightenment of National Education, while the Russians term it as the
struggle against the national romantic. The struggle began, first of all,
for the language of instruction and the official language of the state in
general. While the Russian communists promised a full independence,
all educational instructions were printed in Russian and demanded that
the education of the new man be carried out in the spirit of the communistic society—communism should become an organic part of the
people. The Ukrainian communist authorities in education, under the
leadership of G. Hrinko, wanted to build a communist type of school
but maintain the Ukrainian language. The communist party of Russia,
however, wanted to educate an international proletariat and to maintain
the superiority of the Russian language and culture. Instead of sound elementary and secondary education, they emphasized the *dopomizhni usta-
novy* (relief establishments) and put before themselves the task of
re-educating Ukrainian society. From 1920 on, the most important schools
were not those dealing with general education but those for indoctrinating youth in communist propaganda. There were four types of such
schools: (1) professional schools for workers; (2) general schools for
political knowledge; (3) schools for party members and (4) schools for
mass political education. Only after completing one of these schools could
a student continue his education on another level, for example, agricultural economy (a general three-year program for adults), state and local
administration, or other vocational areas.

In 1929, a Ukrainian communist, Mykola Skrypnyk, attacked the
educational system of Hrinko, saying that it had no national coloring,
and it did not satisfy the Ukrainian needs in education. Skrypnyk, a
friend of Lenin, was quite successful at first in changing the Russian type
of education and in establishing a national-communist educational system
with the emphasis on the Ukrainian language and culture.

For a few years at least, this process affected quite a number of people
at home and abroad. Many emigrés began to change their minds about
Ukrainian Bolshevism and returned home to work for the Ukrainian
national, although communist, culture. Skrypnyk was quite effective in
maintaining and organizing the national cultural reforms at that time.[6]
However, in 1931, eleven top administrators were called to Moscow to
'discuss' the policy of communist revolution. They never came back.
Skrypnyk, together with Ukrainian President Lubchenko, reportedly committed suicide, and thus ended this establishment.

---

[6] Krylov, *Sistema narodnoi osvity v Ukraini*, p. 8–79.

Third Period (1931 and after). This period may be characterized by inconsistency. The Russian communists were advertising 'flourishing' national cultures, but in reality strong Russification trends were continuing.

A typical example of the Bolshevik national policy was seen after the death of Skrypnyk, when all the non-communists were in a very unfavorable position. The national intelligentsia suffered the first blow of the purges introduced by Postishev and Stalin. In 1932, for instance, there were 10,063 scientific workers in the Ukrainian SSR. In 1933, the number dropped to 8,415 and in 1940, to 5,000. What caused such a decrease among the Ukrainian intellectuals? Soviet sources do not explain. The same applies to the number of Ukrainian students at higher educational institutions when the general educational student body increased. For example, in 1940, there were 127,000 students in the general educational system; 275,000 in 1954; and 643,800 in 1965; but the number of the Ukrainian students decreased. (See also Figure 3.)

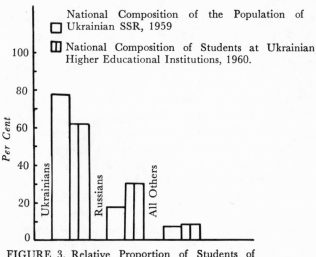

FIGURE 3. Relative Proportion of Students of Higher Educational Institutions in Ukraine.

Calculated from: John Kolasky, *Education in Soviet Ukraine* Toronto: Peter Martin Press, 1968), pp. 214–215.

The development of the national culture, as the Russians advertised it, was not quite logical when one considers the data of various publica-

82   Communist Education

tions. For example, in 1956, the percentage of Ukrainian language periodicals in the U.S.S.R. amounted to less than 10 per cent of the total number of periodicals, while the Ukrainians constituted more than 20 per cent of the population. Furthermore, of 212 different periodicals in 1956, less than 28 per cent were printed in the national languages.

There are about 27 per cent of non-Russians living in the Russian republic, but not a single periodical is printed in the vernacular languages. The number of journals in native languages is entirely disproportionate to those in Russian. Only five republics have some kind of scientific periodical and all important journals are published in Russian. Sometimes the cover is in the vernacular language, but the content of the journal is in Russian.

Status of the vernacular language in books on various branches of the national economy, varied according to the importance of a product or the area of industrial concern. Before World War II, the People's Commissariat of Education recommended to workers certain books for their vocational and industrial training. In the agricultural branch of the economy, we see that only two books were published in the Ukrainian language compared to thirty-six in Russian. There were no books recommended on metallurgy in the Ukrainian language and only one on railroad transportation as compared to seventy-one in Russian. Also, in 1950, the Academy of the Ukrainian Sciences published 210 different books, in 1951, only 180, and in 1952, only 135.[7]

Another aspect of national cultural development policy is noted in the relocation of Ukrainian scientific workers and technological personnel. In 1954, alone, more than 40,000 Ukrainian mechanics, of which 11,000 were agricultural mechanics, were sent to Kazakhstan. This was 10 per cent of all Ukrainian manpower being transposed to this area. In return Russian specialists were sent to Ukraine. They taught in Ukrainian schools and promoted the Russian language. In 1953, nearly 78 per cent of the Ukrainian Higher Educational Institutes were Russified, that is, the use of Ukrainian was prohibited as the language of the school. In the same year in the Western Ukraine not a single college was allowed to use the Ukrainian language as its administrative language. In Kiev, more than 80 per cent of all colleges and technical schools were converted into Russian schools. (See also Figures 4 and 5.)

Considering this data, we can say that the official language of most Ukrainian colleges and universities is not Ukrainian but Russian.

[7] V. Virnyk, *Istoriia Ukrainskoi SSR*, p. 179; Krylov, *op. cit., p. 79; D. Solovei, Natsional'na polityka partii i uriadu v Ukraini* (Munich: Institute for the Study of the USSR, 1956), pp. 113–133.

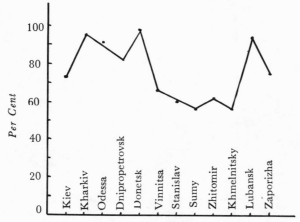

FIGURE 4. Russification of Ukraine: Per Cent of Students in Russian Schools (Out of the Total Student Population of the Ukrainian SSR) in Some Major Cities of the Republic, 1959.

Calculated from: John Kolasky, *Education in Soviet Ukraine* (Toronto: Peter Martin Press, 1968), p. 57.

In other cultural media the process of Russification was taking place. The Ukrainians complained that in 1964, the most important section of the state library in Kiev, the section containing historical documents and archives, was set afire. They claim that all the historical evidences of Ukrainian national movements and Ukrainian history were purposely destroyed by arson. Even in Ukraine, this episode is mentioned "once upon a time," but the reason is not stated. A trial was ordered in 1964, where certain people testified that not they but the communist authorities should be accused.

Ukrainian national museums and churches were either converted to Russian museums or "run down by the tractors and used as fire wood."[8]

Therefore, only after a careful investigation of the Russian cultural policies in non-Russian schools and cultural institutions can one rationally examine the statistical data of the Soviet government. It is true that the number of students had increased from 2.4 million in 1926 to 8.5 million in 1965; (see Appendix, Table 5) but this could have also been

---

[8] *Literaturna Ukraina,* June 18, 1965; *Radianska kul'tura,* May 28, 1964; Solovei, *op. cit.,* pp. 113–133.

84   Communist Education

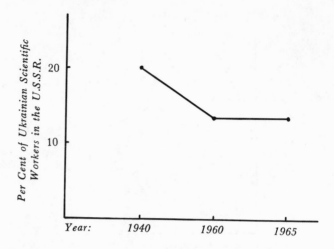

FIGURE 5. Decrease of Scientific Workers in Ukraine

Calculated from: Tsentral'noe Statisticheskoe Upravlenie pri Sovete Ministrov SSSR, *Narodnoe khoziastvo v 1963, 1964, 1965* (Moscow: Gosstatizdat, 1964, 1965, 1966), pp. 592, 702, and 712 respectively.

achieved without the use of terror or the degradation of national culture. The Russian communists do increase the number of students in elementary schools simply because literacy on the part of everyone is required by law; but in higher institutions the situation is entirely different. There the policy of Russification still exists and only trusted students are able to continue in their desired professions.

EDUCATION IN CENTRAL ASIA

As mentioned in Chapter 1, pre-revolutionary Turkestan was divided into several republics during the period of 1924-1936. Their Muslim educational system, too, was changed and religious schools were prohibited by law. The *Jadid* or New Method School—a progressive type of Muslim religious school—was also hindered by Russian laws and was subsequently liquidated.

After the revolution, the Bolsheviks at first prohibited any kind of religious education, including that given in the Muslim schools. Soon after, however, Lenin saw that it was necessary to allow Muslim elementary and secondary schools in order to influence Muslims outside the Soviet Union. At the same time the communists led extensive propaganda designed to liquidate the Muslim religious schools in that region.

By 1928, of 7,000 Muslim schools, 7,417 teachers and more than 100,000 students, nothing was left.

In view of this situation, the Muslim educational and cultural development was quite different from the Russian. The educational development of Central Asia can be divided on the basis of local conditions. Such a division can be categorized into three periods: (1) the revolutionary period lasting until Turkestan was divided into several small republics (1925); (2) the period of co-existence between the Muslim religious schools and the public schools (1923-1928) and (3) the period of Sovietization, or in Soviet Russian terms, the victory of socialism (1928-on).

First Period. Educational developments during the first period were largely influenced by two factors: (1) the 1918 declaration of 'equal' educational opportunity for all peoples; (2) legal provisions for the enactment of the declaration.[9]

In Central Asia, however, only initial steps were taken to organize public education during the period of 1918-1924. The 1918 Turkestan 'Constitution' contained certain clauses which specified educational opportunities for all; to accomplish this a special agency was set up to direct the reconstruction of education. But the traditional native school system was too strong to be radically reorganized or to accept changes in line with Soviet aims. In 1920, Lenin ordered the Turkestan Commission to collaborate with the natives and to engage them in the social and cultural work of the Soviets. He solicited the commission's aid in fighting the Russian *kulaks* of the area and enunciated the proper measures to be followed in the struggle against the clergy and local nationalists.

The pressure the natives put on the Bolsheviks can be observed in the Soviet concessions made in favor of Islam and Islamic schools. The decree of February 14, 1923, ordered local executive centers of Turkestan not to interfere with Muslim religious schools. Furthermore, the law provided certain rights for religious schools and establishments of the Muslim Educational Council, *Makhkamei Shirai,* a legally approved administrative body of Turkestan.[10]

The council was to take necessary measures to spread revolutionary, religious and scientific concepts among the people of Syr-Dar'ia. Cadres of specialists were organized for this purpose.

At the same time 'rights' were granted to Muslim traditional schools, Russian authorities in Uzbekistan began intensive work to create the

---

[9]Boldyrev, *op. cit.,* p. 127; P. V. Gidulianov, *Otdelenie tserkvi ot gosudarstva v SSSR* (Moscow: Gosiuridizdat, 1926), pp. 375–377.
[10] Gidulianov, *op. cit.,* p. 375; K. I. Bendrykov, *Ocherki po istorii narodnogo obrazovaniia v Turkeśtane* (Moscow: APN SSSR, 1960), p. 447.

Soviet educational system in the country. Initial steps toward Sovietization can be seen in 1922, when the Soviet government established twenty-three technical schools which enrolled 2,600 students. Since that year six provinces of Turkestan (Fergana, Samarkand, Amu-and Syr-Dar'ia, Turkmen and Dzhetissiuk) added to the state budget 577 schools, 1,534 teachers and 38,095 students.

Second Period (1925-1928). This was the period of the co-existence of two systems—the Muslim religious and the Soviet public systems. Religious schools were based on the traditional Islamic practices, whereas the Russian communists were trying to establish a school system in Central Asia similar to that in Russia.

Following the Turkestan division in 1924-1925, the People's Commissariat of Education was organized to direct the educational development of that region. Their scope of activities was determined by the Soviet Constitution, as well as by federal laws of the U.S.S.R. The Uzbek, Tadzhik, Turkmen and Kirgiz Constitutions, like the Russian Constitution, promised equal educational opportunities for all regardless of their race, language or economic background. This movement was known as *korenizatsiia,* or the development of the local national cultures. It was national in content and communist in character. But as indicated in Figures 6 and 7, the Muslim population was not too eager to follow the philosophy of Russian communism. The Muslim intelligentsia in particular did not cooperate on a massive scale with the Soviets, and those who cooperated were not given any important positions in the national administrative apparatus (See Figure 7).

The Muslim progressionists, the *Jadids,* were a special case. The Jadids claimed that the German and Russian interpretation of Marxism did not fit their needs. In the early 1920s the Turkestan Muslim leaders decided to protest the Soviet Russian administration. They issued a resolution accusing the Soviets of Imperialism. Sultan Galiev, the leader of the movement and a Muslim communist, had his own ideas about the education of Muslims. Although he accepted the communist world outlook, he wanted to educate the Turkish speaking people of the Soviet Union in terms of their own national culture. He proposed to the Central Committee of the Party that the Muslims of Russia should be organized into one national republic, not included in the borders of the Soviet Union. Galiev thought that such a move would help the development of communism in other Islamic countries. He was arrested in 1923 and is believed to have been executed in 1930.

The consequences of Galiev's proposals were to be noticed in many

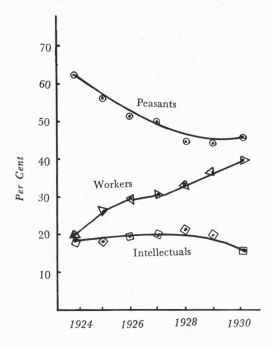

FIGURE 6. Distribution of the Communist Party
membership according to social classes
(Turkestan).

Calculated from: Baymirza Hayit, *Turkestan im
XX. Jahrhundert* (Darmstadt: C. W. Leske Verlag, 1956), p. 235.

areas of Muslim activities. The party accused the Muslims of being Pan-
Turkists, nationalists and other counter-revolutionary enemies of the
Soviet Union. Many of them were accused of supporting the *kulaks,* or
other reactionary groups.

In order to win Muslim support, Soviets began to impose their values
in education. The resolution issued on April 27, 1927, by the All-Russian
Central Executive Committee called for strengthening the work among
the minorities of the Soviet Union and ordered all Union-republics to
cooperate. The issue was that national cultural improvement was not to
be developed in the cultural traditions of a given minority but on imposed communist values. Kalinin, for example, in 1929 said that the
object of the Soviet policy was to teach Kirghiz, Uzbeks, Turkmen and
others the spirit and ideas of the Leningrad workers.

At the same time, children were told to join the various movements

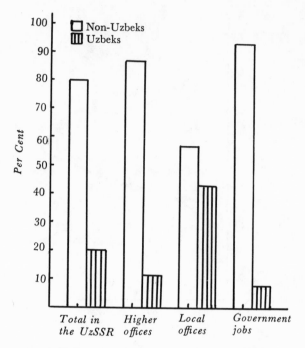

FIGURE 7. Distribution of administrative personnel in the UzSSR, 1930.

Calculated from: Baymirza Hayit, *Turkestan im
XX. Jahrhundert* (Darmstadt: C. W. Leske Verlag, 1956), p. 248.

established for them such as the Octobrists, Pioneers and Communist
Youth League. But the situation was, as of 1927, that the majority of
children did not belong to any organization. For example, in the Tashkent district 24,271 children were not in any organization; 639 were
candidates for the *Komsomol* and 1,116 were *Komsomol* members; 3,246
were Octobrists; and 8,827 were Pioneers. The teachers also did not
yet participate in political organizations, since out of 1,325 teachers in
the Tashkent district (of whom 585 were of Uzbek nationality), only
seventy-one were party members or candidates and thirty-five were in
the *Komsomol* (see Table 11). The communist party did not have at
that time anything like a mass following.

Third Period (1928 and After). After 1928, mere persuasion or any
other peaceful means were no longer used to introduce the communist

TABLE 11

Data on Tashkent District: Number of Public Schools,
Children, Teachers, and Childrens' Movements (1925-27)

Kinds of Activities	Number of Them in:			
	Old City	New City	Dis-trict*	Total
A. 1925-26				
First Level Schools (Grades 1-4) . .	43	14	167	224
Secondary Schools (5-9)	2	14	3	19
Children's Homes	6	14	5	25
Preschool Training Organizations . .	4	15	. . . .	19
Number of Children in Them .	12,028	14,220	10,449	36,697
B. 1926-27				
First Level Schools	44	14	190	248
Secondary Schools	7	18	8	33
Children's Homes	5	14	6	25
Preschool Training Organizations . .	4	14	1	19
Number of Children in Them .	12,676	13,480	11,943	38,099
Total Number of School				
Age Children	32,000	27,000	73,000	132,000
Per cent in Schools	37.5	59.26	16.44	30.3
Of Which:				
a. Male	10,072	6,817	9,028	25,917
b. Female	2,604	6,663	2,915	12,182
c. Uzbek	12,193	963	5,358	18,506
d. Russian	5	9,158	4,518	13,681
e. Other nationalities . . .	478	3,359	2,075	5,915
C. Participation in the				
Childrens' Movements				
a. Octobrists	934	687	1,625	3,246
b. Pioneers	2,653	3,391	2,783	8,827
c. Komsomol Candidates .	236	157	246	639
d. Komsomol Members . .	441	281	394	1,116
e. Not in Any				
Organization	8,412	8,964	. . . .	24,271
D. Public School Teachers:				
1. Total	453	528	344	1,325
a. Male	223	242	119	684
b. Female	130	286	225	641
2. Nationality:				
a. Uzbeks	330	19	110	459
b. Russians	48	412	125	585
c. Others	69	103	109	281

(Continued on next page)

TABLE 11 (Continued)

Data on Tashkent District: Number of Public Schools,
Children, Teachers, and Childrens' Movements (1925–27)

Kinds of Activities	Number of Them in:			
	Old City	New City	Dis- trict*	Total
3. Party Members and Candidates .	38	33	....	....
Komsomol Members and Candidates	19	16	....	....
Non-Party Members	316	479	....	....
4. Level of Education:				
a. Higher	21	186	23	230
b. Secondary	217	333	230	780
c. Elementary	215	9	91	315

Otchet Tashkenskogo Ispol'nitel'nogo Komiteta 2-go Soiuza za 1925–26 god (Tashkent: 1926), pp. 174–181.
* District (*raion*), includes the area of Tashkent and its vicinities.

system of education. All religious schools were prohibited by the law and a compulsory educational system soon began to operate in Muslim regions. At first the development of Muslim public education was not rapid, because, as a Soviet source stated, "many mullas and teachers of the old religious schools were particularly antagonistic to public education and attempted to fight the incoming system." Nonetheless, the most rapid development of Uzbek public education can be documented during 1930-1932. Especially significant was the year 1930, because during that time compulsory elementary education was enforced in the U.S.S.R. This policy had a significant effect on the general school population since in that year the number of students in elementary and secondary schools had increased by 153,000 (see Table 12). The next school year, 1931-1932, the number of students again increased by 125,000.[11] In 1933, nationals of the Uzbek SSR comprised 0.7 per cent of the total number of students in higher educational establishments in the Soviet Union. However, the percentage of natives in higher institutions fluctuated with time. In 1934-1935, for instance, the percentage of Uzbeks studying in Soviet universities dropped from 0.7 per cent in 1933, to 0.55 per cent in 1935 (see Table 13). This indicates that the vast majority

[11] *Narodnoe obrazovanie v Uzbekistane za 15 let*, p. 46; Sharafudinova, *op. cit.*, p. 13.

TABLE 12
Increase in Number of Schools, School Children and
Teachers in the UzSSR, 1929-35

	Year	Schools	Teachers	All Types of Schools for General Education	
				Pupils	
				Absolute figures	Per Cent of 1928-29
A	B	1	2	3	4
UzSSR—Total	1929-30	2,471	6,802	175,750	100.0
	1930-31	4,613	11,129	363,331	206.7
	1931-32	6,531	18,715	642,093	365.4
	1932-33	5,855	18,524	611,853	354.3
	1933-34	5,314	17,004	570,228	324.5
	1934-35	4,968	16,790	584,898	333.4
Cities	1929-30	418	3,780	86,990	100.0
	1930-31	459	4,151	120,181	131.1
	1931-32	682	4,551	158,292	182.0
	1932-33	497	5,434	141,997	163.2
	1933-34	388	3,880	132,370	152.0
	1934-35	374	4,311	141,253	162.4
Rural	1929-30	2,053	3,022	88,760	100.0
	1930-31	4,154	6,978	243,150	273.9
	1931-32	5,849	14,164	483,798	545.0
	1932-33	5,358	13,090	569,856	529.0
	1933-34	4,926	13,124	437,858	493.3
	1934-35	4,584	12,479	444,645	501.0

Central Administration of Economic and Social *Statistics of the State Planning Commission of the USSR, Socialist Construction in the USSR. Statistical Abstract* (Moscow: Soyuzorgouchet, 1936), p. 453.

of students were Europeans—Slavs, not Uzbeks. Although precise data on the ethnic composition of all students at higher levels in the late 1930s are not available to the writer, some data pertaining to particular administrative provinces indicate that the per cent of Uzbeks in higher educational institutions of the republic was very small.

The Uzbeks as of 1935, were still behind other European nationalities as far as higher education was concerned. There were complaints about

TABLE 13

Per cent of Student Body at Factory Schools, Technicums
and Universities: By Nationalities

Nationalities	Factory schools 1933	Tech- nicums 1933	Univer- sities 1933	% of total popul.*
A	1	2	3	4
Russian	66.4	52.7	53.5	52.9
Ukrainian	17.7	19.9	16.1	21.2
W. Russian	2.5	3.0	3.3	3.2
Kazakh	1.1	1.2	0.5	...
Uzbek	0.4	1.6	0.7	2.5
Tartar	1.7	1.8	1.3	3.7
Jewish	4.2	5.3	12.8	3.2
Georgian	0.9	4.1	2.9	1.2
Turk	0.6	1.6	1.4	1.1
Armenian	1.2	2.2	2.3	1.0
Mordovian	0.2	0.4	0.2	...
German	0.3	0.5	0.7	0.9
Chuvash	0.2	0.6	0.4	0.7
Tadzhik	0.1	0.2	0.1	0.6
Bashkir	0.3	0.4	0.2	0.5
Polish	0.4	0.6	0.8	0.4
Turkmen	0.1	0.5	0.1	...
Other	1.7	3.4	2.7	10.3

Calculated from: Tsentral'noe Upravlenie Narodnogo Khoziaistvennogo Ucheta Gosplana SSSR, *Sotsialisticheskoe Stroitel'stvo SSSR* (Moscow: Soiuzorguchet, 1935), p. 617.

* Per cent of total population is based on 1926 census, cited from: Frank Lorimer, *The Population of the Soviet Union: History and Prospects* (Geneva: League of Nations, 1946), p. 51; *Soviet Union Year-Book, 1929.* Compiled and edited by A. A. Santalov (London: George Allen and Unwin Ltd.), p. 22.

the status of educational development in the Central Asian territories.[12] As of that year, the population of Uzbekistan represented nearly 3 per cent of the total population of the U.S.S.R., but only 0.020 per cent of Uzbek students were attending the Higher Educational Institutes. In comparison, Jewish inhabitants of the Union represented fewer than 2 per cent of the total population, but comprised more than 13 per cent of the student body.

Of course, the number of students in all Central Asian republics had increased simply because the population also had increased. In 1939, for

---

[12] Schlesinger, *The Nationalities Problem and Soviet Administration,* p. 223.

example, the Uzbek SSR had 1.2 million students in general types of schools; by 1965, the number had increased to 2.2 million; the Tadzhik SSR in 1939, had 303,115 students in the same type of school and 535,000 in 1965, etc. (See Appendix, Tables 4 and 5.) However, when one considers the number of natives in professional schools, as for example, the number of Uzbek physicians (see Figure 8), the story is quite different. There were only 20 per cent of the native physicians in the Uzbek SSR at the end of the Stalin era, while the ratio in the population is 88 per cent natives and only 12 per cent non-natives of the region.

Unfortunately it is impossible to include all of the other nationalities of the Soviet Union in this type of a book. This would require an encyclopedic type of study. Even the so-called republics (although there is little difference in their political and educational structure) would each require a separate study in order to make an objective analysis of their system or systems.

After World War II, many scholars who were previously Soviet citizens contributed a great deal to the presentation of the real situation in Russia. Many books and periodicals were published in the free world regarding the national cultures and the nationalities of the Soviet Union. All of them stressed one point: the existence of the Soviet Russian communist structure is aimed at the complete destruction, physical and cultural, of the national cultures in the Soviet Union.[13]

In summarizing the general historical trends of Soviet educational developments we note the following facts: the Russian, Ukrainian, Muslim and other nationalities went through three common stages (differing only in the terminology used to describe them): 1) the liquidation of illiteracy; 2) the foundation of the communist educational system; and 3) the liquidation of any national initiative in education and the replacement thereof with communistic ideals. Here it is important to underline that the communist system was quite beneficial for the first group—the Russians—since all other nationalities of the Union were the subjects of physical and cultural assimilation. The fact that there are more students in the schools of the Russian minorities than before 1917 does not justify the pernicious methods of obliterating national school systems. In fact, any country of the 1960s—even those of the primitive African tribes—has increased its number of students and schools. The fact is that the Russian

---

[13] For further information see *Kavkaz* (Munich, monthly), No. 2 and 3, 1951, pp. 12 ff.; *The Voice of Georgiia* (New York, monthly), No. 6, 1954, pp. 10–16; *Belorusskii golos* (Munich, monthly), February 1966; *Milli Turkestan* (Munich, monthly), No. 5, 1952, *passim*.

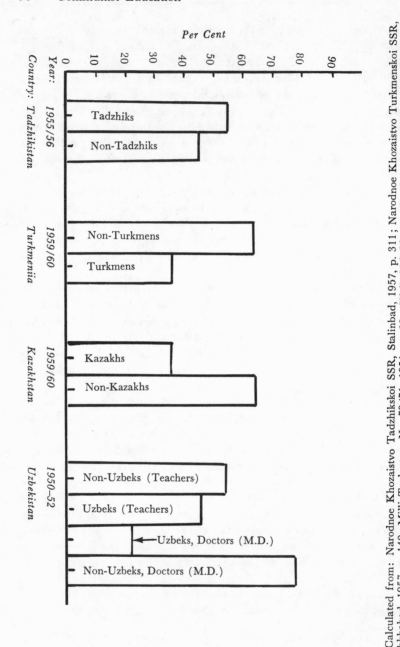

FIGURE 8. Per cent of Turkestanian students in Higher Educational
Institutions; per cent of teachers and doctors in Uzbekistan.

Calculated from: Narodnoe Khozaistvo Tadzhikskoi SSR, Stalinbad, 1957, p. 311; Narodnoe Khozaistvo Turkmenskoi SSR, Ashkhabad, 1957, p. 140; Milli Turkestan, No. 79/71, 1951, p. 32; Kizil Uzbekiston, October 29, 1957; Kazakhstanskaia Pravda, March 18, 1961; also cited by Baymirza Hayit, Turkestan as an Example of Soviet Colonialism, Munich: Studies on the Soviet Union, Vol. 1, No. 2, 1961.

communists condemn those who believe in God as their Creator; they condemn any national cultural or political event which is not pro-Russian; they condemn any national initiative, pride or achievement. These are the important facts to be understood.

The great advances in communications technology are not all beneficial for Soviet citizens because Soviet newspapers, radio and television do not report the full truth about events in non-communist countries. Soviet schools, theaters and cinemas show only the negative aspects of Western culture and keep silent about their own shortcomings. All is aimed at persuading the Soviet people of the 'superiority' of the Russian communist system and purposely manufacturing hate against the West. The Western mass media, as well as many Western scholars, treat the Soviet-Russian system much more favorably than it deserves to be treated. The Russian communists are constantly feeding their people nonsense about the Western world and the 'bourgeois' culture. The Communists always talk about things that do not exist in the Soviet Union (freedom of speech, religion, etc.), but they have yet to develop a set of moral principles which would treat man as man and student as student regardless of his 'bourgeois' origin.

Additional References

Some important sources concerning illiteracy and general education are: Kh. Pulatov, *Kul'turno-vospitatel'na deiatel'nost' sovetskogo gosudarstva v Uzbekistane* (Tashkent: Gosizdat, 1959), especially pages 80–97; *Aziatskaia Rossiia,* vol. 1, pp. 160–258; *Revoliutsionnyi vostok,* No. 1, 1934, pp. 162 ff.; *Soviet Cultural Bulletin,* No. 6, 1931, pp. 18 ff.; Boldyrev, *Direktivi VKP (b) i sovetskogo pravitel'stva po narodnom obrazovanii,* vypusk 2, p. 136; Kary-Niiazov, *Ocherki kul'tury sovetskogo Uzbekistana* (Moscow: AN SSSR, 1955), *passim; Direktivi KPSS po narodnom khoziaistvu,* vol. II, p. 186; G. G. Karpov and others, *Razvitie sotsialisticheskoi kul'tury v soiuznykh respublikakh* (Moscow: Gospolitizdat, 1962); *Sbornik zakonov i razporiadzhenii rabocho-krestianskogo pravitel'stva SSSR* (Moscow: Izdatel'stvo SNK i Soveta trudu i Oborony, No. 39, 1929), pp. 348–349; F. F. Korolev, M. K. Goncharov, *Novaia sistema narodnogo obrazovaniia v SSSR* (Moscow: APN RSFSR, 1960), *passim;* N. DeWitt, *Education and Professional Employment in the USSR* (Washington, D. C.: Government Printing Office, 1962); M. M. Deineko, *Spravochnik direktora shkoly* (Moscow: APN RSFSR, 1955); George Counts, *N. S. Khrushchev and Central Committee Speak on Education* (Pittsburgh: University of Pittsburgh Press, 1959), *passim;* J. V. Stalin, *Sochineniia,* vol. 5, pp. 264–275, vol. 6, pp. 236 ff.; Institute for the Study of the USSR, *Ukrainskii zbirnyk,* book 1 (Munich: Institute for the Study of the USSR, 1957), *passim; Istoriia sovetskoi konstitutsii, 1917–1956* (Moscow: Gosiuridizdat, 1956), pp. 455–473, 484.; G. Wheeler, *Racial Problems in Soviet Muslim Asia* (London: Oxford University Press, 1960), *passim.*

Chapter 5

NEW TYPES OF SCHOOLS vs
NEW DEMANDS

From the very beginning of the Bolshevik regime in Russia, the Soviet government tried to change not only the character of educational institutions but their traditional names as well. The gymnasiums and lyceums were replaced by new terms merely for the reason that these names were used by the czarist authorities. They were motivated by one premise: everything old was to be rejected and everything of communist origin was to be accepted.

Since the communists wanted to educate a new generation—the structure of schools changed from time to time depending on the planning of the national economy and the resolutions of the communist party. Education involving the children in nurseries and kindergarten changed little, but general education was another story. Nine years of schooling was initially required for the secondary school diploma—known as 4:3:2. Later this was extended to ten years—4:3:3; after World War II to eleven years of total training—5:3:3; and in 1964 it reverted to the previous ten year program.

At the higher level, the institutes (colleges) and the universities became the standard types of higher educational institutions.

PRE-SCHOOL EDUCATION

Nurseries. Nursery schools in the Soviet Union were established to help the working parents and they continued to grow in proportion to industrial developments. One of the articles of the Soviet Constitution states: one who does not work does not eat—which of course applies to the working mothers.

Soviet authorities claim that there is an equal distribution of nurseries throughout the Soviet Union, but in reality these schools exist only near industrial establisments. Before World War II only about seven per cent of the children were enrolled in nursery schools, or approximately 800,-000 children. These schools were located near factories or a collective farm and had no more than one single room. Very often they were conducted under trees and were actually a baby-sitting service for working parents.

Teaching personnel ideally required a *med-sister* (nurse), but in most cases an elderly woman did the job. In rural areas and in agricultural establishments the nursery personnel consists of elderly people who are unable to work physically but are healthy enough to perform babysitting functions. Very often these schools have no furniture or toys but are just a tent-type hut with a bundle of hay spread around which serves as mattresses for the children.

The Soviet statistical publications list all these nurseries as pre-school educational establishments regardless of their condition or exact function. In 1964 there were 5,496,000 children in the pre-school establishments, of which 758,700 were in nurseries.

Kindergarten. Soviet schools of this type have very little in common with the philosophy of Froebel, the founder of the kindergarten, who believed in a school where all children regardless of the political affiliation of their parents would play, learn, and share experiences. The Soviet kindergartens, like any of their other schools, must first fulfill all the political obligations of the party. The child is taught atheistic communism as early as possible. The three year old child must be reminded that not God but science is the source of all miracles, and that not God but the party is the source of authority and a sort of mediator between life and death.

The usual practice of kindergartens is to accept children when they have reached three years of age. The school administration provides arrangements for those parents who cannot pick up their children at closing time or those who live too far away. The average stay in school is about nine hours but may be as long as twelve hours. During the day the usual practice is to keep the children outside unless the temperature reaches 10° below zero. Here the children play together and learn how to live socially and, according to the Soviet interpretations, "try to avoid the tiresome play suggested by Montessori or Froebel."[1] Since the basic skills of reading and writing are taught here, the Soviet kindergarten is supposed to be above the Western type of kindergarten.

Elementary school instructions begin for Soviet children when they have reached the age of seven while in the United States and other European countries the age of enrollment is six. Therefore it is not unusual to be able to read at the completion of kindergarten when a child is seven years of age. The Soviet child is taught the principles of ethics that are practiced by the communist societies only. A five year old boy knows only that there is no better school than the Soviet school and that there is no better science than Soviet science. The youngster learns the superiority of the communist system, the heroes of communist social construction and the "evil of capitalism."

The Soviets also believe that it is not a good practice to switch the teachers from one class to another in that a child has no opportunity to become accustomed to one teacher and to gain from the teacher's experiences.

In terms of control, the kindergarten as well as the nurseries are under the administration of local enterprises, factories, or collective farms. These in turn are under the supervision of the Ministry of Health. Some steps have been taken to subordinate all pre-school educational institutions to the Ministry of Education.

In 1965 for example, there were over 49 million children in general schools, of which 5,496,000 were in kindergartens. It is interesting to note that during the year 1940-1941 there were 1.2 million children in Soviet pre-school institutions, but only 266,000 were distributed in the rural areas while the rural population of that time comprised well over 60 per cent of the total Soviet population. In 1945 the number of children increased to 1.4 million but in rural areas only a slight increase was noticed. Even in 1965 only 1,049,200 children were in rural kindergartens while in urban schools there were 5.5 million pre-school children.

---

[1] Medynski, *Narodnoe obrazovanie*, p. 11; Lorimer, *op. cit.*, p. 238; *Uchitel'-skaia gazeta*, August 13, 1964; DeWitt, *Education and Professional Employment in the USSR*, p. 74; *Narodnoe khoziaistvo*, 1964, p. 677.

On the whole as of 1965 only 15 per cent of the kindergarten-age children were able to attend this type of school.[2] It is evident that the establishment of pre-school educational activities is based on two premises: giving help to the working parents, and setting up such schools only in industrial centers.

SCHOOLS FOR GENERAL EDUCATION

The Soviets group under this category two types of schools: primary schools consisting of four years of training and the secondary schools, either incomplete or complete secondary schools, consisting of eight and ten (as of 1964) years of training respectively.

This system witnessed many changes during the early Soviet period of experimentation, i.e., years of schooling were added or subtracted according to the national needs of the Soviet economy and the needs of the political institutions. In 1958, for example, Khrushchev's plan called for the compulsory physical labor on the part of all students who intended to enter higher educational institutions. That meant that actual secondary school training had been cut to nine years instead of eleven years since two years of the secondary school period had to be spent in industrial or agricultural enterprises.

This law was designed to close the gap between the working people and the students in terms of social equality. After all, the goal of the Soviet education is to achieve the status of a classless society.

Polytechnical General Education. The aim of Soviet schools is to educate a well rounded communist individual indoctrinated in the superiority of the Soviet system and above all in hate toward the Western civilization. For this reason religious ideas, especially the Christian ideas, are rejected because Christianity most of all represents the European-American civilization and, of course, is associated with the old Imperial Russian-Christian civilization with which the communists do not want Soviet society to be associated.

The imperial educational theories were rejected by the Soviets primarily because they had their origin in Christian ethics and Christian pedagogical practices. Christian education called for the obedience to God's laws before any other laws. The Soviet pedagogy, on the contrary, calls for blind obedience to the party and the communist state and only after this comes other educational goals.

---

[2] *Narodnoe khoziaistvo,* 1964, pp. 676–677.

Much has been written by Soviet educators about polytechnical education which supposedly should provide answers to educational problems. Soviet educators, like Konstantiov, Korolev, Medynski and others tried to develop sound pedagogical foundations based on Soviet experiments, but they were restricted by the dictates of the political organs.

Early Soviet educators found solutions to polytechnical education neither in the political resolutions of the communist party nor in the traditional Russian theories and practices. So the solution was sought abroad, primarily in the writings and practices of the English socialist, Robert Owen.

Robert Owen holds an assured place in the history of educational experiment. In temperament and theory, Owen was an educational liberal; in economic practice and social experiment, he was a radical socialist; and in vision and character, he was a prophet proclaiming the dawn of a new age.

Regardless of his political ideas, Robert Owen initiated very progressive reforms in Scotland, particularly in his factories where he demanded that each child be taught at least the basic knowledge of industrial needs, also that he be given the opportunity to aspire to all educational levels. His factories at New Lanark became the examples of polytechnical education—a practice which Russians wanted to utilize. A study-work plan was introduced whereby each child was expected to produce some useful contribution to the enterprise and to society in general. Children were allowed to pursue their educational goal while making a living at the same time.

The experiments of Robert Owen became very important as theoretical and practical foundations for many educators, including Lenin's wife Krupskaia. The Russians thought that by taking the practices of English socialism they could change the old Russian traditional practices, and at the same time initiate the first Marxist polytechnical education at the secondary level. But in practical experiences, the polytechnical education was rather slow; it began in 1918 and lasted until about 1930. Then nothing was said about it until 1951-1952 when the old ideas were introduced to the Soviet educational practices. In reality, an intense call for polytechnical education began in 1956 when Khrushchev initiated a work-study plan.

During the periods of 1930's and 1940's the communists wanted to educate not only polytechnical intelligentsia but an atheistic intelligentsia which would reject religious ethical moral principles and accept only the communist "morality." All Soviet textbooks during this period were atheistically oriented.

Soviet schools involved more than merely teaching the necessary subject matter needed for graduation. Military training, for instance, was just as important as the study of Russian language or the appreciation of the Soviet arts, and from the Soviet point of view, was a part of a well-rounded individual.[3]

Enrollment. In theory every Soviet child must be in school until fourteen years of age. In practice most children quit school after completion of the fifth grade because of the unavailability of the semi-secondary education in rural areas.

Soviet sources list the educational accomplishments of each republic beginning in 1914. These look quite impressive but are not quite correct, e.g., the number of schools reported show increases of varying degree, but the Muslim schools or the Russian religious schools (as of 1915) are not mentioned.

In 1965 the number of general schools (elementary and secondary) reached the 218,000 mark and enrollment was over 46 million with 2,435,000 teachers. (See also Table 14.) But when one considers the

TABLE 14

Number of Schools, Teachers and Students in Soviet
Selected Republics: 1965

Republic	Number of:			Students at Higher Educ. Institutions
	Schools	Teachers	Students[1]	
USSR—Total	218,384	2,199,000	46,664,000	3,608,400
Russian SSR	123,007	1,001,713	25,709,000	2,212,900
Ukrainian SSR	35,405	357,010	8,524,000	643,800
Uzbek SSR	8,387	67,112	2,279,000	154,300
Kazakh SSR	10,408	75,683	2,626,000	132,000
Kirghiz SSR	2,064	18,430	583,000	29,000
Tadzhik SSR	2,779	18,731	535,000	26,900
Turkmen SSR	1,590	12,407	402,000	18,500

Tsentrlanoe Statisticheskoe Upravlenie pri Sovete Ministrov SSSR, *Narodnoe Khozaistvo SSSR v 1964 godu* (Moscow: Gosstatizdat, 1965), pp. 674, 681.
[1] The number of students is rounded to the nearest hundred.

number of students in certain grades, the figures are different. For example, in the same year there were 19.9 million students in grades 1-4

[3] Medynski, *Narodnoe obrazovanie*, p. 30; I. T. Ogorodnikov, *Pedagogika* (Moscow: APN RSFSR, 1954), p. 15; N. K. *Krupskaia o kommunistcheskom vospitanii* (Moscow: Gospedizdat, 1958), pp. 350–360.

but in the eighth grade there were 4,671,000 students and in the eleventh grade only 1.4 million students. The logical deduction is that the Soviet secondary schools are not designed for the mass population but for those who can qualify for them, i.e., they are college preparatory schools.

The number of dropouts in secondary schools is high. According to Soviet data only 25 per cent of the eighth graders graduate from the incomplete secondary schools. The completion of secondary education has varied from 10 per cent to 25 per cent. Thus, the Soviet secondary schools are about the same as the German type gymnasia where the screening of students takes place not in colleges but in secondary schools, a practice which is standard in European countries. The Soviets believe that it is too expensive and meaningless to keep a child in school if he does not want to be there.

SCHOOLS FOR WORKING YOUTH, RURAL YOUTH AND TECHNICUMS

In line with other educational establishments, the Soviets established in the early 1920's *fabrichnozavodskie uchilishcha* (schools located at industrial enterprises) designed to help the working youth. Later on another type of school was established especially for rural youth.

This school differed in many respects from the regular secondary school in its content and in its organization of subject matter. The Soviet People's Commissariat before 1946 and the Ministry of Education after that date issued special decrees regarding the structure and organization of the schools for rural youth where the instruction lasted six months or 25 weeks at the rate of twenty hours per week. These schools prepared students for higher educational institutions just as did general secondary schools. In 1965 there were over 26,000 such schools, with an enrollment of some four and one-half million working or rural youth.

Another Soviet type of secondary school is the *Technicum,* a semi-professional educational institution which offers a variety of training. There are medical technicums, pedagogical schools, trade schools, railroad schools, and others. All are under the jurisdiction of the Central Administration of the Working Reserves, a section of the Ministry of Education. These schools have their own plans for particular subject matter as well as standard methods, throughout the Soviet Union.

As a rule the time of study in these professional schools on the secondary level lasts between three and four years. Students are accepted in the age group of fourteen and fifteen with a prerequisite of at least elementary education—four years. But new requirements demand a semi-secondary education or at least seven years of schooling. On the other hand their training period may last longer, sometimes as long as seven years due to the lower social and economic background of their student population. In all semi-professional schools about one quarter of the time is alloted to theoretical knowledge. The rest of the time is devoted to industrial training or a practicum in one's field.

The Soviets also have schools for skilled workers who do not necessarily need a formal type of semi-secondary education to be eligible to enter such schools, because the training varies according to one's specialization. The time of study, or study and work plan, depends on the type of specialization and lasts six months to a year. Most of these students are in the age group of 16–18, and receive vocational education designed for those who cannot compete in high school or professional technicums. This is a very practical educational program because it enables the student to learn the trade he desires. It also helps the teachers to maintain an academic curriculum, and most of all, discipline at the secondary level. Those who do not want to go to school beyond 14 years of age are not forced by law.

The Soviet statistical publications list technicums, factory schools, trade schools, and training school for technicians as the secondary special schools. In 1940 there were 3,777 such schools with 975,000 students. In 1965 there were 3.3 million students divided as follows: 1.6 million day time students; 586,000 evening students; and 1.1 million correspondence students. Most of the students were specializing in mechanical trades; in 1965 over 490,000 were in mechanical training schools, 440,000 in economics, 390,000 were nurses, 265,200 teachers at lower levels, and 126,000 were radio technicians.[4] The number of girls in these schools depends on the type of profession, e.g., ninety-nine per cent of weavers are women, eighty-nine per cent of those in the candymaking business are women; eleven per cent of electricians and ten per cent of the automatic machine tool adjusters are women.

WORKERS' FACULTIES (RABFAK)

In 1919 the Soviets decided not only to change the structure of the old czarist education but to establish a school which would train the future communist leaders. Michael N. Pokrovski, Deputy Commissar of Education, came out with a new idea completely revolutionizing the already existing Soviet system. He and other communist educators, par-

---

[4] *Norodnoe khoziaistvo,* 1964, p. 678. See also Akademiia Pedagogicheskikh Nauk RSFSR, *Razvitie vysshogo obrazovaniia v SSSR* (Moscow: Gosizdat, 1961), p. 195.

ticularly the Commissar of Education, Lunacharski, decided to establish a school for workers and peasants known as the Workers' Faculties in the abbreviated Russian form as the *Rabfak*. Their motive was to give equal opportunities to the lower classes who in the new Soviet structure supposedly represented a leading social class. Before 1917 only five per cent of these were able to enter higher educational institutions.

Such schools began in 1922 and continued until World War II. The major aim of the Rabfak was to educate the communist intelligentsia devoted to the communist party and the world revolution. Children of the previous czarist officers, or the czarist administrators were denied admission to Rabfaks which was a great blow to many children, since most of the university students were taken from Rabfak schools.

The communists went further than that, limiting the educational opportunities to the "sympathetic" members of society, purposely omitting the children of the intelligentsia—children who had nothing to do with the previous regime.

There were several causes for this discrimination. First, the Soviets did not trust the old (pre-revolutionary) teachers and took steps to replace them. The only solution was to train their own people, who might be less qualified, but more dependable. By 1937, the communists were able to substitute the old teachers with the new, thus eliminating the old intelligentsia from important positions. In 1939, Stalin commented that the new education was not a dream but a reality.

The most important prerequisites were that a student be a hopeful candidate for the party and be in the age group of eighteen to thirty. A student was trained two to four years in Rabfak and sent to the university without much trouble since there were no entrance examinations during the early 1920s. The aim of the party was to fill all places at higher level educational institutions with graduates from the Workers' Faculties. Medynski, a Soviet educational historian, indicated that after 1930, the situation at Soviet universities completely changed. For example, forty-two per cent of the student population were children of the proletarian white-collar workers; thirty-nine per cent were the children of workers and sixteen per cent of farmers.

The farmers benefited little from the new schools because the "proletarian" intelligentsia dominated the Workers' Faculties. In 1931, the proletarian class represented over seventy per cent of the students at Soviet higher institutions and in 1936, over eighty per cent, at which time there was no need to continue the Rabfak, because regular secondary schools were obligated to do the same job.

Administration of the Rabfak was under the strict supervision of the party organs. More than any other type of school, they belonged under the control of higher educational institutions since the universities subsequently had to deal with their students.

Political party schools exist at secondary and higher levels, but their number is not always listed accurately. Students in political schools pay no tuition nor do they pay for their room and board. There were over 6,000 such schools at the secondary level in 1954, in addition to the military schools of Nakhimov and Suvorov.[5]

BOARDING SCHOOLS

What is a boarding school? In America almost every higher educational institution is in a sense a boarding school because students live and eat there. In Russia, it is quite different since educational institutions incorporate children into a boarding school atmosphere from the very beginning of the school age. This has tremendous political significance since the child is so indoctrinated that when he leaves the boarding school he is thoroughly imbued in the communist way of life.

Schools of this kind always existed in the Soviet Union but they were schools for orphans, homeless, or delinquent children. In the new system the children stay in school the entire week regardless of the distance to school from their homes. This was calculated by the communist party to educate fanatics of the communist system on one hand and to prevent ideological diversity among students on the other. The Soviets claim that these students are "the best educated builders of communism."

What Nikita Khrushchev and his followers thought about the new educational program remains to a great extent a secret, but we do know that in 1956 at the special meeting between Khrushchev and Suslov, Aristov and Furtzeev—top political figures of the country—the educational programs of the communist indoctrination were discussed. At this meeting it was decided that the work-study plan would be incorporated into the Soviet system and more efficiency would be introduced in educational organization throughout the Soviet Union. Khrushchev supported his thesis by saying that in many homes and schools children lack "warm care and surroundings as well as clothing and furniture sufficient enough for carrying out the educational programs." In reality it was not the

---

[5] Boldyrev, *op. cit.*, (vypusk 2), p. 103; Bereday, *The Politics of Soviet Educa-.
tion*, p. 58; Medynskii, *Noradnoe obrazovanie*, p. 168.

"warm care" but "cold" political care that stimulated the communists to introduce a new system. In his speech, Khrushchev gave examples of the old czarist system where the ruling class had always practiced selective educational privileges, sending their children to schools known as *kadet,* special girls' schools, gymnazia and others. He issued detailed plans for both buildings (planned as an example to all schools in terms of location and instructions) and political indoctrination. Subsequent directives of the twentieth Party Congress called for the rapid spreading of the boarding school system throughout the Soviet Union.

It is very difficult to give an exact estimate of the number of boarding schools because Soviets do not give exact data on them. However, it is a fact that such schools existed before 1956, in most of the Union republics but in another form, that of "special schools." There were over 500,000 such students in the Russian republic alone, and in Ukraine, the number reached the 100,000 mark. The 1964 *Narodnoe Khoziastvo* does not have a separate column for boarding schools. However, many Central Asian republics, as well as the Baltic States, initiated the boarding school program and spent as much money on them as on higher education.

Other schools supported entirely by the states are for crippled children, children with birth defects, the physically handicapped, the mentally retarded and others. In 1965, there were 245,000 students in schools for the handicapped and the retarded.[6]

HIGHER EDUCATION

In Imperial Russia higher educational opportunities were limited to a few select groups of society. On the other hand, the level of higher education in Russia was not too high compared to Germany or America of that time. The Russian Ministry of Education saw deficiencies in its own system and began to send specialists abroad to study European educational systems, primarily those of Germany and Switzerland. As early as 1862, 46 such specialists were sent to Europe to study the educational systems there. During the period of 1863-1875 the Imperial government gave scholarships to 328 Russian students to study abroad. They were to be trained as teachers for Russian universities (there were only seven universities in 1890). The number of students before the Revolution was as follows:

---

[6] *Narodnoe khoziaistvo,* 1964, p. 668; *Radianska Ukraina,* March 17, 1956; Deineko, *Spravochnik direktora shkoly,* pp. 172–178.

Location	1850	1890
Moscow	821	3,257
St. Petersburg	387	1,799
Kazan	309	785
Derptsk	554	1,632
Kharkiv	394	1,330
Kiev	553	2,088
Odessa	. . .	540
Total	3,018	11,431

Total for 1917: 11 universities with 37,000 students.

When one considers the Russian population of the 1890's (over 120 million people) then the number of 11,431 students at the university level is not high. A smaller country, Italy, at the same time had 21 universities with 14,000 students.[7] Italy's total population was then below 30 million.

After the Bolshevik *coup d'etat* in 1917, Lenin and the party promised a complete reconstruction of higher education. They issued a decree on August 2, 1918 on reconstruction of Russian universities, stipulating acceptance of anyone who had reached the age of sixteen and had a full time job. No other credentials were required. The following year, the decree was modified, making provisions for the rapid training of Soviet scientific personnel, but there have been no other radical changes.

Lenin asked the communist party to be careful in liquidating all the old intelligentsia because the future of rebuilding the new education would be in peril. He emphasized that until the new generation was educated, the old one must be tolerated and that only when the new communist generation was ready to take its place in society could the policy toward the old change.

Table 15 shows the growth of Soviet higher education.

NEW DEMANDS FACING TEACHERS' INSTITUTES

The communist party of Russia officially subordinated Soviet teachers to party control. The Law of 1919 stated clearly that the Soviet teacher must consider himself as an agent of the party and communist education.

---

[7] *Zhurnal Ministerstva Narodnogo Prosveshcheniia* No. 6, 1888, p. 106; K. T. Talkin, *Vysschoe obrazovanie i podgotovka narodnykh kadrov v SSSR* (Moscow: Sovetskaia Nauka, 1958), pp. 25, 51.

TABLE 15

Number of Students In Various Educational
Establishments: 1914, 1950, 1964
(Number in Thousands)

	1914/15	1950/51	1964/65
Total Number	10,588	48,770	68,926
Of Which:			
General Schools	9,656	34,752	46,664
Grades 1–4	na	20,023	19,989
Grades 5–8	na	13,705	19,563
Grades 9–11	na	907	6,867
Schools at Factories (FZU)	106	882	1,607
Secondary Special	54	1,298	3,326
Higher Education	127	1,247	3,608

Tsentral'noe Statisticheskoe Upravlenie pri Sovete Ministrov SSSR, *Narodnoe khoziaistvo SSSR v 1964 g.* (Moscow: Gosstatizdat, 1965), pp. 667–668.

In the early beginning of the Soviet regime, the teacher was educated not in terms of quality, but in quantity. The level of education was so low that little other than political indoctrination was taught. Lenin himself constantly reiterated that the teacher was obligated to help the party, and that the curriculum of the teachers' colleges should be communist oriented. Lenin, in 1917, stated that a new army of teachers should be prepared—an army which would interpret for the people "the things that communists do." He also advocated leadership positions only for those who had mastered the practicalities in the area of education.

Lunacharski, like Lenin, emphasized that the Soviet teacher was not a classroom fixture but a participant in the working people's struggle, as well as an agent in the spreading of party programs. The Marxist pedagogue, according to Lunacharski, was the builder of society rather than a product of its past and present.

Pokrovski, the Commissar of higher education after the 1917 Revolution, was faced with a three-fold problem: to train qualified teachers for Soviet schools from peasants and worker classes; to train these teachers in Marxian world outlooks; and to provide opportunities for various types of professional specialization.

Special correspondence courses were offered by the higher educational institutes, designed primarily to fill teaching places that remained critically empty. These courses lasted from six months to two years, often resulting in inadequate qualification of teachers. In 1933-1934, there were

655,636 teachers and by 1936 the number of teachers at elementary and secondary levels had increased to 709,378.[8]

The Teacher vs. the Government. The pressure of the Soviet government upon the teachers has been an endless proposition from the very beginning of the Soviet regime. There is hardly anything the teacher can initiate without consulting the party leaders. One would think that after the death of Stalin and after the exile of Khrushchev, the situation would improve, but in reality the teacher is still—as originally planned by Lenin—an instrument of the party.

The Central Committee of the Russian Communist Party keeps issuing resolutions regarding the Soviet teacher and his duties toward society and the party. Each party congress must, without exception, include some resolution concerning the teacher and his role toward the society. In 1962, for example, the 22nd Party Congress issued a resolution in which it is stated that pedagogy should, above all, educate a new man. What kind of a man will this be? The answer to this question is not a teacher's worry. The party will give the "right" answers as to the tasks and nature of man in general. It requires that the new man be a well rounded individual and a person who helps to create "the material and spiritual wealth of society." But the chief activity of the Soviet teacher is to study that discipline and those experiences which are closely related to the life and practice of building communism.

The Soviet teacher is equally significant in extracurricular activities. There are village meetings of the party, professional unions (to which every teacher must belong), and most important of all, anti-religious organizations. Here the teacher must explain to the people the "hazards" of religion to one's physical health, and must advocate the ideas propagated by the Militant Atheist (now called the Society for Propagation of Scientific and Political Knowledge) and other "voluntary" political organizations.

All subject matter and every method of instruction must be in line with the rules given by the party, which lists the regulations and methods of teaching from the ABC's to one's private behavior. In addition to this supervision, every faculty member must manifest in his lectures loyalty to the government and must actively participate in politics. Those who

---

[8] Tsentral'noe Statisticheskoe Upravlenie pri Sovete Ministrov SSSR, *Kul'turnoe stroitel'stvo SSSR* (Moscow: Gosstatzidat, 1956), p. 80; *Sotsialischeskoe stroitel'-stvo SSSR,* 1935, pp. 602–603; A. V. *Lunacharsky o narodnom obrazovanii* (Moscow): APN RSFSR, 1958), *passim;* Lenin, *Sochineniia,* vol. 32, p. 104; Korolev, *op. cit.,* p. 397.

are indifferent to political questions are listed in the same category as the enemies of the state. The Soviet teacher, by all means, must stress the achievements of the Soviet regime, avoid mentioning the achievements of enemy countries, and be very careful in making remarks about the foreign states. He must denounce all publications disapproved by the party, and must even denounce the works of his colleagues or his own if they happen to fall into the black list of the party.

An enemy is always a necessary tool to continue the class struggle, not only in philosophical theories but in actual teaching routines. Before World War II, Nazi Germany and Fascist Italy were the subjects of attack; after the war, the enemies were the United States, England, and West Germany. The Soviet teacher must advocate a general policy of hate toward these three powers. China is not included in this group because there is a general belief among party leaders that the differences between China and the Soviet Union are not as great as those between the United States and other Western powers. Thus there is nothing surprising that in international disputes regarding the internal affairs of an independent nation (e.g. Vietnam) both countries are in agreement and collaboration with each other.

Administrative officials always find a way to check a teacher if he is not doing his job properly. General party lines must be carried on without the slightest disagreement. It is a common practice for the school director to visit classes and take notes about a teacher's remarks, or to keep a secret agent in a classroom who records remarks and explanations of a teacher. In case the teacher is proven guilty of any deviation the mildest punishment is the public acknowledgement of his own mistakes. More severe would be dismissal from the job which is one of the hardest punishments since no other school may rehire him and psychologically he pays a high price since he must stay away from his friends in order to preserve their own safety. Those who speak to or associate with the enemies of the people are on the black list of the party.[9]

OTHER AREAS OF HIGHER EDUCATION

The Soviet statistical publications as a rule list twenty-two different categories of higher learning. These are the general categories which are subdivided into 550 various professional specializations. The highest number of students, as can be expected, is in education: 748,100. This is

---

[9] Ivan Rozhin, "A University Professor in the USSR," in *Horizon* (New York: Ukrainian Student Review), vol. III, No. 1–2, 1959, pp. 43–47; Ogorodnikov, *op. cit.*, p. 48.

followed by mechanical engineering with 462,400; economics, 355,600 and others (see Tables 15, 16, 17).

TABLE 16

Number of Students In Higher Educational Establishments:
1914–1965

Republic	1914/15	1927/28	1933/34	1964/65 (In 1,000)
Russia—Total	127,423	168,554	458,309	3,608,4
Russian SSR	86,472	114,184	303,173	2,212,9
Ukrainian SSR	35,204	21,141	97,533	643,8
Belorussian SSR	. . .	4,632	10,924	96,3
Uzbek SSR	. . .	3,876	10,865	154,3
Kazakh SSR	. . .	75	3,618	132,0
Georgian SSR	314	10,503	16,555	74,8
Azerbaidzhan SSR	. . .	4,503	9,558	58,7
Lithuanian SSR	. . .	. . .	. . .	42,8
Moldavian SSR	. . .	. . .	492	33,4
Latvian SSR	2,084	. . .	. . .	32,4
Kirghiz SSR	. . .	. . .	413	29,0
Tadzhik SSR	. . .	. . .	654	26,9
Armenian SSR	. . .	1,640	3,261	33,7
Turkmenian SSR	. . .	. . .	1,283	18,5
Estonian SSR	3,349	. . .	. . .	19,9

Tsentral'noe Statisticheskoe Upravlenie pri Sovete Ministrov SSSR, *Kul'turnoe stroitel'stvo SSSR v 1956 g.* (Moscow: Gosstatizdat, 1956), pp. 208–211; Tsentral'noe Statisticheskoe Upravlenie pri Sovete Ministrov SSSR, *Narodnoe khoziaistvo SSSR v 1964 g.* (Moscow: Gosstatizdat, 1965), p. 681.

Note that there were 754 higher educational institutions in the Soviet Union in 1965 as compared to 105 in 1914.

At present, most Soviet students are studying natural science, primarily because the growing economy demands more and more specialists in the natural sciences and there is also some freedom here from political participation. Those engaged in scientific areas are less frequently attacked by communist organizations and are given more time to master their professional pursuits.

Scientific Workers. The Soviets list under the category of scientific workers the following: academicians; members of Academies of Sciences; all who possess Ph. D. degrees or the Candidate of Science degree; all teachers of higher educational institutions; all research personnel (regardless of whether these people in research have an academic degree or not); and specialists in industry who don't have academic degrees.

It is difficult to distinguish the actual scientists from the "statistical"

TABLE 17

Number of Students In Higher Educational Institutions According
to Specialty: 1965 (In Thousands)

Specialty	Number of Students
Total	3,608,4
Of Which:	
Geology	28,2
Archaeology	38,3
Dynamics	83,5
Metalurgy	43,9
Mechanical Engineering	462,4
Electrical Engineering	260,3
Radio Technology	141,5
Chemical Engineering	94,3
Forestry	28,8
Welfare and Supply	54,4
Industrial Management	40,1
Civil Engineering	219,4
Geodesy and Cartography	7,4
Hydrology and Meteorology	7,1
Rural Economy	318,4
Transport	101,6
Economics	355,6
Law	56,3
Health and Physical Education	226,6
Specialties at University levels	262,2
Pedagogical and Library Institutes	748,1
Arts	30,0

Tsentral'noe Statisticheskoe Upravlenie pre Sovete Ministrov SSSR, *Narodnoe khoziaistvoe SSSR v 1964 g.* (Moscow: Gosstatizdat, 1965), p. 679.

scientists. At any rate, the Soviet colleges in 1964-65 graduated 354,000 scientific specialists at the higher level, and 558,300 at the secondary level.

As mentioned before, in 1965 there were 754 higher educational establishments in the Soviet Union with 3.6 million students. In addition to these higher educational institutions there were 4,651 research institutes with 612,000 scientific workers, of which there were 13,700 Doctors of Sciences, 123,900 Candidates of Sciences, and the rest of the scientific personnel were not classified as having academic degrees.

At the present time, the Soviet higher educational institutions together with other research institutes are increasingly engaged in training scientific personnel and in improving methods of research and instruction generally. The number of postgraduate students involved in research is steadily improving compared to 1955-1956 when the postgraduate enrollment was low (29,400 in 1955 and 25,500 in 1956). From 1958 on there has been a decided increase in this area of academic concern.

The leading universities of the Soviet Union have opened special boarding schools for those who are willing to enter postgraduate studies. To their dismay Soviet administrators find that many capable students, after fulfilling their two years of industrial work, decide to stay in industry where the pay is better and the living conditions are more favorable than in the boarding schools. The Minister of Higher Education of the Russian republic has complained that the universities are losing many talented young people because of the inefficiency of graduate programs.

This inefficiency has caused many other problems. For example, the percentage of young people in higher educational institutions is dropping instead of increasing. In 1939 researchers with doctorates (ages 30-39) comprised almost 42 per cent of the total higher research personnel while in 1959 they comprised less than 35 per cent. Persons who teach at the university level and are working for their doctorates do not continue post-graduate work once they are established at a certain university.

The growth of Soviet higher education and the enlargement of its faculties shows a normal increase in proportion to the student population and the growth of the population in general. Soviet data of 1964 indicate that there were 10,500 Doctors of Sciences employed by universities in 1959 and the number increased to 13,700 in 1964; there were 88,700 professors and lecturers in 1959 and 135,500 in 1964.[10] It should be noted that the Soviet universities do not confer so many Ph. D. degrees as the United States (in 1967 more than 18,000 persons in the United States received Ph. D. degrees). (See also Figure 9.) There are no Ph. D.'s in guidance counselling, physical education, etc., which are standard degrees in American universities. In the Soviet Union the number of degrees conferred in education has not increased while the Ph. D.'s in natural sciences have increased from 39 per cent in 1951 to 58 per cent in 1964.

ADULT EDUCATION

The history of adult education in Russia began in the 19th century when in 1860 the *Zemstvo* school was established to provide some education for adults. Also during the 19th century so-called People's Uni-

---

[10] *Pravda*, March 14, 1964; *Vestnik vysshei shkoly* (Moscow, monthly), No. 7, 1962, p. 51; *Vestnik statistiki*, No. 4, 1962, p. 64.

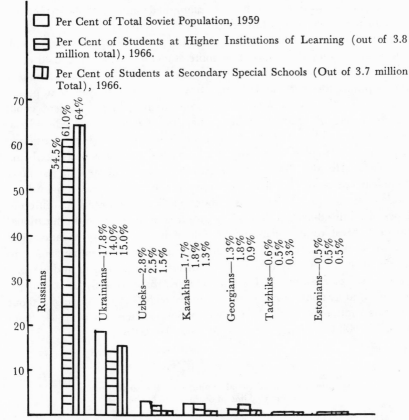

☐ Per Cent of Total Soviet Population, 1959

▤ Per Cent of Students at Higher Institutions of Learning (out of 3.8 million total), 1966.

⊞ Per Cent of Students at Secondary Special Schools (Out of 3.7 million Total), 1966.

FIGURE 9. Per Cent of Students at Higher Educational Institutions and at Special Schools in Proportion to Total Population: Selected Nationalities Only

Calculated from: Tsentral'noe Statisticheskoe Upravlenie pri Sovete Ministrov SSSR, *Narodnoe Khoziaistvo v 1965 g* (Moscow: Gosizdat, 1966), pp. 582, 701; *Itogi vsesoiuznoi perepisi v 1959 g* (Moscow: Gosstatizdat, 1962), p. 185.

versities were founded serving strictly the adult population mostly on a non-credit basis.

In 1919 the Workers' Faculties continued adult education. In 1924 the *Radio University* was established which offered daily instruction for 30 or 45 minutes for the willing listeners who took notes, solved problems, and sent them to a proper university or an adult educational center. In 1926 the Workers' University was founded (replacing the pre-revolutionary People's University) and which accepted students over the age of 18. In 1938 correspondence courses were offered for adults; in 1943 the schools for working youth were established; and in 1956 further improvements concerning adult education were initiated. The reforms of 1958 called for a better relationship between schools and society. They demanded that more students be encouraged to enter educational institutions and to pursue their studies without mandatory interruptions for work in industry. It was also felt during that period that many subjects required much more energy than a student could devote during the daily schooling. Therefore a more liberal educational program was to be made available at adult levels. Khrushchev criticized the school curriculae, especially those on the secondary basis, as being unrealistic. He also demanded that more time be allotted to the polytechnical education in order to improve the educational standards of workers at all ages. A plan was elaborated listing programs for different types of adult education depending on one's occupation and educational pursuits. Most of the planning was done in the area of technological education. Various categories of adult education were implemented in all union republics: day time studies, correspondence courses and evening programs. For example, in Ukraine in 1964, there were 643,800 students at higher educational institutions of which 386,500 were studying without the interruption of work. In the whole Soviet Union as of 1964, there were 506,000 in evening schools. (See also Table 18.)

TABLE 18

Distribution of Students at Higher Educational Institutions
According to Time of Studies (In Thousands)

Year	Total No. of Students	Day-time Students	Evening Students	Correspondence
1940/41	811,7	558,1	26,9	226,7
1945/46	730,2	525,2	14,0	191,0
1947/48	963,6	690,4	15,2	258,0
1949/50	1,132,1	755,9	22,3	353,9
1951/52	1,356,1	886,1	32,1	437,9
1955/56	1,867,0	1,147,0	80,9	639,1
1957/58	2,099,1	1,193,1	127,2	778,8
1959/60	2,267,0	1,145,8	195,8	925,4
1960/61	2,395,5	1,155,5	244,9	995,1
1964/65	3,608,4	1,514,0	506,0	1,588,0

Tsentral'noe Statisticheskoe Upravlenie pri Sovete Ministrov SSSR, *Vysshoe obrazovanie v SSSR: statisticheskii sbornik* (Moscow: Gosstatizdat, 1961), p. 80; Tsentral'noe Statisticheskoe Upravlenie pri Sovete Ministrov SSSR, *Narodnoe Khoziaistvoe SSSR v 1964 g.* (Moscow: Gosstatizdat, 1965), p. 678.

The level of adult education is still much less than desirable. *Pravda* and other newspapers from time to time complain about the lack of qualified instructors, the lack of textbooks and the bureaucracy of educational organs.

In conclusion, it is interesting to note the ratio of students of all kinds in percentage to the total population of various countries. Thus, in the early 1960s the figures were as follows:[11]

The entire world	12.4% of the total population were in schools	
Western Europe	15.5%	" "
Asia	10.3%	" "
Africa	7.2%	" "
South America	12.7%	" "
North America	23.5%	" "

Additional References

Important sources concerning Robert Owen's social and educational philosophy are: *Robert Owen, The New View on Society and Other Writings* (London: J. M. Dent and Sons, 1940); Robert Hill Harvey, *Robert Owen: Social Idealist* (Los Angeles, 1949); *Robert Owen: Pioneer of Social Reforms* (London: 1908; R. F. Pachard, *The Life of Robert Owen* (Philadelphia: 1866).

Other important sources concerning the history and politics of Soviet education are: Maurice Shore, *Soviet Education* (New York: Philosophical Library Press, 1947); J. V. Stalin, *Voprosy Leninisma* (Moscow: Izdat. Ogiz, 1947); Gosplanizdat, *Socialist Construction*, Statistical Yearbook (Moscow: Foreign Languages Publishing House, 1936); *Stenograficheskii report 20-go s'iezda KPSS* (Moscow: Gosstatizdat, 1956), especially pages 81 ff.; F. F. Korolev, *Sistema narodnogo obrazovaniia v SSSR* (Moscow: Gosstatizdat, 1961).

---

[11] Urlanis, *Naselenie mira*, p. 143; *Radianska Ukraina*, October 11, 1965; *Narodnoe khoziaistvo*, 1964, pp. 679-693; Akademiia Nauk SSSR, *Razvitie vysshogo obrazovaniia v SSSR* (Moscow: Gospolitizdat, 1961), p. 155.

Chapter 6

ADMINISTRATION AND CONTROL

At first sight the administrative structure and control of Soviet education would seem to be a very simple process; but close inspection of various divisions of the Soviet political and cultural administrative practice shows the situation to be quite different. The communist party of Russia controls many phases of political and social life; however, there are many educational situations that cannot be within the scope of the party. Some of these are simple classroom situations, problems that teachers may face in schools (regardless of the political orientation of the school or the parents), financial problems, etc. As far as general planning is concerned, the ideology of all education, and more important, the power of appointments, are strictly in the hands of the communist party.

THE ROLE OF THE PARTY

As the political structure of the Soviet government is based on the so-called class of the proletariat, so the educational administration is based on the orders and initiatives of the communist party of Russia. The Soviets theorize that the communist government of Russia is the govern-

119

ment of workers and peasants. But since not all the peasants are able to lead, the party gives them a "helping hand" in all their endeavors. Where does the party get its wisdom? From the writings of Marx, Lenin and other approved Soviet leaders, of course. And why does the party use force in carrying out its policies? Because there are always some individuals who do not agree with the Marxian philosophy of life and who aim to destroy the communist regime. The only Marxian solution to these problems is the use of force if it becomes necessary. But for those who never object to communist decisions, the process of running the country is based on a peaceful coexistence between rulers and subjects. Furthermore, no other political party is as good and as wise as the communist party, nor are there smarter leaders than the communist leaders who set for themselves the task to "establish the Communist system once and for all."

The Soviets also write much about democratic structure in government and of general administrative assignment in various branches of the national economy. The communist party of Russia purposely divided the country into many national autonomous units consisting of various administrative committees and groups. Theoretically, all decisions have their origin in different types of Soviet Councils, but practically all of them applaud only the decisions made by the party.

The most typical feature of the Soviet philosophy of administration is that the main initiative does not come from the administrative people themselves but from special committees of the party. The party's recommendations have a decisive significance on the structure of the educational apparatus and educational decisions. The primary unit of school administration is a branch of the communist party which exists in all schools. Lenin, in 1921, gave the following instruction: "Not a single political or administrative question should be decided without the directive of the Central Committee of the Party."

From the beginning, the party thought its duty was to interfere in educational matters by "suggesting" or directly issuing decrees and laws binding all schools of the Soviet Union. They also stated that only the communist party has the right and the responsibilities for educating a new generation indoctrinated in the spirit of communist ideas and the communist morality. Some basic tenets and practices of the Soviet government's educational administration are as follows:

1. The right to select and promote to important administrative positions the communist-devoted believers who are sufficiently qualified and who have sufficient political knowledge.

2. The party committees of various districts require a report from educators at least once a month.

3. The party committees delegate a party member to a given educational position primarily because he is qualified politically and stays in line with major party policies.

4. All important decisions of public education are carried out only after the party has had a chance to consider them. This consideration may begin at the local level and continue to the national level of discussion.

5. For the proper fulfillment of the decisions of the party, special personnel are to be hired—people who carry out and supervise the decisions of the party and the People's Ministry of Education.

6. The party encourages its members to participate in all decision-making bodies—in all cultural and educational administration such as schools, libraries, cultural committees and others.

7. The party committees report periodically about fulfillment of the duties entrusted to them by higher officials.

In the post-war period there were no educational reforms other than those originated by the party. For example, in 1954-57, the drive toward polytechnical education was initiated by the party. In 1956, and again in 1965, the decision to change the secondary school system was also initiated not by school authorities but by the party.

All of these decisions and school system reconstructions are not referred to as orders but as "help" to the educational institutions and the Soviet teachers. Those who refuse this help or have other ideas about administering school matters are proclaimed the enemies of the people.

It is important to note, therefore, that the philosophy of the party does not change. Only certain leaders are subjects for removal or appointments. Only certain educational or political institutions are changed for the sake of changing their name. We noted earlier the name changing of the Soviet of People's Commissars to the Council of Ministers, of the *Narkompros* (People's Commissariat of Education) to the Ministry of Education—but in its function and philosophy very little changed. The many sections of the administrative apparatus starting from the simple post of a school director on up through the various *oblast'*, regions, *krai*, national republics, Ministries of Education, Council of Ministers and Soviet of Nationalities all take and follow orders in their very detail from one institution: The Central Committee of the Communist Party. There has yet to be a single case in the history of Soviet education of a local branch of education being able to persuade a higher authority to adjust its decisions to local circumstances, nationality interest or the desire of parents to educate their children in the spirit of their own needs and their own beliefs.

In theory, each Union republic has its own Ministry of Education, also every autonomous republic (twenty of them) has its own ministries or other types of educational departments designed to handle its own educational problems and needs. In practice, however, nothing is changed or introduced without the official permission of the Russian communist party.

All major educational decisions are originated in Moscow regardless of the fact that there are fourteen other non-Russian republics and many non-Russian nationalities in the Soviet Union. The reason that the Soviets divide the administrative functions among many districts is quite obvious: Smaller units are more feasible for administering and carrying out central instructions. Dividing the areas into national regions, when these nationalities have nothing to say about decision making in their own districts, is a political device to impress other nations about the Soviet 'democratic' administrative practices.

The higher educational establishments until recently were under a direct control of the Russian Ministry of Education which initiated, "suggested" and supervised all the important decisions made by the Kremlin.

As study of this particular area is continued, one must remember that educational systems don't exist in a vacuum—they are shaped and influenced by a particular society's conditions and needs. This makes the study of the U.S.S.R. difficult because Western observers are sheltered from reality in many of these areas. They must beware of jumping to conclusions. Our standards of judgment very often do not apply to other nations.

Regardless of whether it is obvious or not, the communist party has direct or indirect control of all areas and all phases of educational policy from overall objectives down to day-to-day operations. Communist party central organs formulate policies covering types of schools, curricula, programs, instructional methods, school requirements, etc., and they oversee enforcement of the same. These policies, as mentioned before, originate as resolutions in the Central Committee and then are formally decreed by the Council of Ministers of the U.S.S.R. with or without the "rubber stamp" ratification of the Supreme Soviet.[1] Decisions of the Central Committee are binding even though it appears that much dis-

---

[1] DeWitt, *Education and Professional Employment in the USSR*, p. 40. See also Bereday, *The Politics of Soviet Education;* Bereday, *The Changing Soviet Schools*, p. 111; V. I. Lenin, *Izbrannye stati po natsional'nym voprosam* (Moscow: 1929, *passim;* Lenin, *Izbrannye proisvedeniia*, vol. II. 4th edition, p. 573; V. Skorodumov, *Struktura rukovodstva sovetskoi shkoloi* (Munich: Institute for the Study of the USSR, 1955), p. 2, 12–75; Herbart C. Rudman, *Structure and Decision Making in Soviet Education* (Washington, D.C.: U.S. Office of Education, Bulletin No. 2, 1964), pp. 3–6.

cussion occurs and voting takes place in the Supreme Soviet of the Council of Ministers of the U.S.S.R. The same procedures, voting discussions, etc., take place in the local or union republics regardless of the fact that those who discuss or vote have no right to change a single point without the approval of the Kremlin.

THE FEDERAL CENTRALIZED STRUCTURE

The Soviet centralized educational structure is, of course, similar to the centralized political structure of the Russian Soviet Empire. It would be quite logical to name it the Russian structure since there are no other independent structures. Nonetheless, there are fifteen separate republics in present day U.S.S.R.

Union Republics. What are the rights of a union republic? Each republic has its own constitution, president and ministries, but does not have its own army, foreign diplomats, Olympic participation and many other rights that an ordinary non-Soviet republic would enjoy. According to the constitution, each of the fourteen non-Russian republics voluntarily joined the union and each is free to stay or leave the union contingent on the wishes of the people. Furthermore, at one time or another, each of these republics was "liberated" either from their own dictators or from the foreign imperialists. Each of them is very thankful to the Russian people for their "liberation." The Soviet official source stated that:

> In our country there is no desire to make any separation of national republics because by belonging to the Union each country has gigantic opportunities and gigantic rights for self-determination.[2]

The republics are: Russia, Belorussia, Ukraine, Moldavia, Latvia, Lithuania, Estonia, Georgia, Armenia, Azerbaidzhan, Kazakh, Kirghiz, Turkmen, Uzbek and Tadzhik. All of them have equal representation in the Council of Nationalities and the Supreme Soviet of the U.S.S.R., i.e., the legislative bodies of the Soviet Union. Theoretically, they have their own executive branches of government. In practice, only two non-Russian republics have their own representatives in the United Nations and none of the republics are even allowed such a little thing as send-

---

[2] Nikitin, *Ekonomicheskaia geografiia,* p. 248; T. Reller (ed.), *Comparative Educational Administration* (Englewood Cliffs, N.J.: Prentice-Hall, 1962), p. 116.

ing their own athletes to the Olympic games. All of them have their own educational ministries who are supposed to handle the educational affairs of the country.

Autonomous Republics. There are twenty such republics. The reason for creating such republics is that all are inhabited by other than Russian ethnic groups. Sixteen of these autonomous republics belong to the Russian SFSR and the other four to other non-Slavic regions. They, too, have their own ministries of education. They are the following: Karels, Tatar, Marii, Mordva, Chuvash, Bashkir, Udmur, Kimi, Kalmyk, Dagestan, North Osetin, Kabardin-Balkar, Chechin-Ingursk, Tuvin, Buriat and Iakut. Kara-kalpak ASSR belongs to the Uzbek SSR; Nakhichevan ASSR to Azerbaidzhan SSR; and the last two—Abkhaz and Adzhar—belong to the Georgian SSR.

Krai. This administrative unit involves most of the Asiatic regions of the Soviet Union. These regions are populated largely by ethnically Asiatic groups spread out on a large territory. Each is called a *krai,* which is equivalent to the English meaning of country or territory. It has its own educational board which submits directly to the higher Russian administration. There are six such territories in the Russian SFSR: Altaisk, Krasnodarsk, Stavropolsk, Krasnoiarsk, Khabarovsk and Primorsk (Primorskii krai). Another difference between the *krai* and *oblast'* is that, except the Primorsk krai, each one has in its structure an autonomous *oblast'.* All six of them belong to the Russian SFSR.

Autonomous Oblast' (District). There are many types of districts (*oblast'*) in the U.S.S.R., some of which are regular administrative districts. For example, the Russian RSFR has 49 districts, and Ukraine has 26. The difference between regular districts (such as Moscow, and Leningrad with predominantly Russian population) and the autonomous district is that the latter's population is a non-republic one. Each *oblast'* has its own representative in the Soviet of Nationalities and in the local educational councils. There are eight such autonomous districts, five of them belong to the Russian SFSR: Adigeisk located in Krasnodarsk krai; Karach-Cherkask in Stavropolsk krai; North-Altaisk located in Altai krai; Khakask in Krasnoiarsk krai and Evreisk (Jewish population) located in Khabarovsk. The other three are distributed as follows: South-Osetin belongs to Georgian SSR; Badakhshansk to the Tadzhik SSR; and Karabokhsk to the Azerbaidzhanian SSR.

National Region (Natsional'nyi okrug). The national region is usually smaller than the *krai* and thus it is subordinated either to the *krai* or to a regular district. The reason for such a division is that certain ethnic groups inhabiting an area differ significantly from the majority group living in the area, in their language, culture or national traditions. Most of these groups have their own elementary educational systems in their own languages and have representation in a *krai* or a local district of education. They also have their own representatives in the Soviet of Nationalities. At the present time there are ten such regions, all belonging to the Russian SFSR: Nenets, Komi-Permiats, Iamalo-Nenets, Hanti-Mansiisk, Taimirsk, Evenkisk, Chukotsk, Kuroiaksk, UstOrdinsk and Aginsk-Buriat.

As mentioned before, regular districts are the usual administrative units, like units in any other country, that have local administrative boards and other major offices of the area. It is important to study the U.S.S.R. under these stated divisions because the non-Russian ethnic groups were purposely divided into so-called autonomous regions, ASSR or other administrative units. The Russian republic alone has sixteen autonomous republics, six *krai*, ten national regions and five autonomous districts. The next largest republic is the Ukrainian republic, but it does not have any separate divisions as the Russian republic has. (See also Figures 10, 11, and 12.)

Of course, the most important republic is the Russian republic since it controls and appoints all the important administrators of the Soviet Union, e.g., the Ministry of Higher and Special Education controls all the activities of this area in all republics.

In general, educational policy in the Soviet Union is determined by a relatively small group and then filtered down through succeedingly larger units of administration until it is finally put into practice at the local level. The Central Committee, the Supreme Soviet of the Union and the Soviet of the Nationalities are all supposedly elected by the people, though in actuality, all of them are appointed by the party. All decisions are made by strategic committees.

Functional operation lies in the hands of those who have contact with the masses, namely the party locals. Party locals may have anywhere from three to thirty members depending on the number and size of the area schools. Many teachers belong to the party locals. They have regular meetings, usually three a month with as many as fifteen smaller committee meetings a month. There may also be some closed-door meetings, but the local citizenry is fairly well informed about what goes on. The locals are concerned with party organizational work which includes dis-

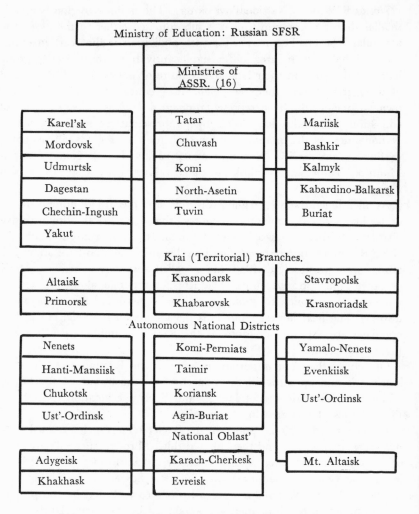

FIGURE 10. Educational Administration of the Russian SFSR.

Calculated from: N. P. Nikitin, (ed.), *Ekonomicheskaia Geografiia SSSR* (Economic Geography of the USSR). Moscow: Izdatel'stvo "Prosveshchenie," 1966.

cussion of party directives with the people, programing activities of the schools and communities and reviewing the school administrative activities. Another very important area of work includes political work and propaganda.

Ministry of Education; USSR

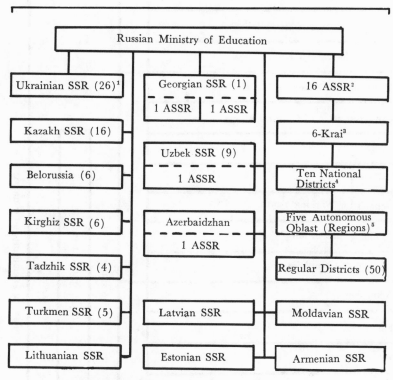

FIGURE 11. Educational Administration of the USSR.

[1] Number in parentheses indicates a regular district.
[2] Autonomous Soviet Socialist Republic.
[3] Administrative Area, usually in Asiatic parts of the USSR.
[4] National district administers various ethnic groups of the area.
[5] Population of the region is that of non-Russian nationality.

THE NARKOMPROS AND THE MINISTRY OF EDUCATION

The communist administration of 1917 did not name the educational authorities the ministries of education because ministry was a term used by the Imperial regime. They used the name People's Commissariat of Education, or in abbreviated form: The Narkompros.

Another reason was that under communist planning the department of education was not yet clearly defined and no exact tasks were entrusted to it by the Russian government. It lacked a clear philosophical foundation and an organizational structure *per se*. The first Commissar

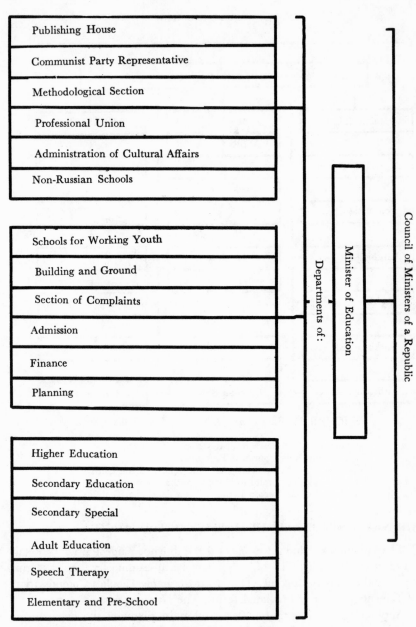

FIGURE 12. Administrative Structure of the Ministry of Education
(Union Republic).

of Education, Lunacharski, was not quite clear about the tasks and the structure of Soviet education when he decided to establish the State Council of Soviet Education.

Soon after the creation of the State Council or committee, which embodied rather broad democratic practices, the Russian government planned the future of communist education using the same techniques as the Imperial regime. They gave certain freedoms but restricted certain activities that were not in line with communist beliefs and practices.

Religious schools, previously under the control of the Holy Synod, were dissolved, and their property became the property of the People's Commissariat of Education. At the same time, Lenin issued a decree whereby the schools were separated from the church and the church from the state.

From 1918 until the end of the Second World War, the Narkompros was the highest educational authority in all republics. There were other administrative units, but major policy-making was divided between the Central Executive organs of the Party and the Commissariat of Education.

Other educational agencies, such as the libraries, museums and theaters were also under the direction of the People's Commissariat of Education. Each school was strictly obligated to keep in line with the educational policies of the central organs, especially after the 1936 reforms when all foreign educational practices were banned in the U.S.S.R.

Soon after World War II, the Soviet government decided to rename the educational offices and they became known as the Ministry of Education. In addition to the Russian Ministry of Education, each union republic and each autonomous republic was given a Ministry of Education. Districts and cities had their own educational boards directly subordinate to regional authorities. At all educational levels, however, the representative of the communist party has his chair; and directors or teachers have to ask him for approval of suggestions or projects.

After World War II, Soviet educational authorities also spread the system of the Academies of Sciences to all the union republics. Previously only more culturally advanced Soviet nations enjoyed the privilege of having their own Academies of Sciences; but after the war, these became standard in all the states.

The primary function of the Soviet Academy of Pedagogical Sciences is the supervision of methodological activities as well as control over research projects. (See Figure 13.)

It is important to note that the publishing of educational material—

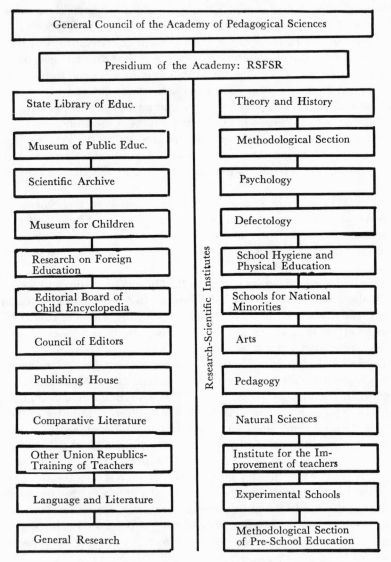

FIGURE 13. The Structure of the Academy of Pedagogical Sciences.

Calculated from: V. Skorodumov, *Struktura rukovodstvo sovetskoi shkoloi* (Munich: Institut po Izucheniiu SSSR, 1955), p. 72 mimeo.

textbooks, literature for children, audio-visual printed material—all belong to the supervision of the Academy of Pedagogical Sciences. It also controls the editing of the Children's Encyclopedia, museums, research institutions and the training and development of teachers. It is imperative that they be consulted in the field of methodology. The Academy of Pedagogical Sciences cooperates with other branches of sciences, especially those related to secondary school disciplines.[3]

The Soviet government from time to time criticizes all levels of educational activities and thus expects better work in educational matters. In the research fields, especially since 1960, special emphasis has been given to the natural sciences, those sciences which supply the needed students for industry and schools. A special committee was established in 1961 to direct all research in the U.S.S.R. The Russian republic, stated *Pravda*, gives all the necessary "help" and supervision to all other union republics in this matter.

FUNCTIONS OF THE MINISTRY OF EDUCATION

One of the most important functions of the Ministry of Education is the supervision of the curricular activities at all levels of the educational system. Here, more than in any other area of education, special care must be taken to educate the children of the proletariat properly. Special *spravochniki* (study plans), which must be followed in detail, are published annually for the various levels of schools.

In 1958, when the work and study plan became effective in all Soviet schools, more intensive scheduling of subject matter was introduced. In 1960, special plans were issued for the Schools of Working and Rural Youth. It was felt that the program of these schools should fit in better with the particular type of student population, and the nature of the work the students were doing. The eleven year program existing in the Soviet Union at that time did not necessarily improve the educational level of the secondary schools because students had to spend two years in industrial or agricultural centers which in reality cut their total time in formal education to a nine year program.

Recently the Boarding Schools received much attention since these are rather new (in their present form). In 1962, there were 700,000 children in these schools which are not only designed to help the work-

---

[3] *Pravda*, April 12, 1964; See also Boldyrev, *Direktivi VKP (b) i sovetskogo pravitel'stva po narodnom obrazovanii*, vypusk 1, 1947, p. 20; Skorodumov, *op. cit.*, p. 7.

ing parents take care of their children, but even more to help the government educate a new generation indoctrinated in the communist world outlook. Children in these schools are more or less cut off from parental influences since they come home only on weekends. The Ministry of Education sends out for each school a special *spravochnik* (study plan) indicating a sequence of subjects to be covered.

General Education. The Ministry of Education has departments to administer the elementary and secondary schools. Preschool education, nurseries, and kindergarten belong under the jurisdiction of the Ministry of Health, although efforts are being made to subordinate these schools to the Ministry of Education. Directors are appointed by the Ministry as well as the inspectors of schools. Both receive their instructions not from local school councils but from the union ministries of education. Regular general schools are of three types depending on the number of grades they teach: grades 1-5; grades 1-8; grades 1-10 or 11. The director of the schools has to answer to the inspector of education who in turn informs the Ministry about the state of the schools in his area of control.

The teachers get their jobs through the Ministries of Education, and salaries are contingent upon the type of teaching, grade level, years of experience, and geographic location, e.g., in northern regions the pay is higher than in central Russia.

The administration in every school must create favorable conditions for the student organization, the Octobrists, the Pioneers, and the Komsomol, who operate on school premises but take their instructions from the communist organizations of the area.

Higher Education. In theory each republic has a Ministry of Higher Education. In practice, as seen at other levels, these ministries take their orders from the Russian Ministry of Education. Actually it was only after World War II that Moscow permitted such offices in other republics. At the present time the Ministry of Higher Education also handles the affairs of secondary special education. As of 1961, thirty-nine universities were supervised by the republic ministries of education. All polytechnical institutes are supervised by the *Sovnarkhoz* (Soviet National Economy Bureau); the transportation institute by the Ministry of Railways; the agricultural institute by the Ministry of Agriculture; and the medical institute by the Ministry of Health.

Other higher educational institutions, such as research institutes and the Academy of Science belong under the jurisdiction of the Ministry of Education. Many *aspirants*—graduate students—work in research institutes while simultaneously pursuing their advanced degrees.

Other Functions of the Ministry. All decisions of the Ministry of Education are in line with other departments dealing with the national economy, national planning, and with technological education.

The Ministry of Education issues instructions regarding entrance examinations to higher educational institutions, giving priority to the workers of "communist construction" and then to the able specialists.[4]

The Ministry of Education also takes care of part-time and evening education. In Ukraine alone, for example, by 1970 more than seventy per cent of the total student population at the higher level will be studying at night or on a part-time basis.

THE SCHOOL ADMINISTRATION

All elementary and secondary schools and institutes are administered by a director who is ordinarily a member of the communist party and who is also trained to be a teacher. The university president, or as the Soviets call him, the rector, is appointed by the Ministry of Education while academic promotion at the university level is decided by the university council and subsequently acknowledged by the Ministry of Education.

Every director has to take certain administrative courses. This, however, should not be compared to European or American administrative training where the administrators must take courses related to their area of specialization. The most important courses for Soviet administrators are those dealing with the policies and practices of the communist party of Russia and the required methods of indoctrinating children in the communist world outlook. About 200 hours are required for a person to be qualified as a school director.[5]

The responsibility of the school director is not only to administer the school business, but most all to follow and explain a definite line set

[4] A. M. Pankratova, *Istoriia SSSR,* 10th edition (Moscow: AN SSSR, 1955), pp. 407–415; *Direktivi KPSS po khoziaistvennym voprosam,* p. 115; N. A. Konstantinov, *Systema narodnogo obrazovaniia* (Moscow: Izdat. Moskovskogo Universiteta, 1956), p. 390; S. Rosen, *Part-Time Education in the USSR* (Washington, D. C.: U. S. Office of Education, Bulletin No. 17, 1965), p. 25.

[5] *Pravda,* April 12, 1961.

up by the party. Therefore, it is important that a position of this kind should be in the hands of a party member because, according to the Soviets, only he can foresee and properly interpret the party's plans and ideas. Only about ten per cent of the Soviet teachers belong to the communist party, but the director of every school is always a party member. This is important because in the Soviet structure some teachers and students belong to the secret police and observe students and teachers alike. It is unlike in the United States, for example, when the Association of Students discovered that certain members belonged to the CIA, and the Association automatically created a furor, almost comparing it to treason for students to belong to an organization such as the CIA. In the Soviet Union, or as a matter of fact, in all European countries, it is considered a privilege to belong to the organs dealing with the security of the state.

Another reason for the mandatory party membership of school administrators is that when the party decrees new laws, these must be carried out by force if necessary regardless of the age of the students or the feelings of the community. Naturally, party members are more responsive to such a task.

As Figure 14 shows, the city or local council enjoys the highest esteem on the top of the administrative pyramid. Next is the director of a school as well as a representative of the local communist party, who in reality runs the school.

THE TEACHER

The Soviet teacher is in a rather paradoxical situation. He is highly respected by the community and the students, yet he has nothing to say about the method of teaching his own subject, conducting his own laboratories or counselling a student. Moreover, the Soviet teacher has no tenure rights.

Teachers of history or literature, as well as many other branches of the social sciences, have a dual task toward the school and the community. They must deliver speeches propagating the new ideas that the party promulgates. No other position is as demanding as the position of a teacher. Lunacharski once said that the teacher is the tool between the party and the community: it is his duty not only to educate young minds but also to influence all the people and explain the new ideas to society.

The Ministry of Education dictates the amount of material to be covered during certain periods of time. It is quite common to see the same subject covered in the same day in the schools of Moscow or Siberia.

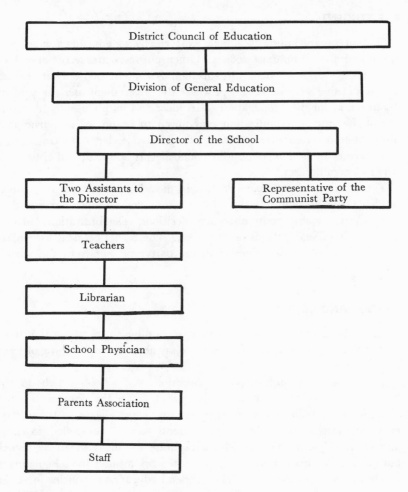

FIGURE 14. Educational Council for Schools of General Education.

Calculated from: V. Skorodumov, *Struktura rukovodstva sovetskoishkoloi* (Munich: Institut po Izucheniiu SSSR, 1955), p. 72, mimeo.

There are strict orders from the Ministry not to deviate from the prescribed lines of instruction. For this reason ideological indoctrinations have no limits. The Soviet teacher must attend very often (every summer) "improvement" schools where he is reminded about the "great achievements" of the party and public education. He is encouraged to join the party and he must believe that he is better trained than the American teacher, or any other teacher outside the U.S.S.R.

THE STUDENT

Student organizations in school exist chiefly to educate a new generation of the communist society. Other purposes are secondary. This aim of the Soviet Student Organization is evident not only in Russia but in all other satellite countries where the government uses the student organization for the propagation of its ideas and its philosophy. A member of the student organization is required to be an active participant of the building of communism, and a progressive leader of the community who devotes himself to persuading nonbelievers about the atheistic doctrines of communism.[6]

There is little student participation in the administration of the school. Students have no right to select a lecturer for a desired topic, nor may they demonstrate against administrative decisions. Demonstrations always support the official policies of the school. The Soviet Student Organization takes all of its directions from the party and not from the school. (See also Figure 15.)

SCHOOL AND SOCIETY

As has been stated before, parents have nothing to say about the structure of the school, and have very little to say about the upbringing of their own children.

There are many professional organizations and schools which do not have a section in their administrative pyramids for the parents. But the niche for the communist party representative must always be there. Parents committees exist only so that parents can be compelled to come and listen to party agitators who paraphrase the ideas stated by higher authorities. Parents may do some physical work around the school premises but may never decide moral or general educational policies for their children.

The whole spectrum of Soviet education reveals the central planning. The Soviets feel their system is best for accomplishing those aims which they themselves set. The totalitarian character of communist education is absolute. The 1946 definition of its general contents has changed very little. It involves the care and supervision of the development of the rising generation and arming it with systematic knowledge, skills and habits necessary for future practical activities. Also involved is training

---

[6] *Sovetskaia pedagogika,* January 1967, p. 138. See also Boldyrev, *Direktivi VKP (b) i sovetskogo pravitel'stva po narodnom obrazovanii,* vypusk 1, p. 128; *Soviet Education,* July 1966, vol. viii, No. 9, p. 3.

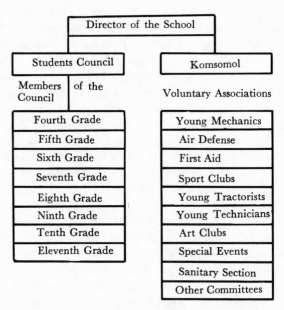

FIGURE 15. The Structure of the Student Government.

Calculated from: V. Skorodumov, *Struktura rukovodstva sovetskoi shkoloi* (Munich: Institut po Izucheniiu SSSR, 1955), p. 72, mimeo.

in the necessary emotions, inclinations and interests, habits of behavior and features of will power and character in accordance with the spirit and principles of communist morality.[7]

EDUCATIONAL EXPENDITURES

Comparing the pre-revolutionary expenditures on education with those of the Soviet government, there is no question that the Soviet government has spent more money on education than the Imperial government. But here, as in other areas, one must be careful in evaluating the Soviet data. The Soviets list and compare only the expenditures of the Ministry of Public Education with those of the Soviet Ministry of Education— purposely leaving out the expenditures on education by the Holy Synod,

---

[7] Bereday, *The Changing Soviet Schools,* p. 138; Akademiia Obshchestvennykh Nauk RSFSR, *Voprosy ideologicheskoi raboty: sbornik vazhneishikh reshenii KPSS,* 1954–1961 (Moscow: AON RSFSR, 1961), p. 229.

local *zemstva* (private economic enterprises) and private endowments. If the Soviets would add all of these funds, the Imperial data would not appear as bad and the Soviet data would not appear as good.

Of course, in many areas the Imperial administration did not care about the education of non-Russians, as can be seen in Central Asia. The Muslim schools depended largely on the *vakuf* endowment properties. Even public schools in Russian Turkestan did not enjoy full financial support from the government. For example, in 1893, Fergana oblast' received 198,277 rubles for education, or 0.02 kopeiki per inhabitant of the region. Samarkand received 141,890 rubles, or 0.4 kopeiki per capita. In 1915, the Imperial government assigned 1,084,800 rubles for educational needs in Turkestan, which was 2.4 per cent of its total budget, or 0.22 kopeiki per capita.

The aid to other regions depended largely upon political aims of the administration. For example, in 1894, the Muslim schools of Kazan received from the local *zemstvo* budget an amount of 1,439 rubles as compared to 6,799,832 rubles to Russian schools of Kazan.

The Russian schools, on the other hand, were supported by the *zemstvo* or by funds from the Ministry of Public Education and the Holy Synod. Although not a huge amount of money was assigned to education, nevertheless, it was subsidized by the state or local budgets. In 1893-1894, e.g., the Russian schools of Zakaspeisk Oblast' received from municipal sources 2,850 rubles, to cover the expenditures for forty-two schools and 1,825 students. Similar amounts were assigned to Samarkand and Syr-Dar'ia. Besides the *zemstvo* funds, the Ministry of Public Education granted some aid to schools.[8] (See Table 19.)

Since 1917, the expenditures on public education increased substantially not because the Soviet government took over, but because many schools were destroyed during the war and revolution and because after World War I, in all states of Europe, formal education received new regard. As Table 20 shows, the expenditures on education depended largely on the location of school programs. For example, in 1934, in the Russian SFSR eleven per cent of the total national budget was spent on education while in the whole U.S.S.R. fourteen per cent of the total budget was allotted to education. In 1965, 21.8 per cent of the Soviet budget was assigned to education. (See Table 21.)

It is interesting to note that after the death of Stalin new types of boarding schools became quite important in the Soviet educational struc-

---

[8] *Nachal'noe obrazovanie v Rossii,* vol. 1, pp. 201–206; Narkompros UzSSR, *Spravochnik instruktsii v avguste 1939 g* (Tashkent: Narkompros UzSSR, 1939), pp. 11–12.

TABLE 19

Expenditures of the Ministry of Public Education on Elementary and Secondary Schools: 1893
(In rubles)

Region	Total Expenditures on Primary and Secondary Education	Secondary-General	Secondary-Professional	Teachers' Institutes and Seminaries	Urban Schools as Specified by decree of 1872	Elementary Education
Kazan'	225,549	91,361	...	79,857	31,101	23,230
Urban	207,889	91,361	...	79,857	31,101	5,570
Rural	17,660	...	...	...	...	17,660
Moscow	612,179	417,835	90,108	46,104	44,117	14,015
Urban	581,466	417,835	90,108	29,406	44,117	...
Rural	30,713	...	...	16,698	...	14,015
Orenburg	164,630	78,946	800	42,119	12,824	29,941
Urban	147,276	78,946	800	42,119	12,824	12,587
Rural	17,354	...	...	...	...	17,354
Zakaspeisk	2,850	...	...	...	...	2,850
Urban	2,850	...	...	...	...	2,850
Rural	...	...	...	...	...	...
Samarkand	13,562	...	...	...	8,087	5,475
Urban	11,572	...	...	...	8,087	3,485
Rural	1,990	...	...	...	...	1,990

(Continued on next page)

TABLE 19 (Continued)

Expenditures of the Ministry of Public Education on Elementary and Secondary Schools: 1893

(In rubles)

Region	Total Expenditures on Primary and Secondary Education	Secondary-General	Secondary-Professional	Teachers' Institutes and Seminaries	Urban Schools as Specified by decree of 1872	Elementary Education
Syr-Dar'ia	121,947	50,716	...	46,144	12,559	12,528
Urban	117,468	50,716	...	46,144	12,559	8,049
Rural	4,479	...	...	...	...	4,479
Fergana	25,209	...	...	...	13,384	11,825
Urban	24,214	...	...	...	13,384	10,830
Rural	995	...	...	...	...	995

Calculated from: Imperatorskoe Vol'noe Ekonomicheskoe Obshchestvo, *Nachal'noe narodnoe obrazovanie v Rossii*, edited by I.Fal'bork i V. Chornolutskii (St. Petersburg: Tipografia Narodnaia Pol'za, vol. 3, 1900), pp. 188–206.

TABLE 20[1]

Expenditures of the Soviet Government on Education, in Selected Republics: 1932–34
(In millions of rubles)

Republic	1932			1934		
	Expenditures			Expenditures		
	Total	Of Which on Education	Per Cent of Total on Educ.	Total	Of Which on Education	Per Cent of Total on Educ.
RSFSR	2,179,0	316,0	15	4,753,8	508,3	11
Transcaucasian SFSR . .	378,5	81,8	22	621,8	134,0	22
Uzbek SSR[2]	263,7	62,4	24	418,0	88,9	21
Turkmen SSR	114,8	25,7	24	172,9	38,9	22
Tadzhik SSR	109,2	19,9	18	150,1	31,6	21
USSR—Total	4,043,2	740,3	18	8,067,9	1,154,8	14

[1]Central Administration of Economic and Social Statistics of the State Planning Commission of the USSR, *Socialist Construction in the USSR* (Moscow: Soyuzorgouchet: 1936), pp. 486–87.
[2]According to Kari-Niiazov, the expenditures of the Uzbek SSR on education equaled 49.4% of the total budget of the republic in 1940 (See Kari Niiazov, op. cit., p. 166).

TABLE 21

Expenditures of the Soviet Government
On Education: 1950, 1965
(In millions of rubles)

Types of Expenditure	1950	1965
Elementary & Secondary: Urban Schools.	651,1	2342,8
Elementary & Secondary: Rural Schools	1287,0	2752,0
Boarding Schools: Urban.	518,0	518,0
Boarding Schools: Rural	. . .	134,4
Homes for Children and Special Boarding Schools . .	462,0	367,9
Higher Education	235,7	1358,6
Technicums: Secondary Level	244,9	746,2

Ministerstvo Finansov SSSR (Ministry of Finance of the USSR), Gosudarstvennyi biudzhet SSSR i biudzhety soiuznykh respublik. (State Budget of the USSR and the Budgets of the Union Republics), Moscow: Izdatel'stvo "Finansy," 1966, pp. 8, 80–88. Note that the total budget for the USSR (1965) was 101,621.2 millions of rubles of which 21.8% was spent on education; 10.7% on health; 12.3% on social security; 22.4% on industrial developments, but the source does not mention the amount of money spent on military matters.

ture. The government spent a substantial amount of money on these schools, designed to educate fighters for communism. As can be noted from Table 21, in 1965 over 652 million rubles were spent on boarding schools.[9] In short, when the Soviet state spends that much money on boarding schools alone, there is a political reason for it.

Additional References

Best sources concerning the educational policies are those edited by the communist party officials, or the authorities of the party, predominantly works of Lenin and Stalin. The most important work is *KPSS v rezoliutsiiakh i resheniiakh s'iezdov, 1917–1952;* Boldyrev, *Direktivi VKP (b) i sovetskogo pravitel'stva po narodnom obrazovanii* (Moscow: Izdat. Sovetskaia Pegagogika, 1947); V. I. Lenin, *Izbrannye proizvedeniia,* vol. II, 4th edition (Moscow: Gospolitizdat, 1949); also V. I. Lenin, *Izbrannye stati po natsional'nym voprosam* (Moscow: 1949).

Other sources are: Nigel Grant, *Soviet Education* (London: University of London Press, 1965); *Narodnoe obrazovanie,* No. 8, 1962, pp. 2–8; *Uchitel'skaia gazeta,* April 10, 1962; Nikolas Hans, *Comparative Education* (London: Routledge and Kegan Paul Ltd., 1955); Vol'noe Ekonomicheskoe Obshchestvo, *Nachal'noe obrazovanie v Rossii* (St. Petersburg: Izdat. Fol'barka, 1900).

---

[9] *Gosudarstvennyi budzhet SSSR v 1966 g* (Moscow: Izdatel'stvo Finansy, 1966), pp. 51, 76–87.

Chapter 7

CURRICULUM POLICIES

In line with the rejection of the Christian theories concerning the nature of man and his relationship to society, the communists rejected many academic subjects taught in the old Russian regime regardless of the fact that these subjects had nothing to do with politics. Further, the Soviets eliminated from their school curriculum the Latin and Greek languages, religion and jurisprudence, replacing them with the study of natural sciences and the study of revolutionary movements.

The Ministry of Education furnishes every single detail of curriculum requirements as well as very detailed plans for teaching all subject matter, so at first glance it seems the educative process is very simple.[1]

---

[1] See, for example, the yearly *spravochniki* and *uchebnye plany* for every school and every grade as well as every subject offered. No teacher has the right to deviate from the plan published by the Ministry of Education. Such plans are: *Ministerstvo Vysshogo Obrazovaniia SSSR* (Ministry of Higher Education of the USSR); *Uchebnye plany pedagogicheskikh institutov* (Study plans for Pedagogical Institutes) (Moscow: Ministry of Education Press, 1966), passim; Ministerstvo Vysshego i Srednego Spetsial'nogo Obrazovaniia; *Uchebnyi plan spetsial'nostei 0201, 0807, passim.* Similar plans are published for humanities and are distributed throughout the Soviet Union for. each school and each area of specialization.

143

On the other hand, the Soviet curriculum policies are more complicated than one may think because such "pedagogical" practices as Sovietization, Russification, and indoctrination of the child in new Soviet philosophy and culture go with them.

We shall first view the curriculum policies on the general level, or in our terms the elementary and secondary education.

ORGANIZATION AND CURRICULUM POLICIES IN GENERAL SCHOOLS: 1918-1941

Curriculum depended on the level of education. Since the old system had been changed in 1918, especially the secondary schools, the curricula were also in the process of experimentation. As mentioned before, the Unified Labor School had consisted of two divisions: five-year elementary education, and four-year secondary education. In 1927, this system too had been changed into the following administrative divisions:

a. elementary school, of the first level, consisting of four years of schooling;

b. incomplete secondary school, consisting of seven years of training, including elementary;

c. secondary school, consisting of a total of nine years;

d. factory schools (FZU—fabrichno-zavodskie uchilishcha) post-primary training with emphasis given to practical needs of the factory;

e. *Rabfak*, a school especially designed for the working classes, aimed at preparing the students for higher educational institutions in a reduced time-period basis.

The guidelines in curricula planning for all programs were the national policies in the economic development of the country, as well as specific projections made by the party and government with regard to education.

In the first period (1917-1920), the Narkompros published new curricula plans for elementary and secondary schools. According to these plans, the first grade of the elementary schools had no divisions of subject matter. It was similar to continuation of a kindergarten situation where children could improve their language skills, familiarize themselves with the natural surroundings, sing and draw, not in the form of subject-matter but in a manner that was termed a "child encyclopedia approach."

In general, the first four years of elementary training were devoted to the mother language, history, physical education, and biology. Grades five to nine included physics (four hours per week), chemistry (three hours per week), mathematics (four to five hours), and foreign languages (two hours per week beginning in the sixth grade).

New Soviet curricula excluded pre-revolutionary subjects such as religion, Latin, law and philosophy, replacing them with aesthetics, chemistry, fine arts, music and physical education. Requirements of physical labor were also included in the school curricula.

Curricula developments during the New Economic Policy (NEP) period (1921-1928) were better organized, although the philosophical concepts regarding the school and society had a share in shaping the Soviet school program. General inclination was toward the natural sciences and to ideological education.

The party required that children be brought up in a Marxian world-outlook and that schools should participate in a struggle against the bourgeois ideology and existing bureaucracy in the Soviet system. Educators were required to discuss important educational issues with the party leaders.

Curriculum development during the period of industrialization, or as the party labeled the times—the period of establishment of proper cultural development—was focused around subjects needed for industrial goals. Preparation of curricula was carried out in terms of the general goals outlined by the Commissariat of Education. The elementary school curriculum, for example, was based on peasant economy and forms of agriculture; the city as a center of industrial development; the plan of great works; Lenin and the party; Komsomol; transition period from capitalism to communism; and so forth.

In 1929 the nine-year schools were extended to the ten-year program schools in RSFSR. After the Soviets launched the first Five Year Plan calling for industrialization of the country, the subject matter shifted more toward natural sciences and physical labor. One can notice this shift by comparing the 1927 curricula and the curricula of 1929. In 1927 physical labor was not required for grades eight and nine, but by 1929, thirteen hours per week in grade eight and fifteen hours in grade ten were devoted to physical labor and fine arts. (See Tables 22 and 23.)

Special schools were established to fulfill the needs of industrial areas. In 1929 the country needed more chemists, especially agricultural chemists, so a special decree was issued on August 29, 1929, authorizing the Narkompros to strengthen technical education on the secondary level, particularly in the field of chemistry. At the same time, the new laws

TABLE 22
Comparison of Curriculum of Boys Gymnasium, 1914, and
Soviet Curriculum of 1920, 1927

Subject	Total Number of Hours per Subject in Grades		
	4–8 1914	5–9 1920	5–9 1927
Russian Language and Literature	640	882	748
Mathematics	640	714	714
Aesthetics	...	578	578
Chemistry	...	306	306
Physics	320	510	612
Social Science	500	816	714
Geography	224	340	240
Foreign Language	928	272	442
Latin Language	800	...	...
Fine Arts	...	408	306
Singing and Music	...	...	272
Physical Education	...	340	272
Labor (Trud)	...	...	306
Astronomy and Meteorology	...	64	...
Law	64	...	...
Philosophy	96	...	...
Religion	320	...	...

F. F. Korolev; T. D. Korneichik; Z. I. Ravkin, *Ocherki po istorii sovetskoi shkoly i pedagogiki, 1921–1931* (Moscow: Izdatel'stvo APN, 1961), p. 81.

stated that students should allot at least 40-50 per cent of school time on practical training (work in industry, agriculture, practice teaching). All republics were ordered to comply with the new regulations.[2]

CURRICULUM IN NON-RUSSIAN SCHOOLS:
UKRAINE AND UZBEKISTAN

Curricular changes like the Russian changes were made in all union republics. In this section we shall take two Soviet republics, Ukraine and Uzbekistan, as a representative sample of non-Russian schools.

The Soviet reconstruction in Ukraine did not start in 1918 because at that time Ukraine was an independent country. The curriculum dur-

[2] Korolev, *Ocherki po istorii sovetskoi shkoly i pedagogiki*, p. 31; *KPSS v rezoliutsiiakh i resheniiakh s'iezdov*, vol. 1, pp. 754–755; *Direktivy KPSS po khoziaistvennym voprosam*, vol. II, p. 115; Boldyrev, vypusk 2, *op. cit.*, p. 14.

TABLE 23

Curriculum of the Soviet Ten-Year Program School,
Distribution of Hours Per Week on Subject Matter:
RSFSR, 1927, 1929

Subject	Grade						
	V	VI	VII	VIII	IX	X	Total
1927							
Social Science	4	4	4	5	4	...	21
Russian Language and Literature	5	5	4	4	4	...	22
Mathematics	4	4	5	4	4	...	21
Fine Arts	3	4	4	3	3	...	17
Chemistry	1	2	2	2	2	...	9
Physics	4	4	4	3	3	...	18
Geography	2	2	2	...	...	...	6
Foreign Language	3	3	3	2	2	...	13
Labor (Trud)	3	3	3	...	...	...	9
Music	2	1½	1½	2	1	...	8
Physical Education	2	1	1	2	1	...	7
Total	33	33½	33½	27	24	...	151
1929							
Social Science	4	4	4	3	4	4	23
Russian Language and Literature	5	4	4	3	3	3	22
Mathematics	6	4	4	3	3	3	23
Aesthetics	4	3	4	2	2	2	17
Chemistry	...	2	2	2	2	2	10
Physics	...	3	4	4	3	3	17
Astronomy	...	...	...	...	...	2	2
Geography	2	2	2	...	...	...	6
Economic Geography	...	...	...	2	...	...	2
Foreign Language	3	2	2	2	2	2	13
Fine Arts	2	2	2	...	...	...	6
Physical Education	2	2	2	2	2	2	12
Labor (Trud)	3	3	3	...	...	...	9
Music	1	1	1	...	...	...	3
Subjects for Upper Level (Grades 8-10) Related to a Type of Activity (Labor or Fine Arts)	...	...	...	13	13	15	41
Total	32	32	34	36	36	36	206

F. F. Korolev, T. D. Korneichik, Z. I. Ravkin, *Ocherki po istorii sovetskoi shkoly i pedagogiki, 1921–1931* (Moscow: Izdatel'stvo APN, 1961), pp. 79–80, 97.

ing the period of 1917-1921 was based on the decisions and recommendations of the *Narodna Rada* (National Council) which tried to establish Ukrainian-type schools with the subjects needed for the newly developed country and the newly developing industry. For obvious reasons, the study of the Ukrainian language was emphasized (it was non-existent before 1917 in the Russian empire), as well as the study of religion, Latin and other classical subjects. In line with these subjects a polytechnical type of curriculum was being developed in the Ukrainian National Republic. As mentioned before, the first Unified Labor Schools were developed in Ukraine and later copied by Lunacharski in Russia.

During the New Economic Policy Period (1921-1928) an attempt was made to establish a communist system which was national in form and communist in character. But as was noted before, Khvilovij, Lubchenko and Skrypnyk—top leaders of the country—committed suicide and their followers were liquidated.

In Uzbekistan, like the Ukraine, there existed until 1926 Muslim religious schools, *mektabs* and *medressas*, which had curriculum based upon Islamic religious practices. By 1928, no religious doctrines were taught in any Muslim schools of the U.S.S.R.

Elementary schools in general were organized on Soviet Russian pedagogical principles, providing specific measures for each ethnic group living in the area. The Uzbek programs for the schools of this first level required quite new methods of approaching a child, taking into consideration the many variables (cultural, social, psychological, etc.) that children exhibit. School was to be related to work and society, and during the very first years of schooling the child had to be acquainted not only with his natural surroundings but also with things that communists do.

The first year of elementary education, according to the program of 1927, was still in a way the prolongation of the kindergarten training, including such topics as home and school conditions; October holiday; acquaintance with the kinds of work in the family and school; family and school collectives; acquaintance with the environment, etc.

The second level involved a knowledge of the society in which they lived. Children were to be acquainted with the study of social conditions and the organization of a collective life; understand the cultural importance of things in the home and school, the things that human labor produced; acquire an elementary knowledge about personal and social property; understand the necessity of rules and order in the classroom; learn to work and play collectively; participate in the work of school (such as being on duty in the classroom, cleaning the blackboards, furniture, etc.); learn to conduct themselves properly in a meeting of their group; discuss problems in a group under the direction of the teacher.

Further, they were to be acquainted with the different organizations in which children participate—Octobrists and Pioneers—which subsequently they were to be prepared to join.

The third level was dedicated to the specific learning of reading and writing, correct pronunciation of words, and general introduction to speech principles. Such principles included the ability of a child to discriminate the word in a phrase, an interrogative sentence from a demonstrative sentence, etc.

A higher level involved subjects dealing with sciences, arithmetic (addition, subtraction, multiplication, division), measurement of weight and length, time, weighing things on scales, or measuring length, basic principles of geometry, measuring and showing the location of a given subject by drawing an approximate picture, etc.[3]

After the New Economic Policy period, the situation changed completely because of two reasons: the Soviet government was against supporting the Islamic educational institutions and did not wish to continue those schools on territory of the Soviet Union; the development of industrialization demanded a new type of curriculum which the native Islamic schools were unable to offer.

The new Muslim schools were established on the basis of Russian historical and cultural developments and disregarded completely native traditions and religious beliefs. As Tables 22 and 23 indicate, the subjects in these schools were similar to Russian schools except that all scientific subjects were taught in Russian. The Uzbek language was to be kept only for local communications but not for sciences.

The period between 1918 and 1940 was generally motivated by two principles: education of the new Soviet man and the adaptation of schools toward industrial needs. Especially after 1936, when the Communist Party rejected foreign influences on the Soviet educational philosophy, the Soviet system went back to such pre-revolutionary practices as sound disciplinary measures and selectivity at higher levels of learning.

GENERAL EDUCATIONAL CHANGES AFTER WORLD WAR II

Curriculum changes after World War II were largely influenced by the new developments in the atomic field and sciences in general. Subjects like physics, mathematics, and chemistry were largely emphasized (see Table 24) while subjects like psychology and philosophy were neglected.

---

[3] K. F. Lebedintsev, *Rukovodstvo po algebre* (Tashkent: Gosizdat, 1927), *passim;* Narkompros UzSSR, *Shkol'noe upravlenie, instruktsii o provedenii soveshchanii uchitelei v auguste 1930 g.* (Tashkent: Narkompros, 1930), p. 13.

In addition to this, the new policy required a polytechnical orientation at all levels of education.

By rejecting Stalin's cult of individualism, Khrushchev not only changed international politics but education as well. Policies initiated by

TABLE 24

Curriculum for Grades IX and X In Ukrainian SSR: 1967–1968

Subject	Number of Hours per Week	
	Grade IX	Grade X
Native Language	...	...
Native Literature	2	2
Russian Language	1	1
Russian Literature	3	3
Algebra	3	2(3)*
Geometry	2	3(2)*
Physics	3	3(4)*
Chemistry	2	2
Biology	2	0
Geography	0	2
History	3	4
Foreign Language	2	2
Drawing	1	1
Industrial Learning	9	9
Physical Education	2	2
Civil Defense	1	0

Calculated from: Ministerstvo Prosveshcheniia Ukrainskoi SSR, *Uchebnyi plan dlia vos'miletnykh i srednikh shkol Ukrainskoi SSR*, No. 7–8 (Kiev: Ministerstvo Prosveshcheniia UkSSR, 1967), pp. 27 ff.
* Indicates the number of hours in the Spring Semester.

Stalin were no longer the supreme laws of the land; new directions were initiated, especially those that Lenin and his wife, Krupskaia, had suggested. After 1956, the most important policy changes were the emphases on polytechnical education. These were as follows:

a. polytechnical training of teachers and students alike,
b. a close cooperation between educational agencies and industrial enterprises,
c. emphasis on that subject matter which could be utilized in the neighboring industrial factories and enterprises.

These ideas were basically practical but their execution was not. The communist party felt that mere issuance of laws regarding polytechnical education would not help the political cause of the party. Therefore, they introduced the previously mentioned work and study plan, which was another failure. The party thought that this combination would strengthen its political position since the students would have the chance to use the same language as the workers and would gain some practical industrial experience. It was soon apparent, particularly after the fall of Khrushchev, that making one's hand dirty does not necessarily make him a communist. The experiences gained while working in factories were not all positive. Drinking and linguistic vulgarity were common among those who became closely associated with factory life.

It became clear to Soviet educational leaders (after Khrushchev's fall) that today's polytechnology is not based on political indoctrination but on the mastery of "learning and doing" techniques. It is true that complex machinery requires more experience than it did in the early 1920s; nevertheless, physical work cannot substitute for basic theoretical knowledge.

One also has to take into consideration the availability of technological instruments and machinery in Soviet secondary schools. Only the best schools in the country can afford the luxury of technological equipment, e.g., secondary schools in Moscow have some facilities in chemistry and physics where students can spend up to two hours a week of extra work in a laboratory, but this is unusual.

At the secondary level, there is not much to be added to the official study plans sent by the Ministry of Education. A review of the study plans from 1940, 1959 and 1966 shows the following:

		Number of Hours			
Number of Lessons	Type of Lessons	Urban Secondary with Industrial Training	Rural Secondary with Industrial Training	Correspondence Evening Schools	Evening Schools Part-Time Only
1	Methods of Descriptive Geometry	26	26	26	26
2	Technical Drawing	12	12	12	12
3	Details of a Drawing	10	7	10	5
4	General Drawing	22	20	22	12
5	Structural Drawing	8	10	10	5

The distribution of time in Soviet schools is divided as follows: between 30-42 per cent is alloted to natural sciences; 36-38 per cent to humanities (languages and social sciences) ; and between 30-33 per cent to vocational activities.[4]

Generally speaking, the students take about 4-5 hours per week in the Russian language (in grades 8-10), six hours per week of mathematics, four hours of history, two hours of biology, and at least three hours per week of a foreign language course which begins at the fifth grade.

Astronomy, physics, chemistry and the Soviet Constitution each occupy between one and two hours per week in the upper grades of secondary education.

CURRICULUM STRUCTURE AT INSTITUTES OF HIGHER LEARNING

The planning of curriculum at the higher level is motivated first of all by the Soviet ideas about the purpose and aims of higher education. Each study plan must underline the necessity of a politically conscious intelligentsia and the task of the high educational institutions to do their best in fulfilling the goals set up by the party. Eliutin, the Minister of Soviet Higher Education, said that development of Soviet higher education paralleled the people's needs and the people's economy. But at the same time Eliutin underlined the importance of the 20th Party Congress which gave opportunities to Soviet higher educational institutions to achieve a better balance between industry and the school. Furthermore, the goal of the higher institutions of learning is to obtain maximum activities and independent work on the part of the students in the framework of Socialist economic and cultural plans.

In line with the fulfillment of political tasks the Ministry of Higher Education requires special courses to be taken by each student regardless of his area of concentration. These subjects are: (1) history of the communist party of the Soviet Union, (2) history of the political economy, (3) dialectical and historical materialism. These three subjects, according to Eliutin, help to educate the new generation in the Marxist-Leninist world outlook, a generation which loves work and is faithful to communist "morality" and other practices of communist society.

The study plans as of 1967, for example, give the general orientation of the curriculum structure. Each plan must be in line with industrial needs and attuned to a better relationship between school and society. They enumerate the necessity of educating the following: (1) highly

---

[4] Eliutin, *op. cit.,* pp. 53 ff. See also DeWitt, *Education and Professional Employment in the USSR,* p. 107.

qualified specialists, (2) highly qualified specialists who also are educated in the Marxist-Leninist philosophy of life, (3) highly qualified workers of the socialist construction in general.

In line with these general instructions Soviet students at higher educational levels have almost no electives. They are so overloaded with the required subjects that the *fakul'tentnye distsipliny* (optional courses) are almost non-existent. Secondly, besides the courses required for one's specialization, courses in Marxian dialectics are very much emphasized. Together with other courses in "scientific atheism" they compose over 15 per cent of the overall school curricula. For example, 500 hours out of 3,908 are required on political subjects. (The department of history demands 574 hours; philosophy, 844 hours; chemistry, 510 hours; biology, 600 hours; and economics, 660 hours.)

The length of training usually determines the shape of the curriculum since different specializations require different amounts of time spent in schools. Pedagogical institutes, for instance, vary from three years to five years, while medical schools require at least six years of training. It should be remembered that medical schools also include subjects in dialectical materialism. Soviet doctors must spend at least 15 per cent of their training on subjects specified by the Ministry of Education. This would cut the six years of training to about five if the subjects not related to the practice of medicine were eliminated.

Medical students have to take during their first and second years 160 hours of the history of the communist party, 90 hours of political economy, 140 hours of dialectical materialism, and 220 hours of a foreign language. Other departments dedicate even more time to political subjects. For example those studying economics spend only 42 per cent on their main subjects while the rest is divided between political subjects and subjects dealing with Soviet affairs. Business administration aspirants spend 32 per cent of their time on political subjects and 16 per cent on modern language.

The discipline of political economy is almost entirely devoted to the knowledge of Marxism-Leninism. The curriculum of this school is as follows: economic theories of Slavic societies, their history and culture, the development of feudalism, late feudalism, the rise of mercantilism, the rise of the bourgeois class (particularly in Great Britain and France), economic theories of Adam Smith and Ricardo, the economic theories of Russian Decembrists, utopian socialists of the West, political economy of the vulgar bourgeois, crisis of capitalism, and others.[5]

---

[5] R. L. Meek, "The Teaching of Economics in the USSR," in *Soviet Studies,* vol. X, No. 4, 1959 (London), pp. 343–349; Rosen, *op. cit.,* pp. 13–17.

Curriculum of Teachers' Institutes. Because of the specific role of the teacher in the Soviet society, the curriculum policies concerning Teachers' Institutes are very much under the strict observation of various party committees. The general idea is that you can't teach the teacher how to teach if you yourself have no experience. The communists believe that the teacher must not only know his subject matter but most of all he must live like a communist and must "teach the youth to work and live in a communist manner." The teacher also must work physically. How else can he teach others to love physical work if he has never worked before or if he hates physical labor? Who other than the teacher, the Soviets ask, "made it possible to produce the Sputnik, and who has made it possible for us to achieve so much in the building of Communism?"

Reality is not always so ideal as the Soviets claim. The Soviet teacher has not always been trained to the utmost of his abilities, nor to an adequate knowledge of his field. In the early period of the Soviet regime, the training of the teachers was truly oriented towards the "building of Communism," as Table 25 shows. Besides political subjects very little else was offered in the pedagogical institutes of the 1920s.

As mentioned before, the educational development in non-European parts of the Russian FSSR, was in critical condition. Soon after the Revolution initial steps were taken to develop a Soviet educational system. For example, Tashkent State University, in 1920, established a pedagogical department designed to train the natives to teach in the public school system. Similarly, other Asiatic cities in the Union began to establish pedagogical institutes either on secondary or higher levels (university).

The Commissariat of Education aimed at converting nearly illiterate persons into elementary teachers, in short courses ranging from as little as 2 months to 3 years. The result, however, was not beneficial for educational standards because such teachers lacked formal pedagogical training. Some teachers with short courses knew only part of the alphabet after one year on the job. The Narkompros complained that many schools were not able to teach children more than ten to fifteen letters during the full school year.[6]

After World War II, the teachers were trained in three different schools: (1) pedagogical schools, (2) institutes, and (3) universities.

The aim of pedagogical schools is to train teachers for kindergarten and grades one through four. Students are admitted to pedagogical schools after completion of secondary education and required to study

---

[6] *Narodnoe obrazovanie v Uzbekistane za 15 let,* p. 98.

TABLE 25

Courses for Teachers in Pskovsk Guberniia: 1923

Subject	Number of		
	Lessons	Seminars	Total No. of Hours
Political Economy	24	16	40
History of Revolutionary Movements in Western Europe	24	16	40
History of Russian Culture	8	16	24
History of Materialism	18	16	34
Youth Movements	8	8	16
Soviet Constitution	8	. . .	8
Land Laws	8	. . .	8
Political Economy	8	. . .	8
History of Science	60	. . .	60
Complex Method	4	16	20
Methods of Russian Language	20	. . .	20
Methods of Mathematics	7	8	15
Pedagogical Psychology	20	. . .	20
Unified Labor School	18	. . .	18
Fine Arts	4	16	20
Total	269	132	401

F. F. Korolev, T. D. Korneichik, Z. I. Ravkin, *Ocherki po istorii sovetskoi shkoly i pedagagiki, 1921–1931* (Moscow: Izdatel'stvo APN, 1961), p. 397.

two years in pedagogical school to qualify for a diploma. Those who finish the course work receive a diploma specifying the exact level of school they are eligible to teach. The top five per cent are encouraged to continue their studies at the Institute level where training is more extensive.

A representative curriculum of pedagogical schools in terms of the total hours per subject is as follows:

History of the Communist Party of Russia . . . . 138 Hours
Child Psychology . . . . 76 "
Child Development . . . . 70 "
History of Education . . . . 66 "
Children's Literature . . . . 99 "
Methods of Teaching the Russian Language . . . . 66 "
Drawing and Modeling . . . . 180 "
Singing and Music . . . . 180 "
Physical Education . . . . 138 "
Practice Teaching . . . . 338 "

Pedagogical institutes, on the other hand, are the institutions of higher learning and the time required to graduate is not less than four years. Some pedagogical institutes even require five years of study to complete the required curriculum.

Students who want to pursue their studies at the pedagogical institute must complete secondary school and must pass an entrance examination consisting of oral and written tests in Russian language and literature as well as in one foreign language. A student may not apply to more than one institute in the same year. Priority is given to exceptional students and to those who have completed two years of physical labor.

As of 1967, most institutes offered five years of training. The curricula depend on the area of specialization, but again, courses dealing with indoctrination are given priority in curricula planning. For example, the general division of subject matter in pedagogical institutes is as follows: Students specializing in literature devote over 1,600 hours of 4,300 to the study of literature; students specializing in history devote 1,682 hours to history. The rest of the time is spent on the subjects like Russian language—416 hours, history of the communist party—220 hours, political economy—150 hours, dialectical materialism—140, instructions in linguistics—72 hours, practical training (teaching and observation)— 1,550, methods of teaching—104 hours, physical education—140 hours, and other subjects.

The purpose of the university is to educate teachers for higher educational positions. Although the admission requirements are the same as those for the institutes, only a few qualify. Only exceptional students or those who have political backing are admitted.

University graduates are eligible either to teach at the institute level or to work in industry and research institutes; however, most are specialists in one discipline. This has been criticized recently by educators and the party. While the institute students spend most of the time on theoretical studies, the university students divide their time equally between theory and practice.[7]

Additional References

Important sections concerning Soviet curricula can be found in F. F. Korolev's writing, such as *Ocherki po istorii sovetskoi shkoly i pedagogiki, passim* and *Novaia sistema narodnogo obrazovaniia v SSSR*. See also E. Moos, *The New Work-Study Plan in Soviet Education* (New York: National Council of American-Soviet Friendship, 1959); S. Rakhimi, *Bukvar' dlia detei* (Samarkand: Gosizdat, 1926), *passim;* G. E. Shulz, "Soviet Medicine and the Communist Party," in *Soviet*

---

[7] Eliutin, *op. cit.,* p. 53; Rosen, *op. cit.,* p. 17.

Studies, vol. II, No. 5, (Munich: Institute for the Study of the USSR, 1965), pp. 13–18; F. Maksimenko, "The Teacher—Decisive Force in the School Organization," in *Education in the USSR,* vol. 1 (Munich: Institute for the Study of the USSR, 1963), pp. 140 ff; *Narodnoe obrazovanie v Uzbekistane za 15 let sovetskoi vlasti* (Tashkent: Gosizdat, 1939), *passim.*

Chapter 8

METHODS OF TEACHING

Early Soviet education authorities rejected almost everything that the old-imperial schools practiced so the Soviets had to look abroad for the solution of methodological problems, especially to America. The Dalton Plan, the project method, the laboratory methods, were all practiced in the Soviet Union even though details of these plans were unknown to the majority of Soviet teachers. The Dalton Plan, for example, was understood as group learning in which the individual did not agree to master the given material—the *brigadir* (leader) was put in charge of each group of students, and his word, not testing, decided the progress or failure of the entire brigade.

As to the method of learning, there was a trend in the early 1920s to follow some of the American patterns in this area, e.g., Pinkevitch was influenced by John Dewey and Lenin's wife, Krupskaia, by William James. Krupskaia seemed to agree with William James concerning the problem of a child's interest. She cited James's idea about the slow learner who after all can learn facts in which he is interested, even better than the brilliant student.

Another problem for the Soviet educators was that of grading. Many of the early Soviet teachers believed that the so-called ABC grading method was not democratic, and many schools began to use other variables of grading such as the individual work-book, a collective diary of the class (kept by the children themselves), *brigadir's* report, and finally, the teacher's observation. The individual work-book was considered to be best since it could serve as an indicator of a student's attitude toward work and society. It consisted of records kept by the student showing which articles he had read, which problems he did not understand and questions he needed to solve.

All of these theories and practices were not the Soviet product but foreign—predominantly American. Not until the late 1930s was the unique Soviet system developed by Anton S. Makarenko.

MAKARENKO'S METHOD

Makarenko discussed very delicately the problems of the obligations of students and teachers in general. He saw in the Soviet system improvements and deficiencies. Under the category of deficiencies, Makarenko listed the following:

a. the lack of proper order in structural and organizational instructions for the teacher;
b. the lack of discipline;
c. the lack of continuity between the educative process and the managing of children's problems;
d. the inconsistency of the educative process.

According to Makarenko, these deficiencies are more serious if we consider the direction and the purpose of educative process. Makarenko criticized foreign educational methods as having no definite system or goal, existing only by chance and being decorated by various kinds of "entertainments" and "progressive approaches to children."

Makarenko recognized that an educative process must also be concentrated around the idea of struggling with evil or improper behavior. But one cannot begin the educative process only when students have committed some error. In such a case, one would envy those who committed some crime because only they would be educated or have an opportunity for education.

Makarenko criticized those educators who spent seventy-five per cent of their time explaining the deficiencies of education and twenty-five per cent on a real situation.

Counselling. The Soviet attitude toward counselling is negative. They do not believe in a degree leading to a counselling profession—every teacher should be intelligent enough to advise in educational situations. Makarenko gave an example from his experiences when counselling techniques were used. He cited the case of a boy who broke a rule and how he should have been handled according to the rules of counselling. The counsellor, according to the theories of guidance and counselling, should never raise his voice or express any emotion because of an incident. He should explain in a low voice, calmly as if it were not his personal interest. Nothing is to be said to arouse emotion, etc. Makarenko criticized this technique, saying that a teacher is thus doing more harm than good. The teacher should include his own feelings about certain behavior because the broken rule is his concern and the concern of the state. Therefore, one should not play an indifferent role or be "cool" just for the sake of appearing to be a gentleman.

Counselling is further attacked because of its impracticality, e.g., a certain boy stole six rubles from a classmate, who subsequently complained to the authorities. The principal of the school reported it to a counsellor who in turn tried to solve the case. The boy's name was not revealed to the public, and the problem was solved only between the boy and the counsellor. Nobody else knew anything about it. After the solution of the problem, the girl still did not get her money back; and the boy, after feeling guilty for a while, was planning the next adventure because no one except himself and the counsellor would know that something was stolen. The boy in time gets used to "verbal" punishments and continues stealing while others suffer the personal loss of property. Makarenko thinks that society is more important than the personal pride of a thief who should be punished openly. Children, too, can learn fast what is legal and what is not, or who knows when and how to act stealthily. Makarenko thinks that to punish a boy who steals is not an act of cruelty, but one of the ways to help the boy and society. Thus, individuality must be subordinated to society.

The Soviets think that reward is not to be used constantly. Punishment has its pedagogical value in many cases as well. Counselling in the Soviet Union is not counselling as it is understood in America. Every child is responsible to all of society. The punishment of a thief is handled publicly. His name is published in the newspaper and very often a "confession" is made before a group. Children realize that school is not only play; it is also a serious process of education.

Makarenko, in general, tried to introduce the old Russian practices, adding to them only the communist coloring but essentially maintaining the old system of methods and practices. The experiments used by the

American progressivists were foreign to the Russian mind; therefore, they were harmful to Soviet society. Counselling is rejected by the Soviet educators because it stresses individuality. Makarenko offered instead mass culture and a collective type of philosophy in terms of ideas, subjects, methods of teaching and the general problem of discipline. It is a careful elaboration of all important sectors of pedagogy starting with the pre-school age up to adulthood.

In his attempt to educate a new Soviet man, Makarenko goes so far as to reject everything that might have some connection with supernatural beliefs of any kind. He is against, for instance, fairytales that mention witches or evil spirits—all that is connected with any spirit—because it conjures up associations with the supernatural. Only those fairytales are acceptable which describe animals, imaginary buildings and social heroes who fought for one's country.

SUBJECT MATTER vs. TEACHER

Much had been written about the role of the teacher in the Soviet society and about the significance of the method of teaching. The Soviets tend to argue that there are no poor students—only poor teachers. In theory, the Russians insist that any child can be educated to his highest capacities if given a proper environment.

The teacher, therefore, has a double task before him: indoctrinating the party's objectives and actual teaching. As an example, in presenting to pupils the political system of the Soviet society, the following set of questions is usually used:

> "What kind of political structure is better: capitalism or socialism?" "Of course, socialism," the student answers. "Now, what methods are used to insure the proletariat in power?" "Force and violence," answers the student, "because until the stage of communism is reached, the dictatorship of the proletariat must prevail, etc."[1]

The teacher further explains the capitalistic danger to Soviet society and the horrible capitalistic exploitation of the lower classes. There is no justice except Soviet justice, and there is no freedom except Soviet freedom—so the young child is constantly told. The brain-washing is a continuous process which changes its form depending on the age of the

---

[1] *Vestnik Instituta po Izucheniiu SSSR*, 1955, p. 131. See also Anton S. Makarenko, *O vospitanii molodezhi* (Moscow: Trudrezervizdat, 1951), pp. 71–73; N. K. *Krupskaia o kommunisticheskom vospitanii*, p. 92; A. I. Lutchenko, *Sovetskaia inteligentsiia* (Moscow: Izdat. Znanie, 1962), *passim;* Korolev, *Sovetskaia shkola*, pp. 180–198.

student. Recently the Soviets have tried to educate Soviet youth in terms of international communist solidarity and communist patriotism.

Soviet methodology in the historical and general social sciences is rather peculiar. It operates on the basis of slogans rather than on the pedagogical principles of the educative process. The teachers are always reminded that they are the army of communism. Many books on teacher training are published; most deal with the "right" method, but this "right" method is not without foreign influences.

After the death of Stalin and the fall of Khrushchev, one finds a different approach in the teaching of various subjects and in the general context of Soviet methodology. We shall examine, therefore, some subjects as described and taught by the Soviets in the 1960s.

Pedagogy and History of Education. Recently a somewhat new approach has been initiated by the Soviet educators in the field of educational matters. It is a combination of two systems: the Western-bourgeois and the communist, or Russian system of education. This is not really new because there has always been an interest in Western education, especially American education. But now such study is not undertaken merely to show it inferior to Soviet accomplishments. Soviet students are seriously pursuing the original writings of educators like Dewey, James, Spencer and a few other individuals approved by the Ministry of Education.

Pedagogy, according to the new Soviet approach, must be related to other disciplines such as philosophy, ethics, physiology, psychology, sociology, aesthetics, logics and anthropology. Second, education should generally influence not only the above mentioned disciplines, but also other organizations participating in the building of communism. Primary concern is given to professional organizations of teachers, writers, scientific workers and others.

As Table 26 shows, the plan is divided into three main areas of concentration: the general background of pedagogy, didactics and theories of learning. To the first category belongs a brief description of pedagogy as a science, but most of this section is concerned with the Marxist-Leninist theories of education dealing with such issues as the development of personality (more so the individualism) and its relationship to education, the individual and the collective in communist education, the goals and task of communist education and many other *communist* tasks. As before, the word communism is used constantly which gives the teacher and children the notion that communism, *per se,* is more important than the child himself. (See also Table 27.)

TABLE 26

Structure of Lectures in Pedagogy and Schedule of Hours

Lecture Number	Lecture Title	Activities and Hours per Lecture	Seminar	Lab.
Part I. General Background of Pedagogy:				
1.	The subject matter of pedagogy	4	...	...
2.	Pedagogy and individual development	6	4	...
3.	The place of collectivism vs. personality	4	...	...
4.	Goals and aims of communist education	4	...	...
5.	System of public education	2	4	...
Part II. Didactics:				
6.	Didactics as a theory of education and learning	2	...	...
7.	Content of education	4	2	...
8.	Basic educative process	4	2	...
9.	Fundamentals of learning	4	...	...
10.	Patterns of learning	4	2	8
11.	Methods of teaching	6	...	...
12.	Evaluation of students	2	...	...
Part III. Theory of Education:				
13.	Foundations of education	2	2	...
14.	General methods of education	6	...	4
15.	Formation of communist world outlook	2	2	2
16.	Moral education	8	2	2
17.	Physical labor	2	...	...
18.	Aesthetic education	4	2	2
19.	Physical education	2	...	2
20.	Teaching children the collective way of life	4	4	...
21.	Leading role of Communist Youth Organization in school collective	2	...	4
22.	Education and the family	4	...	6
23.	The role of the teacher	2	...	4
Total		84	26	36

Sovetskaia pedagogika, No. 1, 1967, p. 41.

The second category, didactics, is even more radical. The teacher has to make sure that the general lines of Marxist-Leninist teaching prevail in his lesson plans and other classroom activities. Specific issues and topics are listed for each lesson, so that in reality, the individual teacher tries to explain in his own way the principles laid down by the higher educational authorities. The fundamentals of any teaching, according to this new view, are to acquire knowledge and to transmit it to others. The task is first to equip students with the right habits and help them form

TABLE 27

Soviet "Commandments" of Moral Behavior

A. Soviet Patriotism: Service to the State.

---

1. The love for one's country and one's native language; the love for distinguished people of the Soviet state. The readiness to defend the great socialist country; willingness to die for it if it becomes necessary. Always be proud of socialism. Soviet socialism is the best in the world. Socialism was first established in the Soviet Union.
2. Hate toward the enemies of the country. Self-confidence.
3. Desire to serve the Soviet country; belief in the communist society; optimism.
4. Subordination of individual interests to the country's interests.

B. Communist Attitude Toward Labor.

---

1. Love for work and respect for work as the prerequisite of communist regeneration of society and the establishment of communism throughout the world.
2. Hate toward the inactive people, the disturbers, and all those who disrupt the establishment of communism.
3. The necessity of labor and the necessity of participation in the social struggle for the sake of constructing socialism.
4. Selfconfidence in labor. Enthusiasm at work. Heroism in productive labor.
5. Will power in overcoming difficulties.
6. Discipline and responsibility at work.
7. Knowledge of collective work: the ability to work with others.
8. Protecting and respecting common property as the property and labor of the Soviet people.

---

communist consciousness, and only then, to help the students to develop their own capacities to learn and create something new. Here again, as in any area, the Marxist-Leninist theory of learning and perception should prevail. In line with this, the plan requires adverse criticism of many bourgeois educational theories, especially Herbart's. After covering these disciplines, topics such as attention, memory, the will, emotion and logical judgments are discussed.

Other essential parts of didactics are preparation of lessons, supervision of students, assignment of proper homework, excursions, laboratory work and work related to the national economy. The last topic is important because it gives children an opportunity to get acquainted with some of the machines used in the national economy and their operation. Programmed learning and teaching machines and their relationship to learning in the United States and the Soviet Union are also discussed.

The third category is the theory of education and its "superiority" over any other existing system. In this context, Western educators are discussed more than in any other section. (Actually, the study of Western philosophy became visible in Soviet schools only after the death of Stalin.)

Of course, all educational authorities whose works are studied are selected by the Ministry of Education and no one is allowed to read beyond the topics or issues stated by this authority. Hegel's works, for example, are never read completely. In fact, his works are not distributed among the students—only selected portions are quoted and discussed.

We note that the plan of 1967 is probably the most liberal in Soviet educational history. A review of the disciplines and the people shows that this area is developing fairly well, although not without the Marxist-Leninist coloring and the ideas of superiority of socialism over any other politico-cultural system. Nevertheless, at least 100 pages of the 1967 Plan are devoted to the study of the foreign educational ideas which are divided into the following categories: (1) education during slavery (this describes educational activities in the Greco-Roman World, mentioning very briefly Aristotle, Plato, Quintilian, and the appearance of Christianity); (2) the second period deals with education and schools during the epoch of feudalism in Western Europe and the education of the elite and the masses during this period. Here such important educators as Erasmus, da Feltre, Montaigne, More, and Campanella are mentioned; (3) the school during the initial stages of capitalism is followed by explanations of general Marxian theories of social and cultural development. Comenius is described in a rather good manner. John Locke is mentioned also. Rousseau is described at length, followed by Helvetius, Diderot, Condorcet, Pestalozzi, Herbart and others. The most important period, of course, is devoted to the teaching of Marx and Engels and their struggle with the bourgeois capitalistic system. The last category is entitled Bourgeois Education during the Epoch of Imperialism, and for some reason John Dewey is considered to be an imperialist. The struggle of the communist parties all over the world for a better education is also described.

The rest of the plan is devoted to the history of education of the people of Russia before 1917. The history of education in socialist countries, a lengthy description of Soviet educational practices during the period of socialist construction, and of the building of communism in the Soviet Union are included.[2]

The new Russian plan in education is important not because of the

---

[2] *Sovetskaia pedagogika*, No. 1, 1967, pp. 44–65. *See also Uchebnye plany na 1965 god, passim.*

large number of topics that it covers but because of the permission given to study, at least briefly, the western educators. The fact that these philosophers are usually explained as the exploiters of society and the fact that only materialistic educators are covered does not brainwash the students as much as previously. New ideas can enter their minds for the control has eased somewhat. This is important because any intelligent student when reading Hegel or Pestalozzi would like to know more about them, and if he has the chance he can read and find for himself that those people were not the representatives of capitalism, but the representatives of education or philosophy *per se*.

It is also true that Soviet teachers are subject not only to indoctrination, but they must also do their share in indoctrinating others, e.g., the Communist Youth Organizations are to be covered in all Soviet schools.

Psychology. The teaching and understanding of psychology is based, more or less, on Pavlovian concepts of psychology with additional interpretations. Soviets study human growth and development as do we, but under different interpretations. They recognize stages of development like infancy, childhood, adolescence, adulthood, etc. However, there is no mention of the will. Instead of the spiritual components of the nature of man, the Soviets strongly underline such things as the concept of debt towards one's country (in particular towards Russia); the proletarian consciousness; the role of the communist party; the danger of the idealistic interpretations of the psychological phenomena; the subordination of one's desires and ethics towards the communist mass psychology; the communist humanity; and others.

It is a general trend of Soviet psychology, as of any other social science, to subordinate the role of the individual to the state. Through collectivity one learns and is influenced in the shaping of his personality. The Soviets do teach, however, that the first task of psychology is to liberate man from such undesirable concepts as hate, sorrow and fear.

It is very important to note the effect of the Soviet psychology on later stages of youth. Children soon find that the idealistic interpretations of society and the glorifications of leaders are nothing but fairytales. When they are confronted with real life situations, they find that there is tremendous conflict between theory and practice, that most Soviet leaders base their theories on false promises and the destruction of those who oppose the dictated way of life. All this inculcates in Soviet youth disrespect for authority, skepticism, hypocritical behavior, egotistical relationships with friends and the lack of independent initiative.

In Marxian psychology there is no room for jokes or laughter during classes or lectures. Humor is rejected by the Marxian psychologists;

tension and caution are required on the part of students. All personality characteristics must be subordinated to the collective spirit, collective discipline and the collective life. Any other behavior is termed bourgeois behavior, dangerous for the building of communism and Soviet society. Therefore, the class struggle has also a psychological impact upon one's personality since nothing can exist without the struggle between the inferior and superior forms or the struggle between people in general.

Obviously we cannot accept such half-truths and suspicious ethics. To the Soviets, only those ideas and things that are originated by the communists are morally correct. Psychology, in short, should serve only the goals of the party inside and outside Russia. Personality, *per se,* is not important; the society is the actual carrier of all values.

Teaching of Philosophy. The Soviets have completely inverted the study of philosophy. Philosophy is not studied from the point of view of values, concepts or metaphysical questions but from the point of view of a historical materialism designed to disprove non-communist philosophies. They favor only extreme materialistic explanations of natural or supernatural phenomena. To the Soviets, historical materialism is an integral part of an individual's world outlook regardless of whether he is a historian, physicist or mathematician.

How does one better understand the philosophical categories? *The Soviet Journal of Higher Education* gives the following example: a student who had the experience of working in the national economy can easily apply his experiences to philosophical problems. He may, for instance, think about the process of loading and unloading economic goods. If the people who are engaged in the process of loading and unloading economic goods have advanced machinery, the job will be done faster and market prices will drop because of the mechanical help.

Atheism. Scientific atheism is a constant reminder to educational institutions and teachers that they must plan their work on the basis of the communist morality. According to the *Journal of Higher Education,* communist morality requires the debunking of the dogmas of religion in order to elucidate the social class importance of idealistic views. The students must participate more than in any other class in discussions, ask relevant questions in regard to religion and be aware of its danger to society.

One of the most popular reference books is the work of the Soviet Academician, E. A. Kosminski. Kosminski related the history of the Middle Ages to the study of religion.

The contentions of Kosminski are as follows: (a) He accuses the church of supporting the feudalistic systems of that time. The orthodox church is accused of being a tool of the Byzantine emperors; the Muslim church is accused of being a passive member of that society and of educating slaves rather than free people; the Catholic Church is accused of supporting the crimes of feudalism. (b) The Catholic church in Bohemia is pictured as the most brutal persecutor of the peasantry. (c) All churches were purported to be based on hypocrisy.

As usual, the most wicked enemy of the "workers and peasants" is the Catholic church. The repetitious attacks on the church have become a stereotyped method which is obviously quite exaggerated.[3]

In reality, however, the aim of the Soviet fight against religion is not to fight religion, *per se,* but to fight certain Western ideas which are related to religion.

METHODS OF TEACHING HISTORY

The teaching of the "right" history was not solved until the late 1930s when the party interfered in the methods of teaching history and rejected previous methods.

During the early period of Soviet educational development, methodological questions were rather neglected. The Soviets had practiced, as mentioned before, American methods of teaching, which did not work simply because of the different nature and goals of Soviet education. After the termination of the New Economic Policy (1928) the Bolsheviks began to work on the methods of teaching, especially the method of teaching Russian or Soviet history. The communist party of Russia began to issue laws and directives in relation to methodology, discipline, subject matter and the general orientation of the student life. The party wanted to inculcate the idea that there can be no scientist other than a Marxian scientist and that there is no better method of teaching than the Soviet method. As to how the process of reconstruction was developed, we shall present the original accepted and rejected Soviet ideas about this subject.

---

[3] Note that almost every page of the book is designed to fight religion. See E. A. Kosminskii, *Istoriia srednikh vekov, uchebnik dlia 6–7 klassov srednei shkoly* (Moscow: Uchpedgiz, 1951), pp. 9–58, 106, 145, 183–201; I. Valenskii, *Akademik E. K. Kosminskii i voprosy interpretatsii istorii srednikh vekov v sovetskoi shkole* (Munich: Institute for the Study of the USSR, 1954), pp. 5 ff.; L. I. Novikov, "Trud i nravstvennoe vospitanie podrostaiushchego pokoleniia," in *Sovietskaia pedagogika,* No. 1, 1967, pp. 104–121; *Voprosy psikhlogii,* No. 1, 1967, pp. 135 ff.; *Vestnik vysshei shkoly,* No. 11, 1959; No. 5, 1960.

Michael N. Pokrovski

Pokrovski was the most important and most controversial Soviet historian. He was born on August 30, 1868, in Moscow, where he also completed his university studies in history under the supervision of two important historians, Pavel Vinogradov and Vasili Kliuchevski. He helped to edit Kliuchevski's *Russian History* as well as his *History of the Middle Ages*. In 1905, Pokrovski sympathized with the Decembrists (December Revolution of 1905) and officially joined the Bolshevik movement after the revolution.

From 1905 on, he either stayed in Russia or in major European capitals, like London and Paris. He never officially escaped from Russia (as did Lenin and Stalin) but collaborated with all socialist movements that were working towards the destruction of the czarist regime.

His works are not primarily concerned with the Marxian interpretations of history but rather with a history of Russia as it existed and as it shaped the destiny of the Russian people. Pokrovski collaborated with many socialistic movements in Europe and in Russia—with Trotsky, Lenin, Stalin, Martov, Lunacharski—regardless of whether they belonged to the *Mensheviks* (minority) or the *Bolsheviks* (majority). His major work was a *History of Russia from the Earliest Times to the Rise of Commercial Capitalism* (in four volumes) which began to appear in 1910. This interpreted Russia in the light of historical and economic materialism, which of course, was in line with Lenin and other Bolsheviks. It was not this history that got him into trouble but the *Brief History of Russia* published in 1920.

Pokrovski occupied various important positions in the Soviet government and in scientific associations. He was a chairman of the Moscow Soviet. He participated in the treaty of Brestlitovsk (he opposed that treaty), established the previously mentioned *rabfak* and helped to establish the Russian Association of Social Science Research Institutes. He served as the President of the Society of Marxist Historians, edited the Journal, *Istorik-Marksist* (Historian-Marxist), published *Krasnyi Arkhiv* (The Red Archive), and from 1918 until his death in 1932, was a deputy Commissar of Education.[4]

What were Pokrovski's theories? First, he believed that many Marxists had not successfully escaped all bourgeois theories concerning the nature of the state and the history of society. Pokrovski also believed that history was more than merely a class ideology. He felt the Marxian conception of history, i.e., strictly from the point of view of economic determination

---

[4] Roman Szporluk, "Pokrovsky and Russian History," in *Survey*, No. 3, October 1964, pp. 107–118; Boldyrev, vypusk II, *op. cit.*, pp. 50, 83–101.

and exploitation, did not always fit reality. He denied that only Marxian science can be called a science and that non-Marxian writings had no scholarly value. When Stalin and other communists initiated a drive to belittle previous Russian accomplishments in culture and science as being parasitic and bourgeois, Pokrovski commented that only a fool would dare to throw away works of Kliuchevski (a historian) and Soloviev (a philosopher). These statements, as can be expected, got him into trouble. The party began to attack him. But since he was a personal friend of Lenin and quite influential as a communist, they left him alone until his death in 1932, after which he was constantly attacked as a stooge of the bourgeois, a non-Marxist and the enemy of the Soviet state. He was officially rejected by the party in 1934. Finally in 1936, Stalin personally attacked his theories as non-Marxian historical theories.

In order to understand Pokrovski's method of research, as well as his method of writing and teaching history, it is necessary to indicate briefly a few basic concepts of Pokrovski's methodology and scientific method.

a) *History vs Sociology.* When the Commissar of Education, Lunacharski, declared that a Marxist pedagogue dares not to move a single step without a sufficient knowledge of sociology, Pokrovski opposed him. He said that sociology is concerned with social norms, values and groups but not with armies, mountains, forests and ravines which are strictly the business of history and not sociology. Furthermore, society is helpless without strong leadership and strong hopes and plans for the future.

b) *The Place of the Romanovs.* Although Pokrovski basically opposed the monarchical system and the right of the Romanovs to decide the fate of Russia, he approached the problem not from an emotional point of view but from its historical importance in relation to space and time. Russia and the Russian czars were to him the same as monarchs were to the early Egyptians, Syrians, Greeks and others. The Russian czars established a fundamental political order based on economic serfdom and a standing army necessary for national defense. The Russian Czar, Peter the Great, was the most progressive and the most patriotic Russian ruler. But on the other hand his aristocratic reign prevented a rapid spread of capitalism in Russia and general industrial development.

c) *The Place of Capital.* Pokrovski basically disagreed with Stalin and others that the prime prerequisite for the world revolution was acceptance by all nations of Marxian theories: basically that political structure would evolve from capitalism to socialism and finally to communism. To Pokrovski this evolutionary theory made no sense. He had his own theories, more or less based on the following: (1) economic conditions; (2) political conditions—always hostile to capitalism; and (3) the role of the leader or ruler of a country. It is true that Pokrovski believed that formation of the Russian empire was influenced by the mercantile capital and not the capitalistic development of Russia's own monopoly as in Europe. In addition to mercantile capital, the shape of Russian history was influenced by the German philosophy of idealism, which indicates that forces behind creating history are three: ideas, man and capital.

One should notice the difference between mercantile interests and industrial capital or the interests of industrial capital. The mercantile system is based on smaller profits and supports serfdom. Industrial capital favors the liberation of peasants, free labor and a free market. Russia was behind most European countries and insisted on the continuation of the mercantile interests rather than large industrial interests simply because Russian bureaucracy did not want to liberate the peasants and to initiate free labor. Therefore, Pokrovski opposed Marx in the peaceful transformation of mercantile capitalism to the industrial type of capitalism. (To Marx this was an automatic process: the replacement of mercantile capital by big capitalistic monopolies causing the revolution and eventually the stage of socialism.) To Pokrovski, Russia was different because the mercantile capital reached its highest stage in the second half of the nineteenth century, while in Europe the big monopolistic enterprises replaced the small merchant-type enterprises much earlier.

d) Imperial Agricultural Policy. To Pokrovski the imperial administration was rather backward in economic development, especially in agricultural reforms. He recognized one exception: Stolypin, who at the end of the nineteenth century initiated some progressive agricultural reforms and abolished the village commune, thus enabling big industrial planning and investment to develop in Russia. To Pokrovski everything follows a natural order and nothing comes by chance.

e) Political Order. As a communist, Pokrovski believed in the communist structure of government, but he had his own explanations of certain historical dates and epochs. To him the Russian Revolution of 1905 could not have been accomplished without the previous political revolts in the 1820s and the economic developments of the nineteenth century. Most important, men—not ideas (as Marx believed)—create and establish the new order. According to Pokrovski, the Bolsheviks could have won the revolution in March, 1917, if only Lenin had been present in Petrograd. He made the analogy that ideas cannot accomplish much without strong leadership. Pokrovski noted the failure of the Kerensky government for the following reasons: the bourgeois intelligentsia were always afraid of peasants; second, the industrialists were never good revolutionists; and the intelligentsia unknowingly promoted capitalism and with it destroyed themselves. Pokrovski believed that the Decembrists could have won the Revolution of 1825, but they were psychologically unprepared. They were afraid that the Czar would conquer them as he did Pugachev, which meant that the intelligentsia had no psychological motives; and they failed to include the peasants in their system as did Lenin.

f) *Methods of Historical Research.* To Pokrovski, man is the creator of history. However, at the same time, the task of history is to describe events not in terms of sociological significance but as political occurrences and support the same with objective evidence. The historian has to look for historical facts and sources and not for the sociological laws and norms that govern certain groups.

g) *The Significance of the Bolshevik Revolution.* Pokrovski described the Bolshevik Revolution as the triumph of courage (muzhestvo). He indicated by many examples that other political movements could have won the battle against the czars if only they had had courageous leadership. He does not mean merely raw courage but the ability of men to make important decisions during a crisis. Lenin, to him, was a great leader because he initiated the land and peace reforms (at least in word since he needed the support of the peasants for their implementation) and signed a treaty with Germany (against the total opposition of his followers) which eliminated Germany from the Eastern front. Not only could the Socialists have won the revolution, but also the Constitutional Democrats. The Revolution of 1905 would have been successful if they had had a man with the ability to make important decisions. A man, as Pokrovski stated, may be an honest man and a good man, but he may not qualify for leadership.[5] In short, history cannot be interpreted purely through simple economic laws.

The Period After Pokrovski

The Communist Party obviously did not stop interfering in educational matters after the death of Pokrovski. They tried to control educational

---

[5] M. Pokrovsky, *Ocherki po istorii revoliutsionnogo dvizheniia v Rossii v 19-om i 20-om v* (Moscow: AN SSSR, 1927), pp. 118–127, 25; M. Pokrovsky, *Brief History of Russia,* translated by D. S. Mirsky, vol. 1 (New York: Vantage Press, 1933), p. 11; M. Pokrovsky, *Istoricheska nauka i borba klassov* (Moscow: AN SSSR, 1933), p. 265.

matters, especially the teaching of history, even more rigidly than during Pokrovski's time.

There were continuous repetitions of communist demands on the teacher and his role in presenting historical material. In 1938, a decree was issued to "strengthen" the party ideas with a newly published book entitled *Short History of the Communist Party*, that demanded that care should be taken to patch the damages done by Pokrovski.

After World War II, the idea of Russian nationalism prevailed in the presentation of historical facts and in the general interpretation of history. History books made vivid and clear the things that the party wanted to push forward, e.g., the Soviet way of life was presented in pictures, figures and all kinds of illustrations.

The method of teaching history in Soviet classrooms is carefully elaborated. Children have to be conscious of the class struggle and imperialistic danger facing the Soviet state. In most studies of history, the stages of communism are to be taught, followed by explanations of Marxian "classics," such as Marx, Engels, Lenin, Stalin, etc. It goes something like this: the teacher should present facts followed by interpretations such as "why not illustrate that the United States spends $100 billion per year just for ammunition and arms . . . compare graphically how many houses can be built for this money." It is further suggested that a teacher should not present facts, but rather emphasize such topics as people's movements, rebellions in various countries, the collapse of colonialism, etc.

Another method is described by Sivodedov, who among other things, suggests that an eleventh grade student should not learn more than two or three new names, and that the main emphasis should be placed upon the personality of those names; or that the history book should first of all represent the might of the U.S.S.R. as the defendant of peace; also, such issues as the crisis of capitalism, the collapse of colonialism, the people's struggle against world war, etc.

There are other approaches to studying and presenting historical facts. They may vary from the class struggle within the Russian society, to the class struggle of the capitalistic society, but the struggle must go on. In recent interpretations of Stalin's epoch, the Soviets although rejecting major points of his methods, basically aver that he was a good communist. All knowledge of history, says *Pravda*,[6] should first serve the struggle for communism. Soviet historians insist that their writings should have international significance and should "enlighten" the way of other

---

[6] *Pravda*, January 30, 1966; *Izvestiia*, January 20, 1966; *Novaia i noveishaiia istoriia*, No. 5, 1960, p. 82; *Istoricheskii arkhiv* (Moscow: AN SSSR, No. 1, 1961), p. 132.

revolutionists who are trying to establish the dictatorship of the proletariat in their particular countries.

And what is the method of this "enlightenment?" Most important, the Soviet historian has to portray the United States as a country "that heads the capitalistic camp by repressing the people ... bloody imperialists, slave-holders, etc."

How does the student know the difference? All that he can read is the communist sources. Thus, the student's knowledge is limited only to the Soviet sources and for this reason the censorship bureau checks every new textbook before it is published. History books are completely distorted and the Soviet children know about World War II only from what communist educators write. A Soviet textbook on history indicated that the atomic bomb was dropped on Hiroshima for the sole purpose "to deprive the Soviet Union of the advantages which victory had brought to it."[7]

TEACHING OF UKRAINIAN HISTORY

The history of the Soviet Ukraine is the most distorted history of the Soviet nationalities. The reason is obvious: Ukraine is the second largest nation of the U.S.S.R. and is agriculturally the most important part of the Soviet Union. The Ukrainian soil is the richest of all Europe. Politically it represents tremendous power with a population of forty-five million; militarily it serves as a strategic wall between Western and Eastern Europe.

The Russian strategy in teaching Ukrainian history is aimed at Russification on the one hand and at proving the hypothesis of Russian "liberation" on the other. Thus, any occupation of Ukraine by Russian forces is interpreted as the policy of liberation and any independent Ukrainian national movement is termed by the Soviet historians as enslavery of Ukraine.

The Soviets tried to prove historical unity between the two nations, starting from the Ukrainian dynasty of Rurik (a Viking who came to Ukraine between the eighth and the tenth century and established the first organized Ukrainian state) and continuing with the Romanovs of 1613. It is clear that the dynasty of Romanov had nothing in common with the dynasty of Rurik. It is true that the Kievan dynasty gave the legal and cultural foundations to the Moscovite state, but this has nothing to do with the hereditary relationship between the two nations. These

---

[7] Gunther, *op. cit.*, p. 263.

relationships are the same as the relationships between the Poles, Czechs, Serbs—in all respects cultural and linguistic.

The official history of Ukraine was presented by M. Yavorski, the founder of the Marxist school of history, who wrote two books on Ukrainian history. One was titled the *History of Ukraine* and the other *A Short History of Ukraine*. Both were published in 1928-29, and accepted by the communist party.

Yavorski's conception of history is as follows: the task of history is to reveal concretely the developmental laws of historical process on the basis of dialectical materialism, as well as those laws that lead classes of society toward social revolutions which will culminate in the establishment of classless society. Yavorski divided Ukrainian history into four categories: (1) the period of feudalism; (2) the period of serfdom; (3) the period of capitalism; and (4) the period of socialist revolution. In addition to these periods, Yavorski describes several concepts designed to interpret the Ukrainian past and present. They are:

The Concept of "Lesser Evil." It was a general tendency in Ukrainian history to interpret the treaty between the Hetman of Ukraine, Bohdan Khmelnitski, and the Russian Czar, Alexi, in 1654, as a treaty of "lesser evil." This treaty, concluded in Pereiaslav, made most of the present day territory of Ukraine a federal state of Russia. It was believed at that time that the war with Poland could not continue indefinitely and since Khmelnitski was very worried about a future attack by Poland, he concluded the treaty with the Russian Orthodox czar. It is true that the nobility of the Ukraine at that time favored neither Poland nor Russia; but because Russia was Orthodox and Poland was Catholic, they thought that Russia was a "lesser evil" than Poland. This term was also accepted by the Soviet authorities at first; but after World War II, the Russians introduced a new idea into the study of history. It was simply that there were never any occupations by Russia. All such maneuvers were made in the interest of the growth of the Russian people and were actually liberations. So the Russians did not occupy the territories of thirty million Muslims, the whole of Siberia, Poland and parts of Romania—they "liberated" them. In the same line, the Soviet historians opposed the term of "lesser evil" because, according to the Soviet interpretation, the treaty of Pereiaslav was a fortunate date because it began the prosperous period of Ukraine.

The Concept of the Older Brother. Pankratova, and other Soviet historians interpret the Russian colonialization of the pre-Bolshevik period not in terms of imperialistic desires of the Russian czars, but in terms of "brotherhood" and "liberation." Since Russia was a society of a "higher order," other nations apparently did not mind being occupied by the more advanced culture. The concept of the "higher order" and the idea of the "older brother" pertains to the Russian people who preserved and cultivated the *right* Marxian interpretation of historical periods and the development of other nations and groups living in Russia. Pankratova especially wanted to prove that the brotherhood of Russian, Ukrainian and Belorussian people always existed and only after the Mongol invasion were the non-Russian people (Ukrainians and Belorussians) created.

It is important to note that the history of the Soviet Ukraine is not a free history, i.e., Ukrainian history is written under pressure and is interpreted not in terms of historical realities but in terms of Russian needs at certain points in time. We find in the concepts of Soviet history various interpretations regarding the non-Russian people: e.g., history is nothing more than an account of great ideas, history is the branch of dialectical materialism which teaches us that the focal points of historical development are the things in themselves, or that history is a contrast of two forces—thesis and antithesis, etc. Regardless of what is behind Soviet-Russian interpretations of the historical method, one thing is clear: Russians dictate the method of writing the histories of other nationalities and select or impose certain historical episodes according to Russian taste. Ukrainian authors have no freedom whatsoever to describe objectively historical events, for they must always add the Russian coloring. Ukrainians, Turkestanians, Latvians, and Estonians cannot speak of Russian occupation of their countries, but must refer to the concepts of "older brother" and "liberation" as having motivated the Russians to enter into their countries.

In this context, *A History of Ukraine* was written by a certain Virnyk, who was given the task of writing Ukrainian history on Russian terms. Thus Ukraine was described from the well known Marxian views: primitive communism and Ukraine; the epoch of feudalism; capitalism; and socialism. Under these four categories the relationship and brotherhood of two nations, Russia and the Ukraine, were studied from the very beginning until the present. Virnyk had to underline the "wholehearted desire of Ukraine to be united with Russia the older brother." At the same time the author of Ukrainian history dares not forget to describe the superiority of Russian culture. He supports this story with much writing about Russian cultural leaders and leaves no room for description of the Ukrainian leaders.

The Nation vs. the Tribe. It is also a duty of the Soviet historian to redefine certain terms. For example, K. Hulysti, a Soviet historian, introduced three definitions: the tribe, the nationality and the nation. Following Marxian dialectics, during the first stage of communism, tribe is the proper term to describe people; during feudalism, nationality is used; and only during the epoch of capitalism is the term nation used. Therefore, the Ukrainian nation did not exist before the epoch of capitalism, but the Russian nation has always existed. In order to be logical, the author of the Ukrainian history goes on to say that during the epoch of feudalism nationalities began to develop their cultures, and the Russian nationality was the most vivid and most progressive.

Method of Writing Ukrainian Textbooks. After the death of Stalin, a new history of Ukraine was published which followed as usual the main concepts of Marxian history. The important thing was not the publication of history but the method of its writing. First, it was not the Ukrainian Academy of Sciences which initiated the move, but the Russian Academy of Sciences and especially the Lenin-Stalin-Marx-Engels Institute in Moscow which lent a "helping hand" in sources and in methods (rather directives) concerning Ukrainian history. The Institute of Slavic Studies and others "offered" help in writing the Ukrainian history.

As one can gather, the writing of the Ukrainian history was not initiated by Kiev, but by Moscow. There were eighteen members of the "historic" committee who helped to write a *History of Ukraine.* One important thing can be noticed: historical and scientific sources were not used for reference material, but the sources of social Marxian philosophy. That book is long—if nothing else—over 700 pages, but the total number of foot notes does not exceed 150, of which 68 refer to Lenin.

The reason for avoiding other sources is obvious: to avoid arrest, one must cite party members and grandly underline their greatness and significance in the history of a non-Russian nation. The Soviet author, in any history book, has to make vivid that Leninism is the highest achievement of the world's culture and of the history of Russia. Furthermore, the appearance of Leninist ideas had a gigantic significance for the whole world as well as for development of the culture of all Soviet nationalities and, therefore, the Ukrainian nation.[8]

The basic policy in writing Ukrainian history is that the author should

---

[8] Krupnitsii, *op. cit.*, pp. 13–65, 136–148.

ɯake it clear to a reader that the only good sources are the Marxian sources and that without these sources one cannot write a book on any subject. They are the bible of communism. Second, one must avoid citing sources of non-communist origin; and if one does so, the purpose must be to make them appear inferior to the Soviet in all ways. (Also, the author must not give the reader the idea of looking elsewhere for verification of his statements.) For example, a section of the Ukrainian history, "The Development of the Ukrainian Culture in the Second Half of the Nineteenth Century" devotes most of its space *not* to a description of the Ukrainian cultural history and its leaders, but to Russian cultural leaders like Chrnishevski, Nekrasov, Chekhov, Tolstoi, Dobroliubov and others.

One of the most popular Moscow approved histories of Ukraine is that edited by O. Kasimenko, which if nothing else, argues and condemns all non-Russian editors of the History of Ukraine. The most condemned is M. Hrushevski, an internationally known Ukrainian historian, a man who tried to present history as a study of nations and individuals and as a free scientific investigation based on facts rather than on propaganda. Hrushevski is presented as "the damned enemy of the Ukrainian and Russian people, a bourgeois nationalist and a liar . . . who wanted to prove that the Russian and Ukrainian people are different." Another Ukrainian historian, V. Antonovich, is represented as a bourgeois nationalist who wanted to defend the monarchy and a wicked enemy of the revolution and the Russian people. He, Hrushevski and all other non-communists were collaborators of Austro-Hungarian nationalism, stooges of nationalism, the most wicked enemies of Ukraine, etc. In short, all who want an independent Ukraine, all who say that Ukraine is not Russia are, as far as Soviet terminology is concerned, liars, stooges, nationalists, etc. This history teaches a young child hate toward all who are not of Russian origin. The well known metropolitan Sheptitsky, a leader of the Ukrainian Catholic Church, is described by the Soviets as a bourgeois nationalist, the biggest enemy of the Ukrainian people, a traitor and many other things.

It is clear that this interpretation of historical facts serves the Russian purpose because the Ukrainian students have no opportunity to read history books other than those published by the Russians. Those Ukrainians who participate in historical writing are only rubber stamps who sign their names to complete falsifications of history designed to erase any traces of Ukrainian national independence and culture.

Another Ukrainian leader, hetman Mazepa, who in 1709 lost the

Battle of Poltava, which meant the subjugation of Ukraine to Russian rule, is described as a traitor, a stooge of the Swedish king, Charles XII, and unfaithful to Peter the Great.

To summarize briefly, in studying Ukrainian history in the Soviet Union, one must use (besides the general Marxian lines) the following criteria: (1) the superiority of Russians over all other nations; (2) the utmost desire of Ukrainians to be united with Russians; (3) the superiority of those Ukrainians who live in the Soviet Union over the Ukrainians living outside the Soviet Union; (4) the goodness of the centralized system; (5) the desire of Ukrainians to be liberated from the Ukraine; (6) the Ukrainian culture is nothing but a part of the Russian culture; and finally, (7) the concept of hate towards non-communists.[9]

TEACHING OF CENTRAL ASIAN HISTORY

The aim of Soviet interpretation of facts concerning Central Asia is, of course, to persuade the world and the native population that the Russians in 1865 did not occupy Turkestan, but liberated it. Any revolutionary uprising on the part of the natives against Russia was reactionary and cannot be approved in any manner by a Russian historian.

This interpretation of Turkestan history is falsification of the native history of the Muslim people. The Muslims complain that everybody talks about English colonialism but no one says anything about Russian colonialism. Any native endeavor to describe history from the viewpoint of Muslim historical significance is termed by Russian communists as the work of nationalism or pan-Islamism.

Central Asian history probably belongs to the most interesting type of educational study. Under the Romanovs the Russians were satisfied to extend their economic influence, but the Soviets wanted to change not only the social system of Turkestanian people but also their attitudes and wanted them to acquire a proper understanding of other powers, especially Britain. The policy of colonialism is widely discussed and studied, but not the Russian colonialism, even though it was performed by the czars.

The conference of historians which took place in Tashkent on March 7-11, 1950, declared that the national movement under czarism was reactionary, since they had insisted on the separation of Central Asia from Russia. In 1954, another conference was held on the history of

---

[9] V. Dubrovskii, *Nainoviisha sovetska kontseptsiia istorii Ukrainy* (Munich: Institute for the Study of the USSR, 1956), pp. 72–100; A. K. Kasimenko, *Istoriia Ukrainy* (Kiev: AN UkSSR, 1955), pp. 86, 295, 685, 723.

Central Asia before the October Revolution. It was decided that the Rebellion of 1916 was partly progressive and partly reactionary, since it embodied nationalistic elements and was anti-Russian. The Ministry of Russian Education elaborated a theory regarding the Turkish nationalities that the "national movements headed by Muslim leaders were reactionary since they were against Russia." They further explain the Revolution in Turkestan (1917-1922) as a reactionary movement organized by "the clique of bandits," who collaborated with "the imperialists of the USA and England and who concluded a conspiratory plot against the country in order to enslave the people of the U.S.S.R."[10]

Additional References

V. P. Petrosiak, "Kakim dolzhen byt' uchebnik," in *Novaia i noveishaia istoriia,* No. 5, 1960, pp. 86 ff.; I. Mishalov, "O podgotovke i usloviiakh raboty prepodavatelei sovetskoi shkoly," in *Vestnik Instituta* (Munich: Institute for the Study of the USSR, 1955), pp. 131 ff; *Sbornik rukovodiashchikh materialov o shkole,* pp. 92 ff; M. O. Mikhailov, "Pro 29 rokovini z dnia smerti V. I. Lenina," in *Visnik Akademii Nauk UkSSR,* January 1953, pp. 6 ff.

---

[10] *Istoricheskii arkhiv,* No. 1, January 1961, p. 132. See also Akademiia Nauk SSSR, *Materialy nauchnoi sesii posviashchennoi istorii srednei Azii v dooktiabrskii period* (Tashkent: AN UzSSR, 1955), p. 584; *Ost Probleme,* No. 32, 1961, pp. 984 ff.; Krist, *op. cit.,* p. 71.

Chapter 9

DIALECTICAL MATERIALISM
vs EDUCATION

Soviet social thought, especially in the area of philosophy, is very complicated. The Communist government does not support study of other than dialectical materialism, thus eliminating any objective research of philosophy in general and the philosophy of education in particular. Free thinking and free research in this area are further complicated by the imposition of certain laws concerning general beliefs and the general orientation of the social sciences. A Soviet philosopher dares not write a book without referring to the works of Lenin. Marx and Lenin are not only political revolutionists but are elevated to the level of supernatural phenomena whose names must be mentioned in all the sciences. In such conditions one obviously cannot blame the Russian teacher or the Russian philosopher because he is limited in his scope of inquiry by political decrees and laws concerning the role and place of philosophy in the communist structure.

GENERAL BACKGROUND

The development of materialism in Russia was not unexpected and not necessarily connected with the Bolshevik success in 1917. The materialistic philosophy of life was evident among the Russian intelligentsia long before the revolution of 1917. One can even trace the origin of Russian materialism back to the time of the Nikon and Avacuum controversy when some Russians decided not to follow either bishop and began to concentrate on the science or simply the negation of any religious beliefs.

Major contributors to the growth of Russian materialism were the political reformers and Marxists, like Plekhanov, Bukharin, Martov, Trotsky, and many others who rejected every single promise of idealistic philosophy. Outside Russia, Marx was the most important. Marx first applied the term "dialectical materialism" to economic conflicts, and later applied it to social conflicts, thus arriving at a doctrine of class struggle. He tried to incorporate this philosophy into history. Lenin criticized him as an inadequate thinker and pointed out that Marx did not understand the Russian political mind, but rather limited himself to an exact observation of French history and the bourgeois machinery of the state.

The Russian Revolution did not follow exactly the Marxian patterns of social change, nor did the philosophical structure follow the French or English examples. Marx generally was wrong about the Russian Revolution. Lenin, however, understood the importance of theory and insisted that the new government needed a different theory, and a different type of education than traditionally had been practiced in Russia. It was his opinion that whoever controlled the theory also controlled the actions produced by these theories. In his *Philosophical Notebook* Lenin referred to Hegel, but not too favorably. Lenin invented the concept of the "materialist-realist" which means that the mind of man not only reflects objective reality, but creates it.

This concept of "reflection and creation" became the motto of early Bolshevik philosophy in general, and their philosophy of education in particular. Stalin ordered that nothing be said about idealistic contributions to Soviet philosophy. (Moreover, Hegel studied from the materialistic point of view.)

A special department under the direction of two physicists, A. Fok and A. D. Aleksandrov, was set up to approve or disapprove philosophical questions. These combined the theory of relativity with the theory of philosophical questions. It reached a point at which Stalin became "god" and the philosophy of dialectical materialism the "gospel" of communism.

After the Second World War, the situation eased a little but was by no means completely free. In 1954, the first Soviet textbook was published, known as *The Foundations of Marxist Leninism,* which was nothing special, but which at least considered philosophy from the *physical* point of view. For the first time Einstein's formula $E = mc^2$ was used, and this was not because the Soviets approved Einstein's theory, but because they wanted to utilize it in philosophical theories in terms of change (the axiom of space and time). *The Foundations of Marxist Leninism* can hardly be considered as a contribution to philosophy. It is a rather extreme critique of the non-Soviet philosophy, in fact, of any philosophy that did not originate in Russia. The book does not seem to recognize any values other than Marxist values. It takes the Bolshevik Revolution as the standard of human morality. Much of its philosophy is based on the critique by Marx of the philosophy of Eugene Duehring who, according to Marx, was inclined to believe in the dynamic and empirical values.

By 1958, *The Foundation of Marxist Leninism* was revised but the superiority of Russian philosophy over any other philosophy was maintained. This work, published by A. D. Aleksandrov, again touched upon the theory of relativity. But Aleksandrov wanted to be different from Einstein: he argued that any theory must first assume or establish the absolute and from there must proceed to the partial or relative.[1] Einstein took the opposite view.

BASIC CRITERIA OF RUSSIAN DIALECTICAL MATERIALISM

The Myth of Superman. In studying the Soviet textbooks, as well as reading the Soviet press and other literary publications one cannot avoid noticing the extreme glorification of Soviet leaders, particularly Lenin, to an almost supernatural level calling them (Lenin, Stalin, and others) the sun, father, brother, the light, and many other things. Reading the Soviet Encyclopedia one can gather from the description of Lenin that he was the greatest genius ever produced by the human race.

The extent to which this glorification of Soviet leaders takes place in Russian society can be seen in the foot notes of any textbook in any field. The previously mentioned work, *Foundations of Marxian Philosophy,* tries to present Lenin as superior to Aristotle, Plato, Descartes, Locke, Kant, and other non-communist philosophers, e.g., the book has 668 pages with over 400 foot notes, of which 170 refer to Lenin, 53 to Engels, 62 to Marx, 2 to Stalin, 4 to Khrushchev, 3 to Mao Tse-tung, 34 to other Russian communist-socialists, and 60 to non-Russian communists. Only a few refer to Western philosophers.

---

[1]V. Ilin, *Martirilog filosofii* (Munich: Institute for the Study of the USSR), No. 4, October-December, 1956, pp. 16–62. See also The Evolution of Lenin's Physics, in *Soviet Studies* (Munich: Institute for the Study of the USSR), vol. II, No. 5, 1960, p. 4.

Matter and Form. The dual and complementary concepts of matter and form are categorically rejected by communist philosophy. They say only matter exists. A man who has views different from the official materialistic philosophy of communism encounters various difficulties and problems in that society. The communists try to picture every important Russian writer as a fighter for materialism and a martyr under the previous regime. Men like Soloviev and Berdyaev, although they were Russians, do not deserve mention by Soviet social scientists simply because they disagreed with official interpretations of the basic philosophical issues on existence of matter and form.[2]

Anti-Westernism. Various schools of Western philosophy are interpreted by the Soviets from a single point of view: reactionary-bourgeois philosophy which is based on the rotten foundations of capitalism. Soviet philosophy, on the other hand, is the "philosophy of workers and peasants which depicts an objective world without any deterioration from the outside."

Soviet writers and teachers must satisfy the communist lines in teaching philosophy. Therefore it is not uncommon to find various falsifications of Western philosophy just to make it inferior to the communist. Hegel and other idealistic philosophers are never interpreted objectively by Soviet philosophers, but their thoughts are always pictured as "bourgeois ideology," and dangerous for the Soviet youth.

One-Sided Knowledge. The Soviets try to find a solution to almost any problem by scientific calculations. Sciences, according to Russian philosophy, will replace the idea of the supernatural (as natural law will replace the tyranny).

In the Russian history of philosophy Soviets maintain that all progressive Russians were materialists. If they were not, they were reactionary philosophers, who were as bad as Kant, Fichte, Schelling—"not worth mentioning."

Lenin in his few remarks on philosophy underlined the significance of a materialistic world outlook for the new communist society. He called it an objective interpretation of natural phenomena to say that "matter

---

[2] I. I. Shchipanov, *Iz istorii russkoi filosofii* (Moscow: AN SSSR, 1959), p. 5. See also V. V. Zenkovskii, *O mnimom materialisme russkoi nauki i filosofii* (Munich: Institute for the Study of the USSR, 1956), pp. 3–8; F. F. Aleksandrov, *Dialekticheskii materializm* (Moscow: AN SSSR, 1954), pp. 29 ff.; F. F. Konstantinov (ed.), *Osnovi marksiskoi filosofii* (Moscow: AN SSSR, 1959), pp. 5–11; *Voprosy filosofii,* No. 7, 1960, p. 15.

is the essence of all things according to which a realistic objectivity can be accomplished and which exists in our consciousness."

But we know that materialism is not a Soviet monopoly. Many European philosophers have expressed the idea of the superiority of the materialistic world over the spiritual world, either in terms of natural science or in terms of positivistic interpretations of natural laws and social conditions. To be different from other materialists, the Soviets define the movement of positivistic philosophy as most widely spread among the idealistic philosophers in bourgeois societies. On the other hand, Soviet dialectics is the science concerning the most common laws of natural developments, society, and condition. Their theory of cognition, and also of logic, follows this premise: private property is the thesis; the proletariat is the antithesis; and the abolition of the private property is the synthesis.

Soviet Optimism. As in any other area, the Soviets are not disturbed by such ideas as original sin, religious commandments, life hereafter. They believe strictly in the scientific laws of evolution and the Soviet revolution. The general trend in philosophy is also to picture man and the universe in an optimistic manner. Important scientists as well as social leaders must underline the facts that "life is better and happier than ever."

Konstantinov claims that only the philosophy of Marxism-Leninism founded on dialectical-historical materialism will be able to survive and surpass all other philosophies, since it has already "withstood with honor the test of time."

MARXISM AND THE NATURE OF REALITY

According to the Soviets, Marxian dialectic explains the many factors of human and natural developments on the basis of objective scientific experimentations. This dialectic studies the most common "laws of nature," i.e., the process whereby old laws must give way to new laws—the process of everlasting innovation.

The basic laws of dialectic are: the law of evolution; the law of contradiction; and the law of negation of negation.

The principle of evolution is based upon change from quantity to quality during which process things and matter of lower origin (too weak to survive) are eliminated, thus giving way to stronger forms and organisms. The second law, also called the law of antithesis, also functions on foundations of natural evolution. There is nothing sacred in the communist dialectic. There are no Hegelian forms of logic (being, nothing and becoming)—there is only a passion for improvement of the social order on the basis of some previous experiences. The Marxists, in using the law of contradiction, do not follow the Platonic method of arguing, i.e., dialogue. Furthermore, they reject the possibility of any true religious prophet and yet they have a "prophetism" of their own based on the socialist revolution. The third law, the negation of negation, characterizes the act of association among various stages of development. It gives the basic value orientation which one must follow in order to be able to solve any problem by natural evolution, i.e., from the simple to the more complex and from a lower type of form (or forms) to a higher.

In addition to these three laws Soviets have various categories such as the categories of form and content, necessity and causality, space and time, understanding and perception, and many others.

The main characteristic of Soviet philosophy lies in the fact that it represents a system of common views concerning man, nature, society, and the world. Every man, according to the Soviets, shapes his own nature independently from supernatural phenomena (God, Spirit, Absolute, etc.) according to general stages of evolution.

The Russians, however, are somewhat confused in explaining the characteristics of two basic concepts: form and matter. The first one is not as simple as they would like. They themselves are not sure whether or not form is a material substance, a process of evolution which is based on the cultural components of human development and which during the evolution has reached the form of a higher stage. But as far as the "right" answer is concerned, "nobody created anything; nature existed always." Furthermore, the world exists apart from man's consciousness. This being so, any associations (connections) between various appearances are not established by man's logical premises—they exist on the basis of objectivity not depending on man's judgments and sensations. Therefore, it is irrelevant for a philosopher to decide what existed first: the mind or the essence (being).[3]

Soviet philosophers further criticize non-materialistic philosophies (or as a matter of fact any non-Soviet philosophy) for being inadequate in solving problems. They maintain that idealistic philosophy rejects the idea of the ability of man to know truth. Konstantinov thinks this is one of the reasons why capitalism is in the process of decline—because capitalism is pessimistic about man's ability to solve his own problems. Konstantinov deliberately neglects to mention what kind of ability and what kind of objective solutions to problems. We know that most Western phi-

---

[3] Lenin, *Sochineniia*, vol. 19, p. 4; Anton S. Makarenko, *Sochineniia*, vol. 7 (Moscow: APN RSFSR, 1952), p. 23; Zenskovskii, *op. cit.*, p. 9; Aleksandrov, *Dialekticheskii materializm*, p. 52.

losophies accept some concept of *a priori*, i.e., there are things that man is unable to prove by logic (morality and ethical norms), but he must accept them as valid or otherwise society would become chaotic and anarchic. Konstantinov does not distinguish between logical and ethical judgments, or between scientific investigations and moral values.

Dialectical materialism is nothing but the "registration of changes" that take place in our world. All these changes are judged by their materialistic causes: conditions of production and the class structure in which certain changes took place. Idealism, therefore, is rejected as a subjective interpretation of the laws of nature.

Why is Idealism rejected? Lenin stated that the communists must use Hegelian dialectics not to praise Hegel but for communistic expediency. As is known the Hegelian system must be viewed as a whole and not in part. The communists, however, take the weaker parts of Hegel and try to base their whole criticism of idealistic philosophy on one man's work. The communist idea of absolute does not mean divine values, but absolute communist values and communist prescribed rules of moral behavior.

Exaggerations of a Struggle

No concept, no moral law, no theory is so important as the concept of struggle. The Soviets include under this term quite a variety of issues, ideas, and notions—everything that involves man and society.

In this struggle, religion must be fought by all the Soviet people and all Soviet power.

Naturally, the communists in power are not interested in philosophical argumentation just for the sake of arriving at an objective end. They definitely want more than dialectical arguments. While most philosophers agree on dialectical methods, communists add the prior necessity of a struggle to make the contradictions (Hegelian) meaningful. By adding the term *materialism* to the *dialectical*, they try to prove that materialism will explain all human phenomena—physical, mental and moral—and all activities of matter. Here the struggle plays an important part, because only through the struggle can one discover the meaning of an idea. Struggle is not included for the sake of arriving at true knowledge. Struggle means the existence or non-existence of the opposition.

Next to the struggle with religion, the communists consider most important the struggle against bourgeois philosophy, meaning idealistic philosophy as the first target and any non-communist philosophy as a second target. Lenin underlined the fact that any present-day philosophy affiliated with a political party begins with the struggle between the two ideas—

materialism and idealism—and ends with a struggle between people. The present epoch, the Russians theorize, is an inevitable struggle between growing communism and dying capitalism. The dialectics are as simple as this: the communists are good people, the non-communists are bad people; all people are equal but the communists are more equal than others. Therefore, Russian materialism is based on *revolutionary* dialectical methods simply because, the Russians say, everything is changing and everything old must be eliminated to give way to the new.

The struggle must also go on against the old method of judgment. The new dialectical method must reflect the laws of the objective world. To simplify, one must consider only the Marxian categories based on the following: money and capital. Thus philosophical reasoning is eliminated because by using the Marxian categories one can use a real example—an example which reflects the objective world.

There are also the "categories" of possibility and impossibility. But nothing is actually impossible if one takes "proper" examples. Never take examples that may be confusing or hard to explain on the basis of pure materialistic formula. For example, the Chinese revolution was impossible in the 19th century, but in the 20th century it became possible.

The struggle must involve not only "matter and form," but logic, metaphysics, Stalin, Khrushchev, heaven—everything that may be used at certain times to promote the Bolshevik cause. As Berdyaev indicated, communists and fascists alike assert that only they know the truth and that it reveals itself in a collective conflict.[4]

THE NATURE OF TRUTH

The communists do not believe in universal principles of ethics or any ethical laws founded on Christian teaching. They consider ethics merely the practices and experiences found in a given society at a given time. Marx and his disciples elaborated ethical categories for the communists which allowed no room for religious dogmas and laws. Marx pictured the communist society as a perfect society without any exploitation of one man by another. Men would work and share the good collectively, working together in a perfect harmony, finding happiness in their work just as artists find happiness in their creative arts, etc. A free man, according

---

[4] N. Berdyaev, *Slavery and Freedom,* Translated from Russian by M. French (New York: Charles Scribner Press, 1944), p. 29. See also Konstantinov, *Dialekticheskii materializm,* p. 17; John La Farge, "The Philosophical Basis of Communism," *Informationes et Notitiae Manuscripti Instar ad USUM Nostrum Tantum,* vol. 1, No. 4 (Washington, D. C.: Georgetown University, 1935), pp. 34–38.

to Marx, needs no rules imposed from above, no authorities, no moral laws, no discipline except the discipline required by the work itself. In such a society, Marx taught, there would be no criminals or conflicts. Therefore, there would be no need for an organized state or an organized code of morals.

Other Marxists have also theorized that during the full stage of communism there would be no organized exploiting administration. There would be only a socialist (collective) management which would depend on a commercial morality such as the morality of utilitarianism or the belief that all things can be treated as a means to an end. Therefore, the real issue of Marxism is not ethics but the consequences that might follow if the communists fail to produce laws similar to commonly accepted universal ethical laws.

Lunacharski and Soviet Marxists drew heavily on the ideas of the German philosopher Nietzsche in rejecting conceptions of moral obligations and divine laws of morality. Moral rules, Lunacharski wrote, "can generate nothing but slaves." The communists think that the new society will produce its own laws and ethics, completely free from any supernatural laws. Man's desires will not be bound by any moral laws and the interests of a man will be in complete harmony with the social interests.

As time went by communists changed their conception of morality and ethics. The destruction of peasants and various liquidations of opposition were explained by communist authorities as truly ethical deeds based on the philosophical conceptions of the nature of the struggle and the nature of the new morality. The party theorist Zalkind, wrote that the proletariat does not recognize any laws stated by metaphysical regulations and beliefs; the proletariat recognizes only the interests of the revolution. Thus, Soviet moral conceptions are based on the October Revolution and the experiences of men who fought during the revolution as well as on the rules laid down by the communist party of Russia.

The Soviets thought that by rejecting religious ethical laws they would also displace religion *per se.* The idea during the 1920s was that once the organized type of economy was introduced and secured, the behavior of man would automatically change according to the laws set by economic survival. To improve the ideological-moral position, the communists would reject money as a means of reward, and regard it only as a unit of account. Furthermore, private property and private enterprise would be displaced in favor of collective property; the family would not be bound by moral laws but merely by the "laws" of affection; and sometimes they would be obliged to bring up children for the benefit of the society; crime would disappear and in case someone did commit a crime he would be treated in a mental hospital. The Communists would have no laws, no formal codes; they would have merely a collective regulation which would help the group to live in harmony and complete freedom in relation to sex and the fulfillment of one's desires.[5]

Makarenko, on the other hand, approached the problem of values from prevailing circumstances of his time. He wrote that there must be a discipline, or some kind of activity dedicated to the improvement of the moral standards among youth. He listed the following moral categories:

a. Discipline is the prerequisite of any social or individual order. The communist society must build its own code of morals in the same way as it builds new homes and new streets.

b. The religious ten commandments must be replaced by the communist commandments founded on the political directives of the communist party. There cannot and should not be any separation between political ethics and pedagogical ethics. All laws must be issued in terms of Soviet demands and Soviet experiences.

c. Soviet theory, as well as Soviet methods, must be founded on the new values; the values practiced by the communists today.

d. The struggle against the old values (religious and social) must go on simply because one can always find some "germ-spreaders" among the old people. Christian values particularly, such as the teaching of Jesus Christ, must be eliminated from the Soviet book of "ethics."

After World War II there were some other theories concerning the standards of Soviet moral behavior. A certain Shishkin published in 1955 the *Foundations of the Communist Morality* (Osnovy kommunisticheskoi morali), and in 1959 another booklet about Soviet ethics. Both were in a way models of the Khrushchevian society since Khrushchev demanded that the Soviet intellectuals produce a book of "morals" in his speech at the 21st Congress of the Communist Party.

From 1960 on the Soviet journal on philosophy, *Voprosy filosofii* (Questions of Philosophy) has dedicated quite a bit of space to Soviet moral and ethical principles. It criticizes Christian ethical norms as offering no practical or moral solutions to existing problems in Soviet society. The Soviets say it is their duty to explain ethical values of socialism and at the same time to "disarm" the bourgeois philosophy. According to the Russian interpretation of ethics, bourgeois ethics are unable to disprove relative values; only communists can do so with "moral education based on the highest principles of ethics—the communist morality."

---

[5] E. Kamenko, "Marx, Marxism and Ethics," in *Survey*, No. 39, 1961, p. 56.

Morality, therefore, is based on the class struggle. There are, however, certain differences between the individual's feeling and the group feeling but these can be cured by one's social consciousness. Therefore no books on ethics are necessary if one senses what is good and what is bad. One must only possess the feeling of conscience, and this will eventually result in social morality.

As the Table of Values indicated (see Table 27, page 165) there are a variety of rights and obligations toward which one must strive. Nothing is mentioned about love for one's fellow man, only love for the communist man and hate for non-communists. The values expressed in the table are the practical Soviet norms being taught in Soviet schools. Humanism, friendship, and socialist humanism are mentioned but all of them are a provincial type of humanism not designed for mankind *per se.*

Aesthetics

In this area the Soviets are quite different from the rest of the world. As in their ethical categories, communists demand that every Soviet citizen and every Soviet child should appreciate Soviet art. Russian art should be especially appreciated by all Russian and non-Russian nationalities.[6]

On the other hand, the value of the Russian-Soviet aesthetics can be seen in its vividness. Thus, it is quite natural for an artist to depict Russian accomplishments on a larger scale than any others, e.g., a sculptor would always present a Russian woman as taller, more beautiful, and stronger than any other Soviet or non-Soviet woman.

Appreciation of art is not based on individual taste and individual ability. The Soviets maintain that appreciation of art has first of all a collective or social coloring and that individual taste follows social taste. The development of aesthetic feeling takes place under two conditions: materialistic features and socio-economic features of human and natural existence. The final "law" on appreciation of art is, of course, the direction stated by socialist realism and the works produced by Soviet leaders. An average book of aesthetics would emphasize that the poor people always dreamed about freedom and about absence of violence, but these came only during the Soviet regime, and more so by the decisions of the 21st Party Congress which gave the directions for the nature of Soviet Aesthetics and its significance to Marxism.

---

[6] M. V. Goncharenko, *Mystetstvo i estetichne vykhovannia* (Kiev: AN UkSSR, 1963), p. 7. See also A. Makarenko, *o vospitanii molodezhi,* p. 239; *Voprosi filosofii,* No. 1, 1962, p. 41; *Filosoficheskie nauki,* No. 3, 1961, pp. 120–125.

PHILOSOPHY AND SCIENCE

Frequently Soviet philosophers get into trouble with the natural scientists because of the inability of the latter to prove that physical phenomena are the same as philosophical phenomena. Engels thought that dialectics was the science of all laws and all motion and extended this concept not only to the natural sciences but to all of human history and ideas. For this reason it was quite natural for the Soviets to work in the general directions given by Engels in his simple generalization concerning the laws of motion and the laws of human thought. Men like Smirnov, Bovin, and Omelianovski, who insisted that Marxism had transformed the previous philosophy into science, began themselves to doubt the possibility of philosophical axioms always having the same value as physical axioms.

The Soviets only lately have accepted the theory of relativity and Einstein's contribution to science in general. Einstein was called a reactionary scientist and the bourgeois philosopher.

The reason for this accusation is obvious: the theory of relativity has revealed facts that were not in line with the Soviet philosophy of dialectical materialism, i.e., the relativity of length of time, even of simultaneity. All these do not fit neatly into the categories of dialectical materialism. Only in 1955 did the Soviets change their minds on the theory of relativity, and as usual, accused Stalin of being against this theory.

The most radical theories of Soviet scientific works were those advocated by Michurin and Lysenko, both of whom insisted that certain features acquired by an organism during its life may be also passed on through heredity. More important, though, Lysenko's theory does not admit any struggle for existence within a species. It recognizes mutual support of certain organisms for the purpose of the continuation of their own race or stock.

As can be expected, dialectical materialism won the struggle with scientists because, according to Soviets, it was Marxism that gave the scientists the rich food for thought.[7]

THE IMPACT OF DIALECTICAL MATERIALISM
ON EDUCATIONAL PRACTICES

During the Soviet "trial and error" period the educational practices varied according to the official lines set up by the communist party. In

---

[7] M. Mikuliak, "Philosophy and Science," in *Survey*, No. 57, July 1964, pp. 147–157; *Kommunist*, No. 5, 1960, pp. 96 ff; G. Wetter, "Dialectical Materialism and Natural Sciences," in *Soviet Survey*, No. 1, 1957, pp. 51–59.

the early period, foreign ideas and practices were used, and after the Khrushchevian period, they were "modified." Obviously, the general value orientation expressed by the philosophy of dialectical materialism had its influence upon educational experiences.

The traditional system was completely rejected and the new philosophy of education was emerging on the Soviet cultural scene. Second, Marxian "classical" ideas were in the process of being tested in the new society. Soviet educators believed that the child must be taught from an early age to work not only with his mind but with his hands as well. Marx pointed out that the child must do physical work at least two hours a day, beginning at the age of nine, and that this kind of work would increase proportionately to his age. He believed that children who study on a part-time basis learn just as much and often more than full-time students.[8]

In the early 1920s, the Soviet educators advocated the concept of dialectical materialism and its application to the philosophy of education. To what extent this philosophy was dialectic and to what extent it was materialistic was and still is problematical. A majority of the Soviet people during the early period of the regime did not know about dialectical materialism, especially in education. Marx himself never wrote much about the philosophy of education and there were no sources available on this subject before the Russian Revolution.

The school in this period was not so much an institution for intellectual development as it was for propaganda. Lenin and other Soviet leaders feared the weakening of the Bolshevik system which would be brought about by a lack of theories, or as John Dewey pointed out, the schools are, in the current phrase, 'the ideological arms' of the Revolution.[9]

The Soviet authorities demanded that educational theory should provide answers to such various questions as: the historical significance of communist education; the necessity of polytechnical training; the preparation of pupils for future leadership (organizing children into pioneer centers and Communist Youth Organizations) which would enable them to take an active role in school matters; anti-religious education; broad international educational perspectives; aesthetic development (arousing an appreciation for proletarian literature, music and arts); physical education; and disciplinary measures allowing the teacher to perform his tasks.[10]

---

[8] Karl Marx, *Sochineniia*, vol. 13 (Moscow: Izdatel'stvo IMEL, 1936), p. 198. See also Wasyl Shimoniak, "Communist Educational Philosophy," in *Catholic Educational Review*, vol. LXV, No. 5, 1967, pp. 312–322.

[9] John Dewey, *Impression of Soviet Russia and the Revolutionary World: Mexico, China, Turkey* (New York: The Republic Press, 1929), p. 61.

[10] *Kommunisticheskoe vospitanie v sovetskoi shkole*, p. 83.

In search of answers to such broad questions, a variety of educational theories and practices were employed in the early Soviet period. One group of Russian educators began to return to reformist pre-revolutionary ideas found in the writings of Herzen, Dobroliubov, Leo Tolstoi, and, especially, Konstantin Ushinski. The latter was the main concern of Soviet educators as he had cited the necessity for vernacular languages in schools, as well as a need to create a national consciousness, developed out of Russia's own educational experiences, and a definite relationship between theory and practice. Another group followed American educational practice, especially American instrumentalists. Pinkevitch, a well-known Soviet educator in the early 1920s, stated that many American educators, Dewey, Hall, Judd, Monroe, Thorndike, and many others who were known to every educator in Russia[11] were sufficient reminders of the tremendous influence which American education has exerted.

The Soviet educators thought, at first, that the new regime would introduce more liberal measures concerning the school educational process, particularly the idea of the development of one's intellectual and physical capacities in terms of universal knowledge. The study of *pedology* (note: not pedagogy but pedology) which deals with a complex variety of subjects—hygiene, genetics, anatomy, embryology, psychology of the child—was especially supported by Krupskaia, P. Blonski, Basov and other important Soviet educators of that time. They all favored the pedological approaches toward the study of the child rather than the one-sided party lines.

There were other factors concerning philosophical questions and the nature of education. For an intelligent observer, even though he was a materialist, it was not enough to state that one must follow a materialistic philosophy of life. The search for authority in Soviet philosophy began. The most important man in the area of Soviet educational philosophy was Anton A. Makarenko.

MAKARENKO'S SYSTEM

The importance of Makarenko's theories lies in the fact that he was one of the first Soviet educators to emphasize the idea of collective spirit and collective process. Every pupil was to be educated in a way that he should feel responsibility to the collective, and contribute something to

---

[11] Albert Pinkevitch, *The New Education in the Soviet Structure*, Translated by N. Perlmutter, edited by G. Counts (New York: The John Day Press, 1929), pp. 117, 240.

the group—either in terms of helping slow learners, or in terms of helping the group to maintain proper order, or in taking care of pupil health. Furthermore, educators should realize that:[12]

> A collective is wholly like a crowd: in its ideal form it is an organization of mutual responsibility, self-governing and self-determining, within which the individual first learns the meaning of moral principles and in their observance finds the security he needs to mature.

Makarenko's collective was designed to give form and style to future life. Education to him meant teaching pupils to live in harmony with their society.

Makarenko was aware of the fact that the desire for security is the chief problem of any child. According to his theories, the only way to achieve this is to put the child into a collective. This was to be done, however, freely and without compulsion. The role of the collective is to develop a sense of belonging, and a sense of loyalty. He said that:[13]

> In the Soviet Union a personality cannot exist outside the collective, and therefore there can be no isolated personal destiny, no personal way, and no personal happiness which is opposed to the destiny and happiness of the collective.

The concept of system of perspective lines is another example of Makarenko's concepts. This was designed to strengthen the relationship of the collective with society. He realized that learning is a conscious intellectual process, but that the motivating forces behind it are moral and emotional. Thus, learning cannot be separated from incentives because these are part of the moral and emotional system of the child. According to Makarenko, a teacher should be flexible in approach, not dogmatic, simply because children vary in their process of development. One can never say that a particular child is good or bad; he is just a child whose will can be influenced in either direction. This is why he thought that the *sense of the mean* is the most important factor in dealing with young children.

Parents must see that the child's character is molded in the right way. Financial agreement should prevail in the family, also the happiness of common sharing. Money can spoil the child. Makarenko stated "of all human inventions, this invention (money) came nearest to the devil."

---

[12] Anton S. Makarenko, *The Road to Life* (Moscow: Foreign Languages Publishing House, 1951), p. 64.

[13] *Ibid.*, p. 34. See also Anton S. Makarenko, *Learning to Live* (Moscow: Foreign Languages Publishing House, 1953), p. 20; Fredrik Lilge, *Anton S. Makarenko* (Berkeley: University of California Press, 1958), p. 2; *Narodnoe obrazovanie*, February, 1960, pp. 1–5.

Many parents are blinded with love toward children, and they fail to see, e.g., that their son has long ago ceased to be affectionate, that he never uses words of welcome, that he has new suits while his father has only one worn outfit. In such cases, the task of the teacher is to straighten out the child's behavior and adjust him to the collective needs. A teacher can always find some path and reciprocal relationship from which the individual can benefit.

We note that the Soviets credited Makarenko with many things, such as being the first man to elaborate the basis for the conscious discipline; with awakening in the child the idea of conscious class-belonging; and with arousing the confidence of the Soviet people. Regardless of what may be behind the lines of Soviet interpretations of Makarenko, his main objective was to demonstrate before the Soviet society that collective discipline can be established and maintained. The fact is that individuals were trained to be capable of absolute loyalty, obedience and responsibility to the Soviet regime—these were qualities that the Soviet authorities wanted.

Additional References

A. A. Maksimov, *Ocherki istorii russkogo materializma v russkom estestvoznanii* (Moscow: Gospolitizdat, 1951); V. I. Lenin, *The Paris Commune*, vol. 5 (New York: International Publishers, 1934; V. I Lenin, *The April Conference*, vol. 10 (New York: International Publishers, 1934); *Kommunist*, No. 13 and 14, 1966; V. I. Lenin, *Sochineniia*, vol. 19 (Moscow: Gospolitizdat, 1954); Konstantinov, *Istoriia pedagogiki, passim;* Akademiia Pedagogicheskikh Nauk, *Konstantin Ushinski* (Moscow: Gosizdat, 1947), pp. 3–30; Anton S. Makarenko, *Pedagogicheskaia poema* (Moscow: Izda. Sovetskii Pisatel' 1940), pp. 4–70; Anton S. Makarenko, *Kniga dlia roditelei* (Moscow: APN RSFSR, 1953); *Doklady Akademii Pedagogicheskikh Nauk RSFSR*, No. 2, 1958; *Izvestiia Akademii Pedagogicheskikh Nauk*, No. 58, 1954; Anton S. Makarenko, *A Book for Parents* (Moscow: Foreign Languages Publishing House, 1953).

Chapter 10

SOME CONCEPTS OF SOVIET
EDUCATIONAL PSYCHOLOGY

Unfortunately Soviet educational psychologists must study the works of Lenin, Marx, Stalin and other "psychologists" before they can study the works of Russian psychologists and physiologists, particularly the works of Pavlov, Sichenev and some other approved scholars. Communist philosophy is overloaded with topics such as class struggle, productive labor, socialist morality, etc., and so are its psychological textbooks. For example, a textbook on educational psychology by Levitov is written in just such a manner. It is somewhat moderate compared to Smirnov's psychology which attacks bourgeois psychology instead of getting to subject matter. Levitov starts his description of the subject of psychology by citing the decision of the Central Committee of the communist party of June 1963. Then he attacks those who want to limit the tasks of the school only to teaching and learning and not to the broad perspectives of general culture.

GENERAL BACKGROUND

One of the early pioneers in educational psychology was Konstantin Ushinski who endeavored to introduce to Russia some basic concepts of psychology, especially those which he found in Germany and Switzerland. However, he did not create new concepts or a school of psychology; he merely emphasized the importance for "the human soul to read psychological works which may help him to develop his own psychological foundations." Ushinski also wrote about the task of psychology, which should study the human soul, the nature of the environment and the scientific definitions of human nature.

Another group of Russian physiologists and psychologists—Bekhterev, Sechenov and Pavlov—were engaged in the behavioristic study of psychological phenomena. Bekhterev and Sechenev were the first Russian scientists who were concerned with the study of human reflexes and their importance in the field of psychology. Sechenev wrote a book, *Reflexes of the Brain*, which provides the foundations for modern Russian psychology.

The Soviet psychologists maintain that Sechenev's work represents an unbreakable chain between the Russian philosophy of materialism and the experimental psychology of his time. However, Sechenev himself was not interested in whether a certain philosophy was materialistic or idealistic. He was concerned about its application in various fields of human endeavor. Sechenev's name is quite frequently cited by Russian psychologists (if only for the reason that the communists want to associate the science of modern psychology with Russian political aims) and the physiologists. In the Soviet conception psychology and physiology are an unseparable chain in studying human behavior.

The Russians also claim that Sechenev is "the first man in the history of mankind to define exactly and *materialistically* the field of psychology."[1] It is true that Sechenev advocated the theory of psychophysical unity, according to which psychological phenomena can exist only when given certain materialistic conditions. At the same time he underlined the fact that psychological and physical forms are not related to each other, but rather represent two different forms.

Obviously, Sechenev did not separate the man from matter, neither did he go to an extreme position in contrasting the physical sphere of influence with the psychological area of activities. The unity between the two exists but one is not the same as the other. Furthermore, Sechenev by his philosophical convictions was a mixture of realist-naturalist and he asserted that psychological appearances (phenomena) represent by far a greater puzzle for the naturalist than for the philosopher-humanist. He further insisted that modern science does not contain a single formula or

---

[1] U. M. Sechinev, *Izbrannye filosoficheskie i psikhologicheskie sochineniia* (Moscow: APN RSFSR, 1947), p. 3; K. Ushinski, *Sobranie sochinenii* (Moscow: APN RSFSR, 1950), p. 48; Shchipanov, *Iz istorii russkoi filosofii*, p. 504.

a single law which would prove that matter is the basis of all existence. He spoke about his reflexes as types of scientific hypotheses but never as scientific laws. According to Sechenev, reflexes of the brain are types of typical psychological phenomena which reflect human thought and human passion, but they do not necessarily appear in some definite spot in the human body.

Other pre-revolutionary Russian psychologists and physiologists that the Soviets want to utilize are men like A. M. Butlerov, V. Markovnikov, D. Mendeleev, A. Stoletov, N. Umov, and most important, I. P. Pavlov. Almost all of them were concerned with the idea of *matter, motion* and *spirit* as the bases of human existence.

Pavlov, as it is known, was interested in physiological research and conducted various experiments in this field on animals, especially dogs. He studied his animals systematically from the very beginning of their lives until the end, collecting and analyzing the data he obtained. Like Sechenev, he maintained that any psychological response is impossible without some sort of stimulus and that human behavior, as well as animal behavior must be associated with conditional reflexes. The behavior of man and animal alike is conditioned not only by their nervous systems but also by various circumstances which affect the organism during a certain activity, i.e., there is always a continuous learning process. Therefore, an unconditional reaction (that is, the unconditional reflex) appears very seldom since the organism always acts in context with the surrounding environment.

Pavlov also worked on the interrelationship of the two signal systems (the first and the second signal system) and their importance in studying the higher nervous system in small children. He further wanted to conduct extensive research on the independence of the two types of higher nervous system vs. the environment. But Pavlov made it clear that the experiments conducted by him on animals are not always applicable to human beings, particularly to small children. He asserted that one cannot be limited to a knowledge of physiological disciplines because there exist many non-physiological phenomena which influence the psyche of the individual.

Further experiments in the field of psychology in Pavlovian behaviorism were conducted during the early period of the Soviet regime when Pavlov himself was in charge of behavioristic research in Leningrad. S. L. Rubinstein tried to apply Pavlovian principles to character education and to indoctrination in the Soviet way of life.[2] However, Soviet psychology is

---

[2] A. N. Levitov, *Problemy razvitiia psikhiki rebenka* (Moscow: APN RSFSR, 1959), pp. 29–30; I. P. Pavlov, *Polnoe sobranie sochinenii,* vol. 3 (Moscow: APN RSFSR, 1951), p. 51.

not merely political manipulation. It is rather a combination of many social and scientific forces aimed at changing the behavior of man. Therefore, it is necessary to pin-point briefly the main features of Soviet psychology.

CHARACTERISTICS OF EDUCATIONAL PSYCHOLOGY

The first characteristic of Russian psychology is its *Russian* content in every scientific investigation. The Soviet psychologists, besides following the various political directives, are required to extol Russian science *per se* before they can study other scientific contributions to the field of psychology. One who studies Russian psychology cannot help noticing the extreme emphasis on Russian contributions to psychological science, mainly the contribution of Pavlov, and the complete neglect of the study of other European or American schools of psychology. Even if a foreign scholar is studied, it is not because the Soviets want to use his theories but because they want to criticize foreign ideas as inferior. In no other country of the free world is such an approach used. In no other country of the world is psychology being applied so totally to the education of the new generation.

The second feature of Soviet psychology is its emphasis on the scientific investigation. It has come to the point that many Soviet and non-Soviet observers tend to believe that science is the religion of the Soviet Union. There is no question that such an attitude is entirely in line with the main philosophy of the government since new psychological investigations reject anything that could be associated with spiritual entities. Marxism views man as the product of his environment. Hence society is responsible for man's character and behavior rather than man's being responsible for society.

The Soviets saw a great deal of promise in the use of scientific methods of psychology in solving social problems. However, constant interference by the party has resulted in a lack of vivid psychological theories or the development of new psychological concepts. Instead of doing new research Soviet psychologists have concentrated on Pavlovian findings and trying to prove that Pavlov was right.

The third feature is the excessive emphasis on the environment to the neglect of the individual in general. The individual is merely the product of his environment. Yet the slow learners and the mentally retarded children are completely neglected by that environment. Pavlovian psychology is being practiced to an extreme in attempting to reduce all human and infra-human behavior to primary reflexes. The party requires that theories of behavior be deterministic, dialectical, materialistic, and most of all must view psychological phenomena from the point of view of genetic and environmental forces. The responsibility of man's action and the shape of his character are entirely attributed to the environment.

The fourth characteristic of Soviet psychology is its concentration on the ideas of consciousness and self-consciousness. This, in a way, serves a useful purpose in the area of discipline and self-discipline. It has resulted in the complete rejection of psychological tests and in the whole area of industrial psychology.

These motives of consciousness and self-consciousness have helped to reduce the extreme application of environmental factors. At present the Soviets are changing the old Soviet two factor developmental theory—nature and nurture—and are replacing it with theories having three or four factors: inheritance, environment, training and self-training.

Finally, in addition to the above mentioned characteristics, the following features are important:

a. emphasis is placed upon natural experiments with application to concrete, practical problems;
b. work and experiments are selected for their practicality, utility and application to educational matters;
c. there is a complete lack of psychometric investigation;
d. animal psychology is quite limited except for the Pavlovian oriented research (on dogs);
e. psychopathology (abnormal psychology) is classified as a branch of medicine because there is supposed to be no continuity between psychology and psychiatry;
f. the field of sensation and perception (psychophysics) receives more than ordinary attention in general psychology.

In general, there are frequent complaints that students are unable to put their theories into practice, their creativity into useful deeds or their psychological knowledge into actual application.[3]

CHILD DEVELOPMENT

The Soviet psychologists must know the ideas of Lenin about child development before they can study the subject from psychological or bio-

---

[3] *Uchitel'skaia gazeta,* August 7, 1962. See also M. Menshunskaia, "Psychology and School Reorganization," in *Soviet Education,* vol. 2, No. 8, 1960, pp. 38 ff.; J. Brozek, "Current Status of Psychology in the USSR," in *Annual Review of Psychology,* vol. 13, 1962, pp. 515–566.

logical points of view. For example, Lenin's theory about the "destruction of the old and the appearance of the new" is the first "scientific" formula that Levitov has used in determining the "dialectic-materialistic conception of child development."

According to this theory of the dialectic-materialistic world outlook, child development—like any other development—occurs in the struggle of contradictions, i.e., when the new forms of life appear, the old ones must be overcome or destroyed. In this process old forms sometimes might be utilized in order to make new forms stronger.

The Soviets divide the development of a child into the following stages: infancy; the pre-school years; the school years (six to eleven); early adolescence (eleven to fifteen) and adolescence (fifteen to eighteen). At each stage the child develops according to the dialectic-materialistic patterns of development. For example, during infancy, the child develops sensual perceptions and speech formation. During the pre-school age (early childhood), the child learns to discriminate between certain subjects and acquires his first abstract concepts.

The official Soviet theory of child development rests upon a behavioristic interpretation of individual mental and physical capacities. The theory asserts that all children are able to accomplish certain desired ends once they are given a proper environment. Sometimes this theory is advocated just for the sake of its difference from non-Russian psychological theories and Soviets often list facts that do not have scientific value in the Western world. Non-Russian psychological accomplishments in the area of educational psychology are criticized as being old-fashioned, superstitious and following only the principle "he was born like this and nothing can help him." Yet Soviets make a big issue of a minor experiment as if they were the only ones who were studying experimental-educational psychology. Each book and each author must underline the fact that the task of Soviet psychology is to fight Western psychology (i.e., any non-Russian psychology) and its points of view.

Child development and its various stages cannot be considered only from an environmental point of view (although this is very important) but must also be viewed from a biological point of view. Soviet educational psychologists tend to disagree with Watsonian theories of development. All these theories are wrong because the central committee of the communist party rejected Watsonian psychology.

The psychological development of a child through all stages must be considered from the point of view of natural surroundings and the innate needs of a child. Thus, when an adolescent changes his attitudes, it is not because certain faculties of his soul command him to behave differently, but because he has been exposed to many scientific subjects—chemistry, physics, geometry, etc.—which determine his outlooks.

In short, Soviet educational psychologists are limited in their endeavors by the party's demands on the nature of psychology in general and the nature of educational psychology in particular.

RECENT EXPERIMENTS IN LEARNING

According to the Soviet view, learning activities depend largely upon various conditions of the nervous system. The theories of learning must be studied from the point of view of four dimensions: 1) the whole *vs.* parts; 2) the assimilation of many activities into a single one; 3) the organism itself *vs.* incoming stimuli; 4) the organism (and with it learning) *vs.* actual conditions of life.

The many components of learning—memory, retention, perception, interest, attitude, emotional stability, etc.—must be seen from the Pavlovian viewpoint, or from the outlook of approved communist scholars in the area of behavioristic psychology.

In recent years the Soviets have conducted many psychological experiments, many concerned with the study of languages and the study of mathematics.

The study of languages is a very important field in Soviet education. Various experiments designed to improve habits of learning are conducted. For example, there is much research in autogenic methods and muscular relaxation. It is believed that by this method learning situations can be improved without causing any adverse effects on the neuropsychological condition of the individual.

Soviets also apply the method of muscular relaxation vs. autogenic training repeatedly on the same group. Unlike the experiments in which the method was used on many groups, one experiment is replicated many times on the same group, which assures the reliability of this method under different conditions. They are trying to prove that by applying some mechanical means together with a purely psychological aid one can improve learning and problem-solving.[4]

In improving the study of modern languages, as well as the natural sciences, a combination of theoretical and experimental training goes hand in hand. Many Soviet educational psychologists believe that the student, by applying some physical activity, such as clenching one's fist, or one's

---

[4] Levitov, *op. cit.,* p. 24. See also R. I. Zhukovski, *Vospitaniia rebenka* (Moscow: APN RSFSR, 1963), p. 6; Ushinski, *Sochineniia,* vol. 8, 1950, p. 395.

teeth, is less subjected to outside interferences, therefore can concentrate better and solve problems faster.

These experiments must be related to the age of children and the material being studied. In languages, for instance, knowledge of certain basic linguistic structures, or previous hearing of some words can accelerate learning and the memorization of vocabulary.

Pavlov, as well as his followers, thought that one must first study the individual and different types of nervous system activity before any choice of subject matter or the definition of a learning situation, can be intelligently stated. Since thinking and learning are to be considered as one educative process, one must choose examples which will not only enrich the child's knowledge of a certain subject (e.g., mathematics) but at the same time will increase his linguistic ability and his development of clear, fluid linguistic patterns.

The Power of Association. According to the Soviet view the relationship between understanding and recall is proportional to the power of association.

An association is related to the individual's experiences. The more an individual is exposed to new experiences the better are his chances for connecting the new experiences with the old ones. Of course, there are cases when there is not always a correct response between associations.

Various levels of understanding are related to associations. The child is not always able to associate correctly previous ideas and experiences with new questions. For example, when a child is asked to define a noun, he may answer in many ways: the noun is homework; the noun is a section of the book; or finally, the noun is "the house, the birds, the book." The logic of the question-answer dialog is that if a child were not exposed to enough experiences, he could not form the proper associations.[5]

THE SUBJECT OF PERSONALITY

Personality and Society. One of the most important areas in the study of personality is the relationship personality has to society. The Soviet communists assert that the individual is only important as long as he contributes to the society in which he lives.

Historical materialism (a term which the Soviets use) studies the individual as a component of a *mass* (society). Kovalev tells us that political economy, for instance, studies the individual as a part of productive labor;

---

[5] *Voprosi psikhologii,* No. 1, January 1967, pp. 107–114; A. G. Kovalev, *Psikhlogiia lichnosti* (Moscow: Izdat. Prosveshchenie, 1965), p. 183.

ethics studies the personality as a bearer of moral principles, habits, norms; jurisprudence studies the legal conditions of an individual; pedagogy investigates the process of education and methods and forms of education; psychology studies the individual from a spiritual point of view—"but all social sciences are founded on one methodology expressed in the works of classical Marxism-Leninism."

In bourgeois society, the Soviets say, only certain people mean something; the rest of the people do not have any particular importance. Only Marxism-Leninism puts the status of workers into a proper perspective. Personality is the indivisible unit of the whole (society), which works in the name of and creates the history of a society. The particular individual traits of a personality are determined by an individual's contribution to society. However, the individual is a conscious being, so he can choose a profession or a path of life which suits his taste—but his taste must be the taste of society. It is also important that each individual possess the idea of guilt or self-criticism, which must be used when the interests of society are at stake.

The Soviets also acknowledge "productive" and "creative" types of personality, but they always associate productivity and creativity with the social norm of productivity. The products of individual efforts are not credited to the individual but to the mass of people, the society in which that individual happens to live.

Development of Personality. The communists theorize about the all-around development of personality. They conceive of a "new man" who will perform a variety of tasks properly and correctly, and who will integrate his spritual wealth with his overt behavior. This necessitates the development of proper individual traits.[6]

According to the Marxian interpretation of personality, the "flowering" of the human spirit is possible only when private property is eliminated. This leads to full liberation and restoration of a true humanity. Khrushchev, in 1959, commented that a man's fame in the U.S.A. is based neither on his labor nor on his intellectual capabilities, but on his capital, and that the average Soviet person stands head and shoulders above many who enjoy fame in the U.S.

From the communist point of view it is important for a person to develop an optimistic attitude towards life. A person must believe in his capabilities. He must believe that he can do something for society, and

---

[6] Akademiia Nauk SSSR, *Pavlovskie sredy* (Moscow: AN SSSR, 1949), p. 580; *Voprosi psikhologii,* No. 1, 1967, pp. 11–16.

that he can do it better than others. All this is on the basis of his labor and not merely theory. Furthermore, the Soviets officially do not recognize any aptitude tests in determining personality traits. Testing is capitalistic, discriminatory, and in Soviet society everyone is just as able as his neighbor or friend.

Methods of Character Education. Most of the methods concerning the development of certain personality traits as well as character education can be found in works of Makarenko. He elaborated the foundations of Soviet educational philosophy along party lines. The most important point of character education rests on the fact that not the family but the state is the model of moral values. Makarenko stated that he admired lads who disobeyed their mothers and fathers because they had much faith in the Soviet state.[7]

The most peculiar feature of Soviet character training is the socialization in the school collective. Contrary to American ideas where the individual is all that matters, the Soviets tend to educate men who will forget about themselves and dedicate themselves to the collective.

Social competition in schools, so common and so natural to the Soviets, is based on competition not between individuals but between groups. A teacher commonly remarks, "let's see which row can finish this assignment faster, or what row can sit the straightest," etc. Thus, the competition between rows in a school situation is a foretaste of future competitions between nations, between social classes and between races.

There are special manuals designed for character education that each teacher must follow. There are no school psychologists but huge charts are kept in each grade and each row in school and results are posted on the walls of the school. Each student can see the progress of his group.[8] Those who happen to be in the top performing group receive a reward— not money but the group's picture might be placed in the school newsletter, or the winning group would be visited by other groups in order to learn from them how to achieve such excellence.

A teacher does not correct a child's behavior by himself. He merely mediates between the offending student and the group. For example, when a student is tardy the teacher would ask the group, "is it helpful to us that this student is late?" The answer from the group would be, of course, no. To remedy the situation the teacher would assign a punctual student to the one who is constantly late and ask them both to help each other.

---

[7] Levitov, *op. cit.*, p. 76.
[8] *Soviet Education,* vol. 4, No. 7, 1961, pp. 12, 16.

If it happens that the next day not only the previously tardy student is late but the punctual one also, the whole group receives a warning. The teacher may test the students in other ways. He may, for instance, come late to school just for the purpose of checking on the whole group, or to check the monitors who supervise the class during the teacher's tardiness.

Another method used in Soviet schools to develop proper personality traits is to have parents report to teachers about their children. Thus, the child is not supposed to behave as he pleases even at home, because if his mother is a sincere Soviet citizen she will report all his misdeeds to the teacher. The teacher in turn has a good picture of the child in relation to his school work. Sometimes a representative of the school will come to the worker's home and observe the children.

An individual's grade to some extent depends on the performance of his group. Therefore, it is imperative that children help each other in school assignments, so the standing of the group can be improved.

The Russians also distribute a set of rules to each school, especially to the boarding schools where the teacher watches the children all day. The instructions emphasize that the peer collective surpasses the family; that the behavior of an individual should be judged from his contribution to the collective; that the rewards and punishments must be meted out to groups rather than to individuals; that the distribution of punishment must be set by the collective in the presence of a teacher; that each member of a collective is to be encouraged to observe and report the deviant behavior of his playmates; that group criticism should be applied because it develops the idea of self-criticism. These rules must be put into practice and results must be reported to the administrative authorities.

All these practices and methods lead to one goal—the formation and education of members of the communist society. The steps may be difficult and complicated, but all these complications depend on those requirements which the communist party sets forth for the personality of the Soviet man.

POLITICAL PSYCHOLOGY

After World War II, a new psychology developed. In non-communist countries, industrial psychology came on the scene and in communist countries political psychology, very often referred to as "brain-washing," made its debut. In general, it followed the idea that truth does not always prevail: Therefore why not use both sides of "truth."

The Russian communists certainly give credit to Pavlov for his work on conditioned behavior and conditional reflexology. As is known, the Pavlovian theory says that man's behavior can be controlled by signals, or in effect, social conditions can be manipulated scientifically. In short, a man can be transformed into another mental being regulated by pre-set conditions (either economic, political or social).

On this basis the communists believe that groups, nations, and social classes can just as well be conditioned as single individuals or animals. It is particularly important "when a human animal is denied food and treated to overdoses of ringing bells."[9] In this process the communists make sure that their subjugated people obey the "signals" of authority.

The communists officially do not accept Freud as a psychological authority but they accept many points of Freudian psychology. Their method of psychoanalysis is designed to function in such a way that it will prove the individual guilty by his own faults. They apply techniques of various kinds: compulsory writing of a diary, group diaries in elementary schools, oral interviews with party members or the secret police and public "confessions." A "guilty" person is required publicly to repeat the phrase, "I am a saboteur and exploiter, I am guilty before the party and the people." This is a kind of hypnosis designed to turn a man into a helpless creature.

In school the child is under the pressure of politico-indoctrinational techniques; in social life he is under the observation of his superiors; in political affairs a man must be tested and controlled until he is indoctrinated to the point that nothing can change his views. It is a common procedure for all those who apply for party membership that they be screened in such a way that they will forget their own past: "he is cutting loose from all the black shadows of the past, and that he desires to sacrifice himself for the cause."[10]

Frustration and guilt are very important points in communist psychology. By engendering frustration the communists try to arouse economic or racial feelings in a given nation (similar to Freudian sex frustration) so it will try for revenge. (Wars are always justifiable as long as they are initiated by the communists in the name of class struggle.) They also try to create frustration in strong non-communist nations, especially dissatisfaction with present political leaders. Subsequently it is hoped that the leaders themselves will feel a sense of inferiority, guilt, and frustration with world problems. This is the way the communists fight religion, because

---

[9] Uril Bronfenbrenner, *Soviet Method of Character Education* (Ithaca: Cornell University Press, 1962), p. 552.

[10] *Ibid.*, p. 555. See also Levitov, *op. cit.*, pp. 217 ff.

religion sensitizes the human conscience and thus undermines the power of the state. As far as the advancement of Soviet political psychology is concerned, the techniques of brain-washing certainly have been used on many political prisoners and prisoners of war. Experiments on individuals frequently apply to groups. The communists foment racial struggle by arousing excessive fears, exploiting calamities, stimulating panicky attitudes, or giving signals for actions against scapegoats or for actions with a symbolic character, or keeping the majority of the population paralyzed.

The most important objectives of communist political psychology may be summarized in the following points: the communists use psychological theories primarily for political needs in helping them to maintain strong leadership; the communists create states of confusion, frustration, pessimism, guilt, fear, hopelessness, etc., among the hostile camps in order to destroy anti-communist leadership; the communists must and always will use the concepts of hate, anxiety, fear of atomic war, and the promise to solve all problems on the basis of the communist "morality" to attain their goals; finally the communists will use any method in order to weaken and destroy national consciences and any opposition to communism.[11]

Additional References

N. A. Bauer, *The Man in Soviet Psychology* (Cambridge: Harvard University Press, 1959); A. Emery, "Dialectics vs. Mechanics, A Communist Debate on Scientific Method," in *Psychology of Science*, II (1935), pp. 9–38; N. F. Poznanski, "Heredity and the Materialist Theory," in *Soviet Psychology: A Symposium*, Forward by R. B. Winn (New York: Philosophical Library, 1961), pp. 49–54; A. A. Smirnov, "The Development of Soviet Psychology," in *Soviet Psychology: A Symposium* (New York: Philosophical Library, 1961), pp. 11–30. A. A. Zalevskaia, "O vospriiatii novoi inoiazychnoi leksiki s razlichnoi informatsionnoi nagruzhkoi," in *Voprosi psikhologii*, No. 1, 1967, pp. 127–135; Makarenko, *A Book for Parents*, pp. 37 ff.; A. N. Levitov, *Detskaia i pedagogicheskaia psikhologiia* (Moscow: Izdat. Prosvishchenie, 1962), *passim*.

---

[11] Ferreus, "The Menace of Communist Psychological Warfare," in *Orbis* (Pittsburgh: University of Pennsylvania Press), No. 1, 1957, pp. 99–119.

Part Two

IMPACT OF COMMUNIST POLICIES
ON THE SOVIET SOCIETY

Chapter 11

BOLSHEVIK
LINGUISTIC POLICIES

Bolshevik policies have tried to achieve the same ends as the Imperial linguistic policies, but with different methods. Imperial Russia openly denied the support of non-Russian languages; the Bolsheviks, on the other hand, openly supported the flourishing of national languages but secretly fought it with more vigor than the Imperial Russians did.

The linguistic policy of the Russian Soviet government is a long-range planned strategy to assimilate slowly all non-Russian nationalities. This policy usually had the veneer of the proletarian culture.

The Bolsheviks continued the same policy of Russification as Imperial Russia with some minor exceptions which favored national languages. The Imperial regime prohibited Ukrainian and Belorussian as the languages of instruction in schools, thus hindering the development of national cultures of those two nations. The Soviets began to revise books in order to slowly assimilate these languages into the Russian language. In rewriting books the Russians included their own vocabulary especially in scientific terminology. Another step, after the scientific terminology, was to penetrate a given language with various kinds of neologisms (usually Russian words), or reject certain letters from its alphabet. For example the Ukrainian language has a letter (g) "ґ" while the Russian language does not have this letter. By combining the letter *h* (г) with the letter *g* (ґ) the Ukrainian language would sound more Russian than Ukrainian: e.g., *hovority* is the Ukrainian word for "to speak"; *govorit* is the Russian word with the same meaning. Thus the many Ukrainian words beginning with the letter *h* would be Russified by pronouncing them with the Russian *g*. The Bolsheviks tried to assimilate the Ukrainian and the Russian infinitives by cutting off their last letter "i" and replacing it with the Russian soft sign, e.g., "to read" in Russian means *chitat́*, but in Ukrainian *chytaty* is pronounced quite differently from the Russian chitat́. Thus, by replacing certain Ukrainian letters with the Russian ones, a young child learning his own language will come closer to the Russian language because his own native language is being distorted. This is done purposely to confuse the little child and to make his native language a sort of "underdeveloped" language.

These examples represent only two of the many grammatical rules of a given native language. There are many similar examples of Russification in the Ukrainian, Belorussian and Turkish languages. The introduction of the modified Ukrainian alphabet and the abolition of the Arabic alphabet of the Muslims was a well-planned linguistic strategy to make those languages, if not dead, at least impossible to develop on a free linguistic and cultural basis. The slow reshaping of a vernacular language creates confusion among the native linguists who find it impossible to resist because of the Russian laws. This is compounded by the struggle between the followers of the Russian reforms and those who oppose the reforms. The old rule—divide and conquer—is applied in the Bolshevik linguistic reforms.

Bolsheviks claimed that they wanted "to make a live language out of dead ones,"[1] but this "liveliness" was not based on the voluntary acceptance of certain neologisms (necessary for any language) but on interference in the linguistic matters of nations.

LANGUAGE AND THE NATION

Language is one of the most important criteria for national independence or self-determination. Language is among the basic essentials for national independence and it is no wonder that great powers have always

---

[1] Akademiia Nauk SSSR, *Kratkoe soobshchenie o dokladakh i polevikh issledovaniiakh instituta istorii material'noi kul'tury* (Moscow: AN SSSR, 1947), *passim.* See also A. Marr, *Etapi razvitiia kul'tury Kavkaza* (Moscow: AN SSSR, 1932), p. 86.

tried to interfere in the natural linguistic development of peoples, e.g., England prohibited Gaelic for the Irish as early as the 16th century and the Austrians prohibited Czech or Serbian as the intellectual languages of those states. The Hungarians prohibited Ukrainian and so did the Russians.

Lenin realized the problem of linguistic struggle and he began to shape his strategies accordingly. At the Seventh All-Russian Communist Congress he declared that one must be insane to follow the old policy of the czar Nicholas. He further stated that if Finland, Poland, Ukraine, or any other nation within the Russian empire wants to be separated from Russia, there is nothing wrong with that desire. Marxism promises complete freedom of political action to all nations.

Other Marxists, Russian and non-Russians, varied on the question of national linguistic and political self-determination. Marx, for instance, favored the self-determination (political and linguistic) of Poland and Ireland but not so much the self-determination of Serbia and Czechoslovakia. He did state, however, that it is a misfortune for a nation to rule over other nations. Plekhanov strongly supported the self-determination of all nations within the Russian empire by stating that if the communists fail to recognize the fact of national independence they may as well give up the slogan "the proletariat of all lands unite!" Other Russian Marxists generally were against self-determination except for a few prominent ones like Chernyshevski and Dobroliubov.

There is no question that Lenin wanted to utilize the unfavorable position of Russian nationalities in rising to power. He initiated a drive for the complete self-determination of each nation in Russia. There was a special section in Lenin's declaration of independence concerning the non-Russian nations. In 1903 Lenin accused the Imperial regime of being nationalistic and chauvinistic, a regime which subjugated other nationalities. Further, he considered the Russians inferior culturally to other nationalities inhabiting Russia—for example, Finland, which "is a democratic country, well developed and more culturally advanced than Russia. In 1915 Lenin further underlined the fact that the national question was very important because only 43 per cent of the population of Russia was Russian; the rest were non-Russians. Those non-Russians, according to Lenin, were not permitted to use their own languages, to develop their own education—"there is no other country in Europe, or even in Asia, which would practice such discriminatory policies as we have in Russia . . . against the Jews, the Poles, and the Ukrainians."[2]

---

[2] Lenin, *Izbrannye stati po natsional'nym voprosam*, pp. 5 ff.

Stalin, as the Commissar of Nationalities, did much work on the different nationalities of Russia. At first, he favored self-determination in the linguistic area, but later on did not. From 1904 on Stalin worked on his *Marxism and the Nationality Question* which became a source book for later official applications when he became the ruler of the U.S.S.R. Skrypnyk, a Ukrainian Commissar of Education, expressed similar ideas in his *Stati i promovy* (Articles and speeches).

The Russian Social Democratic Party (presently communists) from the very beginning incorporated into its body many non-Russian representatives and various ethnic organizations. There were autonomous national organizations within the communist party of Russia—Jewish, Muslim, Armenian and others. Important positions of the party in some areas were occupied by non-Russians, for instance, the Jews—Trotsky, Kamenev, Zinoviev, Lunacharski, Kaganovich; the Georgians—Stalin, Beria; and the Ukrainians—Skrypnyk and Petrovskyj. All of them were encouraged by the Bolsheviks to stimulate national feelings toward a national uprising. Once the struggle was over, these leaders were no longer needed. When they asked Stalin for help he declared that he himself was already Russified.

Actually Lenin and Stalin emerged victorious because they promised more than any other political party. Lenin, when he needed help, called for complete linguistic and political independence and incorporated these clauses into the official Soviet decrees and documents. According to Lenin, no nation has the right to have special privileges over another nation. But at the same time he underlined the fact that communists must use vigorous national sentiments to win the struggle. He called upon the party leaders to utilize the peasants, the non-Russian ethnic groups, and revolutionary peoples in all lands, and to make it clear to them that the only way to liberation and national self-determination is international revolution. In this Lenin opposed Marx who favored the independence of Poland but not of the Czechs and the Serbians. Marx feared that the Czechs and the Serbians would imitate the Russian reactionary practices, and thus would only hinder the proletarian revolution. On the contrary, said Lenin, "We are for assimilation but not for forceful assimilation; and we take from the national culture only those elements that are socialistic and non-bourgeois."

Thus Lenin was not for real independence in any nation, but for the assimilation of the working classes of the whole world into one communist and Russian controlled camp. This policy is seen from the Soviet examples where national questions are only utilized at certain times.[3]

---

[3] *Ibid.* p. 28.

In 1930, Stalin criticized Kautsky who said that socialism will not know national languages and that the aim of socialism is to assimilate all nations into one universal language. Stalin said that the German language cannot be adopted as the language of communism. He opposed the universal German language, but the universal Russian language was a different matter.

Stalin during his life strongly practiced the philosophy of "the survival of the fittest" since he believed that the strong language will always survive. He saw no danger of corruption of the Russian language. On the contrary, he anticipated assimilation of hundreds of non-Russian languages since these lack official support.[4]

During Stalin's rule national self-determination in the linguistic area was fiction since official policy was to construct a language of socialism based on the class struggle. The plan for the universal communist language was as follows: first, "completion" and "enrichment" of existing languages by adding to them a "rich" terminology (Russian); second, the elimination of foreign scientific and religious terms (Arabic ones in Central Asia and German ones from the Baltic states); third, the establishment of Russian as the language of socialism.

This policy was practiced until 1950. Then came a period marked by the Marr controversy. Marr (a Soviet linguist supported by Stalin) advocated the idea that language is only the superstructure which changes as society changes, that certain languages are condemned to fade away because of their cultural inertia, and that the Chinese languages are due to become obsolete. When in 1950 Mao Tse-tung protested against the theories of Marr, Stalin declared that Marr was an idiot who "prostituted" the science of language.

Stalin also defended the thesis of culture and language by saying that culture may be bourgeois and proletarian but a language always remains a national language. Thus, it is clear that the proletarian language will be the language of that nation which conquers the other nations.

THE UKRAINIAN REFORMS

There were many Ukrainians, particularly the intelligentsia, who believed the Bolshevik propaganda and the sincerity of Lenin and his party. They also believed that the Russians were truly communists working for the international proletariat and not for the great Russian empire. There were also some enthusiasts who thought that they really would build an

---

[4] J. V. Stalin, *Marksism i voprosy iazykoznaniia* (Moscow: Gosizdat, 1936), p. 150.

independent Ukraine, free from Russian exploitation of any kind. The Russian communist party promised the Ukrainian communists anything they asked—complete freedom in educational matters, freedom to develop their own national culture, language, and "constitution." The Russians said that they meant free "constitutions" because "only the bourgeois write a constitution for the purpose of deceit, and there will be no such thing in the Soviet Ukraine."

In light of these promises the Ukrainian communists organized certain legal institutions, and introduced the study of the Ukrainian language in all schools and for all who wanted to work in Ukraine. It was stated at first that only those with spare time or those who intended to settle in Ukraine should learn the language. However, the Russian communists began to accuse the Ukrainian communists of chauvinism, nationalism and radicalism. As this situation got worse, the Russian communists began to liquidate those Ukrainian communists who dared to speak Ukrainian at official meetings.

After the establishment of the communist regime the strategy of Russian communists was to secure its cultural and political position in such a way that the Russians would "follow" the rules of the majority, i.e., the non-Russian speaking ethnic groups. Lenin and Stalin declared that communists do not believe in borderlands since the workers do not heed any state, only the solidarity of international friendship. However, for a temporary period, the communists theorized, the state must exist. But this is not because the Russians want it but because non-Russian nationalities desire Russian protection against the future invasion of the capitalists. Therefore, in 1922 Stalin declared that the Ukrainians, Belorussians, and Transcaucasians (predominantly Muslims) wanted to establish the Union of the Soviet Socialist Republics. He stated that these nationalities desired the union because they wished to strengthen their cultural unity with the Russian people and to work together for the accomplishment of the world revolution.[5]

It became obvious to many non-Russian communist leaders that theory was one thing and practice was an entirely different matter. The leading Ukrainian communist, M. Skrypnyk, saw the clever strategy of Russian communists, and began to attack the official line of the communist party. He stated that Ukrainians were united on the national question, and protested the great Russian chauvinism.

There were other complaints against the Russification of the non-Russian population within the Russian republic as well as within other

---

[5] *Ibid.*, p. 109.

areas of the Soviet Union. To solve the problem, the communist party of Russia decided to instruct all national committees responsible for cultural development to introduce the study of vernacular languages in schools. To what extent this was carried out the following points of the directives of the Russian communist party may reveal:

a. In all Union-Republics the Marxist-groups must be organized and Marxian literature must be published in the native language;
b. in the Eastern regions of the Union, the communist party must support the branches of the regional communist parties and help spread massive amounts of communist literature in those national languages;
c. in the area of political education, the Marxian studies must be strengthened in all Union-Republics, and communist work among the youth of various ethnic groups must be intensified.

It became evident that this freedom in regard to language offered nothing in a vernacular except political indocrination. The Russian communist party made it clear that the provisions and the directives of independent linguistic opportunities were not based on a majority of a population speaking a certain language but on a majority's being members of the communist party. Since a number of the communist party members in Ukraine favored the Russian ethnic group, the resolutions and the laws issued in Moscow, of course, favored Russian linguistic freedom. It was a fact that the urban intelligentsia of Ukraine predominantly spoke Russian, but it was also a fact that the incoming peasants and workers from the rural areas wanted Ukrainian to be introduced in all official communications.

The trend of the "Ukrainization" became pronounced in the 1920s when the enthusiastic communists, Skrypnyk and Khvylovy, worked for the realization of the communist ideological programs. The previously cited decision to educate future communists in a vernacular language was utilized by the Ukrainians for the purpose of seeking national independence and the development of a national-communist culture. Skrypnyk and others demanded that all the Communist Youth Organizations in Ukraine must support the study of the Ukrainian language and must introduce it as the official language of the state. Skrypnyk demanded the annexation of the Ukrainian territories, Kuban, Voronezh, and Tahanrih to the Ukrainian People's Republic. He also demanded the right to cultural opportunities for the seven million Ukrainians living within the boundaries of the Russian SFSR. Skrypnyk further criticized the Russian administration for educationally depressing the Ukrainians, since there were only 500 elementary and two secondary Ukrainian schools in the Russian SFSR, obviously quite disproportionate for the several million Ukrainians living in the Russian republic.

For some reason, Stalin favored Skrypnyk's demands and ordered the establishment of Ukrainian schools and other cultural institutions which would use the Ukrainian language as the official language of communication. In 1929 Skrypnyk reported that there were 14,430 Ukrainian schools (out of 20,764) with 1.3 million students; 1,504 Russian schools with 112,735 students, and about 600 other schools on the territory of Ukrainian SSR.

The Period of Russification. While the development of the national-communist culture was going on, the Russian communists prepared certain steps to prevent further Ukrainization of the richest part of the Soviet Union. Not only Ukraine, but all other nationalities witnessed some sort of independence during the New Economic Period.

By 1928, the Russian policy concerning development of national-communist cultures began to change. The Russians began to invade the industrial districts saying that it was not a good policy to have various terminologies. It would be better to replace German, Ukrainian, Latvian, Polish, etc., scientific terms by the Russian terms for unity in "scientific production." The Ukrainians, of course, protested that they could not separate technology from the total national culture and that the Ukrainian terminology did not interfere with production.

Skrypnyk, like Muslim cultural leaders, still believed the principles of communism expressed by Lenin during the revolution, proclaiming that it was inhuman to do otherwise. He also insisted that the Ukrainian population in villages and the workers in factories did not speak Russian and could understand neither political nor technological instructions in Russian. Skrypnyk insisted that the Ukrainian language must be used in all state matters because only the old bourgeoisie spoke Russian and they would misinterpret the communistic design of the state.

The strategy of the Russian communists was to infiltrate the industrial proletariat with Russian culture and then to impose it in all other institutions. In 1930 all official communications were carried out in Ukrainian, although considerable resistance was evident among the higher party members. The Commissariat of Education strictly insisted upon the usage of the Ukrainian language in schools, thus taking the initial steps to educate the Ukrainian-conscious communists.

When the resistance was continued, the Ukrainians in Russian SFSR (not those living in Ukrainian ethnographic territories) supported the cause of Skrypnyk and others began to participate intensively in the cultural organization of the country. B. Kovalenko, for instance, published a book, "The Proletarian Literature in the Struggle for the Leninist National Cultural Construction," in which he tried to defend and to prove the right of one nationality to build her own communism. Zinoviev, Molotov, and other Bolshevik leaders accused the Ukrainians of nationalism and ordered a massive attack on those people who sympathized with the Commissar of Education (Skrypnyk) and other Ukrainian communists.

At the same time the Russian communists began to advocate the existence of two cultures, a *superculture* or the socialist (Russian culture) and the provincial or national type of culture. But like other reforms, the initiative was introduced by Moscow and not by any national groups of the Soviet Union. Later on, after the temporary toleration of the concept of two cultures, the policy was to impose completely a sole language and a sole culture—the Russian one. The Russian communists justified such action by saying that use of the Ukrainian language might bring about a certain type of recession which would hinder the development of communism. The Ukrainian writers, especially M. Khvylovy, protested the policies of the Kremlin, but the Russian communists maintained that struggle was necessary for the survival of communism. Stalin and other communist leaders constantly reminded people that only that language will survive which is able to withstand the attacks made on it and which is culturally stronger. Obviously, the "struggle" was nonsense for the non-Russian nationals because they were not free to compete with the Russians.

When the Ukrainians, especially Skrypnyk, attacked the idea of the linguistic struggle by stating that it was only a trick to subdue other nationalities under the old Russian imperalistic rule, the party not only did not improve the situation, but punished those who opposed it. Skrypnyk argued that the only valid assimilation is a voluntary one. There is no real assimilation when a policy is forced upon a nation and native initiative is suppressed.

In view of these theoretical arguments "practical" measures were taken by the Kremlin. Those who opposed the policy of Russification were liquidated.

All those who participated in the so-called Ukrainian renaissance were defined as *kulaks* or bourgeois nationalists. Stalin himself made a speech on the Ukrainian question accusing of nationalism all those who wanted to use the Ukrainian language in their cultural communications. In 1933, he made a Russian, P. Postishev, the Commissar of Ukraine. Postishev completely liquidated any nationalistic desires and national type of communism. At the same time, Khrushchev was learning the techniques of ruling since he succeeded Postichev as the iron man of Ukraine.

Khrushchev and After. In 1938, Nikita Khrushchev was appointed by Stalin as the Secretary of the Ukrainian Communist Party, in effect the ruler of Ukraine. He followed exactly the policy of his predecessors in liquidating any traces of the Ukrainian national communism. He saw the danger in studying Ukrainian, a danger that might play a negative part in the Russian policy of imperialism. Language to Khrushchev was one of the most important media of communication and the *medium* of the national consciousness.

At the Fourteenth Party Conference, Khrushchev brutally attacked the Ukrainian "nationalists" (communists who disagreed with Moscow) as well as others who supported the separation of the Ukrainian language from the Russian language, a move which Khrushchev considered as the first step of a separation of Ukraine from Russia.

The Russification process began to go wild. For example, in 1939 when the Russians occupied the Western Ukraine, all official communications were carried out in Russian although the native population never in history belonged to Russia and did not know that language. In the Russian SFSR, as mentioned before, more than seven million Ukrainians had settled. But from 1939 on the publication or circulation of any Ukrainian book or newspaper was prohibited. It came to the point that even the Ukrainian journals published in Ukraine, like *Kommunist,* were not allowed to be circulated among those Ukrainians who lived in the Russian SFSR. Ukrainians had to read the Russian newspapers or they could read German, English, or French, but not Ukrainian. After the liquidation of the Ukrainian resistance Khrushchev said:

> Comrades! Now all the nations study the Russian language, because the Russian workers raised the flag of the revolution. The Russian workers showed the workers of the world how one has to fight, how one has to handle the enemies and how one should fight for freedom. Comrades! The Bolsheviks have studied the German language in order that they could read Marx in the original.... Now all the nations are studying and will study Russian in order to be able to read the original works of Lenin and Stalin and to learn how to conquer the enemies.[6]

In countries occupied by the Soviet Union the study of Russian is compulsory. The Hungarians, the Romanians, the Poles and many others,

---

[6] Vasyl Chaplenko, *Bil'shovitska movna politika* (Munich: Institute for the Study of the USSR, 1956, mimeo), pp. 8, 11–59.

have no choice in selecting the language they want. They must study Russian before they can study any other language. The non-Russian languages in the Soviet Union (German, Jewish, Ukrainian, Kalmyk and others) are condemned to die, or will be forcibly eliminated from any important area of contribution in the cultural sphere.

Now the Russian communists are changing the strategy by saying that the Russian language is not the language of the great Russian leaders but the language of the Great October Revolution. In short, a native language can develop just so far, but once it reaches a stage of competition with the Russian language, and is able to handle all the necessary scientific and political literature, that language must be fought. After World War II the Ukrainians in *Ukraine* were afraid to speak Ukrainian in higher educational institutions because they were afraid of being accused of nationalism and conspiracy against the Russian regime.

Since the fall of Khrushchev there is nothing new that would favor development of the Ukrainian language in accordance with national traditions and innate characteristics. The language now is studied from the "scientific" point of view, either to prove its origin or as part of the secondary reflex system (Pavlovian term), or as a development in reaction to certain things. It is true that now there are many journals in Ukraine, but it is also true that their circulation is very limited. The language of these journals is not carefully edited, leaving them purposely in a "broken" Ukrainian in order to force the young Ukrainian generation to seek the proper terms in Russian dictionaries because the Ukrainian ones are not adequate. The Ukrainian press here and there dares to criticize the poor writing in certain textbooks, especially a new dictionary for the secondary schools, but nothing is done about it. The "Ukrainian" dictionary is more Russian than Ukrainian, e.g., such words as *Parikmakher, pereulok, diadia Misha, povar, probka,* all are Russian words. The Ukrainian Academy of Sciences has nothing to say about it. The Ukrainian literary and linguistic journals operate on the basis of great slogans, such as "the Ukrainian literature is dedicated to its people, to the communist party and to the great ideas of Leninism . . ." But as the Chinese proverb says: "you give us plenty to swallow but nothing to eat."[7]

Ukrainian literature must praise the accomplishments of the Russian people before it can praise the accomplishments of its own people. Lenin and some other Russian members of the communist party are extolled as heroes, but famous Ukrainians and great humanitarians may not be

---

[7] *Literaturna Ukraina,* January 27, 1967, p. 3; *Molod' Ukrainy,* March 17, 1965.

mentioned. The linguistic journals are dedicated to "satisfy the scientists and wide circles of our populations,"[7] but in case they do not "satisfy" the wide circles, they will be discontinued as was the *October* (Zhovten') in Lvov.

In short, the present day linguistic status of Ukrainian in the Soviet Ukraine can be described as being in a *state of inertia*. There are no developments that would annoy the Kremlin nor anything that positively contributes to the development of the Ukrainian language. Russian propaganda says that there are over seventy "official" languages on the territory of the Soviet Union. In reality most of these are being slowly squelched.

LINGUISTIC REFORMS IN CENTRAL ASIA

The situation of the Muslim linguistic reforms was somewhat different since most of the Muslims had no alphabet of their own and very often they did not know their ethnic origin. Nevertheless, the Muslims in this respect were similar to the Ukrainians because they, too, were subjects for Russification and assimilation with the "older brother."

Historical Background. The first traces of script used by the peoples of Central Asia were found in the seventh century when the Mongolian alphabet was used. This script, however, was based on the Syriac alphabet which had been used by early Christians in the Eastern Roman (Byzantine) Empire. Subsequently the Syriac script was taken by the Sogdians, an Iranian people, and later by the Turkish Ujgurs who made some adjustments suitable for Turkish languages and used it until the end of the thirteenth century.[8]

When Timur began his campaign for world domination, the Ujgur alphabet also began to lose its significance. This time, the Arabic script became more popular since it represented the symbolic attachment to Islamic religion as opposed to Mongolian script, which at that time represented the Buddhist religion.

Another peculiarity among the ethnic groups of Central Asia was their disregard for specific ethnic origin. Although there are linguistic differ-

---

[8] Important sources concerning Soviet linguistic policies toward Muslim peoples are: I. Malov, *Pamiatniki drevno-russkoi pis'mennosti* (Moscow: 1951), passim; I. Malov, *Pamiatniki pis'mennosti Turkov* (Moscow: AN SSSR, 1952); J. Wurm, *Turcic Peoples of the USSR* (London: Central Asian Research Center, 1954), p. 12; Paul B. Henze, "Politics and Alphabet in Inner Asia," in *Royal Central Asian Journal*, vol. XLIII, January 1956, p. 29.

ences between the Persian-speaking Tadzhiks and the Turkish-speaking Uzbeks, this does not seem to be as significant as is geographical location. Some Iranians adopted Turkish speech and customs, while some Turkish elements, in particular the Sarts, adopted Iranian speech and ways of life. Still others used both languages in their social interaction.

Three different trends affected the establishment of a unified language for all the ethnic groups inhabiting the region. The first trend was represented by the nomadic tribe, Shabanids (Shaibani Khan who invaded the region of Uzbekistan in the sixteenth century) ; the second group, sedentary peoples, Sarts, used both languages—Iranian (Tadzhik) and Turkish; the third group, a pre-Shabanid Turkish nomadic people—different from the nomadic Uzbeks and the sedentary Sarts—who called themselves Chagatais, or identified by the names of their tribes (Kurluks, Kipchaks, Turks, Kurams, etc.).

When Russians occupied this area in the nineteenth century they saw the lack of linguistic unity and they began to work on Russian-Latin script for natives, hoping at the same time to convert some of them to Christianity, e.g., Ilminski's Institute in Kazan had worked on linguistic matters of Muslim nationalities. But the central idea of Ilminski's Institute was the propagation of Orthodoxy. Although provisions were made to educate Muslims on the same level as Russians, the Muslims were not eager to accept these ideas since they regarded the Arabic script as the holy script of Islam, in which the Koran was written.

The second half of the nineteenth century indicated some progressive trends in linguistic development of Muslim Central Asia since the natives themselves began work on a united script. The major initiative stemmed from the Muslim social and literary people of Kazan (Tatars), leading personalities of which were men like Arkhundov, Mikumi and Furkat, and most important Gasprinski, the founder of the Jadid movement in the Russian Empire.

After the Revolution of 1917, the Kazan-Tatars again gained a substantial influence over the peoples of Central Asia. They proposed changing the Arabic script into Latin letters, but again a variety of opinions and ideas on the new alphabet hindered rapid progress. Leading Muslim reformers wanted to maintain the Arabic alphabet, allowing for some modifications suitable for the Uzbek language, but retaining the script as a whole. This group succeeded to the extent that in 1923 the modified Arabic alphabet became the official script of the region. The second group, Chagatais, wanted to reform the Uzbek language on the basis of classical Chagatai language (influenced by Iranian). Others thought that a modern Uzbek language should be based on the Turkish language; still others maintained that a modern Uzbek language should be a composite of local dialects, permitting,[9] however, one dialect to dominate and ultimately play a leading role in the formation of the Uzbek language.

All of these linguistic theories, then, were centered mainly around two factors: modified Arabic, the language of Islam; modified Turkish, the language of pan-Turkism. The Soviets were not in favor of either plan. They began to elaborate a linguistic theory which would eliminate both Islam and pan-Turkism by putting emphasis on local language. Such plans to change the Arabic script into Latin began in 1920 when the first Oriental Congress met in Baku. The important issue of the above Congress was not the imposition of the Cyrillic script upon Muslim peoples, but the Latin one which was favored by Muslims themselves.

In 1921, Stalin advocated (as part of national policy) that the communist party should take a lead in linguistic controversy and that the party should promote local languages, should establish a local press in a language understandable to the people, and should promote and organize educational, cultural, and other institutions for this important cause. In 1922, the twelfth Party Congress made a major point of the need to bring into Soviet administration local people who knew the native languages, customs, life, and habits of the minority peoples; and also the need to pass laws (*obespechivaiushchie zakony*) guaranteeing the use of native languages in "all organs and enterprises serving the local native population."

In 1925, Stalin further outlined the following main goals in his speech to the Fifteenth Party Congress:

a. Establishment of non-party clubs and educational institutions in local languages;
b. Attracting "loyal" teachers of local origin to teach in Soviet schools;
c. Creation of a network of informational agencies to disseminate literacy instruction in local languages;
d. Providing means for publishing facilities in local languages.[10]

Thus, the use of the Arabic alphabet by many Muslim ethnic groups of the Soviet Union became the subject not only of Muslim reformers but

---

[9] M. A. Shcherbak, "K istorii obrazovaniia uzbekskogo narodnogo iazyka," in *Voprosy iazykoznaniia*, No. 6, 1954, p. 114. See also Caroe, *op. cit.,* p. 156; A. K. Borokov, "Ocherki istorii uzbekskogo iazyka," in *Sovetskoe vostokovedenie* (Moscow: Institut Vostokovedeniia, 1949), *passim;* Alexandre Bennigsen and Chantal Quelquejay, *The Revolution of the Muslim Nationalities of the USSR and Their Linguistic Problems* (Oxford: St. Anton's College Press, 1961), p. 35.
[10] Stalin, *Sochineniia,* vol. V, p. 298.

also of the communist authorities. Up to 1925 many foreign materials were sent to Muslims of the Soviet Union by other Islamic countries, but the law of August 1925 prohibited any further imported materials printed in the Arabic alphabet.

At the same time that the linguistic controversy was going on, the Soviets had worked on methods aimed at persuading the Muslim population to favor the change. They emphasized the idea that the Arabic script had limited possibilities in expressing scientific terms, especially those related to technical sciences, and that the Arabic alphabet was not suitable for all the Turkish dialects,[11] because

> "Words are written from right to left while figures are written from left to right, making their simultaneous use very difficult."

Similar critiques of the Arabic alphabet were launched by other Muslims of the U.S.S.R. The result was that Azerbaidzhan, the first Soviet Muslim country, accepted the Latin alphabet. In 1922 they established a journal in Latin script known as *Joni Jol* (*Iangi Iul* in Uzbek version), "New Road," which had the following circulation: September 1922, 200 copies (weekly) ; 1924, 1800 copies (becoming a daily paper) ; in 1926 the circulation reached 6,000.

This was significant because step by step other Muslim ethnic groups changed their respective journals into Latin. By 1926 all necessary steps had been taken to prepare the Muslim population to favor the new script. When the Congress of Orientalists (initiated by the Soviet government) met in Baku, the Muslims of the U.S.S.R. generally favored the reforms because similar changes were in stages of development in Turkey, also an Islamic country. But the Soviets surpassed the Turks in this "linguistic race" and when the Baku decision was reached, accepting the Latin script, *Pravda* commented on the situation stating that the decision of the Baku Congress (1926) had not only a great linguistic significance but also a political one.

In 1926, the Supreme Soviet of the U.S.S.R. established a state body to supervise the introduction of the Latin alphabet into Turkish tongues. This legal Committee was labeled as the "All-Union Central Committee on the New Turkish Alphabet" (Vse-Sciuznyi Tsentral 'nyi Komitet Novogo Tiurskogo Alfavita-VTsKNTA) with headquarters in Baku. On August 7, 1929, the VTsKNTA and the U.S.S.R. Sovnarkom decreed the Latin-type alphabet to be introduced in all Turkish institutions and ordered the

---

[11] Thomas Winner, "Problems of Alphabetic Reforms Among the Turkic Peoples of Soviet Central Asia," in *The Slavonic and East European Review*, vol. XXXI, No. 76, 1952, p. 136.

seizure of the Arabic script, at the same time prohibiting any importation of materials printed in Arabic. In November 1930, the Sovnarkom of the Uzbek SSR officially ordered all cultural and educational establishments of the republic to use the Latin script as the alphabet of the state. By 1930, thirty-six minority languages serving about thirty million Muslims used the Latin script.

The change from the Arabic into the Latin script did not last long; by 1936 Russian linguists took steps to change Latin into the Russian Cyrillic. It became evident that the change from Arabic into Latin was primarily political. They did not want to frighten the native population immediately with the Russian script. The final goal was realized in 1939 when the Supreme Soviet issued a law prohibiting the use of Latin for the Muslim people, and introducing the Russian script instead.

During the war there was little argument about the Russian script, and after the war few of the old Muslim reformers were around to resist the change. In 1950 Stalin came up with a new idea in linguistics when he decreed that language must be studied from two angles: the class dialect and the territorial dialect. But this was merely an addition to the already existing Marr theories. The class dialect was to be associated with the Russian language, and the territorial dialect with the native languages. New grammars and new dictionaries were written on the basis of the assimilation of two languages. They were Uzbek-Russian, Kazakh-Russian, Tadzhik-Russian, Kirghiz-Russian and Kalmyk-Russian; in short, all languages were dominated by the Russian language.

The Mongolian People's Republic—the first Russian satellite—was also forced to accept the Russian alphabet as their alphabet. The natives of Turkestan often complain about the policy of Russification and about the excess of instruction in the Russian language in their schools. All this was carried out, of course, on a "voluntary" basis as the Soviet Encyclopedia has described:[12]

> The Latin alphabet played an important part in the development of national languages and in the process of liquidating illiteracy. But in time these languages became inadequate for the future development of Soviet culture. In all the nations comprising the Soviet Union there is a strong desire to learn the Russian language and to read the Russian classics in the original . . . the peoples of the USSR are desperately anxious to learn the Russian culture, to enrich their language with Russian words, and to get acquainted with the most progressive culture of the world.

---

[12] Chaplenko, *op. cit.*, pp. 64–65; Kary-Niiazov, *op. cit.*, p. 260; *Pravda,* March 3, 1926.

As Table 28 indicates, the study of a native language decreases as the age of the child increases. In all respects the Muslims have particular difficulties coping with the Russian curriculum—they must study three or more foreign languages since the Russian language is also foreign to them.

Another point is that the native languages, either the Central Asian ones or Azerbaidzhanian are loaded with Russian grammatical forms, Russian diminutives, and Russian politico-scientific expressions. In literature the Russian impact has been very powerful.

TABLE 28

Distribution of Class-Hours Per Native and Russian Languages
1930s

Grade	Native Lang.	Russian Lang.
	(Hrs./wk)	(Hrs./wk)
2	5	5
3	4	6
4	3	5
5	3	5
6	4	5
7	2	4
8	2	5
9	3	4
10	2	6

Baymirza Hayit, *Turkestan in XX Jahrhundert* (Darmstat: C. W. Leske Verlag, 1956), p. 353.

The Goals of the Soviet Linguistic Reforms. Regardless of linguistic controversies, the important issue was the following: by the end of the nineteenth century Turkish nationalists had planned to establish a great state unifying all Turkish peoples, or even all the Muslims of the world, into a vast empire. In 1920, Enver Pasha had a similar idea. The Jadids, also, were optimistic about the possible creation of a huge Islamic state hoping that Kazan would be the capital of the Muslim communist world.

As mentioned before, Soviet leaders sought to oppose Islamic as well as new pan-Turkish influences in the area. To counter effects of this upon the Muslim population, the Soviet government began to concentrate efforts on neutralization of Turkish influences rather than unification of all Turkish peoples. The Soviets promoted the local languages for many ethnic groups of Turko-Tatar origin, thus reducing the impact of Turkish unity by putting a linguistic block between elements working for Turkish political unity.

As a result of Soviet efforts many linguistic changes were made during the 1920s and 1930s. The Russian language came to exercise considerable influence, e.g., during 1923-1940 the quantity of Russian words in the Uzbek language had increased from 2.0% (in 1923) to 15% (in 1940), while the Persian-Arabic words in Uzbek decreased to 25% in 1940 as compared to 37.4% in 1923.[13]

Additionally, use of local languages made it impossible for many ethnic groups to preserve their national unity, e.g., the urban Uzbek-Tadzhik group, who for centuries were allied culturally, but differed linguistically and economically, were approaching a stage of assimilation. As one investigation has indicated, the Tadzhiks living in Uzbekistan "are condemned to absorption by the Turks among whom they live." This trend is pronounced in the rural areas where the Tadzhik language has disappeared—only large cities can maintain the old Tadzhik linguistic and cultural habits. (See also Table 29)

Turkish-speaking peoples of Tadzhikistan who also came under the dominant influence of the Tadzhik language had the same problem. Territorial demarcations and opposition to Islamic influences in the area certainly helped the Soviet plans to promote national languages. The policies forestalled an unexpected spread of Turanianism or other pan-Islamic or pan-Turkish ideas. Moreover, it obliged the native population to look to Russian as a major modern language.

In general, a change in alphabet to Latin meant that school children would be learning—especially in cities where many natives could read—a "new" language very unfamiliar to them, hence there would be a gap between parents and children. The schools had few materials in either alphabet, and changing to Latin meant that existing Persian-Arabic literature would soon become "foreign" to the youth—thus facilitating rapid educational changes away from traditions. Therefore, in Turkestan an evolutionary method rather than a revolutionary one was employed.

Obviously, the introduction of Russian was hindered in those languages not suited for the Cyrillic alphabet. It is impossible to express the exact meaning of many words using the Russian alphabet. Uzbek, Kazakh, Uigur, Buriat and other languages must use either Latin signs such as *h*, and *j* or they are unable to express meaning clearly.

The Soviets also wanted to go further than that. They wanted to in-

---

[13] Shcherbak, *op. cit.*, p. 115; Benningsen, *op. cit.*, p. 36; Wetter, *Dialectical Materialism*, p. 110.

TABLE 29

Nationalities of the Uzbek SSR According to the Language
They Speak: 1960

Nationality	Number of People (In Thousands)	Language Spoken in Per Cent of Total[1]	Per Cent of Total
Total of UzSSR	8,106	95.3	100.0
Of Which:			
Uzbek	5,038	98.6	62.2
Russians	1,091	99.6	13.5
Tatars	445	89.0	5.5
Kazakhs	335	86.4	4.1
Tadzhiks	311	94.9	3.8
Karakalpaks	168	95.3	2.1
Koreans	138	81.8	1.7
Jews	94	50.0	1.2
Kirghiz	93	92.3	1.1
Ukrainians	88	40.6	1.1
Turkmen	55	92.3	0.7
Azerbaidzhanians	41	91.3	0.5
Armenians	27	58.9	0.3
Turks	21	86.9	0.3
Greeks	20	84.3	0.2
Uigurs	19	60.0	0.2
Germans	18	64.0	0.2
Others	104	. . .	1.3

Pravda Vostoka, July 31, 1960, p. 6.

[1] The remaining per cent of given ethnic groups "accepted" as their own the Russian language. From this, it can be seen that the policy of Russification still exists and is widely felt.

troduce the Russian *ʺ*, a hard sign which does not exist in many languages. It is somewhat similar to the German *umlaut* (ü, ö), or the Hungarian *ö*. It is impossible to introduce it, because the sound is totally foreign to many languages. It would be like trying to impose the English *th* sound into Spanish.

At present, however, the struggle for the alphabet is over. The natives of Turkestan and other Islamic peoples have to study the nature of society from the communist point of view, as outlined by Mikoyan at the 25th Congress of the Oriental languages. The emphasis is on study of oriental languages, and also national movements in capitalistic countries (Gafurov, former Secretary of the communist party of Tadzhik SSR, has outlined the study of languages in terms of national uprisings).

By 1964 Russification accomplished its ends. For example, the *Teacher's Gazet* stated the following:[14]

Upon the request of parents, all schools of Karelia, many Tatar schools in twenty-three regions of the RSFSR, as well as a great majority of national schools of Dagestan, Kabardino-Balkaria and Kalmykia—have adopted the Russian language as the language of education maintaining the native language as a separate subject.

The same source further states that more and more schools in the territory of the Soviet Union are adopting the Russian language as their own. It is in this framework of Russian policy that the national cultures are "flourishing," a policy which is aimed at the complete destruction of national cultures. As a result the Russian population had increased from 43 per cent before the revolution to about 55 per cent in 1959, while the Kazakhs decreased by 21 per cent and the Ukrainians by more than 10 per cent. These examples make it clear that when Russian communists speak about self-determination, freedom, and development of national cultures, what they really mean is native acceptance of the Russian language and culture, completely foregoing a nation's desire for independent cultural development.

Additional References

Arnold Klees, "Ethnogenese—Eine neue sowjetische Wissenschaft," in *Osteuropa*, Heft 3, June 1954, pp. 165–173; E. Girchak, *Na dva fronta v bor'be s natsionalizmom* (Moscow: Gosizdat, 1930); Laurat Lucien, *Staline la linguistique et l' imperialisme russe* (Paris: 1951), pp. 77–91; Roman Smal-Stocki, *Ukrains'ka mova v pid-sovietskii Ukraini* (Warsaw: 1936); Roman Smal-Stocki, *Nationality Problem of the Soviet Union* (Milwaukee: Bruce Publishing Co., 1950); *Ukrainska mova i literatura v shkoli* (Kiev: monthly journal, Published by the Ministry of Ukrainian Education); J. V. Stalin, *Sochineniia*, vol. 5, especially pages 5–30; *Millij Turkistan*, March 1951, No. 70–71, pp. 12 ff; *Millij Turkistan*, August 1952, p. 28. (Part of the material on Central Asia in this chapter has been published by the author, Wasyl Shimoniak, in the *Ukrainian Quarterly*, Vol. 24, No. 4, 1968, pp. 361–368. Reprinted with permission.)

---

[14] *Uchitel'skaia gazeta*, March 12, 1964; Bennigsen, *op. cit.*, p. 31; *Voprosy iazykoznaniia*, No. 5, 1957, pp. 18–31.

Chapter 12

RELIGION AND COMMUNISM

The Soviet reforms concerning religion have been conducted in about the same patterns as the reforms concerning language, methodology, literature, education, i.e., on the basis of new laws and directives issued by the communist party of Russia. In theory, the Bolsheviks guaranteed freedom of religion by law but in practice the followers of any particular religion faced prosecution from the same Soviet laws.

There were various religions in Imperial Russia which the Soviet government wanted to change or to eliminate from society. Many of these religions played an important part in a national cultural development. The Muslim religion, for instance, was more than merely a religious organization. To the Muslims Islam meant a national way of life, economic orientation, a scheme of self-determination and legal provisions concerning the whole of man's life. The abandonment of Islam meant abandonment of their nationality as well. Christianity, in the view of many Christians, is not only a promise of life hereafter but also a set of moral rules that each must follow and for which no "ism" (Communism, Nazism, Fascism, etc.) can substitute.

During the czarist regime, the Christian religion developed freely; the Jews were persecuted; and the Muslims had their own religious courts. When the communists came to power they began to fight religion by every possible means. Force, violence, persuasions, propaganda, promises of the bright future for those who would follow Bolshevism—everything that was beneficial for the communists was tried. The communists also demanded from every intelligent person—regardless of his profession, whether physician, chemist, or teacher, etc.—participation in anti-religious propaganda and "explanation" to people of the "hazards" of religion. The struggle against religion was carried out under the following programs: (1) development of the theoretical foundations of atheism; (2) legal decisions in regard to religion; (3) methods used in fighting religion; (4) techniques used in fighting individual religions; and (5) the present policy of coexistence.

FOUNDATIONS OF ATHEISM

The Bolshevik philosophy of atheism is found primarily in Marx and Lenin. Other social philosophers were not as effective on the Russian mind as were these two men. Moreover, Western socialists and communists had very little influence in the shaping of the atheistic mind of the Soviet Union. Besides Marx and Lenin there were a variety of administrative supplements in Stalin, Khrushchev and other Soviet leaders.

Marx, as it is known, elevated matter to the supreme level and made economic conditions the very basis of all existence. According to Marx, man sets up his own nature as God, and religion becomes the product of human needs and wishes. Religion to him is the opiate of the masses and the sooner mankind gets rid of religion the better it is for the prosperity of man. Lenin, like Marx, insisted that religion had to be replaced by new Soviet values, values based on the communist practices. Lenin believed in group values and temporary ethical standards, but there was nothing for him that existed a priori or outside human society.

The Christian principles of morality and ethics were rejected by the Bolsheviks. Universal love for one's fellow man does not exist in the Soviet society; love can only exist for the communist "fellow man." The Soviet leaders, past and present, are trying to establish a communist "humanism" which is as follows:

Proletarian humanism requires undistinguishable hate toward the capitalist government, toward its representatives, toward the Fascists, toward the traitors of the working classes, toward everything that forces man to suffer, toward all those who live from other people's suffering . . .[1]

What is life? The communists answer that in this life on earth man remains completely alone and that he is confronted by a mysteriously silent and empty universe. The world may from time time be mysterious, or the concept of eternity may from time to time puzzle man. Nevertheless, "the meaning of our life is to be found in life itself . . . man is the creator of life, and this is our principle and understanding of life."[2]

The purpose of life is to be found in two sets of values. The first set involves such things as labor, health, glory, honor, fame, money, ambition, happy family relations, struggle for peace, building the new society. To the second category belong ideas about self-improvement, spiritual health, self-sacrifice and other kinds of "selfs." Friends are helpful only when one has a need for them.

Atheism rests upon the denial of the existence of God. But the Russian communists go beyond the denial of God. They want to "liberate" man "from the very notion of God," and try to prove that moral standards and norms are to be found not in religion but in the Soviet society itself.

LEGAL LIMITATIONS OF RELIGIOUS FREEDOM

The Bolsheviks wanted to destroy religion, and primarily the Christian religion, since the majority of the *Politburo* members were not Christians (Trotsky, Zinoviev, Bukharin, Kamenev, Lunacharski, Kaganovich). Thus it was not surprising that Saturday was declared as the official day of rest, rather than the customary Sunday.

The Soviet hatred toward religion could be seen as early as 1917 with passage of the first law regulating state and social affairs. A few days after the Bolshevik *coup d'etat,* Lenin wrote a rough draft of the law known as the Separation of the Church and State and the School from the Church. The law provided freedom of religion for every Soviet citizen, but at the same time prohibited stores from selling anything to the churches. It stated that "freedom of religion is permitted only when its exercise does not prejudice the republic," and also announced confiscation of all church property.

---

[1] The Soviet "Humanism" further accuses, in vulgar manner, western societies of being rotten societies and the enemies of Russia. See, for example, *Robitnicha gazeta,* February 1, 1966. See also Lenin, *Sochineniia,* vol. 31, p. 261.

[2] *Nauka i religiia,* No. 7, 1965, p. 7.

The paragraph concerning freedom of belief was deceptively ambiguous because the law of 1918 demanded that each priest must have a full time job assigned by the Commissariat of Internal Affairs, thus limiting freedom of the clergy to perform the usual duties.

There were many other restrictions on religious freedom, such as prohibition of religious teaching to children. At least twenty-five signatures had to be collected before a group could ask for permission to open a "prayer-house." In 1919 the Party stated the following: [3]

> In relation to religion the Russian communist party does not limit itself to the already decreed separation of Church and State and of the Schools from the Church; the Party strives toward a complete destruction of the relation between the exploiting class and the organization of religious propaganda, thus affecting the actual liberation of the toiling mass from religious prejudice and toward organizing a most extensive scientific educational and anti-religious propaganda.

Extensive propaganda was conducted by the communists to eliminate all religious teaching anywhere. The Soviets reiterated that the teaching of religion only results in stupidity. The clergy were told that the government would prohibit teaching of religion to children.

In 1923 the criminal code of the Russian republic provided punishments for those who practiced any religion. They appointed a Commissar of Justice, M. A. Reisner, who was responsible for the administration of the laws.

This prohibition greatly affected the Muslims, who began to revolt, causing the Soviets to be more careful in Central Asia. As early as 1921, the Soviets began to shift policies when the Muslim intellectuals refused to support the Soviet regime if persecution of Islam continued. Upon evaluation of the situation, Lenin did not apply the 1917 law to the Muslims, and even permitted them to celebrate Friday as their official day of rest and to keep their religious schools open.

The concessions were nothing but false promises because the Soviets had the power of appointment and were the administrators of the schools. No school and no church operated unless a representative from the Ministry of Justice and a local representative of the Secret police were present.

After the Muslim population was calmed down with Soviet promises the communists began to liquidate the leading Muslim religious clergy and

---

[3] *KPSS v rezoliutsiiakh, postanovleniiakh i resheniiakh s'iezdov,* vol. 1, p. 420; Gidulianov, *op. cit.,* p. 368; M. M. Persits, *Otdeleniie tserkvi ot gosudarstva i shkoly ot tserkvi* (Moscow: AN SSSR, 1958), p. 105. See also Wasyl Shimoniak, "Destruction of Islam in Uzbekistan," in *The Ukrainian Quarterly,* vol. XXI, No. 3, 1965, pp. 232–246.

intelligentsia. By 1928 no religious school existed in the Soviet Union. The law of April 8, 1929 stated that any religious prayer, any financial aid to religious organizations, any use of buildings for religious purposes—were punishable by the criminal law of the Soviet Union. Other Muslim republics—Uzbek, Tadzhik, Turkmen, Kazakh—followed the Russian example by decreeing that anyone who did not comply with the new law of 1929 would be punished with a minimum of three years imprisonment to the maximum measure of the socialist defense—"death by shooting."

In the meantime the party leaders "guaranteed" religious freedom as long as the Muslims obeyed the general Soviet laws. There was complete contradiction between the Soviet laws and their speeches; nevertheless the "freedom" of religion was to go on. Kirov, for example, declared that as long as the Muslims kept the portrait of Lenin on the walls of their courts instead of the portrait of Nicholas II, the party would not object.

It soon became evident that the Soviet regime intended to liquidate all religions in its territory. By 1928-29 the Bolsheviks promised the people that by the end of the second five-year plan religion in the U.S.S.R. would be exterminated. All clergy were liquidated or sent to Siberia where they had no influence or opportunity to continue religious duties.

During World War II the communists ceased to persecute religion, but right after the war they strongly attacked the Catholic Church, especially the Ukrainian Uniate Catholic Church. They demanded complete surrender to the Moscovite Patriarchate. The Church was labeled as the servant of bourgeois nationalism and the Vatican was called a cradle of fascism.

Under the pressure of the Western powers, especially the United States and England, freedom of religion was again promised by new Soviet laws. Before long, however, as soon as the promises were forgotten, the communists again closed churches and theological seminaries, and strictly prohibited any publication of religious literature. In 1965 the Moscow court tried a group of people for "illegal activities" because they secretly printed the Holy Bible and other religious books.

Soviet libraries keep a special catalog of the names of children and adults who are associated with any kind of religious organization.[4]

---

[4] *Sotsialisticheskaia kul'tura,* September 12, 1964. See also Pravda, August 13, 1964; N. A. Smirnov, *Ocherki istorii izucheniia Islama v SSSR* (Moscow: AN SSSR, 1954), p. 141; Walter Kolarz, *Islam and Communism in the Soviet Union, 1917–1960* (Karachi Dacca: Pakistan Committee Congress for Cultural Freedom, 1960), p. 15; Boleslaw Szczezniak, *The Russian Revolution and Religion: A Collection of Documents Concerning the Suppression of Religion by Communists, 1917–1925* (Notre Dame: University of Notre Dame Press, 1959), p. 113.

THE SCOPE OF ANTI-RELIGIOUS PROPAGANDA

The scope of anti-religious propaganda in the U.S.S.R. is about equal to the scope of the Soviet propaganda abroad which is designed to praise the "peaceful coexistence" of the Soviet government and the dictatorship of the Kremlin. In the field of anti-religious propaganda everybody participates and everybody participates "voluntarily." The propaganda organs include the communist party, the press, the Soviet youth, the Soviet physicians, scientists, and above all, the Soviet educators.

The methods used depend on the religion and on the area in which it operates. In general the following method was used in restricting Christianity:

a. depriving the church of property and material possessions that could be used for maintaining the church;

b. reducing priests to a socially inferior status; prohibiting participation in elections or holding governmental positions for persons associated with church administration;

c. destroying religious influence upon children by strong propaganda and the prohibition of religious teaching;

d. physical liquidation of bishops and priests—thus making it impossible for the Orthodox and Catholics to perform their religious duties on a large scale.

The methods used among the Muslims varied according to their cultural level. In many cases the Muslim women were trained and organized to carry out the job, or young children already indoctrinated in schools began to work for the communists.

Of course there were many Muslims who entirely opposed the anti-religious propaganda and asked the atheist lecturer such questions as: "who created you if not God?" or "how can one live without religion?"

The Russians knew that they would not be successful in Central Asia if they did not include the natives in their anti-religious propaganda. They selected one man, Sultan Galiev, who was considered by many Muslims as the foremost leader of the Islamic people and an excellent social reformer. He wrote a special book on how to fight Islam and elaborated methods for doing so. He concentrated on three points: use of Muslims themselves to carry out the anti-religious propaganda; a guarantee from the Russian communists that they had no connections with former missionary groups; the use of propaganda only and not force and violence.

Galiev's plans were carried out even though the party arrested him in 1923. He succeeded to the extent that on May 23, 1923, the President of

Central Administration of Religious Affairs of Muslims in European Russia, Riasidin Rakhertdinov, issued a proclamation to all Muslims in the world, stating, among other things:[5]

> At present our co-religious in India and Arabia are oppressed by England and many of them are suffering in prisons. . . . The Muslims of the whole world must not forget this and must thank the Soviet Government. We, the Muslims of Russia, consider the Soviet Government the protector of the oppressed and declare to the 400 million Muslims of the world the necessity of full support of the Soviet regime.

Further, the resolution called to the attention of the Muslim peoples the fact that it considered the administration of religious affairs by the Soviet government correct because the Soviet government had always shown care for the needy Muslim people.

In 1931, the party dedicated a special section of its schedule to fight religion. Yaroslavski, a Soviet specialist in anti-religious propaganda, wrote a whole series of works on the subject. Leninism, according to Soviet specialists, was the fight against any religion, and the final goal was atheism.

The Soviet leaders adjusted their propaganda to the traditional behavior of ethnic groups or nationalities. Some people, even members of the communist party, put attendance at church before attendance at party meetings. There were also some who at first believed the sincerity of Soviet laws and even compared important religious writings to the Communist Manifesto. On the other hand, the majority of the people were opposed to cooperating with communists in the field of atheistic propaganda.

The Press. The Soviet press does not generally serve the public but the party. It is the duty of the press to inform citizens in such ways as Soviet leaders dictate. The daily newspapers are obligated to print atheistic propaganda and all scientific journals have been ordered to fight religious "intoxications."

There are journals established by the communists for the sole purpose for fighting religious beliefs among Soviet citizens. These journals, where possible, are printed in vernacular languages and their circulation is not necessarily based on subscriptions but rather on "donations." They are distributed in all parts of the Soviet Union. There are also journals meant for only certain areas, such as *Novyi vostok* (The New East), *Koloniial'nyi vostok* (The Colonial East), *Fen-em-din* (Science and Religion in Tatar Language), *Khudosizlar* (Atheist in Uzbek language), *Zhisn' natsional'-nostei* (The Life of Nationalities), and many others.

---

[5] Szczezniak, *op. cit.,* p. 65; Timachev, *op. cit.,* p. 24.

The duty of the Soviet press is also to educate people in the atheistic world outlook and to participate in seminars sponsored by educational institutions. The press also serves as the "watch-dog" for those who break the Soviet laws. Often one finds that a father broke the law because "on the advice of a priest he decided to baptize his child" in a Christian rite.[6]

In 1965, a new Ukrainian journal was dedicated to anti-religious propaganda. It was called *"Liudyna i svit"* (The Man and the World), and was assigned the task of explaining the "teaching of religion and science and about the meaning of life." It was also the duty of the journal to investigate the number of saints in the Orthodox Church. In January, 1965, the journal stated that the Orthodox Church had over 500 saints of which 13 per cent were kings and princes; 2.8% aristocrats; 45.1% bishops; 32.7% monks; only 0.3% peasants and 6.1% unknown.

Among the Muslim population Soviet propaganda stresses the weak points of Muslim traditions, namely the inferiority of Muslim women in the social and administrative system before the Bolshevik Revolution. The press pictures women participating in elections or women judges, or women in other important positions. It illustrates how the Muslim women, for instance, are engaged in pig breeding (prohibited by the Koran) and how the Tatar women have conquered Allah, the Prophet, the mullas and the kulaks.[7]

The Youth. Although official Soviet sources state that there is no religious survival among Soviet youth, the same leaders frequently underline the fact that one must fight the religious survival that exists among the youth. Khrushchev called upon Soviet society to help the party fight religion because "studies of laws of nature should have no room for God," and because Soviet children must be educated in the principles of the October Revolution.

The question arises: if there is no religious survival among the Soviet youth, why fight and against whom? Religious survival can be illustrated from the Soviet press, e.g., a literary journal, *Zvezda* (The Star), points out that in Soviet life more and more of these problems arise "... the problem of the spiritual life, which nowadays occupies a great significance." Similarly, the article "Let It not be Painful and Harmful" written by V. Bavina, discusses a problem having to do with a quite important and difficult situation, even in the Soviet society, such as the matter of life and death.

---

[6] *Trud*, August 4, 1964; Smirnov, *op. cit.*, pp. 150–161.

[7] Ili Kantemir, "The Muslims," in *Religion in the USSR* (Munich: Institute for the Study of the USSR, 1960), No. 59, July 1960, pp. 143–150; Radianska Ukraina, February 27, 1964.

It is very important that the teacher be aware of parents' views toward religion and their effect on a particular child. The teacher should emphasize to youngsters that belief in God is not compatible with a strong body and care for one's health.[8]

Soviet propaganda has no limits in its attacks against religion. It is active in all parts of the Soviet Union and in all denominations. The communists issue pamphlets and other illustrated literature picturing the "horrible time of the past" when people were affected by religious superstitions and awaited miracles instead of searching for answers in the sciences. The atheistic agitators in Central Asia are criticized by the Russian communists for insufficient efforts among the Muslims since "the representatives of Muslim intelligentsia consider it their duty to keep up with national traditions."

It is logical to assume that only a small percentage of Soviet youth is religiously oriented and the government does much to insure atheistic education of the young generation. Literature, the press, the theaters—all media of communication—participate in this effort. Russian communists use such greetings as "there is no God!," or poetry designed to belittle religion:

> Doloi, doloi monakhov, ravvinov i popov!
> My na nebo zalezem, razgonim vsekh bogov!

An English translation would be as follows:

> Down, down with the monks, the rabbis and the priests,
> We shall climb into heaven and disperse all the gods,

It is hard to determine the success of such propaganda, but it may be supposed that any extreme attitude creates a reaction. We find this in Soviet society where the young generation disagrees with much propaganda, not necessarily because they are religious, but because of the exaggerated position taken by the party in regard to the dangers of religion. For example, the *Komsomolaskaia pravda* printed a letter of a certain Leonid who stated that "all around me, people say one thing and do another."

The Scientists and Professional Workers. Frequently the party accuses Soviet scientists of inactivity in the anti-religious struggle. Even doctors are required to participate in the anti-religious struggle if only for the reason that most of the people see physicians frequently. Doctors should explain religious hazards to patients.

---

[8] Soviet Education, December 1960, vol. III, No. 2, pp. 2–6. See also *Zvezda*, June 1961, pp. 196–204.

Soviet engineers and professors of higher educational institutions are by all means obligated to lecture in such a way that one can see a direct disproportion between science and religion. Although from time to time one may mention that there might be some ethical principles found "in some parts of the Bible," basically one should be guided by the party's decisions and recommendations.

Soviet artists are encouraged to find artistic plots, ideas, and inspirations among the experiences gained by anti-religious propagandists, and they are encouraged to attend meetings and gatherings of the anti-religious "scientists."

More recently the journal *Nauka i religiia* (Science and Religion) suggested that Soviet scientists should work together in every situation; but most important, they should write a basic reference source of anti-religious propaganda to be entitled "The Encyclopedia of Atheism." As a matter of fact such an "encyclopedia" already existed on the subject of Islam. Five special theories dedicated to the elimination of Islam were created by the Soviet orientalists. The first, elaborated by M. A. Reisner, endeavored to prove that Islam was only the ideology of commercial capitalism, and that its original strength was developed in Mecca during the bourgeois commercial development. The second, elaborated by N. A. Roshlov, tried to prove that Mohammedanism was a movement that caused the overthrow of the feudal systems. The third theory, propagated by N. L. Tomar, indicated that the reason for the birth of Islam was the poverty of the population in Khidzhar. N. A. Morozov went even further, claiming that such personalities as Mohammed and the first Caliph were mystical (*mificheskie*) individuals. The final theory, elaborated by S. P. Tolstov, maintained that the cause of Islam and its spread among Arabs and other nations was the class structure of Arabic tribes. This class structure, according to Tolstov, was feudal and slave-oriented; therefore, Islam was the result of socioeconomic events.

Such literary works, according to Smirnov, tremendously helped the Muslim people in their struggle to overthrow "religious slavery." Any religion, in terms of Soviet interpretations, was the product of economic development and it was always in service for bourgeois dominated classes.[9]

Propaganda and Education. School is the most important center of Communist propaganda either for training future propagandists or for supervising activities of teachers.

---

[9] *Nauka i religiia*, No. 12, 1966, pp. 40–41; see also Smirnov, *op. cit.*, p. 236. *Sovetskoe zdravokhranenie*, No. 8, 1966; *Komsomol'skaia pravda*, October 19, 1965; *Leningradskaia pravda*, June 19, 1965.

Almost every party congress has dedicated time to the issuance of decrees or resolutions concerning anti-religious education. They also made practical "recommendations" on patterns of education and of propaganda. Teachers were required to do anti-religious work not only in classrooms but also on every occasion they deemed practical or necessary. The teachers especially had to make sure that every student was in school during religious holy days.

In 1958, a special program was initiated by the party for training active propagandists of scientific atheism. Some points of this program are as follows:

a. The curriculum must include an explanation of the philosophical nature of atheism from the beginning to the present, utilizing the best instructors from the departments of philosophy, history and sciences.

b. The lecture plan must include a historical presentation of important individuals in the field of materialistic philosophy. Men like Wan Chun, Xenophones, Heraclitus, Democritus, Epicurus, Holbach, and Marx (and other Marxists) must be systematically analyzed and presented to students. A special text is used for the teaching of Christianity, "*The Origin of Christianity and its Nature.*"

c. The economic significance of religious problems must be underlined with the lecturer concentrating on major social and economic revolutions and their causes, such as the English bourgeois revolution, the French revolution, and the Russian revolution. The present day economic structure of the Christian parties of Germany, Italy, and France is discussed.

d. The scientific approach must be used, i.e., the subject must be well documented, analyzed and proven correct in all its details. Examples should be taken from Lenin's legal decisions, such as the law, "On the Separation of the Church from the State and of the School from the Church."

e. The instructors must use a literary approach to atheistic problems, i.e., the works of important literary people must be analyzed and discussed. These works include Diderot, Voltaire, Radishchev, Lomonosov, Chekhov, Maiakovski, and other atheistic writers.

f. Economic geography must be included in a study plan, primarily the descriptions of certain cities—Jerusalem, Mecca, Medina, Benares, Lhasa and other religious centers.

g. Finally, atheistic lectures should include discussions of certain topics with all participants of a group. The teacher should stimulate students to ask questions about key ideas, e.g., Lenin and his ideas about private property, Lenin's evaluation of the philosophy of Hegel, Lenin and the October Revolution, etc.

Students are also required to attend special seminars called atheistic evenings where the problem of religion is discussed in relation to physics or other sciences. These seminars, arranged to fit several levels of education, must be carried out in a proper methodological way so that the relationship between physics and religion may be explained by the physicists, and history and religion by the historian. A book published in 1965 by a group of instructors from the Pedagogical Institute in Moscow under the title *Questions of Scientific Atheism and Atheistic Education,* supposedly helps fight "underground literature such as the Bible."

In Ukraine alone, the members of the atheistic organization *Znannia* (Knowledge) gave over 222,000 lectures in 1963 in every school and among all the strata of the population. At present, an "All-Ukraine Evening University of Atheism" is being established to train highly qualified atheistic lecturers.

Those who do not take anti-religious instructions seriously, or who believe in God, are expelled from higher educational institutions. The journal *Molodoi kommunist* reported that three students, V. Khazanov, V. Krutikov, and V. Chigan, asked the local priest in Moscow to accept them as members of the Catholic Church because they wanted to be priests. The journal accused them of "trading their country, their honor, and their future for Catholicism." At the same time the Pedagogical Institute expelled them from school. Many similar examples can be cited from the Soviet press regarding the fate of students and other people who accept Christianity.

THE FATE OF INDIVIDUAL RELIGIONS

The Greek Orthodox Church. Before the Bolshevik Revolution, well over 90 per cent of Russians belonged to the Orthodox Church. After 1917 constant pressure was put on the church, which resulted in its liquidation.

After World War II, when the Russian Orthodox Church was in a way "restored," the party required that its administration be of a totalitarian character, i.e., all religious matters must be controlled by the Patriarchate of Moscow. Thus, the Russian Patriarch in Moscow was also the head of all Orthodox Churches of the Union.

S. Krushel graphically describes the number of churches liquidated in

Moscow, Ukraine, Siberia and other parts of the Union. The Ukrainian Orthodox Church is strictly subordinated to Moscow, and the so-called "exerchate in Ukraine" is only a fiction, and it is very doubtful whether it has anything to do with religion.

Since the Orthodox bishops and clergy were liquidated before World War II, and all theological seminaries were dissolved, it was not difficult for the communists to "reestablish" the church in 1945. We know that in the early 1920s, 34 bishops and 1223 priests in Ukraine alone were brutally murdered. In all parts of the Soviet empire, a total of 217 bishops and 27,000 priests were liquidated.[10]

Soviet laws limit religious believers in the pursuit of equal economic opportunities. The laws introduced in 1917 and 1925 still bind all citizens in regard to religious freedom, e.g., the constitution of the Russian republic (1925), section 69, prohibits the right of priests and religious servants of any religion to vote or to be elected to public office. All those who belong to any religion must be registered at the local police station.

The Catholic Church. As mentioned before, the Russians as of 1917 were predominantly Orthodox, but they represented only 43 per cent of the total population. If the Eastern Ukrainian Orthodox Church is included, the Orthodox Church represented about 66 per cent of the total population, while the Western Ukraine and Poland were over 90 per cent Catholic. There were over eleven million Roman Catholics in Russia as of 1897, and about two million Catholics of Byzantine rites who were completely ignored by the Imperial census and were listed as Orthodox. The Mohylev diocese (Ukraine) alone had over one million Uniates (Catholics) in 1917.

After World War II, more than four million Ukrainian Catholics were annexed to the Soviet Union. The data of 1939 and 1953 show the following for the Ukrainian Catholic Church:

---

[10] It is hard to determine the number of believers in the Soviet Union because Soviet data do not list people according to their religious denominations. It is also true that the people are afraid to register as believers because of the persecutions by the government. In Georgia, for instance, the bishop Katolikos was killed after the war simply for having a conference with the Bishop of Salisbury. See the *Voice of Georgia*, No. 1, June 1953, pp. 12–14; R. F. McCullaugh, *The Bolshevic Persecution of Christianity* (New York: Dutton Press, 1924), pp. 285–294; James Zatko, "The Catholic Church and Russian Statistics," in the *Polish Review*, vol. VI, No. 1, 1960, pp. 35–52; *Radianska osvita*, June 5, 1965; *Radianska Ukraina*, May 10, 1964; *Radianska Ukraina*, January 27, 1965; *Molodoi kommunist*, January 31, 1965; *Nauka i religiia*, April 12, 1965; Soviet Education, vol. 11, No. 5, 1959, pp. 48 ff.

In 1939 there were:	*Status of Church in 1953*
Five Diocese	Liquidated
Two Territories of Apostolic Administration	Liquidated
Ten Bishops	All liquidated
2950 Secular Clergy	50% of them imprisoned; 20% hidden; 13% forced into schism.
520 Regular Clergy	All imprisoned
4,283,000 Faithful	Many imprisoned, no exact data available.

The Ukrainian Catholic authorities in Rome gave the following data on the fate of the Ukrainian Catholic Bishops: Bishop Khomyshyn died in prison in 1946; Bishops Latishevskyi, Chrnytskyi, Kotsilovskyi and Lakota died in prison in 1945; Bishop Romzsa was murdered in 1948 and others were deported to Siberia.

The Catholic Church—all rites—from 1917 until 1959 within the borders of the Soviet Union and countries occupied by the Russians since 1917, has suffered the following losses: 55 bishops, 12,500 priests and monks have been killed; 199 bishops, 15,700 priests and about 10 million Catholics were either deported to Siberia or to labor camps elsewhere in the Soviet Union.[11] The Catholic church is officially prohibited inside the Soviet Union, with the exception of diplomatic missions; and the Catholic faithful are once more forced to turn to the catacombs for religious services.

Other Christian Churches. Protestants in Russian RSFR were not numerically significant, so not as much resistance was noted. After World War II, the Soviets occupied the Baltic states and a part of Finland, both of which areas had a considerable Protestant population. There are well over a million Protestants in these areas, but unfortunately the lack of reliable data precludes further treatment of this topic, and the Baltic area would in itself require a separate study. Some sources indicate that various Protestant communities do exist within the U.S.S.R., among which are Baptists, Lutherans and Reformed (Trans-Carpathian Ukrainian). The Russian *dukhobory* (similar to the American Quakers who are opposed to

[11] *Shliakh (The Way)*, February 16, 1964 (Philadelphia: *Ukrainian Catholic Daily*). J. Buchko, Ti. Bishop of Cadi (ed.), *First Victims of Communism* (Rome: OSMB Press, 1953), pp. 83–85.

bearing arms) were completely liquidated in the 1920s, even those who came from Canada as a result of Russian propaganda.

The attitude of the communists toward Christians is reflected in an article in the communist Journal of October 9, 1964 which accused Christians of being drunkards, traitors and a "kind of people who are engaged in immoral ways of life."

Islam. Since Islam is closely related to civil life, as well as to the religious behavior of Muslims, it is hard to determine on what grounds many millions of Muslims have perished during the Soviet regime. We know that in the early 1920s more than three million Central Asian Muslims were liquidated (see chapter one), but it is hard to determine the percentage liquidated for religious reasons.

The "peaceful" liquidation of the Muslim religion and the Muslim way of life continued from the very beginning of Bolshevik rule. In 1928, for example, in Crimea alone over 14,000 mosques were closed; in Bukhara not one mosque was left by 1928 and by 1932, 2,700 mullas (religious clergy) had been liquidated.

In 1937 the communist party of Russia began to accuse the native leaders of Uzbekistan, Tadzhikistan, and Turkmenia of associating with religious Muslim leaders abroad as well as collaborating with foreign espionage. All were removed from office including some high-ranking cabinet members.

In other Muslim districts of the Soviet Union the same policy of liquidation is practiced. In the Northern Caucasus, for instance, in 1921 there were 10,000 religious clergy and by 1941 only 150 were left; in Idel-Ural there were over 18,000 Muslim religious clergy and only 250 were left in 1941; in 1921 there were 6,000 Metchets in Idel-Ural and only 200 remained in 1941; and of 7,000 religious schools in 1921 none were left by 1941.

At the same time the Russian communists forced the Muslims to equate the writings of the Koran with communist writings, and to deliver extensive propaganda lectures on the problems of religion. In 1961 alone over 570,000 atheistic brochures were published and distributed among Muslims of Uzbekistan and 243 anti-religious centers were in operation.

The Jews. The Soviet Jews have problems with obtaining religious books. The Soviets say that Jews can use the Christian Bible (the Old Testament) and there is no need for a special Jewish edition. Jews do not agree. Furthermore, no Jewish rabbi may obtain a visa to travel abroad.

Russians impose their way of life upon the Jews and forbid the young Jews to attend religious services. Most Russian Jews do not admit their Jewish background for fear of being persecuted. Synagogue attendance shows only the old people at Jewish religious services. In the city of Kishiney which has a Jewish population of about 30,000, only between 100 and 150 are practicing Jews. Those who admit their religion, as in the case of the composer David Hershfeld, are accused of anti-Soviet activities.[12]

An example of Soviet policy toward religion and nationality is seen in Soviet Uzbekistan where only fifty per cent of the Jewish residents admit a knowledge of Yiddish and adherence to Judaism.

Buddhism. The Buddhists in the Soviet Union are numerically very small. However, their fate was like that of the Orthodox and Catholics. There were only three Buddhist districts: Buriatiia, Tuva and Kalmykiia, and these were wiped out completely. According to the Soviet journal *Nauka i religiia* there were 36 Buddhist monasteries with 16,000 lamas before the Revolution. In Tuva there were 22 monasteries and 4,000 lamas. By 1960 only three monasteries are reported to exist and no more than 30 lamas. In Kalykiia none of the religious monasteries or lamas were left by 1960.

Hinduism. Hindus are insignificant in number in the Soviet Union. Soviet sources do not even include the Hindu religion as a target of the anti-religious campaign. However, they are opposed to Hinduism as they are to any religion simply because it is contrary to the philosophy of Marxism-Leninism. Before Indian independence, Ghandi was accused by Soviet sources of being the stooge of English imperialism and the enemy of the Indian people.

IS RELIGION DEAD?

Regardless of the fact that millions of believers have disappeared during the communist regime, it would be incorrect to say that religious life under communism does not exist. It is true that the majority of the present Soviet citizens are educated in such a way that they do not feel any

---

[12] *Komsomol'skaia pravda,* March 29, 1964; *Oktiabr,* No. 9, 1964, pp. 10 ff.; see also Institute of Jewish Affairs, *The Institute Annual,* 1956, Religious Life in the Soviet Union, pp. 360–378; *Vestnik Instituta po izuchniu SSSR,* No. 3, 1954, pp. 42–55.

connections with any religion, but the fact is that for some people religion lives in the cult of the saints, in the observance of holy days, in national traditions, and in many other ways.

According to the Soviet press, almost every social group contains some people who believe in God. *Partiinaia zhizn'*, for example, bitterly complains that even some communists do not understand the nature of the anti-religious propaganda and they often break the laws by going to church or by observing the holy days or keeping ikons in their homes. Some Soviet intelligentsia maintain that sciences are meant for the brain and the Bible for the human heart.

The Soviet journal, *Sovetskaia Moldavia* (Soviet Moldavia) also complained that the party cannot handle the problem of religion. When a reporter was asked to list the number of believers, he listed most of the people as some kind of believers although their belief might have been associated with reaction to Soviet propaganda. Many youth are dissatisfied with propaganda which aims to belittle everyone and everything not Soviet. Many students maintain that people like Tolstoi, Pushkin, Radishchev, and Dostoevski believed in God, but at the same time they were good Russians and good revolutionists.

The Leningrad *Pravda* published a letter of a certain Andreieva who accused the propaganda agency of harm with its attitude toward religion. She asked the question: What is this all for? Why spend so much effort on anti-religious propaganda when only a few people among the younger generation attend church and the future Soviet generation will not attend at all? Even if they do attend, there is no evil done because church attendance does not require money. The propaganda agency should concentrate its efforts on attendance at taverns. These are places where one needs money to go and to stay. The tavern, not the church, is the carrier of infections. Further, the anti-religious agitators are defined as being naïve if they think that they can extinguish in fifty years all the ideas and beliefs that mankind has held sacred for two thousand years.[13]

In conclusion, we may cite the teaching of Jesus Christ who said to Peter: "You are Peter and upon this rock I will build my church and the gates of hell shall not prevail against it."

---

[13] *Izvestiia,* March 24, 1964. But not only the *Izvestiia,* the whole Soviet press is designed to fight religion. See for example, *Partiinaia zhizn',* November 1, 1964; *Nauka i religiia,* No. 2, 1967; *Sovetskaia Moldaviia,* July 11, 1964; *Sovetskaia Rossiia,* May 12, 1964; *Komsomol'skaia zhizn',* No. 15, 1963; *Leningradskaia pravda,* March 11, 1964; *Komsomol'skaia pravda,* January 16, 1964; *Radianska Ukraina,* February 12, 1965. See also Walter Kolarz, "Religions of the East," in *Survey,* No. 43, August 1962, pp. 130–138; *Pravda vostoka,* July 31, 1960, p. 6.

Additional References

Julius Hecker, *Religion and Communism* (New York: Wiley and Sons, 1934), especially pages 225 ff; *Studies on the Soviet Union* (Munich: Institute for the Study of the USSR), vol. 13, No. 2, 1966, pp. 26–30; *Nauka i religiia*, No. 7, 1965, pp. 10 ff; *Komsomol'skaia pravda*, May 29, 1966; S. Timashev, *Religion in Soviet Russia* (New York: Sheed and Ward Press, 1942); E. S. Bates, *Soviet Asia: Progress and Problems* (London: Jonathan Cape, 1942); *Izvestiia*, March 31, 1964; Vason-Girei, "Sovetskii Soiuz i Islam," in *Vestnik Instituta* (Munich), No. 3, 1954, pp. 42 ff.; *Sotsialisticheskaia kul'tura*, September 12, 1964; N. Irkolin, "Religioznoe nastroenie sredi sovetskoi molodezhi," *Vestnik Instituta* (Munich), No. 6, 1954, pp. 124–132; *Osteuropa*, Heft 6, December 1954, pp. 412–421; James Zatko, *Descent into Darkness, The Destruction of the Roman Catholic Church in Russia, 1917–1923* (Notre Dame: University of Notre Dame Press, 1965), pp. 172 ff.; *Osteuropa*, Heft 3, June 1955, pp. 222–227; *Sovetskaia Latviia*, March 19, 1964; *Izvestiia*, June 19, 1963.

Chapter 13

WOMEN AND COMMUNISM

From the very beginning of our history men have philosophized about the position of women in society. The ancient Greek philosophers maintained that three things are dangerous for man: water, fire and women. But even before Greek times social philosophy concerning the status of women was anything but favorable. The Chinese considered a woman without ability a normal thing; Hindus considered infidelity, violence, deceit, and envy as the natural faults of woman. The Romans regarded most women as housekeepers who engaged in physical work, except those of wealth who did not work but were kept in seclusion.

With the rise of the industrial revolution more emphasis was given to the education of girls and to woman's role in society in general. French social reformer and philosopher Condorcet demanded equal rights for women and the English social reformer, Mary Wollstonecraft, wrote "A Vindication of the Rights of Women" (1792) protesting the existing status of women in English society at that time. However, it was not until the late 19th century that women were given the right of suffrage and in some European countries not until the beginning of the 20th century.[1]

---

[1] *Encyclopaedia Britannica* (1949 ed.), vol. 23, p. 704.

THEORETICAL FOUNDATIONS

Engels' "The Origin of the Family, Private Property and the State" is the most important work written by any communist social philosopher on woman's role in society. In it, Engels theorized that women were equal in the era of primitive communism: they partook of all that was beautiful—flowers, gardens, et cetera—while men hunted for food. When they got together in this primitive stage, they treated each other as equals. But—said Engels—women began to lose their freedom and equality with the initiation of private property. During the stage of feudalism, woman was treated as a slave, the upkeeper of the family who did all the heavy work while men were fighting and struggling for private property. Thus, man became the master and "woman was his housekeeper and the slave."

Another cause of inequality is to be found in the Greek and Roman social philosophy which ruined the *lus matris* in favor of the *ius patris* (father as the head of the family). Woman became more and more dependent upon economic support from man and as a result was lowered to the position of slave or merely served the purpose of recreation for man.

During the period of industrialization, especially in England, the position of woman was further belittled because she was engaged in twofold work: in industry and at home. Engels criticized the English system of employing women in industry as entirely contrary to the communist understanding of labor. Engels supported his thesis with many examples referring to the condition of women in English factories and the fate of children improperly cared for because of women's inability to stay at home with their children. In one district of Manchester county 225 children died tragically because their mothers were working in industrial enterprises.

Women were further exploited in another way. Engels pointed out the common practice in 19th century England of arranging marriage contracts not on the basis of agreement of two young people but on the basis of an agreement between their parents. Such marriages often resulted in misery and prostitution, affecting not only the immediate family, but the whole community as well.

In addition to Engels and Marx, Robert Owen spoke about conditions of women in England. He felt that girls should be taught in school to read well and to understand what they read; to write a good legible hand; and to comprehend and use with facility the fundamental rules of arithmetic. The girls should also be taught to cut, sew, and make up useful family garments, and after a sufficient knowledge of these, they should learn to prepare wholesome food in an economical manner and to keep a house neat and well arranged.[2]

In Russia, neither Marx nor Owen was taken as guides for the emancipation of Soviet women. In Russia the needs of the revolution stimulated the Bolsheviks to introduce new reforms. Women were mobilized to do all kinds of work for the production of war materials needed for the Red Army. Lenin praised this accomplishment in 1920 when he said that in Petrograd, Moscow, and other towns the women workers acted splendidly during the revolution, and without them there would not have been victory.[3]

Lenin and other Bolsheviks actually sought utilization of women in the national economy. Since the country needed a huge army of workers, women worked in various agricultural centers, in the food industry and in cafeterias serving food to the Red Army. It was this kind of emancipation to which Lenin called women in order to break the routine of "the deadening atmosphere of household and kitchen."

In reality the position of Soviet women in the early period of the regime was anything but fortunate. There were frequent abuses, rapes, and exploitations of women, especially those who held property before the revolution. Abortion was legalized; the family as a unit was actually broken, and young and old alike followed the idea that sex is as simple as drinking a glass of water. It came to the point that party officials had to interfere—not because of their moral beliefs but because it was too expensive for the government to support illegitimate children and to cure various venereal diseases. Lenin said that such intervention had nothing in common with the free love which the Bolsheviks accepted.

Marx and Engels as usual emphasized the idea that the causes of the unjust position of women could be found in the economic structure of society. Marx insisted that women should be completely emancipated, receive "equal pay for equal work," and engage in state administration. He was in favor of eliminating any special privileges for men before the law.

Lenin approached the problem of emancipation in terms of equal rights and equal obligations, rather than in terms of equal pay for equal work.

---

[2] Robert Owen, *The New View of Society and Other Writings* (London: J. M. Dent and Sons, Ltd., 1949), p. 48. See also Society for Cultural Relations with the USSR, *Women and Communism* (London: Lawrence and Wishart, 1951), pp. 9–37.

[3] V. I. Lenin, *Sochineniia,* vol. 32, pp. 138–140; *Women and Communism,* pp. 27–29, 89–90.

Because women's role in the Soviet society was deemed important, Lenin applied a utilitarian method for the purpose of accomplishing emancipation principles. His policy was to employ women in the political system, stating that it was impossible to drive the masses into politics without including women.

Lenin was not as much concerned about the theoretical questions of emancipation as about the practical application of these theories. He saw women as important agents who would help the Soviet regime in educating the new Soviet man. For example, in 1919 he stated that women should not only work in factories, but should also carry out active propaganda in society. Lenin further theorized that the only way to improve women's conditions was to give them experience in social life, and that "the proletariat cannot achieve complete freedom, unless it achieves complete freedom for women."

There were also many other factors which determined the scope of reform concerning women. Russian women had an opportunity to participate in the Russian cultural structure, but the women of Central Asia were deprived of such opportunities before the Bolshevik Revolution. Lenin met radical opposition, even from the Muslim communists, who insisted on maintaining their Islamic way of life and argued that the political state of affairs should not interfere in religious beliefs. Therefore, Lenin changed his policies in regard to Muslims; they were allowed to continue their traditional way of life, and to treat the women as they did before the revolution.

Stalin, like Lenin, took advantage of the status of women in pre-revolutionary Russia and used women for promoting his cause. He wrote about the inferior position of women in the bourgeois society and their bright future "under the victory of socialism." Stalin further theorized about the rights of women on the basis of Marxian dialectics and the Marxian understanding of society. The fate of women throughout history, according to Stalin, depended largely on the development of society (according to the communists: primitive communism, slavery, feudalism, capitalism, socialism, and communism) and the economic division of labor. In practice, however, Stalin was interested in the army of workers that the women represented in the Soviet reconstruction of society and culture.

WOMEN AND THE PROPAGANDA APPARATUS

The rights of women are one thing but their obligations toward Soviet society are another. The position of Russian women before the Bolshevik Revolution was not much different from that of other European women.

In Russia, as elsewhere, the role of the woman was first to educate the children and to care for the family. The role of man was to work for the "daily bread and butter." Many Europeans still believe that a wife should not have an outside job, that families should manage on the husband's salary. Therefore, it was not the law that regulated the behavior of women, but the accepted norms of society. In 19th century Austria and Poland, those men whose wives worked were regarded by the rest of the society as "good for nothing" men since they were apparently not able to support their families. The duty of a woman was to be religious, tender, and nice. If she wanted to go to a university she could do so. But heavy physical work was regarded in many European countries as an exploitation of woman, an inhuman practice that a civilized family should avoid.

Russian, Ukrainian, Latvian and other women in the European parts of the Soviet Union bitterly protested the emancipation practices of the Soviet government. They did not regard as progress the government requesting school attendance but prohibiting church attendance. Nor did they see as a progressive reform the Soviet demand that each person works or does not eat.

In order to strengthen the relationship between women and the party, the Bolsheviks began to demand inclusion of women in all economic, political and cultural life. Under the supervision of Russian women, other nationalities began various organizations designed for the "building of communism in one's own country." Special emphasis was given to the organization of women into communist-controlled *zhenotdely* (women's groups) particularly among the non-Russian women. These groups soon increased in number and were drawn into participation in the politico-economic program of the party. *Zhenotdely* work consisted in gathering women into small groups to explain the party's emancipation objectives. Women were offered equal opportunity in all fields of the national economy, in education, in the departments of justice and political organizations.

The prospect was obviously beneficial for the Soviets, especially among Muslim women who for the first time in history were promised positions equal with men. Native women—Uzbek, Tadzhik, Turkmen, Kazakh and other ethnic groups—began to participate in professional organizations, Communist Youth Organizations and were delegates to the communist party conference and congresses.

The Soviet media, especially illustrated journals, pictured native women training for a new life—showing pictures in which the new contrasted with the old system, e.g., an old fashioned spinning wheel and a new Singer-type sewing machine; a woman talking to Kalinin, a top party official; a man working at a hand loom while girls gain experience at the technical school, etc.[4]

Women were pictured in many parts of the Soviet Union as real contributors to the new reforms as well as the real movers in social organizations. Communist propaganda focused on the Muslim nationalities because there are about 30 million Muslims in the U.S.S.R. and from an economic point of view, it was important that the Muslim women be recruited. It is also true that the position of women in Muslim society was below human dignity; they were exploited, sold into marriages, treated as slaves and forbidden to attend higher educational institutions, and any change represented progress.

With the prohibition of religious holidays the Russian Communists introduced a state holiday designed particularly for women, known as the International Women's day. This falls each year on March 8.

Women's Day and Muslim Women. In order to change the traditional habits of life Russian administrators found it most effective to mobilize the native women into the communist propaganda apparatus. By promising women certain privileges and by reducing the rights of Muslim men— state, economy, courts and family life—Muslim women began to participate in Soviet reforms.

Muslim women were called upon to celebrate the solidarity of all women as well as to protest against their own traditions. The first major celebration of the International Women's Day took place in Uzbekistan in 1927, when mass demonstrations were organized. In 1928 a similar event took place in Bukhara where veils were publicly burned, and 100,000 women renounced the veil. It seemed, at first, that such demonstrations would finally put an end to the practices of veiling women and to the *shariat (Koranic laws)*. But after the demonstration, only 5,000 women remained unveiled, the rest being afraid to do so. As a result, fanatical opposition was aroused in some circles of the Muslim population. They considered a woman who dared to throw off her veil no better than a prostitute and punished those who participated. Many of those who organized the demonstration, pioneers of the communist-directed emancipation drive, were either beaten, raped or killed.

The struggle against "The International Women's Day" was carried on throughout the 1920s with similar attacks on those women who participated in the communist campaign and those who denounced the traditional Muslim laws. The Russians then took the situation into their hands

---

[4] *Iangi iul* (In arabic script), No. 10, 1927 *Soviet Union Yearbook* (London: Unwin Press, 1927), p. 497, *Women and Communism*, p. 61.

and punished those who broke the Soviet laws, e.g., in Kaska-Dar'ia province, seven men were shot, 13 exiled, and 60 men were given ten years' imprisonment.

Resistance to the Soviet laws was largely broken by the early 1930s and there was none after World War II. If any resistance was noticed among the Muslim women it was not based on religious principles but on political and economic ones. By the end of the 1940s the newly produced intelligentsia was indoctrinated in new sets of values which had little or nothing in common with the laws of the *shariat* or the Koran.

Women's Day and the European Soviet Women. In the European parts of the U.S.S.R. the Women's Day is nothing other than a strengthening of the "spiritual" powers of the Soviet Union. From its origin to the present, the communist party has directed every single step of the activities on Women's Day. Leaders of the Women's Day organization have always been told exactly what to say in their speeches. The major aims of Russian propaganda are set forth as are the goals of the communists at certain periods of time. Soviet women have been required to emphasize that only the Great October Revolution brought them happiness and that the Russian revolution "gave women complete equality with men in the home, in social and political life and in production." Thus, in this respect, Russian women work in a broader framework of ideas—communist world domination—than do the Muslim women who were once limited to provincial activities.

In almost all publications, one notes the general idea that everything that moves, exists, or develops does so because of the "wise leadership" of the communist party. The party leaders are always pictured as the defendants of the rights of women, children and justice. At special occasions distinguished Soviet women read speeches prepared for them by the party. Current popular Soviet strategy is to extol women's contribution to the advancement of Soviet science, especially the woman astronaut Valentina N. Tereshkova. She spoke at the International Women's Day in 1967 underlining the fact that her success must be attributed to the communist party. She also spoke about the suffering of women under the czarist regime.

Soviet propaganda also emphasizes the solidarity of all communist women. In all journals, regardless of the subject matter, Soviet women are required to attack American imperialists, the enslavement of women by bourgeois society and the "atrocities perpetrated there against innocent women, children and old people." The medal of the Hero of Socialist Labor is given yearly to more than 3,000 women who receive it for their part in building communism.

An international women's gathering convenes periodically in Moscow. In 1967 more than 80 different countries sent their delegates to the International Women's Day, but the Soviets never allow non-communist women to attend and represent non-communist Soviet women.[5]

General Tendencies. The program of Soviet leaders tends to instruct women to do the political job of praising communist accomplishments. Nothing is said about other responsibilities of women, such as the moral education of children, the moral standards of women themselves, responsibilities of a woman to her family, physical looks, fashion, etc. Those who read Russian sources, especially daily newspapers and journals, note that in no other country of the world are words like *freedom, liberty, peace, opportunity,* etc. so frequently used and so misused as in the Soviet Union. It is like a hungry man who does not have food but talks only about food—food that he can only imagine. On the other hand, credit must be given to the Soviets for enabling women to become doctors—over eighty per cent of the physicians in Ukraine are women—and to be participants in the national economy.[6] Forty-four women are members of the Supreme Soviet of the U.S.S.R. and 154 members of the Supreme Soviet of the Ukrainian SSR are women.

The number of women in important political office in Ukraine is disproportionate, however, as is illustrated by the fact that of 176 communist party secretaries who are responsible for district administration, only *four* are women, while over 10,000 women work as official party representatives.

Over 45 per cent of all workers are women and this is not something about which the women are proud and happy, for it means that someone else is assigned to educate and care for their children.

Women in Communist Youth Organization. The task of the woman is not necessarily to take care of her own family but the Soviet family in general. The Communist Youth Organization is a "voluntary" organization to which every school girl must belong in order to participate in group or individual music, theatrical, or other extra-curricular activities. This movement began in 1917 when the Communist Party of Russia de-

---

[5] *Moscow* (Moscow: weekly newspaper designed for non-Soviet people), No. 9, 1967, p. 3; *Moscow,* April 1, 1967; *Moscow,* March 18, 1967. Sources pertaining to the status of Muslim women in the early 1920s are: *Iangi iul,* No. 19, 1928, pp. 18 ff, Hecker, *op. cit.,* p. 226; V. Hale, *Frauen des Osten* (Zurich: 1928), pp. 150–152.

[6] *Robitnicha gazeta,* March 8, 1967.

creed that Soviet youth had to be educated in socialist world-outlooks, to be conscious of the class struggle, to fight chauvinism, etc. A few years later the 15th Party Congress again underlined the importance of political education.

Special methods were elaborated for work among Muslims. The Soviet leaders saw the importance of an organization that could work both within the local schools and also in the community. This organization promised complete freedom to schools and students to organize such movements or not. But regardless of the "freedom" of choice, strict supervision and control were provided by the Central Committee of the party, and special workers were assigned among Muslim women. Membership in the Communist Youth League was reserved to those who accepted communism as their creed, and the party hoped to attract women into the party itself.

During the early 1920s this movement was unpopular and its growth depended on the political developments of the country. The organization of women into communist associations developed with difficulty in many areas, e.g., in 1923 about 23 per cent of the members of the Communist Youth Organization were women, in 1924 only 14 per cent regardless of the fact that the total number of members had increased by 100 per cent.

In February 1924, a special resolution was issued by the Central Committee of the party on the organization of girls into political propaganda units, especially in cities (*agitpropaganda v gorode*). According to this resolution, girls were to establish a proper relationship with working women and Komsomol organizations; further, they were to take advantage of existing clubs for youth, to fight sentimental bourgeois literature, and to conduct political work among working people's families.

Experienced party members, who were also specialists on local affairs, prepared special seminars for the work among girls. Questions on local issues were discussed on levels determined by the girls' educational levels, their family backgrounds, and the general psychology of the younger generation.

Another 1924 decree, designed to increase women's participation in the Komsomol in the Soviet east, stated that special lectures must be prepared for the women, that the largest possible number of women be mobilized for them and that each ethnic group must have its own section in the Komsomol.[7]

---

[7] Otdel rabotnits i dekhkanok TsK KP Uzbekistana, *Buleten' rabory v zhenskikh klubakh Uzbekistana* (Samarkand, 1927), No. 1 and 2, p. 62; *KPSS o komsomole i molodezhi* (Moscow: Izdatel'stvo Molodaia Gvardiia, 1958), pp. 75–153; A. Mal'chikov, *Pervoe desiatiletiie komsomola* (Moscow: Molodaia Gvardiia, 1929) pp. 93, 194.

WOMEN IN THE NATIONAL ECONOMY

The most important duty of women is work in the national economy where Soviet women really are equal in all areas of employment. They work in construction, as carpenters, bricklayers—all sorts of physical labor —an "equality" that American women would not prefer. Of course there are many women employed in areas of non-manual skills. No large statistical columns are needed to show this (the Soviets try to show the increase of women in clerical work) because in any country the women represent a potential power in the field of non-manual work.

Work is often a necessity. Present family or individual living standards continually require more money to maintain, and in Soviet society, the necessities of life have always been minimal. The majority of Soviet women do not wear such luxurious clothes as European women, nor do they worry about current fashions, as do American women.

The proportion of women in the national economy has grown according to the industrial development of the country. For example, in 1940 the women comprised 38 per cent of the total working force of the Soviet Union; in 1959 they represented 47 per cent and in 1965, 49 per cent. When we distribute the women-workers according to their occupational pursuits, the Soviet women represent 46 per cent of the industrial workers; 29 per cent of the construction workers; 25 per cent of the transport industry; 76 per cent of those in the field of health; and 11 per cent in higher education.

The Bolshevik reforms involved many areas of national life, such as drafting women into the state administration and engaging them in party meetings and administrative decisions. Some success was apparent because by 1930, women in the Uzbek National Assembly totalled 3,890 delegates, twelve per cent of the total seats, compared to only forty-nine in 1924.

Coming back to the whole U.S.S.R., the most striking example of the Soviet policies toward women can be seen in medical professions. In 1913, only ten per cent of the 2,800 physicians were women; in 1965, seventy-four per cent of the 396,200 physicians were women.

The number of women who work as scientific workers (this term includes teachers, research workers, scientists and helpers in academic or research institutions) totalled 230,200 (from a total of 612,000) in 1964.

If we consider the total number of scientific workers—612,000—then the distribution is not equal in terms of nationalities. For example, in 1965 the Russians had 404,170 scientific workers, the Ukrainians had 65,094 and the Jews had 50,915. Women represented twenty per cent of the total administrative power of the secondary schools.

Elementary and Secondary Education. In the early period of the communist regime there was not much talk about secondary education for all students, because there were no teachers and furthermore, the war against illiteracy was the most important project. In 1897, literate women in Central Asia were barely 2 per cent of the population, and the average for the whole Russian Empire was barely 12 per cent.[8] In 1926, the rate of literacy in most areas of Central Asia was still low: 14 per cent of the men and 6.5 per cent of the women, an improvement of just over 4 per cent. But during 1926-1939, according to the Soviet sources, the situation had changed: the ratio of literacy jumped to over 61 per cent, a 55 per cent increase during this 13 year period.

In other educational areas, such as technical training and higher education, enrollment of women increased. In 1928, girls constituted about a third of the students in the Technicums, for the whole Soviet Union and by 1932, this increased 45 per cent (see Tables 30 and 31).

The number of girls in the rural schools of Central Asia also equalized by 1939. Distribution of total primary school population in the five major provinces of Turkestan (Tashkent, Samarkand, Fergana, Bukhara, and Khiva) showed that girls represented about 43 per cent of the total school population.

In the whole U.S.S.R. in 1928 women represented 13 per cent of students in engineering institutes; they exceeded men in physical education—52 per cent; and in medical schools, women represented 45 per cent. By 1935 they comprised 38 per cent of all university students in education, and 44 per cent in all fields. (See Figure 17.)

Higher Education. In 1918 the Soviets initiated reforms in higher education, demanding that universities accept students regardless of sex and social origin. In 1925 a similar law was passed by the *Sovnarkom* to the effect that anyone 17 years of age can be admitted to a university.

The percentage of women in higher educational institutions increased in certain areas of specialization. In 1926, for example, women comprised 30 per cent of all students, in 1936 they comprised about 42-45 per cent, and in 1965, 43 per cent.

The percentage of native women increased in all fields. Such areas as Uzbekistan, Turkmenistan, or Kirghiz, areas that never in history offered women any higher educational opportunities, seemingly benefited from the

---

[8] *Narodnoe khoziaistvo,* 1964, pp. 552 and 735; *Narodnoe khoziaistvo,* 1955, p. 552; *Iangi iul,* No. 10, 1928, pp. 2–3; Hecker, *op. cit.,* pp. 225–226; Otdel rabotnits i dekhkanok TsKP UzSSR, *Materiali i programi delegatskogo i kishlaknogo sobraniia* na 1926/27 god (Tashkent: 1927), p. 162.

TABLE 30

Distribution of Population of the Uzbek SSR According to Major Occupations: 1926, 1939

Occupation	1926	1939	
		Total	Per Cent of Women
A. Manual Workers			
Woodworking	4,813	20,806	9
Textile	37,299	28,167	55
Construction	13,764	49,960	2
Agriculture	1,673,762	1,878,652	47
Railroad	6,040	12,931	10
B. Professional Workers			
Agronomists, Zoo Technicians, Veterinarians, Foresters. . .	4,176	8,547	9
Physicians	905	2,852	56
Physicians in Charge of Hospitals or Medical Centers . .	57	487	33
Dentists	155	299	70
Fel'dshers,* Midwives . . .	933	2,371	68
Nurses	558	4,451	95
C. Educational Personnel			
Professors of Higher Education and Directors of Research Centers	332	3,093	28
Teachers	4,841	52,053	50

TABLE 30 (Continued)

Distribution of Population of the Uzbek SSR According to Major Occupations: 1926, 1939

Occupation	1926	1939	
		Total	Per Cent of Women
D. Judicial Personnel (Judges and Prosecutors)	719	1,966	14
E. Others			
Trade and Welfare Workers. . .	29,265	15,640	40
Timekeepers & Accountants . .	7,004	45,104	29

Tsentral'noe Statisticheskoe Upravlenie pri Sovete Ministrov SSSR, *Itogi vsesoiuznoi perepisi naseleniia 1959 goda*, Uzbekskaia SSR (Moscow: Gosstatizdat, 1962), pp. 112–126.

*Fel'dsher are medical workers who do not have a medical degree but whose training exceeds the training of nurses.

TABLE 31

Per Cent of Student Body at Higher Schools of All Types,
Technical Schools ("Technicums") and Workers'
Faculties: By Sex

Educational Institutions	Per Cent of Women				
	1928	1931	1933	1934	1935
I. Universities	28.1	28.3	33.3	36.5	38.0
1. Industrial & building construction . . .	13.4	15.5	19.8	22.4	23.3
2. Agricultural	17.4	25.4	30.6	32.1	31.8
3. Socio-economic . . .	21.1	24.8	34.9	36.0	39.0
4. Pedagogical	48.7	44.4	49.3	50.2	48.4
5. Medical	52.0	58.0	71.4	75.1	71.2
II. Technicums	37.6	38.8	41.7	43.9	44.1
1. Ind. & build. construction . . .	9.5	25.8	28.5	30.1	29.6
2. Agricultural	15.4	31.0	33.3	30.1	31.6
3. Socio-economic . .	36.3	48.2	51.9	54.5	54.6
4. Pedagogical	53.5	51.9	54.1	54.6	55.2
5. Medical	89.3	87.3	85.6	80.7	79.7
III. Workers' Faculties . . .	15.6	24.8	34.0	36.9	36.6

Central Administration of Economic and Social Statistics of the State Planning Commission of the USSR, *Socialist Construction in the USSR. Statistical Abstract* (Moscow: Soyuzorgouchet, 1936), p. 457.

Soviet reforms because by 1958 the number of women in such schools was almost equal to the number of men. The women of Uzbekistan (Russian and non-Russian) as of 1958 comprised 40 per cent of the total student population at higher levels, while Kirghiz women comprised 42 per cent compared to 48.2 per cent of the Russian women. The average for the Soviet Union as of 1958 was 46.7 per cent.

By 1965 women represented 63 per cent of the personnel in secondary special educational establishments. Also they constituted 83 per cent of the teachers who had no more than secondary educational training. (See also Figures 16 and 17 and Tables 30, 31, and 32.)

According to the Soviet sources, the percentage of women in higher schools of learning in various countries, as of 1960, was as follows: 44 per cent in the U.S.S.R.; 23 per cent in China; 36 per cent in the United States (except for the junior colleges and community colleges which Soviet statisticians do not consider to be on the higher educational level), 29 per cent in Italy; and 24 per cent in England. The ratio of students at higher

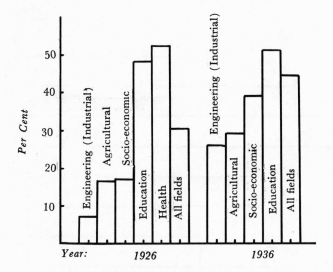

FIGURE 16. Relative proportions of women among regular students in Soviet Higher Education (per cent of women enrolled), 1926, 1936.

Calculated from: Nicholas De Witt, *Education and Professional Employment in the USSR* (Washington, D. C., National Science Foundation Press, 1961), p. 654.

technological institutions is in favor of the Soviets since they represent nearly 30 per cent as compared to about one half of one per cent in the United States.[9] (See Tables 33 and 34.)

IS THE SOVIET WOMAN HAPPY?

The statistical data concerning the percentage of all women directly engaged in the national economy are not always a measure of happiness of the Soviet woman. In the first place, the so-called emancipation drive has placed a tremendous burden upon Soviet women since they now have to perform the same physical work as men. Second, it is hard to prove the accuracy of the Soviet statistical data. Third, a great percentage of Soviet women would not work if they could survive on their husband's salary. Also, from *time to time the Soviet press complains about the

---

[9] *Vysshoe obrazovanie v SSSR v 1960 g*, pp. 254; Konstantinov, *Sistema narodnogo obrazovaniia*, p. 6; *Itogi vsesoiuznoi perepisi 1959 g.*, p. 89; *Narodnoe khoziaistvo*, 1964, p. 690.

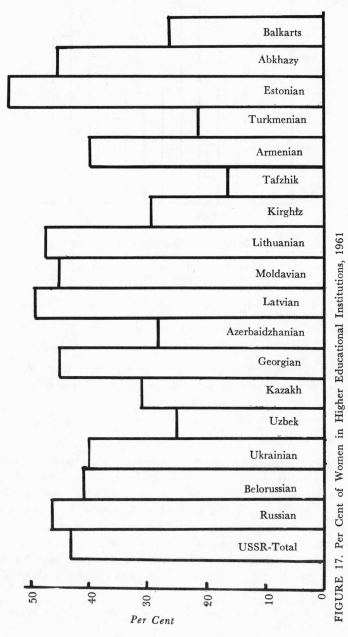

FIGURE 17. Per Cent of Women in Higher Educational Institutions, 1961

Calculated from: Tsentral'noe Statisticheskoe Upravlenie pri Sovete Ministrov SSSR, *Vysshoe obrazovanie v SSSR* (Moscow: Gosstatizdat, 1961), p. 85.

Balkarts

Abkhazy

Estonian

Turkmenian

Armenian

Tafzhik

Kirghłz

Lithuanian

Moldavian

Latvian

Azerbaidzhanian

Georgian

Kazakh

Uzbek

Ukrainian

Belorussian

Russian

USSR-Total

50   40   30   20   10   0

Per Cent

TABLE 32

Per Cent of the Student Body at Higher Schools of All
Types, Technical Schools ("Technicums") and Faculty
Schools: By Nationalities

Nationalities	Rabfaks		Technicums			Universities		
	1928	1933	1928	1933	1935	1929	1933	1935
	Per Cent of Total Number of Students							
	1	2	3	4	5*	6	7	8*
Russian . . .	74.4	66.4	55.6	58.0	55.8	56.1	56.0	54.4
Ukrainian . .	10.9	17.7	11.2	15.8	18.1	14.6	15.5	14.3
W. Russian .	0.9	2.5	2.4	2.5	3.2	2.9	2.7	3.0
Kazakh . . .	0.2	1.1	1.3	0.6	0.8	0.2	0.3	0.4
Uzbek	0.5	0.4	1.9	1.4	0.6	0.3	0.9	0.5
Tatar	0.9	1.7	3.3	1.8	2.0	0.8	1.4	1.3
Jewish	6.5	4.2	8.2	5.8	4.9	13.5	12.2	13.3
Georgian . .	0.9	0.9	3.0	3.5	3.5	2.4	2.7	3.5
Turkish . . .	0.5	0.6	3.0	1.4	1.9	1.1	1.5	1.3
Armenian . .	1.0	1.2	1.9	1.8	2.0	2.0	2.0	2.3
Mordva . . .	0.05	0.2	. . .	0.5	0.4	0.2	0.3	0.3
German . . .	0.3	0.3	0.7	0.7	0.7	0.5	0.5	0.7
Chuvash . . .	0.3	0.2	0.9	0.7	0.8	0.5	0.5	0.5
Tadzhik . . .	0.05	0.1	0.2	0.4	0.3	0.05	0.1	0.1
Bashkir . . .	0.2	0.3	0.5	0.4	0.4	0.1	0.2	0.2
Polish	0.9	0.4	0.8	0.6	0.5	0.6	0.8	0.7
Turkmen . .	0.1	0.1	0.3	0.6	0.3	0.05	0.1	0.1
Other	1.4	1.7	4.8	3.5	3.8	4.1	2.3	3.1

Tsentral'noe Upravlenie Narodno-khoziaistvennogo Ucheta Gosplana SSSR, *Sotsialisticheskoe stroitel'stvo SSSR* (Moscow: Soiuzorguchet, 1935), p. 617.

* Central Administration of Economic and Social Statistics of the State Planning Commission of the USSR, *Socialist Construction in the USSR, Statistical Abstract* (Moscow: Soyuzorguchet, 1936), p. 457.

"liberation" of women from work, which in effect means that there is a shortage of jobs. The government actually cannot provide enough jobs for needy women.

The Soviet press once in a while describes the position of women as it actually exists. For example, a certain Eduard Shim wrote in the *Literary Gazette* about the hardships of women who are employed as cement workers, carpenters, construction workers and the like. The opinion of the paper was that such practices were permissible during the war but why employ them in 1967. Apparently the situation has not changed, since the

TABLE 33

Number of Women Specialists With Higher and Secondary
Special Education: 1964

	Number of Specialists In Thousands	Per Cent of Women
Total Number of Women with Higher Education . . .	2,394,3	53
Of Which:		
Engineers	460,3	31
Agronomists, Zoo Technicians &		
Veterinarians	116,8	41
Economists, Statisticians, Quality		
Control Workers	191,2	63
Physicians *.	354,2	74
Teachers and Librarians	1,173,3	68
Total Number of Women Specialists		
with Secondary Special Education	4,216,2	63
Of Which:		
General Technicians	1,013,9	38
Agronomists, Zoo Technicians,		
Veterinarians' Helpers	195,9	44
Statisticians and Quality Control Workers	530,4	76
Medical Workers (Including Dentists)	1,279,3	92
Teachers and Librarians	1,026,3	83

Tsentral'noe Statisticheskoe Upravlenie pri Sovete Ministrov SSSR, *Narodnoe
Khoziaistvo SSSR v 1964 godu* (Moscow: Gosstatizdat, 1965), p. 566.
* Does not include dentists.

Soviet woman works as before in the most difficult divisions of labor.
When one takes into consideration women's work after a regular factory
job, the Soviet woman, as *Pravda* indicated, works 16 hours a day.

The 1967 Soviet Statistical Bulletin shows over 37.7 million women
employed in the national economy. This is 49 per cent of all workers.
Soviet statistical data did not include the number of women working on
agricultural collective farms. Obviously if complete data were available
women workers in the Soviet economy would outnumber men. The
Literaturnaia gazeta candidly complained "for how long will a woman
work on construction while a certain red-head sells beer in taverns?"

Women in Concentration Camps. The exact number of people in Soviet
concentration camps is hard to determine but at various times the number
has reached twenty million. Khrushchev released some in 1958, but in

TABLE 34
Number of Students In Communist Countries vs.
Some Other Countries

Country	Elementary & Secondary (In Thousands)	Number of Students at Higher Educational Institutions (1963)		
		Students	Per 10,000 of People	Per Cent of Women
A. Communist Countries				
Albania	340	12	69	18
Bulgaria	1,281	78	96	41
Hungary	1,648	82	82	35
E. Germany	2,265	114	67	32
N. Vietnam	2,600	26	16	na
China	102,900	na	na	na
N. Korea	1,990	214	188	na
Mongolia	134	10	100	na
Poland	5,693	209	68	35
Rumania	3,020	113	60	33
Soviet Union . . .	42,442	3,944	132	43
Czechoslovakia . . .	2,368	138	99	37
Yugoslavia	3,096	160	84	29
B. Other Countries	Per Cent of Students in Schools, Age 5–19 (1960)			
Austria	59	43	60	23
Belgium	72	41	45	26
England & Wales . .	81	238	45	na
Spain	60	na	na	18
Italy	50	192	39	28
France	76	230	50	38
W. Germany	80	217	40	24
India	29	913	23	15
Japan	73	758	80	20
United States . . .	81	2,222*	119	37

B. Urlanis (ed.), *Naselenie mira* (Moscow: Gospolitizdat, 1965), pp. 144, 146–147, 149, 150.

* The Soviet source does not include the first two years of American colleges in the category of university education. According to Soviet standards the first two years are listed as the upper grades of secondary education (Ibid., p. 149).

their place people like the Hungarian revolutionists of 1956 were sent to Siberian concentration camps as well as a constant "supply" of newly convicted persons. The fact is that *twenty* per cent of the convicted persons suffering in Soviet concentration camps are women. Out of the four million women in concentration camps, two million are Ukrainian women. This is ten per cent of the total female population of Ukraine.

The working conditions in concentration camps are very difficult. For instance, a woman working in a Siberian mill has to carry each day 120 bags of grain, each bag weighing 220 pounds. Women who work at distribution centers have to unload eleven tons of potatoes or nine tons of packaged food. In cutting timber a woman has to fulfill the norm of six cubic yards per day. If a woman cuts six trees in a prescribed time, she can warm her hands at the fire.[10]

Additional References

Pertaining to sources of Marxist-Leninist social philosophy in regard to women are: F. Engels, *The Origin of the Family, Private Property and the State* (New York: 1942), especially Chapters II and IX; Karl Marx, F. Engels, *Capital and the Communist Manifesto and other Writings* (New York: 1942), Chapters II, IV and V; V. I. Lenin, *Sochineniia,* vol. 32, pp. 138–140; *Stenograficheskii otchet 15-go s'iezda VKP* (b) (Moscow: Gospolitizdat, 1961), pp. 103 ff.; Gosstatizdat UzSSR, *Vsesoiuznaia perepis naseleniia 1926 g.* (Tashkent: 1931), vol. 32, pp. 118–135; E. Cherniavskii, *Prazdnyk vyborov* (Tashkent: Gosizdat, 1927); Tsentral'noe Statisticheskoe Upravlenie pri Sovete Ministrov SSSR, *Vysshoe obrazovanie v SSSR v 1960 g* (Moscow: Gosstatizdat, 1961), pp. 48–127.

---

[10] Kanadiiske Naukove Tovaristvo im. Shevchenka, *Zbirnik materiialiv naukovoii konferentsii K. NTSh v oboroni ukrainskoi kul'tury i naroda* (Toronto: Homin Ukrainy, 1966), pp. 41–43; See also *Literaturna gazeta,* February 1, 1967; *Vestnik statiztiki,* No. 1, 1967, pp. 40 ff; *Pravda,* January 16, 1967.

Chapter 14

SOME CONCEPTS OF
SOVIET CULTURE

In this chapter we shall present some fundamental concepts of Soviet cultural policies based, according to the Soviets, on the revolutionary experiences of Soviet society. Russian communists have rejected most Western socialistic theories of any kind: philosophical, psychological, sociological and others. Lenin and other Soviet leaders did not want to create a national culture or national-communist states but one Russian state where the Russian predominance would be visible in all areas. For this reason the early Bolsheviks rejected the humanitarian-socialist theories of Kautsky, who compared the policies of the Bolsheviks to the policies of the Jacobins during the French Revolution and said that "Lenin and Stalin knew the Soviet peoples only as trembling slaves."

The process of building the one socialist culture was not developing as expected because the party was too eager to give "a guiding hand" to the workers of the new society. Lenin, however, was consistent—when force was necessary, force was applied. But in cultural affairs he insisted that intellectuals cannot be forced to glorify the Soviet regime. He stated that "one can force a man to be afraid to join the White Army—this we are doing very well," but to force a man to build the culture of a new society is another story.

The Bolsheviks of 1917 initiated a different set of cultural criteria, e.g., Plekhanov emphasized a culture without the state and without class division. The Bolsheviks used the term *kul'tura* as a revolutionary slogan to influence the illiterate masses with something new, not necessarily something better. It was first known as the Russian culture, and later was called the Soviet culture with the dominant influence understood to be Russian. The cultural revolution was designed under the following program:

a. liquidation of all previous cultures on the territory of czarist Russia, national or religious;

b. spread of the *only culture*, first known as the proletarian and later on as the socialist; the latter to be built on national principles, with the provision that nationality had to be replaced by internationality;

c. construction of a Marxist ideology of culture; i.e., doctrines of materialism in philosophy, dictatorship in politics, collectivism in ethics, and

d. replacement of the belief in God with an absolute belief in science.

These concepts were the main guide lines of the Soviet reformers. Any deviation was not tolerated by Soviet leaders. The points outlined by the party had to be accepted as dogmas. Stalin himself defined them as being the "axioms of Bolshevism."

SOVIET CULTURE vs. NATIONAL CULTURE

The Marxian thesis of a superstructure was definitely applied in Soviet society, with the exception that the Russian culture was regarded as the culture of socialism. The Russian communists used extensive propaganda to persuade other nationalities that there was no need to argue for any ethnic-national culture because the communists did not care about borders of any kind. The terms nationality and national culture were "bourgeois inventions" and Soviets reject anything of that origin. The communists further theorized that there would be no more struggle between *nationalities,* but there would be struggle among *classes.*

Stalin from the very beginning of the Revolution played an important part in the building of the communist culture in the Soviet Union, since he was Commissar of Nationalities. He was non-Russian, so he had a tremendous influence upon other non-Russian nationalities. As early as 1918, Stalin spoke of the need to educate the masses in the new demands set forth by the Soviet government.

Although theoretically socialist culture was based on given national traditions, the Russian communists took great care to see that there was

little or no native representation in the non-Russian communist governments. For example, the early communist government of Turkestan, in
Tashkent, had not a single Muslim serving in it. The Russian communists
kept saying that the struggle between nationalities is bourgeois and that
the struggle between classes should be encouraged. Nevertheless they did
include in their thinking the struggle among various non-Russian nationalities and prohibited any struggle against the Russian nationality. They
made it clear that "the most important power of the new system was the
Russian worker."

At the same time the Russian communists were making every effort to
belittle all minority cultures, but not the Russian national culture. They
thought the idea of national culture was not in line with communist
principles and was old fashioned. Non-Russians were obligated to support
Russian ideas by giving examples of the inferiority of their native culture,
e.g., "man had the right to kill a woman, but now with the help of great
Russian people the Muslims constitute a first class socialist society . . ."[1]

LITERATURE IN THE SOVIET SOCIETY

One of the most important means of penetrating the hearts of the young
are literary works. It is not only Soviet society that stresses the importance
of literature in schools—all cultures and civilizations do the same thing.

It is not the purpose of this study to describe the trends in Soviet literature or to illustrate its major goals. It is rather to consider the major
themes that the Soviet government, during its fifty years of strict control
over any literary genre, has tried to impose upon Soviet writers.

During the revolution and a short period after the revolution, extreme
patriotism was the most popular literary theme. There were no formal
rules and regulations concerning the style of writing, or literary and aesthetic forms. In short, everyone wrote as he pleased. The old intelligentsia
refused to write praise of Lenin and Stalin, and the young ones (except
for a few) were unable to communicate with the masses. A few gifted ones
were Alexander Blok, Sergei Esenin and Vladimir Mayakovski. All three
were endowed with great talent and ability and all three belonged to the
communist movement. Blok's future was finished when he wrote the poem
The Twelve in which he depicted the communist Politbureau as the

---

[1] *Istoriia sovetskogo gosudarstva i prava Uzbekistana*, p. 507; Kary Niiazov,
op. cit., p. 85; Urazov, *op. cit.*, p. 203; Z. Radzhabov, *Iz istorii obschestvennoi
mysli tadzhikskogo naroda* (Stalinbad: Gosizdat Td. SSR, 1957), p. 443. See also
Lenin, *Sochineniia*, vol. 16, p. 124; Karl Kautsky, *Bolshevism at a Deadlock* (New
York: Rand and Sheed Press, 1931), p. 128; S. R. Tomkin, *The Russian Intelli-
gentsiia* (Norman: University of Oklahoma Press, 1957), p. 246.

twelve apostles. Blok pictured the communist leader in an idealistic-romantic way; no matter what they did—murder, shooting, killing—Christ was following them because they did it in the name of Russia. The party condemned this poem because it incorporated a religious motive. The second poet, Esenin, a very gifted man, was a socialist. He lived for a while in New York, came back to Russia and became very famous with his new style of impressions. He was very much disappointed with things that the Bolsheviks did. Ultimately, he committed suicide in 1925, after writing his last poem with his own blood, a poem that every Russian knew—*Goodbye, my friend, goodbye*. Five years later, early in 1930, one of the greatest Russian-communist poets, Mayakovski, a representative of futurism, also committed suicide. There may have been other motives for his death, but nevertheless he too was disappointed with the new culture. Other great authors like Boris Pasternak and Anna Akhmatova kept silent until 1956.

With the beginning of the NEP period, there was a trend toward literary renaissance among the non-Russian nationalities. The strongest and most active group was the Ukrainians who produced such excellent writers as Khvylovyj, Zerov, and the whole school of proletarian writers, of whom almost all were killed or deported when the NEP was over. The same fate met many Russian writers who believed in the Bolshevik propaganda and returned from exile to work for the Soviet literary cause. Stalin and his associates forced many of them to work and write on party directives. One such convert was Tychyna, a Ukrainian who decided to write as the party wanted. One of his well known anti-religious poems is a story about a mother and son in which the mother tells the son to fear God, and the son answers that her priests and religious superstitions do not scare him. The motive was clear here: to contrast the old and the new; mother and God; the man and the revolution.

Similarly, Muslim poets were forced to write on behalf of Soviet leaders, especially Lenin and Stalin. In 1927 a certain Kokushkin wrote a poem about Lenin in which he said that Lenin was sent by God, and now that Lenin is dead, he is with Allah but he has left the world free and liberated. Another writer, Zade, glorified with a poem and song the confiscation of land.[2]

After the NEP, Maxim Gorky and others initiated the new literary movement in the Soviet Union: socialist realism, which in some ways is still predominant in Russian writing at present. The main characteristics of

---

[2] *Pravda*, January 4, 1926. See also *Izvestiia*, January 21, 1927; George Van Rouch, *A History of Soviet Russia* (New York: F. Praeger Press, 1962, V-514), pp. 403–405.

this new trend are the following: supreme fidelity to the regime; elimination of any weaknesses in describing the heroes of socialistic realism (the new Soviet man is a strong character, realistic, etc.); praise of "wise leaders" of the party (novels of this period choose a party man as a leading personality); praise of the heroes of the industrial revolution; being strictly anti-religious, especially anti-Christian; belief in a bright future; and self-criticism.

Only during the war was this trend somewhat modified. Then Russian nationalism was stressed because the party needed patriotic youth to fight for Russia. Right after the war there was once again strict control. This time it was known as "Zhdanovshchina," bearing the name of its innovator, the party Commissar, Zhdanov. The first targets of the new revision were Ukrainian writers who were ordered during the war to write patriotic works but after the war became enemies of the revolution, e.g., Sosiura who wrote the poem *Love Ukraine* (Liubit' Ukrainu) which brought him into disgrace with the party.

Zhdanov first attacked a Soviet writer in his speech to the Central Committee in September 1946, where he strongly criticized deviations from socialist realism and stressed the fact that the duty of a Soviet writer is not to imitate the West but to teach the West new morals and ethics. Writers Zoshchenko and Akhmatova, the philosopher Varga and the psychologist Arbeli were all accused of "showing a little too much independence."

After the death of Stalin, Khrushchev began the liquidation of the "cult of individuality." He needed the Soviet writers to help. Here, for the first time, we see changes in Soviet literature. For the first time, party leaders were criticized in novels, e.g., *Not by Bread Alone, The Thaw*. But as soon as this movement began to grow, the party attacked the authors of these two books, accusing them of being bourgeois writers and enemies of the Soviet people.

After a "gentle" attack, in May 1956 a stronger pressure was put upon the writers and they were accused of liberalism. They were told to see the difference between good and bad literature.

On the other hand, the Soviet writers were not satisfied with the party's delineation of good and poor literature. One of the best expressions of the Soviet "care" for Soviet writers can be found in a diary by Ukrainian Vasyl Symonenko, *The Diary that Terrified Moscow*.

Symonenko in his diary expressed one idea: in order to get ahead in Soviet society one has to lie and do all kinds of immoral things as long as the communist party benefits from them. Cheating and deceit are approved as long as they serve communist goals.

Regardless of the suffering of Soviet writers, the communist party of

Russia spends a tremendous amount of money on propaganda to spread communist culture abroad. After many failures to sell the ideas of Soviet culture to Western Europe, North America and even to the Russian satellites, the Russian communists are making every effort to sell the ideas of the "most advanced" culture to the underdeveloped nations of Asia and Africa. Many of these peoples know nothing about the real situation in Russia. For example, a novel by the revolutionary writer Ostrovski, *Kak zakalialas' stal'* ("How the Steel was Tempered"), was translated into 42 different languages of India and Africa. The new Russian "messianism" is not based on the old religious doctrines but on the doctrine of internationalism and Soviet humanism.

Inside the Soviet Union the trend is to imitate "the older brother" in all literary endeavers and ideas. Estonians, for instance, write stories about the struggle between the old and the new.

Political motive must always be present in all communist literature. For example, Vosznesenski wrote a poem, "Walky-Talky," in which he tried to portray the idea of the danger of the yellow race. Blok called Russia a shield against two hostile camps: Europe and the Mongols. Voznesenski called upon the Russian people to defend Europe against the Mongol invasion since the Chinese want again the territories Russia conquered before 1917.

SCIENTIFIC COMMUNISM

The application of the scientific method to social problems existed long before the Russian Revolution. The French social philosophers, especially de Maistre and August Compte, maintained that there is a natural evolution of society, then a consensus of all social phenomena; and finally a subordination of the individual to society takes places.

Marx and other communists saw the evil of all existence in private property. Private property was seen as the origin of all injustice and exploitation. The only solution to these problems was to nationalize all private property. The Russian communists went further than that. Property, they maintained, is truly the origin of all evil, but nationalization of property does not necessarily provide a scientific basis for social revolution. In the process of social revolution one needs "aspirations and enthusiasm which can only be acquired by the living ideas of Lenin and Stalin."[3]

After the death of Stalin the situation changed somewhat but the main lines of scientific communism were kept. Soviet social and intellectual

---

[3] *Pravda*, January 3, 1953; *Znamia*, No. 1, 1967, p. 246; *Novii mir*, No. 11, 1966, pp. 225–243.

workers still complain that there is too much rhetoric and too little actual work in subordinating individuals' needs to the needs of society. But this rhetoric is also a part of scientific communism which must be visible in all areas and all actions. We shall, therefore, list some of the concepts of scientific communism.

Science and Traditions. As previously mentioned, the Soviets try to solve all issues by the use of science. Almost all speeches or lectures say something about the importance of science and the hazards of the old traditions. This scientific communism, as *Voprosy filosofii* stated, cannot tolerate religion and traditions connected with religion. The Marxists regard the Christian churches as dangerous organizations which serve only capitalistic infiltrations into various countries. But as usual, with the help of science, communism will triumph over all sorts of traditions that originate in religious beliefs.

Science and Ideas. Since the death of Stalin Soviets have approached the study of social phenomena from a twofold view: a materialistic explanation of human nature and an idealistic explanation of Marxism. Furthermore, the old party line, explaining all social and natural phenomena on a purely scientific basis derived from experiments in physics and chemistry, is no longer the tack of modern Soviet scientists. The Fok-Aleksandrov theories of dialectical materialism are revised in such a way that predominance is, of course, given to the materialistic explanation of man, but at the same time the idealistic interpretations of the Marxian movement are tolerated and supported.

Science and Art. In the Soviet understanding of art one should never create something that would confuse the viewer or put him in a state of doubt. Modern art as prevalent in Western societies is not tolerated. Art must propound the idea that the only movement is movement of *socialist realism* with no room for experimentalism, formalism, or any sort of abstractionism. In short, art must represent people, the things that communists do, and revolutionary movements, but must stay away from symbolic or religious issues and subjects.

Science and History of Philosophy. The only true explanation of historical and philosophical phenomena are the Marxian interpretations. All other views, especially non-communists critiques of Marxian philosophy, are labeled as vulgar caricatures of the West, and anti-Soviet. The study of non-Russian and non-communist philosophies are included only for the sake of degrading them. There is, however, some interest among the Soviet philosophers in the philosophy of neo-positivism and the study of linguistic philosophy and semantics. The main portion of Soviet social philosophy still must be dedicated to study of the Great October Revolution, experiences of Soviet leaders and the history of the communist party. All these are the norms which Soviet philosophers cannot neglect.

Science and Mankind. According to Soviets, the only way to survive and to bring happiness to mankind is to follow the Marxian experiences. Further, the history of mankind is the history of the struggle between private property and the exploited classes. All efforts made by man in the past and present are concentrated around the development of socialism and the transition to communism, which is the highest stage of social development. The future of mankind will be safeguarded only when communism triumphs over all the globe.

Science and the Family. The family as a unit, according to Soviets, does not mean much unless it is able to produce something useful for the collective. The Small Soviet Encyclopedia described the future of the Soviet family in the following way: all children will be sent to nursery schools and later on to boarding schools where they will stay 24 hours a day. The married couple will stay together as long as the bonds of love unite them. Once the "fire of love" is extinguished the family as a unit will disappear by joining the larger family, i.e., the collective where adult people will live together and will be free from the burden of educating children. The children belong to the state and the state will educate them in a way most profitable for the state.

To what extent this philosophy is applied in the Soviet Union, and more important, to what extent it is successful is hard to determine. The fact is that questions are always raised in such a way that blame is fixed upon the Soviet regime for destroying the family unit. "My brother has been killed . . . my father was prosecuted . . . my mother and four sisters went to Tiflis and we were split in that way . . ." These anguished comments picture the fate of the family as the primary social unit.

The young generation is free of any moral rules, e.g., one hears frequent complaints made by the older generation that a certain girl student "renders services to many foreigners," or that "unfortunately, we, too, have spiritual paupers, engaged in prostitution." The press bitterly attacks the problems of immorality without any substantial results. The *Komsomolskaia pravda* really pictured the situation of the family when it stated that under communism there will be no family and the word family will disappear. The words husband, wife, and marriage will also disappear and there will be only a union of free "hearts" and no restrictions of any kind.

What good is such morality? Even the Soviet communist press has acknowledged the fact that Soviet youth has no moral restrictions and the communist "morals" do not influence the younger generation. There is a lack of parental supervision, and frequently, older people take sexual advantage of youths. The Komsomol organizations are unable to give children the love, affection, sincerity, and feelings of guilt, which a family normally does.

Why is the divorce rate comparatively low? The answer is simple. There are heavy financial penalities levied by the government on those who marry and leave their children and spouse without financial help. Most people cannot afford a divorce. Even though there are people that marry as many as four times, the divorce rate is lower than in the United States (according to Soviet sources). It is only 1.3 per 1,000 people while in the United States it is 2.24 per 1,000.

Although communists maintain that "religions melt away like mist," and that individual values slowly are disappearing from the Soviet scene,[4] the fact is that the formulae of scientific communism cannot substitute for such values as family attachments, moral laws, love for each other, and most of all, the love of parents for each other and their children.

THE CLASS STRUGGLE

In the long history of Russia the state has never been controlled by a majority of the people. During the Imperial regime a small minority, not even one per cent, was able to impose its will upon the Russian and non-Russian inhabitants of the empire. The social composition of Russian society in 1897 was as follows:

Social Class	Per Cent of the Total Population
Nobility	0.97
Office Workers	0.50
Clergy	0.42
Distinguished Citizens	0.27
Merchants	0.22
Middle Class	10.66
Workers and Peasants	86.96

[4] Edward H. Carr, *The Soviet Impact on the Western World* (New York: The Macmillan Press, 1948), p. 99; Urlanis, *op. cit.,* p. 140; *Izvestiia,* January 4, 1962; *Komsomol'skaia pravda,* January 7, 1963.

Inside Russia, or inside the Soviet Union, there were many nationalities who had their own national social classes apart from the common super-structure. The Poles, for example, had their own *shliakhta* (nobility), and the Muslims had their own *beys* and religious hierarchy. When Lenin came to power he promised to follow the Marxian patterns of class struggle. Marx in his work, the *Communist Manifesto,* stated that the exploitation of one individual by another would be eliminated in the same way as the exploitation of one nation by another. But Lenin went further, calling for the elimination of nationality interest and its replacement by class interest. This policy was followed by Stalin and other communists, although not without some additional coloring in the name of Lenin and the proletariat.

There is, however, a great inconsistency in Soviet logic. They maintain, in the first place, that there are no classes in Russian society, but at the same time they extensively propagandize for initiation and creation of the class struggle in the U.S.S.R. and other satellite countries. Soviet statistical data show that there are no more exploiting classes in the new society. For instance, the *Narodnoe khoziaistvo* listed the following figures on the status of social classes:

	1928	1937	1939	1955	1965
Workers and Salaried Employers	17.6	36.2	49.8	58.3	75.1
Peasants Working in the Collective Economy	2.9	57.9	46.5	41.2	24.8
Peasants not belonging to the Collective Farm System	74.9	5.9	3.0	0.5	0.1
Merchants, *kulaks*, and others	4.6	. . .	0.7	. . .	. . .

As the data show, it is easy to see the disappearance of classes like merchants, property owners, or the old Russian intelligentsia. But Soviet data do not list separately the merchants of the present-day Kremlin as well as the leading party members and police force who really represent a separate class, since beside the Russian language they have very little in common with the Russian people.

The most important social class in Soviet society is comprised of the various executive committee members of the communist party. Although the Soviet structure has many branches of government and various types of *Soviets,* in reality no member of the Soviet executive apparatus is elected by the people. The so-called *nomenclatura* is the system whereby all administrative persons are appointed by the Central Executive Organs of the communist party.

The Soviet *nomenclatura* is similar to the Imperial Office of Appointments through which the czar approved every important member of internal and external affairs. *Nomenclatura* power rests in the hand of the Central Executive Committee where the secretary performs the functions of the czar. All members of the Supreme Soviets, the members of the Soviet of Nationalities (the Soviet Parliament), all ministers of internal and external affairs, all secretaries of the Union Republics—in short all those in important administrative positions—are appointed by the Central Committee of the communist party.

These conditions in Soviet class structure clearly indicate that there is no need for popular elections or democratic procedure in winning a political or economic administrative office. Although the Soviet data indicate that there is a division of labor, but no division of classes, the 34 million *kolkhoz* workers, as the *Narodnoe khozaistvo* listed them, have nothing to say about the representation of their interests in the Soviet higher administrative apparatus. The previously stated figure of 0.97 per cent of the population that constituted the Imperial elite ruling class still holds true at present where no more than that control the Soviet empire.

Cadre is the term used in an official Soviet index for all those who qualify for administrative office. The party keeps an exact account of all those people who are recommended by the local branches for future political and economic needs. Although the Large Soviet Encyclopedia describes the Soviet class structure as one based on friendship of the peoples of the U.S.S.R. and motivated by moral and political unity of the Soviet society, the real political bureaucracy has all the characteristics of the czarist regime.

Obviously persons having political appointments are in the upper economic brackets. There are frequent complaints among Soviet citizens that the politically appointed persons tend to exploit others. For example, *Pravda* cited a case where a chairman of a *kolkhoz* received 12 times as much money and 6.5 times as much grain as the ordinary worker. Most of these "sympathetic" members of the political bureaucracy own property and sometimes hundreds of animals. In line with the political privileges, these people have more security and better pensions.

Along with economic wellbeing the policy of prestige is also practiced in the Soviet classless society. There are frequent complaints among idealistic communists about the unequal treatment of other fellow men. People who hold high administrative positions do not wish to travel in the same car with working people, as was pointed out by V. Soloukhin in the *Journal of Literary Russia*. Here the rule of "classless" society certainly does not apply since the political bureaucrats not only have special privileges but they exploit others in the area of "equal distribution to the individual needs." Peasants in particular complain that they receive less than they deserve.[5]

SOVIET INTELLIGENTSIA

Second to the political hierarchy is the class of Soviet intelligentsia which includes party and non-party members. They *ipso facto* represent the social elite, a class which in the theoretical framework of communism should be fought in order to maintain the class struggle. But in the Soviet understanding of the class struggle they must be left outside.

The Soviet definition of intelligentsia is rather complicated. To this group belong all political workers—regardless of their level of education—all types of scientific workers, army officers, police, all white collar workers and those who have completed secondary or higher educational institutions. The Soviets also put the intelligentsia into one common group, the communist intelligentsia—regardless of nationality.

Policies regarding the intelligentsia have been elaborated by the same political organ, the Central Committee of the communist party, which preaches classless society. At the beginning of the Soviet regime, the communists devised three ways of handling the old intelligentsia: 1) attracting them into the Soviet camp; 2) exploiting them for communist purposes; 3) re-educating those who could be re-educated.

This plan became standard communist policy toward the old intelligentsia. There were many resolutions and directives issued by the party regarding the intelligentsia educated in the new world outlooks. In only one academic year (1930-1931) did the communist party demand that the higher educational institutions increase their percentage of communist students to 70 per cent. By this, they hoped to create a new class, attached to the people on and yet able to "provide the brains and the organizing ability required by the Soviet regime."

---

[5] *Narodnoe khoziaistvo*, 1964, p. 63; Inkeles, *op. cit.*, p. 301. See also *Pervaia obshchaia perepis'* (The 1897 Census), pp. xviii, 10. Note that the social structure in certain regions was very disproportional. For example, the middle class of Central Asia represented only 1.97%; in Siberia 5.62% and only in Polish regions did it represent 23.53%. See also A. Avtorkhanov, *Tekhnologiia revoliutsii* (Munich: Institute for the Study of the USSR), 1956, p. 406; *Pravda*, Jan. 16, 1963.

The Soviets wanted to utilize the intellectual elite in building communism, but they also wanted to avoid the error of the Imperial regime—creation of a special privileged class solely to serve the czardom. Yet in the Soviet example there is some similarity. During the Imperial regime most intellectuals tended to agree with Imperial policies because they benefited materially and monetarily more than the peasants. So do the communist intellectuals. Second, the new Soviet intelligentsia practice the Great Russian nationalism (which attracts many young people). With this they have better opportunities in their own pursuits and are able to live substantially better than other social classes. Therefore, there is little desire to initiate a new revolution since economically they are better off than the few intellectuals during the Imperial regime who opposed the rule of the czar.

As far as the non-Russian intelligentsia are concerned the situation is not exactly always favorable for the Russians. There are examples in history of many colonial powers that educated the native intelligentsia who then refused to serve colonial purposes. Educated Turks and educated Africans opposed colonial rule once they were better able to see the value of freedom and the consequences of assimilation with a colonial power.

It is an undeniable fact that during the entire Soviet period in Russia, the selection of intellectual cadres (the future intelligentsia), has always been made with great care. Undesirable people were rejected from higher educational institutions on the grounds of being descendants of the bourgeois social class, or on grounds that their parents cooperated with some enemy of the Soviet regime. The old intelligentsia were forced to work for the new regime, and most were treated like slaves and threatened with liquidation.

The position of the non-Russian, nationally-conscious individuals, is very difficult. It is very dangerous in the Soviet Union to admit belonging to the non-Russian intelligentsia, because those people are frequently accused of being nationalists and fascists, even though they are communists. For example, when the Russian satellites wanted to rule their own states and educate their own intelligentsia the nationally conscious communists were prosecuted. Beginning in 1948, native intelligentsia in satellite countries were eliminated from important positions when they disagreed with the Russian communists. A long time friend of Russia and a devoted communist, Dimitrov, the Bulgarian Secretary of the communist party, was called to Moscow and never came back. Xoxe, the Albanian chief of the party, was hanged because he opposed the Russian communist rule. The head of the Hungarian communist party, Rajk, was hanged. The Polish head of State, Gomulka, was sent to prison. The president of Czechoslovakia and the foreign Minister, Jan Masaryk, "jumped from a window and committed suicide." In short, all non-Russian communists who opposed Russian imperalism were liquidated.

Inside Russia, the many nationalities were treated in the same way. A. Bennigsen, a specialist in Soviet affairs, has made a study of the fate of Muslim intelligentsia who, like other non-Russian intelligentsia, became the subject of Russification. In the words of Bennigsen, the political police and the director of the State Security in any Muslim country, "is always and everywhere a Russian."[6] Other important ministries of the so-called Central Asian Republics, such as the Ministry of Economic Affairs, the Ministry of Communications, local industry, etc., are always in the hands of Russians.

CONCLUSIONS

One may wonder what is happening to the "flourishing" cultures during the Brezhnev-Kosygin regime? It is common knowledge that during the 1965-1968 period many writers were persecuted for demanding more freedom for the Soviet literary intellectuals. Although some of the names of more important writers who became the victims of the new trials were revealed by the Soviet press, the less known writers, in particularly those of non-Russian nationality, were not publicized either inside or outside the Soviet Union.

Recently a White Book concerning the trials of non-Russian intellectuals has been smuggled out of Ukraine. Viacheslav Chornovil compiled this evidence on the basis of his own experiences. Chornovil, a member of the communist party, was dissatisfied with Russian policies in Ukraine where the Ukrainian intellectuals were persecuted only for the reason that they demanded freedom of expression as well as the freedom to develop the national communist culture based on the Ukrainian culture and its development. When he began writing petitions and requests addressed to the Ukrainian Ministry of Interior as well as to the Ministry of Education (aimed at defending freedom of expression) he, too, was jailed and secretly tried in Lvov in November, 1967.

The Ukrainian intellectuals demanded cultural opportunities not only

---

[6] V. Bennigsen, "The Muslim Intelligentsia in the USSR," in *Survey*, No. 28, 1959, p. 7. See also B. Shiriaev, N. Koshevati, *K problemam intelligentsii SSSR* (Munich: Institute for the Study of the USSR, 1955), p. 41; Hugh Seton-Watson, "The Role of the Intelligentsia," in *Survey*, No. 43, August 1962, pp. 23–30; Rauch, *op. cit.*, p. 391.

for the Ukrainians but also for other non-Russian nationalities who were persecuted by the Russian communists. The Jews, for example, although comprising over 150,000 people in Odessa have not a single Jewish school, and they represent no more than 5 per cent in higher educational institutions of the region.

Further, Ukrainian libraries are not allowed to order books without approval of the Russian authorities. There are books in German, French, and English but very few books in the Ukrainian language, in particular those books that may reveal facts other than the Russian communists supply. For example, in 1965, the Ministry of Education authorized the following distribution of titles for the Ukrainian school libraries: 117 titles printed in English, German and French; 111 in Russian and only 99 in Ukrainian. Of the 99, most were related to the communist "classics" (works of Lenin, Marx, and other approved writers). Further, in upper grades of secondary education, the Ukrainian language has been eliminated from the school curriculum while Russian and other foreign languages are still taught.

There are many other evidences of the supression of non-Russian nationalities in the Soviet Union. In 1965 the Ministry of Education of the U.S.S.R. prescribed 1,874 various books for the Soviet *technicums* and all but 269 books in Russian. In 1960 there were only 81 Ukrainian students (at higher levels) per 10,000 inhabitants while in the same year and at the same level there were 177 students per 10,000 inhabitants; as of 1967 there was not a single Ukrainian school for the Ukrainians living in the Russian SFSR (over seven million Ukrainians lived there in 1930 and about four million in 1959) nor is there any choir, newspaper or any other cultural organization. There are almost no Ukrainian textbooks at the higher technological educational level, and the president of the Ukrainian Communist Writers' Association, Oles Honchar, has said that the Ukrainian language often finds itself in a worse position than the foreign language.

In conclusion, the new concepts of Russian communist culture are entirely different than theorized by the Marxian idealists. The use of force, violence, inversion of facts, suppression of non-Russian cultures, liquidation of religion—are all designed to build Russian communism. In spite of all this, *Pravda* maintains that "only Marxism-Leninism correctly solves individual problems. Real freedom is only possible in those countries where the individual has ceased to be a slave of capitalism."[7]

---

[7] *Pravda,* November 29, 1966. See also John Kolasky, *Education in Soviet Ukraine* (Toronto: Peter Martin Press, 1968), pp. 68–202; *Svoboda,* March 30, 1968.

Additional References

N. Bukharin, *Azbuka kommunizma* (Moscow: Gosizdat, 1923); Goiuridizdat, *Istoriia sovetskoi konstitutsii* (Moscow: Gosiuridizdat, 1957), pp. 62–64; Walter Laquer (ed.), *The Soviet Cultural Scene* (New York: F. Praeger Press, 1958); A. Filipov, *Nauchnii sotsializm i nauka o obshchestve* (Munich: Institute for the Study of the USSR, 1960), pp. 129–131; *Izvestiia,* May 26, 1963; *Izvestiia,* January 28, 1962; Leon Trotzky, *The Class Nature of Soviet State* (Ceylon: Lanka Samasamaia, 1952); *Molodoi kommunist,* No. 1, 1963; *Sotsialisticheskaia zakonnost,* No. 1, 1963.

Part Three

SCHOOL AND SOCIETY IN OTHER COMMUNIST COUNTRIES

Chapter 15

EDUCATION IN CZECHOSLOVAKIA

Historical Background. The people of Czechoslovakia comprise two major Slavic groups, the Czechs and the Slovaks. Except for the Hungarians, other nationalities represent only tiny fractions of the total Czechoslovakian population.

Historically the Czechs, known as the Bohemians, settled in the region of present Czechoslovakia in the 5th century A.D. and led a tribal-nomadic life as of that time. By the end of the 9th century the Czechs were able to organize themselves into a powerful country known as the Moravian Empire where the Czechs and the Slovaks were united. This union, however, was interrupted in the 11th century when the Hungarians came to the Danube region and conquered Slovakia. From that time on until 1918 the Slovaks were under Hungarian domination, although culturally they always were united with the Czechs and other Slavs.

In 863 two monks from Salonica, Cyril and Methodius, arrived in Moravia where they laid foundations for the Slavic culture and Christianity in general. The alphabetic script invented by Cyril became the corner stone for the Eastern Slavic languages—Russian, Belorussian, and Ukrainian, while Czechs decided to use the Latin script.

The ruling families of Bohemia were, first, the Premysl and the Luxemburgs. The Luxemburgs began their rule in the 14th century producing such famous leaders as King Charles IV who in 1355 became also the Emperor of the Holy Roman Empire. In 1348 Charles IV established the University of Prague which became the cultural center not only of Bohemia but also in Europe.

The history of the Czech people was greatly influenced by the European religious struggle but it took a different form in Bohemia. While the Protestant movement in England, Germany or Switzerland was carried on a strictly religious basis, in Czechoslovakia the struggle was interwoven with Czech nationalism. The burning of Jan Hus at the stake in Constance aroused not so much revolt against the Roman Catholic Church as revolt against the German-Hungarian neighbors who favored the liquidation of the anti-Catholic movements in Bohemia. In the midst of this struggle a national uprising occurred which no longer was purely religiously oriented. It was rather a Slavic-Czech uprising against the Germanic states. Under the leadership of Zhishka the Hussites were able to defeat the German armies and establish sound political control of the state.

After the death of George of Podebrady (1471) the Bohemian gentry elected the Polish-Lithuanian Jagello as king. During the dynasty of the Jagellonians the Bohemian people were able to maintain control over their own cultural and political affairs but after the death of Louis II the throne fell under the Hapsburg domination.

Louis II perished at the battle of Mohacz, and the Czech people fell under direct control of the Austrians who elected a new king, Ferdinand I (1526), and by so doing subordinated the country to Germanic rule. From that time on the Czechs remained under Austrian domination until the end of World War I and the Slovaks stayed under Hungarian rule. Although there were several revolts against the German-speaking Austrians, the people of Bohemia were unable to overthrow the regime since they were opposed not only by the Austrians but also by all great powers of Europe who favored the monarchical type of government. Czech history refers to the period of the 17th and the 18th centuries as the Dark Ages of Bohemia because Czech culture was then suppressed and persecuted.

At the beginning of the 19th century the Czechs began to struggle again for their independence, but as before, the coalition of Russia-Austria-Prussia prevented success in their drive for autonomous government. When the 1848 revolutionary uprisings appeared in major parts of Europe, the Czechs and Slovaks unsuccessfully tried again to restore their statehood. Not until 1918, under the leadership of Thomas G. Masaryk, was Czechoslovakian independence proclaimed.

Between the period of the two world wars the young country was comprised of Czechs, Slovaks, Germans and Ukrainians of the Carpathian mountains.

From 1945 on the Russian communists maintained a strong control over the country and except for a brief period (1945-1948) of semi-independence, the communist party of Czechoslovakia, first under the leadership of Gotwald and later under Novotny and Dubcek, became a puppet of the Soviet Union.

Population. The area of present-day Czechoslovakia covers 49,372 sq. miles with a population of 14,004,000. Out of 14 million people the number of Czechs is 9.1 million and the number of Slovaks is 3.8 million. The largest minority group, over 500,000, is the Hungarians while the number of Russians, Germans and Ukrainians is relatively small.

The annual increase in the population presently averages 7.4 per 1,000 inhabitants. The average geographic density is 107 people per sq. km.[1]

CULTURE AND EDUCATION BEFORE 1945

Although the Czechs were under the political and military domination of Austria, they managed to resist the German cultural offensive for three centuries. Not only that but they led the Slavic nations in cultural endeavors until the end of World War II.

Historically the Bohemian culture had its origin in Latin Rome. The Czechs, like many other nationalities, tried to learn from ancient Rome a philosophy of government as well as the art of writing. It was during the 14th century that the Latin *Alexandreid* was translated into Czech. Some of the foundations of modern Czech literature are laid in the work of *Dalimil's Chronicle*. The anti-German character of this work became a guide for later Czech reformers.

During the period of the reformation and the counter-reformations the Czech people did not stay aloof from the struggles. They participated in the religious struggle on both sides: with Catholics and Protestants. The religious wars turned out to be fatal for the Czechs since at the battle of White Mountain they lost not only religious freedom but also political independence. During the period of Austrian occupation there was one man especially noted for his brilliance in the educational and cultural Czech renaissance, the famous pedagogue John Amos Comenius.

Comenius not only tried to establish a modern educational system, but

---

[1] Vaclav Strako, *Czechoslovakia Today* (Brno: Y. Tiisk, 1964), pp. 1–5; V. Busek, *Czechoslovakia* (New York: Mid European Studies Center, 1957), pp. 5 ff.; *Czechoslovakia, A Handbook of Facts and Figures* (Prague: Orbis Press, 1964), pp. 2–21.

he also tried to preserve the Bohemian people from possible German assimilation. As the Bishop of the Moravian Brethren, Comenius established schools on religious foundations but did not exclude secular subjects from the school curriculum. He was especially known in the field of education because of his new approaches to teaching and learning in which certain objects were used as the means of better communication between teacher and student. His method soon became known as the *sense realism* and was predominantly outlined in his book *Orbis Sensualium Pictus* (1654), the first children's book of its kind. Some of his other works were *Janua Linguarium Reserata, Magna Didactica*, the *Labyrinth of the World and the Paradise of the Heart*, and *Martyrologium Bohemicum.*

Since the Austrian government did not allow the education of the Czech people in their own national traditions and culture, Czech culture had to find other ways for surviving. Among prominent leaders of the Czech enlightenment were writers like Dobrovsky, Palacky, Jungmann, Shafarzik, Chelakovsky, Havlichek, Bozhena Nemcova, Jan Neruda, Moravky, Sladek, and many others. Two famous persons in music should be mentioned, Smetana and Dvorak.

National education developed only after the First World War when Czechoslovakia gained her independence. Many of the philosophical foundations of Czech education were based on Western achievements in education, especially German, French and American. The leading scholar and president, Masaryk, always kept his people away from Russian dictatorial ideas and was not eager at all to follow imperial Russian or communist educational practices.

There was a tremendous influx of English and French philosophical ideas upon the Czech people before World War II, influencing free societies, Czechoslovak education, literature, arts and technology.

The Czech government issued a law in 1922 compelling all parents to send their children to school for a minimum of eight years. This law played a tremendous part in the educational development of Slovakia and the Carpathian region since the cultural level of these regions was very low.

The Masaryk government made further democratic reforms by establishing schools in ethnic languages for every major nationality of the republic. There were four major school systems in pre-World War II Czechoslovakia: the Czech, the Slovak, the German and the Carpato-Ruthenian (Ukrainian). All these nationalities had their own schools on all levels, and all were supported by the government and were given scholarships on an equal basis.

In terms of vocational education the Bohemians tried to adapt themselves to the industrial needs of the country. Czechoslovakia of the 1930s constituted the most industrialized nation in Central Europe and had one of the best agricultural research facilities in Europe. Their industry played an important role in World War II, especially in producing war machinery for the German armies. The vocational schools were fairly well developed especially on the secondary level for the training of specialists in the technical fields. As of 1938 there were 763 such schools with 75,522 students.

The higher educational reforms were conducted on the same democratic basis as the other educational reforms, e.g., the German minority of Czechoslovakia (about two million people) had three universities (while the Ukrainians in Poland—seven million of them—had no university); also for the about 800,000 Ukrainians of Czechoslovakia there was one Ukrainian university in Podebrady and one technological institute.[2]

During the German occupation the Czechs had limited freedom in educational affairs while the Slovaks were independent as far as education was concerned.

SOCIAL FOUNDATIONS OF COMMUNIST EDUCATION

Needless to say that the philosophical and psychological foundations of the Czech schools dared not deviate from the Russian philosophy of education. All basic ideas, concepts, and psychological experiments in the area of education were borrowed from Russian practices.

Studying the Czech educational philosophy one needs only to see the source material that Czech educators use. A certain Polashek, for example, discussed in the Czech *Journal of Education and Psychology* the idea of character training and the importance of the proper world outlook. The story Polashek wrote contained nothing new, and one needs only to go to the Russian sources, Korolev, Konstantinov and Makarenko, to find out that the idea of the new *world outlook* is not Czech.

The idea of the communist world outlook is not limited to a certain educational level; it reaches the whole system of education from the kindergarten to higher institutions. The child must be educated in the spirit of Soviet Russian patriotism, love for the socialistic countries, and finally love for the Czechoslovak republic.

---

[2] N. Apanasewicz, M. Rosen, *Education in Czechoslovakia* (Washington, D. C.: U. S. Office of Education, Bulletin No. 27, 1963), p. 78. See also R. Stransky, *The Education and Cultural System of Czechoslovak Republic* (Prague: 1938); Slovak Studies, *Historica* (Rome: Slovak Institute, 1965); Ludvik Nemec, *Church and State in Czechoslovakia* (New York: Vintage Press, 1954), pp. 92 ff.; *Encyclopedia Britannica* (1949 ed.), vol. 6, pp. 955 ff.; V. Pelisek, *Czechoslovakia* (Prague: Orbis Press, 1965), pp. 6–30.

It is currently quite common for Czech teachers to persuade the children that the only "true" democracy is Soviet democracy. Czech history books describe the Soviet Union as "the example of the true democracy enjoying the highest human freedom and the brotherhood of nations . . ."

The Czech textbooks blame the Western powers (England, France, and the United States) for Hitler's agression on Czechoslovakia in 1938 and they try to justify the last minute Russian withdrawal by blaming the Western powers because, according to the Czech sources, the Soviet Union was willing to send troops to Czechoslovakia but England, France and other bourgeois countries opposed Soviet help.

The Czech history books try to present the Soviet Union as a most moral country, the liberator of the enslaved, the country of supreme freedom where no failures or concentration camps exist and nobody was ever punished because of political reasons. In this area the Czechs truly surpassed the Russian communists themselves who tell the Czechs what to praise and how much to color it.[3]

To make sure that the young Czechoslovakian children inherit no Western thought, the Soviet educators initiated an extensive drive among the Czech educational research institutes to master the theories of Pavlov and other Russian psychologists. At the present time the psychological foundation of Czech education is 100 per cent Pavlovian-Soviet with no interpretations of general Czech psychological research. Man is considered purely a materialistic outcome of evolution and learning is only dependent on the environment. The concepts of conditional and unconditional reflexes are the only ones that matter in modern Czech psychology.

The general lines of the Czech psychological foundations are the same as the Soviet—extreme control by the state. Psychological experiments are conducted on groups of children and on animals (as in the Soviet Union), but the experimenters do not want to recognize any contributions of non-communist psychologists to the field of educational psychology. All reference material is from Soviet psychologists only.

General Education. The system of general education involves preschool, elementary and secondary education. The elementary and secondary systems were changed in both their structure and their orientation.

---

[3] *Czechoslovakia—A Handbook of Facts and Figures,* pp. 131–134; *Sbornik vysoke skoly pedagogicke* (Prague: Statni Pedagogicke Nakladatelstvi, 1955), p. 15; *Sbornik vysoke skoly pedagogicke v Olomouce,* vol. II, 1956, pp. 23–40; Captive European Nations, *Human Rights in Communist Controlled East-Central Europe* (New York: Captive European Nations, 1966), p. 5.

Before 1948, the educational system consisted of kindergartens (usually available in urban areas), eight years of elementary education and the gymnasium which was the most popular form of secondary education. But in between the elementary and the secondary, another type of educational activity existed before the war, the *Mescanka,* or civic school. Training here consisted of three or four years, and students were accepted from the fifth grade of elementary schools. The objective was to train lower level specialists needed in industry and general office work. At the higher secondary level there were academies and teachers' *seminariums,* both for those who had four years of training beyond elementary education.

The new communist system after 1948 was reorganized on Soviet patterns. With few exceptions the system of education in communist Czechoslovakia parallels the Soviet system. The basic general schools are also known as the nine-year schools offering educational training for boys and girls regardless of the social or financial standings of their families. All children attend school six days a week and follow the same curriculum. Religious education is non-compulsory. There is special emphasis on the study of the mother tongue, mathematics, and the basic natural and social sciences.

Apprentice training centers and apprentice schools are administered according to a uniform policy by the Ministry of Education and Culture. The apprenticeships are actually operated by business enterprises, and the larger ones combine practical work with technical and general education and also include all out-of-school activities. The smaller enterprises work with apprentice schools run by the national committee. Foremen, teachers and youth workers cooperate and meet regularly with parents to discuss the children's progress. Incentive is offered in the form of wages. The training is free and lasts about three years. Two year agricultural apprenticeships are offered at state farms.

Vocational schools have courses lasting either three or four years. They provide for technical and vocational education in various areas of industry, agriculture, forestry. Completion of the nine-year general school is a condition of admission.

The general secondary schools from classes ten to twelve provide a curriculum which prepares the student for the university. Even in this school there is some time given to manual work.

Czechoslovakian education today is controlled by the Ministry of Education and Culture. The law regulates cooperation between the parents and the school, the national committees and other public organizations.

The entire concept of Czechoslovakian education is traced to two articles of the Constitution of Socialist Czechoslovakia, adopted on July 11, 1960 (and like all Soviet Republics, has identical articles and sections relating to Socialistic philosophies of education).[4]

> Article 1-Section 1: The Czechoslovak Socialist Republic is a Socialist state founded on the firm alliance of the workers, farmers and intelligentsia, with the working class at its head.

> Article 16-Section 1: The entire cultural policy of Czechoslovakia, the development of all forms of education, schooling and instruction shall be directed in the spirit of the scientific world outlook, Marxism-Leninism, and closely linked to the life and work of the people.

> Article 16-Section 2: The State, together with the people's organizations, shall give all possible support to creative activity in science and art, shall endeavor to achieve an increasingly high educational level of the working people and their active participation in scientific and artistic work, and shall see to it that the results of this work serve all the people.

Education at general schools, including vocational, is free. There are no registration or examination fees, and all expenses are borne by the state. Textbooks are free at the basic nine-year schools, apprentice training centers and schools, and at all secondary schools.

The attendance data show that between 1953 and 1963 there was an increase in both the number of classrooms and students, e.g., in 1953 there were 50,697 classrooms and 1.7 million students for the basic 9-year schools while in 1963 the number increased to 75,333 classrooms for 2.3 million students. The number of students in general secondary schools more than doubled during that ten year period, reaching the 104,484 mark in 1963-1964 as compared to 50,471 in 1953. (See Table 35.)

In terms of vocational education an intensive effort was made to supply needed specialists for the new Czech-Soviet industry. The number of students in vocational schools increased over 300 per cent between 1948 and 1963.

University Levels. This is a vague classification for within its scope are general universities, technical universities and colleges, art schools and teachers training colleges. Studies usually last five years (except teacher training and art academies which are four years; medicine and architecture are six years). Practical work is very much a part of the university level training, and all universities studies are completed with examinations.

Any university graduate may go on for higher degrees such as the Candidate of Science, in which the student works independently on some

---

[4] *Czechoslovakia—A Handbook of Facts and Figures,* p. 24.

TABLE 35

Educational Development in Czechoslovakia:
1937–1964

School Year	Schools	Classes	Children
A. Nursery Schools			
1936/37	2,698	. . .	104,615
1948/49	4,664	6,107	205,416
1963/64	7,254	11,700	317,205
B. Elementary Schools			
1950/51	15,395	50,697	1,685,875
1953/54	12,142	54,708	1,786,790
1963/64	11,782	75,333	2,295,686
C. Secondary* Schools			
1950/51	251	1,769	50,471
1953/54	308	1,490	50,529
1963/64	385	3,390	104,848
D. Vocational Schools			
1936/37	764	2,604	75,522
1948/49	643	3,115	92,610
1963/64	680	10,956	302,224
E. Universities and Colleges			
1936/37	13	. . .	27,068
1948/49	22	. . .	64,703
1963/64	48	. . .	141,943

Czechoslovakia, A Handbook of Facts and Figures (Prague: Orbis, 1964, Second Edition), pp. 135–36.
* These are general secondary schools. There are also other types of secondary schools, such as technical and higher vocational schools.

scientific problem and then defends his thesis. After completion of the Candidate of Science degree, a student may go for a Doctor of Science, a top academic accomplishment.

As of 1963-1964 the number of students at higher educational levels had been increased to 141,943 as compared to 27,068 in 1937, and the number of institutions of higher learning reached 48 compared to 13 during the period of 1936-1937.

RELIGIONS AND OTHER REFORMS

The people of Czechoslovakia are predominantly Catholics. Before World War II about 75 per cent of the people (nearly 10 million) belonged to the Roman Catholic church. The church had 7,000 priests and many religious orders. The Protestant churches comprised about 15 per cent of the population; the rest were Jews or non-believers.[5]

The communists used a variety of methods to fight the Roman Catholic church in Czechoslovakia. Most of these were not entirely new Czech communist tactics because Russian experience in the anti-religious struggle proved important in eradication of religious life in Czechoslovakia. The communist Czechs organized a group called Progressive Catholic Action under the leadership of an excommunicated priest, Josef Plojhar. The aim of this organization was to unbalance the Catholics of the country, as well as to "attract the progressive clergy" to enter into the service of "Catholic Action."[6]

The government issued special laws concerning the future of the Catholic church and its clergy. The law stated that those priests who cooperated with the state would receive a monthly salary from the state, but in return they would have to oppose the Vatican and the Holy See. As it turned out, the "Catholic Action" was prohibited by Rome and the "progressive" priests were nothing but spies for the communist party. However, many young people entered the "progressive" priesthood in order to protect the church from the rising number of communist "priests" who were specially trained by the party to destroy the true essence of Catholicism. The party further ordered the clergy to submit every letter and every sermon to censorship before communication to the people.

From 1949 on all private schools, especially religious schools, were nationalized and their property was confiscated by the state. The government further imposed an official oath upon all the new clergy, demanding their supreme fidelity to the state. The church had to report all budget planning and could not execute any economic policy without getting state approval. As a result, the church completely lost freedom in its own affairs.

From 1950 on, mass trials were ordered by the communist party, with the result that the Greek Catholic Church of Slovakia was completely destroyed; its head, Bishop Gojdych, was sentenced to life imprisonment (he died in prison soon after his 1950 trial) and the clergy was forced to accept a union with the Russian Orthodox church (which was party controlled). In 1951, more than 3,000 Catholic priests were arrested along with 6,000

---

[5] *Ibid.*, p. 135; Apanasewicz, *op. cit.*, p. 21.

[6] Assembly of Captive European Nations, *Bulletin* (New York: ACEN, 1956), p. 52. See also Nemec, *op. cit.*, p. 65; *Trial of the Treasonable Slovak Bishops: Jan Vijtasek, M. Buzalka, B. Goidich* (Prague: Ministry of Information Press, 1951), passim; *Proces proti Vatikanskym agentum* (Prague: Orbis, 1950); *Red and the Black: The Church in the Communist State* (New York: ACME, 1953).

nuns. Archbishop Beran was sentenced to 25 years imprisonment along with many other bishops of the country.

In 1966, government officials complained that there was still insufficient propaganda in the anti-religious struggle, and that more people now practiced their religion than before World War II because the people (contrary to the desires of the party) liked the idea of a "forbidden fruit" more than when that fruit was free.[7]

In 1967 there were some progressive reforms initiated by the new secretary of the party, Alexander Dubcek, not only in terms of religious freedom but also in terms of political independence. However, in September 1968, the Kremlin decided to stop the liberal flow of ideas into any part of the Russian communist world. Czechoslovakia was occupied by the Russians and the so-called Warsaw Pact troops, thus terminating any deviation from Kremlin policy.

There may be many reasons for the Russian move into Czechoslovakia, but the most important include the following: the Kremlin leaders were afraid of the spread of liberalism into other parts of satellite countries, and in particular into the Soviet Ukraine; Brezhnev wanted to show that the policy of force and violence did not die with Stalin and that that policy will always be used in order to promote Russian imperialism as far westward as the West will allow; the Kremlin leaders did not want the free press reporting many acts of Russian communists in satellite countries; the Kremlin did not want to see any closer assimilation of religion and Czech liberalism; and finally, the fear of East German liberalism may cause a serious threat to the existence of communism not only in satellite countries themselves but within the Soviet empire as well.[8]

Additional References

Vasyl Pachovskii, *Istoriia Karpatskoi Rusi-Ukrainy* (Regensburg: Ukrainian Technological Institute, 1948, mimeo); H. Ripka, *Czechoslovakia Enslaved* (London: Galanz Press, 1950); B. Blunden, *Eastern Europe: Czechoslovakia, Hungary and Poland* (New York: Time Incorporated, 1965); Tomas G. Masaryk, *The Spirit of Russia*, two vols. (London: Allen and Unwin Press, 1938); Tomas G. Masaryk, *Die philosophischen und sociologischen Grundlagen des Marxismus* (Vienna: C. Konegen Verlag, 1899); Tomas G. Masaryk, *Ceska otazka* (Prague: Nakl. Pokrok, 1908); P. Stephen, *Slovakian Culture* (Cambridge: Harvard University Press, 1954); Otto Friedman, *The Break-up of Czech Democracy* (London: Galanz Press, 1950).

---

[7] Assembly of Captive Nations, *Religion and Communism* (New York: Assembly of Captive European Nations, 1966), p. 23; *Bulletin of ACEN,* 1956, pp. 52–55.

[8] For further information see Oscar Mochatka, "Masaryk and His Impact On Today's Czechoslovakia," in *ACEN News* (New York: ACEN Press, 1968), September 1968, pp. 1–26; Institute for the Study of the USSR, *Bulletin* No. 9, vol. XV, September 1968, pp. 5–22.

Chapter 16

EDUCATION IN POLAND

Historical Background. Poland is located between two powerful countries, the Soviet Union on the north and east and Germany on the west. The territory of Poland covers 119,800 square miles in Central Europe and is populated by over thirty-one million people. While many factors shaped the development of Polish history and culture, geographic location has always been a dominant factor in Poland's growth or decline.

Throughout history Poland has served as a block between the East and the West. Although Poland belongs to the Slavic world, her culture is of Western origin, and her people, predominantly Catholics, have contributed a great deal to the cultural growth of the West as well as the East.

During the reign of Mieszko I (960-992) Poland accepted Christianity via Bohemia, another Slavic nation. Mieszko took steps to strengthen the union between Western Slavs and to oppose German expansion eastward.

The most important epoch in the history of Poland was that of the fourteenth and sixteenth centuries when the Jagellon dynasty ruled over the people. The Jagellon dynasty began in 1386, when Jadwiga, daughter of the Polish-Hungarian king, Louis I, married the Lithuanian king,

Jagello. The marriage between two royal families at the same time united the two countries which extended from the Dnieper river on the east to the Baltic sea on the north and to the rivers Oder and Neissa on the west. During this period (1386-1572) Poland expanded her influence upon many other nationalities and was also able to withstand the Turko-Tatar invasions from the Crimean regions and the general Mongol threat to Europe.

After the fall of the Jagellon dynasty, the Polish throne was either elected by the people or chosen by the gentry. In 1573, for example, Henry of Valois, the third son of Henry II of France, was chosen by the gentry as the King of Poland. Henry II, however, ruled only one year. He resigned the throne in 1574 to become king of France upon the death of his brother, Charles IX. From 1575-1586, the throne was in the hands of the Transylvanian Prince Stefan Batory and later in the hands of Sigismund III, the King of Sweden. After that the famous military leader, John Sobieski, ruled. Sobieski defeated the Turks (1683) and saved the Christian civilization of Europe.

During the seventeenth century an important development occurred in Eastern Europe, namely, the separation of some Ukrainian territories from Poland. Due to several factors, the Ukrainians rebelled against the Poles, eliminating for later centuries Polish influences upon that area. In 1648, the hetman of Ukraine, Bohdan Khmelnitski, waged war against Poland, thus further diminishing Polish influences in Eastern Europe. In 1654, the hetman and the Russian czar, Alexis I, concluded a treaty of mutual assistance against the Poles which put eastern Ukraine under Russian rule from that time on.

Eighteenth century Poland witnessed many disasters since her Slavic neighbor to the north was anything but a Slavic friend. The Russian czars kept a constant pressure on Poland and in reality precipitated the first partitioning of the country in 1772. In 1793, there was a second partitioning and in 1795, a third. Each time Russia, Prussia and Austria divided Poland among themselves and the Polish people were completely subjugated. In 1918, largely because of Anglo-American assistance, the Democratic Republic of Poland was established.

From 1918 until 1939, Poland was again ruled by military men. Particular note should be taken of Pilsudski, who established a semi-dictatorship in 1922. Although Poland was a combination of many nationalities—more than 13 million non-Poles—the internal structure of the state was such that very little freedom was given to non-Polish ethnic groups. The appointed presidents like Narutowicz (assassinated in 1922), Wojciechowski and Mosciski were puppets of General Pilsudski and his successors.

After the Second World War, the Poles were unable to organize a democratic government because of Russian pressure. The Poles who had fought in the English armies in Africa, Italy and other parts of Europe were considered enemies by the Russian communists. A few persons led by Mikolajczyk opposed the communists and returned to Poland, but very soon, together with Mikolajczyk, they were forced to escape.

Poland lost most of its eastern territories which were populated by non-Polish-speaking people, and got instead parts of Prussia which again extended Polish borders up to the Oder-Neisse shores. Although the western borders of Poland were not recognized by the United States, England and France, nevertheless, present day Poland is on the map of Europe.

The Poles cannot forget that the Russians killed over 10,000 Polish officers in 1939, just because they were Poles, as well as purposely letting the Germans slaughter over 300,000 Poles during the Warsaw uprising (1944) while the Russian armies merely watched. All this was done purposely by the Russians since they did not want to see a democratic Poland.[1]

The present government headed by Gomulka is surprisingly much more democratic than the Czech, Bulgarian or Hungarian governments and has much more power than the so-called republics inside the Soviet Union.

EDUCATION BEFORE THE COMMUNIST TAKEOVER

Historically, Poland served as the cultural bridge between the East and the West and between Roman Catholicism and Greek Orthodoxy. In educational matters the Polish influence upon Ukrainian and Russian education was quite significant since the early brotherhood schools operated in the Polish-Lithuanian state and were to some extent oriented toward the Latin West.

When the University of Krakow was established by King Casimir the Great (1364), the cultural enlightenment followed not only in Poland but in other parts of the Slavic states. The Poles were the first among the Slavs to introduce Western ideas among the people of Eastern Europe. Their literature began as early as the 10th century; and by the middle of the 16th century, they equalled many West European nations not only in literature but also in music, science and technology. In the first half of the 16th century, the very distinguished Polish writer, Mikolaj Rey, gave

---

[1] Clifford R. Barnet, *Poland: Its People, Its Culture and Its Society* (New Haven: Hrat Press, 1958), pp. 7–33. See also Richard F. Starr, *Poland, 1944–1962* (New Orleans: Louisiana State University Press, 1962), passim; Universitet Warszawski, *Zeszyty Historyczne* (Warsaw: 1963); S. Sharp, *Poland White Eagle on a Red Field* (Cambridge: Harvard University Press, 1953).

solid foundations to Polish literature while Copernicus proved the validity of the helio-centric system in astronomy. In later centuries Madame Curie-Sklodowska distinguished herself in natural sciences; Sienkiewicz and Reymont—both Nobel Prize winners in literature—made a tremendous contribution not only to Polish literature but to world literature as well.

On the basis of these contributions, Polish education was developed. There were, however, some weak points in the historical development of Polish culture, but these must be attributed to the political situation inside Poland and to the partitioning of Poland by her neighbors.

General Background. Historically, education in Poland was designed for the upper classes. Until the latter part of the eighteenth century, when an important educational reorganization plan was carried out, almost all education in Poland was classical. Principal subjects of study were history, philosophy, languages, theology, the arts and sciences. Development of individual critical ability and independence of thought were encouraged. In 1773, the National Commission of Education was created.

During the time of her partitioning among Prussia, Russia and Austria (1795-1918), Poland was subject to three different educational policies. Russia made little provision for educating children; Prussia maintained an eight-year compulsory system, and only Austria permitted the use of the Polish language in teaching and under her administration, the University of Krakow remained the center of Polish culture. There were no universities in the Prussian and Russian sections, but qualified students could attend German or Russian universities.

On February 7, 1919, the government issued a decree for compulsory education for all between the ages of seven and fourteen. Educational management for the whole country was centralized in the offices of the Ministry of Education in Warsaw. The seven-year compulsory school system was finally established by the law of March 11, 1932. This law is sometimes referred to as the School Reform Bill of 1932, or the National Education Act of 1932.

From the social point of view, Poland had a dual educational system: one for the low and another for the higher strata of society. In an educational system such a structure set definite limits to the occupational and distributional functions of schools. Such a system worked not for the improvement of social mobility, but primarily for the maintenance of the existing order—hierarchy and stratification of social classes.

After 1926, the intelligentsia, particularly the school bureaucracy, affiliated chiefly with the well-to-do and with the Roman Catholic Church, was the chief social force molding the Polish school system.

Before the war, there were over a million school-age children not attending school. Most children in rural areas could take advantage of schools only on the lower level. It usually took seven years to cover a four-grade program. As a result, twenty-five per cent of the total population over ten years of age could neither read nor write.

For economic, political and social reasons, it was difficult for working class and peasant children to obtain admittance to secondary and higher schools. They constituted fewer than 14 per cent of all secondary school pupils, and the percentage was even lower in institutions of higher education.

School buildings presented a second major problem for the Polish people. In 1919, 100,000 units of school space were needed. By 1936, 45,000 classrooms were still needed. When the Second World War began, many schools in Poland were still in private homes which had been converted for school use.

Public school education was free. The elementary public school system was uniform throughout the entire country, so that after completion of the sixth grade, all graduates had identical educational backgrounds.

General Education. In general the elementary school program in Poland was similar to the United States primary school. The stress was on the acquisition of fundamentals of general education, rather than certain special subjects. Compulsory elementary schooling in America begins one year earlier and ends one year later than in Poland. The compulsory Polish elementary school was for a seven year period of time, while the American elementary school is an eight year program.

The educational system of Poland consisted of the following divisions: kindergartens for children aged three to seven, elementary schools with a seven year program, and secondary schools. These secondary schools were divided into two levels: The first four years were called gymnasiums and the last two years were called lyceums. Higher educational institutions consisted of four to six years of training.

Minority Schools. The Polish government before World War II permitted only elementary schools. For 13 million non-Poles there was not a single higher educational institution in the country. Those minority group members who completed school abroad or in Poland, could not find a position because of the discriminatory policies against them. Ukrainians were transferred to Poland to teach or work in given professions and Poles were transferred to Ukrainian territories, thus negatively affecting cultural development.

Teacher Training. The training of elementary school teachers was not as good as could be desired. The standard teachers' training was as follows: seven years of elementary education followed by four years of *Seminarjum nauczycielskie* (Teachers Seminarium). After that training, teachers in urban areas occasionally took some courses during the summer. Not until 1930 was an additional year added to the pedagogical training.

The training of secondary school teachers was much better. The usual sequence of teachers' training at secondary level consisted of six years of elementary education, four years gymnasium, two years of lyceum and the usual training (four years) at the university level in a given specialty.

Higher Education. Before the First World War there were just two centers of higher education. The Austrian government permitted university instruction in the Polish language at the University of Krakow and the Institute of Technology at Lvov.

In 1916, during the German and Austrian occupation the Warsaw University and Institute of Technology were Polonized. Shortly afterward two new state universities were established, one in Poznan and another in Vilna. The Vilna University was an old university established in 1579, but closed by the Russians in 1831. Additional professional schools of veterinary, mining, medicine, rural economy, fine arts and so on were established in the larger cities like Warsaw and Krakow. At this time several private schools of higher education were established like the Catholic University of Lublin.

Again in the early years of independence, one of the major problems of the universities was the number of professors available. Up to 1937-1938, there were approximately 50,000 students and 1,000 professors in all thirty-two institutions of higher learning.[2]

EDUCATION UNDER COMMUNISM

General Education. As in other communist countries, educational opportunities have become available to almost all the social classes. In most areas of educational endeavor the increase in the number of schools, students, teachers and scientific workers cannot be disputed.

In line with the increase of schools and students, communists demanded that the philosophy of education be changed. They insisted that there

---

[2] Seymour M. Rosen, N. Apanasewicz, *Higher Education in Poland* (Washington, D. C.: U. S. Office of Education, Bulletin No. 19, 1963), p. 8; Barnet, *op. cit.,* pp. 331–348; Sofia Skubala, *Polish Universities* (Warsaw: Polonia Press, 1959), pp. 25, 120.

should be no emotional ties between Roman Catholicism (which was so inseparable from the Polish way of life) and the philosophy of education, as well as no ties between Polish patriotism and communism, *per se*. The extreme political indoctrination was not limited to the classrooms but was extended to the factories, farms, clubs, children and adult organizations— any situation which might have been favorable for performing a political job.

Education is similar to other Soviet schools, with the exception that after 1956, religious instruction was permitted. All Polish youth received a compulsory seven year education in an elementary school. Pupils start school at age seven and complete the seven year (in some cases eight) elementary school at age fourteen. There are also nursery schools which start pupils as early as age three.

There are various types of secondary education offered in Poland today. The main type is a four year general education *lyceum,* grades eight to eleven, for youths fourteen to eighteen. From the *lyceum,* pupils may go on to technical schools, any of many types of colleges or academies or the universities. After completion of grade seven, youth has several alternatives: one may go to a five year normal school, then take two additional years of courses for teachers and go on to Teacher's College; or one may go on to a five year technical school and then continue in higher technical education; or he may decide upon a three year basic vocational school, followed by three more years in a technical school and then higher technical education, or he may opt for a five year secondary art school which can be followed by higher education at an academy of art.

It is hard to compare the number of students in 1939, to that in 1967, because the territory of Poland changed. As mentioned before, there were almost 5 million children in elementary schools as of 1939, and this did not change in 1960. But by 1964, the situation changed rapidly since there were 7.5 million pupils in elementary schools of all kinds and 631,259 in secondary schools (see also Table 36).

There was great need to improve the standards in vocational education. As of 1961, the vocational student had two choices: he could begin directly after completing elementary schools; or he could attend the four year *lyceums* (secondary schools) and then go to a higher vocational school. As of 1963, there were 1,183,595 students in all kinds of vocational schools in Poland as compared to 207,529 in 1939.[3]

---

[3] *Twenty Years of the Polish People's Republic* (Warsaw: Wydawnystvo Ekonomiczne, 1964), pp. 195–197. See also Z. Dwojat, "Dobre perspektywy rozwoju warstatow szkolnych," in *Szkola zawodowa,* No. 3, 1966, pp. 18–20; Colliers Encyclopedia, vol. 19, p. 198.

TABLE 36

General Development of Education in Poland: 1963–1964

Type of School	Schools	Teachers	Students	
			Male & Female	Female Only
Preschool	10,101	24,786	532,650	na
Primary	26,506	170,360	5,181,679	2,491,138
Secondary	852	18,256	378,464	252,785
Technical	5,677	92,382	775,350	341,430
Teacher Training . . .	216	5,917	74,162	57,416
Higher	74	21,817	212,558	74,759

United Nations Statistical Yearbook (New York: United Nations Service, 1965), p. 710. Note that there were some improvements made in general education, especially in the area of adult education. In 1965, for example, there were special secondary schools for adults incorporating 116,500 students. The number of students in general secondary schools also has been increased to 405,212 of which 272,785 were girls; in higher educational institutions there were 231,224 students (compared to 212,558 in 1963) of which 83,653 were women. For further information see *The International Yearbook and Statesmen's Who's Who*, 1966 (London: Burke's Peerage Ltd., 1967), p. 412; *United Nations Statistical Yearbook*, 1966 (New York: United Nations Service, 1967), p. 738.

HIGHER EDUCATION AND TEACHER TRAINING

Higher Education. The lack of personnel in higher education was the most important and unique problem of the communist educational system. In the first place, more than 20,000 teachers lost their lives as a consequence of German purges during the war. Further, many teachers refused to work for the communists and either worked in industry or migrated to England or other democratic countries. The University of Warsaw alone lost 160 staff members.

The communist reforms touched upon many areas: reorganizing higher educational institutions, broadening areas of specialization, increasing the number of students in higher institutions of learning, and most important of all (as can be expected) increasing the number of communist students at higher institutions of learning. The schools also had to be coordinated with the industrial needs. According to Polish communist sources, the number of trained scientific workers had increased from 3,000 in 1939, to 16,000 in 1958. Also, the number of students in proportion to the population increased: in 1938, there were fourteen students per 10,000 people (in Italy as of the same year there were seventeen and in France twenty-three students) ; but in 1957, there were forty-five students per 10,000 people in higher educational institutions.

Another important area of the Polish communist reforms is the training of physicians. As in the Soviet Union, the number of doctors has substantially increased, e.g., between 1944 and 1955, more than 15,000 students finished medical school, increasing the number of doctors to 18,273 or one doctor per 1,500 people as contrasted to one doctor per 2,700 people in 1938.

In 1939, only nine per cent of university students were from the working class; in 1958, there were 32 per cent of the students from the working class, 21 per cent from the peasant class, 42 per cent from professional workers, and 5 per cent from other strata of the population. While in 1939, 69 per cent of all students studied at their parents' expense, only 22 per cent were supported by parents in 1955. As of 1964, there were 75 institutions of higher learning in Poland with 35,000 staff members and 287,317 students, or 57 students per 10,000 people.

Control of Education. The Minister of Education establishes the program of study, approves textbooks and teaching aids, establishes the criteria for acceptance and transfer of students, and establishes the methods of examination and procedures for granting titles and diplomas.

Local school administration is supervised by the People's Council, that in turn is subordinate to the Council of Ministers. The People's Council secures living quarters for teachers and other school workers, finds locations for schools, furnishes and equips local schools, directs the general activities of the schools and provides other financial aid. Superintendents of school districts, who are under the supervision of the People's Council, are responsible for the general working conditions in the schools and the maintenance of the physical plants. The superintendents of the school districts are responsible to the Ministry of Education on matters of organization and methods of educational work.

The chief authority over higher education is the Ministry of Higher Education. The Polish state also exercises ultimate control over the higher non-state schools. A higher non-state school must operate according to statutes drawn up by the Minister of Higher Education. These statutes determine, among other things, the program of study, the rights and obligations of students and graduates, the units of the school and methods of operation, and methods of appointing scientific and other workers. The only higher non-state school remaining is the Catholic University of Lublin.

The general trend is to remove the technical faculties from the university and increase the number of higher technical schools. The universities are primarily concerned with the theoretical sciences and the humanities. The number of faculties in technical and other specialized schools now far outnumbers those in the universities, and about half of the students in higher education are in specialized schools.[4]

Teacher Training. The most crucial problem facing Polish higher education was the shortage of teachers. Over 40 per cent of the teachers at the higher educational level were lost as a consequence of the Second World War. Still another problem was that the industry demanded some redistribution of professional man power and as a result many teachers chose industrial employment over teaching.[5] The number of teachers, as of 1963, show the following ratios:

Type of School	Male	Female
Primary	170,360	126,180
Secondary	18,256	9,523
Technical	92,382	30,186
Teachers' Colleges	5,917	2,535
Higher Education	21,817	5,792

OTHER REFORMS

Women and Society. The place of women in pre-war Poland was about equal to that in any other European country. Most women did not work simply because there was no work available. Poland was predominantly an agrarian country, so women either worked in the fields or helped those who could afford to hire labor. It was not exactly exploitation as Polish communist sources labeled it, but rather that the general social conditions of the country could afford so much and no more. There were very few industrial establishments that could employ large numbers of people. Therefore, it was not the intentional policy of the pre-war Polish government to pay women less, but the national economy was such that it could not afford to pay any more.

---

[4] For further information see J. Rabasztyn, *Formy podnoszenia kwalifikacji inzynierow gornictwa* (Katowice, 1966), *passim.* Information concerning the function of the Ministry of Education can be found in *Zarazadzenie Ministra Szkolnictwa Wyszego z dnia 19 stycznia 1966* (Warsaw: Ministry of Higher Education, 1966), *passim;* Skubala, *op. cit.,* pp. 135–140.

[5] *International Yearbook and Statesmen's Who's Who* (London: Burke's Press, 1966), p. 412.

The number of women attending educational institutions—particularly at the higher levels—was low, as it was in other European countries. The percentage of women in professional schools over the years can be seen in the following table:[6]

Profession	Total Per Cent of Students in an Area of Concentration		Per Cent of Women	
	1936	1956	1936	1956
Technology	10.9	41.3	1.6	17.5
Agronomy	8.1	14.0	5.0	14.4
Law and Economics	40.6	8.8	26.8	10.3
Humanities	16.2	6.0	30.4	9.1
Natural Sciences	7.4	5.0	13.0	8.8
Medicine	15.9	21.8	21.7	35.0
Arts	0.9	3.1	1.5	4.9

Religion. Since Poland is about ninety-five per cent Catholic, the communist pressure against religion was not as great as in other countries where the communists used one religious denomination to fight another. In Poland, because of several internal and external factors, there was less killing and shooting of clergy than, for instance, in Ukraine or Rumania. However, there were many policies aimed at the destruction of Catholicism in Poland.

First of all, the communists published laws which guaranteed to all citizens freedom of conscience and religion, but in actual situations the story was different. The government vigorously supported the leading anti-religious leaders of the country. It became evident, especially after 1948, that communism and religion could not coexist.

The communists also used former Nazi collaborators to fight Catholicism, one of whom was Boleslaw Piasecki, a fascist who favored German occupation of Poland, but who was able to persuade the Russians that he could be "useful" to them. Piasecki headed a militant atheist group that worked intensively to destroy the prestige of the church and to create the impression outside Poland that Polish Catholics supported the communist regime.

The communists not only used persons like Piasecki but also organized "Progressive Catholicism" which included the "training" of "progressive" clergy who were in reality agents of the communist party. When the

[6] *Twenty Years of the Polish People's Republic*, p. 66; *Social Achievements of People's Poland:* Labor Protection for Women (Warsaw: 1954), p. 47.

Stockholm Peace Appeal—initiated by Moscow in Sweden—was distributed in communist countries, the Polish Catholics as well as their clergy were forced to assist in distribution of the "Peace Appeal." Those who refused to do so were arrested, persecuted and displaced. In 1950, between 200 and 300 Catholic priests were arrested and another 500 were displaced. To impose the will of the party, all Catholic hospitals and all Catholic schools (except one university in Lublin) were nationalized.

Third, the communist party invented espionage charges against the Polish clergy. One martyr was Bishop Kaczmarek, who was sentenced to twelve years of prison on grounds that he was a spy for the United States. When Cardinal Wyszynski protested, he too was arrested in 1953, and spent five years in prison. After arresting the cardinal, the purge against the clergy and the believers began. Not until 1956 was any relief evident and this was due to the pressure of several international situations (e.g., the Hungarian Revolution). Finally, Moscow not only decided to stop the purges against the Polish Catholics, but to permit religious instruction for those children who wanted to have it.

This concession was by no means a sign of complete freedom of religion in Poland, but in general, the situation was better than in the Soviet Union. Although the government kept accusing the religious believers of bourgeois habits and forced many of them to accept the communist "morality" in order to survive, there has been no radical force applied since 1959. Educational institutions, as in other communist countries, are required to educate conscious workers of socialism[7] and to profess love for all communist nations, especially Russia.

Additional References

B. Schmitt (ed.), *Poland* (Berkeley: University of California Press, 1945); S. Arnold and M. Zynchowski, *Outline History of Poland* (Warsaw: Polonia Publishing House, 1965); Oscar Halecki, *History of Poland* (New York: F. Praeger Press, 1956); N. Apanasewycz, William K. Medlin, *Educational System in Poland* (Washington, D. C.: U. S. Office of Education, Bulletin No. 12, 1959); Z. Parnowski, *Education in Poland* (Warsaw: Polonia Publishing House, 1958); H. Barycz, *The Development of University Education in Poland* (Warsaw: Drukaria Naukowa, 1957); Ministry of Higher Education, *Higher Education in Post-War Poland* (Warsaw: Polonia Publishing House, 1961).

[7] *The Church and State Under Communism, Committee on the Judiciary, United States Senate,* vol. V, *Poland* (Washington: U. S. Printing Office, 1965), pp. 7–9; *Polish Review,* vol. XI, No. 4, 1966, p. 85; Assembly Of Captive European Nations, *Bulletin* (New York: ACEN Press, 1966), pp. 66 ff.; "The Catholic Church in Poland," 1945–1966, in *The Polish Review,* vol. XI, No. 4, 1966, p. 77.

Chapter 17

EDUCATION IN BULGARIA

Unlike the People's Republic of Yugoslavia, Bulgaria is a homogeneous nation which is 88 per cent Bulgarian, 8.6 per cent Turkish, 2.6 per cent Gypsy plus small minorities of Armenians and Jews.

The population of Bulgaria was 8,078,000 in 1963, with male and female population almost equally distributed. Since the end of World War II the tendency of the population has been to shift toward urban areas where the possibility of employment is better. In 1956, e.g., the rural population represented about 66 per cent of the total and by 1963 the percentage had dropped to about 60 per cent.

Except for the Turkish minority the nationalities of Bulgaria have learned to live together—contrary to the Serbs and Croats, or the Russians and Ukrainians in their respective countries—sharing the common burdens of the developing country. Only the Turkish minority of Bulgaria presented some real problems—the communist regime was not able to solve the Turkish-Muslim demands. The Bulgarian communists, therefore, deported 250,000 Turks to Turkey which created some tension between the two rival neighbors. The Macedonians, a Slavic group, present a complicated problem, since both the Bulgarians and the Serbs claim the Macedonian territory. Tito established independent Macedonia, however, the Bulgarians claim that Macedonians living in Yugoslavia are in reality a part of Bulgaria because they speak almost the same language as the Bulgarians do.[1]

GENERAL BACKGROUND

Through the centuries the Greeks, the Romans, the Bulgarians and the Turks each had demanded rule of the Balkan peninsula, and through the centuries the only solution of this problem was war among them. Even during the time of Constantine the Bulgarians participated in the struggle for Byzantium, a city whose name Constantine changed to Constantinople, and which was later the capital of the Eastern Roman Empire.

One of the brightest Bulgarian historical moments belongs to the year 811 when the ruler Khan Krum defeated the Byzantine Emperor Nicephorus I.

With the acceptance of Christianity in the 9th century, the Bulgarians made an important contribution to the rest of the Slavic world with their written language and the style of literary writings. They were the first to oppose Latin in the liturgy which became a factor of dispute in later centuries among the Eastern Slavs. The Bulgarians were able to penetrate with their culture the Eastern Slavs (the Russians, the Ukrainians, and the Belorussians), all of whom accepted Old Bulgarian as the language of the Orthodox Church.

The Bulgarians were not only the first Slavic nation to accept Christianity but they were the first missionary nation to spread it among other Slavs living in Central Europe (Moravia and Bohemia). They sent the two famous monks—Cyril and Methodius—to Kherson (present day Ukraine), an area occupied by the non-Slavic peoples.

Bulgarians are proud of the fact that the early bishops of Kiev or Moscow were not Russian nationals but Bulgarians, and that they gave to the Russians the idea that the mission of Russia was to convert Latin Europe to Orthodoxy.

From the 14th century, Bulgarians were victims of Turkish expansion and for five centuries they were under direct control of the Turkish sultans. Only after several wars between Russia and Turkey were the

---

[1] *East Europe,* vol. VII, No. 1, 1958, p. 28. See also Nikolai Todorov, *Bulgaria: Historical and Geographical Outline* (Sofia: Foreign Language Press, 1965), pp. 1–5; Central Board of Statistics, *People's Republic of Bulgaria: Statistical Manual* (Sofia: Foreign Language Press, 1965), p. 5; H. Kostanick, *Turkish Resettlement of Bulgaria,* 1950–1953 (Berkeley: University of California Press, 1957), pp. 65–163.

Bulgarians able to gain independence via Russian assistance. Although there are frequent misinterpretations of Bulgarian history by Russian and Bulgarian communists, nevertheless Bulgarians recognize that their heroes during the Turkish occupation were not the servants of the bourgeoisie (as the Russians claim them to be) but real Bulgarian patriots. Rewriting of history, however, is a well known communist tactic aimed at the complete inversion of the historical facts.[2]

During World War I the Bulgarians fought on the German side and during World War II they tried to maintain neutrality but were unable to do so because of German pressure. At the end of the war they declared war against Hitler as a means of trying to improve Bulgarian-Russian relations.

EDUCATION BEFORE 1945

Unfortunately Bulgarian education before the 19th century had little to offer. The bright period of the 9th century—the foundation of the Cyrillic script by two Bulgarian monks—did not continue. Due to internal struggles, the Bulgarians were unable to establish an educational system in the early part of the Middle Ages, and after the 14th century Turkish domination prevented significant cultural growth. There were some parish schools designed to train young boys for the priesthood but no elementary schools organized on Bulgarian cultural traditions. A priest, Paisi, in 1762, wrote *A History of the Bulgarian People: Tsars and Saints* which touched on educational problems. Between 1760 and 1830 education was conducted on a bilingual pattern, i.e., Greek and Bulgarian were used as the cultural languages. In 1834 new national education began with the publishing of the first Bulgarian ABC book, *Bukvar*.

After the Congress of Vienna, Bulgarian cultural enlightenment grew very rapidly. As a matter of fact, the Bulgarian people had a higher literacy rate than any other Balkan nation and were generally better educated. The school system was supported both by private individuals and the state and the jurisdiction of the latter increased by the end of the 19th century.

In 1879 an important educational program was introduced, one of the first programs aimed at free compulsory elementary education. In 1888 the first institution of higher learning, the University of Sofia, was established. By 1910 the Bulgarian educational system consisted of four

---

[2] S. Runciman, *A History of the First Bulgarian Empire* (London: Bell Press, 1930); L. A. Dellin, "Bulgarian History Revised," in *Survey*, No. 39, 1961, pp. 105–112.

years of elementary school, three years of pro-gymnasium, and five years of gymnasium.

Just before the outbreak of World War I the literacy rate of Bulgarian people was as follows:

Area	Female	Male	Total
Urban	24.5	36.7	30.5
Rural	38.5	57.8	48.1
Total	35.5	53.3	44.4

It was further indicated that during World War I only 5 per cent of the Bulgarian soldiers were illiterate and by 1934 illiteracy dropped to only about 10 per cent of the total Bulgarian population.

Several educational measures taken by the pre-World War II Bulgarian government aimed at extending compulsory education to at least eight years of schooling, as well as improving the school curriculum in line with economic developments. There were no important industrial enterprises in the country which could employ the graduates after completion of secondary schooling, so subjects dealing with humanities predominated in Bulgarian elementary and secondary education. The most common languages taught were Old Slavonic, German, French and Greek along with classical subjects dealing with the philosophy and literature of Christian civilization.

As of 1939-1940 there were the following types of schools:[3]

Types of Schools	Number of Teachers	Number of Students
Total	31,825	1,071,874
General Education	28,625	1,009,690
Vocational-Technical	2,261	41,094
Special Schools	422	10,118
Semi-higher Schools	64	803
Higher Education	453	10,169

[3] N. Apanasewiscz and M. Rosen, *Education in Bulgaria* (Washington, D. C.: U. S. Office of Education, 1965), pp. 5–7; L. D. Dellin, *Bulgaria* (New York: Mid European Studies Center, 1957), p. 194. See also S. Evans, *A Short History of Bulgaria* (London: Lawrence and Wishart, Ltd., 1960).

In terms of vocational education there were several courses offered by the Bulgarian professional schools which usually consisted of two years of training. There were no highly qualified teachers in these schools, since the teacher training was not good. Most teachers were either from vocational trade organizations or were students who had completed vocational schools.

The opportunities for completing the higher educational institutions were rather slim. Only 10,169 students pursued higher educational careers before the World War II out of almost 8 million people. Requirements for entering the university were two: highly academic training in pre-college school, and a high social class. By 1940 there were eleven institutions of higher learning in Bulgaria.

THE PERIOD OF RECONSTRUCTION

Education in Bulgaria since 1944-1945 can be usually studied under two periods: the period of reconstruction (or the period of establishing the socialist system of education) from 1944-1959, and the period of the new era in education (the period of the Communistic system of education from 1959 on).

After World War II, Bulgarian communists under the leadership of Dimitrev wanted to establish a system of education similar to that of the Soviet Union but at the same time they wanted to maintain the national spirit of Bulgarian culture. Bulgaria was a small nation so was not enthusiastic about international communism or giving up her own national identity. She simply wanted to democratize the educational system without Russification of it.

There were many enthusiastic ideas about education, such as reconstructing the schools so as to unite theory and practice, giving opportunities to lower classes who were deprived of educational opportunities, and raising the standards of education in terms of the new technological demands and industrial needs.

Taking their instructions from the Russian communists, the Bulgarian educators had little to say about communist education in their country. General Marxism-Leninism philosophy prevailed in all educational institutions at every level. Instead of establishing and building new schools the communist authorities in education began to build communist centers, central Leninist party schools aimed at educating communist propagandists. During the five year period 1945-1950 more than 130,000 students attended these schools and in 1950 alone 5,600 "experts" graduated from the Leninist schools. Most of these schools were, however, one-teacher schools which tried to influence the people with communist Russian ideology. By 1954 there were more than 27,000 trained propagandists whose job was to remold the minds of the Bulgarian people.

Changes in General Education. There were three levels that were generally considered the general educational structure, i.e., preschool education, elementary education and secondary education. The most noticed change at any level was made in the curriculum. The old type of religious-moral education was abolished and the new "morality" was introduced. Latin and Greek were not to be taught at the secondary level. Instead of these subjects, the new lines fell into a general context of physical and intellectual development. As in Russia, physical education was introduced at all levels of education and in the upper grades military training was introduced. It was supposed to educate a "healthy soul in a healthy body" based on the concepts of communist progress, technology, industrial demands and political requirements of the party.

The Russian language, culture and literature were introduced at the fifth grade of the elementary schools. New subjects like astronomy and hygiene were added to the upper grades of the elementary schools or to the junior secondary schools.

From 1949 on education was based on the Russian system in terms of curriculum as well as in terms of general structure. The length of time at the elementary-secondary level was reduced to eleven years (instead of the twelve years before that date) and the first four years were compulsory.

Not only was the entire system reorganized, it was reconstructed philosophically. Preschool educational demands were specifically listed by the party: the Bulgarian child must be educated early in national consciousness and his responsibilities to the people; children must be taught work and study habits as often as possible. The party stated that the type of citizens educated and the speed of reconstruction depended on the work done by the Bulgarian schools.

The primary aim of Bulgarian communist educational authorities was to increase the number of students at each educational level. No questions were asked about the quality of education since the majority of teachers either needed special training in the new state demands or there simply were no qualified teachers. Bulgarian statistical data indicate that during the school year of 1939-1940 there were 1,072,250 students in all types of schools in 7,891 different educational institutions. By 1965 the number had not been doubled but it was larger than in 1939. For instance, in the 1963-1964 school year there were 1,613,266 students in all types of educational institutions.

There is no question that progress has been made in particular educational areas. There were only few schools for mentally and physically handicapped children before the war—blind, deaf-mute, handicapped and delinquent children—but in 1964 there were 83 such schools with 9,984 students compared to 5 such schools with 376 students in 1940. A tremendous leap forward was made in secondary education compared to the pre-war period. In 1964 there were 8,131 secondary (vocational and special) schools with 162,365 students as compared to 422 such schools in 1939 with 10,118 students. (See Tables 37 and 38.)

TABLE 37

General Development of Education in Bulgaria: 1940, 1957, 1965

Number of Schools, Teachers, Students	1939/40	1956/57	1964/65
A. Total:			
Schools	7,891	7,113	5,856
Teachers	31,889	55,001	74,781
Students	1,672,250	1,249,589	1,613,266
Students per 10,000 People . .	na	1,649	1,997
B. General Schools (Elementary & Secondary)			
Schools	7,455	6,773	5,157
Teachers	28,625	46,627	55,137
Students	1,009,690	1,126,061	1,281,684
C. Vocational			
Schools	385	133	277
Teachers	2,261	1,743	4,171
Students	41,094	20,100	61,969
D. Higher			
Schools	5	20	25
Teachers	453	3,026	5,359
Students	10,169	36,705	77,507
Students per 10,000 People . .	16	48	96

Central Board of Statistics at the Council of Ministers of the People's Republic of Bulgaria, *Statistical Manual* (Sofia: Foreign Language Press, 1965), pp. 152–153.

Higher Education. Higher education was another target of the communists who wanted to improve it for several reasons. First, the universities of Bulgaria paid too much attention to the old classical curriculum and neglected the education of the technological intelligentsia. Second, the social

TABLE 38

General Educational Polytechnic Schools: 1940, 1957, 1965

Number of Students, Teachers, Schools	1939/40	1956/57	1963/64
A. Students:			
Grades 1–4	638,719	614,122	603,544
Grades 5–7	288,311	346,576	533,169
Grades 8–9	82,660	165,363	144,971
B. Teachers:			
Grades 1–4	17,258	21,638	21,446
Grades 5–7	8,266	17,539	26,485
Grades 8–9	3,101	7,450	7,206
C. Schools:			
Grades 1–4	5,298	2,946	1,713
Grades 5–7	2,023	140	82
Primary 1–7	*	3,328	3,074
Secondary 1–9	134	359	288

Central Board of Statistics at the Council of Ministers of the People's Republic of Bulgaria, *Statistical Manual* (Sofia: Foreign Language Press, 1965), p. 154.

*After World War II the Bulgarian school system was reorganized according to the Soviet pattern of education. The seven-year school system was added after 1945.

composition of students was not always favorable to the working classes, and third, the relationship between work and school was distant.

The communists also claimed that the old distribution of specialists at the higher levels was neither planned nor organized. They blamed the bourgeois regime for not introducing new reforms. A frequently cited example was that the number of doctors in pre-war Bulgaria was disproportionate to the total population. In 1944 there were 3,516 physicians or only one for every 1,966 persons while 1963 there was one doctor for every 623 persons or a total of 3,022 physicians in Bulgaria. The distribution of dentists was no better since there were only 824 dentists in 1944 compared to 2,830 in 1963.

General enrollment increased rapidly in higher educational institutions, e.g., there were only five institutions of higher learning in pre-war Bulgaria, and by 1964 there were 25 with 77,597 students. The ratio changed from 16 students per 10,000 people in 1940 to 96 in 1963. (See Table 39.)

TABLE 39

Development of Higher Education in Bulgaria
(1940, 1957, 1965)

Number of Schools, Students, Teachers	1939/40	1956/57	1964/65
A. Schools:			
Total Number	5	20	25
Faculties-Total	7	32	44
Engineering	. . .	7	18
Agriculture	2	4	4
Economics	. . .	8	6
Medical	1	3	3
Fine Arts	. . .	5	5
Others	4	5	8
B. Students:			
Total Number	10,169	36,705	77,597
Engineering	. . .	9,645	30,671
Agriculture	826	6,822	10,005
Economics	3,229	6,217	9,113
Medical	1,021	5,687	6,548
Fine Arts	380	1,133	1,478
Education	2,839	5,817	16,589
Sport	. . .	773	1,842
Law	1,878	611	1,351
C. Teachers:			
Total Number	453	3,026	5,359
Professors	140	410	460
Readers	60	335	579
Assistants	177	1,331	2,978
Instructors	76	960	1,342

Central Board of Statistics at the Council of Ministers of the People's Republic of Bulgaria, *Statistical Manual* (Sofia: Foreign Language Press, 1965), p. 159.

THE PERIOD OF SOCIALIST EDUCATION

There were no major changes in the educational system in methods or in curriculum in 1959, nevertheless a new phase in Bulgarian education began.

There were several reasons for the changes in educational structures and in general approaches to education. The main change was in the political structure of the Kremlin since Stalin's death. Other reasons were the

Polish and Hungarian uprisings, the problems inside the communist bloc, and the internal situation in the Soviet Union.

The Bulgarian school system changed in the transition from capitalism to socialism, but much more in the transition from theoretical to practical types of schools. Referring to the Soviet reconstruction in 1956-1959 we note that a similar plan was introduced in Bulgaria. It was designed to strengthen the ideological relationship between the party and the people by requiring each student to work physically at least two years before entering any higher institution of learning. In Bulgaria, just as in the U.S.S.R., the law of 1959 demanded establishment of a closer link between education and practical life.[4]

In 1964, however, the general lines of the Khrushchevian reforms changed. It was no longer demanded that each student had to work physically; it was rather demanded that each student approach every situation on the basis of the logical requirements of his profession vs. national needs of the Bulgarian economy.

Bulgarian education returned to the twelve-year traditional general educational system with the only exception that polytechnical aspects of education were underlined. Bulgarian and Russian languages were not excluded but were treated in terms of their importance to one's specialization. The polytechnical schools demanded all-around educational development. Each individual was required to be well trained in theoretical and practical aspects of his profession as well as in the Bulgarian traditions and culture. We should, of course, not confuse ourselves with the idea of democracy in Bulgarian schools because they are far from that. They just simply changed as did the Russian schools but both systems are still very much controlled by the party and the central system of education. Students still must have a good recommendation from the Communist Youth Organization as they did in early periods of the communist regime.

Emphasis on vocational education is a general characteristic of the post-1959 period in Bulgaria. Considerable improvement has been made in industry, thus the school of the 1960s can be more realistically adjusted to industrial needs in both theory and practice. We note that in 1956 there were only 2,979 students in technical schools (industrial, building, agricultural, transport, economic, medical and Public Catering) as compared to 8,131 in 1964. The number of graduates from these schools, as well as from others, has increased each year since then. (See Table 39.)

---

[4] Apanasewicz, op. cit., p. 13. See also Central Board of Statistics, Statistical Manual, 1965, p. 152; Tudor Zhuvkov, On the Pioneers and Youth (Sofia: Narodna Mladezh, 1963), p. 13; UNESCO, World Survey of Education (Paris: UNESCO Press, 1955), p. 178; The Yearbook of Education, 1948, p. 503.

The 1959 reforms made it easier for Bulgarian students to study abroad, but most of the non-communist students are still not free to travel or study in non-communist countries. Opportunities for contact with foreign students are still restricted even in the 1960s.

The 1959 reforms also made it easier for students in vocational schools to enter higher educational institutions. Prior to that year these students were limited to their specific vocations since they encountered several difficulties when they wanted to enter a university. The 1959 reforms gave them some opportunities to study at higher educational levels.

Bulgarian statistical data list separately the semi-higher institutes (in the American system these would be equivalent to junior colleges) and the institutes of higher learning. As of 1964 there were general improvements in both—enlargement of their research facilities and an increment of higher educational faculties and students in them. (See Table 39.)

Education of the New Man. The education of the new man in Bulgaria undertakes the same processes as the education of the New Soviet man with the exception that in the former case the education of the new *Bulgarian* man is emphasized.

The school curriculum must be so organized as to achieve the training of the new man. All roads, the communists insist, must lead to communism. History must be taught (as in the Soviet Union) from the Marxian interpretations of history, i.e., following the communist pattern of historical developments: primitive communism, slavery, feudalism, capitalism, etc. Geography must be taught from the economic vantage of "capitalism," and the "neo-colonies" of American imperialism, but nothing is ever said about Russian presence in Bulgaria or in the Asiatic parts of the Soviet Union.

The new Bulgarian man must have some foundations for psychological reorientation, so the Bulgarians introduced the early Russian practice of the so called *udarnik* which meant simply that the individual who overproduced his working norm without demanding extra pay for it became a hero.

One of the best methods of educating the new man is to keep him away from parental influences. For this reason the communists in charge provide many opportunities for children to be educated collectively. Since 1960 (as in Russia), popular centers known as *zanimalna* and *internate* for child care have been established. The *zanimalna* literally means to be busy or to be occupied by something. They provide special help for children whose parents are at work. Children usually stay in this school as long as necessary. Under the special supervision of an adult teacher they do their homework or play collectively. The *internate* are the boarding schools, similar to the Soviet schools, where children stay in school for six days and come home during the weekend. Thus, they lose complete contact with their parents and are not influenced by the "old-fashioned" ideas. The Ministry of Education planned in 1960 to increase the number of students in the *zanimalna* and *internate* to one million by 1980. This means that all children will be in these types of schools.

There are several types of youth organizations which are assigned the task by the communist party to educate the Bulgarian youth in the communist world outlook. The Pioneers and the Young Communist League are the most effective groups. They provide several activities for all school children. In theory these organizations have nothing to say about the education of children, but in practice at each school the head of the Young Communist League has much to say about the nature of instruction and of extracurricular activities. The Young Communist League is in charge of special events like the celebration of national holidays, presenting certain plays, organizing sport clubs, etc.

The general idea of the communist authorities is to educate the children so that they realize that labor, communism and patriotism are inseparable. The party vigorously tries to implement such plans whereby good specialists will be good communists and at the same time Bulgarian patriots. In the future, according to the communist party program, the country will need a great number of such specialists educated in the *troika* concepts (labor, communism and patriotism).[5]

OTHER REFORMS

Religious Policies. When in 1947 Georgi Dimitrov returned from Moscow and became the real dictator of Bulgaria the purge against religion began. Dimitrov was trained by the Russian anti-religious propagandists. He applied the same methods in Bulgaria as the Russians did in the Soviet Union. It is hard to list in such a brief review all the methods that the communists used in liquidating religious influences upon the people, but they included every means the state had in its power or at its disposal. They established many organizations dealing with the anti-religious struggle, published books and periodicals, organized workers and peasants into special "re-educational" communes, imposed an anti-religious philosophy upon the League of the Young Communists, and engaged the teachers in anti-religious propaganda.

---

[5] Communist Party of Bulgaria, *Directives of the Eighth Congress of the Bulgarian Communist Party* (Sofia: 1963), p. 34. See also *Survey*, No. 39, 1961, pp. 80–85.

The population of Bulgaria was about 85 per cent Greek Orthodox, 14 per cent Muslim and one per cent Catholic. The Orthodox church for centuries was the protector of Christian civilization in Bulgaria and the preserver of the Bulgarian nation *per se*. Since Bulgaria was for five hundred years under Turkish rule, the Orthodox church did not manage to hold any important property and generally was poor. The clergy before 1944 were paid by the state and were allowed to teach in the public schools.

Dimitrov first wished to create hatred among the Christian churches. He thought that by disuniting them the struggle against Orthodoxy would be easier. The Catholics were accused of being collaborators with the old regime and spies for the United States. The Protestants (a very small group of Calvinists) were accused of anti-communist activities, being supporters of the Lutheran countries, etc. The Orthodox church, the communists thought, could be dissipated if the top religious authorities were belittled or forced to accept state superiority over religious matters.

When the people failed to respond favorably to the communist propaganda, the government began to use the most effective communist methods of persuasion, force and violence. In 1949, for instance, 15 leading Protestant clergy were tried for anti-government activities; 40 Catholic priests were sentenced to heavy labor in prison; Bishop Basilkov and three priests were sentenced to death. The Orthodox clergy also were not omitted from the communist persecutions, although a majority of the people thought that the communists would not touch the Orthodox religion, which is the religion of Russia and Bulgaria alike. But in 1950-1952, the purge against the Orthodox began.

After the death of Stalin there was a respite in property destruction by the party but propaganda was intensified. Religious holy days were always interrupted by party fanatics and such celebrations as Christmas and Easter were frequently interrupted by indoctrinated communist agitators.

Women and the State. After 1945 an intensive effort was made to include more women in the national economy and in political organizations. Propaganda was stepped up, especially among the Muslim Albanians to liberate women from Muslim religious laws. Women were required to participate in all events which would have been unthinkable before the communist regime. They also were included in all Communist Youth organizations. The number of women in school, in the national economy, and in the party was almost equal to the number of men by 1965.

Economic Reforms. Private property, of course, was nationalized by the communists in 1944-1945 and the Soviet economic patterns have been introduced. The continuous Five Year Plans have been incorporated into the Bulgarian economic system as part of the Bulgarian national tradition. The economic situation obviously was not solved by merely passing official decrees and initiating new plans. The country was for centuries an agricultural-pastoral country which could not have been changed in a short period of time. The communists wanted first to modernize the agricultural industry, and second to build up heavy industry. The promised Soviet help did not materialize, so Bulgaria sought advice and aid in many Western countries, e.g., Italy, Germany and the United States.[6]

Since 1939 there has been a decrease in agricultural production and in the breeding of livestock, e.g., in 1939 Bulgaria had 10.3 million sheep and in 1961 only 9.2 million; they had 1.9 million cattle in 1939 and 1.7 in 1961.

In other developments, transportation, industry, and the national economy generally suffered severe blows due to unrealistic planning by communist economists.[7]

Additional References

Roger L. Wolfe, *The Balkans in Our Times* (Cambridge: Harvard University Press, 1956); Akademiia Nauk SSSR, *Osvobozhdenie Bulgarii ot turetskogo iga* (AN SSSR, 1961), especially vol. II; Boris Ivanov, *Sudurzhanie i formi na politechnicheskoto obuchenie* (Sofia: Narodna Prosveta, 1960); Tudor Ganev, *Nauchni subrania na Bulgarskata Akademia na Naukite* (Sofia: Bulgarska Akademia na Naukite, 1958); N. Papazov, *Results of the Reorganization of Public Education and Our Future Tasks in Bringing the School Closer to Life* (Sofia: Narodna Prosveta, 1963), pp. 30 ff.; Dimitrovski Kommunisticheski Mladezhski Soiuz, *Materiali ot deveti kongres na DKMS* (Sofia: Narodna Mladezh, 1958); D. Kosev, *A Short History of Bulgaria* (Sofia: Foreign Languages Publishing House, 1963).

---

[6] J. Kalo, "The Bulgarian Economy," in *Survey*, No. 39, 1961, pp. 86–94. See also Assembly of Captive European Nations, *Bulletin* (New York: ACEN Press, 1956), p. 50; Dellin, *Bulgaria*, p. 192; *Osteuropa*, June 1955, p. 227.

[7] *East Europe*, Vol. 13, No. 2, 1964, p. 35; Kalo, *op. cit.*, p. 92.

Chapter 18

EDUCATION IN YUGOSLAVIA

Yugoslavia is one of the newest European countries, having come into existence after World War I, and embodying several Slavic and non-Slavic nationalities in one federal state. Serbs, Croats, Slovenians, Macedonians and others are included.

The Yugoslav territory is spread between the Adriatic Sea, and the Rumanian and Hungarian valleys, occupying some of the richest soil in Europe. A chain of big rivers, the Danube, Tisa and Drava, provide excellent water transportation as well as irrigation for fields.

The population of Yugoslavia is by no means homogeneous. Serbs represent a minority in the total population, but as far as control of the state is concerned, they predominate. Not unlike Russia in composition, Yugoslavia of today has the following distribution of population:[1]

---

[1] For further information see Josef Hecimovic, *In Tito's Death Marches*, translated and edited by John Precela (Chicago: Croatian Franciscan Press, 1961), pp. 12–102; I. Udich, *Sposterezhenia z Yugoslavii* (New York: Dnipro Press, 1957), pp. 14–16. See also Federal Statistical Office, *Statistical Pocketbook of Yugoslavia*, 11th Edition (Belgrade: 1955), pp. 18 ff.

329

Republic	Area in Sq. km	Population (In Thousands)	Inhabitants per sq. km.
Bosnia and Herzegovina . . .	1,129	3,278	64.1
Montenegro	13,812	472	34.2
Croatia	56,538	4,160	73.6
Macedonia	25,713	1,406	54.7
Slovenia	20,251	1,592	78.6
Serbia	88,361	7,642	86.5
Total	255,804	18,550	72.5

Almost 90 per cent of the population is of Slavic origin. The non-Slavs are settled in Bosnia and Herzegovina, the Turks in Montenegro, and the Albanians around the Albanian borders. The Slavs, although linguistically similar, have great political differences and live like "cat and mouse," especially the Serbs and the Croats (like the Russians and the Ukrainians in the Soviet Union). It has to be noted that non-communists suffered heavy losses after World War II when the Titoists liquidated many people.

The over-all increase of the Yugoslavian population has not been rapid. A Serbian source estimated that the population of Yugoslavia was 19,-279,000 in 1964; by 1975 it will reach 21,732,000.

Historical Background. The history of Yugoslavia is the history of a captive nation. Serbs and other Slavs living in the Danube basin were the first target of the Turco-Tatar invasions. They were later subjugated by the Turks. From 1389 on, when the Serbs lost the battle at Kosovo, Serbia became a vassal principality of Turkey while the Slovenians and most of the Croats were subjugated to the Austro-Hungarian rule. Political divisions of this kind were reflected later on in the history of the Southern Slavs and in the mentality of certain ethnic groups. Thus the Serbs, being under Turkish occupation, appropriated many behavioral characteristics of the Turks, while the Slovenians and Croats followed more or less the behavior of the Germans and Hungarians. We note this from the fact that Serbians, accepted the Greek Orthodox religion—a heritage of the Greek Byzantine Empire—while the Slovenians and the Croats became Catholics. Even today the present day Yugoslavia is divided religiously as follows: About 50 per cent of the population belongs to the Greek Orthodox religion; 38 per cent to the Roman Catholic (Croats and Slovenians); and about 12 per cent are Muslims.[2]

---

[2] Vera Tomich, *Education in Yugoslavia and the New Reforms* (Washington: U. S. Office of Education, Bulletin No. 20, 1963), pp. 3–4; *Statistical Pocketbook*

The Slovenians and the Croats were under German-Hungarian rule from the 12th century on. Only before 1102—the year when the Croats lost their independence and became the subjects of Hungarian exploitation —did the Croats and Slovenians have their own state, while the Serbian independence lasted until the end of the 14th century. Serbs and Croats are similar linguistically; Slovenians differ substantially.

The Montenegrins, like the Serbs, enjoyed independence until the Turks occupied the country. However, the geographic condition of Montenegro was quite different from Serbia since Montenegro was located in a mountain region, along the coast of the Adriatic Sea. Therefore, they were less exploited by foreign rule, namely, Turkey. In reality Turkey was never able to control the situation in the mountains where the Montenegrins lived, and finally granted freedom to these people in 1799, partially because the area was not strategically important for the Turks and partially because of the pressure of Turkish wars with Russia.

The most controversial Slavic part of Yugoslavia is the region of Bosnia and Herzegovina which, although it was under the Turkish rule until the Congress of Berlin (1878) and was given to Austria after that date, remained a very unique area in social and political aspects. This area accepted the Islam religion while maintaining the Serbo-Croatian language and culture. About 30 per cent of the population of the region are Muslims.

The Macedonians represent another complicated problem for the Yugoslavian state since the people of this region are the most racially mixed of all Yugoslavia. The region is surrounded by Albania, Greece, and Bulgaria. For centuries it was under the influence of Slavic, Greek and Turkish cultures. Linguistically, the Macedonians are associated with the Serbians, and both nations belonged to the same state during the Middle Ages. Both were conquered by Turkey in the 14th century.

The Yugoslavian struggle for independence actually began in the 19th century and was due to Russian pressure on the Turkish empire. Like the Romanians and Bulgarians, the peoples of Yugoslavia awaited the outcome of Turco-Russian relations and the subsequent destruction of the Ottoman empire. From these the subjugated Balkan nationalities tried to benefit. K. Petrovic and M. Obronevic, leaders of the struggle for Serbian independence, organized resistance to the Turks in the early part of the

---

of Yugoslavia, 1965, p. 19; T. H. Hammond, "A Brief History," in R. Byrnes (ed.), *Yugoslavia* (New York: F. Praeger Press, 1957), p. 2; H. C. Darby and Seton-Watson, *A Short History of Yugoslavia* (Cambridge: Harvard University Press, 1966), pp. 13–23; Fred Warner Neal, *Titoism in Action, The Reforms in Yugoslavia after 1948* (Berkeley: University of California Press, 1958), *passim.*

19th century. Gradually the struggle became uncontrollable for the Turks. Under the constant pressure of the Russian armies and with the Russian occupation of Turkestan in 1865, the Turks lost the battle and were forced to grant freedom to most of the Balkan states in 1878. As a result of the treaty of Berlin, Serbia became independent, but was not without fear of invasion by Austro-Hungary, the new protector of the Balkan states. The clash came in 1908 when the Hungarians occupied Bosnia and Herzegovina. This slowly led to the Sarajevo incident in which Prince Ferdinand was assassinated, and World War I began. Only after 1918 was Yugoslavia completely free from the Turkish-Hungarian rule.

When World War II began, Yugoslavia was a weak spot for German aggression since the Serbs and Croats were fighting each other. The Germans made the most of this situation. In 1941 the Germans established an "independent" Croatia while most of the country was either following the national liberation movement led by Joseph Broz, known as Tito, or the democratic revolution under the leadership of General Mihajlovic. Only a very small minority of the population believed that the young King Peter (born in 1923) could offer any reasonable solution to the Yugoslav problems. After the war the king escaped to London while the forces of Tito-Mihajlovic were fighting on two fronts: against each other and against the Germans. Due to the English and American recognition of Tito, the communist dictatorship was established in Yugoslavia.

EDUCATION BEFORE THE COMMUNIST TAKEOVER

During the Turkish and Hungarian occupations, the educational level was anything but sufficient. Most of the people were illiterate or had no more than an elementary education. Only Slovenians were equal to the Austrians in literacy. The Croats enjoyed moderate success in educational matters. Like the Slovenians, the Croats use the Latin alphabet. This gave them access to European contributions to education, and at the same time made it possible for many Croats to study abroad. In Croatia, also the Roman Catholic church provided for some basic educational needs, especially religious training. The Serbians, however, used the Cyrillic alphabet (the same one as the Russian) and their association with the Latin West was not as close as that of the Croats.

Between the two world wars the monarchal government of Yugoslavia did very little to improve the cultural level of the people. Data from 1930 show that over 50 per cent of the female population was illiterate, and that varied substantially from region to region. For example, as of 1931, 46.9 per cent of the total population was illiterate; in Croatia 31.5 per cent; in Bosnia and Herzegovina 70 per cent; and in Macedonia 67.5 per cent.

The average for the whole country was 32.3 per cent of the men and 56.4 per cent of the women. In some parts of the country the situation was even more serious, e.g., in Bosnia and Herzegovina, 84 per cent of the women were illiterate and in Macedonia about 82 per cent.

Elementary and secondary education was reorganized after the first World War. The law of 1929 provided for universal compulsory elementary education, though in reality this never came into existence, since most children quit school after completing four years. However, some improvements were apparent as the following data indicate: the percentage of children in the age group of 7-14 attending elementary schools varied from 21 per cent in Bosnia and Herzegovina to 55.8 per cent in Croatia, and an average of 50.1 per cent for the whole country.

By 1939 the situation had not improved substantially. There were slightly over 9,000 elementary schools with 1.5 million pupils for a population of 14 million. There were only 88,000 students in the vocational schools and 125,000 students in the secondary schools of the country. The last category was almost in line with the national needs because most of the Yugoslavs were engaged in agriculture (76.3 per cent) and only 10 per cent were in industry.

Before World War II extreme selectivity as to higher educational opportunities was practiced by the Yugoslavian regime. There were only 17,000 students in institutions of higher learning for the whole country. Places like Bosnia and Herzegovina and Montenegro had no institutions of higher learning and Macedonia had only one establishment for higher education.

Schools for national minorities hardly existed. The Macedonians, the Bulgarians, and over 500,000 Albanians had no schools in their native tongues of any kind. The same policy applied to Turks living in Yugoslavia, also Czechs and Italians. Hungarian, German, Romanian and Slovak nationalities, however, enjoyed equal rights along with the Serbs since they had their own elementary and secondary schools in areas populated by these ethnic groups. There were 183 Hungarian elementary schools with 27,915 students as of 1939. All other nationalities had only 266 schools with 41,974 students.[3]

SOCIAL FOUNDATIONS OF EDUCATION AFTER 1945

During the first few years the Serbs copied almost everything from the Russian communists. The school system was organized on patterns similar

---

[3] *Statistical Pocketbook of Yugoslavia,* 1965, pp. 19–92. See also *Osnovni Statisticki Podaci i Stanju Skolstva u Federativnoi Narodnoi Republici Jugoslavii* (Belgrade: Komisia za Reformu Skolstva, 1957), p. 9; Tomich, *op. cit.,* p. 6.

to those of the Russian communist system. Also the agencies of control were very similar to the Russian administration. Until the split between Belgrade and Moscow the Serbs were especially pro-Russian. The new educational system was to be based on the policies and practices of the early Bolsheviks: national in form and communist in character. Since the social conditions of Yugoslavia were similar to the social conditions of Russia—several nationalities with different linguistic and cultural backgrounds—the Tito regime promised complete cultural freedom to the peoples living in Yugoslavia.

After a few years with the "Russian brothers" the Yugoslavian communists began to doubt the Russian interpretation of Marxism. In the course of ideological polemics a positive philosophical movement took place in Yugoslavia; that is to say, the Yugoslavian intellectuals began to approach the Marxian doctrines from a critical point of view, just as Marx and Lenin approached the social problems of their times from different points of view.

School and society were considered from the socialistic point of view. Serbian-Croatian educators began to discuss whether or not the socialism predicted by Marx was possible at all. If the situation and present day conditions are different, why not adapt the socialistic ideas to the present world rather than the present world to the socialistic ideas?

The Yugoslavian intellectuals also considered the school from the communist point of view but with one exception, i.e., if the interests of social classes are not to be in conflict in the new society, then it is logical to presuppose that the interests of the government should not be different than that of the classes. In short, there should not be two kinds of needs —one for the workers and another for those who control the workers; nor should there be two kinds of ethics—one for the communists and another for non-communists.

A further point that the Yugoslavian intellectuals raised was the problem of morality and its relationship to the school situation. The question was asked whether or not the study of history should replace the ethical and moral principles of mankind, or whether it is more desirable to base morality on the modes of behavior displayed in a revolution (e.g., the Russian Revolution). The problem that confused many people (not only philosophers and intellectuals, but also party politicians) was the problem of eternal values. Even among communists one finds serious consideration concerning the notion of infinity and temporality. What is the goal of life? Once one accepts the idea of infinity, the notion of Being must make some sense, for without an Infinite Being the existence of man makes no sense.

The Soviet ethical principles, "the end justifies the means," was also a subject of criticism. Scholars who argued about the validity of that premise, pointed out that there must be a difference between the means and the ends. One cannot solve every problem according to one single theory.

What actually are the Serbian scholars trying to do? The answer is that they are trying to avoid the mistakes made by the Russian communists, or as Stajonovic called it "the ethical tragedy of socialism." From the Yugoslav viewpoint, to be a "revolutionary being" one should not favor only certain historical ends, but one should adapt his behavior to those ends. The principle "I serve only my party" can be very ambiguous and therefore dangerous.

School Reform Movement. There is no question that philosophical ideas combined with political events of the Tito-Stalin-Khrushchev regimes made a tremendous impact on the new communist education of Yugoslavia. Since the school must serve the collective, the role of the individual was interpreted somewhat differently from the role of the individual in the Russian collective. The same applied to the educational institutions. The role of the school was not only to train people in technological skills but to indoctrinate them with party philosophy. The Educational Law of 1958 required that the school educate the children in a socialistic world outlook but at the same time it must care for the personality of the individual.

The Yugoslav educational reforms endeavored to reorganize the system in such a way as to educate a well rounded individual fit for the new society. There was no radical change from the previous system since there was no need to expand the school reforms to every level of professional pursuit—there were not sufficient openings for all the graduates from existing schools. There were efforts to provide vocational opportunities for those willing to learn a trade, since technological education had been neglected during the short history of Yugoslavian independence.

Tito's reforms also aimed at improving the poor relationship between intellectuals and manual workers, a condition common to most European countries. For this reason, he appointed the School Reform Commission, and as a result of this committee's work, the schools were reorganized in 1958 in the following manner: first four years, between the ages of three and seven, were termed preschool education; from seven until fifteen, elementary education; from fifteen to nineteen, secondary education; and from nineteen to twenty-two or twenty-five (medical schools), higher education. At the same time the Federal Council of Education was set up (similar to the Ministry of Education in the U.S.S.R.), under whose authority all national, regional, district, and city educational boards were subordinated.[4]

GENERAL EDUCATION

Schools of general education include the kindergartens, elementary-secondary schools and vocational schools. The Yugoslav general law outlined for each area certain provisions designed to improve the system.

Since most young people were unable to attend higher educational institutions, the general law made it clear that the education of the Yugoslav youth should be socialist oriented—should be related toward the choice of profession (either a trade or a professional specialty)—and should bring happiness to the individual and the society in which he lives.

Compulsory eight-year education is required by Yugoslavian law for all children regardless of sex, creed, or race.

Elementary Education. Yugoslavian children begin elementary school when they reach seven years of age. Although there are pre-elementary institutions, such as nurseries and kindergartens, these are not compulsory schools. They are designed especially for the working parents, and are "baby-care" establishments.

The school administrators, as well as the teachers, are encouraged to orient children in the direction of a future vocation according to their interests and abilities. No plans are made for an individual's future profession, but it is generally believed that with proper motivation, the child might choose a future occupation even while of elementary school age.

It is interesting to note that Yugoslav communist education is not based on the same social foundations as is the Russian communist system. Soviet children are taught to respect authority, but only communist authority. They are taught to respect mother and father, but to denounce them before the communist authorities in case of anti-Soviet activities. The Yugoslavian educational authorities do not specify two types of ethics. They maintain that a child must be educated in humanistic principles and *not* in "communist humanism" only.

The Yugoslav teachers are required to act for the interests of the children and to help every child in all possible ways. However, there are no guidance programs, no counseling services, and no measurement of child's

---

[4] *Ibid.,* pp. 62–110. See also *Praxis,* Philosophical Journal (Zagreb), No. 1–2, 1966, pp. 66–151; *Praxis,* No. 3, 1966, p. 67; *Praxis,* No. 4, 1966, pp. 162 ff.

interests and emotions—practices that are common in America. The Yugoslav teacher has to perform these functions as best he can. The teacher is encouraged to do his best in the name of socialistic society, humanity, civilization, and other grand generalizations.

Disciplinary problems are handled by the school teachers, not counselors or parents. The child is well disciplined, but the Yugoslav child, unlike the Soviet child, is not subjected to collective punishments or confessions. Old practices which demand that the school must handle the children properly in every possible pedagogical way are not entirely rejected. There are no religious commandments on the walls of educational institutions, but the socialist discipline requires that every child be educated in universal brotherhood, respect for authority, for his fellow-man and for other peoples.

There has been a substantial increase in the number of students in elementary education since 1939. As mentioned before, only 50 per cent of the school age children were able to attend schools during 1939-1940. In 1964 there were 14,568 elementary schools with almost three million pupils as compared to 9,190 schools with less than one and one-half million pupils in 1939. There was about equal distribution of primary school students in all regions of the republics. The tremendous increases in this twenty-five year period may be clearly seen in Tables 40 and 41. (See Table 40 and 41.)

Secondary Schools. The most common secondary school is the four-year gymnasium which children enter after completion of the eight-year elementary schools. The last four years of elementary school are considered as junior high school, since before the communist takeover the secondary school lasted eight years as it did in Europe. Due to the expansion of compulsory education to eight years, elementary training is supposedly raised to a higher level than before the war.

There are other secondary schools, very often termed vocational schools, where the students take courses suited for their future occupations. The gymnasium, on the other hand, is designed for those students who do not intend to go to higher institutions of learning.

The study plans issued by the educational authorities in Belgrade are the same for all schools. The students at the secondary level have no choice but to take those subjects listed by the study plan. There are electives (of minor significance) and included may be music, foreign languages, or sometimes extra work in some scientific laboratories. Due to technological development and the ever-growing demands of industrial society, the es-

TABLE 40

Educational Development in Yugoslavia: By Republics; 1939, 1964

Republic	Number of Students		Number of Teachers	
	1938/39 (000 omitted)	1963/64 (000 omitted)	1938/39	1963/64
A. PRIMARY SCHOOLS . . .	1,471	4,980	34,663	96,370
Bosnia & Herzegovina. . . .	148	575	4,203	13,876
Montenegro	44	90	1,080	3,176
Croatia	385	630	9,181	20,848
Macedonia	101	253	1,693	8,694
Slovenia	182	244	5,651	9,418
Serbia	611	1,188	12,855	40,358
B. VOCATIONAL	88	361	7,908	18,462
Bosnia & Herzegovina. . . .	12	47	890	2,354
Montenegro	3	8	366	487
Croatia	20	88	1,942	4,992
Macedonia	7	26	670	1,259
Slovenia	10	38	962	1,968
Serbia	36	154	3,078	7,402
C. GENERAL SECONDARY SCHOOLS	125	142	5,607	7,404
Bosnia & Herzegovina. . . .	15	21	640	1,096
Montenegro	10	6	425	278
Croatia	30	36	1,417	1,891
Macedonia	11	19	495	876
Slovenia	13	11	542	712
Serbia	46	49	2,088	2,551
D. HIGHER	27	159	1,204	15,002
Bosnia & Herzegovina. . . .	. . .	20	. . .	1,793
Montenegro	. . .	2	. . .	117
Croatia	6	37	508	4,402
Macedonia	. . .	9	29	821
Slovenia	2	14	143	1,752
Serbia	19	77	524	6,117

Statistical Pocket Book of Yugoslavia, 11th edition (Belgrade: Federal Statistical Office, 1965), p. 92.

sentials of scientific knowledge are necessary for all children regardless of their area of concentration.[5]

[5] Gymnaziia u novom sistemu obrazovania i vaspitania (Belgrade: Commission for School Reforms, 1954), p. 4; B. R., "Brez teorije ni prakse," in Prosvetni delavec (Liubliana: 1966), No. 10, p. 1.

TABLE 41

Number of Schools, Students, and Teachers in Yugoslavia
(1939, 1964)

Type of Schools, Students & Teachers	1938/39	1963/64
A. SCHOOLS:		
Primary Schools	9,190	14,386
Schools for Skilled Workers	766	629
Adult and Vocational Schools	4	40
Technical Schools	53	516
Secondary Art Schools	5	48
General Secondary Schools	205	337
Other Schools	66	1,222
Teachers' Schools	37	99
B. STUDENTS (000 omitted)		
Primary Schools	1,471	2,980
Schools for Skilled Workers	70	153
Adult and Vocational Schools	0	3
Technical Schools	11	172
Teachers' Schools	4	29
Secondary Art Schools	1	5
General Secondary Schools	125	142
Other Schools	9	93
C. TEACHING STAFF		
Primary Schools	34,663	96,370
Schools for Skilled Workers	6,174	5,499
Adult and Vocational Schools	23	400
Technical Schools	879	9,791
Teachers' Schools	555	1,698
Secondary Art Schools	136	1,074
General Secondary Schools	5,607	7,404
Other Schools	684	7,603

Statistical Pocket Book of Yugoslavia, 11th edition (Belgrade: Federal Statistical Office, 1965), p. 9.

Note that there were 14,386 primary schools as compared to 9,190 in 1939; there were 1,332 vocational schools in 1964 compared to 881 in 1939; there were 337 general secondary schools in 1964 and 205 in 1939; and there were 260 high and higher schools in 1964 as compared to 26 such schools in 1939.

Attendance increased slowly in general secondary schools. Data show that in 1964 there were 142,000 students as compared to 125,000 students in 1939, and the reason for this slow increase was the great expansion in other secondary schools (technical, vocational, and teachers' schools) after 1945.

The curriculum in the gymnasiums is very uniform throughout the country. For example, an average of 31 hours per week is required from all students attending the gymnasiums. The subject matter is divided approximately thus: the mother language is offered for four credits throughout the four year period; two hours of art; a foreign language is offered for one or two credits; 3 credits of mathematics and physics are offered in each semester; etc. The Latin language is included in the secondary school curriculum, but religion is not. Physical education as well as military training are compulsory disciplines.

Other Secondary Schools. There are several types (other than gymnasium) of secondary education which are called vocational schools or schools for professional education. The 1964 statistical yearbook of Yugoslavia lists the following types: schools for skilled workers; administrative and medical institutes at the secondary level; technical schools; teachers' schools; secondary art schools; schools for adults; and schools for supplementary education.

The time required to graduate from the Yugoslav secondary schools is usually four years but it can be longer. Some technical specialties require more time and some teachers' schools graduate teachers after only two years of training beyond the eight years of elementary education.

Curriculum is regulated by the section of the Central Educational Council responsible for the given level, e.g., the physics curriculum would be mostly oriented to natural sciences, or the modern languages major has the opportunity to master a given language. But, in all areas of study, physical education, military training and, in most cases, Latin, are included.

It has to be noted that elementary school teachers do not have a diploma from a higher educational institution. Most have only four years of training beyond the elementary level, or (in rural areas) only two years. Secondary school teachers, however, do attend higher educational institutions and most have a diploma in one specific field (e.g., physics or mathematics but not both, or modern languages but not a native language).

The data from 1964 show that there were 153,000 students in schools for skilled workers as compared to 70,000 in 1939; there were 172,000 students in technical schools as compared to 11,000 in 1939; 29,000 in teachers' schools as compared to 4,000 in 1939; there were 93,000 in adult secondary schools as compared to 9,000 in 1939, etc.

Schools for national minorities also increased after 1945. Prior to 1945 there was only one Hungarian vocational secondary school with 82 students; by 1964 there were 89 vocational schools with 11,724 students; there were only four secondary general schools in 1939 (two Hungarian, one Romanian and one Slovak) while there were 31 such schools in 1964 with 4,902 students. It should be noted that among the national minorities are Bulgarian, Czech, Slovak, Italian, Hungarian, Rumanian, Ukrainian (Ruthenian), Turkish, and Albanian.

HIGHER EDUCATION

One of the most important communist reforms is that concerning higher education. Almost in every country the communists control, they issue special directives on the nature of higher educational institutions and require compliance.

The Yugoslavian reforms were not much different from those of the other communist countries. All wanted to eliminate the social barrier, i.e., privileges given to upper classes and certain nationalities. The Yugoslav laws of 1945, 1956, and 1958 called for the higher institutions of learning to give special attention to the education of new leaders for the new society. All schools were required to relate school life to the life of society and theory to practice.

Priority in schools was given to those sympathetic to the new regime as well as to the children of working parents. But, regardless of attitudes, the new laws required increased knowledge of socialistic disciplines. All students were required to study the revolutionary movements of socialistic countries and the communistic designs of the future state.[6]

The most crucial problem of Yugoslavian education was the training of teachers for the secondary and higher educational schools. (As mentioned before, elementary school teachers are trained only on the secondary level and no higher education is required.) By 1960 the situation due to the consequences of war had more or less ameliorated, e.g., there were 18,462 teachers in vocational and technological schools as of 1964 as compared to 7,908 in 1939; there were 7,404 teachers in general secondary schools in 1964 compared to 5,607 in 1939; and there were 15,002 teachers at higher educational establishments in 1964 compared to 1,204 in 1939.

The number of students at institutions of higher education increased very rapidly. For example, in 1939 there were only 26 higher educational institutions in Yugoslavia with 16,978 students while in 1964 there were 260 higher educational institutions with 160,959 students. The proportion

[6] V. Puzevski, "Shkola s produzenim boravskom-zahtiev naseg vremena," *Zivot i skola*, No. 1, 1966, pp. 21–36. See also *Statistical Pocketbook of Yugoslavia*, 1965, p. 93.

of Yugoslav students to the total population is much higher than, for instance, the proportions of English, French, German or Italian students to their respective countries. (See Table 40.)

OTHER DEVELOPMENTS

There are several educational-political implications of Titoism in Yugoslavia. First, the communists realize that education of youth is one of their most important goals. Without the youth there would be no safe future for communism in Yugoslavia. In order to keep things under control, the Yugoslav director established the League of Communists which occupies the most important political place in the country. In educational matters the League of Communists serves as the "advisory" body to all educational institutions of the country. But in reality, they lead education, "suggest" new laws and reforms, and issue directives and other ideological decrees. Most important, the League is concerned with the education of youth outside school activities.

One such organization under communist control is the Pioneer organization—quite similar to the Soviet Pioneer organization—to which all children aged 7-15 are to belong. Their program is directed by the communist party, which tries to educate children in the spirit of international brotherhood and love of one's own country.

The second organization of the Yugoslav youth is the People's Youth of Yugoslavia. It is an identical copy of the Soviet Communist Youth Association (Komsomol), has the same educational platforms and goals, and is comprised of all students aged 15-25 who attend secondary and higher educational institutions.

Another important development in communist Yugoslavia is the extensive propaganda system dedicated to strengthen the relationship between the leaders and the masses. The Yugoslav press has substantially increased since 1945 and there are many newspapers in the minority languages, e.g., in 1964 there were 23 different major newspapers in six official languages as well as newspapers edited in Italian, Hungarian, Bulgarian, Turkish and Czech.

Yugoslav communists did the same as the Russians to emancipate women. True, women are in all branches of the national economy but they also work on construction, do heavy factory work and other jobs that women in Western European societies do not usually do. The number of women students varied according to the area of concentration, e.g., there were more women in the medical professions than men, especially on the secondary level. In economics there were three times as many females as males; in the technical fields only about 10 per cent of the students are women, e.g., in engineering, mining, etc.

In religious freedom, Yugoslavia is second only to Poland among the Soviet satellites. Except for a brief period of 1944-1946 when the clergy and the Catholic believers were liquidated, freedom of religion is relatively great.

The Yugoslav communists took an entirely different view of the state and society. They were the first communists who dared to criticize Marx as being impractical because he was dealing with the analysis of the concept of labor, not practice.[7] After all, Marx lived in a century that was entirely removed from Yugoslavia's existence.

The success of the Titoists in Yugoslavia can be attributed to many factors. First, they used extremely brutal force and violence (as the Russians did) and made it impossible for other groups to strike back. Second, American economic help saved Tito from political starvation, and third, Tito—unlike Benesh of Czechoslovakia or Mikolajczyk of Poland (who flew from London to take office at home)—came to political office with the help of the army. Tito won his office on the battlefield of Yugoslavia. Fourth, Tito was clever enough to look beyond the war. He envied Lenin and Stalin because of their ability to rule, so he imitated them on the road to power.

Tito also saw that the concepts of full communism and the complete nationalization of man's property were too utopian. He was first among the communist dictators to allow private ownership of plots of land and private farming. The latter was on a small basis (not more than 24 acres of land could be owned by one farmer), nevertheless it was a beginning. Tito also allowed workers to participate directly in controlling factories and and getting some share of the common profits. All these things were later introduced in the Soviet Union. He also demanded that primary loyalty should be given to the state and only after that to the party.

There are no free elections, of course, but at least there is some freedom to work in various areas of the national economy. In the words of Petrovich:

> Despite its advances toward increased human freedom and individual dignity, there is one thing Tito's system cannot do—give up power. Tito's communists can try to do many things for their people, but they can never set them free ... But the people of Yugoslavia would like best of all to be free for this is the greatest certainty of all.[8]

---

[7] *Ibid.*, p. 95; Tomich, *op. cit.*, p. 47; *Praxis,* No. 6, 1965, p. 49.

[8] Michael Petrovich, *Titoism* (Milwaukee: Marquette University, Slavic Institute Papers, No. 3, 1958), p. 49.

Additional References

Francis Eterovich and C. Spalatin, *Croatia: Land, People and Culture* (Toronto: University of Toronto Press, 1964); A. Daskalakis, *The Hellenism of Ancient Macedonians* (Chicago: Institute for Balkan Studies, 1965); E. Kofas, *Nationalism and Communism in Macedonia* (Washington: Georgetown University Press, 1964); Thyllis Auty, *Yugoslavia* (New York: Walker Press, 1965); J. Arnovljevic, "Za pravilni tretman mesta i uloge akolskog pedagoga," in *Prosvetni preglad* (Cultural Review), Belgrade: 1966), No. 19, pp. 77 ff.; G. Ernjakovich, *The Yugoslav Educational System* (Belgrade: Commission for School Reforms, 1959), *passim*.

Chapter 19

EDUCATION IN EAST GERMANY

The East German Democratic Republic, as the Russians have baptized it, was a creation of fear and hurry. After the war the Russians intended to dominate Western Europe and to expand their influence far westward, even to other continents. When the Western powers began to do something about this expansion, the Russians organized the democratic eastern European states into the Warsaw pact and added to this pact the Republic of East Germany in October, 1949.

For the last 20 years, East Germany has not had to worry about an over-population problem (probably the only country in the world) because since the "free" republic was established the population of East Germany has decreased substantially. It dropped from 19 million in 1946 to 17 million in 1957. The number of *Flüchtlingen* (displaced persons and escapees from the East) is constantly increasing. The West German government has a real problem with this massive inflow. In addition to those evacuated from the Polish occupation and the Sudetenland (Czechoslovakia), the number of *Flüchtlingen* increases yearly, e.g., in 1950 over 197,000 escaped to the West; in 1955 over 255,000; in 1961 over 207,000.

GENERAL POLYTECHNICAL EDUCATION

Under the term of general polytechnical education belong elementary education and a general ten-year program of secondary education. The educational system of East Germany is as follows:

a. Primary school: the first three years of training;
b. Middle school (Mittelstufe): the fourth, fifth and sixth grades;
c. Secondary polytechnical: ten-year school.
d. Complete secondary school where the students who pass all the required exams receive their diplomas or *Abitur*. This training lasts two years longer than the preceding, or a total of 12 years.

The East Germans, like other communists, have three types of instruction, i.e., daytime, evening, and correspondence school. Many schools carry on instruction on a parttime basis, especially for those who work full time and for those who are working for a degree on the secondary level or higher. The most common type of schooling is daytime schooling but evening education is growing steadily. There were 2.4 million children in schools of all types (elementary and secondary levels) in 1965, of which, according to an East German statistical source, about 20 per cent were learning a vocation.

The aim of East German Communist education is the same as that of any other communist satellite. Children must be educated in the Marxist world outlook and the school should leave no room for religion. Quite often the idea of communist humanism is underlined. Scientific education is intended to replace an idealistic or religious orientation. Under the common denominator of Marxism-Leninism, the school has to educate a new youth capable of the realization of the communistic design of the future state (Russian German state) and the youth must be indoctrinated in the spirit of anti-militarism and the *demokratisierung* of the German nation.[1]

The reason that the term polytechnical education is used is simply because the Russian pattern of a school system must prevail in any structural

---

[1] *Neues Deutschland,* December 16, 1966. See also *Ein Taschen und Nachschlagenbuch ueber die Sowjetische Besatzungszone Deutschlands* (Berlin: Tempelhof Verlag, 1966), p. 127; *Statistisches Jahrbuch der deutschen demokratischen Republik* (Berlin: Deutscher Verlag, 1966), p. 463; H. Wittig, *Plane und Praktiken der polytechnishcen Erziehung in Mittledeutschland* (Harzburg: Wissenschaft Verlag, 1962), *passim;* Bundesministerium fuer gesamtdeutschen Fragen, *Ein Taschen und Nachschlagebuch ueber die sowjetische Besatzungszone* (Bonn: Deutscher Bundes Verlag, 1966), p. 145.

design. The work and study plan must be in line with the planning of the general Russian-German communist economy and the general political structure. For the East German, the term education alone is insufficient; it must be "socialist education" and "socialist culture."

SOME PROBLEMS BEYOND THE SECONDARY LEVELS

There were many problems facing the East German educational authorities after World War II. One most crucial problem was the organization of educational institutions beyond the secondary level. Most of the institutions fell under the American or British occupational zone. Vocational training at higher levels was also similarly affected.

For the sake of comparison we shall indicate the level of higher education in West Germany. Most of the fourteen universities existing during the Third Reich are located in the West, e.g., in 1960, West Germany had seventeen universities and about one hundred other higher educational institutions with 217,000 students in 1960 and about 250,000 in 1965-1966.

In East Germany, educational authorities wanted to revise the nature of German education and then to expand the educational system. In the East German study plans one could have found not only academic requirements, but also the aims and objectives of communist education.

The annual statistical data published by the Ministry of Education attempts to show that the West Germans and their achievements in this area have been surpassed. They compare the numbers of pre-war Germany with data of the present day, which of course is higher because the nazi system cared largely for the education of the nazi elite. Here the communists differ from the nazis because they give the opportunity for higher education to many more people than the nazis, although they also destroy opportunities for those who do not believe in the communist way of life.

Teacher Training. Soviet authorities screened all the former teachers in their part of Germany, and rejected almost 80 per cent as unsuited for teaching in the schools of the East German communist state. In order to staff the classrooms, in the early days following the war, politically reliable individuals were recruited from other fields, regardless of educational background. When possible, they were supervised by an experienced teacher. Within a few months, short courses in teaching methods were set up to help these novices become adjusted to their new roles.

The problem was particularly difficult because there was no official curriculum, and no textbooks were available. Teachers in the year after the end of the war harked back to the ideas of older educational leaders and it wasn't until mid-1946 that education faculties were established in institutions of higher learning, and the School of Education at Potsdam did not open until October, 1948. In August of 1949, East German education took a major turn in direction at the Fourth Pedagogic Congress, held in Leipzig. At this meeting, the government stated that Soviet education and Soviet texts would henceforth be the standard for education in the German Democratic Republic. Soon after that, translations of Soviet educational works began to appear in East Germany, and remained the basic tools of the classroom through the 1950s.

In the area of higher education, the communist East Germans have 46 institutions of which there are *hochschulen,* offering training in several different branches of natural sciences; the rest are divided between such disciplines as zoological technology, agronomy, agricultural economics, pedagogy, political science and law. In addition to these, there is a School of Mines and six major universities.

In 1952, for instance, there were 35,976 students at higher educational institutions, of which 24 per cent were women; in 1958 there were 64,106 students, of which 30.7 per cent were women. This latter percentage is not too high since one of the Soviet republics, Uzbek SSR, had at that time almost 100,000 students in higher schools and with 8 million inhabitants instead of the 18 million of East Germans. In 1965 there were 76,888 students in the higher schools of the country of which 24,190 were freshmen, or newly admitted and 20,190 were *absolventen,* or those who were to graduate at the end of the year. (See also Tables 42, 43.)

TABLE 42

Development of Elementary and Secondary Education in East
Germany: 1955–1965

Year	Schools	Teachers	Students
1955	11,007	75,572	1,883,400
1960	9,729	86,250	2,059,043
1961	9,750	101,693	2,158,891
1962	9,519	104,542	2,265,231
1963	9,496	113,122	2,345,728
1964	9,155	118,005	2,395,672
1965	8,883	121,580	2,425,582

Statistisches Jahrbuch der deutschen demokratischen Republik, 1966, p. 10. Jahrgang (Berlin: Staatsverlag, 1966), p. 463.

TABLE 43

Development of Higher Education in E. Germany:
1965

Area of Specialization	Total Number Students
Agriculture	8,208
Medical	13,630
Of Which in Dentistry	2,040
Economics, Law and Journalism	15,867
Philosophy, Speech, History & Music	2,618
Arts	1,604
Sculpture	1,117
Theology	642
Education	31,162
Total	76,888

Statistisches Jahrbuch der deutschen demokratischen Republik, 1966, p. 10. Jahrgang (Berlin: Staatsverlag, DDR, 1966), pp. 476–477.
Note that the distribution of East German students according to time studies was as follows: 74,418 studied on fulltime basis; and 29,549 on parttime basis, i.e., evening and correspondence schools.

The communists want to show that the state is really in the hands of the workers and peasants because the number of students from these classes is the highest. In 1965 over 40 per cent of the student population in universities was from the working class, 24 per cent from the non-manual workers and 18.75 per cent from the intelligentsia[2] (although the source does not define the term intelligentsia).

MORAL EDUCATION

The concepts of moral education are found in works of Marx, Lenin, Stalin and other Marxists approved by Moscow. German children, like any other communist children, are taught blind obedience to the communist regime, especially to the Russian regime, and the equality of all people, but most of all the equality of the communist people.

---

[2] *Statistiches Jahrbuch der DDR,* p. 477. See also Helmut Arnts, *Tatsachen ueber Deutschland* (Wiesbaden: Steiner Verlag, 1960), p. 212; Joseph S. Roucek, *Behind the Iron Curtain* (Coldwell, Idaho: The Caxton Press, 1964); Walter Stahl, *Education for Democracy in West Germany* (New York: F. Praeger, 1961); P. Bodenman, *Education in the Soviet Zone of Germany* (Washington, D. C. U. S. Office of Education, Bulletin No. 26, 1961).

The agency which is responsible for the moral upbringing of children is not the school, but the Communist Youth Organization, established in March 1946, and labeled as *Freie Deutsche Jugend* (Free German Youth) based on the Russian Komsomol. Predictably, the Youth Organization, the child of the communist party, takes its orders from the party, not from the schools.

One of the focal points of communist moral education for the whole German population is the idea of world peace. Into this "peace" movement, Soviet propaganda includes the whole of national and cultural life.

The Idea of the Bright Future under Communist Regime. The communist party of Germany wants to demonstrate to the German people that they are truly representative of a united Germany and the carriers of the old German idealistic philosophy of life. The party endeavors to prove to the people that communists are militant fighters against injustice and that they are the agents through which Germans can hope to unite with their brothers in the West. But to achieve this, one must do everything possible to help the Soviet Union in her fight for "peace." A German child would learn: "Let us go with Pushkin's nation, people of art and mind creation. . . . We'll drink your vodka; take our wine."[3]

The idea of the bright future and patriotism can only be possible through the Soviet mirror: only he who loves the Soviet Union above all else can love his own nation truly.

Hate for the United States. Like Soviet indoctrinational patterns, East-German propaganda is focused on the United States. In Germany, the communists try to prove that the development of the American culture and society underwent quite different patterns than those of Europe. While in Europe the people built cathedrals and museums, in America the drive was for gold and automobiles. The communists further claim that the government of the United States does not interfere with trusts exploiting people, but it does strictly control the private life of its people, such as "who kisses whom" or "what one should or should not drink," and that the American imperialists are thinking of the restoration of Prussian militarism.

---

[3] Peter Grothe, *To Win the Minds of Men* (Palo Alto: Pacific Books Publishers, 1958), p. 51; E. J. Salter, *Deutschland und der Sowjet-Kommunismus* (Munich: R. Piper Verlag, 1960); M. Lange, *Dokumente zuer sozialistischen Kulturrevolution* (Berlin: Aufgabe Verlag, 1960); Bodenman, *op. cit.*, p. 112; *Die Pionierorganizationen "Ernst Thaelman" in der Sowjetzone* (Bonn: 1957), pp. 14 ff; J. Beggenkampf, *Die sowjetische Erziehung: Dokumente* (Dusseldorf: Potmos Verlag, 1961), *passim*.

Providing the Right Weltanschauung. For this cause every means of propaganda and every branch of educational activities is involved. The press especially is loaded with teaching as to how to achieve the perfect man and the perfect communist society. It goes to such an extreme that there is hardly any area of occupational pursuit in which the idea of the right *Kultur* is not mentioned. Even the sports reporters must undergo strict training in Marxist-Leninist sport-journalism. For example, when a bicycle race was held in 1956 from Warsaw to East Berlin, the news media reported that it was not only a bicycle race, but also a "peace race."

A young person trying to become a journalist must first be trained in the philosophy of Marxism before he can pursue his profession. The Institute of Journalists in Leipzig has a special program in Marxist-Leninist theories of journalism and reporting, which leaves little time for the study of the objective subjects of this discipline. The *Neue Deutsche Presse* stated that the task of the journalist is not only to report facts, but also to form the people's opinion in achieving goals. In addition to the people's "opinion," financial help is always appreciated, e.g., German newspapers publicized at length the efforts of some young people at Herzstadt who collected 1,388 marks for the war in Vietnam.

Happiness is the New Idea of East Germany. The prospect of a bright future must be reflected in every possible human social and intellectual endeavor. Poems and songs are composed to reflect the new Germany. Songs like this one: "My Heinz is a tractorist. He plowed the land for us. . . . 'I am protecting our harvest now,' he said with happy eyes, 'so that it will bloom and grow just like our Republic does.' " To insure the *right* happiness the whole governmental apparatus works to help the party persuade the young masses of the bright future and the eventual surpassing of the American economy.

New Trends in German Literature and Music. The communists are aware of the fact that any successful movement must have its culture, history, heroes, and other cultural phenomena. Since East Germany is a rather new creation, the historical figures of German culture must be converted to communism. The Soviet-German communists even go so far as to try to interpret Goethe from the Marxist-Leninist point of view. Works that can not be converted into communistic ideology are removed from the library shelves. In 1952 alone some 7,000 libraries were cleaned up and about nine million volumes were discarded. The communists further say that such musicians as Beethoven and Shubert can only be appreciated in peace-loving countries, and that the music of Schubert gave much hope to a 19th century people living under the worst feudal and reactionary forces.

The painter, Bachmann, painted a picture and gave it to the exhibit in Halle. A critique stated that the picture has several deficiencies because the story is not complete. According to the communist critique, "Poppy before Blooming" (the title of the picture) should have been changed in the following way: Instead of the three red dots in the middle of the picture, an illustration of the Communist Youth should have been used.

Methods of Imposing New Values. The most successful way to introduce any value is through the school system. The communists in power, especially those responsible for the writing of new textbooks, are actually slowly trying to change human nature, particularly through the education of the young generation.

At the elementary level when the children learn German grammar, the method of teaching is quite different from that used in other countries. A standard type of instruction and the way of presenting complicating problems of tenses looks like this: up to 1945 the war was waged, many people suffered, etc.—this was the past tense. Now we are rebuilding Germany to a more beautiful state than ever before—this is the present tense. We shall see that the Five-Year Plan is fulfilled so that the future will be bright for us—this is the future tense.

Furthermore, if the children have problems in using certain prepositions, such as *for, against,* which require the accusative case, one has to give a practical example. The preposition "for" can best be learned by using such a phrase as "we work *for* peace, happy future *for* the children . . . ." and the preposition against is better learned by memorizing such sentences as "fight *against* the warmonger," etc.[4]

RELIGION AND SCHOOL

The place of religion in East German society is rather pessimistically viewed. The East German authorities in education use the same methods as the Russians, emphasizing the need for strong political propaganda to replace religious beliefs. Science is supposed to answer all the problems one has in finding happiness here and "out there." In case of any doubts the works of the Marxists should supply the answers. The Roman Catholic

---

[4] Grothe, *op. cit.,* pp. 112–169. See also A. Buchholz, *Neue Wege sowjetishcer Bildung und Wissenschaft* (Koeln: Verlag Wissenschaft und Politik, 1963); *Neue Heimat,* April 1967, p. 13.

religion is the most persecuted, but no religion escapes. As of 1965, East Germany had over 17 million inhabitants of whom 13.5 million were Evangelicals and 1.9 million Catholics. The rest of the people belonged to Protestant churches.

Churches are under great pressure from the government, and religious activities are quite restricted. Statistical data indicate that in 1965 there were a total of 642 theological students of which only 80 were able to complete their education. Further, many churches are nationalized and believers are denied their "constitutional" right to belong or not to belong to a religious organization or a church.

In 1958 the Ministry of Culture ordered an extensive struggle against the church and asked parents to explain the danger of religious instructions to their children as well as the physical hazards that may follow religious practices. The government further closed religious schools for children and prohibited any missionary society in East Germany. In industrial centers, no religious organization is allowed to function.

Communists further explain that there is nothing in peace treaties (Potsdam, and others) that would force the government to support a church. On the contrary, the communists say that the church is against socialistic progress and its practices are against the Marxist doctrine; therefore it must be fought. They say this fight must be carried on by propaganda, and the East German Republic will not use force to liquidate the church. According to the Constitution, any person has the right to belong or not to belong to any religion.

Important universities, especially those devoted to social sciences, have established special departments for the study of scientific atheism (as in the Soviet Union) and the liquidation of religious "prejudices." A department of scientific atheism was established at the University of Jena.

Although party propaganda and the party's secretary, Ulbricht, maintains that church membership is a purely personal matter, nevertheless children of religious ministers have difficulty in entering higher educational institutions. In all schools religious symbols have been removed and replaced with pictures of communist leaders. In classes, the communists emphasize the points that (a) the Bible is a collection of myths; (b) only old people who expect to die believe in religion; (c) students must abandon religious thinking, since this is not what educated men should believe.

Religious literature, of course, may not be distributed among children and the religious press can hardly function under such conditions.

What is all this leading to? As one German author put it: The dog hears the bell, and he secretes saliva. The indoctrinated East German hears the word "America" and he generates hate. Why? Because when one goes he hears the words, "American warmongers," "imperialists," "barbarians," and "militarist America," etc.[5]

WOMEN IN EAST GERMAN SOCIETY

The high position of women is always emphasized in the communist societies. Communists proudly pinpoint the number of women in different departments of higher education, especially in the natural sciences where the percentage seems to increase yearly in every communist country.

In East Germany the position of women is rather unique because after the war there were two million more women than men. Therefore, it is quite natural that the proportion of women in schools and the national economy would increase. Women were also asked not only to go to school but to join professional organizations such as trade unions, which had two million members in 1958. Women working in such positions as typists, clerks and others totalled to 200,000.

The East German government makes big issue of the number of women employed in various branches of the national economy. In most occupations, there is a political friendship group designed to socialize the women and thus bring them closer to the idea of Marxism.

The number of women in the various branches of higher educational specialization is not as impressive as in the Soviet Union. Only 25 per cent of the total student body at higher educational establishments is female.[6]

Additional References

Statistisches Jahrbuch der Deutschen Demokratischen Republik (Berlin: Staatsverlag, DDR, 1966), pp. 517 ff.; T. Schieder (ed.), *The Expulsion of the German Population from the Territories East of the Oder-Neisse Line* (Bonn: Federal Ministry of Refugees and War Victims, 1954); W. Wagner, *The Genesis of the Oder-Neisse Line* (Stuttgart: Brentano Verlag, 1964); Staatssecretariat fuer die Hoch und Fachschullwessen, *Hochschulfuehrer der DDR* (Berlin: Deutscher Verlag, 1960); H. Schulte, *Pramissen und Maximen Kommunistischer Pädagogik*

---

[5] Grothe, *op. cit.*, p. 216. Other sources on religion are S. Brant, *The East Germans Rising* (New York: F. Praeger Press, 1953); Martin Ruber, *Die Evangelische Kirche in Berlin und Mittledeutschland* (Berlin: Eckert Verlag, 1955); *Der Kamf gegen Religion in der sowjetischen Besatzungszone Deutschland* (Berlin: Morus Verlag, 1966). See also *Neue Heimat*, February 1966, p. 3, concerning the freedom of the press.

[6] *Ein Taschen und Nachschlagebuch*, p. 152; *Statistisches Jahrbuch der DDR* (1966), p. 474.

(Munich: 1960); L. Froese, *Sowjetiesierung der deutschen Schule, Entwicklung und Struktur des mittledeutschen Bil dungswessens* (Frieburg: Herder Verlag, 1962); E. Wiekerkehr, *Jugend im Bannkreis der roten Moral* (Berlin: 1958); Max Lange, *Totalitäre Erziehung* (Berlin: Frankfurter Verlag, 1954); Gerhard Mobus, *Psychologie und Padagogik des Kommunismus* (Koeln: Westdeutscher Verlag, 1959); G. Mobus, *Erziehung zum Hass* (Berlin: Moris Verlag, 1961).

Chapter 20

EDUCATION IN HUNGARY

Historical Background. The Hungarians belong to the Ural-Altaic race, to the same branch of people as the Turks, Mongols, Huns and others. Anthropologists divide the Ural-Altaic peoples as follows:

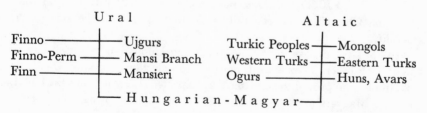

Although the Hungarian nation of today is under Slavic domination, its historical and cultural development is quite different from that of Russian or other Slavic peoples. Except for a brief period during the 11th century when Hungarian and Kievan princes intermarried, Hungarians and Slavs were enemies. Only Poland (for a brief period) kept friendly relations with the Hungarians.

During the migration of nations, the Hungarians came to Europe from Central Asia, mainly from the Syr Darya and Fergana regions. They first settled in present day Ukraine and then migrated to the west between the rivers Tisa and Danube. In 896, under the leadership of King Arpad (who was also the founder of the Arpad dynasty which lasted until the 14th century) they crossed the Carpathian mountains and settled within their present day boundaries.

Before the Magyar arrival, the territory was occupied by another Mongolian tribe, the Huns. They were under the leadership of Attila, whose home was someplace between the Tisa and Danube. After the death of Attila, the Huns went back to Central Asia, while the other Mongolian group, the Avars, were destroyed by Charlemagne.

The Magyars, or Hungarians, were a fighting nation, which to some extent determined the shape of their history. Only after their defeat near Augsburg by the German king and the Emperor of the Holy Roman Empire, Otto the Great, did they learn that it is better to live in peace than in a constant state of war. Unlike the Huns, they began to collaborate with the Christian monarchs of that time. Under the leadership of Prince Géza, and more particularly under the reign of his son, St. Istvan (Stephen), they accepted Christianity. During the same time, (1001) Pope Sylvester II sent a golden crown to the Hungarian king (St. Istvan) and gave him the title of the Apostle which became a symbol of Hungarian power and Hungarian Christian traditions. In 1083 St. Istvan was canonized, which added a special prestige to the Hungarian people.

After the death of St. Istvan, the Hungarians had to withstand the Mongol invasion and to defend Christianity against Muslim-Turkic attacks. They tried first to settle the differences between several princes of their own stock. The *Golden Bull,* issued in 1222, was a Hungarian "Magna Charta" which generally gave more power to the gentry and nobility.

In 1304 the dynasty of Arpad ended and Hungarian princes began to fight each other. They agreed, however, on election of a king, Charles I of Anjou, who proved to be better than expected. His son, Louis the Great, led the Magyars to the peak of their history by occupying many Slavic lands and conducting wise diplomatic relations with those whom he could not conquer. He also became the king of Poland. After his death, Sigismund I also quite effectively ruled the nation. He became not only the king of Hungary and Bohemia, but also the Emperor of the Holy Roman Empire (1387-1431).

From the 14th century on, the war with Turco-Tatar tribes slowed down the politico-cultural process of the Hungarian princes. They finally met total defeat at the battle of Mohach, 1526. They shifted their attention toward the Austrian monarchy and soon the two nations were under the same crown, but separated internally. From the 16th century on, the Hapsburg dynasty ruled the two nations until the end of the Austro-Hungarian monarchy. Although there were some wars between Germanic Austria and the Hungarians, they managed to live together. In 1848 under leadership of Lajos Kossuth, the Hungarians began a revolution against Austria. Eventually they suffered defeat, not so much from the Austrians, but rather from the Russian armies who came to help the Austrian crown. The Russians liquidated the rebellion by shooting 13 Hungarian generals, something the Magyars never forgot.

Even after this defeat the Hungarians were able to rise again. In less than twenty years they gained full independence. In 1867, an agreement was reached between the Austrian throne and the Hungarian crown on the future of the Hungarian people. The *Ausgleich* or compromise not only gave the Magyars full power within their own domain but also made many Slavic peoples subject to Hungarian rule. Some of the Ukrainian people (Carpathian Ukraine), the Slovakians, Bosnians, Croatians, and some Serbs became subjects of Hungarian political and cultural control. Ultimately not a single non-Hungarian cultural institution existed. There was extreme nationalistic suppression and economic exploitation of non-Hungarians. Furthermore, the Ukrainian population of the Carpathian region had no right to call themselves Ukrainians, but a new term, "Magyar-orosz" (Hungarian-Ruthenian), was used. Even as late as 1940, anybody who called himself a Ukrainian was arrested.

After World War I, the Hungarians lost their Slavic territories, as well as those in Transylvania, but in spirit they always kept the borders of the 11th century. Nothing could persuade a Hungarian that the borders of 1001 had no legal or political effect. In all political and geographical maps they used the old borders of 1001 and supported them with the slogan "Mindent vissza" (Everything back)—regardless of the fact that the Hungarian nationality represented only a fraction of the population. Hungarians remember this occasion with great feeling, e.g., they claim that after World War I, "the country lost 71.4 per cent of its total territory and 61 per cent of its total population. . . . 31.5 per cent being annexed to Romania, 19.6 per cent to Yugoslavia, 18.9 per cent to Czechoslovakia, 1.2 per cent to Austria, or three million Magyars." An objective look at the situation shows that Yugoslavia of today has over 19 million people; Czechoslovakia, 14 million; Romania, 19 million. This is a total of more

than 52 million people, of whom three million are Hungarians. Logically
and legally, the impracticality of incorporating the remaining 49 million
under the rule of three million as it was before 1914 seems obvious.[1] There
must be a reason for calling the pre-World War I Austro-Hungarian
monarchy a prison of nations.

EDUCATION BEFORE 1945

Formal education came very late to Hungary. Prior to the late 19th
century there were a few religious schools in the country—predominantly
Roman Catholic ones, since about 70 per cent of the country was Roman
Catholic. However, some schools were established by the Calvinists, the
Lutherans (in Transylvania) and the Unitarians. The Greek Orthodox
church had little influence on the philosophy of Hungarian education or
on the whole Magyar philosophy.

Initial steps to improve the educational system were first taken in 1868
(after the revolution against the Austrians), when a public law established
universal compulsory education for all children in the age group of six to
twelve years. The school was called *népiskola* (public school) and was
founded on the pattern of the German *Folkschule,* a new and quite impressive system of education of that time. The law also provided special
regulations on improvement of secondary education and continuation of
elementary education beyond the four-year period.

In 1883, other laws further improved secondary education. Actually,
what the law provided was a clear division between the three types of
gymnasiums: the "real" gymnasium emphasizing the study of natural
sciences and modern languages; the classical type of gymnasium stressing
the study of classical subjects; and a third type of secondary school (the
Polgari iskola), a sort of higher elementary school designed to give basic
vocational knowledge to craftsmen and others. But nothing was done
throughout the entire history of Hungary to improve education at the
secondary level.

Higher education before 1945 was definitely oriented toward the upper
classes. As late as 1939 only four per cent of the working classes were able
to attend secondary school. The status of the working people was such
that not only were they deprived of higher educational opportunities, but

---

[1] Julius Kornis, *Education in Hungary* (New York: Columbia University Press,
1932), pp. 75 ff.; *Narodnoe khoziaistvo,* 1964, pp. 782–793; Ernst Helmreich
(ed.), *Hungary* (New York: F. Praeger Press, 1957), pp. 3–5, 200; Imre Kovacs,
Facts About Hungary (New York: Hungarian Committee Press, 1958), p. 19.

a boy from a peasant home would never dare to invite a girl to a dance if that girl happened to be a daughter of an office worker or a higher administrative officer. These, of course, are only a few of the causes of the radical European movements that tried to remedy or improve the position of the lower classes.

The theorized compulsory elementary education of 1883 in reality never was implemented on a large scale. The rate of illiteracy before World War I was as high as 50 per cent in Central Hungary and up to 80 per cent in the Carpathian regions. School attendance data before World War II indicate that out of eight million people, only 1,096,300 children attended the elementary schools; only 52,300 were in secondary schools, and 12,000 in higher educational institutions. Some vocational schools were established by the law of 1920 under the direction of Kuno Klebelsberg, the Minister of Education.

There were also so-called "continuation schools" for children who could not attend school beyond the age of twelve. In 1938 there were 395 such schools, of which 160 were state, 101 communal, and 101 denominational. At the secondary level there were 35 gymnasiums of the classical type, 75 of the natural sciences and modern languages, and 47 lyceums for girls. As of 1938 there were only 18 technical secondary schools. There were also commercial schools, often called the academies, which trained students for commercial or the office-type work.

Higher Education. University education in Hungary began very early compared to other countries in that area. Even during the reign of St. Istvan steps were taken to establish a sound foundation, if not in the actual organization of universitiy education, at least in establishing libraries associated with religious orders. One such institution was the Benedictine Abbey founded by St. Istvan near present day Budapest. It is known as *Mons Sacer Pannoniae* in memory of St. Martin of Tours, the Apostle of France, who was born near Budapest, according to tradition. This monastery was a sort of Monte Cassino for the Hungarians, serving not only religious purposes but cultural ones as well. Even now it has a library of more than 300,000 volumes.

The first university, however, was established by King Louis the Great in 1367 in Buda. Pope Urban V, by a special charter issued in Avignon in 1367, recognized this university as the best higher school of learning at that time. In 1388, Sigmund I founded the second university of Hungary in Obuda (near Budapest), and the third one in today's capital of Slovakia, Bratislava, in 1467. By the end of the 19th century only the Univer-

sities of Budapest and Cluj (Romania) survived. In 1900, there were
three universities and one technological school of higher learning. By 1939
six universities and several academies existed. At the same date (1939) the
Catholics had 15 seminaries, the Lutherans had one college and the Calvinists had three. In Budapest there were three Academies: the Academy
of Applied Arts and Crafts, the Academy of Dramatic Arts, and the
Academy of Music. Also some lower level agricultural schools and junior
colleges were controlled by the Ministry of Agriculture.[2]

EDUCATION UNDER THE COMMUNISTS

The Russians wanted primarily to change the social structure of Hungarian society and the structure of the student body at higher educational
levels. The most important aim of communist education was reeducation
of Hungarian youth in the spirit of Soviet communism. This general value
orientation involved many social and educational reforms in Hungarian
institutions.

Goals of Hungarian Education. The philosophy of communist authorities, educational and others, is in Hungary essentially the same as elsewhere: everything from matter to people is the property of the state;
there can be no other authority than the communist authorities; youth
must be educated so that no religious authority supersedes state authority
and no parents may decide the future of the young generation.

We have seen that communism involves the whole of man's life. Since
the young generation is educated in the spirit of world revolution, they
must also be educated in the philosophy of dialectical materialism. No
subjects can be taught without reference to the works of Lenin, Stalin, and
other communist leaders. But, more important, a youngster must be able
to understand the plans of the party, the future of the state, and the nature
of society. The school alone cannot do all these things and so is forced
to invite the party representative (and indeed incorporate him) into its
educational structure. The party works through the Pioneers and the Communist Youth Organization to help educators regenerate society.

---

[2] D. Heckenast, "Hungarian Universities—Past and Present," in *Etudes Slaves et
Est-Europeennes,* vol. II, Fasc. 1 (Montreal: Publication du Centre d'Etudes
Slaves de l'Universite Montreal, 1957), p. 31; Helmreich, *op. cit.,* p. 194; A.
Macarthy, D. Litt, *Hungary: A Short History* (Chicago: Aldine Press, 1962), p.
239; F. Fejtoe, *Behind the Rape of Hungary* (New York: David McKay Co.,
1957), pp. 80 ff.

The young Hungarian children are cut off from Western influences since communists do not believe in exposing the children to other ideas or other cultures before they are trained in such a way to believe that "the voice of the party is the voice of God." In the process of this education family influences must be eliminated as much as possible until the youngster becomes a party fanatic. Incredible as it is, the Hungarian child is more aware of the danger of American imperialism than the Soviet child. The Hungarian official sources picture the American school as a "horrible place where the teacher roars at children and very often beats them . . .;" and that all students must go to a police station to have their fingerprints taken "like ordinary criminals so that in war their corpses can be identified."[3]

Hungarian girls are taught that the supreme purpose of life is not to keep their bodies and souls clean but to work for a socialistic society. The role of a woman is not the upbringing of children but the construction of a socialist society. Any work that may deviate from this general direction is considered to be a degenerate relic of bourgeois society. The woman in Western societies, particularly American society, is pictured in an "atmosphere of barbarism, ignorance and anxiety."

The goal of the school is also to develop a sense of sympathy and love for the Soviet Union, its people and places. The Hungarians applaud any decision of the government which schedules meetings—youth or any other type of conferences—in Moscow. The Soviets give them a "helping hand" in such endeavors and illustrate in their press the friendship of two nations. For example, a Soviet periodical stated that "the Hungarian workers are very happy to have their next Congress of Workers in Moscow, the city of communism, the city of brotherly love toward the Hungarians. With pride and joy, the Hungarian people look upon Soviet progress in science, technology, culture. . . ."

The history books in Hungarian schools praise the accomplishments of Hungarian communists, particularly those who were fortunate enough "to have been buried long enough to be praised as progressive in their own time."[4]

---

[3] William Juhasz, *Blueprint for the Red Generation* (New York: Mid-European Studies Center, 1952), p. 24.

[4] One of the books that the communists praise was the work of Ervin Szabó, *Százforduló: A második reformnemzedék története* (Hungarian Turn of the Century: History of the Second Reformed Generation) (Budapest: 1961), *passim;* see also *Bulletin for the Study of the USSR,* vol. 13, December 1966, pp. 27–37; *Sovetskie profsoiuzy,* No. 23, December 1961, p. 15.

GENERAL AND SECONDARY SCHOOLS

Since 1945, the term "general schools" has applied to all types of elementary schools existing before the war. The program offers eight years of compulsory education and incorporates to some extent subjects previously taught in first years of secondary education (first four years of gymnasium).

Whatever the communists did in other branches of social and individual life, they certainly improved the standards of education in every country they have occupied. This of course applies to Hungary because Hungarian education was anything but progressive. The Hungarian communists, following the Russian example, introduced a Five Year Plan (1949) designed both to change the structure of the school system and to educate the proletarian intelligentsia. As mentioned before, prior to World War II, educational opportunities were available only to upper classes and education of common people was completely neglected. During that five year period (1949-1954) the number of pupils in nurseries rose by 20 per cent; the number of children in primary schools grew 50 per cent; and the number of secondary school graduates increased by 73 per cent. Although there were 1.1 million students in elementary schools in 1938 and only 1.2 million in 1954 (see Table 44), this does not mean there was no increase. First of all, the Hungarian population decreased after the war, and Hungary lost some of its territorial regions (parts of Slovakia); second, more than 60 per cent of the Hungarian children before the war never went beyond four years of elementary education.

Another important development in Hungarian education is the distribution of students in general schools, e.g., over 75 per cent of the Hungarian population belongs to the working class, and in schools as of 1954, this class represented 64 per cent of the students. The number of secondary school students increased from 52,300 in 1938 to 162,000 in 1954-1955 and to 210,683 (secondary regular and secondary technical) students in 1964.

The curriculum of secondary schools was (as is usual in all communist countries) also changed. The previous study of classical languages was replaced by study of natural sciences and modern languages. Great attention was given to adjusting the school curricula to meet the industrial needs of the country, allotting much of the school time to subjects dealing with current industrial requirements.

It is important to note that the Russians did not change the name of the secondary educational institutions, i.e., the gymnasia system remained unchanged. But the curriculum was altered entirely compared to the prewar period. In 1954, the structure of secondary education was thus:

Type of Schools	1937–38 (in per cent)	1953–54 (in per cent)
General Gymnasia	56.1	43.0
Industrial	2.2	27.0
Agricultural	1.5	6.0
Economics (business)	22.1	14.0
Normal (teachers')	17.2	7.5
Teacher Training Institutes for Nursery Schools	0.9	2.5

There were 285 secondary schools in 1938, 441 in 1954, and 536 in 1964.[5]

Vocational Education. Many secondary schools after the 1945 reforms began to offer vocational educational courses either part-time or in evening programs. The communists claim that during the period of 1947-1954 more than 1.8 million workers acquired vocational skills and more than 113,000 young workers were able to learn important trades through industrial apprenticeships. Vocational education tended to involve more than regular work skills. In many cases, the vocational trades included subjects which required additional training at higher educational institutions.

Higher Education. The Hungarian educational reform and policies were based on the following principles. First, the number of higher educational institutions was to be expanded throughout the country and the student population was to be enlarged by drawing students from the working classes. Second, the educational reforms would contribute very little to the reconstructed society if they omitted the technological necessities of the time, so the many specializations of higher education were to be expanded. Third, the training of teachers was to be the focal point of the new educational programs. Teachers were to be educated in the Marxist world outlook as well as a sufficient knowledge of their given subject matter.

The Hungarian educators began to develop a socialist culture in the framework of the new demands and the new philosophy of education. Many times, especially during the early period of the Russian occupation, ideological knowledge came before subject knowledge. Students were

[5] *Sztatistikai szemle* (Budapest, 1954), No. 1, p. 199; Helmreich, *op. cit.*, p. 109; *U. N. Statistical Yearbook*, 1965, p. 704.

TABLE 44

Educational Development in Hungary
(1949–1965)

Type of	Schools	Teachers	Students	
			Male & Female	Female Only
1956				
Preschool	2,509	6,030	167,849	na
Primary	6,273	52,516	1,255,001	na
Secondary	476	7,935	172,693	na
Higher	31	na		na
1965				
Preschool	3,131	9,776	184,345	89,898
Primary	6,162	61,518	1,458,683	710,179
Secondary . . .	337	7,092	139,763	88,832
Technical	199	3,539	82,280	30,653
Higher	90	6,947	70,920	30,012
Special	101	1,779	21,683	na

United Nations Statistical Yearbook, 1957, 1965 (New York: United Nations Service), pp. 619 and 704 respectively.

Note that in 1937 there were 1,096,650 children in schools, of which 52,300 were in secondary schools, and over 12,000 in higher educational institutions. Only four per cent of the students at higher educational levels were from the working classes. In 1949 there were 1.4 million students in schools of which over 93,000 were in secondary schools; in 1954 there were 122,627 students in secondary schools and about 50,000 in higher educational institutions of Hungary. See *United Nations Statistical Yearbook* (New York: United Nations Service, 1954), p. 581; *U. N. Economic Bulletin for Europe*, vol. VI, No. 2 (August 1955), p. 99; F. Fejto, *Behind the Rape of Hungary* (New York: D. McKay Co., 1957), pp. 80–81; E. Helmreich (ed.), *Hungary* (New York: Praeger Press, 1957), p. 203.

admitted to higher educational institutions not necessarily on the basis of academic excellence but on the basis of political recommendations by certain communist organizations. Priority, of course, was given to workers and peasants who did not have sufficient background due to the discrimination of the previous regime.

Accelerated enrollment at higher educational institutions can be noticed during the early period of the Hungarian communist regime, in a comparison of the number of students in higher institutions in 1938 with 1954 or 1964. One hundred and one special research and technological institutions were established that enrolled 21,683 students. The government gave special subsidies to more than 80 per cent of Hungarian students who could not otherwise afford the luxury of a college education.

New teacher training schools also rapidly expanded. In 1952 there were 31 higher educational institutions, and by 1964 there were 90 regular schools of higher learning and 101 special research schools. The number of teachers, at all levels, was distributed fairly well according to sex. There were 61,518 teachers in 1963 at the elementary level of which 3,342 were women; and 6,947 at the higher levels of which 1,386 were women.

The communists also paid particular attention to areas of specialization, e.g., most students in Hungarian universities before World War II were predominantly humanistically oriented. Very few students, especially few females, registered for subjects like electronics, engineering, and other natural sciences. In 1938 more than 37 per cent of the students registered in law school as compared to 9.1 per cent in 1950; in 1938, those in engineering represented 9.6 per cent of all students while in 1950 the percentage increased to 28.9 per cent; in medical schools, 13.5 per cent in 1938 as compared to 15.1 per cent in 1950. In education, arts, and economics no significant changes were seen.[6]

OTHER REFORMS

Religious Reforms. Hungary was no exception in the Soviet design to exterminate all religions. When the Red Army moved in, the anti-religious propaganda followed.

Before the war the Hungarian population, in terms of religious denomination, was as follows: 67 per cent Catholic, 20.8 per cent Calvinist, 6 per cent Lutheran, 2.5 per cent Greek Catholic, the rest belonged to smaller denominations.

In 1945 the communist authorities began to limit church influence on public and political life. At first they limited themselves to "persuasion," but when this failed, legal provisions were passed by the communist government of Hungary setting up a special department to control religious life. It was known as the State Office for church affairs, and the Christian churches rested under its legal authority.

Education and the religious institutions became separate. No church, especially the Catholic church, had the right to own property or to organize educational institutions. Nearly 3,000 Catholic grammar schools were

---

[6] Helmreich, *op. cit.,* p. 204; Fejtoe, *op. cit.,* p. 81; *U. N. Statistical Yearbook,* 1965, p. 701.

taken over by the government by 1949 and only eight of 1,117 Calvinist schools functioned as before. Lutheran and Uniate educational institutions were also closed.

The most radical reforms began in 1948 when the Hungarian Catholic Church proclaimed the year 1948 as the year of the Virgin Mary to contrast the communist proclamation of the 100-year anniversary of the 1848 revolution. This served as a clash between the state and the church. Cardinal Mindsenty was arrested and sentenced to life imprisonment; so were the Protestant bishops who opposed joining the "Priest Committee of Peace" specially established by the communists to disrupt the church hierarchy.

As in other communist countries the Hungarian communists organized a massive propaganda campaign against the clergy and all religious believers. Not only that, but they opened new theological seminaries accepting only persons "sympathetic towards the government." Those who graduated as "priests" served as tools for the communist propaganda machinery, did everything that the party ordered, and disobeyed that which higher church authorities demanded.[7]

Ideological Orientation. Ideological indoctrination is the most important part of Soviet reforms. Stalin, Lenin, and other Soviet leaders were fully aware of the importance of ideological views and did everything possible to strengthen the ideological struggle inside and outside Russia. This struggle for the right world outlook was first carried on at the theoretical front, but if things did not work on the theoretical front attention was applied to the practical front, i.e., they arrested those who disagreed with the Soviet interpretations of Marxism.

The Russians approached the Hungarian problems from many angles. They spoke of the glories of international communism and claimed that they were true friends of the Hungarian people. Intensive propaganda was launched explaining the ideas of communism from the idealistic point of view, from Soviet experiences, from the anthropological causes of revolution and in many other ways. Hungarian literature, science, educational and social organizations had to help the Soviet authorities in Hungary in the politico-cultural work. Those who resisted were arrested,[8] and

---

[7] Assembly of Captive European Nations, *News Bulletin* (New York: ACEN Press, 1965), pp. 58–60. See also Miklos Vetö, *The Catholic Church in Hungary* (New York: F. Praeger Press, 1962), *passim;* I. Kadar, *The Church in the Time* (Budapest: 1958); J. Mindsenty, *Dokumentation* (St. Polten: Verlag der Pressfereins-Drukerei, 1956), *passim.*

[8] *East Europe,* vol. VII, No. 18, 1956, p. 15; Kovrig, *op. cit.,* pp. 73–105.

in 1956 alone the Russians deported to Siberian concentration camps 50,000 Hungarians. When the Hungarian revolution broke out in 1956, the Russians blamed the intelligentsia for it. In reality, however, the data indicate quite a different picture. For example, persons arrested in connection with the revolution during the period of November-August 1957 represented the following classes: 199 industrial workers; 48 persons who were either policemen, writers, artists, or teachers; 44 students and 22 others.[9] The data show that the bourgeois students did not initiate the revolution. Rather it was the working people who were disappointed with the Russian type of communism.

Additional References

Ferenc Eckhart, *Magyarorszag toertenete* (Budapest: 1958), *passim;* Bela Kowrig, *Four Meanings of National Communism* (Milwaukee: Marquette University Press, Slavic Institute Papers, 1958), *passim;* Andor Heller, *No More Comrades* (Chicago: Henry Regnery Co., 1957); J. Michenev, *The Bridge at Andau* (New York: Random House, 1957); E. Pfeifer, *Child of Communism* (London: Weidenfeld Press, 1958); *Czalad és iskola* (Budapest: January 1965), *passim;* V. V. Bodrin, *Vengerskaia Narodnaia Respublika* (Moscow: Gosizdat, 1962); Imre Nagy, *On Communism: On Defense of the New Cause* (New York: F. Praeger Press, 1957).

---

[9] Institute for the Study of the USSR, *Bulletin,* No. 12 (Munich: Institute Press, 1966), vol. 13, p. 29.

Chapter 21

EDUCATION IN ROMANIA

Historical Background. The country of Romania is located between the Tisa, Danube and Prut rivers and the Black Sea. Her geopolitical location is not as fortunate as the Romanians would like, for their area is surrounded by the Slavic world except for a small part neighboring on Hungary.

The Romanians belong to the Romance linguistic group. They are the descendants of the old Romans who settled in the region between 50 and 150 A.D. During the barbarian attacks the Romans were forced to abandon the region whose population in later centuries was subject to several influences: Russian, Hungarian, Greek, Polish and Ukrainian. Therefore, the language of Romania is not as pure as Italian or French. It is heavily mixed with Slavic words.

Like the Ukrainian principalities of the Kievan period, the Romanians established several principalities during the 13th century and were strongly attached to the democratic traditions of the old Rus, although linguistically they were different. We find in the Romanian structure the same type of internal security, *boyar,* an Old-Slavic word meaning a knight, which is one of many indications of Slavic influence on the region. The most important influence was, of course, acceptance of the Greek Orthodox religion and rejection of Roman Catholicism in the early stages of Romanian Christianity. The Orthodox church had much in common with Slavic philosophy and social structure. The previously mentioned Metropolitan Peter Mohyla was born in Moldavia and influenced both nations— Ukraine and Romania—in the field of religion.

From the time of the fall of Constantinople in 1454, the Turkish influences are noticeable but not as much as the Slavic ones since religiously Romanians had nothing in common with Muslims or their social and religious practices. Under the Mongol invasion, the Romanian nation began to lose its initiative and leaders went as far as selling the throne to the Greeks. Not until 1821 did Tudor Vladimirescu restore the Romanian nation by establishing a native government. From this time on, the region became very much Russian-oriented and depended mostly on Russia for political and military safety. During the Russo-Turkish wars (1826 and 1877), Romania supported Russia and as a result of this support the Romanians were able to proclaim their independence in 1881, headed by King Carol I.

After World War I the Romanians not only regained their independence but they also occupied non-Romanian territories such as the Ukrainian Bukovina, parts of Bessarabia, Hungarian Transylvania and parts of the Carpathian region, the area around the Marmoros-Siget. The ethnic groups of these regions were denied any sort of autonomy. Romanians during this period, 1918-1940, ignored any national self-determination and forgot that they were themselves subject to foreign rule. Between the years of 1918-1939 they followed either the French or German political and cultural examples. During World War II Romania fought on Hitler's side, especially on the Russian front. (The areas of Ukraine and others around the Black Sea were promised them by Hitler as a reward for participating in the war against the Allied powers.) With the end of the war in sight, and after the Russians had occupied most of their country, Romania "declared" war against Germany at the end of 1944. From that year on, there was a power struggle between the communists and the non-communists headed by the puppet king Michael I who figured as the "head" of state until 1948. In 1948 the communists, under the direction of the Russian foreign minister A. Vyshinski, completely dominated all political positions in this state.

During the Chinese-Soviet "friendship" the Romanian communists kept on the Soviet side although they were eager to join Albania or Yugoslavia in the communist bloc of nations. Even today the Romanian communists like to quote Marx who in his time could well have said that it would be better for the Bessarabians to be under Romanian domain rather than under the Russian. But at the same time the Romanians underline the great importance of the Russian occupation ("liberation") of Moldavia, and other previously held Romanian regions.

In 1964 the Chinese dictator, Mao Tse-tung, declared that the Russians had no right to be in Moldavia and other previously held Romanian territories. This confused some Romanian communists as to the side to which they should belong. In the same year, the Romanian Academy of Sciences sent a noted professor, A. Otetea, to Amsterdam to find an exact quotation of Marx who at one time wrote about the Romanian right to stay in Bessarabia. During the crisis between Israel and the Arabic world (June 1967), the Romanian representative voted, for the first time, against a Russian proposal.

According to the first communist census of Romania in 1956, the population of the country amounted to 17,489,450, of which almost 15 million were Romanian, 1.6 million were Hungarians, 385,000 German, 146,000 Jewish, 104,000 gypsies, and other ethnic groups numbered below one hundred thousand.[1]

Religiously most of the Romanians belong to the Greek Orthodox religion, while the Germans, Hungarians and Ukrainians living in the area of Marmoros Siget are either Catholic or Protestant.

EDUCATION BEFORE 1948

Before World War I Romania was one of the most backward countries in Europe, second only to Albania. There were hardly any schools before the Spring of Nations (1848) except for a few theological seminaries, and public schools were nonexistent before 1830.

The development of public education in Romania did not stem from Romanian initiative but from Russian. In 1832 the Russian prince Kisseleff organized the first public schools in Wallachia and Moldavia, more or less on the Russian model. Since both nations belonged to the Greek Orthodox religion, many similarities can be found in the educational systems of Russia and Romania. Between 1830 and 1864 there were 288 primary schools in Wallachia and 55 in Moldavia.

---

[1] *Anuarul Statistic al R. P. R.,* 1960 (Bucharest: Directia Centrala de Statistica, 1960), p. 69. See also Randolph L. Braham, *Education in Romanian People's Republic* (Washington, D. C.: U. S. Office of Education, Bulletin No. 1, 1964), pp. 1–2; M. Rura, *Reinterpretation of History as a Method of Furthering Communism in Romania* (Washington: Georgetown University Press, 1961), pp. v–vii; *Sovetskaia Moldaviia,* November 23, 1966, p. 45.

The educational structure during the 19th century consisted of four years elementary education and three years secondary education. The following three years were called *gymnazia*. (This was quite different from the European gymnazium which consisted of eight years.) After completing the seven year program the student would either go to the lyceum for another four years, or to a technical school.

Attendance data show that during the period of 1929-1939 not more than 13 per cent of Romanian children were in the kindergartens and only 5.4 per cent continued beyond the fourth grade. Before World War II there were 5,537 students in secondary schools and 39,250 students in various vocational trades representing a country of twenty million people. At higher educational institutions, pre-communist Romania had 26,489 students in 33 different colleges.[2]

THE COMMUNIST REFORMS: 1948

After the communist takeover in 1945, a Romanian government was formed under the leadership of Petru Groza and, of course, the Russian armies stationed in Romania. King Michael I "abdicated" and the new government took over. Here, as in other satellite countries like Czechoslovakia, Poland, and Hungary, the Kremlin did everything possible to exterminate not only the non-communist opposition to the regime but also the nationally conscious communists. Everything was to be reconstructed on the blueprint of Russian revolutionary practices.

As is known, the education of youth is one of the most important of communist plans because the youth are given the task of continuing the class struggle for the sake of the world revolution. A new educational program was therefore initiated in 1948, which was designed to change not only the school system as such but to change also the child's mind. A decree of August 3, 1948 stated that every citizen of Romania had the right to an education, as provided by the constitution, and that education at all levels was the responsibility of the state. The decree, Number 175, further specified the following objectives: eradication of illiteracy; democratization of education—giving opportunities to all social classes; education of youth in the spirit of the people's democracy; guiding extracurricular activities of children; training needed industrial specialists at all levels; training of scientific workers needed for social institutions and research; and training the teachers for many levels of education.

Regardless of all the intentions specified by various decrees and resolu-

---

[2] *Anuarul statistic al R. P. R.*, 1960, p. 354; Braham, *op. cit.*, pp. 8–11.

tions, the most important need was to eliminate illiteracy. More than 38 per cent of all Romanians were illiterate and in certain districts (Maramures and Vlasca) illiteracy reached 60 per cent. In view of these circumstances, educational policies were aimed at liquidation of illiteracy first. Romanian law required that all people in the age group 14-55 must attend school, and in 1948-49 about one million people per year attended the schools for illiterates.

Reforms in General Education: Elementary and Secondary Schools

The 1948 educational reform and the subsequent application of these reforms in 1949 were based entirely on Russian educational structure, curriculum, practices, and most of all, on the Russian philosophy of education. It was almost an identical copy of the Soviet system, e.g., elementary education is scheduled for four years, grades one through four. Semi-secondary additional consists of three years and the complete secondary education consists of ten years (after 1956, eleven years), followed by higher educational programs scheduled anywhere from three to six years.

In terms of the goals of Romanian education, the communists did not forget to include the most important Soviet clause, i.e., education must be so designed as to prepare conscious workers of socialism. Other aspects of communist indoctrination were equally underlined by the new reforms, such as education of students in the spirit of socialist patriotism, development of a proper relationship between the school and society, and inculcation in the atheistic attitude toward life. In all, the Romanian educational programs were nothing else but copies of the Soviet programs.

A more practical point of Romanian educational reforms was the introduction of technological training (very much neglected during the Romanian monarchal regime) and the stress on industrial subjects in both theoretical framework and vocational orientation. The Romanian schools, in accordance with their economic capabilities, included in their programs field trips, laboratory exercises, industrial arts, and practical experiences. In addition, education of the "new Romanian communist man" was very much emphasized. In the last year of secondary education acquisition of Marxist knowledge is heavily stressed. The study plans issued by the Ministry of Education require that 62 hours per year be spent on scientific socialism, of which 51 hours are to be allotted to the following: Marxism-Leninism as the revolutionary theory of the working class; dialectical materialism; historical materialism; the class struggle; Marxism-Leninism teaching on the dictatorship of the proletariat; socialist revolution; and the Great October Revolution.

Other subjects of the school curriculum are strictly prescribed by the Ministry of Education and nothing can be changed without official permission from higher educational authorities. No school director has the right to change subjects or methods, but he may suggest ideas in written statements as may any teacher. Humanities are centered around the history of Romania and the U.S.S.R., the constitution, and modern languages which begin in the fifth grade. As a rule Russian is the first language taught. French follows in the seventh grade. Latin and Greek are not offered. Priority is given to natural sciences, shop work and physical education.

In the schools for national minorities, especially the large Hungarian group, about the same curriculum is followed except that the Hungarian language is added. It is more difficult for the Hungarian child to succeed in school because he has to take three foreign languages instead of two as do the Romanian children, i.e., the Romanian language is also foreign for the Hungarian child.

The number of children in schools for national minorities stays relatively the same. For example, in 1951 there were 244,649 children in these schools of which 160,631 were in elementary schools (grades one-four); over 11 thousand in technical schools; and 3,253 in higher educational establishments.

A comparison of the 1939 data with 1963 shows that in 1939 there were 1.6 million children in schools for general education—elementary and secondary schools—and by 1963-64 there were 2.7 million children in elementary schools and 376,620 in secondary schools. In technical education (on the secondary level) there were 14,746 in 1939 and 60,030 in 1964; there were 90,787 children in pre-school education in 1939 and 1.9 million in 1964.[3]

Vocational Education

Vocational education in Romania began somewhat late compared to other countries. Even now Romania is far behind other European countries and the United States. In Romania the people are still predominantly engaged in agriculture, sheep breeding, and woodworking. Only lately

[3] *Ibid.,* p. 354; U. N. *Statistical Yearbook,* 1965, p. 710; A. Kashin, "Romania and Polycentrism," in *Studies on the Soviet Union,* Bulletin No. 10, vol. 13, October 1966, pp. 430–49; *East Europe,* June 1959, pp. 46–48; Central Statistical Office, Romanian People's Republic: *Statistical Pocketbook* (Bucharest: Central Statistical Office, 1961), p. 370; UNESCO, *The Liquidation of Illiteracy in the Romanian People's Republic: Fundamental and Adult Education* (Paris: UNESCO Press, 1958), vol. X, No. 4, p. 146.

have industrial enterprises developed. In 1955 as in 1939, the people in villages had no electricity, no large industry, no natural gas distribution for daily uses. Romanians still have to depend on importing major appliances, machinery and electronic equipment.

In 1948 through Russian efforts the Commission on the Coordination of Vocational Education was established to organize vocational education according to the needs of industry. Its primary responsibility was to organize basic training centers for skilled labor and incorporate students into these centers. The age requirement for students was set at 14 and the training was to be for two years as factories hired people at 16. Special provisions for rural youth helped to train some 45-55 thousand students in this age group in 1951. In 1955 the curriculum of secondary schools was expanded to allow 25 per cent of time for technical education.

Care should be taken in tabulating data regarding technological or vocational education in underdeveloped countries like Romania because included in their statistical tabulations is training that in advanced countries is usually done by factories, e.g., in the United States, tool and die makers, milling machine operators, punch press operators, etc. are trained on the jobs. But because these occupations are highly complicated for an underdeveloped nation, they are listed as parts of an educational system and fall directly under the Ministry of Education.

The statistical data issued by the Romanian statistical bureau show that during a 10 year period vocational education increased by about 70 or 80 per cent. In 1948-49 there were 511 schools of vocational learning with 61,372 students and in 1959-60 there were 505 schools and 102,012 students. Most of the students learning a vocational trade were engaged in the agricultural industry (29,760 as of 1960), followed by general machinist training and construction work (26,948 as of the same year compared to 39,894 in 1949).

HIGHER EDUCATION

Higher education in Romania began very late compared to other European countries. It was only in the late 19th century that a considerable effort was made by the nationally-conscious Romanians to organize and expand the educational system on the higher level, distributing the students into specialties that were essential for maintaining and improving the national economy. Before 1940 the educational pursuits on this level were conducted primarily in Bucharest, Iasi, Timisoara, Chernivtsi (a Ukrainian city without a Ukrainian university during the Romanian occupation) and in Clij, a Hungarian city. Most of the students before World War II were studying the humanities. In 1939, ten thousand out of a total of 26,489 students in higher educational institutions were in law schools. (See also Table 45.)

TABLE 45

Development of Education in Romania: 1939, 1960, 1964

Type of School	1938/39	1959/60	1963/64
A. Preschool			
Schools	1,577	6,837	7,633
Pupils	90,787	315,998	372,430
Teachers	1,819	11,326	*
B. Primary & Secondary			
Schools	13,865	15,600	15,469
Pupils	1,604,481	2,388,447	3,058,339
Teachers	46,435	97,907	125,671*
C. Teacher Training			
Schools	55	13	17
Students	5,537	5,246	10,498
Teachers	na	na	472
D. Technical			
Schools	142	268	817
Students	14,746	46,853	260,212
Teachers	3,871	3,355	13,626
E. Vocational			
Schools	224	505	na
Students	29,250	102,012	na
Teachers	896	6,081	na
F. Higher			
Schools	33	88	171
Students	26,489	61,980	112,611
Teachers	2,194	8,041	11,155

Anuarul statistic al R. P. R., 1960 (Bucharest: Directia centrala de statistica, 1960), p. 354; *United Nations Statistical Yearbook* (New York: U. N. Service, 1965), p. 710.
* The 1965 data include the total number of teachers at all educational levels of the general education, i. e., kindergartens, elementary and secondary education.

The reforms of 1948 (the previously mentioned decree No. 175) elaborated rules and regulations on the future of communist higher education, and once again, the Soviet structure and control was taken as an example. The Romanian schools of higher learning were opened to all classes of the population. Strong emphasis was placed upon the relationship of theory and practice as well as upon the relationship of subject-matter with productive labor. The last category was reinforced in 1957 when the communist party of Romania demanded from the higher educational institutions the following: socially useful labor at all levels and specializations at higher institutions of learning; improvement in the social composition of students, i.e., priority given to students recommended by the communist party and to students belonging to communist party organizations; mandatory political participation in social organization of all students; teaching staffs reorganized in light of the new demands set by the party; and the improvement of the financial status of schools.

By these and other decrees, the independence of the Romanian higher educational institutions was definitely limited. The communist party of Romania demanded that university education be entirely submitted to party control either directly or indirectly, through the power of appointments and "recommendation" of certain faculty members. In the social sciences, particularly in the teaching of history, the party controlled the educational endeavors of a university. Special instructions were issued regarding methodological questions at higher educational institutions, demanding that each school underline the importance of the "socialist" achievement in science, particularly the "achievements of Soviet science and technology." Furthermore, the university had to assure the political authorities that the ideological teaching was functioning properly, i.e., nothing but the works of Marxist-Leninist social philosophy were taught. Books and teaching material must be approved by the party, and all publications were subject to approval or disapproval by the party. All research was to be organized in such a manner that the basic concepts of "scientific socialism" would be clear in all areas of scientific endeavors. The party decrees demanded that all Romanian changes must be attributed to "innovators in the U.S.S.R. and the Romanian People's Republic."

Academic improvement in many areas, however, was not perceptible. There were complaints that the schools could not handle properly the academic requirements of a university plus the requirements made by the party simply because many "politically progressive" students were unable to cope with academic subjects. We can note this in enrollment statistics, e.g., in 1939 there were 26,489 students at Romanian universities; 48,614 in 1949; 61,123 in 1951-52; 80,593 in 1953. Enrollment then dropped to 67,849 in 1958-59 and finally to 61,980 in 1960 as stricter academic requirements were set up. By this time the political fever was more or less over and school administrators were able to impose their own ideas on the future of higher education in Romania. As Table 46 indicates there were

TABLE 46

Number of Students at Romanian Universities: By Area

City	1938/39	1953/54	1959/60
Total	26,489	80,593	61,980
Of which in:			
Bucharest	17,791	46,531	32,488
Cluj	3,544	11,725	11,220
Iasi	4,093	8,489	8,464
Timisoara	463	4,469	4,164
Brazov	...	3,582	1,976
Craiova	...	1,454	1,453
Galati	...	1,346	781
Tirgu Mures	...	1,012	727
Petrosani	...	990	707
Arad	...	986	...

Anuarul statistic al R. P. R., 1960 (Bucharest: Directia centrala de statistica, 1960), pp. 386–87.

also basic structure changes, such as discontinuing schools because of financial difficulties or lack of teaching personnel. (This happened in the schools of Brad, Cimpulung, Moldovenesc and Constanta.)

Length of studies was modeled on Russian experiences. The study of medicine was extended to six years and other areas of concentration averaged between four and five years. In 1960 there were 38 higher educational establishments in the People's Republic of Romania, most located in Bucharest, Cluj, and Iasi, with about 80 per cent of all students in these three cities. The largest single university is the I. Parhon university in Bucharest, which had over 11,000 students in 1965. The next biggest is the A. I. Guza university at Iasi with about 3,000 students. Third is Victor Babes University in Cluj (Hungarian district of Romania), and it is particularly important because of a historic struggle between the Hungarians and the Romanians over the territory of Cluj and its surrounding areas. Over 90 per cent of the people are Hungarian but somehow it belongs to the Romanian People's Republic.

During the Hungarian revolution in 1956 there was a quite open and active student movement in support of it. There were evidences of Romanian nationalism both before and after the communist takeover of the country. Laszlo Banyai, a director general in the Ministry of Education, in 1957 expressed the view that the educational opportunities in Romania were unfair as far as non-Romanian nationalities are concerned. Banyai said that before the communist regime only 41 per cent of the Ukrainian, 53 per cent of the Turkish, and 68 per cent of the Russian children had been able to graduate from the elementary schools of the first level (first four grades).

Educational development in Romania was slow and came very late. The first school of medicine was opened in 1869 in Bucharest and it did not actually operate properly until 1918. The first polytechnical institute was established in 1920 in the city of Timisoare, and other colleges and universities were established only in the 1930's, or after the communist takeover.[4]

TEACHING PROFESSION

The distribution of teachers depends, first, on the level of training, and second on sex. Most teachers in pre-primary education are women who have successfully completed the teachers institute at the first level (usually two years of training).

There are three major divisions in terms of rank: professors, master instructors, and the regular teachers. These ranks are basically determined by special examinations, and not necessarily by seniority rule. In Romania there are 10 separate grades for evaluating an individual's performance in school. The grade of 10 is equivalent to the American "A" and the grade of 5 is a failing grade. The lower numbers, 4, 3, etc., are designed for those who fail *for sure*—which cannot be explained in terms of American or Russian standards. In the teaching profession, a grade of 7 must be secured for the lowest type of teaching position; a grade of 8 for the number two spot; and an average of 9 must be secured to qualify for the number one degree.

In terms of the distribution of work, i.e., the number of hours of teaching for a particular category, a usual load for the professor (not a university professor, but elementary or secondary teacher who is by Romanian standards called a professor) is three hours a day or 18 hours per week; for the master instructor the load is five hours a day or 30 hours per week; and for the regular teacher (usually a beginner) six hours a day or 35 to 42 hours per week.

The Romanian teacher has no worry about the method of instruction because the Ministry of Education takes care of it. Like the Soviet Union, every methodological problem is decided not by the individual teacher or

---

[4] Braham, *op. cit.*, p. 108; *Anuarul statistic,* 1960, p. 386; David Froyd, *Romania, Russia's Dissident Ally* (New York: F. Praeger Press, 1965), pp. 1–14.

school director but by the Ministry of Education which publishes annually instructions regarding methodological problems and questions. In theory, each school has its own method council, but in practice their duty is to fulfill the directions sent from above.

The teacher who did an excellent job during a school year is not given more money, but instead gets a medal or an honorary title, such as "leading teacher" or "leading professor"; then he is congratulated for doing an outstanding job.

At the secondary level most of the teachers are men, although the situation has improved since 1948 when women became eligible to obtain teaching positions at all levels. The communists must be given credit in this area since they did improve the status of Romanian women in general and female teachers in particular. The educational programs were planned in such a way that in the future both sexes would enjoy equal opportunities in the teaching professions. The number of girls in rural schools, as of 1960, was as follows: in grades one through four, 575,514 out of a total of 1,183,600; in grades five through seven, 183,505 out of a total of 422,-015; in grades eight through eleven, 7,784 out of 20,313. The urban school population was much lower in the elementary grades but much higher in the upper grades. In the same year, the number of urban children in grades one through four was only 324,801 of which 159,018 were girls; in grades five through seven there were 204,987 students of which 96,746 were girls. In grades eight through eleven (secondary education) the total number of students was 182,731 in urban schools as compared to a total of 20,313 in rural schools. Therefore, most of the educational activity on the higher level is still predominantly in urban centers.[5] By 1967 the number of teachers, based on the above statistical data, was fairly equal as to distribution of teachers by sex. (See also Table 47.)

OTHER COMMUNIST REFORMS

The population of Romania is distributed, according to religious affiliations, as follows: 72 per cent are Greek Orthodox, 10 per cent belong to the Uniate (Catholic) church (predominately the Ukrainian and Hungarian population of Romania), 7 per cent are Roman Catholics, and the Protestants represented about 6 per cent of the total population (20 million as of 1966).

From the very beginning the policy of the communist regime was to liquidate all religions as soon as possible, but primarily minority groups.

---

[5] Braham, *op. cit.*, 162; *Anuarul statistic*, 1961, pp. 74–76.

TABLE 47

Elementary and Secondary Education in Romania
(1939, 1960)

Type of Education	1938/39 No. of Students	1959/60 No. of Students
A. Schools:		
Four Year Schools	12,884	9,957
Seven Year Schools	770	5,130
Eleven Year Schools	211	517
B. Pupils in Schools:		
Grades 1–4	1,456,367	1,508,401
Of Which Girls	703,426	734,532
Grades 5–7	119,110	627,002
Of Which Girls	53,540	280,251
Grades 8–11	29,004	203,044
Of Which Girls	11,834	92,260
C. Graduates of:		
Four Year Schools	236,991	285,356
Seven Year Schools	17,225	116,698
Eleven Year Schools	4,200	53,033
		30,731
D. Teachers in:		
Grades 1–4	36,665	53,033
Grades 5–11	9,770	44,874

Anuarul statistical R. P. R., 1960 (Bucharest: Directia centrala de statistica, 1960), pp. 356–363.

The government first began to change the administrative pattern of the church. Until 1920 the Romanian Orthodox church was affiliated with the Patriarchate of Constantinople and after that date it was independent. In 1948 the communists established a special bureau, the Ministry of Cults, to deal with the religious problems of Romania. Furthermore, they controlled the power of appointments of all religious authorities. Thus in 1949 they appointed a pro-communist patriarch, Justinian Marian, who declared that Marxism and Leninism have features in common with the Christian Gospel.

The major communist attack, however, was directed against the Catholic church. In 1948 alone 92 Catholic priests were arrested. In that same year, strong propaganda was initiated against the Catholic church proclaiming that the policy of the Vatican was against the spirit of the Christian faith and that the Romanian state could not stay aloof in these problems.

Between 1947 and 1949 more than 600 Catholic priests and all Catholic bishops were arrested which left the church without leadership. In 1950 a congress of the Romanian Orthodox church held in Bucharest laid plans to take over the Catholic church.

At first the Romanian communists tried to persuade the clergy to accept the communist union. Then, they arrested the religious leaders of both the Ukrainian and the Hungarian Uniate churches, confiscated the church property and completely closed the churches. The communists subdued the Catholic church on October 1, 1948 in Cluj. They then elected delegates by fraud and force and proclaimed to the people that the decision to unite the two churches under the Orthodox rule had been accomplished "unanimously and with great enthusiasm."

The fate of the Protestant church and the Jewish community in Romania was identical to that of the Catholic church under the communist regime.[6]

Language and Literature. At the present time Soviet linguistic policies in Romania are concentrated upon a study of a mutual relationship between the Russian and Romanian languages. The Romanian Linguistic Institute at the University of Bucharest publishes a biennual study called *Romanoslavica* designed to prove that the Romanian language has much in common with the Russian language and other Slavic languages, and that the Romanian culture is greatly influenced by Russian Slavic culture. Even the origin of some Romanian cities has a Slavic root. According to Professor Petrovich, the city of Tirnava (the word, of course, is of Slavic origin) was established by some Slavic tribes.[7]

Additional References

S. Fischer, *Romania* (New York: F. Praeger Press, 1957), pp. 1–30; N. O. Iorga, *A History of Romania: Land, People and Civilization* (London: T. F. Unwin, 1925); Seton-Watson and R. William, *A History of the Romanians* (Cambridge: Harvard University Press, 1934); A. Cretzianu, *Captive Romania* (New York: F. Praeger Press, 1956); Henry Markham, *Romania Under the Soviet Yoke* (Boston: Maedon Press, 1949); N. Buhler, *Discrimination in Education in the People's Democracies* (New York: Mid-European Studies Center, 1955); Asociatia Slavistilor din Republica Populara Romina, *Romanoslavica* (Bucharest, No. 1, 1958), pp. 9 ff.

---

[6] Assembly of Captive European Nations, *Bulletin*, 1956, pp. 42–69.
[7] *East Europe*, No. 7, 1963, p. 51; *Survey*, No. 55, 1965, pp. 38 ff.

Chapter 22

EDUCATION IN ALBANIA

Albania is the smallest country of the Balkan peninsula. It is located on the shores of the Adriatic Sea and borders on Bulgaria, Greece and Yugoslavia. Although the country covers less than 11,000 square miles and has a population of less than two million, it plays an important part in the European community of nations, especially since the government of Albania decided to follow the Chinese path of building socialism.

Historical Background. Although numerically and geographically small, the country of Albania played an important role in the shaping of the history of Southern Europe. For centuries the country was a target for the aggression of foreign powers like the Romans, the Greeks, the Sicilians and most important by the Turks, who eventually occupied the area in the fifteenth century and held it for the next five centuries. There was, however, an important uprising against Turkish domination in 1458, led by George Castriota (known as Scanderbeg), but it was only briefly successful since the Turks overcame the Albanian forces.

During the course of Turkish occupation, the Albanians learned to adapt themselves to the military regime of the Ottoman Empire. They not only were able to preserve their national identity, but they were selected by the Turks as the elite of all the soldiers in the Empire defending the palaces of high Turkish officials and very often, even the safety of the Sultan himself. An honor guard of Albanian soldiers was selected to guard the Sultan's palace of Constantinople.

After the Congress of Berlin (1878), most of the Balkan countries were declared to be free from Turkish influence. However, at that time, the Albanians preferred to stay with Turkey rather than with the new regime of Montenegro. When the Congress of Berlin decided that the larger part of the Albanian population should be assigned to Serbia, the Albanians refused to cooperate with other Balkan nations and formed their own military league known as the Albanian League. Only after the Turks were defeated in many areas of the Balkan states did the Albanians decide to declare their independence in 1912. The leader of the Albanian independence movement, Ismail Kemal, was unable to do much because of the opposition of other Balkan nations, especially Serbia, which wanted some parts of the disputed territory.

After World War I, there was confusion as to who had the right to control the business of the state. At one time Bishop Fan Stylian Noli was president of the country (1924), but was unable to retain power because of larger opposing political forces. Ahmed Zog, a pro-Italian Albanian, took control of the country and established a dictatorship which lasted until the beginning of World War II. Zog was clever enough to avoid direct war with the Italian and the German forces. He skillfully maneuvered politically in dealing with the Italians and the Germans in such a way as to avoid a direct participation of Albania in the war. When the Germans finally occupied the area, Albania became a good partisan fighting ground for both Albanians and Serbs. During the war, due to Serbian and Russian influences, the Albanian National Freedom Movement was organized and proclaimed Albanian independence from Germany-Italy in 1944.

From 1945 on, the power of the government rested in communist hands. There was, however, some dispute as to what type of communism the new government would adopt, but since Tito's men were already there during the war, the Albanian communists favored the Serbian brand of socialism over the Russian. The Albanian communist leader Xoxha (Hoxha) proclaimed independence, but as a result of Russian "advice" Xoxha was shot in 1949 as an enemy of the Great October Revolution. From that time on, the leading Albanian communists tried to seek the solution for their internal and external problems from their new ally, Red China.

Population. As of 1964, the total population of the Albanian People's Republic amounted to 1,814,432, of which 881,570 were female. Most of the Albanian population lived in rural areas (1,212,907) since there was no significant industry in the major Albanian cities to attract the rural population. Population density is very low; an average of sixty-three persons occupy one square kilometer.

The urbanization processes are rather slow. The major Albanian cities are as follows:[1]

City	Population	
	1916	1939
Tirana (capital)	1,200	35,000
Scutari	na	30,000
Koritsa	11,000	22,500
Bertrat	8,500	11,000
Durazzo	600	9,000

Much of the Albanian population, over 700,000, lives in Yugoslavia. There are only 50,000 Albanians in exile, predominantly in the United States.

EDUCATION AND CULTURE BEFORE 1945

Albania was one of the most backward countries of Europe before 1945. About 85 per cent of the people could neither read nor write, and as of 1940, Albania had no encyclopedia, no national dictionary, and no Bible had been translated into Albanian.

Linguistically, the Albanians still have not reached an agreement on the exact literary language of their state. Although they belong to the Indo-European group of languages, the Turkish occupation of the region played an important part in shaping of the modern Albanian language.

There are not sufficient data available on the history of the language, but according to sources available, modern Albanian is the product of two ancient languages, Illyrian and Thracian. Historically these languages influenced each other to the extent that it is hard to distinguish one from the other.

---

[1] S. Starvinos, *The Balkans Since 1453* (New York: Holt, Rinehart and Winston, 1961), p. 731. See also Henry Hamm, *Albania: China's Beachhead in Europe* (New York: F. Praeger, 1963), pp. 2–5.

Even today there is no standard Albanian literary language. Two dialects are used as equal components of the linguistic media: the Geg dialect in the north and the Tosk dialect in the south.

The first traces of the Albanian alphabet are not too old either. In 1908, the Albanian alphabet was established by some enlightened intellectuals who accepted the Latin script rather than the Arabic (holy to the Muslims) or the Greek.

In terms of educational enlightenment little was done before the twentieth century. Several religious missionaries, however, were active in the region, but only the Catholics initiated progressive educational reforms. In 1920, the Congress of Lushnje ordered all schools to introduce the modern Albanian language. By 1933, education was nationalized and the system, introduced by the Minister of Education, Dr. Ivanaj, consisted of the following divisions:

a. elementary education lasted from four years of age (in rural areas from seven) through fourteen, while there was no exact division between the pre-school education and the elementary schooling *per se;*
b. gymnasium, the secondary school, was divided into four years at the junior level and four years at the senior level. The *lycee,* a prestige secondary school, was operated on French educational standards even using the French language;
c. normal schools served for the training of teachers at the elementary and secondary levels;
d. commercial and technical institutes, although listed in the program, hardly existed before World War II.

There was no higher educational institution in pre-war Albania.

As of 1937/38, there were 642 elementary schools with 1,350 teachers and 54,000 students for a population of 1.5 million people. At the secondary level there were 261 teachers with 5,677 students.

Education After 1945

Social Foundations. The social foundations of Albanian education must be considered in regard to two categories: Russian contributions until 1961 and Chinese influences upon the philosophy of education after that date. The philosophy of Albanian education is materialistically oriented and does not allow for religious influences upon the child's mind.

There were important influences on the Albanian philosophy of education made by Tito's government, but due to the Serbo-Albanian border disputes, the Serbian line of socialism was replaced by the Russian and, occasionally, the Chinese version. There was a trend in 1952 to study the origin of the Albanian language in the light of Stalin's work on linguistics; however, after Stalin's death the policy of the relationship of the Russian and Albanian languages was abandoned. It was soon found out that the so-called Albanian Soviet Friendship Society was an agent of the Russian linguistic offensive whose purpose was to Russify the small Albanian nation.[2]

General Educational Reforms. One of the basic educational reforms after 1945 was the change in the philosophy of education. As stated before, the value orientation of communist education has to be altered to political ends. Education was assigned the task of training new, dependable leaders for the future communist society in Albania. Elementary school children were indoctrinated to absorb communistic ideas, as is the usual pattern.

The new reforms subordinated every activity of a teacher to the power of the state. Obviously, the state controlled the whole educational process, as in any other communist country.

The first law on compulsory elementary education was passed on August 17, 1946. It required that every person aged twelve to forty years must learn to read and write and every child between the age of seven and twelve must attend a school for elementary education.

During the first five years of the new regime, several other measures were introduced. An exact copy of the Soviet educational system was adopted. Elementary education began at the age of seven and was completed at the age of twelve. The secondary school consisted of two levels: the junior (three years) and the senior (three years). The whole system was 5:3:3.

There were, however, a variety of secondary educational institutions established, if not in quality at least in quantity. These were technicums, such as medical, technological, handicrafts, lower vocational schools, middle schools, higher secondary schools and others. The law of 1950 provided emergency measures for the training of teachers so that only a minimum of schooling and experience was required. Very often elementary school teachers had no more than two or three years of total training. Although there was a higher pedagogical school in Tirana, it was unable

---

[2] Roucek, *op. cit.,* pp. 125–146; *Vjetari Statistikor I. R. P. Sh., Vjetari Statistikor Republikes Popullore te Shqiperise* (Tirana: 1965), p. 271; Stravo Skendi, *Albania* (London: Atlantic Press, 1957), p. 300.

to produce teachers in a short period of time. The pedagogical institute, also patterned on the Soviet model, had five departments: Albanian language and literature, Russian language and literature, history and geography, physics and mathematics, and biology and chemistry.

The data of 1964 indicate that there were 23 pre-schools in 1939 and 429 in 1965; on the elementary level there were 649 schools with 55,404 children in 1939, and 3,332 schools with 378,924 children in 1965. In the lower vocational and secondary levels there were proportionate increases. (See Table 48.)

TABLE 48

Educational Development in Albania
1938–1965

	1938/39	1955/56	. 1964/65
A. Pre-School Education			
Schools	23	155	249
Children	2,434	10,004	23,024
Teachers	40	297	1,108
B. Elementary & Secondary			
Schools	649	2,222	3,332
Students	55,404	172,831	378,924
Teachers	1,477	4,942	13,209
C. Lower Vocational			
Schools	11	8	20
Students	2,056	1,045	4,121
Teachers	109	34	159
D. Higher Vocational			
Schools	5	17	31
Students	879	4,818	22,078
Teachers	34	171	748
E. Higher Education			
Schools	—	1	8
Students	—	304	11,937
Teachers	—	13	732

Vjetari Statistikor I.R.P. SH., *Vjetari Statistikor Republikes Popullore te Shqiperise* (Tirana: 1965-Statistical Yearbook of the People's Republic of Albania), p. 357.

Higher Education. The most drastic changes were made in the area of higher education. In 1945, the communists established the first Albanian university (with 53 students) at Tirana, and by 1965, they had eight higher educational establishments with 11,937 students.[3]

___

[3] *Vjetari Statistikor,* pp. 357–373; Skendi, *op. cit.,* p. 278.

The reforms in higher education were not without a policy of discrimination, however, for the children of pre-war high officials were not accepted. Priority was given to those of the working classes and to those who were able to produce a certificate of national security, which of course, was related to membership to the communist party. There is no doubt that progress in raising the level of higher education has been made. This is the policy of the party and its administrators since the government needs people who can bring home to others the ideas of communism.

An intensive effort has been made to increase the number of teachers at the secondary level. Since the end of the war the number of teachers graduated from pedagogical institutes has increased fourteen times, e.g., there were 298 teachers in middle schools in 1939, and the number increased to 4,228 in 1965.

According to Albanian communist sources almost every student at a higher educational institution receives a scholarship, e.g., 11,937 students received scholarships in 1965, the identical number of students who attended higher educational institutions that year. Apparently not a single student paid his own way through college (see Tables 49, 50).

TABLE 49

Distribution of Albanian Students at Higher Institutions of Learning: By Sex (1964–65)

	Male	Female
A. Full and Part-time		
1946/47	38	15
1950/51	243	61
1955/56	2,915	496
1962/63	9,462	2,225
1964/65	9,507	2,430
B. Day Time		
1964/65	4,948	1,435
C. Evenings		
1964/65	354	38
D. Correspondence		
1964/65	4,205	957

Vjetari Statistikor I. R. P. SH., *Vjetari Statistikor Republikes Popullore te Shqiperise* (Statistical Yearbook of the People's Republic of Albania) (Tirana: 1965), p. 371.

TABLE 50

Number of Men and Women Graduated from Higher Educational Institutions:
1955, 1965

Faculty of Department	1955		1965	
	Male	Female	Male	Female
Total for Albania	199	41	1,320	343
Of Which in				
A. Tirana				
University	126	19	724	162
Law	...	...	35	9
Economics	...	...	89	19
History	58	12	129	38
Engineering	55	2	166	6
Geology	...	...	79	8
Geophysics	...	...	11	0
Medicine	...	...	85	33
Sciences	12	5	141	49
B. Agricultural Institute . .	34	8	196	2
C. Arts Institute	...	...	7	...
D. Drama School	...	...	19	...
E. Physical Culture	...	...	15	1
F. Physical Education . . .	...	...	22	...
G. Two Year Pedagogical Institute .	39	14	337	181

Vjetari Statistikor I. R. P. SH., *Vjetari Statistikor Republikes Popullore te Shqiperise* (Statistical Yearbook of the People's Republic of Albania) (Tirana: 1965), p. 372.

The Education of Girls. Before the communist takeover only thirty per cent of all the girls attended elementary schools. The secondary schools were predominantly for boys.

According to Albanian communist sources there were fewer than 16,000 girls in the elementary schools of Albania and 1,425 in all secondary schools in 1939. By 1965, the situation had changed as follows: in grades one through four, there were 109,563 girls out of a total of 231,479 students; in grades five through seven, there were 47,617 girls out of 117,662; in grades eight through eleven, there were 18,704 girls out of 50,203 students. The number of teachers in these grades was as follows:[4]

---

[4] *Vjetari Statistikor*, p. 367.

Grade		Number of Teachers as of	
		1939	1965
1 through 4	Male	991	3,580
	Female	358	3,623
5 through 7	Male	65	3,457
	Female	17	1,521
8 through 11	Male	42	769
	Female	4	259

In 1965 there were more women students in the pedagogical institutes for lower elementary classes than men (4,228 women and 3,138 men). The ratio between the males and females on other educational levels was fairly equal.

Policies Toward Religion

The people of Albania had contact with Christianity at the very beginning of its recognition by the Roman Emperor Constantine. Although there are no exact accounts on the status of Christianity during the early period of its existence, we do know that in 732, Leo III (the Isaurian) detached the present region of Albania from Rome and subordinated it to the Patriarchate of Constantinople. After the Great Schism (1054) the northern part of the country remained with Rome and the southern part followed the path of Constantinople and the Orthodox religion.

When the Turks occupied the region in the late 14th century, the population was subjected to Turkish political and religious rule. Force and violence were used to convert the Albanian Christians to Mohammedanism. As a result by the end of the 19th century, the population of Albania was religiously distributed as follows: 70 per cent Muslim, 20 per cent Orthodox and 10 per cent Catholic.

The fate of religion during communist domination in Albania was similar to that of the Soviet Union. As a matter of fact, Albania was second only to communist Russia in the destruction of organized religion by force and violence. According to data given by the former Minister of Education (before 1945), Dr. Rexhep Krasniqi, the Catholic church suffered the following losses in 1952 alone:

Type of Religious Person	The Measures Taken by Albanian Communists
1. Regular Clergy . ، . . (Including Bishops)	93 Total, of which
	13 were executed
	39 imprisoned
	11 drafted into the army
	10 died
	3 escaped
	13 remainer unharmed
2. Jesuits	94 Total, of which
	16 were shot
	16 expelled
	35 imprisoned
	13 went into hiding
	6 died
3. Nuns	200 Total, of which
	85 were expelled
	43 imprisoned
	remainer unknown

The elimination of the Catholic clergy began in 1948, and was "completed" in 1952. During this period the most brutal measures were used to liquidate the Catholic church from Albanian soil. To name just a few, among the victims of communism were the bishops Prennushi, Volaj, Gjini, and Thaci.

It is estimated by Albanian scholars that over 200 religious persons of all denominations were killed. Among these were three Muslim leaders of Islam, six Orthodox bishops along with many members of their respective clergy.

Any religious teaching was prohibited and severe punishments were imposed upon those who dared to break the law. The youth, until 1961 (when Albania became pro-Chinese), were educated in the spirit of Marxism-Leninism-Stalinism; and, after 1961, in the spirit of Stalinism and Mao Tse-tung-ism.

There is no indication of any let-up in the persecution of religious believers, e.g., in 1961 a Catholic priest was sentenced to jail because of illegal activities—printing the Holy Bible.[5]

Additional References

Assembly of Captive European Nations, *Facts on the Captive Countries* (New York: Assembly of Captive Nations Press, 1961), *passim;* Joseph Rouchek, *Balkan Politics* (Stanford: Stanford University Press, 1948); V. Robinson, *Albania's Road to Freedom* (London: George Allen and Unwin Ltd., 1941).

---

[5] R. Krasniqi, "Persecution of Religion in Communist Albania," in *Assembly of Captive European Nations* (New York: No. 128, March-April, 1967), pp. 17–21; Skendi, *op. cit.*, pp. 285–295.

Chapter 23

THE SCHOOLS OF CHINA

Both the fortunes and misfortunes of China are bound up with her gigantic size and population as well as her geographic location in Asia. The idea of progress, as the Western world conceives it, was strange to most of the Chinese. The China of today threatens the existence of the Soviet Union, the safety of all other neighboring non-Chinese people and even the future of the human race.

There is difficulty in estimating accurately the number of people inhabiting China since there has never been an exact census of the population. We know, however, that in 1953, there were approximately 583 million Chinese and in 1960, the number increased to 655 million. The growth of the population is extremely rapid and there is little reason to believe that the present government of China will introduce effective measures to curb it. The Chinese claim that the present net annual increase in population amounts to 2.5 per cent while the birth rate is estimated to be in the vicinity of forty-five per 1,000 people.

Accurate estimates are very difficult, due to the inconsistency and inadequacy of statistical and general data. The facts are, however, that given the present conditions and the present rate of increase, the population of China will reach the one billion mark by the end of this century. There is presently quite an improvement of health, social and educational conditions in China. While the mortality rate was about twenty-eight per 1,000 in 1953, and the infant mortality rate was very high (200 per 1,000), the population has never suffered such losses as did the Soviet population during the communist regime.

The unity of race is a favorable feature of the Chinese nation. Ninety-four per cent of the people belong to the Chinese or Han group while the other small minorities represent no monolithic unity. Again, when we compare the Soviet population, with 180 different ethnic groups and only about 50 to 52 per cent of the total population being Russian, we see that the Chinese are much better off in terms of future growth. Small ethnic groups like Mon-Khmer, Shan, Tibeto-Burman, the Mongols and Tungus, and a few thousand Turks and Ujgers are the only small minorities threatening the mainland.[1]

Linguistically the Chinese also represent the most unified group in all of Asia, since most of them belong to the Han linguistic block. China faces no linguistic revolution as is possible in India or in some African countries.

Religiously, the Chinese fit the communist pattern of life better than any other nation if only for the reason that most of the people of China historically have had no religion. A minority followed the Buddhist path of salvation while the majority followed the humanistic philosophy of Confucius who is not regarded as a prophet or a saint.

Education Before 1949

Chinese philosophy of education reflects, first of all, the philosophical thought of Confucius (551-479 B.C.) and to some extent that of Buddhism and Taoism. The most profound influence is seen in the combination of Chinese legalism and Confucianism, which for centuries changed little or not at all. Like the Hindu, Chinese educational philosophy is based primarily on humanitarian and moral concepts, but, again like the Hindu, divisions between social classes were for centuries very rigid. Confucius was never clear about his attitude toward the supernatural. On the contrary, he expressed the idea that he himself had enough trouble in this world and was unwilling to predict the future of the next world. In his

---

[1] John S. Cramer, G. S. Browne, *Comparative Education* (New York: Harcourt and Brace, 1965), pp. 531–532; Leo. A. Orleans, *Professional Manpower and Education in Communist China* (Washington, D. C.: U. S. Government Printing Office, 1960), pp. 1, 125; Urlanis, *op, cit.,* p. 314.

Four Books, which serve as a type of Bible for the Chinese people, there is no mention of heaven.

In one of the Four Books, the *Great Learning,* Confucius describes the main criteria of great learning, such as virtue and wisdom; but his wisdom is designed to help one to control his own affairs such as his own family and his surroundings. Confucius saw no great learning beyond this world and thought man would do best to concentrate on the moral issues of the day rather than programming the far-reaching concerns of tomorrow.

There were four types of traditional Chinese schools: (1) family schools, similar to the early American dame schools, where rich families hired a tutor for educating their children; (2) the clan schools, designed to provide opportunities for learning the skills possessed by one clan and strictly controlled by its elders (the "teaching staff" of the clan school consisted of clan elders); (3) the rural schools, designed to give basic skills to youngsters of settled tribes; (4) the private academies, the highest level of the old Chinese education, designed to educate the select classes of the population. Teachers of the academies were usually nationally known scholars who offered their knowledge to a group of students on a voluntary basis.

More important than the structure of the old-Chinese education was its purpose. With the exception of the academies, the imperial schools all prepared students for the imperial examinations. These were set up by the government to select students from the privileged classes, and those who passed the local examination were given the certificate or *Hsiu-ts'ai,* as the Chinese called it, which qualified students for entering the provincial examination held every three years. In theory every Chinese could take the examination but in practice only a few hundred of the students qualified. Upon completing the exams, students were assigned to governmental or other higher positions in the economy or the state. This educational evaluation was abolished in 1905.

The actual enlightenment in Chinese education can be noticed in the second half of the 19th century when the Chinese intelligentsia began to see the vital necessity of accepting Western ideas in order to survive culturally. From 1860 on, there are continuous evidences of Chinese participation in Western intellectual endeavors. Numerous educational institutions began to appear in China offering much more variety in educational training. In 1862, the first foreign language institute was opened in Peking, in 1866, the first technical school in Fukien, and in 1881, the first naval academy was opened in Tientsien.

A more modern and rapid development of education followed the Sino-Japanese War of 1894-1895, when the Chinese government, realizing the necessity of it, introduced a new system, somewhat along the Japanese pattern. Thus, a long isolation from the West was about to end. The period of compromise followed by the period of acceptance of Western ideas dominated the beginning of 20th century Chinese thought.

By 1922, China had thirty-three universities, seven medical schools, and thirteen technological schools. There was a total of 125 higher educational institutions with 5,613 teachers and 34,880 students.[2]

Communist Educational Reforms

As early as the late 1930s, the communist leader Mao Tse-tung spoke of education as being part of the political and ideological revolution. Mao Tse-tung further called for a complete reconstruction of traditional Chinese education and a repudiation of Western educational practices. He stressed the importance of the Chinese cultural-educational heritage. The nationalistic concept was fully utilized by the communists. The new education was to be free from all foreign elements. All non-communist products were eliminated. All foreign schools or traditional schools were labeled as decadent bourgeois survivals, agents of imperialism and hotbeds for the spread of individualism. The education of the New Democracy was to be built on the following principles: (1) the application of dialectical materialism in the search for the right knowledge; (2) the idea that true knowledge can be found only through practice; and (3) the development of the proletarian culture (or as it was later termed, the cultural revolution).

In 1951, the school system of China was changed to the following levels: nurseries and kindergarten in the age brackets of three to seven; primary schools from seven to twelve; followed by the junior middle schools of three years and the senior middle schools of another three years (4:5:3:3). Higher education began after the student finished eleven years of total schooling and lasted three to five years. There were also lower technical professions requiring only two or three years of training (similar to Soviet technicums) and research institutes (graduate schools) controlled by the Academy of Sciences.

In 1958, this system was changed somewhat but the structure remains basically the same except elementary education was extended to six years.

---

[2] Chung Shin, *Education in Communist China* (Hong Kong: University Research Institute, 1958), *passim;* Chang-Tu-Hu, *Chinese Education Under Communism* (New York: Columbia University Press, 1962), p. 12; Hsi-en Chen, *Teacher Training in Communist China* (Washington, D. C.: U. S. Office of Education, mimeo, 1960), pp. 1–24.

Spare Time Schools were operated on the same structure with the exception that there were no age requirements since the students of these schools were working people.[3]

Following this structural pattern, the Chinese began to implement educational ideas and curricula designed for re-educating the old and new generation. Like the early Soviet experiments, the Chinese regarded as good, valid, scientific, and useful only education originating in the communist bloc.

Social Foundations of Chinese Education

Chinese communist education, like Soviet communist education embraces the concept of political socialization as well as the concept of atheistic indocrination.

In the last respect communist China is far ahead of the Russia of 1917 because there were never any strong religious foundations in China. In Russia, even today, the government spends a tremendous amount of money and time fighting religious beliefs while in China there is no need to fight Buddhism or Taoism.

As in other communist countries, one of the most important goals of Chinese education is to educate a "new Chinese man," a man who will follow the decisions and orders of the party without question. With this general principle, the communists plan to upgrade the general cultural level of the nation and inculcate the ideas of the famous past, the great history of the Chinese nation, and Chinese civilization. National pride is, therefore, the first motto for Chinese cultural reconstruction.

Motivated by the need to educate the masses, the communist authorities in China have certainly raised the level of education and increased the enrollment of various schools. In 1953, for example, more than fifty million Chinese children were in primary education on a full-time basis and a quite impressive number of people—over 100 million—attended the so-called spare-time educational institutions. By 1958, the Chinese initiated the policy known as the "great leap forward." It was designed to arouse a national pride and a national consciousness based on Chinese historical and educational developments. In less than ten years of the communist regime in China, the number of children in elementary schools has increased to 60 million, and the percentage of students in higher educational

---

[3] E. Cressy, *Understanding China* (New York: Thomas Nelson and Son, 1957); see also Chang-Tu-Hu, *op. cit.*, p. 25; Chang-Hu, "Higher Education in Mainland China," in *Comparative Education Review,* vol. 4, No. 3, 1961, p. 163; Mao Tse-tung, *Selected Works* (New York: International Publishers, 1954, vol. 3), p. 145.

institutions has increased over 500 per cent when compared to the 1948 level.

The new Chinese man is not the same type as the new Russian man since, except for Lenin and Stalin, no other Russian communist is thought to be worthy of study. Also, the children of communists must realize that all the decisions of the party are wise, good and must be carried out. When the party required each student to work physically at one time or another during his school career, this decision was widely supported by the students who felt this would help industrial development and also help to get rid of the old class structure. Today's China is a mass of semi-educated Chinese, but these Chinese are part of the common people who share the same experiences and hardships of social situations. The intelligentsia, no longer aloof, is representative of the newly educated generation.

When the Great Proletarian Revolution began, in roughly April, 1966, a new method was used to educate the new man, a method of ruthless attack on those who thought that coexistence was feasible. Even Russian communists are labeled as the stooges of capitalism. The present policy of the communist regime is "to criticize reactionary academic authorities, criticize the ideologies of the bourgeoisie, all exploiting classes, and persons in power who have wormed their way into the party and are taking the capitalist road."

One of the most important goals of education is to develop a new technological intelligentsia, particularly atomic scientists who will be able to overtake the West in the atomic race and raise Chinese military power to first place in the world. School authorities are constantly reminded that this is the primary goal of the new government.

In order to achieve the desired industrial improvements, communist leaders involved all the people. This was the goal of Mao Tse-tung and his trusted friend, Liu Shao-Chi'i, the Chairman of the People's Republic of China. Both of them proclaimed that in the future several tens of millions of peasants would enter cities and factories.

We often find in speeches of Liu Shao-Chi'i references to the Great Learning (book of Confucius) for the foundations of the new communist generation. Liu Shao-Chi'i was quite active in educating the new communist youth before he got into trouble with the party.

The Chinese communist leaders fully realize that China must increase her industrial output and improve her production and distribution techniques before the term "great step forward" will have any meaning. Without industrial potential, China cannot compete with her neighbor, Russia, or any other country to which she tries to sell her ideas.

There were many faults in the communist planning, such as a too rapid transition from a pastoral to an industrial society, the failure of the "great leap forward" in 1962, and the terror behind the "new cultural proletarian revolution." All of these steps are explained, however, as essential steps on the road to communism.

Another goal of Chinese education is to produce a large social-political intelligentsia. Progress has been made in quantity but not in quality. Many teachers, clerks, technical workers and others barely know how to read and write; their only qualification is faithfulness to the party and the new regime.[4]

The following data are available on the status of Chinese education:

Type of School	Number of Schools	Year	Number of Students
Pre-School	2,758	1955	561,594
Primary	530,000	1955	53 million
		1959	90 million
Secondary	5,120	1955	3.9 million
		1959	8.5 million
Technical	...	1955	
		1959	850,000
Pedagogical Schools	551	1955	280,203
		1959	620,000
Higher Education	151	1955	205,000
		1959	810,000

As can be expected, there is little or no mention about Chinese failures inside and outside China. Mao Tse-tung, like the Russian communist leaders, is not subject to any criticism for mistakes. Mao himself tried to prevent such occurrences by purging people who disagreed with him. The Red Guards were instigated to wipe out all those who disagreed with the principles of the great proletarian revolution. Mao decides who will succeed to the post of presiding over the communist party of China.

In Peking the cultural revolution always must be more vivid than any other place since it is the cultural and political center of China. The communists in power are trying to do many things in a short period of

---

[4] There are many teachers who do not know how to read or write, but since their political qualifications are sufficient they are allowed to teach. See *Teacher Training in Communist China*, p. 48; *U. N. Statistical Yearbook*, 1955, p. 578.

time such as creating a new culture and building a platform of the new and young generation. This is necessary since no big power can be effective without its own heroes, its cultural and scientific accomplishments, its great poets, writers and politicians. All of these are a part of politico-cultural revolution that China has needed so badly for the last one thousand years.

ORGANIZATION AND CONTROL

There are similarities between the Russian and Chinese structures of education. Both employ the centralized system of control; both systems have extensive departments for administering schools at all levels. The Ministry of Education is expected to control, organize, plan and supervise all educational endeavors; it is a tool through which the party programs are carried out.

The Academy of Sciences oversees all research and scientific programming and Russia and China differ greatly in the administrative structure of this institution. As mentioned in the section on Russian administration, the Soviet Academy of Sciences has many rights and responsibilities, such as methodological questions, organization and planning of research activities, cultural planning (e.g., museums and literature for children) and press and scientific publications in general. In addition, the Soviet Academy has branches in each of the Union Republics with about the same scope of activities as the Russian Academy of Sciences. The Chinese Academy of Sciences on the other hand is quite limited in its planning and its area of concentration, per se. The highest legal body over the educational matters which the Academy handles is the Chinese State Council on Science and Planning. Then there are in descending order the Council of the Academy, the Science Publishing House, the general library, followed by five major departments: biological sciences, physics-mathematics, geology-geography, philosophy and the technical sciences. The Academy has branches in the major districts of China as well as in individual institutes in certain places of the country.

Spare Time Education. Organization and control of the spare-time educational system is divided between the management of an industrial enterprise and the communist party. The party, regional or local, is responsible for political education of youth, but a school administration takes responsibility for industrial matters. Further, the administrative staffs of factories—engineers, technicians—are assigned as teachers. They teach in their "spare time" in addition to holding their regular jobs. In 1960, some

430,000 teachers participated in the program on the spare time basis, in addition to some 60,000 full-time teachers.

Trade union officials are also responsible for political education, thus the union is also a major factor in the education of workers.

It is difficult to estimate the precise number of students in spare-time schools. Statistical sources vary as much as 100 per cent. The following data are available on the number of workers attending spare-time classes:[5]

Year	Number of Students
1949	276,432
1950	764,199
1951	2,026,381
1954	3,050,000
1959	13,000,000
1960 (August)	25,000,000

As this data indicates, the number of students in spare-time schools as of 1960 totalled twenty-five million. But if one compares the spare-time schools with the schools for the illiterates, one notes that the number of students in schools for illiterates exceeded the number of students in all schools of spare-time education. In 1957, there were 72 million in schools for illiterates, in 1958, 40 million; there was no proportionate increase in the spare-time schools. The authority of the trade unions and factory management in spare-time education increased greatly after the 1958 reforms. The party continues its close supervision and inspection in every area.

The factors are conspicuous in a comparison of the Russian and Chinese educational structures; the Chinese are less efficient and they are less complex.

Like those in many other undeveloped countries, Chinese schools had to overcome the key problem of general illiteracy. To remedy this, Chinese authorities organized part-time schools for the specific purpose of eradicating illiteracy. However, these schools soon began to offer other subjects on a very low academic level dealing with the major needs of the industry. They were presented at such a level that a semi-literate person was able to follow some of the "scientific" disciplines, at least in terms of operating and handling a certain type of machine. Most were becoming literate, but

[5] *Ibid.* U. N. Statistical Yearbook, 1966, p. 729; Orleans, *op. cit.*, p. 30; State Statistical Bureau, *The Great Years* (Peking: State Statistical Office, 1960), p. 20.

there were also those who were continuing their studies in some type of technological field. A special school, "Red and Expert School," similar to the early Bolshevik schools, was established to train the proletarian intelligentsia. The Ministry of Education reported that by 1958 more than sixty-six million Chinese had been taught to read and write.

Pre-Schools and Elementary Schools. The communist government also began a massive effort to include pre-school children in some kind of educational activities. Nurseries, almost non-existent before the communist period, began to appear, e.g., in 1951, there were 2,700 nursery schools in the country with 99,000 students; in 1958, the number increased to 3.2 million units with over forty-seven million children. The kindergarten movement spread equally well throughout China. There are no statistical data on this type of school during the school year of 1949-1950, but in 1951, there were already 1,800 such establishments with 140,325 students; and in 1959, according to Chinese statistics, the number of kindergarten establishments had reached 4,980,000 incorporating 67,700,000 students.

The development of primary education also witnessed some rapid changes. In the early years of communist education, reforms were focused on the introduction of general compulsory elementary education throughout the whole country. There were twenty-four million children in elementary schools as of 1949, and the number increased to ninety million in 1960. The rate of graduation and enrollment looks somewhat different since in 1949 only two million children (out of twenty-four million) completed elementary education as compared to sixteen million in 1960.

The general pattern of communist education in China is similar to that of other communist countries. Socially useful labor is required at a pre-school age, e.g., children in kindergarten are taught to respect physical labor and to contribute some themselves according to their capabilities. A Chinese child is required to do some practical work—such things as sweeping the floor, wiping tables and chairs, irrigating plants, etc. Children in rural areas, on the elementary basis, are expected to do some physical work and help their elders in farming.

Secondary Schools. Secondary education in China is divided into two groups: the general secondary schools and the specialized secondary schools. The latter is further divided into the following categories: normal or teachers' schools and vocational schools, primarily those of industrial training. The average age of children in these schools is between thirteen and eighteen. The last three years are considered to be the senior level of secondary education.

General schools are somewhat like the European gymnasiums—they are college preparatory schools. The Chinese at the present time are trying to produce quantity and not necessarily quality in students. There is a drive throughout China to expand secondary education to all the children in the age group of thirteen to eighteen years. When we compare the number of students in the secondary general schools during the ten-year period, 1949-59, we see that the number of these students increased eight times, e.g., in 1949 there were 1,049,000 students in secondary schools of which 296,000 graduated; in 1959, the number increased to 8,520,000.

The specialized secondary schools are of two types: the normal or teachers' schools and the vocational schools. The prerequisite to enter normal school is the completion of the six year elementary education. Those who enter the normal schools are required to spend six years of studying to qualify for a teaching position in the elementary schools. But this too changes. After a teacher has taught a certain amount of time in the elementary school, he will be transferred to the junior secondary school system. Here it is important to note that the training of teachers is of much lower quality than the American training. Ideally, the Chinese teacher would have to complete his elementary education (six years) and then attend the secondary schools for six years. But in practice many teach after completing only nine years, i.e., six years of elementary and three years of secondary education.

Vocational schools are focused on five major areas: engineering; agriculture and forestry; public health; finance and economics; and the fine arts. In 1949-1950 there were over 21,000 students in engineering or 27 per cent of the total number of students at the secondary level while in 1956, the number of students had increased to 177,600 or 55.8 per cent of the total number of students in engineering schools. There are no exact data on the number of students in Chinese educational institutions, and those that are available must be treated with some reservation because there are always some discrepancies in communist statistical publications, e.g., the Chinese statistical bureau gave different sets of data for the number of students in their technical schools of this (vocational) type. In 1955, according to the United Nations Yearbook, the number of students reached 280,203, while the *Jenmin Shou-ts'e* (People's Handbook), Peking, 1957, gave the figure of 318,000. The following data are available for the number of graduates from technical and industrial courses of secondary vocational schools.

Year	Vocational Schools (in thousands)		Technical & Industrial Courses (in thousands)	
	Enrollment	Graduation	Enrollment	Graduation
1949–50	77.1	25.0	24.4	7.0
1950–51	97.8	21.0	29.0	6.2
1952–53	290.4	54.0	111.4	20.7
1953–54	299.4	76.0	129.7	31.8
1955–57	337.0	81.0	207.8	50.0
1957–58	458.0	112.0	282.6	69.1

Higher Education. As mentioned previously, development of higher education in China was very slow. The first university established in 1898 in Peking was called the Capital University and consisted of four major faculties: medicine, law, philosophy and arts. By 1922, there were 108 institutions of higher learning, of which fifty were private, thirty-one provincial and twenty-seven national.

The Nationalist government tried to implement some educational reforms, but in general these were not designed to include large masses in higher educational institutions, neither were they designed to expand in a variety of technological sciences. In the early 1940s there were 143 institutions of higher learning: 39 universities, 50 independent colleges and 54 technical institutes. During the last phase of the Nationalist regime, the number of educational institutions was expanding so rapidly that by 1947 there were 207 institutions of higher learning with 155,036 students.

When the communists came to power, they followed typical communistic patterns of reform. They first implemented policies regarding the structure and content of philosophical requirements. Then they expanded the school system on this newly developed philosophy of education. In 1957-1958, the party introduced other changes in connection with the "great leap forward." In 1960, the "great leap forward" collapsed. In April, 1966, the "great proletarian cultural revolution" began.

In 1958, there were 236 different higher educational institutions divided among several specialties. The most important institution and one of the best Chinese universities is the University of Peking with 13 different departments and 1,600 staff members. The university has special renown in nuclear physics and nuclear engineering, technical physics and applied geophysics.

Since 1958, there have been several reorganizations in the Chinese higher educational structure, particularly in the curricula of the schools.

At the beginning of the communist regime, the emphasis was on political knowledge, e.g., throughout the period of the 1950s a student had to spend between 560 and 600 hours on subjects dealing with the policies of the communist party, the history of the Chinese revolution, the history of the international communist movement, political economy and philosophy. Furthermore, a part of his curricular activities belonged to the field of socially useful labor. A Chinese student usually has a thirteen hour workload. He spends four hours in the classroom, four hours in the field (physical or experimental work), four hours at independent work and one hour is devoted to physical and military training.

The expansion of higher education can be seen from the following figures: in 1950-1951 there were 137,000 students at higher educational institutes of which 19,000 graduated that year; in 1957-1958 there were 441,000 students, 72,000 of which received diplomas; in 1959 there were 660,000 students and 62,000 graduated. Although the number of students entering universities has increased annually, the number of graduates does not always keep the same pace. By the late 1950s, the educational authorities raised standards of admission which, of course, lowered the number of graduates and the number of qualified students to be admitted.

The distribution of Chinese students by professional pursuits is as follows:[6]

Types of Studies	Per Cent of the Total	
	1948/49	1957/58
Engineering	23.2	24.3
Science	7.8	6.4
Agriculture & Forestry . . .	8.1	4.9
Health	12.5	7.5
Education	6.4	43.9
Finance & Economics	19.1	3.3
Literature & Arts	11.4	5.7
Others	11.5	4.0
Total Number of Students . .	19,000	72,000

From time to time educational authorities complain to party officials that policies implemented by the party are not realistic and that changes must be made to improve the level of education. Also, from time to time

[6] Orleans, op. cit., pp. 49–126; Paul Harper, *Spare-Time Education for Workers in Communist China* (Washington, D. C.: U. S. Office of Education, 1964, Bulletin No. 30), p. 24.

the party agrees to change administrative or curricular programs in other than political fields. Like the Russian problems in agriculture (e.g., Khrushchev in 1958 complained that the Russian agricultural institutes gave diplomas to engineers who are afraid of cows), the Chinese complain about the lack of equipment in schools and the overloading of students with subjects not necessarily related to their specialization. In China it is worse than in Russia because many universities that already are functioning do not know what their specialty should be.

Most research and scientific investigations are carried out by pre-revolutionary graduates who are able to stay in China and continue their work. Although many teachers and scientists either were liquidated during the revolution or escaped abroad, potential scientific power still belongs to this group. It is interesting to note that the rate of survival among the pre-revolutionary specialists is low—as is expected in any communist country. There were 6,013 graduates of higher educational institutions from 1913-1917 who by 1960 were in the age group of 65-69, but only 2,928 survived; in 1923-1927, 12,229 people graduated from higher educational institutions who were in the age group of 55-59 in 1960 and of whom 8,426 survived; those who graduated during the period of 1943-1947, and by 1960 belonged to the age group of 35-39, did not seem to lose much since the data available indicates that 74,409 of the total number of 82,311 graduates survived.

As a rule research programs are carried out by the Academy of Sciences. The number of research institutes as well as the number of the scientific workers is hard to determine. Available data indicate that in 1952, there were 31 research establishments employing 5,239 workers. By 1958, this number had increased to 170 institutes and 28,300 scientific workers. It is hard to determine the number of Soviet scientific personnel in China since neither Chinese nor Soviets give an exact account of the nationality of researchers in China. We do know that many Soviet engineers have been sent to China and many Chinese students and scientists have been trained in Russia. In 1957, the Chinese admitted that the Soviet Union "has sent us more than ten of their finest scientists to assist us."

Teacher Training

In present day China, there are three types of teachers' training institutes: the junior normal school, the normal school and the normal college or university. The junior normal schools are designed for the elementary school teachers who complete six years of elementary schools and three years in the junior normal schools, a total of nine years. Normal school training consists of a similar pattern with the only difference an additional three years in the normal school, which qualifies them to teach in the upper level of the elementary and the secondary schools. The highest level of teachers' training institutes is the higher normal college or the university, where the student must have six years of elementary schooling, six years of secondary and four years of university training. Those who finish the university either teach at the secondary level or at the college level.

The curriculum of a normal school, of course, depends on the level of training. An average load for Chinese students is 30 hours of classes per week. A student would spend 4 semester hours on Chinese literature, 2 hours on language training, between 2 and 3 hours on mathematics, 2 hours on physics, 2 hours on history, 2 hours on physical activities, etc.

Political education, as mentioned before, is a compulsory subject at all levels. Students usually spend 2 hours per week on subject matter dealing with political knowledge and indoctrination. The most common program, set up by the Ministry of Education, includes the following: (1) direct education in communist morality in order to cultivate in students the proletarian concepts of morality; (2) basic policies of the party in terms of foreign and domestic affairs; (3) elementary knowledge of the "right" world outlooks and methods of scientific thinking. The whole educational program includes a general knowledge of proletarian teaching methods and proletarian culture. For each political subject there is a specific and detailed plan as to how it is to be taught. If there is an insufficient number of teaching personnel in this area, then the trade unions assist.

The status of teachers in the communist Chinese society was similar to that in the early Soviet period—they were dishonored, belittled and ignored. It was not until the new communist generation was educated that the status of the teaching profession was appreciated and respected. In China, the old-type teachers are very often accused of bourgeois manners and morals. The teachers educated during the Chinese communist regime are upgraded to an idealistic position in society and are praised as the builders of communism.

The monetary reward for teaching is very small; the average teacher in China gets about twenty-two dollars (forty to fifty *yuan*) per month and often less. Although there is a teachers' union representing them before the economic authorities, it does little to provide higher salaries for the teachers. The union is primarily responsible for the political "dependability" of the teachers, and has little influence on materialistic improvements.

There is little to encourage a teacher to do a better job, and there is an insufficient number of new candidates for teaching professions. In short, the training of teachers in communist China is on a much lower level than in advanced European countries or the United States. Even Chinese authorities complain that there are teachers who themselves hardly know how to read. An illiterate teacher whose only qualification is his membership in the communist party is not unusual.[7]

METHODOLOGICAL PROBLEMS

When in 1956, Khrushchev initiated the so-called work and study plan, the Russian secondary schools (especially the upper grades) were responsible for its implementation. The law applied chiefly to those students who wanted to enter the higher educational institutions. The Chinese went further than this, including in their work and study plan not only the secondary schools but also the elementary schools. The children of China are really following the Marxian concepts of polytechnical education and the necessity of child labor. Today the schools of China are located close to industrial enterprises or agricultural centers. It makes no difference whether or not they are located in healthy surroundings or whether these schools are convenient for the working parents. The most important thing is that they must be close to factories where children can get firsthand experience in the production of goods.

Educational authorities in communist China are adopting plans similar to those of Soviets in the field of general teaching methods. The *sprovoch-nik* or study plan (as mentioned in the Soviet section) is quite common in China. Subject matter is listed in study plans and the methods of covering these subjects is provided. More noticeable is the stress on "proper" methodology which is found in higher education, especially that of the training of teachers.

In the Teachers' Institutes, regardless of the level of the institute, the communist authorities supply the schools with supplementary methods—referred to in the instructions as "walking on two legs"—where each subject area is described in terms of the desired method to be followed or the extent of the subject to be studied. In addition to the study plans, each teacher is usually sent to a better school to observe the teaching of his own subject or to learn more about the subject method itself. This is supposed to improve the level of teaching and secure better cooperation between the children and the teacher.

---

[7] Hsi-en-chen, *Teacher Training in Communist China*, pp. 31–48; Stewart Fraser (ed.), *Chinese Communist Education: Records of the First Decade* (Nashville: Vanderbilt Union Press, 1965), p. 192; Harper, *op. cit.*, pp. 6 ff.

Much emphasis is given to the concept of "Red and Expert" which means that the student must first be "red" and then expert. In one of the Chinese provinces, a network of "Red and Expert" teacher training agencies was established. The aim of this type of educational program is primarily to educate active fighters for the world revolution. It is for this reason that the selection of students is mainly from the proletarian classes. Lin Feng, a member of the Central Committee of the Chinese communist party, called for an all-out effort in the cultural revolution to promote education among worker-peasant classes. For example, in 1952-1953, 20 per cent of the university students were of the lower classes (the total number of students from the class of worker-peasant equaled 40,000 in 1952); in 1956, the percentage increased to 29 or the actual number of 80,000 students; in 1958, to 160,000 or 36 per cent.[8]

Other Problems

The Status of Women. The number of Chinese women in educational institutions is not as impressive as one may expect from a communist country. The movement has been intensive but not as rapid as the worker-peasant movement in Chinese communist history. In 1932, women represented only 12 per cent of the college students and in 1940 only 19 per cent, in 1943 18 per cent and in 1946 the same. In 1949, women represented 19 per cent of the total number of students at higher educational institutions; in 1952, they reached the level of 23 per cent which remained the same throughout the 1950s.

At the secondary level, girls comprised on the average 25 per cent during the period of 1949-1957, with about 27 per cent in secondary specialized schools and 31 per cent in secondary general schools. As of 1958, the girls represented 38.5 per cent of the students in the primary schools.

The percentage of women in the national economy has not shown a rapid change. For instance, in 1949, there were 600,000 women in the Chinese national economy or 7.5 per cent; in 1955, the number increased to 2.4 million or 13 per cent, and in 1958, to 7 million or 15.4 per cent.

Progress and Problems. It is a general belief that the Chinese communists have improved the economic conditions of the country as well as having incorporated large masses of the population into the cultural-politi-

---

[8] Fraser, *op. cit.*, pp. 27-92.

cal front. But still it cannot be called a complete success or a progressive movement since progress in a civilized society is that which is accomplished without the use of terror.

One thing is common to all communists: the method of force and violence is the only "progressive" method of the proletariat revolution. Furthermore, China is trying to establish a communist culture rejecting any accomplishments of non-communists even if these are Chinese. Mao Tse-tung has not exactly followed the Russian example. He did utilize some Russian experiences in building communism in China. He said that China will follow Marxism-Leninism, but he will also never reject the old glory of China. Marxism, according to Mao, "must be integrated with the characteristics of the nation and given a definite national form before it can be useful."[9]

From the preceding example, we can see that the communist movement does not have an international set of laws for all communist nations, but is designed by two big centers: Moscow and Peking.

Additional References

Fred Greene, *The Far East* (New York: Holt and Winston Press, 1961); David Rowe, *Modern China: A Brief History* (Princeton: D. Van Nostrand Press, 1959); Karl A. Wittfogal, *Oriental Despotism: A Comparative Study of Total Power* (New Haven: Yale University Press, 1957); Fung-Yul-Lan, *A Short History of Chinese Philosophy*, Translated by D. Bede (New York: The Macmillan Press, 1948); Hu-Chang-Tu, *China: Its Culture, Its Society* (New Haven: HRAF Press, 1960); O. Briere, *Fifty Years of Chinese Philosophy: 1898–1950*, Translated from French by L. Thomson (London: Allen & Unwin, 1956); Chang Hen-Chil, *Communist China's Rural School and Community* (Boston: Christopher Publishing House, 1960); H. Creel, *Chinese Thought from Confucius to Mao-Tse-tung* (Chicago: University of Chicago Press, 1953); Chow Tse-tung, *The May Fourth Movement: Intellectual Revolution in Modern China* (Cambridge: Harvard University Press, 1960); Charles Want, *The Control of Teachers in Communist China* (Lackland, Texas: Training Research Center, 1955); Wen-ham Chang, *The Ideological Background of Chinese Student Movement* (New York: King and Crown Press, 1948).

---

[9] Chang-Tu-Hu, *op. cit.*, p. 76. For further information see John H. Kautsky, "Russia, China, and Nationalist Movement," in *Survey*, No. 43, August 1962, pp. 119–129; "The Soviet Leaders and the Chinese Dilemma," in *Studies on the Soviet Union*, vol. VI, No. 1, 1966, pp. 10–19; Orleans, *op. cit.*, pp. 144–172.

Chapter 24

EDUCATION IN OTHER
COMMUNIST COUNTRIES

The purpose of this chapter is merely to introduce some of the educational problems in four countries: Cuba, Mongolia, North Korea and North Vietnam. Obviously, the importance of these countries is great in cultural and political spheres, but since proper information is not published by the respective educational departments it is impossible to present an objective study of the individual systems. Therefore, only an outline of the historical significance of their cultural reforms will be presented.

It can be stated, however, that educational policies go side by side with political and military policies. One may gather some information by studying these in other Communist countries. It can be also stated that in countries that were entirely dependent on Russian mercy (like Mongolia for instance), the educational developments were somewhat different than in Korea or North Vietnam, where two powers wanted to influence the same nation.

EDUCATION IN CUBA

Educational development in Cuba went hand in hand with other political developments at certain historic times. During the colonial period, edu-

415

cation was not a concern of the Spanish administrators. Those Cubans who wanted education had to hire special tutors, and the more affluent traveled to Spain, North America or Mexico.

Educational developments during the 19th century were not too significant. The Catholic church was the sole owner of the schools, libraries and cultural institutions of the country. One social organization worth noting is the *Sociedad Economica de Amigos del Pais,* a liberal intellectual organization which established two schools in Havana in 1793. This organization played an important role in the cultural and national awakening of the island although not without a definite nationalistic coloring. They established schools in many parts of Cuba and taught the Cubans—white and Negro—the essentials of reading and writing, and a sense of national consciousness. The social revolutionist José Marti, celebrated hero of the Castro regime, was among many patriotic youth thus educated.

Although the Catholic church opposed other private schools, by 1825 the *Sociedad Economica* managed to establish a modern educational system in hundreds of schools throughout the island. The University of Havana began offering courses in anatomy, political economy and other branches of the social and natural sciences. By 1842, with help from the United States, the University of Havana became a secular university offering courses in many areas of specialization.

In other areas of education several plans had been made during the 18th and 19th centuries but hardly anything significant had been accomplished. There was no compulsory elementary education during these periods although several laws had been passed to initiate such a policy. Only after the liberation of Cuba from the Spaniards (1898) were the Cubans able to introduce some basic educational improvements. In 1909 the first effective measure was taken to compel all children between the ages of six and ten to attend some kind of school—either state or private.

The Catholic and Protestant churches alike led an intensive struggle against the backward population. They gave financial help to those who could not afford schooling for their children. Until the 1930 Revolution almost all secondary schools were privately owned, and were financially assisted by United States religious organizations. But after 1930 an intensive effort was made by the state to organize public education on the island. Many secondary general schools were established and the upper elementary schools were enlarged in various parts of the country. Also, several vocational schools were established for agriculture, commerce, industrial training and other subjects. By 1950 there were six secondary agricultural schools offering three-year programs. Only boys who had already completed five years of elementary education were accepted in these schools. Other schools, as of 1950, had also been expanded. For example, in that year there were over 7,000 kindergartens with approximately 100,000 pupils and 20,000 teachers; there were 43 technical schools with 17,500 students and 1,584 teachers; there were 13 teachers' training schools with 492 teachers and 8,650 students.

By 1953 elementary education also was reorganized and pre-school education was also changed. For instance, there were only 1,757 pre-school institutions in 1940 compared to over 7,000 in 1950. Elementary and secondary education was substantially improved since there were over 7,000 elementary schools with 669,610 boys and 343,630 girls in these schools, and there were 129 secondary schools with 30,076 boys and 13,049 girls in them. While before World War II there was only one university in Cuba, by 1953 there were four higher institutions of learning with 19,842 boys and 8,501 girls in them.

During the Batista regime some rural schools were established but in general, educational progress was slow. There were José Marti rural educational schools which trained agricultural teachers on rather low educational standards.

Educational progress has been slow during the entire history of the Cuban people. For example, in 1953, 25.9 per cent of Cuban men and 21.2 per cent of the women were still illiterate. In the age group of 10-14 the percentages were even more startling, with 35 per cent of the boys and 28 per cent of the girls being illiterate.[1]

Castro's Reforms

When Castro made his victorious entrance into Havana on January 8, 1959 he promised to change radically all social and cultural institutions existing during the dictatorship of General Batista.

Like other communists, Castro wanted to educate the new followers of communism by all means and at any cost. Like the Soviets, Castro's Cuba approached the educational problems from the political point of view. There were few cultural activities on the island without some concomitant political indoctrination.

The first target of Castro's reform was to eliminate any religious influence upon educational matters. He prohibited religious schools of all kinds

---

[1] Jean Haiken and others, *Twentieth Century Cuba* (New York: Doubleday Press, 1965), p. 183. See also *U. N. Statistical Yearbook* (1950), p. 611; *U. N. Statistical Yearbook*, 1957, p. 600.

and blamed them for "being in the hands of those who made the students instruments of capitalism and imperialism. Only the rich were educated properly—and to no good ends."

Campaign Against Illiteracy. Following the Russian patterns of educational reforms Castro realized that without education there could be no politics. Therefore, he proclaimed the year 1961 as the *año de educación* (the year of education) with the following objectives:

a. To offer primary education from 1962 on to all those of school age and to those not of school age who had already begun their primary education in 1961;
b. To provide a 6 year course for all those included in the preceding category;
c. To offer basic secondary education to all those who have completed primary education from 1966 on;
d. To provide enough intermediate technical instruction facilities to cover the requirements of the economic development of Cuba.

These objectives were to be carried out by the army of education or *alfabetizadores.* Castro closed all the public schools from the 6th grade through high school for eight months, so that personnel for this army could be recruited and his ideas imposed on the whole educational system. With the 100,000 student teachers and 35,000 professionals united under the cry *patria o muerto* (country or death), the year of education began. Subsequent statistics claim that the army of *alfabetizadores* enrolled nearly 1 million adults and that more than 700,000 learned to read and write during the year-long effort. On the basis of this statistic we conclude the illiteracy rate dropped from 23 per cent to 3.9 per cent.

As expected, no educational reforms went without political coloring. The teachers of the illiterate were told to carry on the anti-American reforms as well as to indoctrinate the students (of all ages) in the new spirit of communism. A cheap type of political poetry was imposed upon students. They were obligated to memorize the verses of something like this: "I swear to you, Uncle Sam" . . . that "we will bury the dollar and the Ku Klux Klan . . ."[2] Hatred toward the United States was very much emphasized.

In order that the reforms would go rapidly, Castro reorganized com-

---

[2] *Wall Street Journal,* March 17, 1961; *Saturday Review,* March 21, 1964, p. 64; *Newsweek,* April 3, 1961, pp. 51–57; UNESCO, *International Yearbook of Education:* 1961–1965, p. 102.

pletely educational control by setting up the Central Planning Board which was responsible for all educational activities. Municipal districts were divided into 24 regional educational zones not in terms of the classless society but in terms of the social regeneration of the classes. The various levels of educational activities, including the *Alfabetizadores,* were not permitted to introduce their own ideas without first conferring with regional authorities.

Elementary and Secondary Education. Castro wanted to enroll as many children in elementary and secondary state schools as possible and at the same time minimize the importance of the religious schools. He also wanted to put into practice the existing theory of six year elementary compulsory education for all who for one reason or another were not able to attend any school.

Many educational materials were imported from Russia, especially films dealing with communist propaganda which Castro got via Mexico. However, in later years Castro did not follow entirely the Russian patterns of communist educational reforms, but combined them with Cuban needs and Chinese ideas for building socialism in one country.

The curriculum of the new schools tried to follow a socialistic content. Russia was much more advanced in technological and ideological aspects of education so the Cuban reformers did not copy everything Russian simply because they could not place their graduates in the same occupations.

The secondary school system of Cuba basically starts after a student has completed six years of elementary education. It is divided, like the American system, into two categories: three years each at junior and senior levels. Each school, unlike the Soviet example, has a school psychologist who provides general orientation in all educational matters.

As of 1963 there were over 700,000 children in Cuban elementary schools; 211,996 in secondary schools; 74,479 in special secondary schools and 48,407 in teachers' training schools. Comparing these data to the pre-Castro period there was a general increase at educational levels (See Table 51.)

Propaganda and Education. In communist countries, the educational system always has to follow political directives. The political implications of education in Cuba constituted one of the most important educational reforms. The Cuban teacher has to carry the political message of Castro to all strata of the population. The slogan *alfabeticemos* ("let's make literate") meant in reality the political indoctrination of the people.

It was not unusual for the Cuban teachers in primary schools, especially

TABLE 51

Educational Development in Cuba: 1953, 1963

Types of Schools	Schools	Teachers	Number of Students	
			Total	Female Only
1953				
Pre-school	1,757	2,604	92,311	46,744
Primary	7,560	18,419	669,610	343,630
Secondary	129	2,041	30,553	13,049
Technical	48	1,699	17,553	6,489
Teacher Training .	38	1,369	10,230	9,600
Higher	4	711	19,842	8,501
Special	5	71	351	205
1963				
Pre-school	13,922*	2,510	86,647	42,653
Primary		34,531	1,194,407	583,799
Secondary	330	7,748	137,930	74,066
Technical	122	3,367	51,502	22,977
Teacher Training .	15	1,123	26,726	21,681
Higher	3	1,987	22,128	8,193
Special	26	355	1,802	681

United Nations, *Statistical Yearbook:* 1957, 1965, 1966 (New York: United Nations Service Press), pp. 611, 701, & 729 respectively. Note that there were no rapid increases or decreases in the educational development of Cuba during 1964–1966. For example, in 1963 there were 1.9 million students in elementary schools and about the same number of students in 1966; there were 137,930 students in secondary schools as of 1963; the number, however, dropped to 135,000 in 1966; there were 22,128 students at higher institutions of learning in 1963 and 23,284 in 1966. (See U. N. *Statistical Yearbook*, 1966, p. 729.)

*Include primary and pre-schools.

those dealing with illiterate adults, to use political textbooks having nothing to do with elementary school subjects but having the political message of the regime. The "textbook" *venceremos* ("we shall win") became a standard type of reference for all teachers in schools for illiterates.

Strong emphasis was placed on technological subjects. The Cubans believed that once industrialization was introduced they would be able to smash the United States "imperialism." Needless to say, in introducing any new subject emphasis was placed on the political relationship between the reforms and international communism.

As soon as the new reforms were introduced the communists tried to color them with sentimentality and make them emotionally arousing. By doing this they expect improvement in a certain scholastic area. They also require a positive attitude toward school, work, industry—anything that is new is good and anything that is old is bad—a pattern so widely used in early Soviet experiences.

It must always be underlined, in curriculum and in the teachers' manuals, that the old system of education served capitalistic ends and exploited workers and peasants. The young Cuban must be taught to remember the hazards of the old traditions and practices and they should not be allowed to creep into one's mind. By emphasizing the wrongness of the old and the goodness of the new the Cuban communist reformers believe that political ends will be served and teachers will be helped in motivating the children.[3]

Higher Education. Higher educational institutions train qualified specialists but also train qualified political workers. After 1959 Castro demanded that students participate in the socio-political activities of the country to further the socio-political revolution that was taking place. He also promised to expand the number of higher educational institutions throughout the country via Russian assistance. But as time went by, not everything old was rejected and not everything new was installed, e.g., the University of Havana (the country's largest, followed by Oriente and Las Villas) is a mixture of modern and old architecture. The classrooms seat 150. The labs and book shelves are sparsely furnished. As a matter of fact (as part of the Bay of Pigs prisoner exchange) the Cuban government asked for a complete set of modern U. S. published medical textbooks.

The curriculum looks the same as in any Western university except that Marxist dialectical materialism and history is a required course for all students at the university no matter what the field of study.

The University of Havana's catalog reads like a political document. It begins with a 22 page history of "reforms" in higher education. The professors are either young or old; the middle aged ones showed little affection for the new government and were quickly removed from their positions.

As of 1964 there were 2,000 Cubans studying in Russia but no Russians studying in Cuba. This gives us an indication of the quality of the education.[4]

---

[3] *U. N. Statistical Yearbook,* 1963, p. 701; Richard R. Fagen, *Cuba: The Political Content of Adult Education* (Stanford: Stanford University Press, 1964), pp. 6–15, 33–61.
[4] *International Yearbook of Education,* 1964, p. 92; *Saturday Review,* March 21, 1961, p. 64.

As of 1963 there were 22,128 boys and 8,193 girls attending the higher educational institutions of Cuba. The number is not too impressive for a country of 7.5 million, but nevertheless it is slightly better than during the Batista regime. (See Table 51.)

EDUCATION IN THE MONGOLIAN PEOPLE'S REPUBLIC

The country and the people of Mongolia are the ancestors of famous Genghis Khan who in the 13th century came close to world domination. Throughout the centuries Mongols lived in their own ghetto and stayed away from any contact with Western culture. Only through the mediation of the Chinese merchants did the Mongols come in contact with the Buddhist religion and Chinese culture. Basically, they remained for many foreigners a puzzle incapable of solution.

When Russia began to enlarge her borders the Russians, among other things, tried to gain a market for their products. However, their influence on the Mongolian way of life was insignificant not only because of great differences in religion, language and culture, but also because of the Mongolians' unsophisticated manners, poor craftsmanship in goods traded, and inefficient handling of commercial problems. The Chinese, on the other hand, had a great influence on the Mongolian intelligentsia and linguistically dominated the upper classes of the population.

Until the 20th century Mongolia lacked most of the characteristics necessary for statehood: no efficient army, no industrial potential, no great cities of cultural and industrial attractions, and most important, no diplomatic contact with the Western world. Until 1920 the Mongols were known outside Mongolia only because of their strategic geographic importance in the rivalry between China and Russia.

Russian Intervention

The Bolshevik Revolution in Russia stimulated some Mongolians to action but not on behalf of communism. It was rather a nationalistic desire of the Mongols to separate themselves from Chinese cultural influences. By no means was there any interest in communism especially the Russian brand. Here, however, credit must be given to Russians who were able to take advantage of the Mongolian internal situation. They promised full support to the Mongolian nationalists and by doing so "hooked up" the Mongolian people subconsciously. At the same time the communist "advisers" to Mongolia had infiltrated every important political position. Eventually they were able to put the huge non-communist masses under their influence.

The communists continued in Mongolia the Imperial Russian strategy concerning the future of Outer Mongolia. Sources indicate that czarist government had long planned the infiltration and the subsequent occupation of Outer Mongolia.

During the Bolshevik revolution of 1917 the communists did not anticipate that political events would be so favorable. Only after the indifference of the Western powers toward the Asiatic peoples, especially in remote places like Mongolia, did the situation change. Lenin immediately appointed a special committee to "help" the Mongolian people. When in 1920 the forces of General Kolchak (White Army) were defeated, an officer serving under General Kolchak, Baron von Ungern-Sternberg, organized a garrison of no more than 1,000 men and occupied the major city of Urga. He established a stronghold against the communist forces in Siberia, and subsequently regained the lost territories of Russia. Lenin, however, took advantage of the Chinese-Mongolian dispute to publicly announce that a Mongolian "liberation" army would be established. What actually happened was that the Mongolian National Army consisted of 400 native men and the rest of the "Army" consisted of the Russians or the Buriat Mongols conscripted by force to fight for the communist cause. As a result of this "liberation" the Russians occupied the major Mongolian cities and established a puppet government in 1921.

From 1921 on the Mongolian People's Republic became the first Russian satellite. It was completely sealed from all outside influences; even Soviet citizens were prohibited from traveling in Mongolia. Since China was too weak to interfere in Mongolian matters, the Russian communists ruled the Mongolian people as they saw fit. Not only that, but they occupied the Chinese city of Tuva, made it an eastern Russian fortress, and subsequently colonized it with a Russian population.

From 1921 on Mongolian history was not written by the natives but by the Russian communists. In all Mongolian people's histories one finds only extreme praise for the Russian "liberation" together with spurious revolutionary heroes, denunciation of capitalistic exploitation, and admiration for brotherhood with the Russian people. The countless foreign agents, military interventions, the total liquidation of any opposition and the shooting of all religious leaders are not mentioned, but instead voluntary support of the Mongolian people is emphasized.

Casual observance of the economic and cultural development of Mongolia shows that it is an exact replica of Soviet cultural and economic policies. The Mongols are encouraged to kill non-communists and to build socialism in their own country.

In economic affairs, the Mongols are predominantly engaged in agriculture. There was no industry before 1900 and only a small amount of manufacturing was developed by the Chinese. The communists built some plants but concentrated mainly on the dairy industry which still provides the major source of income for most of the Mongol peoples.

After World War II some factories were built in the Mongolian capital of Ulan Bator, and the first railway was constructed between the capital and the coal mines of Nalaikha. The Five Year Plan of 1960-1965 called for a large capacity increase in the agricultural industry, and for a large increase in the number of livestock. The plan was to increase the number of livestock to 30 million head, compared to 26 million in 1940.[5]

Educational Developments

Only during the famous period of Genghis Khan did Mongols have organized cultural activities. With the exception of a few historic periods, they have led a nomadic way of life and have had no use for an organized educational system. While Mongol hordes kept invading neighboring territories, cultural interactions with other nations were almost nil. We find some cultural enlightenment only in the 13th century. After the death of Kublai Khan there was very little done to attract the attention of other peoples to the Mongolian culture. It is believed that Kublai Khan was the first and the last to build an astronomic observatory in Mongolia. His predecessors used Christian or Chinese scholars to carry on cultural relations with the West.

In the early 1920s almost the entire population was illiterate. But, due to the Russian influence, the Mongols were forced to change their nomadic way of life, and as in the Soviet Union they began to wage war against illiteracy. Techniques similar to those in other satellite countries were used to fight the general educational backwardness of the population. The Russians imposed upon the Mongols the Cyrillic alphabet and the general Russian culture. Thus, the People's Republic of Mongolia was the first nation to be a subject of the Marr (mentioned previously in Russian linguistic policies) linguistic offensive. True, the Mongols had little to offer any cultural revolution, but to the Mongols the Russian alphabet was just as strange as the Chinese alphabet would be to the Russians.

To implement the reforms designed by Moscow, the Mongolian People's

---

[5] Robert Rupen, *The Mongolian People's Republic* (Stanford: Stanford University Press, 1966), pp. 14–106; A. Makhnenko, *Gosudarstvennyi stroi MNR* (Moscow: Gosizdat, 1955), *passim;* B. Shyrendyb, *Narodnaia revoliutsiia v Mongolii i obrazovanie MNR* (Moscow: AN SSSR, 1956), *passim;* Peter S. Tang, *Russian and Soviet Policy in Manchuria and Outer Mongolia, 1911–1931* (Durham: Duke University Press, 1959), pp. 413–415; George S. Murphy, *Soviet Mongolia* (Berkeley: University of California Press, 1966), pp. 4 ff.

Revolutionary Army was created, which not only was trained in military but also in cultural affairs. The Russian command in Mongolia decreed that every literate soldier of the Mongolian Army must participate in the war against illiteracy. The Mongolian educational authorities believed that soldiers are better teachers than civil servants because soldiers, in addition to reading and writing, could teach the children how to handle knives, rifles, cannons and sometimes could even show the students how to fly an airplane.

General Education. Most of the Mongolian educational reforms were focused on the introduction of elementary education. After 1921 intensive steps were taken by the Russian communists to change the Mongol's way of life through education. While more than 98 per cent of the people were illiterate in 1921, the situation was not much better in 1940, since fewer than 10 per cent of the people in the Mongolian People's Republic were literate. The Mongols were just not eager to learn or to improve their cultural situation. Furthermore, most of the people lived in rural areas and led a nomadic way of life, so it was unfeasible for a youngster to go to school every day. Although the Mongols do not think it unusual to send an eight year old child on a 15 mile ride by himself, his education does not thus improve too much. After 1945, increasing efforts were made to improve the situation because there was a danger that China would take advantage of Russian cultural weaknesses in the area.

The educational development of Mongolia is as follows:[6]

Type of School	Number of Schools	Number of Students	Year
Elementary	1	40	1921
Elementary	122	na	1930
Elementary	385	na	1940
Middle (age 11–17)	1	50	1942
Elementary and Secondary . .	434	100,000	1961
of which secondary . . .	94	na*	1961
Elementary and secondary . .	504	107,648	1963

*Not available.

As of 1965 one out of every six Mongols attended some kind of school. Improvement has definitely been made, e.g., in 1920 there were no ele-

[6] Murphy, *op. cit.,* p. 145; *U. N. Statistical Yearbook,* 1966, p. 736; Owen Lattimore, *Nomads and Commissars: Mongolia Revisited* (New York-London: Oxford University Press, 1962), p. 169; Rupen, *op. cit.,* p. 38/39.

mentary schools of any kind, but by 1963 there were over 400. In addition, there are current efforts to improve technological education for basic industrial needs. In 1963 there were 15 technological schools specializing in such areas as medicine (on the secondary level), teaching and mechanics.

For curriculum the Russians supply the major "advice." Following the Russian work and study plan, Mongolian children of today are trained both theoretically and practically. At the elementary level the curriculum is oriented toward the mastery of natural surroundings and improving knowledge of the native language. The Russian language is compulsory for all students at the age of 10 and exceptions are made only if there is a lack of teachers.

Educational policies are copied from Russian policies to the last detail. Although the Mongolian People's Republic has its own Ministry of Education, the major decisions are not made in Ulan-Batur, but in Moscow. As of 1960, the Minister of Education was Professor Khorlo. His control was rather surprising since he did not know even how many colleges were in the Mongolian People's Republic.

Higher Education. The first Mongolian University was established in 1942 in Ulan-Bator but the actual development of Mongolian higher education did not begin until the late 1950s. In 1957 the law on compulsory elementary education was still not passed, although the Second Five Year Plan (1952-1957) made some provisions for it.

Due to these reasons the development of higher education could not grow as rapidly as the party planned, e.g., in the 1940s, the university had no students to register since there were no native students prepared to begin higher education, and this continued into the late 1950s.

With the changes in Russian education the Mongolian educational system began to develop. When Khrushchev introduced the work and study plan in the Soviet Union requiring at the same time an increase in the number of specialists with higher educational training, similar measures were taken in Mongolia. The communist party of Mongolia issued a resolution in 1957 to speed up educational development. Their demands were fulfilled, since by 1960 there were five higher educational institutions including one university with 37,000 students.

In 1961 the Academy of Sciences was established in Ulan-Batur with several sections of research and higher educational specializations. The Medical School at Ulan-Batur is the center of medical research and is directly subordinated to the Academy of Sciences. There are also branches of the Academy dealing with agricultural improvements and general technological needs.

The reforms in education are again undoubtedly a strong communist point, since many Asiatic nations for the first time in their history are able to benefit from the cultural contributions of more advanced nations. In the case of Mongolia, for the first time in Mongol history, a Mongol can now become a physician without leaving the country.

Religious Reforms. After 1921 freedom of religion was greatly suppressed. The usual communist pattern prevailed; at first, legal decrees were issued on the status of religion; later strong propaganda measures were used and in the early 1930s force and violence were used.

Needless to say, no religious school could have been established in Mongolia. The Mongols, however, were not satisfied with legally controlling the Buddhist religion by a secular agency; they wanted to liquidate all Buddhists. Therefore, the number of lamas declined from 112,700 in 1924 to 75,500 in 1930 and to 17,000 in 1936. In 1938-39 the communists initiated the trials against the lamas and as a result in only one year as many as 30,000 of them were killed. Those who survived the purges "supported" the communist regime.[7]

EDUCATION IN NORTH KOREA

The Russian communists had long planned to infiltrate the Korean way of life with Russian ideas of world revolution, particularly because the territory was important for its strategic location in the Far East. Stalin hoped to make Korea identical to his other republics.

General Background. Cultural influences upon the Korean people were generally derived from two sources: the Chinese and the Japanese. Only after 1945 was the Russian influence apparent in the North Korean regions.

Even before the Yi dynasty (1302-1910) the Chinese cultural expansion was quite evident in both Koreas. When the Japanese occupied Port Arthur and other islands in 1905, the autonomy of the Korean nation was directly endangered by Japanese Imperial expansion. During the occupation the Koreans offered small resistance against the strong Japanese culture.

After the Russians occupied North Korea in 1945 they imposed their culture upon the Korean people. The Russians wanted to impose two

[7] J. Bisch, *Mongolia: Unknown Land* (New York: Dutton Press, 1963), p. 80; W. Kolarz, "Religions of the East," in *Survey*, No. 43, 1962, pp. 135–136; Rupen, *op. cit.*, p. 28.

things: a socialistic orientation aimed at the re-education of the Korean people and the Marxist social concept of *learn and study.*

The Koreans took some concepts from the Marxist theories and practices but also followed their own leader, Kim-il-song, who called for Koreans to respect their own tradition and to develop a communist culture with Korean characteristics. The Korean people were for centuries either under their own feudal system, or under the Japanese occupation, so it was only natural that a type of national sensitivity had to be developed before any ideology could work effectively.

As in all communist countries, the individual was required to do some kind of socially useful labor, usually physical labor. In order to change the agricultural society into a semi-industrial one, the government tried to implement certain policies on the one hand and to familiarize the people with the basic concepts of polytechnical culture on the other.

General Concepts of Educational Developments

North Korean communist education was not created by the Koreans, rather it was imposed by the Russians after the 1945 occupation. The Korean communists had little or no knowledge of the theoretical and practical foundations of the communist educational system. After the war, Russian educators came and established the school system based on Russian patterns and Russian Marxist practices.

As a matter of fact all the textbooks were written in a Russian manner, i.e., dealing with Russian methodological and psychological practices. The Koreans apparently preferred the Russian technical terms (actually they had no terminology for technical subjects). The Koreans even hung pictures of Russian war heroes on the walls of their classrooms. It came to the point that the secretary of the Korean communist party complained about his inability to educate Korean youth in the national spirit.

One of the first things the communists did when they came to power was to replace the Chinese and Japanese alphabets by introducing the Korean phonetic alphabet, *Hangu.* This simplified the attack on illiteracy. In Korea, as in Russia, the war against illiteracy was launched all over the country. Private or religious schools were prohibited and state controlled public schools were closely supervised by the educational authorities. The goal of the Korean educational administration was to liquidate illiteracy. In 1944 more than 2.3 million Koreans could not read or write. During the Japanese occupation only 35 per cent of school age children went to school and only 18 per cent of these graduated from elementary schools.

During the Korean war more than half of all students were mobilized for war. Those pursuing higher degrees were sent to the Soviet Union and other communist countries for continuation of their education. All, both at home and abroad, were indoctrinated in the party spirit and in blind obedience to the regime. Students abroad, over 5,000 of them, were predominantly pursuing technological know-how. After the Korean war all of them came back from the various communist countries and began to work for the improvement of Korean education. As a result of this, and some legislative provisions, the first Academy of Korean Sciences was established in 1952.

Party and educational authorities called for more polytechnical education (more or less imitating the Soviet patterns), emphasizing the necessity of labor and the appreciation of labor by the younger generation. The party chief, Kim-il-song, also stressed the importance of developing national polytechnology and general culture, rather than merely imitating Chinese or Russian patterns.[8] The three year plan of 1954-1957 made important provisions for rebuilding the pre-Korean war educational systems, primarily building of new schools and introduction of compulsory elementary education for all children in grades I-IV. (See Table 52.)

The Educational System after 1960. The structure of Korean education after 1960 is somewhat different than that of Soviet or Chinese education. It has four basic divisions:

1. The nursery schools, located in industrial centers and large settlements, for children aged 3 to 7;
2. The standard, or general educational schools, divided into the following:
   a. People's school: four years of elementary school
   b. Middle school (semi-secondary): three years
   c. Technical school: two years
   d. Senior technical school: two years
   e. University and pedagogical schools: four to five years
   f. Research institutes: four years
3. Specialized education: These schools are designed for students in music, ballet, arts, drama and languages and last eleven years (ages 7-19).
4. Adult education. This is usually conducted in the evenings and the

[8] Robert A. Scalopino, "The Origin of the Korean Communist Movement," in *Journal of Asian Affairs*, vol. XX, No. 1, 1960; R. Scalopino (ed.), *North Korea Today* (New York: F. Praeger Press, 1963), p. 125; *Facts About North Korea* (Pyongyang: Foreign Language Publishing House, 1961), pp. 1–20.

TABLE 52

Educational Development in N. Korea
(1946–1964)

	1946	1953	1964
Total number of Students	1,289,000*	1,776,000*	2,638,000*
Of which in Higher Educational Institutions . . .	2,731	8,957	114,000
Number of Higher Institutions of Learning	3	11	97

International Yearbook and Statesmen's Who's Who (London: Burke's Press, 1966), p. 323. There are no exact data on the development of the North Korean educational system. Some sources indicate that there were 97 higher educational institutions in 1964 and other sources indicate that there were 115 such establishments. Also, the number of students at higher educational institutions is not exactly stated by the North Korean sources. See R. Scalopino, *North Korea Today* (New York: Praeger Press, 1963), pp. 125 ff.; *United Nations Statistical Yearbook* (New York: United Nations Service, 1966), p. 730.; *International Yearbook and Statesmen's Who's Who* (London: Burke's Press, 1965), p. 381. According to the above sources, as of 1964, there were 2.5 million students of all kinds in the North Korean People's Republic in 9,407 different types of schools. The most puzzling indication is the rise of the higher educational institutions and the number of students. According to the Soviet source, B. Ts. Urlanis (ed.), *Naselenie mira* (The Population of the World) (Moscow: Gospolitizdat, 1965), pp. 148, in 1956 there were only 22,428 students but in 1964 the number increased to 114,000. The same thing applies to the number of higher educational institutions, which is not exactly stated, i.e., it varies from 97 in one source to 115 in another source.
* Rounded to the nearest hundred.

courses range two to four years beyond the seven years of elementary education.

It has to be noted that the Korean communist educational authorities pay special attention to the training of teachers, their educational standards and their political indoctrination. In the first years of the Korean communist regime these teachers were trained in China or Russia and they often brought with them a foreign educational heritage which was not exactly the aim of Kim-il-song. The educational level of teachers who never left Korea was not too high since many had only an elementary education, and most had no more than a secondary education. Efforts were made to improve this, especially in technology where the teachers' training schools require some basic knowledge of technical subjects. The University of Pyongyang has the best pedagogical school and has the facilities to train teachers in many professional fields.

Higher Education. Higher education in the Korean Republic began after World War II. Prior to that period Korean students pursued professional education abroad, usually in Japan. In 1946 there were three institutions of higher learning in North Korea. By 1963 this number increased to 97.[9]

There are many research institutes at industrial establishments as well as at major universities, with much emphasis given to technological research and industrial needs.

Special educational services are offered for those who work full time or those who wish to work toward a professional degree on a part-time basis. A variety of such training is offered at Kim-il-song University which is considered a prestige university like the University of Moscow for Russians or the University of Peking for Chinese. In 1962 Kim-il-song University had 12,000 students.

Position of Women. The role of women in communist society is always important. Korean women have their duties and responsibilities in the new system, e.g., in education there are about an equal number of males and females on the elementary level, but on the secondary level women constitute only 25 per cent of the total student population.

Another unique feature of Korean communist youth is that they do not have to wear the communist youth uniforms, as is the practice in Russia, but instead they are obligated to wear their own traditional dresses. The female student population is only a part of the total picture since in many other positions they have to do the same work as men do.

The total picture of North Korean education is as follows:[10]

No. of students	Year		
	1946	1953	1964
Total number of . . . . students of which	1,289,000	1,776,000	2,638,000
in higher education	2,731	8,957	114,000
No. of higher educational institutions	3	11	Between 97 and 115

[9] *Report of the U. N. Commission for the Unification and Rehabilitation of Korea* (New York: U. N. Press, No. 12 (A)-1881, 1951), pp. 59–60; Robert Rigg, *Red China's Fighting Hordes* (Harrisburg: Military Service Co., 1954), *passim.*

[10] *International Yearbook of Statesmen's Who's Who*, 1966, pp. 323 ff.; *U. N. Yearbook*, 1966, p. 730; *The China Quarterly* (April-June, 1961), pp. 15–28; Scalopino, *op. cit.*, pp. 136–188.

It is estimated that nearly one quarter of the Korean population is in school, or about 2.6 million people out of 11.5 million are attending some kind of educational institution.

NORTH VIETNAM

For centuries the Vietnamese people were under the direct political and cultural influence of China. When European colonization spread within Asiatic countries, Vietnam (or, as the Europeans named it, French Indo-China) fell first under Spanish influence and later under French occupation.

Religiously, the Vietnamese belong either to the Buddhist religion, to Taoism—a religion of primitive simplicity—or to Catholicism. There is also a great influence from Confucian philosophy, which the Vietnamese adopted while under Chinese domination (until about the 9th century).

When in the second part of the 17th century the Christian missionaries moved in, the Vietnamese at first opposed their ideas but later on began to favor the reforms introduced by Christian missionaries. One of the most important contributions to the Vietnamese people was the introduction of the Latin alphabet by Father A. de Rhodes in 1651, which facilitated communication. At the end of French domination there were over one million Catholics in Vietnam.

There were always revolutionary uprisings against the French but never big enough to do any damage. The majority of the people were united by nationalistic ideas, in a manner similar to Europeans and their wars of liberation. From 1918 until 1929 there were several strong nationalistic uprisings calling for the union of all Asiatic peoples against European domination. When in 1940 Japan occupied Vietnam the Vietnamese joined the China mainland in the struggle against the occupancy.

In 1945 Vietnam declared its independence against the French will and became permanently involved in a liberation war. By this time the communist minority group managed to obtain support from other communist countries, primarily Russia, and waged a total war against the French. In 1954 the Geneva agreement divided the country into two parts, South Vietnam and North Vietnam, dividing the 30 million people about equally.

The Russian Influence. The Geneva agreement to divide the country of Vietnam into two different parts was one of the biggest mistakes made by Western diplomacy. Regardless of the fact that there were already two Koreas, two Germanies, and two Chinas, the West failed to realize the danger of communism to its civilization. All this served the growth of

Russian communism and the decay of Western ideas in the backward minds of many Asiatic peoples.

It became evident after the Geneva agreement that the Russian communists were not satisfied merely with the division of the country into two parts. They began to train communist leaders (in Russia), military personnel, underground fighters, propaganda agents, and others for the takeover of South Vietnam. It did not take even five years to start a full-scale program in the South of terrifying the people with murders, kidnapings, and the liquidation of all who opposed the communist dictatorship—even women and children. By 1960 the Saigon government was able to control about 40 per cent of the people. Twenty per cent were directly involved in guerrilla warfare and the rest either were indifferent to any regime or were under the policy of pacification by the Saigon government.

The Russians began to collaborate with the Chinese communists in training top notch underground fighters, supplying them with the latest weapons of underground warfare. They also initiated chaos within the Saigon regime by supporting or denouncing certain political figures at certain times, and other such maneuvers which created favorable conditions for a communist takeover. The communists took advantage of the religious diversity of the population and began to lead an intensive struggle against the Catholic Church and later on against the Buddhists. Both were aimed at degrading the religious foundations of the social system. By 1965 the communists were able to infiltrate the South with more than 160,000 Vietcong by the additional "recruiting" of 100,000 men from among the South Vietnamese population.

As a result of the communist infiltration of South Vietnam, Soviet "trade" began to grow daily. For example, the Russians not only gave aid to North Vietnamese but they also forced their satellites to do likewise. In 1959 alone the Soviets supplied the Vietnamese with various goods worth 400 million rubles; Czechoslovakia gave the equivalent of 150 million rubles, Poland 30 million, Hungary 8 million, East Germany 60 million, and Communist China 900 million.

At the same time China and the Soviet Union began to fight for military, economic and political control of the country. From 1959 on the Chinese supported the North Vietnamese armies together with Russia although there were some differences between them. Nevertheless in one year alone China supplied North Vietnam with 515 million dollars worth of military and economic goods.[11]

---

[11] Ellen Hammer, *Vietnam Yesterday and Today* (New York: Holt, Winston and Rinehart, 1966), pp. 40–41; *Studies on the Soviet Union,* vol. VI, No. 2, 1966, pp. 25–57; Gerard Tonges, *L'enfer communiste an Nord Vietnam* (Paris: Les Nouvelles Editions Debresse, 1960), *passim.*

Educational Foundations

Since China was in a backward cultural position from the 13th century on, very little help could have been obtained from her. Although there always existed an emotional tie between the two countries the Vietnamese people had long been under the direct cultural influence of France or Spain. After 1900 some provisions were made by Dong Du for a Pan-Asian movement, but in reality no substantial progress was achieved.

Most Vietnamese students had no opportunity to complete higher educational institutions since the university established in Hanoi by the French occupational forces served only a select few. The well-to-do people went to Europe or the United States to obtain a higher education degree.

With the political changes inside Vietnam the communists initiated a new drive for raising the level of education in the area of political education, e.g., before a child was taught any history or scientific subjects he had to be aware of social conditions in the country and must be indoctrinated in the Marxist world outlook.

Historical Background. As in many other countries the original founders of the educational institutions were mostly religious persons. In Vietnam in the 11th century the Buddhists came and taught the people by the sword. They killed over 50,000 Vietnamese, but at the same time established an educational system for the religious elite. There are evidences, however, that some lower classes were able to attend these "higher schools of religious doctrines." The Buddhists, primarily Chinese, also began to establish general schools for secular learning and went as far as granting diplomas, even doctoral decrees.

In the 19th century an attempt was made to reintroduce the old Vietnamese education and culture, especially during the leadership of Minh Mang who tried to establish schools for training future leaders. This effort in reality was nothing more than a conditioning in the spirit of Confucianism, for the subject matter in these schools never went beyond memorization of Confucian classics. Some composition of prose and poetry and some writing was about all that was taught.

In 1868 a Catholic from Nghe, Nguyen Truong Tu, proposed the establishment of a modern European educational system. But it was not too successful since the royal courts were against such reforms. They did, however, translate college and other textbooks from Western languages, especially French. A strong move against Chinese writing and for *quoc ngu* (Latin alphabet) was introduced.

After World War II the leader of the communist minority, Ho Chi Minh, rejected the French patterns of education and introduced educational programs on the Soviet pattern. Ho Chi Minh changed the educational structure in the following way: elementary education consisted of 2 levels, a 4 year session and a 3 year one; and then another two years were allotted for secondary education.

Before Vietnam was divided there were 3,246 elementary schools in the area with 196,067 female students, and a total of 605,009 students. The teaching staff numbered 11,279, of which 2,978 were women. There was one university in Hanoi with 89 teachers and 1,729 students and of the latter there were only 33 women. (See also Table 53.)

TABLE 53

Educational Development in Vietnam: 1952–1965

Types of Schools	Schools	Teachers	Students Male & Female	Female Only
1952 (North and South Vietnam)				
Primary	3,246	11,279	605,009	196,067
Secondary	119	1,352	38,763	9,150
Technical	68	270	5,403	2,234
Higher	1	. . .	1,728	33
1963 (South Vietnam)				
Pre-school	20	579	28,433	13,576
Primary	6,528	27,519	1,574,679	651,252
Secondary	544	8,739	295,693	101,206
Technical	24	780	6,733	795
Teacher Training .	5	46	2,122	421
Higher	19	810	20,848	4,396
Special	2	8	79	15

| 1960–1965 (North Vietnam) | | | |
1960	1961 (In Thousands)	1962	1965
General Educ. . .	1,900	2,386	2,558	4,000
Technical	26	35,5	53,1	85
Higher	12,3	17,9	25,7	40

International Yearbook and Statesmen's Who's Who (London: Burke's Press, 1966), p. 604; United Nations, *Statistical Yearbook*, 1953, 1965 (New York: United Nations Press), pp. 580, 714 respectively.

By 1960 the situation had improved since there were already over 1.9 million students in different schools, of which 26,000 were in secondary education and 12,350 in higher educational institutions. In 1963 there were 2.7 million students in general educational schools which is more than four times as many as in 1939. By 1964 the number of students at the secondary level had increased to 85,000 students. The party hoped to reach 4 million, or about one fourth of the total population, i.e., on all educational levels.

Vietnamese higher education is lowest among the communist countries. The ratio of Vietnamese in schools for higher learning is only 16 students per 10,000 people compared to 26 students in Cuba, 84 in Yugoslavia, 64 in Mongolia, and in Korea 188 per 10,000 people—the largest ratio in any communist country.[12]

Comparing the data on the secondary level with South Vietnam, there were 6,528 elementary schools in South Vietnam in 1963 with 1.6 million students and 27,519 teachers. On the secondary level South Vietnam had 295,693 students of which 101,206 were women; in technical schools, a total of 6,733 of which 795 were women; and in higher education there were 20,848 students with 2,122 teachers. (See Table 53.)

It has to be noted that there are no religious schools of any kind in North Vietnam and that most of the Catholic population has been persecuted by the Ho Chi Minh regime. Well over half of the Catholic population migrated to the South after the partition of Vietnam. On the other hand, the communists sent large masses of able students abroad, especially to Russia, China and France where they obtained technological training.

Political Indoctrination

Political training is the most important phase of communist education in Vietnam, and it is probably the reason that other educational endeavors are not growing rapidly. As one of the leaders of Vietnam put it: "The aim of the present revolution is that the entire people and particularly the working people should thoroughly absorb the socialist ideology."

There are special schools in Vietnam, which in essence are quite different from any other schools in the communist bloc. They are correctional training schools, a Chinese educational invention, aimed at the complete indoctrination of the people with communist ideas and beliefs. They were established in 1949, although their history begins in the late 1920s when

---

[12] Haong Van Chi, *From Colonialism to Communism: A Case History of North Vietnam* (New York: F. Praeger, 1964), pp. 17–98; Hammer, *op. cit.*, pp. 70–71; Urlanis, *op. cit.*, p. 144.

Nguyen Son, a rival of Ho Chi Minh, first thought about such schools. His theories were so successful that Mao Tse-tung adopted this philosophy and imposed it on all politically "minded" personnel.

Students of the correctional technical schools are divided into four groups according to their political role. To the first group belong the high ranking members of the party (like Russian schools for the party and the political elite). Here the most highly regarded teachers lecture, including (upon occasion) Ho Chi Minh himself. To the second group belong the middle ranked members of the party, who are later responsible for the indoctrination of others in a particular area of concern. The third group of students consists of the lowest ranking leaders who function in small provinces and villages. The fourth group is devoted to the education of workers and peasants.

These schools are organized any place at any time. Those students who live in urban areas have some hope for a better future, i.e., to become teacher-propagandists; but in rural areas the education goes on "under a tree." Evenings and rainy days are usually devoted to this type of training.

The method of instruction varies according to the type of students. Teachers generally encourage criticism and self-criticism, and accept some suggestions on the future training of communist leaders. Although these suggestions do not usually mean much, nevertheless from the political point of view they are important. After the lecture, the student body is divided into small groups, usually three members, and the material is thoroughly discussed along with examples and explanations. The students discuss all the material paragraph by paragraph, and if it is necessary countless repetition follows.

When the lessons are completely mastered, the student makes a partial confession, i.e., each student admits in front of his group his previous errors and demonstrates before the group how "smart" he is now by having had the opportunity of acquiring an education.[13]

Additional References

F. Batista, *The Outgrowth and Decline of the Cuban Republic* (New York: The Devin Press, 1964); L. Hubernan, *Cuba: Anatomy of a Revolution* (New York: Monthly Review Press, 1961); Manuel L. Lleo, *Fidel Castro and Company Inc.: Communist Tyranny in Cuba* (New York: F. Praeger Press, 1964).; K. Rozschin, *Sotsialisticheskii ustav v ekonomike MNR* (Moscow: Gosstatizdat, 1958); Moskovskii Gosudarstvennyi Universitet, *Noveishaia istoriia stran zarubezhnogo vostoka* (Moscow: AN SSSR, 1953); McCune, *Korea Today* (Cambridge:

---

[13] Haong Van Chi, *op. cit.*, pp. 130–135. See also Bernard Roll, *The Two Vietnams* (New York: F. Praeger Press, 1963), *passim; Studies on the Soviet Union*, vol. VI, No. 2, 1966, pp. 68 ff.

Harvard University Press, 1950); *Economic Statistical Information of North Korea* (Washington, D. C.: Joint Publications Research Center, June 1960), pp. 120 ff.; U. S. Department of State, *North Korea: Case Study in the Techniques of Take-over* (Washington, D. C.: Department of State Publications, 7118, 1961); P. Huard, *Connaison du Vietnam* (Paris: Imprimere Nationale, 1956); D. Lancaster, *The Emancipation of Indochina* (Oxford: University Press, 1961); Bernard B. Fall, *The Viet Minh Regime* (New York: Cornell University Press, 1954).

Chapter 25

SUMMARY AND CONCLUSION

From the very beginning of the history of mankind, progressive individuals have sought to improve the general conditions of masses and at the same time to limit the power of the few exploiting those masses. In this historical process, communism, like many other political ideologies, sought to improve the living standards of the average man. But several things are common to all ideologies: none guarantees the behavior of individuals who come to power as a result of supporting a certain ideology, and none can forecast the fate of the masses who happen to fall under such influences at any certain period in history. There is no formula for controlling the power-hungry individuals who, once they have come to power, practice the same methods of dictatorship as their predecessors. There is a psychological phenomenon which directs the human animal in certain subconscious activities in his individual life as well as in his social life. A dictator by nature most of the time will remain a dictator regardless of what ideology he may follow. Most dictators become as ruthless as their predecessors and forget completely the noble ideas of the ideology they espouse.

Considering the tactics and methods of communist reforms there are many facts that prove the similarity between the imperial power structure

439

and the new communist structure. There are many evidences of cruelty in achieving their desired ends. As we have seen, the chief motive behind the communist revolution was a thirst for power in many varieties. There are also some things common to all communists (regardless of their nationality) in their controlling of a nation or nations. In this section we shall pin-point the major events—whether negative or positive—and the tactics of the communist reforms.

Communism and the People. From the Russian Revolution of 1917 until recent days the fate of many was determined by a few individuals of the communist party or parties. There is hardly any other historical epoch in which so many have been liquidated for almost no reason whatsoever. The force that the Russian communists used from the very beginning of their administration was dictated by the Russians for many other communist countries. As described before, many people perished not because they did anything against the regime but because they thought differently than the communists did.

We have indicated in the first chapter the fate of many inside the Soviet Union who have perished during the Soviet regime. The horrible methods of liquidation exceeded even those of Nero during the persecution of the early Christians. Artificial famine was used to liquidate over five million Ukrainians and over two million Kirgiz-Kazakhs and inhabitants of Baltic nations. Burning people inside buildings, torture inside prison cells, deportation to Siberian concentration camps or to Manchuria, liquidation of parents which left small children to die of starvation—all were quite common practices of the communists.

The acts committed by communists forced many people living inside the communist states to doubt the sincerity of the communists. The people were not sure that the persecutions of the 1930s in the Soviet Union, the one of 1945 in Yugoslavia, the one in Poland in 1945-1948, China's in 1948-1950 and those in other countries, would not recur. How can they trust a government that liquidated their relatives?

One thing is evident in the study of the population living under communism; the ruling nation always suffered less than the subjugated nationality, e.g., the Russian people gained numerically, increasing from 43.5 per cent in 1918 to 54 per cent in 1960 while other nationalities decreased as much as 20 per cent (see tables on population in Chapter One and the Appendix).

It is also ethically wrong to force people to leave their homes and native countries and migrate to unknown areas. The communists displaced millions from Poland, Czechoslovakia and millions of others inside the Soviet

Union to Siberia and other northern regions where no climatic or cultural attractions would motivate a person to settle. In short, when considering communist progress one should always ask, what happened to the people, and why did it happen?

Administration and Control. Some centuries ago an Italian, Machiavelli, outlined the strategy of a prince who wants to stay successfully in power. Those who are familiar with *The Prince* can easily compare the tactics of the communists to those outlined by Machiavelli who pictured *The Prince* as a man who should not be restricted by laws, morals or ethics in his quest for power.

Administrative practices of the Soviet Union are twofold. For example, they always appoint a native as the head of some organization, but the secretary must always be a Russian. The security officers (police, detectives, militia) are always controlled by the Russian communists. We have seen many evidences in previous chapters, e.g., a Ukrainian or an Uzbek served as the president of his country but all powers belonged to the Russians. The Ukrainians, the Uzbeks and the Finns were nothing but rubber stamps. All decisions were made in Moscow and all were imposed upon the so-called republics.

Educational control is carried out in Moscow. The Russian communists decide all major policies and order other republics to follow their directives. It is for propaganda reasons only that the so-called republic exists, but it has no real power.

Statistical Reliability. As mentioned before, the most unethical example of handling statistical data was that of the 1937 census when the Census Bureau was purged because it revealed the loss of population due to the communist atrocities in territories occupied by the Russian communists.

Since the communists insist that they will overtake the capitalistic countries in economic and cultural affairs, they want to be consistent in publishing various "increases" in population and other achievements, e.g., the general situation in Albania, according to the Albanian communist sources, is better than in the United States. The Albanians, or the North Koreans, or the Serbians have more students in their higher educational institutions, they have more industrial output, their people live longer, etc. All sorts of fictitious data are published in order to disorient and deceive those people who may be blinded by communist propaganda. There is no question that progress has been made in many areas, especially in education, but there is also no doubt in anybody's mind that, for instance, Albania is still quite behind the U.S.A. in industry, education, economics, and many other areas of human concerns. Nevertheless, the propaganda goes on, since the communists in power believe that there always will be some people (including intellectuals) who will be sold on the imaginary numbers. It is for these people that the Soviets, the Chinese, the Serbians, the Albanians, etc. prepare such statistical data. Those people who do not know much about the psyche of a given nation or the strategies of the communists may think communist statistical data are more important than facts.

The communist publications of most dubious accuracy are those prepared for foreign consumption. The English publications in Bulgaria, Poland, Russia, China, and others are produced solely for propaganda purposes and very often are in disagreement with the original sources. It takes a specialist to read what is really behind the lines of the communist statistical "handbook."

Education and Marxism. It is incorrect to call Russian Soviet education pure Marxist education because it deviates in many cases from the Marxist theoretical lines. It is more proper to call it Russian communist education.

Credit must be given to some communist countries which introduced a new type of education based on a classless approach to education. It is a known fact that pre-World War II educational systems of Europe were anything but democratic. There was always much social discrimination, especially in the lower social classes. Children of working families in prewar Hungary, Poland, Yugoslavia, China, Russia, etc., had very little opportunity to obtain an advanced degree. Not only that, but they were rejected from many social events (dances, plays, social gatherings). Such matters, of course, only paved the way for radical forces such as communism, nazism, fascism or other radical political organizations. The communists removed this social block in most cases, but at the same time the children of the party members were always able to move ahead faster— even without a good scholastic record to back them up.

Another important feature of communist educational policies was extension of higher educational opportunities to all. Here we must add that many other non-communist countries (e.g., South Korea, West Germany, Switzerland, Sweden, Denmark, etc.) achieved the same without using a policy of force and violence.

The boarding school is another communist invention and is used in many communist countries. Here the communists want to completely separate a child from his mother and father and subordinate him to the will of the party. A small child, for instance, spending six days a week in a boarding school is very likely to be indoctrinated in those ideas that the communist party promotes. Parents very often are called unprogressive and old-fashioned, especially those parents who are not communists. The communist methods are similar to those of the Turks in the late Middle Ages. At that time the Turks captured many Christian children and re-educated them in the spirit of Islam and then sent them to fight their own people. The Russian communists further imposed their educational policies, methods, and curriculum upon all their European satellites. Each European communist country must praise the accomplishments of the Russian people before their own. All students must study Russian before they can study any other language. Each country must use the Russian method of teaching. The Russians certainly have imposed their cultural way of life upon many other nations of Eastern Europe.

The Communist Youth Organizations. Every school in a communist country must organize the youth in collective types of associations designed to work for the fulfillment of socialism in their own country—and subsequently all over the world.

The youth organizations are very important since they take orders directly from the communist party. Every administrative unit dealing with education must have a member of the Communist Youth Organization and he must be present for all decisions which deal with youth.

The leading communist propagandists work together with the youth organizations in order that a definite ideological line is maintained and fulfilled. The young communists must be well indoctrinated in an anti-religious spirit, in a love for labor, and most of all, and in a love for the Soviet Union—regardless of their nationality. The poem cited before "away, begone, you cheating priest . . ." is not only impressive in poetical rhythm, but it is also an important model for the reeducation of children who happened to be born under a communist regime. Young children are very well supervised by trained adults and no uncensored comics or literature are permitted.

The youth are taught to respect the communist authorities, their teachers, and the public officials. This in turn helps the government to maintain order in a country.

The Curricular Changes. There is no room in a modern communist curriculum for Latin or other classical language. Instead, emphasis is placed on the sciences. Today the young Chinese, the young Koreans, the young Albanians are taught that miracles are performed by scientists and not by saints. Science will lead men to a better understanding of each other, to a happier life among nations, and at the same time it will help the proletariat to win the world revolution which is a goal of every communist country.

Every communist country includes in its school curriculum the military training of youth and provision is made for teaching the basics of chemical warfare and antiaircraft defense. Physical fitness is always included in the school curriculum. The general curriculum must be so organized as to combine the teaching of the ideas of communism and patriotism with the willingness to work for the socialist cause.

Methods of Research and Teaching. No research is possible inside the Soviet Union without conferring with the Russian Academy of Sciences. Textbooks, especially in non-Russian countries, must be so written as to satisfy the major goals of Russian policies. No book may be written without citing the works of Lenin and other approved communists. Physics, chemistry, and many other branches of the natural sciences must first "explore" the works of Marx, Engels and Lenin before they cite other books in their area of concern.

The other feature of Soviet research is that every scholar must first give credit to the Russian contributions in the field of sciences, and non-Russian scientists must recognize the fact that the Russian communists are the best scientists. Also all pre-communist important Russian people—writers, scientists, etc.—were exploited by the regime and they all were really following the philosophy of materialism. Only under the leadership of the communist party can the real Russian science be developed.

The most abused science is the discipline of history. In writing the history of Ukraine, Poland, Hungary, and other countries one must first ask the Russian Academy of Sciences for sources and "advice," e.g., the previously mentioned textbooks, *A History of Ukraine* (see Chapter 8) and the *History of Poland* sound like a history of Russia. Nothing is mentioned about the Russian liquidation of the Polish rebels during the partitions of Poland or the Russian liquidation of the non-communist Poles. The Polish history book purposely omits important parts of Polish history which would show children that Poland was a great country. Instead they are taught that they must be satisfied with living second best and that the Russians always gave a "helping hand" to the needy Polish people. The treaty between the Polish general Pilsudski and the Ukrainian leader Simon Petlyura is described as a bourgeois imperialistic trick and the armies of both nations are described as bandit-kulaks searching for adventures.

In teaching history one must always be careful not to mention certain historical facts which cast a negative light on the Russian people or the communists. The treaty between Mazepa (Ukraine) and Charles XII is described by the Russian historians as banditry because it aimed at the separation of Ukraine from Russia. In Central Asia, the Turkish people are not allowed to praise their own historical leaders, but must praise the Russians who "liberated" them although they were non-communists. In short, Russian imperial or Russian communist occupation of any country is not labeled as an occupation but as a liberation of the people from their own bureaucrats.

In teaching other subjects a teacher must always use charts which contrast the American "imperialists" with the "peaceful" Soviet Union. History textbooks must by all means include pictures of cannons and machine-guns as properly characteristic of the American people. The American Negro is pictured in such a way as to arouse the emotional feelings of other people and arouse hatred against America. Hate toward America is always first and hate toward China is second. In Russian movies about America the Americans generally look like morons and the working people look like slaves during the early period of the Roman empire. For children who have never traveled abroad this kind of teaching accomplishes what the communists wish to achieve with it.

Social Foundations of Education. This means the philosophical and psychological foundations of education. In all communist countries the official interpretation of the nature of man is explained on a purely materialistic basis. There is no soul, and since there is no soul, there is no need to worry about life hereafter. Man is purely the outcome of evolutionary changes just as any other animal with the only exception being that man's reflexes are more highly developed.

Both philosophy and psychology are taught at higher educational institutions from a strictly behavioristic point of view. There is no discussion and there can be no doubt about the correctness of the official lines of Marxism-Leninism-Mao Tse-tungism. Not only children, but all the people should know that the power of life and death rests with the Central Committee of the communist party. All new philosophical and psychological ideas must be first explained not to the people but to the party officials responsible for the cultural revolution.

Linguistic Problems. The most peculiar reforms in regard to linguistic policies were carried out in the Soviet Union. The Russians wanted to increase their empire by all possible means. To do this, they needed more people. Therefore, the Russian linguistic policies were aimed simultaneously at decreasing the non-Russian nationalities and simultaneously increasing the number of Russian speaking people. The new policies aimed at limitation of national language at the high administrative level, but at the same time they promoted national languages at a *local* or provincial level. This policy served two purposes: first, the world could see that there was freedom to use one's native tongue in communist countries; second, by imposing Russian in schools (especially on the higher educational levels) the number of people who speak Russian as their ordinary language has greatly increased. During the past fifty years the new intelligentsia has preferred the Russian language instead of a given ethnic language because by accepting Russian they had more opportunities to advance in state and political administration. Also by prohibiting certain languages (Arabic, for example) the Russians put a linguistic block between religion and nationality.

Outside the Soviet Union the Russians imposed the Cyrillic alphabet on the Mongolian people and have introduced the compulsory study of Russian in every country of their influence.

The previously mentioned Marr theories were designed to make the Russian language the language of communism and hoped to eliminate Chinese as a cultural language, as well as some African languages (which have had no opportunity to develop). The Soviet press frequently maintains that the Russian language is the language of the most progressive people and that the language of Lenin (and to some extent Stalin) should be studied if only for the reason that Lenin spoke it.

Religion and Communism. Those who want to remain religious and at the same time good communists are deluded. The communist party of any country is constantly fighting religion and wishes to eradicate all religious organizations. In the Soviet Union a member of a religious organization cannot be a member of the communist party.

Since religion, predominantly the Christian religion, preaches universal brotherhood, universal love and a universal system of ethics there can never be any agreement between the communists and the Christians. The communists preach two types of ethics: one for communists and another for non-communists. It is not wrong for a communist to kill someone if he does it in the name of the world revolution or in the name of national liberation.

Culture and Communism. At the present time there are two types of communist cultures, Chinese and Russian. Each tries to dominate a given area or a given nation. The Chinese, for example, want to limit the Russian influences in Asia, and they want to influence the Asiatic people inside the Soviet Union who were the subjects of Russian colonialism from the very beginning of the Russian domination of the Siberian regions.

The Russians want to impose their own culture on others, not necessarily the communist culture but the culture of Peter the Great, or as mentioned in the chapter on East Germany, the culture of Pushkin. By doing so they try to elevate the Russian nation to a more prominent status in the eyes of the world. For this reason they support the cultural revolution with many statistical data. They raise the status of women (especially in underdeveloped countries) to even status with men; they publish many books and journals dedicated only to the Russian communist cause; they "inform" the outside world about the achievements of the people's democracies and they blame the American "imperialists" when the "people's democracies" do not produce sufficient results.

In brief, the language of communism cannot be trusted. Russian and Chinese communism are not the types of communism that were dreamed of for many centuries. As seen in every country where the communists came to power, the individual lost his freedom not to the state, but to a few dictators, who were power-hungry individuals. There can be no two political parties, there can be no more than one representative in an "election," and there cannot be division of power between God and the ruler.

At the same time the communists realize that the only way to stay in power is to educate their own intelligentsia, their own leaders and their own children. For this reason, the number of schools has increased in every country they have occupied.

APPENDIX (Comparative Tables)

Author's Note

Those who have gathered or compiled statistics will appreciate the problems inherent in the task. Even when accurate, current and complete figures are available, there is still an irreducible minimum of human error. When the problem is futher complicated by the complexity of the structure of the U.S.S.R., the reluctance of communist authorities to release information, and the incomplete data available, the problem is compounded, as indeed the original inaccuracies of the data may be.

The student of communist education is cautioned, therefore, to regard this information as a conscientious effort at the best possible approximation of the facts. Every effort has been made to insure that the data as presented are correct, complete and useful.

TABLE 1

Distribution of the Available Total Population of the Russian Empire and the USSR (1897–1959)

A. 1897[1]

Region	Population			Per cent of:	
	Male	Female	Total	Urban	Rural
Empire	62,477,348	63,162,673	125,640,021[2]	13	87
European Part	45,749,575	47,693,289	93,442,864	13	87
Polish Regions	4,712,090	4,690,163	9,402,253	22	78
Caucasus	4,886,713	4,402,651	9,289,364	11	89
Siberia	2,964,419	2,794,403	5,758,822	8	92
Central Asia	4,164,551	3,582,167	7,746,718	12	88

B. 1926[3]

Region	Male	Female	Total	Urban	Rural
USSR	71,043,352	75,984,563	147,027,915	17.9	82.1
Russian SFSR	48,170,635	52,720,609	100,891,244	17.3	82.7
Including:					
Kazakh ASSR . . .	3,331,097	3,171,909	6,503,006	8.3	91.7
Kirghiz ASSR . . .	516,392	476,609	993,004	12.2	87.8
Ukrainian SSR	14,094,592	14,923,595	29,018,187	18.5	81.5
Belorussian SSR . . .	2,439,801	2,543,439	4,983,240	17.0	83.0
Uzbek SSR (including Tadzhik ASSR) . . .	2,797,420	2,475,381	5,272,801	20.9	79.1
Tadzhik ASSR . . .	na	na	827,167	4.9	95.1

TABLE 1 (Continued)

Distribution of the Available Total Population of the Russian Empire and the USSR (1897–1959)

Region	Population			Per cent of:	
	Male	Female	Total	Urban	Rural
Azerbaidzhan SSR	1,212,859	1,101,712	2,314,571	28.1	71.9
Armenian SSR	448,674	431,790	880,464	19.0	81.0
Georgian SSR	1,347,513	1,318,981	2,666,494	22.3	77.7
C. January 17, 1939 (In Thousands)[4]					
USSR	na	na	170,467	33	67
RSFSR	na	na	109,279	33	67
Ukrainian SSR. . . .	na	na	130,969	36	64
Belorussian SSR . . .	na	na	5,568	25	75
Azerbaidzhan SSR . .	na	na	3,210	36	64
Georgian SSR	na	na	3,542	30	70
Armenian SSR . . .	na	na	1,282	29	71
Kazakh SSR	na	na	6,146	28	72
Kirghiz SSR	na	na	1,459	19	81
Uzbek SSR	na	na	6,282	23	77
Tadzhik SSR	na	na	1,485	17	83
Turkmen SSR	na	na	1,254	33	67

(Continued on next page)

TABLE 1 (Continued)

Distribution of the Available Total Population of the Russian Empire and the USSR (1897–1959)

D. December, 1939[5]

Region	Population			Per cent of:	
	Male	Female	Total	Urban	Rural
USSR	91,404,452	99,273,438	190,677,890	32	68
RSFSR	51,101,667	57,277,114	108,378,781	33	67
Ukrainian SSR[6] . .	19,362,060	21,106,788	40,468,848	34	66
Belorussian SSR . .	4,315,726	4,594,268	8,909,994	21	79
Uzbek SSR	3,272,212	3,063,705	6,335,917	23	77
Kazakh SSR . . .	3,168,500	2,925,007	6,093,507	28	72
Georgian SSR . . .	1,764,967	1,775,056	3,540,023	30	70
Azerbaidzhan SSR .	1,642,612	1,562,538	3,205,150	36	64
Lithuanian SSR . .	1,381,300	1,498,700	2,880,000	23	77
Moldavian SSR . .	1,214,489	1,237,534	2,452,023	13	87
Latvian SSR . . .	886,181	998,575	1,884,756	35	65
Kirghiz SSR . . .	742,169	716,044	1,458,213	19	81
Tadzhik SSR . . .	769,425	715,015	1,484,440	17	83
Armenian SSR . . .	648,614	633,724	1,282,338	29	71
Turkmen SSR . . .	645,280	606,603	1,251,883	33	67
Estonian SSR . . .	489,250	562,767	1,052,017	34	66

TABLE 1 (Continued)

Distribution of the Available Total Population of the Russian Empire and the USSR (1897–1959)

E. 1959 (In Thousands)[7]

Region	Population			Per cent of:	
	Male	Female	Total	Urban	Rural
USSR	94,050	114,777	2,208,827		
RSFSR	52,425	65,109	117,534		
Ukrainian SSR. . .	18,575	23,294	41,869		
Belorussian SSR . .	3,581	4,474	8,055		
Uzbek SSR . . .	3,891	4,215	8,106		
Kazakh SSR . . .	4,422	4,888	9,310		
Georgian SSR . .	1,865	2,179	4,044		
Azerbaidzhan SSR .	1,757	1,941	3,698		
Lithuanian SSR . .	1,245	1,166	2,711		
Moldavian SSR . .	1,334	2,555	2,886		
Latvian SSR . . .	919	1,174	2,093		
Kirghiz SSR . . .	975	1,091	2,066		
Tadzhik SSR . . .	964	1,016	1,980		
Armenian SSR . .	842	921	1,763		
Turkmen SSR . . .	730	786	1,516		
Estonian SSR . . .	525	672	1,197		

(Continued on next page)

TABLE 1 (Continued)

Distribution of the Available Total Population of the Russian Empire and the USSR (1897–1959)

[1] Pervaia Obshchaia Perepis' Naseleniia Rossiiskoi Imperii, *Obshchei svod po imperii rezul'tatov razrabotki dannykh pervoi vseobshchei perepisi naseleniia*, 28-go ianvaria, 1897 g. (St. Petersburg: Tipografia N. L. Nyrkina, 1905), p. 1.

[2] The 1897 census did not include the population of Khiva and Bukhara (about 3.1 million inhabitants of which 50,000 were Russians —see *Aziatskaia Rossiia*, vol. 1, p. 168), as well as the citizens of Russia who lived in Finland (40,661).

[3] Tsentral'noe Statisticheskoe Upravlenie Gosplana SSSR, *Vsesoiuznaia perepis' naseleniia 1926 goda* (Moscow: Gosstatizdat, 1930), vol. 17, p. 233.

[4] Frank Lorimer, *The Population of the Soviet Union: History and Prospects* (Geneva: League of Nations, 1946), p. 162. Note: This was the third census of the Soviet regime; the second census, 1937, is not available because the entire census bureau was purged. The result of the 1937 census showed a tremendous decrease of the population (1932/33 famine and collectivization); see Bertham D. Wolfe, *Six Keys to the Soviet System*, Boston: The Beacon Press, 1956, p. 126. The Soviets explain that the central statistical administration was unable to apply basic statistical methods "because of difficulties involved in dealing with enemies of the people" (See J. Santin, *Vsesoiuznaia perepis' naseleniia 1937 g.* (Moscow: Goizdat Politicheskoi Literatury, 1938), pp. 19–29).

[5] Tsentral'noe Statisticheskoe Upravlenie pri Sovete Ministrov SSSR, *Itogi vsesoiuznoi perepisi naseleniia 1959 goda* (Moscow: Gosstatizdat, 1962), pp. 19–29.

[6] Data on the Ukrainian SSR include the peoples and the territories occupied by the Soviet Union during the months of September through December, 1939 (about nine million people).

[7] *Vestnik Statistiki*, No. 3, 1962, p. 91; Tsentral'noe Statisticheskoe Upravlenie pri Sovete Ministrov SSSR, *Narodnoe Khoziaistvo SSSR v 1960 g.* (Moscow: Gosstatizdat, 1961), p. 8.

TABLE 2-A[1]

Estimated Deficit of the Population of the USSR, 1926, Attributed to Effects of War and Postwar Conditions (In Thousands)

Approximate Birth Years	Age at Census, 1926	Expected Population	Observed Population	Difference	Deficit as % of Exp.
1897–1901	25–29	13,770	12,045	1,725	13
1902–1906	20–24	15,620	13,822	1,798	12
1907–1911	15–19	17,609	16,986	623	4
1912–1916	10–14	19,630	17,101	2,529	13
1917–1921	5–9	21,988	15,279	6,709	31
1922–1926	0–4	26,517	22,336	4,181	16
Total: 0–29	0–29	115,134	97,569	17,565	15
Males, 30 & Over		30,431	23,141	7,290	24
Females, 30 & Over...............		31,090	26,318	4,772	15
Both Sexes, 30 & Over		61,521	49,459	12,062	20
Total, All Ages		176,655	147,028	29,627	17

TABLE 2-B[2]

Deficit of the Population of the USSR, 1926–1939, Attributed To Purges and Forceful Collectivization (In Thousands)

Age	Expected Population Jan., 1939			Observed Population Jan. 17, 1939			Discrepancy[3]		
	Male	*Female*	*Total*	*Male*	*Female*	*Total*	*Male*	*Female*	*Total*
Under 12	931,849	31,343	63,192	...	...	48,089	...	...	15,103
12 & Over	61,195	66,715	127,910	...	...	122,378	...	...	5,532
Total	93,044	98,058	191,102	81,665	88,802	170,467	11,379	9,256	20,635

TABLE 2-C⁴

Distribution of Population Under and Over 15 Years of Age, By Sex: USSR, 1926–1939
(Estimated)

	Age					
	1926			1939		
Sex	Under 15 Years	Over 15 Years	% Under 15	Under 15 Years	Over 15 Years	% Under 15
Total	54,682,717	92,345,198	37.2	61,499,513	108,967,673	36.1
Males	27,530,718	43,512,634	38.8	30,962,729	50,702,252	37.9
Females	27,151,999	48,832,564	35.7	30,536,784	58,265,421	34.4
% Males in Total Population	50.3463	47.12	...	50.3463	46.53	...

[1] Frank Lorimer, *The Population of the Soviet Union: History and Prospects* (Geneva: League of Nations, 1946), p. 39.

[2] Official Soviet publications estimated that the population of the Soviet Union should reach the 180 (+) million mark by 1938 (instead of 147 million as the actual census data revealed). The Second Five-Year Plan also predicted the rise in the birth rate increasing the population from 165,700,000 as of January 1, 1933, to 180,700,000 as of January 1, 1938—average annual increase of 17.3 per thousand. The Soviet demographic data also admit that there were 5.5 million more deaths between 1926–1939 (those who were registered—and many were not) than had been expected (for further information see: Lorimer, *ibid.*, pp. 112–113; S. A. Novosel'skii, V. V. Paievskii, "O svodnykh kharakterikakh vosproizvodstva i perspektivnykh ischisleniiakh naseleniia," *Trudy demograficheskogo instituta*, vol. 1: Leningrad: Akademiia Nauk SSSR, 1934, p. 16; *The Second Five-Year Plan for the development of the national economy of the USSR, 1933–1937*, New York: International Publishers, 1937, p. 458).

[3] Lorimer, *op. cit.*, pp. 112–113.

[4] Note that the proportion of men, 15 years and over, is lower in 1939 than in 1926. This indicates that men suffered heavy losses during the forceful collectivization and deportations to various Far-Eastern regions. (See Lorimer, *ibid.*, p. 142.)

TABLE 3

Rate of Literacy According to Ethnic Groups of the UzSSR: 1926

Region	Total No. of Literates	In Per Cent to Total Population			Uzbeks		Tadzhiks		Other Natives		Russians	
		Male	Female	Total	Male	Female	Male	Female	Male	Female	Male	Female
Khiva	10,317	5.2	1.1	3.2	4.1	0.4	21.4	25.0	3.8	0.4	83.7	65.6
Urban	5,249	31.3	8.7	20.7	23.5	2.7	33.3	33.3	29.5	2.4	85.8	70.5
Rural	5,098	3.0	0.4	1.8	2.6	0.2	...	...	2.6	0.4	79.0	51.3
Bukhara	24,909	9.0	3.4	6.4	4.8	0.7	4.4	0.6	12.6	1.9	78.5	58.4
Urban	18,982	41.2	19.7	31.2	26.5	5.8	21.9	3.5	39.8	7.6	80.0	60.7
Rural	5,927	3.0	0.4	1.8	2.3	0.1	1.3	0.1	4.4	0.7	71.1	42.9
Zeravshan	9,105	5.1	1.1	3.3	3.2	1.1	4.0	0.2	6.5	0.8	81.4	53.3
Urban	4,185	31.6	12.2	22.9	14.2	1.1	9.7	1.3	37.1	6.5	85.9	63.1
Rural	4,916	3.2	0.4	1.9	2.6	0.1	3.7	0.1	3.0	0.1	72.9	39.0
Samarkand	49,093	12.1	6.1	9.3	5.5	0.7	11.6	2.2	18.6	2.6	75.8	58.7
Urban	39,814	37.0	22.1	30.1	19.8	3.5	17.8	3.3	34.0	4.8	76.8	61.0
Rural	9,279	3.8	0.7	2.3	2.8	0.2	5.5	0.8	6.4	0.8	66.9	37.9
Tashkent City ...	135,925	50.1	33.3	42.0	29.7	8.2	36.4	3.4	53.2	21.4	76.8	61.8

TABLE 3 (Continued)

Rate of Literacy According to Ethnic Groups of the UzSSR: 1926

Region	Total No. of Literates	In Per Cent to Total Population			Uzbeks		Tadzhiks		Other Natives		Russians	
		Male	Female	Total	Male	Female	Male	Female	Male	Female	Male	Female
Tashkent Oblast'	169,100	30.5	19.1	25.1	19.3	4.3	6.8	0.3	8.2	0.8	73.2	57.5
Urban	140,689	50.3	33.5	42.2	29.7	8.3	28.0	3.8	54.0	20.1	76.4	61.2
Rural	28,411	11.7	4.5	8.3	8.2	1.3	3.6	0.2	5.7	0.2	58.5	38.6
Fergana	53,627	11.3	4.2	7.9	7.5	1.1	7.9	1.1	4.9	1.5	79.2	59.4
Urban	38,197	35.7	17.0	26.8	22.7	4.1	16.6	3.0	44.0	18.3	79.7	60.0
Rural	15,430	4.8	0.7	2.9	4.5	0.5	5.4	0.5	1.8	0.1	73.5	53.3
Andizhan	41,230	7.7	2.2	5.1	6.2	2.7	4.3	0.6	3.6	0.3	75.9	56.1
Urban	23,534	21.5	8.5	15.3	13.6	1.7	5.0	...	11.4	3.6	76.7	57.8
Rural	17,696	4.6	0.6	2.7	4.3	0.5	4.2	0.6	3.3	0.2	46.8	39.4
Surkhan Dar'ia	10,245	8.3	1.2	5.0	1.3	0.1	2.1	0.0	3.5	0.0	89.2	57.5
Urban	7,301	79.3	44.2	72.1	31.9	12.0	19.6	2.2	17.7	0.6	89.0	56.2
Rural	2,944	2.7	0.3	1.6	1.1	0.0	2.1	0.0	2.6	0.0	89.8	63.5
Kashka Dar'ia	8,596	4.1	0.7	2.5	2.0	0.1	1.3	0.0	2.0	...	81.2	53.2
Urban	5,630	26.3	6.5	17.6	10.1	1.0	30.1	3.4	13.7	...	84.8	54.7

(Continued on next page)

TABLE 3 (Continued)

Rate of Literacy According to Ethnic Groups of the UzSSR: 1926

Region	Total No. of Literates	In Per Cent to Total Population			Uzbeks		Tadzhiks		Other Natives		Russians	
		Male	Female	Total	Male	Female	Male	Female	Male	Female	Male	Female
Kashka Dar'ia Rural	2,966	1.7	0.2	1.0	1.3	0.0	1.1	0.0	0.9	0.0	80.8	48.6
Kara-Kalpak Autonomous Region . .	534	4.1	0.5	2.3	2.8	0.1	3.6	...	3.5	0.1	88.9	71.8
Total-UzSSR	376,786	11.9	5.5	8.9	6.5	1.0	5.7	0.7	6.4	0.7	76.0	57.8
Urban	283,585	39.3	22.1	31.2	22.0	4.6	17.9	3.3	35.3	6.1	78.2	60.6
Rural	93,201	4.5	0.9	2.8	3.3	0.3	3.4	0.3	4.1	0.2	65.2	41.1

Gosudarstvennaia Planovaia Komissiia UzSSR, Ekonomiko-statisticheskii Sektor, *Raiony UzSSR v tsifrakh* (Samarkand: 1930), pp. 44–57.

TABLE 4

Per Cent of Literates in the Age Group 9–49 in Selected Republics: 1897–1936[1]

Republic	Both Sexes			Male			Female		
	1897	1926	1939	1897	1926	1939	1897	1926	1939
Empire—USSR	28.4	56.6	87.4	40.3	71.5	93.5	16.6	42.7	81.6
Urban	57.0	80.9	93.8	66.1	88.0	97.1	45.7	73.9	90.7
Rural	23.8	50.6	84.0	35.5	67.3	91.6	12.5	35.4	76.8[2]
RSFSR	29.6	60.9	89.7	44.4	77.1	96.0	15.4	46.4	83.9
Urban	61.1	85.0	94.9	71.0	91.9	98.1	48.5	78.4	91.8
Rural	24.6	55.0	86.7	39.5	73.3	94.8	11.0	38.8	79.3
Uzbek SSR	3.6	11.6	78.7	5.6	15.3	83.6	1.2	7.3	73.3
Urban	15.9	39.8	86.8	22.5	49.6	90.4	6.6	28.6	82.8
Rural	1.1	3.5	76.1	1.9	5.5	81.4	0.2	1.2	70.2
Tadzhik SSR	2.4	3.8	82.8	3.9	6.4	87.4	0.3	0.9	77.5
Urban	9.8	19.5	86.8	15.7	29.2	90.5	2.9	6.6	82.2
Rural	1.8	2.0	81.8	3.2	3.6	86.6	0.2	0.3	76.5
Kazakh SSR	8.1	25.2	83.6	12.0	35.4	90.3	3.6	14.5	75.8
Urban	34.7	61.0	87.5	43.5	70.3	93.4	23.8	51.6	80.8
Rural	6.3	21.6	81.9	9.9	31.9	89.1	2.3	10.6	73.7
Kirghiz SSR	3.1	16.5	79.8	5.0	23.9	84.9	0.8	8.4	74.4
Urban	13.2	41.3	85.6	18.9	50.3	89.5	6.0	31.0	81.0
Rural	2.3	13.0	78.3	3.9	20.1	83.7	0.4	5.3	72.7
Turkmen SSR	7.8	14.0	77.7	11.5	18.3	83.0	2.7	8.8	71.9
Urban	49.3	65.6	85.4	52.4	73.8	89.4	37.1	54.4	81.0
Rural	2.5	4.6	73.2	4.1	7.6	79.2	0.6	1.3	66.5

[1] Tsentral'noe Statisticheskoe Upravlenie pri Soviete Ministrov SSSR, Itogi vsesoiuznoi perepisi naseleniia 1959 goda, SSSR (Moscow: Gosstatizdat, 1962), p. 89.

[2] Data on western regions of Ukraine, Belorussia, Lithuania, Latvia, Moldavia, and Estonia were estimated by the Soviet Census Bureau.

TABLE 5

Development of Public Education in Selected Republics: 1914-1940[1]

A. 1914

Region	No. of Teachers	No. of Schools	Total No. of Students	In Grades:		No. of Students in VUZ[2]
				1-4	5-10	
Empire[3]	231,007	105,524	7,896,249	7,030,257	635,591	127,423
Urban	78,633	11,754	1,779,028	965,235	621,012	
Rural	152,374	93,770	6,117,221	6,065,022	14,579	
Of which:						
RSFSR	160,740	75,385	5,483,426	4,909,027	426,720	86,472
Urban	51,777	7,793	185,037	646,368	415,774	
Rural	108,963	67,592	4,298,389	4,262,659	10,946	
Ukrainian SSR	48,403	20,197	1,728,313	1,532,484	149,541	35,204
Urban	17,787	2,586	392,976	209,358	145,908	
Rural	30,616	17,616	1,335,337	1,323,126	3,633	
Uzbek SSR	704	160	17,299	10,970	4,632	...
Urban	622	108	14,271	7,942	4,632	
Rural	82	52	3,028	3,028	...	
Kazakh SSR	3,325	2,011	105,239	96,103	3,996	...
Urban	1,069	250	25,058	16,347	3,996	
Rural	2,256	1,761	80,181	79,729	...	

TABLE 5 (Continued)

Development of Public Education in Selected Republics: 1914–1940[1]

Region	No. of Teachers	No. of Schools	Total No. of Students	In Grades:		No. of Students in VUZ[2]
				1–4	5–10	
Kirghiz SSR	216	107	7,041	5,519	100	...
Urban	73	20	1,738	1,216	100	
Rural	143	87	5,303	5,303	...	
Tadzhik SSR	13	10	369	369	...	...
Urban	8	6	196	196	...	
Rural	5	4	173	173	...	
Turkmen SSR	272	58	6,783	4,416	1,379	...
Urban	222	31	5,283	2,984	1,379	
Rural	48	27	1,500	1,432	...	
B. 1927–1928						
USSR	365,056	118,558	11,368,678	9,910,407	1,458,271	168,554
Urban	127,785	11,006	3,159,611	2,126,439	1,033,172	
Rural	218,708	107,552	8,209,067	7,783,968	425,099	
Of which:						
RSFSR	228,169	80,265	7,386,281	6,426,599	959,682	114,181
Urban	83,060	6,697	2,020,881	1,319,598	701,283	
Rural	145,109	73,568	5,365,400	5,107,001	258,399	

(Continued on next page)

TABLE 5 (Continued)

Development of Public Education in Selected Republics: 1914–1940[1]

Region	No. of Teachers	No. of Schools	Total No. of Students	In Grades:		No. of Students in VUZ[2]
				1–4	5–10	
Ukrainian SSR	70,172	20,463	2,437,224	2,137,308	299,906	29,141
Urban	23,967	2,128	622,142	438,139	184,003	
Rural	46,205	18,335	1,815,082	1,699,169	115,913	
Uzbek SSR	5,387	1,933	139,616	126,155	13,461	3,876
Urban	3,239	462	79,557	66,396	13,161	
Rural	2,148	1,471	60,059	59,759	300	
Kazakh SSR	7,900	3,944	272,804	249,815	22,989	75
Urban	2,535	326	70,168	53,241	16,927	
Rural	5,365	3,618	202,636	196,574	6,062	
Kirghiz SSR	1,147	515	41,454	39,439	2,015	...
Urban	370	74	11,483	9,798	1,685	
Rural	777	441	29,971	29,641	330	
Tadzhik SSR	543	336	13,785	13,349	336	...
Urban	164	48	3,470	3,134	336	
Rural	379	288	10,315	10,315	...	
Turkmen SSR	1,298	508	31,868	27,240	4,628	...
Urban	768	86	18,936	14,308	4,628	
Rural	531	422	12,932	12,932	...	

TABLE 5 (Continued)

Development of Public Education in Selected Republics: 1914–1940[1]

C. 1940–41

Region	No. of Teachers	No. of Schools	Total No. of Students	In Grades:		No. of Students in VUZ[2]
				1–4	5–10	
USSR	1,215,967	191,545	34,510,266	21,375,172	13,135,094	811,680
Urban	374,045	21,498	10,668,450	5,334,529	5,333,921	
Rural	841,922	170,047	23,841,816	16,040,643	7,801,173	
Of which:						
RSFSR	699,763	113,880	20,138,422	12,256,944	7,881,498	478,077
Urban	220,394	125,111	6,546,731	3,254,876	3,292,855	
Rural	479,356	101,369	13,591,711	9,002,066	4,589,643	
Ukrainian SSR	251,276	30,881	6,615,147	3,880,644	2,734,503	196,775
Urban	83,683	4,564	2,164,239	1,034,102	1,130,337	
Rural	167,593	26,317	4,450,908	2,846,542	1,604,366	
Uzbek SSR	35,160	4,838	1,241,494	877,783	363,711	19,061
Urban	8,937	516	277,326	160,639	116,687	
Rural	26,223	4,322	964,168	717,144	247,024	

(Continued on next page)

TABLE 5 (Continued)

Development of Public Education in Selected Republics: 1914–1940[1]

Region	No. of Teachers	No. of Schools	Total No. of Students	In Grades:		No. of Students in VUZ[2]
				1–4	5–10	
Kazakh SSR	44,597	7,827	1,142,618	672,615	470,003	10,419
Urban	11,363	824	349,034	177,010	172,024	
Rural	33,234	7,003	793,584	495,605	297,979	
Kirghiz SSR	11,484	1,645	326,217	220,262	105,955	3,043
Urban	1,980	119	61,939	34,165	27,774	
Rural	9,504	1,526	264,278	186,097	78,181	
Tadzhik SSR	12,972	2,628	303,115	254,751	48,164	2,343
Urban	1,741	127	45,376	29,151	16,225	
Rural	11,231	2,501	257,739	225,739	32,139	
Turkmen SSR	8,549	1,254	237,677	162,267	75,410	2,990
Urban	2,527	179	68,234	40,473	27,761	
Rural	6,022	1,075	169,443	121,794	47,649	

[1] Calculated from: Tsentral'noe Statisticheskoe Upravlenie pri Soviete Ministrov SSSR, Kul'turnoe stroitel'stvo SSSR, statisticheskii sbornik (Moscow: Gosstatizdat, 1956), pp. 80–115; 122–130; 208–211.

[2] Higher Educational Establishments.

[3] The 1914 data for each Union Republic are calculated by the Soviet Census Bureau.

TABLE 6

Distribution of Students in Higher Educational Institutions According to Nationality
and the Per Cent of Women: 1960, 1966

Nationality	1960–1961[1]		1965–1966[2]
	Total No. of Students	Per Cent of Women	Total No. of Students
Total	2,395,500	43	3,860,700
Russian	1,479,500	46	2,360,000
Ukrainian	393,600	42	558,600
Belorussian	63,700	40	114,600
Uzbek	53,500	25	95,600
Kazakhs	40,700	32	69,900
Georgian	48,400	45	70,100
Azerbaidzhanian	28,400	28	54,000
Latvian	16,400	48	42,800
Moldavian	11,900	45	22,900
Lithuanian	25,800	47	21,400
Kirghiz	9,900	29	16,200
Tadzhik	11,900	16	17,500
Armenian	36,700	40	61,800
Turkmenian	9,400	21	15,600
Estonian	12,900	48	18,800
Abkhazy	1,100	45	1,600
Balkarts	0,700	26	1,000
Buriiat	4,500	42	8,300
Bashkir	6,200	39	11,800
Ingush	0,700	18	1,300
Kabardinian	2,000	34	3,800
Kalmyk	0,900	45	1,800
Karakalpak	1,800	19	3,300
Karelian	0,800	44	1,400
Komi	2,900	51	4,100
Maritsi	2,300	34	4,000
Mordva	4,200	34	9,300
Dagestanian	7,300	26	14,800
Osetin	5,500	43	11,000
Tatar	4,000	44	67,700
Udmurti	3,200	46	5,700
Chechintsi	1,400	14	3,500
Chuvashi	8,100	34	16,200
Jakuty	2,800	38	4,700
Jews	77,100	41	91,600
Others	28,000	39	5,900

[1]Tsentral'noe Statisticheskoe Upravlenie pri Sovete Ministrov SSSR, *Vysshoe obrazovanie v SSSR*, Statisticheskii Sbornik (Moscow: Gosstatizdat, 1961), p. 85.
[2]Tsentral'noe Statisticheskoe Upravlenie pri Sovete Ministrov SSSR, *Narodnoe khoziaistvo SSSR v 1965 godu* (Moscow: Gosstatizdat, 1967), p. 701.

TABLE 7

Distribution of Students in Soviet Higher Educational Establishments by Republics;
1915, 1934, 1966 (In Thousands)

Republic	1914/15[1]	1933/34[1]	1965/66[2]
USSR–Total	127,4	458,3	3860,5
Russian SFSR	86,4	303,1	2353,9
Ukrainian SSR	35,2	97,5	690,0
Belorussian SSR	...	10,9	104,0
Uzbek SSR	...	10,8	165,8
Kazakh SSR	...	3,6	144,7
Georgian SSR	0,3	16,5	76,6
Azerbaidzhan SSR	...	9,5	67,0
Lithuanian SSR	...	...	46,4
Moldavian SSR	...	0,4	46,4
Latvian SSR	2,0	...	33,1
Kirghiz SSR	...	0,4	32,2
Tadzhik SSR	...	0,6	30,4
Armenian SSR	...	3,2	38,9
Turkmenian SSR	...	1,2	19,8
Estonian SSR	3,3	...	21,4

[1]Tsentral'noe Statisticheskoe Upravlenie pri Sovete Ministrov SSSR, *Kul'turnoe stroitel'stvo SSSR v 1956 g.* (Moscow: Gosstatizdat, 1956), pp. 208–211.

[2]Tsentral'noe Statisticheskoe Upravlenie pri Sovete Ministrov SSSR, *Narodnoe khoziaistvo SSSR v 1965 g.* (Moscow: Gosstatizdat, 1967), p. 691.

Note that there were 756 higher educational institutions in the Soviet Union in 1965/66 as compared to 105 in 1914.

BIBLIOGRAPHY

Books. Russia-USSR

Official Government Reports, Decrees, Party Resolutions and Reports of
Original Investigations by pre-Revolutionary or Soviet Authors. Sources
are in Russian, Ukrainian, Belorussian, Polish, German, French, English,
Uzbek and Arabic.

Akademiia Nauk SSSR (Academy of Sciences of the USSR). *Istoriia sovetskoi
konstitutsii v dekretakh i postanov-leniiakh sovetskogo pravitel'stva,* 1917–
1936 (History of Soviet Constitution in Decrees and Decisions of the Soviet
Government, 1917–1936). Moscow: Izdatel'stvo Ogiz, 1936.

——. *Materialy nauchnoi sesii posviashchennoi istorii Srednei Azii i Kazakhstana
v dooktiabrskii period* (Data of the Scientific Council Dedicated to the
History of Central Asia and Kazakhstan Before the October Period).
Tashkent: 1955.

——. *Materialy vsesoiuznoi shkol'noi perepisi* (Data on All-Union Educational
Census). Samarkand: 1930.

——. *Nauchnye kadry v SSSR* (Scientific Cadres in the USSR). Moscow:
Izdatel'stvo AN SSSR, 1959.

——. Konstantinov, F. V. (ed.). *Osnovy marksiskoi filosofii* (Foundations of
Marxist Philosophy). Moscow: Gospolitizdat, 1959.

——. *Trudy etnografii. Novaia seriia,* XXI. (Ethnographic Works. New Serias,
XXI). Moscow: 1954.

——. *Pavlovskie sredy* (Pavlovian Environment). Moscow: Izdat. AN
SSSR, 1949.

————. TsK KP, *O programe KPSS* (Central Committee of the Communist Party of the Soviet Union: Programs of the Communist Party of the USSR). Moscow: Izdatel'stvo VPS i AON, 1961.

Akademiia Pedagogicheskikh Nauk RSFSR (Academy of Pedagogical Sciences of the Russian SFSR). Boldyrev, N. I. (ed.). *Direktivy VKP (b) i postanovleniia sovetskogo pravitel'stva o narodonom obrazovanii za 1917–1947* g. (Directives of the Communist Party (b) and Decisions of the Soviet Government Concerning Public Education). Moscow-Leningrad: 1947.

————. *Kommunisticheskoe vospitane v sovetskoi shkole. Sbornik statei* (Communist Education in the Soviet School. Collection of Articles). Moscow: Izdat. APN RSFSR, 1950, four vols.

————. *Natsional'nye shkoly RSFSR* (Schools of Russian Minorities in the Russian RSFSR). Moscow: Izdatel'stvo APN, 1962.

————. Boldyrev, N. I. (ed.). Prilozhenie k zhurnalu Sovetskaia Pedagogika za 1952 g. *Sbornik rukovodiashchikh materialov o shkole* (Collection of Decrees on Education). Moscow: APN RSFSR, 1952.

————. *Konstantin Ushinskii. Izbrannye sochineniia* (Konstantin Ushinskii. Selective Works). Moscow: Gosizdat, 1947.

Akademiia Nauk Ukrainskoi SSR (Academy of Sciences of the Ukrainian SSR). *Istoriia Kieva* (History of Kiev). Kiev: Vidavnitstvo AN UkSSR, 1960.

Akademiia Nauk Uzbekskoi SSR (Academy of Sciences of the Uzbek SSR). *Istoriia sovetskog gosudarstva i prava v Uzbekistane, 1917–1924* (A History of the Soviet State and Law in Uzbekistan, 1917–1924). Tashkent: AN UzSSR, 1960.

Aleksandrov, F. F. *Dialekticheskii materialism* (Dialectical Materialism). Moscow: AN SSSR, Institut Filosofii, 1954.

Alekseev, S. P. i Kortsov, V. G. *Istoriia SSSR. Navchal'na knyha dlia 4-ho kliasa* (History of the USSR. Textbook for the Fourth Grade). Kiev: Vidavnitstvo "Radianska Shkola," 1963.

Bakaev, N. K. "Tatarskaia shkola za sorok let sovetskoi vlasti," in *Natsional'nye shkoly RSFSR* (The Tatar School during the Forty Years of Soviet Regime, in The School for the Minorities of the Russian SFSR). Moscow: APN, 1961.

Bartold, V. V. *Istoriia kul'turnoi zhizni Turkestana* (History of the Turkestanian Culture). Leningrad: 1927.

————. *Sochineniia* (Collective Works). Vol. i, 6th ed. Moscow: Izdatel'stvo A. Mamontova, 1888.

Bendrikov, K. I. *Ocherki po istroii narodnogo obrazovaniia v Turkestane, 1865–1924* (A Short History of Turkestanian Public Education, 1865–1924). Moscow: APN RSFSR, 1960.

Bilodid, K. I. *Kurs istorii ukrainskoi movy* (History of the Ukrainian Language). Kiev: AN UkSSR, 1959.

Bol'shaia Sovetskaia Entsiklopediia (Large Soviet Encyclopedia), 2nd ed. Moscow: Izdatel'stvo Bol'shoi Sovetskoi Entsiklopedii, 1954.

Chrniavskii, E. *Prazdnyk vyborov* (The Celebration of Elections) Tashkent: Gosizdat UzSSR, 1927.

Deineko, M. M. *Sorok let narodnogo obrazovaniia v SSSR* (Forty Years of Public Education in the USSR). Moscow: Izdatel'stvo Ministerstva Prosvishcheniia RSFSR, 1957.

————. *Spravochnik directora shkoly* (The Handbook for the Director of a School), 2nd ed. Moscow: APN RSFSR, 1955.

Direktivy KPSS i sovetskogo pravitel'stva po khiziaistvennym voprosam. Sbornik dokumentov, 1917–1957 (Directives of the Communist Party of the Soviet

Union and Soviet Government on the National Economy: Compilation of Documents, 1917–1957). Moscow: Gospolitizdat, four vols., 1957.

Dobroliubov, D. I. *Polnoe sobranie sochinenii* (Complete Collected Works). St. Petersburg: 1894.

Eliutin, V. P. *Vysshaia shkola strany sotsializma* (Higher Education of the Country of Socialism). Moscow: Izdatel'stvo sotsial'no-ekonomicheskoi literatury, 1959.

Fal'bork, G. A., i Chrnoluzskii, V. *Vseobshchoe obrazovanie v Rossii* (General Education in Russia). St. Petersburg: Imperatorskoe Izdatel'stvo, 1895.

Galkin, K. T. *Vysshoe obrazovanie i podgotovka narodnykh kadrov v SSSR* (Higher Education and the Training of National Cadres in the USSR). Moscow: Izdatel'stvo "Sovetskaia Nauka," 1958.

Georadze, W. *Razvitie natsional'nogo voprosa* (Development of the Nationality Questions). Moscow: Gospolitizdat, 1952.

Gerasimov, T. A. *Kabinet istorii v shkole* (The Chair of History in School). Moscow: Uchpedgiz, 1959.

Gidulianov, P. V. *Otdelenie tserkvi ot gosudarstva v SSSR:* polnyi sbornik dekretov vedomostnykh rasporiadzhenii i opredilenii Verkhsuda RSFSR i drugikh sovetskikh sotsialisticheskikh respublik; UkSSSR, BSSR, ZSFSR, UzSSR i Turkmenskoi (Separation of Church and State in the USSR: A Complete Collection of Decrees, Departmental Orders and Decisions of the Supreme Court of the Russian SFR, and Other Soviet Socialist Republics; Ukraine, Belorussia, Uzbek, Turkmen and Transcaucasian SFSR), 3rd ed. Moscow: Iuridizdat RSFSR, 1926.

Girchak, E. *Na dva fronta v borbe s natsionalizmom* (The Struggle with Nationalism in the Two Fronts). Moscow: Gosizdat, 1930.

Goncharenko, M. V. *Mistetstvo i estetichne vikhovannia* (The Arts and Aesthetic Education). Kiev: AN UkSSR, 1963.

Gosudarstvennoe Iuridicheskoe Izdatel'stvo (Department of Justice Press). *Istoriia sovetskoi konstitutsii v dokumentakh* (History of the Soviet Constitution in Documents). Moscow: Gosiuridizdat, 1957.

————. *Sobranie postanovlenii i rasporiadzhenii pravitel'stva SSSR* (Collection of Decrees and Orders of the Soviet Government) Moscow: Gosiuridizdat, 1944.

Gosudarstvennoe Izdatel'stvo Nauchno-tekhnicheskoi i sotsial'noekonomicheskoi literatury (The State Publishing House of the Scientific-technological and Socio-economic Literature). *Nauka v SSSR za 15 let* (Education in the USSR During the 15 Years). Tashkent: 1939.

Gosudarstvennoe Izdatel'stvo Politicheskoi Literatury (State Publishing House of the Political Literature). 21-oi chrezvichainyi kongres KPSS. *Stenografi-cheskii otchet,* vol. i (The Twenty-First Extraordinary Session of the Communist Party of the Soviet Union.) Stenographic Report. Moscow: Gospolitizdat, 1959.

————. *Razvitie vysshego obrazovaniia v SSSR* (Development of Higher Education in the USSR). Moscow: Gospolitizdat, 1961.

Gosplanizdat, *Socialist Construction. Statistical Yearbook.* Moscow: Gosuchplanizdat, 1936.

Gosudarstvennyi Biudzhet SSSR v 1966 g. Statisticheskii sbornik. (The National Budget of the USSR in 1966. Statistical Handbook). Moscow: Izdatel'stvo "Finansi," 1966.

Gosudarstvennaia Planovaia Komisiia UzSSR: Ekonomiko-statisticheskii sector (The State Planning Commission of the UzSSR: Economic-statistical Section). *Raiony UzSSR v tsifrakh* (Districts of the UzSSR in Figures). Samarkand: 1930.

Herzen, A. I. *Sobranie sochinenii* (Collective Works), vol. VII. Moscow: AN SSSR, 1955.

Imperatorskoe Vol'noe Ekonomicheskoe Obshchestvo (The Imperial Free Economic Society). *Nachal'noe obrazovanie v Rossii* (The Elementary Education in Russia). St. Petersburg: Tipografiia Fol'barka, 1900, vol. 3.

Institut Marksa, Engel'sa, Lenina i Stalina. *Kommunisticheskaia Partiia Sovetskogo Soiuza v rezoliutsiakh i resheniiakh s'iezdov, konferentsii i plenumov TsK, 1898–1953* (The Communist Party of the Soviet Union in Resolutions, Decisions of Congresses, Conferences and Meetings of the Central Committee, 1898–1953). Two vols. Moscow: Gospolitizdat, 1953.

————. *15-yi s'iezd KPSS* (Fifteenth Congress of the Communist Party of the Soviet Union. Stenographic Report). Moscow: Gospolitizdat, 1960.

————. *11-yi s'iezd KPSS. Stenograficheskii otchet* (Eleventh Congress of the Communist Party of the Soviet Union. Stenographic Report). Moscow: Gospolitizdat, 1922.

Institut Gosudarstva i Prava (Institute of the Government and the Justice). *S'iezdy sovetov v dokumantakh* (Congresses of the Soviets in Documents). Moscow: Gosiuridizdat, 1962.

Kaftanov, S. *Vysshoe obrazovanie v SSSR* (Higher Education in the USSR). Moscow: APN RSFSR, 1955.

Karakhanov, Murtaza. *Kul'tura sovetskogo Uzbekistana* (The Culture of the Soviet Uzbekistan). Tashkent: Gosplanizdat, 1957.

Kasimenko, O. K. *Istoriia Ukrainy* (History of Ukraine). Kiev: AN UkSSR, 1955.

Karpov, G. G., and Others. *Razvitie sotsialisticheskoi kul'tury v soiuznykh respublikakh* (Development of the Socialist Culture in Union Republics). Moscow: Gospolitizdat, 1962.

Kedrov, B. M. (ed.). *Dialektika: teoriia poznaniia* (Dialectics: The Theory of Knowledge). Moscow: Izdatel'stvo "Nauka," 1964.

Khvilia, A. *Znyshchity korinnia ukrainskoho natsionalizmu na movnomu fronti* (The Ukrainian Nationalism Must Be Destroyed in the Linguistic Front). Kharkiv: OVOU, 1933.

Kovalev, A. G. *Psikhologiia lichnosti* (Psychology of Personality). Moscow: Izdatel'stvo "Prosveshchenie," 1965.

KPSS o Komsomole i molodezhi (The Communist Party of the Soviet Union Concerning the Communist Youth Organization and Youth). Moscow: Izdatel'stvo "Molodaia Gvardiia," 1958.

Konstantinov, N. A., Medynskii, E. N. *Istoriia pedagogiki* (History of Pedagogy). Moscow: APN SSSR, 1959.

————. *Sistema narodnogo obrazovaniia* (The System of Public Education). Moscow: Izdat. Moskovskogo Universiteta, 1956.

Kornilov, A. A. *Obshchestvennoe dvizhenie pri imperatore Aleksandre* (Social Movement During the Reign of the Emperor Alexander II). Paris: 1905.

Korolev, F. F. *Novaia sistema narodnogo obrazovaniia v SSSR* (The New System of Education in the USSR). Moscow: APN RSFSR, 1960.

————. and Others. *Ocherki po istorii sovetskoi shkoly i pedagogiki* (A Short History of Soviet Schools and Pedagogy). Moscow: APN RSFSR, 1961.

————. and Others. *Sovetskaia shkola v period sotsialisticheskoi industrializatsii* (The Soviet School During the Period of Industrialization). Moscow: Gospedizdat, 1959.

Kosminskii, E. A. *Istoriia srednikh vekov. Uchebnik dlia 6-7 ikh klasov srednei shkoly* (History of Middle Ages: A Textbook for the Sixth and Seventh Grades of Secondary Schools). Moscow: Ministerstvo Prosveshcheniia RSFSR, 1951.

Kostenko, Lev. F. *Turkestanskii krai*. Opyt voenno-statisticheskogo obozreniia turkestanskogo voennogo okruga. Materialy dlia geografii i statistiki Rossii, tom i. (The Country of Turkestan). St. Petersburg: Tipografiia Transbeliia, 1880.

Krasnogorskii, N. I. *Trudy po izucheniiu vysshei nervovoi deiatel'nosti cheloveka i zhivotnykh* (Works Concerning Activities of the Higher Nerve System of the Man and Animals), vol. 1. Moscow: Izdatel'stvo Medgiz, 1954.

Krupskaia, N. K. *Bibliograficheskii ukazatel* (Bibliographical Index. Works of Krupskaia). Moscow: APN RSFSR, 1959.

_____. *O kommunisticheskom vospitanii* (Krupskaia's Views Concerning the Communist Education). Moscow: Izdat. "Moldaia Gvardiia," 1956.

Kshibekov, D. *O feudal'no baiskikh perezhitkakh i ikh preodelenii* (Overcoming the Difficulties of the Feudal-bay Prejudices) Alma-Ata: AN Kazakh SSR, 1957.

Kuchkin, A. P. *SSSR v period vostanovleniia narodnogo khozaistva, 1921-1925* (The USSR During the Period of the Establishment of the National Economy, 1921–1925). Moscow: AN SSSR, Institute of History, 1955.

Khul'kov, I. *Lenin o druzhbe s narodami vostoka* (Lenin Concerning the Friendship with the Peoples of the East). Moscow: Gospolitizdat, 1961.

Kuzmin, O. P. *Iz istorii revoliutsionnoi mysli Rossii* (A history of the Russian Revolutionary Thought). Moscow: AN RSFSR, 1961.

Lenin, V. I. *Izbrannye proizvedeniia v 2-okh tomakh* (Selective Works in Two Volumes). Moscow: Gospolitizdat, 1929.

_____. *Izbrannye stati po natsional'nomu voprosu* (Selective Works Concerning the Nationality Question). Moscow: Gospolitizdat, 1929.

_____. *Nekotorye voprosy stroitel'stva partii* (Some Questions Concerning the Party Structure). Moscow: AON i VPSL, 1961.

_____. *Sochineniia,* vol. XX (Collective Works, vol. XX). Moscow: Gosizdat, 1927.

Lenin, V. I. *Sochineniia* (Collective Works. Translated by J. Kunits). New York: International Publishers, 1929.

_____. *Sochineniia v 35 tomakh* (Collective Works in 35 Volumes). Moscow: Gospolitizdat, 1952.

_____. *The Paris Commune,* vol. V. New York: International Publishers, 1934.

_____. *The April Conference.* New York: International Publishers, 1934.

Leontev, A. N. *Problemi razvitiia psikhiki* (Problems of Psychological Development). Moscow: APN RSFSR, 1959.

Levitov, N. D. *Detskaia i pedagogicheskaia psykhologiia* (The Child and Educational Psychology). Moscow: Izdat. "Prosveshchenie," 1961.

Lunacharskii, A. V. *O narodnom obrazovanii* (Lunacharskii Concerning the Public Education). Moscow: APN RSFSR, 1958.

Makarenko, A. S. *Bibliograficheskii ukazatel'* (Bibliographical Index on Makarenko). Moscow: APN RSFSR, 1959.

_____. *Izbrannye pedagogicheskie proizvedeniia* (Selective Pedagogical Works). Moscow: Uchpedgiz, 1946.

_____. *Kniga dlia roditelei* (The Book for Parents). Moscow: APN RSFSR, 1953.

_____. *O vospitanii molodezhi* (Concerning the Education of Youth). Moscow: Trudrezevizdat, 1951.

_____. *Pedagogicheskaia poema* (The Poem of Education). Moscow: Izdat. "Sovetskii Pisatel," 1940.

_____. *Sochineniia* (Collected Works). 7 vols. Moscow: APN RSFSR, 1952.

Maksimov, A. A. *Ocherki po istorii bor'by za materialism v russkom estestvoznanii* (A Short History of the Struggle for Materialism in Russian Natural Sciences). Moscow: Gospolitizdat, 1947.

Malaia Sovetskaia Entsiklopediia (Small Soviet Encyclopedia). Moscow: Izdat. Bol'shoi Sovetskoi Entsiklopedii, 1931.

Mal'chikov, A. *Pervoe desiatiletie komsomola* (The First Ten Years of the Komsomol-Communist Youth Organization). Moscow: Izdat. "Molodaia Gvardiia," 1958.

Malov, I. *Pamiatniki drevne-turkskoi pismennosti* (The Relics of the Ancient-Turkish Writing). Moscow: Gosizdat, 1951.

————. *Eniseiskaia pismennost'* Turkov (The Writings of the Enisei Turks). Moscow: Gosizdat, 1952.

Marx, Karl. *Das Kapital*. Moscow: Gospolitizdat, 1949.

————. *Sochineniia* (Collected Works). Moscow: IMEL, 1936.

Medynskii, E. N. *Bratskie shkoly Ukrainy i Belorussii* (Brotherhood School of Ukraine and Belorussia). Moscow: AN RSFSR, 1954.

————. *Narodnoe Obrazovanie v SSSR* (Public Education in the USSR). Moscow: APN RSFSR, 1952.

Ministerstvo Vysshego i Srednego Obrazovaniia (Ministry of Higher and Secondary Education of the USSR). *Uchenbye plany srednykh shkol* (Study Plans for Secondary Schools). Moscow: MVO, 1966.

————. *Uchebnye plany pedagogicheskikh institutov* (Study Plans of Pedagogical Institutes). Moscow: MVO, 1959.

————. *Shkol'nye programy na 1965 god* (Study Plans for 1965). Moscow: MVO, 1965.

Ministerstvo Finansov SSSR (Ministry of Finance of the USSR). *Gosudarstvennyi budzhet SSSR* (The State Budget of the USSR). Moscow: Izdat. "Finansy," 1966.

Nalivkin, V. P. *Chto daet sredno-aziatskaia musul'manskaia srednaia shkola v obrazovatel'nom i vospitatel'nom otnoshenii* (What Does The Central Asian Muslim School Give in Cultural and Educational Aspects?). St. Petersburg: Turkestanskii Literaturnyi Sbornik v Pol'zu Prokazhenykh, 1900.

————. *Histoire du Khanat de Khokand*, trad. du Russe por A. Dozon. Paris: Ledorix, 1889.

————. *Ocherki byta tuzemnogo zhenskogo naseleniia Fergany* (A History of the Social Condition of Women in the Fergana District). Kazan: 1886.

Narodnyi Komissariat Prosvescheniia (People's Commissariat of Education). *Uzbek SSR. Narodnoe prosveshchenie za 15 let* (Public Education in the Uzbek SSR During the Fifteen Years, 1924–1939). Tashkent: Izdat. Narkomprosa, 1939.

————. *Programa dla shkol pervoi stupeni* (Programs for Schools for the First Level). Samarkand: Gosizdat, 1926. In Uzbek Language.

Nepomnin, V. I. *Ocherki istorii sotsialisticheskogo stroitel'stva v Uzbekistane* (A Short History of the Socialist Construction in Uzbekistan). Tashkent: AN UzSSR, 1957.

Nikitin, N. P. (ed.). *Ekonomicheskaia geografiia SSSR* (The Economic History of the USSR). Moscow: Izdat. "Prosveshchenie," 1966.

Nikoforova, R. P. *Obuchenie konstruktsionnoi igry detei* (Teaching the Children the Constructive Work and Play) Moscow: APN RSFSR, 1958.

Niiazov Kary, T. N. *Ocherki kul'tury sovetskogo Uzbekistana* (A History of the Uzbek Culture). Moscow: AN SSSR, 1955.

Ogorodnikov, I. T. *Pedagogika* (Pedagogy). Moscow: APN RSFSR, 1954.

————. *Buletin raboty v zhenskikh klubakh Uzbekistana* (Schedule of Works in Women's Club of Uzbekistan). Samarkand: 1927. In Arabic Script.

Oshanin, L. V. *Antropologicheskii sostav naseleniia Srednei Azii* (Anthropological Composition of the Peoples of Central Asia). Erevan: Izdat. Erevanskogo Universiteta, 1957.

Ostroumov, N. P. *Etimologiia sartovskogo iazyka* (Etimology of the Sart Language). Tashkent: Tipografiia General-gubernatora, 1910.

————. *Etnograficheskie materialy*. *Obshchei ocherk* (Ethnographic Materials. General Description. Sarts). Tashkent: Izdat. Sredne-aziatskaia Zhizn', 1908.

Ostroumov, L. N. *Skazki Sartov* (Sart Fairy-tales). Tashkent: Tipografiia Okruzhnogo shtaba, 1906.

Pankratova, A. M. *Istoriia SSSR* (History of the USSR), 10th ed. vol. 3. Moscow: AN SSSR, 1955.

Pavlov, I. P. *Polnoe sobranie sochinenii* (Complete Collective Works), vol. 3, 2nd ed. Moscow: AN SSSR, 1951.

Pereselencheskoe upravlenie glavnogo upravleniia zemleustroistva i zemledeliia. *Aziatskaia Rossia: Liudi i poriadki za Uralom* (Asiatic Russia: People and Systems Beyond the Ural). Three vols. St. Petersburg: Pereselencheskoe Upravlenie, 1914.

Persits, M. M. *Otdelenie tserkvi ot gosudarstva i shkoly ot tserkvi v SSSR* (Separation of Church and State and the School from Church in the USSR). Moscow: AN SSSR, 1958.

Pervaia obshchaia perepis' naseleniia rossiiskoi imperii. Troinitskii, N. A. (ed.). Obshchei svod po imperii resultatov razrabotki dannykh pervoi vseobshchei perepisi naseleniia, 28-go ianvaria, 1897 goda (Results of the First Russian Census, January 28, 1897). St. Petersburg: Typografiia Nyrkina, 1905.

Pisarchik, A. K. "Stroitel'nye materialy i konstruktyvnye priemy narodhykh masterov ferganskoi doliny v 19-om in nachale 20-ikh v." in Tolstov, S. P. (ed.), *Sredno-aziatskii etnograficheskii sbornik* (Collection of Central Asian Ethnographic Materials). Trudy instituta etnografii imeni M. Miklaia, novaia seriia, XXI. Moscow: AN SSSR, 1954.

Pokrovskii, M. N. *Istoriia Rossii* (A History of Russia). Moscow: AN SSSR, 1932.

Ponomarev, B. N. (ed.). *Istoriia KPSS* (History of the Communist Party of the USSR). Moscow: Gospolitizdat, 1959.

Priduvalov, F. M. *Otnoshenie sovetskogo gosudarstva k religii* (Position of the Soviet Government Toward Religion). Moscow Izdatel'stvo "Znanie," 1952.

Radykov, U. P. *Sotsialisticheskaia zakonnost' v sovetskom ugol'nom protsese* (The Socialist Jurisdiction in the Soviet Criminal Law). Moscow: Gosiuridizdat, 1959.

Radzhabov, Z. *Iz istorii obshchestvennoi politicheskoi mysli tadzhikskogo naroda v 2-oi polovine 19-go i v nachale 20-go v.* (A History of the Tadzhik Social and Political Thought in the First Half of the 19th Century and the Second Half of the 20th Century). Stalingrad: AN TSSR, 1957.

Rakhimi, Sh. *Bukvar dlia detei* (ABC Book for Children). Samarkand: Gosizdat, 1926. In Arabic Script.

Razumnyi, V. *Eticheskoe i esteticheskoe poniatie v iskustve* (Ethical and Aesthetical Appreciation of Arts). Moscow: Gosizdat, 1959.

Samarin, Iu. F. *Sochineniia* (Collected Works). Vol. VII. Moscow: 1897.

Santin, J. *Vsesoiuzna perepis' naseleniia 1937 g.* (All-Union Census, 1937). Moscow: Gosstatizdat, 1938.

Sarkysyanz, E. *Geschichte der Orientalischen Völker* (History of the Oriental Peoples). Munich: R. Oldenbourg Verlag, 1961.

Sbornik zakonov i razporiadzhenii raboche-kretianskogo pravitel'stva v SSSR (Collection of Laws and Decrees of the Workers and Peasants Government of the USSR). Moscow: SNK SSSR, 1929.

Sechenev, I. M. *Izbrannye filosoficheskie i psikhologicheskie proizvedeniia* (Collection of Philosophical and Psychological Works). Moscow: APN RSFSR, 1947.

Sharafudinova, R. *Shkol'noe obrazovanie v UzSSR* (Education in the Uzbek SSR). Tashkent: AN UzSSR, 1961.

Shchipanov, I. Ia. (ed.). *Iz istorii russkoi filosofii. Sbornik statei* (From the History of Russian Philosophy. Collection of Articles). Moscow: AN SSSR, Institut Filosofii, 1951.

————. *Russkie prosvititeli ot Radishcheva do dekabristov* (Russian Educators from Radishchev to Decembrists). Moscow: Izdatel'stvo "Mysl", 1966.

Shkolnoe Upravlenie UzSSR. *Spravochnik instruktsii v avguste 1939 g.* (Study Plan and Instructions, August, 1939). Tashkent: Narkompros UzSSR, 1939.

Skrypnyk, M. *Stati i promovy*, tom II. (Articles and Speeches, vol. II). Kharkiv: Vydavnytstvo DVOU, 1931.

Smirnov, V. Z. *Khrestomatiia po istorii pedagogiki* (Readings in the History of Pedagogy). Moscow: Gospedizdat, 1961.

Smirnov, N. Z. *Ocherki istorii izuchennia Izlama v SSSR* (A Short History of Islamic Studies in the USSR). Moscow: AN SSSR, 1954.

Sobranie zakonov i rasporiadzhenii raboche-krestianskogo pravitel'stva SSSR (Collection of Laws and Decrees of the Workers and Peasants Government of the USSR). Moscow: Izdat. SNK, 31-go dekabria, 1929, No. 76, otdel pervoi.

Soviet Union Yearbook. 1927–1929. London: G. Allen & Unwin, 1929.

Sovetkaia Bibliografiia (Soviet Bibliography). Moscow: Ministerstvo Kul'tury SSSR: Vsesoiuznaia Knizhnaia Palata, 1960. (Ministry of Culture of the USSR).

Sovetskoe Stroitel'stvo (Soviet Construction). Zhurnal Tsentralnogo Izpolnitel'nogo Komiteta SSSR (Journal of the Central Executive Committee of the USSR). Moscow: 1926–1932.

Spravochnik direktora shkoly (School Director's Handbook). Sbornik postanovlenii, prikazov, instruktsii i dr. rukovodiashchikh materialov o shkole. 2nd ed. Ministerstvo Prosveshcheniia RSFSR, 1950.

Stalin, J. V. *Marksizm i voprosy iazykoznaniia* (Marxism and Linguistic Questions). Moscow: Gosizdat, 1950.

————. *Marksizm i natsional'no-kolonial'nyi vopros* (Marxism and the National-Colonial Questions). Moscow: Partizdat, TsKKP 1935.

————. *Sochineniia* (Collective Works). Moscow: Izdatel'stvo Ogiz, 1947.

————. *Voprosy Leninizma* (Problems of Leninism). Moscow: Izdat. Ogiz, 1947.

Talkin, K. T. *Vysshoe obrazovanie i podgotovka narodnykh kadrov v SSSR* (Higher Education and Training of National Cadres in the USSR). Moscow: Izdat. Sovetskaia Nauka, 1958.

Timasheff, N. S. *Religion in the Soviet Union* (New York: Sheed and Ward Press, 1942.

Tokarev, Sergii, A. *Etnografiia narodov SSSR* (Ethnography of the Peoples of the USSR). Moscow: Moskovskii Universiter, 1958.

Tolstov, S. P. *Narody Srednei Azii i Kazakhstana* (Peoples of Central Asia and Kazakhstan). Moscow: AN SSSR, 1962.

Tsentral'noe Statisticheskoe Upravlenie pri Sovete Ministrov SSSR (Central Statistical Administration of the Council of Ministers of the USSR). *Dostizhenie sovetskoi vlasti za 40 let v tsifrakh* (Accomplishment of the

Soviet Government During the Forty Years, in Numbers). Moscow: Gosstatizdat, 1957.

_____*Itogi vsesoiuznoi perepisi naseleniia 1959* g. (Totals of the All-Union Census, 1959). Moscow: Gosstatizdat, 1962.

_____. *Kul'turnoe stroitel'stvo SSSR.* Statisticheskii zbornik. (Cultural Construction of the USSR. Statistical Handbook). Moscow: Gosstatizdat, 1956.

_____. *Narodnoe Khozaistvo SSSR, Statisticheskii ezhegodnik* (National Economy of the USSR. Statistical Yearbook, 1950–1966). Moscow: Gosstatizdat, 1950–1966.

_____. *SSSR v 1961* g. (The Soviet Union in 1961). Moscow: Gosstatizdat, 1962.

_____. *Sotsialisticheskoe stroitel'stvo SSSR* (Socialist Construction of the USSR). Moscow: Tsentral'noe Upravlenie Narodnogo Khoziaistva Ucheta Gosplana SSSR, 1935.

_____. *SSSR v tsifrakh v 1960* g. (The USSR in Figures in 1960). Moscow: Gosstatizdat, 1961.

_____. *Vsesoiuznaia perepis' naseleniia 1926* g. (All-Union Census, 1926). Moscow: Gosstatizdat, 1931, otdel 2-oi, vol. 32.

_____. *Vysshoe obrazovanie SSSR v 1960* g. (Higher Education of the USSR in 1960). Moscow: Gosstatizdat, 1961.

Trotsky, Leon. *The Class Nature of Soviet State* (Ceylon: Lanks Samasamaia, 1952.

_____. *The Real Situation in Russia.* New York: Harcourt Brace, 1928.

Turzunov, Kh. *Obrazovanie v sovetskom Uzbekistane* (Education in Soviet Uzbekistan). Tashkent: AN UzSSR, 1957.

Ushinskii, K. D. *Sobranie pedagogicheskikh sochinenii* (Collection of Pedagogical Works). St. Petersburg: 1875.

_____. *Sochineniia* (Collective Works). Moscow: APN RSFSR, 1948.

_____. *Sobranie sochinenii* (Selective Works). Vol. 8. Moscow: APN RSFSR, 1950.

Urazov, S. Z. *Turkestanskaia SSSR i ee gosudarstvenno pravnye osobennosti* (The Turkestanian SSSR and its Legal Position) Tashkent: AN UzSSR, 1958.

Urlanis, B. Ts. *Naselenie mira* (Population of the World). Moscow: Gosstatizdat, 1965.

Ustav Akademii Pedagogicheskikh Nauk, 1944 (The By Laws of the Academy of Pedagogical Sciences, 1944). Moscow: APN RSFSR, 1944.

Uzbekistan za sorok let sovetskoi vlasti (Uzbekistan During the Forty Years of the Soviet Regime). Tashkent: Gosstatizdat, 1958.

Uzbekskaia SSR. Statisticheskoe upravlenie. *Materialy vsesoiuznoi shkol'noi perepisi za 1927* g. (The All-Union Educational Census, 1927). Tashkent: 1930.

Vinogradov, V. V. *Velikii russkii iazyk* (The Great Russian Language) Moscow: Izdat. Ogiz, 1945.

Vyrnyk, D. F. *Ukrainskaia SSR.* Kratkii istorichesko-ekonomicheskii ocherk (The Ukrainian SSR. A Short Historico-economic Survey). Moscow: Gospolitizdat, 1954.

Vitkovich, Victor. *Puteshestvie po sovetskom Uzbekistane* (A Tour of Soviet Uzbekistan). Moscow: Foreign Languages Publishing House, 1954.

Voprosy ideologicheskoi raboty. Sbornik vazhneishikh reshenii KPSS: 1954–1961 (*Questions of Ideological Work.* Collections of the Most Important Decisions of the Communist Party of the Soviet Union: 1954–1961). Moscow: Gospolitizdat, 1962.

Zhirov, B. E. *Voprosy planirovaniia kul'turnogo stroitel'stva v SSSR* (Problems of the Planned Cultural Construction of the USSR). Moscow: Gospolitizdat, 1958.

478   Communist Education

Zhitov, K. I. *Sorok let sovetskoi vlasti v Uzbekistane* (Forty Years of Soviet Administration in Uzbekistan). Tashkent: AN UzSSR, 1957.
Zhukovskii, R. I. *Vospitsnie rebenka* (Education of the Child) Moscow: APN RSFSR, 1963.

U.S.S.R.: Books. Other Books by Soviet and Non-Soviet Authors.

Agabekov, George. *OGPU-The Russian Secret Terror.* Translated by Henry W. Bunn. New York: Brentano's Press, 1931.
Avtorkhanov, A. *Tekhnologiia revoliutsii* (The Technology of the Revolution). Munich: Institute for the Study of the USSR, 1954.
Berghoorn, Fredrick. *The Soviet Cultural Offensive:* The Role of Cultural Diplomacy in Soviet Foreign Policy. Princeton: Princeton University Press, 1960.
Bartold, V. V. *Muslim Culture.* Translated from Russian by S. Suhrwordy. Calcutta: University of Calcutta Press, 1934.
————. *Turkestan Down to the Mongol Invasion.* London: Oxford University Press, 1928.
Bates, E. S. *Soviet Asia—Progress and Problems.* London: Jonathan Cape, 1942.
Bauer, R.; and Others. *How the Soviet System Works.* Cultural, Psychological and Social Themes. Cambridge: Harvard University Press, 1956.
Benningsen, Alexander. *Les Mouvements Nationaux ches les Musulmans de Russe, le "Sultangalievisme" au Tatarstan.* Paris: Mouton-La Haye, 1960.
————. *The Revolution of the Muslim Nationalities of the USSR and Their Linguistic Problems.* Oxford: Soviet Affairs Study Group, 1961.
Bereday, George Z.; and Others. *The Politics of Soviet Education.* New York: F. Praeger, 1960.
————. *The Changing Soviet Schools.* Boston: Houghton-Mifflin Press, 1960.
Berdyeev, N. *The Russian Idea.* New York: The Macmillan Co., 1948.
————. *Slavery and Freedom.* Translated from the Russian by R. French. New York: Charles Scribner's Press, 1944.
Branfenbranner, Uril. *Soviet Methods of Character Training.* Ithaca: Cornell University Press, 1963.
Caroe, Olaf. *Soviet Empire: The Turks of Central Asia and Stalinism.* London: The Macmillan Co., 1953.
Counts, George S. *The Challenge of Soviet Education.* New York: McGraw-Hill, 1957.
————. *Khrushchev and Central Committee Speak on Education.* Pittsburgh: The University of Pittsburgh Press, 1959.
Chaplenko, Vasy. *Bil'shovytska movna politika* (The Bolshevik Linguistic Reforms). Munich: Institute for the Study of the USSR, 1956.
Chokai-ogli, Mustafa. *Turkestan pod vlastiu Sovetov* (Turkestan Under the Rule of the Soviets). Paris: Iam Turkestan, 1935.
Churchill, Winston. *The Second World War,* vol. IV. London: 1951.
Coates, William. *Soviets in Central Asia.* New York: Philosophical Library Press, 1951.
Dewey, John. *Impression of Soviet Russia and the Revolutionary World-Mexico-China-Turkey.* New York: New Republic, Inc., 1929.
DeWitt, Nicolas. *Education and Professional Employment in the USSR.* Washington, D. C.: National Science Foundation Press, 1961.
Dubrovskii, V. *Nainoviisha sovetska kontseptsiia istorii Ukrainy* (The Newest Soviet Conception of the History of Ukraine). Munich: Institute for the Study of the USSR, 1956.

Encyclopedia Britannica. Published by the University of Chicago Press, 1948 edition.

Eversmann, Edward. *Reise fon Orenburg nach Bukhara.* (The Voyage from Orenburg to Buchara). Berlin: In Verlage EHG Christiani, 1823.

Fischer, Ralph T. *Pattern for Soviet Youth:* A Study of the Congresses of the Komsomol, 1918–1954. New York: Columbia University Press, 1959.

Fitzsimmons, Thomas. *USSR: Its Society, Its People, Its Culture.* New Haven: Human Relation Area Files, 1960.

Graham, S. *Through Russian Central Asia.* New York: The Macmillan Press, 1916.

Grant, Nigel. *Soviet Education.* London: University of London Press, 1965.

Gunther, John. *Inside Russia Today.* London: H. Hamilton Press, 1958.

Halecki, Oscar. *Borderlands of Western Civilization.* New York: The Ronald Press, 1952.

Hans, Nicholas. *Comparative Education.* London: Routledge Press, 1955.

Hayit, Baymirza. *Turkestan in 20. Jahrhundert* (Turkestan in the Twentieth Century). Darmstadt: C. W. Leske Verlag, 1956.

Hecker, Julius S. *Religion and Communism:* A Study of Religion and Atheism in Soviet Russia. New York: Wiley and Sons, 1934.

Horecky, P. (ed.). *Basic Russian Publications.* Chicago: University of Chicago Press, 1962.

Hrushevsky, M. *A History of Ukraine.* New Haven: Yale University Press, 1941.

————. *Istoriia Ukrainy* (A History of Ukraine). New York: "Knihospilka" Publishers, 1951.

Inkeles, Alex; Bauer, R. *The Soviet Citizen.* Cambridge: Harvard University Press, 1959.

Institute for the Study of the USSR. *Bol'shevizm v revoliutsionnom dvizhenii Belorussii* (Bolshevism in the Revolutionary Movement in Belorussia). Munich: Institute for the Study of the USSR, 1956.

————. *Reports on the Soviet Union in 1956.* Munich: ISU, 1957.

Ionesco, Teofie Archimandrite. *La vie et l'oeuvre de Pierre Mohyla (Movila).* Paris: 1944.

Irkolin, N. *Religioznoe nastroenie sredi sovetskoi molodezhi* (Religious Attitudes Among the Soviet Youth). Munich: Vestnik Instituta po izucheniu istorii i kul'tury SSSR, No. 6, 1954.

Johnson, H. E., *Russia's Educational Heritage.* Pittsburgh: Carnegie Press, 1950.

Juhasz, William. *Blueprint for the Red Generation.* New York: Mid European Studies Center, 1952.

Kautsky, Karl. *Bolshevism at a Deadlock.* New York: Rand Scheed Press, 1931.

Kish, Eugen. *Changing Asia.* New York: Knopf and Co., 1935.

Kohn, H. *Nationalism in the Soviet Union.* London: Routledge, 1933.

Kolarz, Walter. *Islam in the Soviet Union, 1917–1960.* Karachi-Dacca: Pakistan Committee Congress for Cultural Freedom, 1960.

————. *Die Nationalitätenpolitic des Sowjetunion.* Frankfur/M: Europeische Verlagsanstalt, 1956.

————. *Russia and Her Colonies.* London: Philip & Sons, 1952.

Kolasky, John. *Education in Soviet Ukraine.* Toronto: Peter Martin Press, 1968.

Korol, A. *Soviet Education for Science and Technology.* Cambridge: The Technology Press of MIT, 1957.

Krylov, I. *Sistema osvity v Ukraini* (The System of Education in Ukraine, 1917–1937). Munich: Institute for the Study of the USSR, 1956.

Krist, Gustav. *Alone Through Forbidden Land: Russian Central Asia.* Translated by O. Lorimer. London: Faber and Faber Press, 1939.

Krupnitskii, B. *Ukrainska istorichna nauka pid sovetami* (The Ukrainian Historical Science Under the Soviets). Munich: Institute for the Study of the USSR, 1957.

Lansdel, N. Henry. *Russian Central Asia,* two vols. Boston: Houghton-Mifflin & Co., 1885.

Laurat, Lucien. *La Linguistique et l'imperialisme russe.* Paris: 1951.

Leites, N. *A Study of Bolshevism.* Glencoe: The Free Press, 1953.

————. *Ritual of Liquidation.* Glencoe, Illinois: The Free Press Company, 1954.

Lorimer, Frank. *The Population of the Soviet Union: History and Prospects.* Geneva: League of Nations, 1946.

Mager, N. H.; Katel, J. *Conquest Without War.* New York: Trident Press, 1961.

Mehnert, Klaus. *Soviet Man and His World.* New York: F. Praeger Press, 1962.

McCullagh, Francis. *The Bolshevik Persecution of Christianity.* New York: E. P. Dutton and Co., 1924.

Medlin, K. William. *Soviet Education Programs.* Bulletin No. 17. Washington, D. C.: Department of Health, Education and Welfare, 1960.

————. "The Union of Soviet Socialist Republics," in *Comparative Educational Administration,* Reller, T. (ed.). Englewood: Prentice-Hall, 1962.

Mirchuk, Ivan. *Geschichte der Ukrainischen Kultur* (A History of the Ukrainian Culture), vol. 12. Munich: Izar Verlag, 1957.

————. *Ukraine and Its People.* Munich: Ukrainian Free University Press, 1949.

Mirsky, D. S. *A History of Russian Literature From Its Beginning to 1900.* New York: Vantage Books Co., 1958.

Mishalov, Iu. *O podgotovke i usloviiakh raboty prepodavatelei sovetskoi shkoly* (Preparation and Working Conditions of the Soviet Teachers). Munich: Institute for the Study of the USSR, 1955.

Nol'de, B. *Iuris Samarin i ego vremia* (George Samarin and His Epoch). Paris: 1926.

Olzsche, E. Reiner. *Turkestan.* Leipzig: Koehler Verlag, 1942.

Olufsen, O. *The Emir of Bukhara and His Country: Journeys and Studies in Bokhara.* London: W. Heineman, 1911.

Owen, Robert. *The New View of Society and Other Writings.* London: J. M. Dent & Sons, Ltd., 1948.

Park, Alexander. *Bolshevism in Turkestan, 1917–1927.* New York: Columbia University Press, 1957.

Pierce, Richard. *Russian Central Asia, 1867–1917.* A Study of Colonial Rule. Berkeley: University of California Press, 1960.

Pinkevitch, Albert. *The New Education in the Soviet Structure.* Translated by M. Perlimutter, edited by G. Counts. New York: The John Day and Co., 1929.

Pokrovskii, M. N. *Brief History of Russia.* Translated by D. S. Mirsky, vol. I. New York: 1933.

Rauch, George. *A History of Soviet Russia.* New York: F. Praeger, 3rd ed., V 514, 1962.

Russischer Kolonialismus in der Ukraine. Berichte und Dokumente. (Russian Colonialism in the Ukraine. Reports and Documents.) Munich: Ukrainischer Verlag, 1962.

Schapiro, Leonard. *The Communist Party of the Soviet Union.* New York: Random House, 1960.

Schlesinger, Rudolf. *The Family in the USSR.* Documents and Readings. London: Routledge and Kegan, 1949.

————. *The Nationalities Problem and Soviet Administration.* London: Routledge and Kegan, 1956.

Schwarz, Franz V. *Turkestan: das Wiege der Indogermanischen Völker.* Vienna: Herdersche Verlangshaulung, 1900.

Shimoniak, Wasyl. *The Reforms of Peter Mohyla.* Milwaukee: Marquette University Slavic Institute Papers, No. 20, 1965.

————. *A Study of Soviet Policies in Uzbekistan and Their Implications for Social and Educational Change.* Ann Arbor: Ph. D. Dissertation, mimeo, 1963.

Shore, Maurice. *Soviet Education, Its Psychology and Philosophy.* New York: Philosophical Library Press, 1947.

Shumilin, I. M. *Soviet Education.* New York-Munich: Institute for the Study of the USSR, No. 67, 1962.

Smal-Stocki, Roman. *Nationality Problems of the Soviet Union.* Milwaukee: Bruce Publishing Co., 1952.

————. *Ukrainska mova v pid-sovetskii Ukraini* (Ukrainian Language in the Soviet Ukraine). Warsaw: 1936.

Solovei, D. *Natsional'na politika partii i uriadu SSSR v Ukraini v svitli deiakikh nainoviishikh faktiv. Ukraina: Zbirnik, kniha 6* (The Politics of the Communist Party and the Soviet Government Toward the Nationalities of the Soviet Ukraine: In the Light of the Latest Facts). Ukraine: Collections, Book No. 6. Munich: Institute for the Study of the USSR, 1956.

Spector, Ivar. *An Introduction to Russian History and Culture.* New York: D. Van Nostrand Co., 1954.

————. *The Soviet Union and the Muslim World, 1917–1958.* Seattle: University of Washington Press, 1958, mimeo.

Strauss, W. *Ukraine: Die Ukraine und Ihre Mutigen Literature.* Munich: Institute for the Study of the USSR, No. 37, 1966.

Struve, Gleb. *Soviet Russian Literature, 1917–1950.* Berkeley: University of California Press, 1955.

Szczezniak, B. *The Russian Revolution and Religion.* A Collection of Documents Concerning the Suppression of Religion by the Communists, 1917–1925. Notre Dame: University of Notre Dame Press, 1959.

Timasheff, S. *Religion in Soviet Russia, 1917–1942.* New York: Sheed and Ward, 1942.

Tompkins, Stewart. *The Russian Intelligentsia.* Norman: University of Oklahoma Press, 1957.

Ukrainian Congress Committee of America. *Massacre in Vinnitza.* New York: Ukrainian Congress Committee of America Press, 1953.

Valenskii, Iu. *Akademic E. A. Kosminskii i voprosi interpretatsii istorii srednikh vekov v sovetskoi shkole* (Academician E. A. Kosminskii and the Question of Interpretation of the History of Middle Ages in Soviet Schools). Munich: Institute for the Study of the USSR, 1954.

Visitator Apostolicus pro Catholicis in Europa Accidentoli, J. Buchko, Tit. Bishop of Cadi, Apostolic Visitator (ed). *First Victims of Communism.* Rome: Published by OSBM, 1953.

Wetter, A. Gustav. *Dialectical Materialism.* A Historical and Systematic Survey of Philosophy in the Soviet Union. London: Routledge and Kegan Ltd., 1958.

Wheeler, Geofrey. *Racial Problems in Soviet Muslim Asia.* London: Oxford University Press, 1960.

Wolfe, Bertham. *Six Keys to the Soviet System.* Boston: The Beacon Press, 1956.

Women and Communism. Society for Cultural Relations with the USSR. London: 1951.

Woody, Thomas. *New Minds: New Men?* New York: The Macmillan Press, 1932.

The World Federation of Ukrainians. *The Black Deeds of the Kremlin. The Great Famine in Ukraine, 1932–1933.* Detroit: Dobrus Press, 1955.

482   Communist Education

Yakovlev, V. *Kontsentratsionnye lageri SSSR* (Concentration Camps in the USSR). Munich: Institute for the Study of the USSR, 1955.
Zatko, Zanes. *Descent into Darkness.* The Destruction of the Roman Catholic Church in Russia, 1917-1923. Notre Dame: The University of Notre Dame Press, 1965.
Zenkovsky, Sergii. *Pan-Turkism and Islam in Russia.* Cambridge: Harvard University Press, 1960.
Zhitov, E. K. *Sorok let sovetskoi vlasti v Uzbekistane* (Forty Years of the Soviet Regime in Uzbekistan). Tashkent: 1957.

U.S.S.R.: Newspapers, Articles and Periodicals. Soviet and Non-Soviet Journals Dealing with Soviet Affairs.

Alkin, I. "Kolkhoznoe stroitel'stvo v Tadzhiskoi SSR," in *Revoliutsionnyi Vostok* (Collective Construction in the Tadzhik SSR, in the Revolutionary East). No. 1, 1934, pp. 161–178.
Amerika (America): A Catholic Daily for the American Ukrainians (Philadelphia).
Bakalo, Ivan. "Post Graduate Research in the USSR," in *Studies on the Soviet Union,* vol. VI, No. 3, 1966, pp. 84–91.
Benningsen, A. "The Muslim Intelligentsia in the USSR," in *Survey,* No. 28, 1959, pp. 3–11.
Berdimurat, A. "Islam and Communism in Turkestan," in *Soviet Studies,* 1960, pp. 160–168.
Bobrovnikov, N. "Russko tuzemnye uchilishcha i mektaby i medressi v Srednei Azii" (Russian Native Schools and the Mektabs and Medressas in Central Asia), in *Zhurnal Ministerstva Narodnogo Prosveshcheniia,* Novaia Seriia, XLV (Journal of the Ministry of Public Education, New Series, XLV), No. 6, 1913, pp. 189–241.
————. Sophy. "Muslims in Russia," in *The Moslem World.* A Quarterly Review of Christian Missions in Moslem Lands. Edited by Rev. S. Zwemer. London: The Nile Mission Press, vol. 1, 1912, pp. 5–31.
Borokov, A. K. "Ocherki istorii Uzbekskogo iazyka" (A History of the Uzbek Language), in *Sovietskoe vostokovedenie* (The Soviet East), 1949.
Brozak, J. "Current Status of Psychology in the USSR," in *Annual Review of Psychology,* XIII, 1962.
Chokaev, M. "Turkestan and the Soviet Regime," in *Journal of the Royal Central Asian Society,* vol. 18, 1931, pp. 403–420 (London).
Deshirev, I. D. "Razvitie malopismennykh iazykov narodov SSSR v sovetskuiu epokhu" (Development of Semi-Literacy Languages of Soviet Nationalities during the Soviet Epoch) in *Voprosy iazykoznaniia* (Questions of Linguistics), No. 5, 1957, pp. 18–31.
Dimanshtein, S. M. "Narodnoe obrazovanie natsional nostei SSSR i zadachi vostokovedenia" (Public Education of National Minorities in the USSR and the Administrative Problems of the East), in *Novyi vostok* (The New East), No. 25, 1925, pp. xxxiv–1.
"Falsification of Turkestanian History," in *Millij Turkistan,* No. 74 B, 1951, pp. 11–16.
Ferreus, B. "The Menace of Communist Psychological Warfare," in *Orbis:* A Quarterly of World Affairs, vol. 1, 1957.
Filosoficheskie nauki (Philosophical Sciences). Moscow: Zhurnal Ministerstva obrazsvaniia (Journal of the Ministry of Education), 1, 1960–1962.

Frey, Richard. "The Historical Impact of Islam in the Soviet Union," in *Islam and Communism* (Munich: Institute for the Study of the USSR), 1960, pp. 5–10.

Fritseev, Iu. R. "Kommunisticheskoe vospitanie" (Communist Education), in *Voprosy Filosofii* (Questions of Philosophy), No. 5, 1961.

Gafurov, B. G. "O perspektivakh razvitiia sovetskogo vostokovedeniia" (Perspective Development of the Soviet Eastern Administration), in *Sovetskoe vostokovedenie* (Soviet Eastern Administration), No. 3, 1957, pp. 10–17.

Gegenwartsfrager der Ortodoxen Kirche (Temporary Problems of the Orthodox Church), in *Osteuropa*, Heft 3, June, 1965.

Gulian, L. V. "Marksistskaia etika i problema tsennosti" (Marxist Ethics and the Problems of Value-judgement), in *Voprosi Filosofii* (Questions of Philosophy), No. 1, 1962, pp. 40–42.

Hayit, B. "Turkestan as an Example of Soviet Colonialism," in *Studies on the Soviet Union*, vol. i, No. 2 (Munich, 1961), pp. 1–18.

Henze, Paul. "Politics and Alphabet in Inner Asia," in *Royal Central Asian Journal*, vol. XLIII (London, January, 1956), pp. 28–33.

Iangi-Iul (monthly), in Uzbek Language. Tashkent: 1926, 1928.

Der Islam. Bond 37 (October, 1960). Berlin: 1960–1964.

Iunost (Youth). Moscow, vol. 2, 1962 (monthly).

Institute of Jewish Affairs: The Institute Annual, 1956. Religious Life in the Soviet Union, pp. 360–378.

Istoriia SSSR (History of the USSR). Moscow, monthly, 1960–1964.

Izvestiia (News). Moscow, daily, 1924–1927; 1960–1967.

Kamenka, E. "Marx, Marxism and Ethics," in *Survey* (London: 1961), No. 39, pp. 49–60.

Kantemir, Ali. "The Moslems," in *Religion in the USSR* (Munich: Institute for the Study of the USSR, July, 1960), No. 59, pp. 143–150.

Karelin, P. N. "Training Active Propagandists of Soviet Atheism," in *Vestnik Vysshei shkoly* (Journal of Higher Education) (Moscow), No. 11, 1959.

Kolarz, Walter. "Religions of the East," in *Survey*, No. 43, August, 1962, pp. 130–135.

Kosomolskaia Pravda (The Komsomol Truth). Daily newspaper (Moscow), 1963–1964.

Kommunist, No. 4, 1963 (Moscow, monthly).

Krushel, S. "Razgrom pravoslavnykh khramov v SSSR" (The Liquidation of the Orthodox Churches in the USSR), in *Vestnik Instituta* (Bulletin of the Institute). Munich: Institute for the Study of the USSR, 1954, pp. 110–111.

La Farge, John. "The Philosophical Basis of Communism," in *Informationes et Natitae Manuscripti. Instar ad Usum Nostrum Tantum.* Vol. 1, No. 4, 1935, pp. 34–38.

Leningradskaia pravda (Leningrad Truth). Leningrad, daily, 1965.

Literaturna Gazeta (Literary Gazette). Moscow; 156 issues per year 1960, 1966.

Literaturna Ukraina (Literary Ukraine). Kiev (weekly).

Literaturnaia Rossiia (Literary Russia). Moscow (weekly).

Levshin, L. "All-Round Development of Personality," in Narodnoe Obrazovanie (Public Education), No. 12, 1961. Translated by the staff of *Soviet Education*, vol. V, No. 7, 1962.

Menzel, Theodor. "Turkologische Kongress in Baku," in *Der Islam* Jahrbuch, 1927, pp. 1–16.

Mikhailov, M. O. "Pro 29 rokoviny z dnia smerti V. I. Lenina" in *Visnyk Akademii Nauk UkSSR* (The 29th Anniversary of the Death of Lenin, in Bulletin of the Ukrainian Academy of Sciences) (Kiev), January, 1953.

Mikulak, M. "Philosophy and Science," in *Survey*, No. 57, July, 1964, pp. 147–157.

Mitin, B. N. "Sovetskoe gosudarstvo i stroitel'stvo komunizma" (The Soviet State and the Building of Communism), in *Voprosy Filosofii* (Questions of Philosophy), October No. 10, 1961, pp. 10–39.

Molod' Ukrainy (Youth of Ukraine) (Kiev, weekly), June, 1965.

Motylevo, T. "Glazami druzei i vragov" (Through the Eyes of Friends and Enemies), in *Novii Mir* (New World). Moscow, monthly, No. 11, 1966.

Murgaev, E. F. "Atheism and Religion," in *The Soviet Review*, vol. II, July 1961, No. 7, pp. 41–57.

Nauka i religiia (Science and Religion) (Moscow, monthly), 1965.

Novaia i noveishaia istoriia (The New and the Newest History) Moscow, quarterly, 1960–1964.

Novikova, L. I. "Trud i nrastvennoe vospitanie podrastaiushchego pokoleniia" (Labor and the Ethical Education of the Young Generation), in *Sovetskaia Pedagogika*, June 1967, pp. 104–121.

Ogonek (Light) (Moscow: weekly), 1966–1967.

Ogorodnikov, I. I. "Zadachi i sistema pedagogiki v pedagogicheskikh institutakh" (The Tasks and System of the Pedagogy in Teacher Training Institutes), in *Sovetskaia pedagogika* (Soviet Education), No. 2, 1962.

Oktiabr (October) (Moscow, monthly), 1960–1964.

Ostroumov, N. O. Musul'manskaia vysshaia shkole Madressa (Muslim Higher School, Madressa) in *Zhurnal Ministerstva Narodnogo Prosveshcheniia*, (Journal of the Ministry of Public Education), Sentiabr, 1906, pp. 114–156.

————. "Narodnoe obrazovanie: musul'manskie maktaby i russkotuzemnye shkoly v Turkestanskom krae" (Public Education: Muslim mektabs and Russian Schools for Natives in the Country of Turkestan), in *Zhurnal Ministerstva Narodnogo Prosveshcheniia* (Journal of the Ministry of Public Education), No. 2, part 4, 1906, pp. 113–166.

Orientale Christiana. "The Orthodox Confession of Peter Mohyla, Metropolitan of Kiev" (1633–1646), vol. X, No. 39, October, 1927.

Pankratova, A. "Nauchnye voprosy sovetskoi istoricheskoi nauki" (Scientific Questions of the Soviet Historical Science) in *Kommunist*, No. 6, 1953, p. 63.

Partiinaia Zhizn' (Moscow, weekly), 1964–1966.

Pavlovish, M. "Reforma alfavita v Turtsii" (The Reforms of the Alphabet in Turkey), in *Novyi Vostok* (The New East), No. 25, 1925, pp. 244–257.

Petrosiak, V. P. "Kakim dolzhen byt' uchebnik" (What a Textbook Should be Like), in *Novaia i noveishaia istoriia* (The New and the Newest History), No. 5, 1960.

Pipes, Richard. "Muslims in the Soviet Union," in *Islama and Communism*. Munich: Institute for the Study of the USSR, 1960, pp. 11–19.

The Philosophical and Psychological Foundations of Soviet Atheism (editorial), in *Studies in the Soviet Union*, vol. XIII, No. 2, 1966 (Munich: Institute for the Study of the USSR), pp. 26–30.

Poznanskii, N. F. "Heredity and the Materialistic Theory," in *Soviet Psychology: A Symposium* (New York: Philosophical Library, 1961).

Pravda (Truth) (Moscow: daily newspaper), 1917–1927; 1958–1967.

Pravda Vostoka (The Eastern Truth) (Tashkent; daily newspaper), 1960.

Pickthall, M. "Muslim Education," in *Islamic Culture*, No. i, vol. 1, 1927, pp. 100–109.

Probst, A. N. "O dal'neishei proizvodstvennoi spetsializatsii raionov Srednei Azii" (Industrial Specialization Concerning the Central Asian Regions), in *Izvestiia Akademii Nauka SSSR* (Bulletin of the Academy of Sciences of the USSR), No. 5, 1961, p. 76.

Radianska kul'tura (Kiev: Ukrainian monthly), 1960–1966.
Radianska osvita (Soviet Education) (Kiev: Ukrainian monthly), 1967.
Radianska Ukraina (Soviet Ukraine) (Kiev: Ukrainian daily), 1954–1967.
Robitnicha gazeta (The Workingman's Newspaper), weekly, Kiev, 1965.
Rosler, Roman. "Lage der Ortodoxen Kirchen in den Slavischen Landern" (Conditions of the Orthodox Church in Slavic Lands), in *Osteuropa* (Eastern Europe), Heft 6, 1954, pp. 412–421.
Rozentsveig, Milan. "Nekotorye teoriticheskie voprosy formirovaniia uchashchikhsia srednei shkoly" (Some Theoretical Problems of Forming a World-Outlook in Secondary School Students), in *Sovetskaia pedagogika* (Soviet Education), January 1967, pp. 94–103.
Rozhin, Iven. "A University Professor in the USSR," in *Horizons* (New York: Journal of the Ukrainian Student Association of America), vol. iii, No. 1–2, 1959, pp. 38–49.
Rudman, Herbert. "Structure and Decision Making in Soviet Education," in *Bulletin No. 2.* Washington, D. C.: U. S. Office of Education, 1964, pp. 30 ff.
Russian Review (New York, monthly), vol. 8, 1925.
Shcherbak, M. A. "Kistorii obrazovaniia ubekskogo narodnogo iazyka" (History of the Development of the Uzbek national Language), in *Voprosy iazykoznaniia* (Questions of Linguistics), No. 6, 1954, pp. 107–116.
Shimoniak, Wasyl. "The Destruction of Muslim Religion in Uzbekistan," in *The Ukrainian Quarterly* (New York: vol. XXI, No. 3, 1965), pp. 232–246.
————. Bolshevism in Turkestan: "The Establishment of the Soviet Regime in Central Asia, 1917–1939," in *The Ukrainian Quarterly* (New York: vol. XXII, No. 4, 1966), pp. 351–364.
Shliakh (The Way). Philadelphia (Ukrainian Catholic Daily), 1964.
Shulz, G. E. "Soviet Communist Party," in *Soviet Studies,* vol. 11, No. 5, 1965.
Skotkin, M. N. "Nakazanie i prakticheskie raboty uchashchikhsia" (Punishment and a Practical Work of Students), in *Izvestiia Akademii Pedagogicheskikh Nauk RSFSR* (Bulletin of the Russian Pedagogical Sciences), No. 58, 1954, pp. 12 ff.
Smirnov, A. A. "The Development of Soviet Psychology," in *Soviet Psychology: A Symposium* (New York: Philosophical Library, 1961).
Seton-Watson, H. "The Role of Intelligentsia," in *Survey,* No. 43, August 1962, pp. 23–31.
Sereda, K. "Problema pamiati i obucheniia" (Problems of Memory and Learning), in *Voprosy psykhologii* (Questions of Psychology) January, 1967.
Sovetskaia kul'tura (Soviet Culture) (Moscow: biweekly), 1965.
Sovetskaia Rossiia (Soviet Russia) (Moscow: daily), 1964.
Sovetskoe stroitel'stvo (Soviet Construction) (Moscow: No. 37, 1929), p. 110.
Sovetskoe zdravokhranenie (Soviet Health) (Moscow: monthly), No. 8, 1966.
Soviet Union Review (Published by the Soviet Information Bureau). Washington, D. C.: monthly, 1932.
Stalin, J. V. "On the Problem of Technical Intelligentsia i the USSR," in *Soviet Cultural Bulletin,* No. 5, 1931, pp. 1–5.
Sukhalminskii, V. "Vazhnye problemi teorii i praktiki pedagogiki" (Urgent Problems of the Theory and Practice of Education), in *Narodnoe obrazovanie,* No. 10, 1961.
Svoboda (Freedom). New York: Published by the Ukrainian Congress Committee of America. 1950–1967 (daily).
Symonenko, Vasyl. "A Diary Which Horrified Moscow," in *The Ukrainian Quarterly,* vol. XXII, No. 2, 1966, pp. 164–169.

486   Communist Education

Szporluk, R. "Pokrovsky and Russian History," in *Survey,* No. 53, 1964, pp. 107–118.
Tschokaeff, A. M. "Fifteen Years of Bolshevik Rule in Turkestan," in *Journal of the Royal Central Asian Society,* vol. XX, 1933, pp. 351–359.
Tobolev, K. "O natsional'nykh kadrakh" (On National Cadres), in *Sovetskoe stroitel'stvo* (Soviet Construction), No. 7–8, 1933, p. 15.
Trud (Work). (Moscow; daily), 1964.
Triforov, I. V. "Obzori i zametki" (Notes and Reviews), in *Istoricheskii arkhiv* (Historical Archives), No. 1, 1961, p. 132.
Uchitel'skaia gazeta (Teacher's Gazette) (Moscow: biweekly), 1960–1967.
Ukaz Prezidiuma Verkhovnogo Soveta SSSR ot 31-go maia, 1941 g. (Decree of the Presidium of the Supreme Soviet of the USSR, May 31, 1941), in *Vedomosti Verkhovnogo Soveta SSSR:* Ugolovnyi kodeks RSFSR (Bulletin of the Supreme Soviet of the USSR: Criminal Code of the Russian SFSR). Moscow: Gosiuridizdat, 1952, pp. 83–84.
Ukrainskii samostiinik (The Ukrainian Independent). Munich: 1964–1967.
Ukrainska Vil'na Akademiia Nauk: naukovyj zbirnyk (Ukrainian Free Academy of Sciences: Scientific Works). New York: No. 1, 1952.
Ukrainska mova i literatura v shkoli: Metodichnyi Zhurnal Ministerstva Osvity UkSSR (Ukrainian Language and Literature in School: Methodological Journal of the Ministry of Education of the Ukrainian SSR). Kiev: No. 1, 1967.
Ukrainskii zbirnik: knyha 1 (Ukrainian Collection: Book 1). Munich: Institute for the Study of the USSR, 1954.
Uzbekiston (monthly, in Uzbek and Russian languages, Tashkent), 1962.
Vasileeva, N. "Kogda govorit vremia" (When the Time Speaks), in *Znamia* (Moscow), No. 1, 1967.
Vason-Girei Dzhabash. "Sovetskii Soiuz i shkola" (The Soviet Union and the School), in *Vestnik Instituta po izucheniiu SSSR* (Bulletin of the Institute for the Study of the USSR), No. 3, 1954.
Vestnik statistiki (Statistical Bulletin), Moscow: monthly, 1959–67.
Vestnik vyssdhei shkoly (Bulletin of Higher Education). Moscow, monthly, 1959–1966.
Vitchizna (Fatherland). Kiev: monthly, January 1, 1965.
The Voice of Georgia (New York: Quarterly), No. 2, 1957.
Voprosy istorii (Questions of History) (Moscow: monthly), 1960–65.
Voprosy filosofii (Questions of Philosophy) (Moscow: monthly), 1961–1967.
Wetter, G. "Dialectical Materialism and Natural Sciences," in *Soviet Survey,* 1957, pp. 51–59.
Winner, Thomas. "Problems of Alphabetic Reforms Among the Turkic Peoples of Soviet Central Asia," in *The Slavonic and East European Review,* vol. XXXI, No. 76, 1952.
Zaporozhets, A. V. Razvitie vospriiatiia i deiatel'nost (Development of Perception and Activity), in *Voprosy psikhologii* (Questions of Psychology), No. 1, 1967, pp. 11–16.
Zatko, James. "The Catholic Church and Russian Statistics, 1804-1917," in *The Polish Review,* vol. V, No. 1, 1960, pp. 35–52.
Zhovten' (October). Lvov, No. 2, 1965 (Ukrainian monthly).

Albania

Hamm, Henry. *Albania, China's Beachhead in Europe.* New York: F. Praeger Press, 1963.

Krasniqui, R. "Persecution of Religion in Communist Albania," in *ACEN News,* No. 128, 1967, pp. 17–20.
NDARJA Administrative el R. P. Sh., *Vjetari Statistikor Republikes Populore te Shqiperise* (Statistical Yearbook of the People's Republic of Albania, 1965) (Tirana: 1965).
Rauchek, Joseph S. *Balkan Politics.* Stanford: Stanford University Press, 1948, pp. 125–146.
Robinson, V. *Albania's Road to Freedom.* London: George Allen and Unwin, Ltd., 1941.
Stavrianos, S. *The Balkans Since 1453.* New York: Holt, Rinehart & Winston, 1961.
Skendi, Stavro. *Albania.* London: Atlantic Press, 1957.

Bulgaria

Akademiia Nauk SSSR. *Osvobozhdenie Bulgarii ot turetskogo iga* (Liberation of Bulgaria from the Turkish Yoke). Moscow: AN SSSR, 1961.
Apanasewicz, Nellie. *Education in Bulgaria.* Washington, D. C.: U. S. Department of Health, Education, and Welfare, 1965.
Central Board of Statistics. People's Republic of Bulgaria—*Statistical Manual.* Sofia: Foreign Language Press, 1965.
Dellin, L. D. *Bulgaria.* New York: Mid-European Studies Center, 1957.
Dmitrovski komunisticheski mladezhki soiuz. *Materiali ot deveti kongres na DKMS sustoial ot 27. XI do 1. XII. 1958* (Data From the Ninth Congress of the Bulgarian Communist Youth Association in m. to Dimitrov, Held Between November 27-December 1, 1958). Sofia: Narodna mladezh, 1958.
Evans, S. *A Short History of Bulgaria.* London: Lawrence and Wisharb, Ltd., 1960.
Ganev, Todor. *Nauchni sobraniia na Bulgarskata Akademiia na naukite,* 1947–1954 (Scientific Sessions of the Bulgarian Academy of Sciences, 1947–1954). Sofia: Bulgarska Akademiia na Naukite, 1958.
Ivanov, Boris D. *Sudurzhanie i formi na politechnicheskoto obuchenie* (Content and Form of Polytechnical Education). Sofia: Narodna Prosveta, 1960.
Kossev, D. *A Short History of Bulgaria.* Sofia: Foreign Language Press, 1963.
Kostanick, Huey I. *Turkish Resettlement of Bulgarian Turks, 1950–1953.* Berkeley: University of California Press, 1957.
Papazov, Nacho. *Results of the Reorganization of Public Education and Our Future Tasks in Bringing the Schools Closer to Life.* Sofia: Narodna Prosveta, 1962.
Pavlov, N. and others. *Arithmetic: A Textbook for Grade One of the General Polytechnical School.* Sofia: Narodna Prosveta, 1963.
Runciman, Steven. *A History of the First Bulgarian Empire.* London: Bell Press, 1930.
Todorov, Nikolai. *Bulgaria: Historical and Geographical Outline.* Sofia: Foreign Language House, 1965.
Wolf, Robert L. *The Balkans in Our Times.* Cambridge: Harvard University Press, 1956.

China

Briere, O. *Fifty Years of Chinese Philosophy, 1898–1950.* Translated from the French by L. Thomson. London: Allen and Unwin, Ltd., 1956.
Bulletin, vol. XIV, No. 1, 1967. *Studies on the Soviet Union.* Munich: Institute for the Study of the USSR.

488   Communist Education

Chang Jen-chi. *Pre-Communist China's Rural School and Community.* Boston: Christopher Publishing House, 1960.

Chang Tu-hu. *Chinese Education Under Communism.* New York: Teachers College, Columbia University, 1962.

Chen, William Jun-Tung. *Some Controversies in Chinese Education and Culture.* New York: Columbia University, unpublished Ph. D. dissertation, 1951.

Chiang, Wen-han. *The Ideological Background of the Chinese Student Movement.* New York: King's Crown Press, 1948.

Cramer, John; Browne, G. *Contemporary Education.* New York: Harcourt, Brace and Ward, 1965, pp. 531–542.

Cressy, Earl H. *Understanding China.* New York: Thomas Nelson and Sons, 1957.

Day, Burton C. *The Philosophies of China.* New York: Philosophical Library Press, 1962.

Elegant, Robert S. *The Center of World Communism and the Mind of China.* Garden City: Doubleday Co., 1964.

Fraser, S. (ed.). *Chinese Communist Education, Records of the First Decade.* Nashville: Vanderbilt University Press, 1965.

Greene, Fred. *The Far East.* New York: Holt, Rinehart and Winston, 1961.

Harper, Paul. *Spare-Time Education for Workers in Communist China.* Washington, D.C.: U.S. Office of Education, Bulletin No. 30, 1964.

Hsi-en Chen, Theodore. *Teacher Training in Communist China.* Washington, D.C.: U.S. Office of Education, mimeo, 1960.

Hu Chang-Tu. *China: Its Culture, Its Society* (New Haven: HRAF Press, 1960).

Orleans, Leo A. *Professional Manpower and Education in Communist China.* Washington, D.C.: U.S. Government Printing Office, 1960.

Rowe, David N. *Modern China: A Brief History.* Princeton: D. Van Nostrand, 1959.

Wittfogal, Karl T. *Oriental Despotism: A Comparative Study of Total Power.* New Haven: Yale University Press, 1957.

Wung, Y. C. *Chinese Intellectuals and the West.* Chapel Hill: University of North Carolina, 1966.

Cuba

Batista, Fulgencio. *The Growth and Decline of the Cuban Republic.* New York: The Devin Co., 1964.

Draper, Theodore. *Castroism; Theory and Practice.* New York: Praeger Press, 1965.

Fagen, Richard R. *Cuba: The Political Content of Adult Education.* Stanford: Stanford University Press, 1964.

Haiken, Jea; and Others. *Twentieth Century Cuba.* New York: Doubleday Press, 1965.

Hubernan, L. *Cuba, Anatomy of a Revolution.* New York: Monthly Review Press, 1961.

Lleo, Manuel U. *Fidel Castro and Company Inc., Communist Tyranny in Cuba.* New York: Praeger Press, 1964.

Czechoslovakia

Apanasewicz, Nellie. *Education in Czechoslovakia.* Washington, D.C.: U.S. Office of Education, Bulletin No. 27, 1963.

Assembly of Captive European Nations. *Bulletins,* 1956–1967. New York: Captive Nations Center.

Blunden, G. *Eastern Europe: Czechoslovakia, Hungary and Poland.* New York: Time Incorporated, 1965.

Busek, V. *Czechoslovakia.* New York: Mid-European Studies Center, 1957.

Chlup, Otokar. *Skolsky zakon za dne 21 dubna 1948, c. 95* (School Law of April 21, 1948, No. 95). Vyklad zakona a prov. predpisi. Prague: Orbis, 1949.

Czechoslovakia, *A Handbook of Facts and Figures.* Prague: Orbis, 1964.

Dvornik, Francis. *Sv. Vojtech, II. biskup prarsky.* (St. Vojtech, II. Bishop of Prague). Chicago: Bohemian Benedictine Press, 1950.

Holas, E. "K otazce aplikace Pavlovova uceni na cloveka" (Problem of Application of the Pavlovian Teaching on Human Beings), in *Sbornik Vysoke Skoly Pedagogicke v Olomouce* (Bulletin of the Higher Education in Olomouc, Section of Pedagogy and Psychology). Prague: Statni Pedagogicke Nakladatelstvi, 1956, pp. 23–53.

Masaryk, Thomas G. *Cesta otazka* (The Czech Question). Prague: Nak. Pokrok, 1908.

Masaryk, Thomas G. *Die philosophischen sociologischen Grundlagen des Marxismus* (Philosophical and Sociological Foundations of Marxism). Vienna: Konegen Verlag, 1899.

_____. *The Spirit of Russia,* two vols. London: Allen and Unwin, 1938.

Nemec, Ludwig. *Church and State in Czechoslovakia.* New York: Vintage Press, 1954.

New Family Legislation in Czechoslovakia, Translated from Czech by F. O. Stein. Prague: Ministry of Information and Public Culture, 1950.

Otto, F. *The Break-up of Czech Democracy.* London: V. Gallancz, Ltd., 1950.

Polasek, Alois. "Prispevek k otazce svetovoho nazoru" (Some Questions Concerning the World Outlook), in *Sbornik Vysoke Skoly Pedagogicke,* 1955, pp. 15–35.

Proces proti Vatikanskym agentum v CSR (Process Against the Vatican's Agents in Czechoslovakia). Prague: Orbis, 1950.

Red and the Black: The Church in the Communist State. New York: The National Committee for Free Europe, 1953.

Ripka, H. *Czechoslovakia Enslaved: The Story of the Communist Coup d' Etat.* London: Gallancz Press, 1950.

Slovak Studies, Historica. Rome: Slovak Institute, 1961–1965.

Slovakia, vol. XV, No. 38, 1965. Middletown: The Slovak League of America.

Strako, Vaclav. *Czechoslovakia Today.* Brno: Tiisk, 1964.

Trial of the Treasonable Slovak Bishops: Jan Vojtassak, Michael Buzalka, Pavel Goidich. Prague: Orbis, 1951.

Ucitelske noviny (Teacher's Journal). Prague: 1960–1964.

East Germany

Bodenmann, Paul. *Education in the Soviet Zone of Germany,* Washington, D. C.: U. S. Office of Education, 1959.

Brant, Stefan. *The East German Rising.* New York: Praeger Press, 1953.

Buchholz, Arnold. *Neue Wege sowjetishcer Bildung und Wissenshcaft* (New Ways of Soviet Education and Science) Koln: Verlag Wissenschaft und Politik, 1963.

Bundesministerium fur Gesamtdeutschen Fragen, *Ein Taschen und Nachschlagbuch über die sowjetishce Besatzungs Zone Deutschland* (A Handbook of Facts Concerning the Soviet Occupational Zone of Germany). Bonn: Bundes Verlag, 1966.

490   Communist Education

Froese, L. *Sowjetisierung der deutschen Schule, Entwicklung und Struktur des mitteldeutschen Bildungswessen* (The Sovietization of German School, Development and Structure of Mid-German Schooling). Freiburg: Herder Verlag, 1962.

Germany in a Nutshell. Bonn: Press and Information Office of Federal German Government, 1958.

Grothe, Peter. *To Win the Minds of Men.* Palo Alto: Pacific Books Publishers, 1958.

Neuman, Gunter. *Die Pionier-Organization in der Sowjet Zone* (The Pioneer Organization in the Soviet Zone). Koln: 1959.

Helmut, Arnts. *Tatsachen uber Deutschland* (Facts about Germany) Weisbaden: Steiner Verlag, 1960.

Henning, Frank. *Zwanzig Jahre Zone-Kleine Geschichte der "DDR"* (The Twenty Years Zone). A Short History of DDR. Munich: Goldman Verlag, 1965.

Hansen, Ulrich. *Frühgeschichte und Forschung und Lehre in der sowjetischen Zone Deutschland* (Free History and the Research and Science in the Soviet Zone of Germany) Berlin: 1964.

Hartman, G. *Der Kamf gegen Religion* (Struggle Against Religion). Stuttgart: Quelle Verlag, 1966.

Karisch, Rudolf. *Die Katholische Kirche in Berlin und Mittledeutschland* (The Catholic Church in Berlin and Mid-Germany). Berlin: Morus Verlag, 1966.

Lage, M. *Zur Sozialistischen Kulturrevolution* (Toward the Socialist Revolution). Berlin: Afbau Verlag, 1960.

Lange, M. *Totalitäre Erziehung* (The Totalitarian Education) Berlin: Frankfurter Verlag, 1954.

Moebus, G. *Erziehung zum Hass* (Education for Hate). Berlin: Phorus Verlag, 1966.

————. *Psychologie und Pädagogik des Kommunismus* (Psychology and Pedagogy of Communism). Köln: Westdeutschen Verlag, 1957.

Die Pionierorganization "Ernst Thaelman" in der Sowjetzone (The Pioneer Organization in the Soviet Zone). Bonn: Bundesministerium fur Gesamtdeutschen Fragen, 1957.

Salter, Ernest. *Deutschland und der Sowjet Kommunismus* (Germany and the Soviet Communism). Munich: Piper, 1961.

Staatsecretariat fur das Hoch-und Fachschulsessen, *Hoch-schulführer der deutschen demokratischen Republik* (Highschool Leader of the German Democratic Republic) Berlin: Deutscher Verlag, 1960.

Statistisch Zentralverwaltung für Statistik, *Statistiches Jahrbuch der DDR,* 1966 (Statistical Yearbook of German Democratic Republic). Berlin: 1966.

Wagner, W. *The Genesis of the Oder-Neisse Line.* Stuttgart: Brentanos Verlag, 1964.

Ziemer, G. *Education for Death.* New York-London: Oxford University Press, 1941.

Hungary

Andis, E. *A Magyar munkasmozgalom az 1914–1918 és Vilaghaboru alott* (Hungarian Labor Movement During the 1914–1918 World War). Budapest: 1950.

Bodrin, V. V. *Vengerskaia narodnaia respublika* (Hungarian People's Republic). Moscow: Gosizdat, 1952.

Czako, Elemer. *A Magyarsag néprajó* (Hungarian Ethnography) Budapest, 1965.

Czalad és Iskola (Schools and Family). Budapest: Monthly Journal Published by the Ministry of Education, 1965.

Eckhart. Ferenc. *Magyarország története* (History of Hungary). Budapest, 1940.
Fejtö, F. *Behind the Rape of Hungary*. New York: David McKay Co., 1957.
Heckenast, Desidor, "Hungarian Universities-Past and Present," in *Slavic and East European Studies*. Montreal; University of Montreal, 1957, vol. II. Part I.
Helmriech, Ernst C. *Hungary*. New York: Praeger Press, 1957.
Heller, Andor. *No More Comrades*. Chicago: Henry Regnery Co., 1957.
Juhasz, William. *Blueprint for the Red Generation*. New York: Mid-European Studies Center, 1952.
Kadar, J. *The Church in the Time*. Budapest: Bibliotheca, 1958.
A Kereszt (The Cross). Budapest: Hungarian Catholic Monthly, 1958, 1962.
Kornis, Julius. *Education in Hungary*. New York: Columbia University Press, 1932.
Kovrig, Bela. *Four Meanings of National Communism*. Milwaukee: Marquette University Press, Slavic Institute Papers. Paper No. 5, 1958.
Kovacs, Imre. *Facts About Hungary*. New York: Hungarian Committee Center, 1958.
Macarney, C. A. *Hungary: A Short History*. Chicago: Aldine Publishing House, 1962.
Nagy, Imre. *On Communism: In Defense of the New Cause*. New York: Praeger Press, 1957.
Pfeifer, E. *Child of Communism*. London: Weidenfield Press, 1958.
Stalte, C. "The Hungarian Revolution: Ten Years Later," in *Bulletin No. 12*, vol. XIII, 1966. Munich: Institute for the Study of the USSR.
Statistikai Tajeköztató (Statistical Bulletin). Budapest: monthly, 1966.
Szabad Ifjuság (Free Youth). Budapest: daily newspaper of the Communist Youth Organization, 1961.
Vetö, Miklos. *The Catholic Church in Hungary*. New York: Praeger Press, 1962.

North Korea

Bradbury John. "Sino-Soviet Competition in North Korea," in *The China Quarterly*. April-June, 1961, pp. 15–28.
Cune, N. *Korea Today*. Cambridge: Harvard University Press, 1950.
Economical and Statistical Information on North Korea, Washington: D. C.: Joint Publications Reserve Service, 901-D, January 15, 1960.
Facts About Korea. Pyongyang: Foreign Language Publishing House, 1961.
Report on the United Nations Commissions for the Unification and Rehabilitation of Korea. New York: U. N. General Assembly. Supplement No. 12 (A), 1881, 1951, pp. 59–60.
Rigg, Robert B. *Red China's Fighting Hordes*. Harrisburg, Penn: Military Service Co., 1951.
Scalopino, Robert A. *The Origin of the Korean Communist Movement*, in *Journal of Asian Studies*, vol. XX, No. 1, 1960, pp. 162–168.
Seton-Watson, Hugh. *From Lenin to Khrushchev: The History of World Communism*. New York: Praeger Press, 1960.
U. S. Department of State. *North Korea: A Case Study in the Techniques of Takeover*. Washington, D. C.: Department of State Publications, 7118, 1961.

Mongolia

Bisch, Jorgen. *Mongolia: Unknown Land*. Translated from Danish by R. Spink. New York: E. P. Dutton Co., 1963.

Blagoveshchenskki. *Mongolskaia narodnaia respublika* (Mongolian People's Republic). Moscow: Gosizdat, 1950.
Grofitt, William E. *The Sino-Soviet Rift.* Cambridge: The M. I. T. Press, 1964.
The International Yearbook and Statesmen's Who's Who. London: Burke's Press, 1966.
Lattimore, Owen. *Nomads and Commissars: Mongolia Revisited,* New York: Oxford University Press, 1962.
Makhnenko. A. *Gosudarstvennyi stroi MNR* (Political System of the MPR). Moscow: Gosizdat, 1955.
Moskovskii Gosudarstvennyi Universitet. *Noveishaia istoriia stran zarubezhnogo vostoka* (The Current History of the Foreign East). Moscow: M. Universitet, 1955.
Murphy, George S. *Soviet Mongolia.* Berkeley: University of California Press, 1966.
Rupen, Robert. *The Mongolian People's Republic.* Stanford: Stanford University Press, 1966.
Tang, Peter S. *Russian and Soviet Policy in Manchuria and Outer Mongolia,* 1911–1931. Durham: Duke University Press, 1959.

Poland

Apanasewicz, N. Medlin, William K. *Educational System in Poland.* Washington, D. C.: U. S. Office of Education, Bulletin No. 12, 1959.
Assembly of Captive European Nations. *Religion in Poland.* New York: Assembly's Bulletin, 1956.
Arnold, Stanislaw. *Outline History of Poland.* Warsaw: Polonia Publishing House, 1965.
Bartecki, Jan. *Aktiwizacja procesu nauczenia poprzez zespoly uczniowkie* (The Role of Pupils' Teams in the Teaching Process). Warsaw: Wyd. Naukove, 1966.
Barycz, H. *The Development of University Education in Poland.* Warsaw: Drukarnia Naukowa, 1957.
Barnet, Clifford R. *Poland; Its People, Its Society, Its Culture.* New Haven: Grat Press, 1958.
Concise Statistical Yearbook of the Polish People's Republic 1961. Warsaw: Central Statistical Office, 1961.
Central Statistical Office. *Poland in Figures.* Warsaw: Central Statistical Office, 1959.
Dowjat, Z. Dobre perspektywy rozwoju warsztatow szkolnych (Future Development of School Workshops). *Szkoya Zawodowa,* No. 3, 1966, pp. 18–20.
Halecki, Oscar. *History of Poland.* New York: Ray Publishers, 1956.
Handbook for Candidates to Higher Schools for the 1962/63 School Year. Warsaw: Ministry of Higher Education, 1961.
Higher Education in Post-War Poland. Warsaw: Ministry of Higher Education, 1961.
Karski, Stefan. *Poland Past and Present.* New York: G. F. Putnam's Press, 1933.
Paschalska, Maria. *Education in Poland.* Warsaw: Polonia Publishing House, 1962.
Parnowski, Zygmunt. *Education in Poland.* Warsaw: Polonia Publishing House, 1958.
Monticone, Ronald C. "The Catholic Church in Poland, 1945–1966," in *The Polish Review,* vol. XI, No. 4, 1966, pp. 75–92.
Rosen, S. *Higher Education in Poland.* Washington, D. C.: U. S. Office of Education, Bulletin No. 19, 1963.

Sharp, Samuel L. *Poland's White Eagle on a Red Field.* Cambridge: Harvard University Press, 1953.
Skubala, Sofia. *Polish Universities.* Warsaw: Polonia Publishing House, 1959.
Social Achievements of People's Poland, *Labor Protection for Women.* Warsaw: 1954.
Starr, Richard F. *Poland, 1944–1962.* New Orleans: Louisiana State University Press, 1962.
United States Senate, Committee on Judiciary, *Hearings.* Washington, D. C.: *The Church and State Under Communism,* vol. V. 1965.
Wydaunistwo Ekonomiczne, *Twenty Years of the Polish People's Republic.* Warsaw: 1964.
Zeszyty Historyczne, III. Warsaw: Uniwersytet Warszawski, 1960–1963.

Rumania

Anuarul Statistic al Republica Populara Romina, 1960. Bucharest: Directia de Statistica, 1960.
Assembly of Captive European Nations. *Persecution of Religion in Romania,* Bulletin No. 1, 1956, pp. 68–71.
Asotiatia Slavistilor din Republica Populara Romina. *Romanoslavica,* Bucharest, 1958.
Braham, R. *Education in Romanian People's Republic.* Washington, D. C.: U. S. Office of Education, Bulletin No. 1, 1964.
Central Statistical Office of Romania. *Romanian Statistical Pocketbook.* Bucharest: Central Statistical Office, 1961.
Cretzianu, A. *Captive Romania.* New York: Praeger, 1956.
Cretzian, A.; Froyd, David. *Romania, Russia's Dissident Ally.* New York: Praeger Press, 1965.
Fischer, S. *Romania.* New York: Praeger Press, 1957.
International Yearbook of Education, vol. XIX. Paris: 1957. pp. 146–147.
Iorga, N. *A History of Romania: Land, People and Civilization,* London: T. F. Unwin, 1925.
Kashin, A. "Romania and Polycentrism," in *Bulletin for the Study of the USSR,* vol. XIII, 1956, pp. 43–49.
Markham, Henry R. *Romania under the Soviet Yoke.* Boston: Maedor Press, 1949.
Reichman, E. "The Literary Scene in Romania," in *Survey,* No. 55, 1965, pp. 38–51.
Seton-Watson, Hugh. *A History of the Romanians.* Cambridge: The University Press, 1934.
Thomson, J. "Romania's Struggle with Comecon," in *East Europe,* vol. 13, No. 6, 1964, pp. 2–9.
UNESCO. *The Liquidation of Illiteracy in the Romanian People's Republic.* Paris: UNESCO, vol. X, No. 4, 1958, p. 148.

North Vietnam

Ballis, William B. "Relations Between the USSR and Vietnam," in *Studies on the Soviet Union.* Munich: Institute for the Study of the USSR, vol. VI, No. 2, 1966, pp. 43–57.
Buttinger, Joseph. *The Smaller Dragon.* New York: Praeger Press, 1958.
Fall, Bernard B. *The Viet Minh Regime.* Ithaca: Cornell University Press, 1954.

Grossman, B. "The Influence of the War in Vietnam on the Economy of Communist China," in *Studies on the Soviet Union*. Bulletin of the Institute for the Studies of the USSR, vol. 6, No. 2, 1966.

Hammer, Ellen. *Vietnam Yesterday and Today*. New York: Holt, Rinehart and Winston, Inc., 1966.

Haney, P. J. "North Vietnam Today," *China Quarterly* No. 9, London, 1962.

Haong, Van Chi. *From Colonialism to Communism: A Case History of North Vietnam*. New York: Praeger Press, 1964.

Lancaster, D. *The Emancipation of Indochina*. Oxford: University Press, 1961.

Roll, Bernard. *The Two Nations-Vietnams*. New York: Praeger Press, 1963.

Tonges, Gerard. *L'enfer communiste au Nord Vietnam*. Paris: Les Nouvelles Editions Debresse, 1960.

Yugoslavia

Byrnes, Robert F. *Yugoslavia*. New York: Mid-European Studies Center, 1957.

Darby, H. C. *A Short History of Yugoslavia*. Cambridge: Harvard University Press, 1966.

Dascalakis, A. P. *The Hellenism of the Ancient Macedonians*. Chicago: Institute for the Balkan Studies, 1965.

Development of Schools in Yugoslavia. Belgrade: Information Service Yugoslavia, 1957.

Ernjakovic, G. *The Yugoslav Educational System*. Belgrade: Information Service Yugoslavia, 1959.

Eterovich, Francis and Ch. Spalatin (eds.). *Croatia: Land, People, Culture*. Toronto: University of Toronto Press, 1964.

Federal Statistical Office. *Statistical Pocketbook of Yugoslavia;* 11th edition. Belgrade: 1965.

Fetscher, Irving. "Historische Voraussetzungen des Sozialismus," in *Praxis*. Zagreb: Philosophical Journal, 1966, No. 1, pp. 151–158.

Gimnaziia u novom sistemu obrazovanja i vospitanja (Gymnazium in the New System of Upbringing and Education). Belgrade: Komisija za Reformu Skolstva, 1957.

Hecimovic, Joseph. *In Tito's Death Marches*. Translated and edited by John Pracela. Chicago: Croatian Franciscan Press, 1961.

Heller, Agnes. "Wert und Geschichte" (Value and the History), in *Praxis*, No. 1–2, 1966, pp. 91–101.

Kagraga, M. "Was Denkst du, Philosoph" (What Do You Think, Philosopher?) in *Praxis*, No. 1, 1965, pp. 87–105.

Kofas, E. *Nationalism and Communism in Macedonia*. Washington, D. C.: Georgetown University, 1964.

Mitrovic, Darinka. "Razvoj i savremeni problemi obrazovanja nastavnika (Development and Contemporary Problems of Teacher Training)," in *Zivot i skola*, No. 2–3, 1966, pp. 105–123.

Neal, F. W. *Titoism in Action*, The Reform in Yugoslavia After 1948. Berkeley: University of California, 1958.

People's Youth Organization in Yugoslavia. Belgrade: Information Service Yugoslavia, 1957.

Petrovich, Michael. *Titoism*. Milwaukee: Marquette University Slavic Institute Papers, Paper No. 5, 1958.

Slijepchevich, Boko. *Istorija srpske pravoslavne tsrkve* (History of the Serbian Orthodox Church). Munich: 1966.

Tomich, Vera. *Education in Yugoslavia and the New Reforms.* Washington, D. C.:
    U. S. Office of Education, Bulletin No. 20, 1963.
Udich, Ja. *Sposterezhennia iz Yugoslavii* (Observations in Yugoslavia). New York:
    Dnipro Publishers, 1957.

INDEX

Academy of Pedagogical Sciences, 131
Academy of Ukrainian Sciences, 83
administrative structure, 119–142
adult education, 114–116
aesthetic education, 193
Aksakov, T., 32
Akhmatova, A., 277
Albania, 385–396
  geographical density, 387
  education before 1945, 387
  general education, 389
  higher education, 390
  historical background, 385
  Jesuits, 394
  linguistic reforms, 387ff.
  Ministry of Education, 388
  National Freedom Movement, 386
  Ottoman Empire, 385
  population, 387
  religious purges, 393ff.
  statistical data, 390ff.
  women and education, 392
Aleksandrov, A. D., 184
anti-religious propaganda, 240
  (*see also* religion)
Anglo-American Imperialism, 63
Arpad dynasty, 358

Asiatic Russia, 5, 457ff. (*see also* Turkestan, Central Asia and Uzbek)
Otetea, 373
atheistic propaganda, 54
Attila, 358
Avacuum, 25–29

Balkan nationalities, 331
Baltic nationalities, 10, 468
Batista, F., 417
Belinski, V., 34
Blok, A., 61, 275
Bolsheviks, 184ff. (*see also* communism, Soviet, Marxist-Leninism)
  ethnic groups, 19
  regime, 52
  Uzbek questions, 19
boarding schools, 31, 106
Brezhnev, Leonid, 286
brigadir, 159
brotherhood schools, 24–38
Buddhism, 250
Bulgaria, 315–328
  aims of education, 320
  compulsory education, 317
  Communist Youth League, 324
  curriculum, 320
  Christianity, 318

Cyril and Methodius, 316
Byzantine Empire, 316
education before 1945, 317
enrollment, 322
economic situation, 328
Five Year Plan, 328
general background, 316
higher education, 321
history, 316, 325
language, 318
Leninist schools, 318ff.
Ministry of Education, 326
Marxism-Leninism, 318
Muslim groups, 327
party indoctrination, 320
polytechnical education, 324
religion, 327
Russian language, 320
statistical data, 321
women and education, 327
Bukharin, Nicholas, 54

Candidate of Sciences, 112
Carol I, king of Romania, 372
Castriota, George, 385
Catholics, 303–305 (*see also* religion and individual communist countries)
Catholic church, purges, 247ff.
counselling, 161
Census Bureau, 10
Central Executive Committee, 86 (*see also* communism, and individual communist countries)
Central Asia, methods of teaching Muslim history, 181
Chagatai, 227
character education, 208–210
Charles IV, king of Bohemia, 4, 358
child development, 203
China, 397–414
birth rate, 397
communist education, 400ff.

curriculum, 411
Confucius, 398–400
education before 1949, 397
foreign languages, 399
general education, 406ff.
higher education, 408
Japan, relations with, 399
Marxism, 414
Ministry of Education, 407
population, 397
organization and control, 404
philosophy of education, 409
political education, 401
"Red and Expert," 413
Red Guards, 403
Russian relations, 416
statistical data, 403
Soviet Union, 397
Spare Time Schools, 404ff.
teacher training, 410–412
traditional schools, 399
vocational education, 407
western ideas, 399, 413
Christianity, 244
Christian ethics, 100
Church Slavonic, 25
class struggle, 59, 281
control of education, 119–142 (*see also* individual countries)
Congress of Baku, 220–229
Congress of Vienna, 317
Comenius, John A., 293–295
communism:
control of education, 441 (*see also* Soviet and other communisms)
population, 20
education, 222, 442
ethics, 447
linguistic problems, 215–234, 445
Communist Manifesto, 282
morality, 56
reliability of data, 441

religion, 235–251, 446
science, 278
Communist Youth Association, 56,
    221, 443
Cuba, 415–422
    alfabetizadores, 418
    Catholic church, 416
    Castro, 417
    Bay of Pigs, 421
    elementary education, 417
    higher education, 421
    propaganda, 419
    Russian influence, 419–421
    Sociedad Economica, 416
    statistical data, 420
    University of Havana, 416
    United States of America, 416
    vocational education, 416
curriculum (*see also* individual
        countries) :
    Muslim, 146ff.
    non-Russian schools, 146
    Ukrainian schools, 146
    Uzbek schools, 150ff.
culture: Russian vs. national, 274
    Soviet vs. national, 274
Curie, Sklodowska, 306
Cyril and Methodius, 291
Czechoslovakia, 291–302
    battle of the White Mountain,
        293
    Beran, Archbishop, 301
    Brezhnev, L., 301
    Bohemians, 291
    Carpathians, 294
    constitution, 298
    culture, 293
    freedom, 296
    history, 292
    Moravian Brotherhood, 294
    population, 294
    Progressive Catholic Action, 300
        (*see also* Vatican)
    psychology, 296
    religion, 292–299

schools, 295ff.
Slovaks, 291
statistical data, 298
textbooks, 296
vocational education, 297

Dalimil's Chronicle, 293
Danilevski, N., 32
Dewey, John, 74ff., 159
dialectical materialism:
    criteria of dialectical material-
        ism, 185ff.
    class struggle, 189
    nature of truth, 190ff.
    educational implications, 183
    nature of reality, 187
Dimitrov, George, 285, 318
Drohobitski, Jurij, 24
Dubcek, A., 293
Doctor of Sciences Degree, 112
Dr. Zhivago, 55

education, Soviet, 23–50 (*see
        also* areas of education)
education in Central Asia, 84ff.
education, Soviet general, 70ff.
education of the world, 117
Eastern Slavs, 291
Eliutin, 152
Engels on education, 51
Esenin, S., 275
expenditures on education, 137ff.

family values, 280
Federal   Centralized   Structure,
    123ff.
Flüchtling, 345
Fok, A., 184
Freud, S., 210

Galiev, Sultan, 86, 240
Genghis Khan, 422
German Democratic Republic,
    345–356
    constitution, 353

Communist Youth Association, 352
Freie Deutsche Jugend, 350
history, 345
idealistic philosophy, 350
Kultur, 351
literature and Marxism, 351
Marxist–Leninism, 346
Ministry of Education, 347
moral education, 349ff.
new values, 352
pedagogy, 348
polytechnical education, 346
population, 349
religion, 352ff.
teacher training, 347
theology, 353
West Germany, education in, 347
United States, relations with, 350
women and education, 354
Golden Bull, 358
Gomulka, W., 286
Greco-Latin-Russian Institute, 28
Great Proletarian Revolution, 402
Great Russian nationalism, 285

Han language, 389
Hangu alphabet, 428
Hapsburg dynasty, 359ff.
hate, philosophical concept, 62ff.
Havlicek, 294
Heder (khadera), 50
Hegel, J., 184
Holy Synod, 28, 129
Ho Chi Minh, 434
Hungary, 357–370
Ausgleich, 359
Calvinism, 360
Catholic Church, 368
Christianity, 358
communist reforms, 366
Communist Youth Organization, 362
deportation to Siberia, 369
education before 1945, 360
general education, 354
goals, 362
higher education, 361–365
history, 357ff.
Priest Committee of Peace, 368
religion, 367
research, 367
statistical data, 365ff.
Turco-Tatar wars, 358
workers, 363
vocational education, 364
Huns, 358
Hus, Jan, 292

illiteracy, 67ff. (see also individual countries)
Imperial elite, 283
Imperial Office of Appointments, 283
Imperial Russia, 235 (see also Russia)
Islam, 249
Islamic schools, 41–50 (see also Muslims)
Ivan the Terrible, 4

Jadid, 84–86
Jewish education, 82, 286
Jewish purges, 49
Jesuits, 251 (see also Academy of Peter Mohyla)

Kaczmarek, Bishop, 314
Kalmiks, 4
Kalinin, Michael, 58, 257
Kasimenko, O., 179
Kazakh SSR, 1
Kazakh population, 11
Kazakhstan, 7
Kazan-Tatars, 227
Khadera (Heder), 50
Khan Krum, 316
Khmelnitski, Bohdan, 4, 26

Khomiakov, A., 32
Khrushchev, Nikita S.:
  cult of personality, 77
  educational programs, 58
  boarding schools, 106
  compulsory education, 100
  criticism, 77
  linguistic goals, 224
  nationality questions, 78
  new generation, 58
  work and study plan, 77, 150
Khvylovi, Mykola, 223–276
Kievan Ruś, 23ff.
Kim-il-song, 428
Kirov, Sergi, 239
Kosygin, Alexei N., 286
Klebelsberg, Kuno, 361
Kliuchevski, V., 170
Kolchak, G., 423
kolkhoz, 283
komsomol, 88
Korean People's Republic:
  educational system, 429
  higher education, 431
  history of North Korea, 427
  illiteracy, 428ff.
  Japan vs. Korea, 428
  Marxism-Leninism, 428
  political indoctrination, 430
  Russian occupation, 427
  statistical data, 430
  women, education of, 431
Korolev, F. F., 74
Kosminski, A. F., 168
Kossuth, L., 359
Krupskaia, N., 107, 159
Kremlin, 122 (see also Soviet)
Kublai Khan, 424
kulaks, 85

Language and Soviet policies, 216,
  231, 283
Lenin, Vladimir Ilyich:
  aims of education, 51

army of teachers, 109
Christianity, 236
control of education, 120
cultural reforms, 273
dialectical materialism, 184
child development, 203
eighth party congress, 72
God and society, 52
higher education, 108
linguistic problems, 217ff.
liquidation of old intelligentsia,
  108
Muslim language, 216
Muslim peoples, 84
nationality problems, 8, 217
religion, 73, 237
self-determination of nations, 18
Ukrainian problems, 216
women and society, 255
Lexicon of Slavic Affairs, 27
Linguistic policies of Bolshevism,
  215–234
Lin-Shao-Chi, 402
Lomonosov, Michael, 29
Lunacharski, A., 105
Lysenko, Mykola, 194ff.

Machiavelli, 441
Makarenko, Anton:
  aesthetic education, 193
  counselling, 161
  dialectical materialism, 192, 197
  discipline, 160
  educational policies, 160
  educational system, 197ff.
  method of teaching, 161ff.
  parents vs. school, 198
  personality problems, 197
  punishment, 161
  Soviet patriotism, 196
Makhkamei Shirai, 85
Mayakovski, V., 275
Marr, Nicholas Y., 219
Marti, Jose, 416

Marx, Karl:
  dialectical materialism, 183
  ethical categories, 190
  educational structure, 51
  linguistic problems, 217
  women and society, 254ff.
Marxism-Leninism:
  ideology, 75, 164
  superiority of Russian Marxism,
    166
  theories of learning, 165
Masaryk, Thomas G., 292
Mazepa, hetman, 4
Mao Tse-tung, 399–413
medressa, 41
Medynski, E. N., 68
Mendeleev, D., 201
methods of teaching:
  history, 169–175
  psychology, 167
  Stalin's views on methods, 174
mektab, 41
Mieszko I, king of Poland, 303
Mikoyan, A., 232
militant atheist, 110
Ministry of Education:
  Russian control, 98
  higher education, 132
  Narkompros, 127
  spravochniki, 131
Mohylian Academy:
  curriculum, 26
  Catholicism, 25
  Peter I and the Academy, 27
  Polish relations, 26
  Pope Urban VI, 27
  St. Thomas, influences, 25
  works of Peter Mohyla, 26–27
Mon-Khmer-Shan, 398
Mongolian People's Republic:
  army, 423
  Buddhism, 422
  China's influence, 423
  curriculum of general schools,
    426

elementary education, 424
higher education, 426
religious reforms, 427
Russian intervention, 422
Soviet reforms, 423
Mongol invasion, 23
moral behavior, 165
Moravian Brotherhoods, 24
Mordva ASSR, 11
Moscovites, 23
Muslim (see also Islam):
  anti-religious propaganda, 249
  Arabic script, 227
  before 1917 (in Russia), 40
  Bukhara, 55
  clergy, purges of, 53
  concessions to Islam, 85
  industrialization, 149
  intelligentsia, 286
  Kazan Muslims, 48
  linguistic problems, 226–234
  New Method Schools, 84
  national movements, 86
  Pan-Turkism, 87
  people, 5
  purges of Muslims, 249
  Russko-tuzemnye shkoly, 48
  traditional schools, 40–47, 85
  Turkestanian Muslims, 49
  unity of Islam, 18
  Uzbek language, 227

Narkompros, 74
Nemcova, Bozena, 294
New Economic Policy, 10, 145
Neruda, Jan, 294
New Soviet Man, 51, 161
Nguyen Truong Tu, 434
Niecephorus I, Byzantine Emperor, 316
Nikon, 25, 29
nomenclatura, 283
non-Russian nationalities, 285,
  450, 467

Obronevic, M., 331
Otto the Great, 358
Owen, Robert, 75, 101

Paisi, 317
Pasternak, Boris, 276
Pavlov, I.:
  conditioning, 210
  methods of study, 205
  research problems, 201
Pedagogical Institute, 156
People's Commissariat of Education, 68, 73
personality, 206ff.
Peter the Great:
  church and state, 29
  cultural reforms, 28
  western ideas, 27
Pirogov, N. A., 38
Podebrady, George, 292
Poland:
  Catholic church, 305ff.
  Catholic University of Lublin, 308
  communist party, 310
  control of education, 311
  educational statistics, 310ff.
  history, 304ff.
  Jagellon dynasty, 303
  King Louis I, 303
  language, 306
  minority schools, 307, 311
  National Education Act, 1932, 306
  Oder-Neissa, 304
  Pilsudski, General, 304
  population, 10
  Progressive Catholic Action, 313
  teacher training, 308–312
  women, education of, 312ff.
Pokrovski, Michael:
  Bolshevik Revolution, 173
  capitalism and Bolshevism, 171
  interpretations of history, 171ff.
  opposition to Marx, 172

Polotski, S., 27
Postishev, M., 81, 222
population in communist countries, 20
population trends, 3–18
Psychology (Soviet):
  educational, 202
  child development, 203
  experimental, 204
  political, 209ff.
  Western, 204

rabfak (see also Workers' Faculties), 104
Radio University, 115
Rajk, 285
Reflexes of the Brain, 200
Rey, M., 305
Rhodes, A., 432
Role of the Communist Party, 119ff.
Romanov dynasty, 180
Rousseau, J. J., 166
Rubenstein, S. L., 201
Russification policies, 18, 38, 82, 215
religion and communism, 235–252
  atheism, 236ff.
  Islam, 244
  legal provisions, 237ff.
  press, 241ff.
  Vatican, 239
Romania:
  administration and control, 379
  Catholic church, 383
  Carpathian region, 372
  Christianity, 372
  communist party, 379
  education before 1945, 373
  education after 1945, 381
  educational structure, 374
  higher education, 377
  history of Romania, 371ff.
  King Michael I, 372

language, 384
Marxism-Leninism, 375
population, 6, 373
Soviet assistance, 379
statistical data, 383
training of teachers, 381–382
vocational education, 376
Russian Soviet Federated Socialist
    Republic: Russian policies:
assimilation of nations, 93
Decembrist movement, 153
domination over others, 20ff.
education of nobility, 31
enlightenment, 30ff.
European influences, 34
expansion, 4
Muslim problems, 240ff.
political psychology, 209
patriotism, 53, 63
social classes, 282
Ukrainian relations, 29
Ukrainian Catholic Church, 239

Safarik, J., 294
Salonica, 291
Sarts, 8
Sarajevo, 332
St. Martin of Tours, 361
scientific atheism, 246
scientific communism, 278
science and ideas, 279
schools (Soviet):
boarding schools, 106ff.
higher schools, 107
polytechnical, 100ff.
types of schools, 97ff.
working youth, 103
Serbo-Croatian education, 334
Sheptitski, A., Metropolitan, 178
Siberia, population, 7
Sichenev, M. V., 200
Simonenko, V., 63
Skrypnyk, M., 220
Slavophils:
liberal Slavophils, 32

mission of Slavs, 32
philosophy, 32–33
Sosiura, V., 53
Soviet Union, issues:
abnormal psychology, 203
bureaucracy, 283
cadres-specialists, 283
China vs. U.S.S.R., 110–111
cultural offensive, 67–96
curriculum in general schools,
    144
dialectical materialism, 188
executive offices, 282
English colonies, 61
goals of education, 51–65
humanism, 57
imperialism, 86
intelligentsia, 283ff.
literature, 275ff.
Marxism, 51
Nazi alliance, 110
materialistic philosophy, 188
New Economic Policy, 145
Nietzsche's influence, 191
patriotism, 61
political psychology, 209
slave labor, 63
republics, 450–466
statistical data, 282, 467
Stalin, Joseph V.:
census policies, 10
changes after 1953, 110
classical communism, 174
dialectical materialism, 183
establishment of Central Asian
    republics, 19
Hitler vs. Stalin, 6
linguistic policies, 218
Marxist doctrine, 256
new Soviet society, 256
Pokrovski's repudiation, 170ff.
Skrypnyk vs. Stalin, 222ff.
Uzbek language, 228
women and Soviet society, 256
Stockholm Peace Appeal, 314

Sudetenland, 345
Syriac alphabet, 226

Tadzhik SSR, 93
Tashkent, 89
Teacher's role:
    American and Soviet teacher,
        135
    atheism, 169
    duties vs. the state, 135
    history-teaching, 134
    obligations, 162
    training of teachers, 108ff.
Technicums, 102
Tolstoi, Lev N., 36
Turco-Russian relations, 331
Turkestan:
    before 1917, 14
    constitution, 85
    division of Turkestan, 18, 86
    education, 42–50
    Central Asia, 134, 180
    population, 5, 11
    Soviet interpretation of history,
        180

udarnik, 324
Udmurs, 4
Ukrainian SSR-issues:
    administration, 123
    Christianity, 27
    concept of "lesser evil," 176
    deportation, 12
    decrease of scientific workers,
        81
    dictation of history, 176
    dictionary, 225
    higher education, 112
    intelligentsia, 39, 81, 286
    indoctrination, 61
    Jesuit influence, 25
    language, 287
    linguistic reforms, 218ff.
    method of teaching history, 175
    method of writing history, 178

national anthem, 62
Narodna Rada, 148
purges of religious believers, 247
reforms of 1875, 39
Russification, 78–80, 220
Volga regions, 13
Ulan-Batur, 424
Union of Brest, 25
Unified Labor School, 71
U.S.A. in Russian propaganda, 57
U.S.S.R., ethnic groups, 9
    (*see also* Soviet Union)
Ushinski, Konstantin:
    American Negro worker, 35
    physical labor, 35
    psychology, 36
    teacher's role, 35
    Switzerland and Russia, 34
Uzbek SSR, issues:
    education, 84
    European nationalities in Uz-
        bekistan, 91
    illiteracy, 93
    increase of Russian words in
        Uzbek language, 232
    korenizatsia, 86
    population, 4, 90
    purges, 229
    religious freedom, 148
    Tashkent district, education, 88

Valois, Henry, 304
Vietnam, North:
    alphabet, 432
    Catholic church, 433
    French occupation, 432
    higher education, 436
    Ho Chi Minh, 434
    Japanese occupation, 432
    political indoctrination, 436
    population, 433
    Russian help, 432
    secondary education, 436
    statistical data, 435
Vilborg, 11

Wallachia, 373
Watson, John, 204
window to Europe, 24
women and communism: 252–
    272
  Communist Youth Organiza-
      tion, 260
  concentration camps, 270
  economy, 265
  education of women, 263ff.
  International Women's Day,
      258
  Muslim women, 256
Westernites, 33
Wollstonecraft, Mary, 253
Workers' Faculties (rabfak), 71,
    104
Wyszynski, Cardinal, 314

Xoxe (or Xoxho), Koci, 285

Yavorski, M., 176
Yi dynasty, 427
Yugoslavia:
  Bosnia and Herzegovina, 331

Broz, Josef (known as Tito),
    332
curriculum, 340
communist party, 334
education after 1945, 333
Education Law of 1958, 335
elementary education, 336
ethical principles, 334
higher education, 341
history, 330
Islam, 331
intelligentsia, 334
Komsomol, 342
Macedonia, 331
population, 329
statistical data, 336
teachers, 341
Titoism, 330
Turkish minorities, 330

zemstvo, 138
Zhukovski, A., 30
Zinoviev, Gregory I., 237
Ziska, J., 292

PRINTED IN U.S.A.

COMMUNIST EDUCATION:

ITS HISTORY
PHILOSOPHY
AND POLITICS

This book presents the aims and methods of communist education in terms of historical and philosophical perspectives as well as academic and administrative requirements. It is approached in terms of the entire Soviet sphere of influence—not solely Russia.

One of the greatest values of the book is its presentation of the projection of the Soviet system to other lands, and description of the initial aim of this projection—control of education. Each country is studied on the basis of its dependency on or independence from the big powers, Russia and China.

Several of the smaller countries— Albania, Cuba, North Vietnam, North Korea and others—have not previously been covered in a textbook. Students of Comparative Education and Communist Education will find this book a rich resource, especially as it includes newly translated statistical and demographic data.

Wasyl Shimoniak is a native of Carpathian Ukraine and was educated in Soviet schools. He came to the United States in 1951 and became a citizen in 1956. He received his PH. D. in Social Foundations of Education and Russian Area Studies from the University of Michigan and is currently Associate Professor of Education at Marquette University.